Student Solutions Manual

to accompany

Beginning and Intermediate Algebra:

The Language and Symbolism of Mathematics

Third Edition

James W. Hall
Parkland College

Brian A. Mercer
Parkland College

Prepared by
Mark W. Smith
College of Lake County

The McGraw-Hill Companies

Student Solutions Manual to accompany
BEGINNING AND INTERMEDIATE ALGEBRA: THE LANGUAGE AND SYMBOLISM
OF MATHEMATICS, THIRD EDITION
JAMES W. HALL AND BRIAN A. MERCER

Published by McGraw-Hill Higher Education, an imprint of The McGraw-Hill Companies, Inc., 1221 Avenue of the Americas, New York, NY 10020. Copyright © 2011, 2008, and 2003 by The McGraw-Hill Companies, Inc. All rights reserved.

♻ This book is printed on recycled, acid-free paper containing 10% post consumer waste.

1 2 3 4 5 6 7 8 9 0 WDQ/WDQ 10 9 8 7 6 5 4 3 2 1 0

ISBN: 978–0–07–729692–6
MHID: 0–07–729692–3

www.mhhe.com

Preface

This Student Solutions Manual contains worked-out, step-by-step solutions to odd-numbered end-of-section "Exercises", all "Quick Review", all "Cumulative Review", all end-of-chapter "Review Exercises", and all end-of-chapter "Mastery Test" problems contained in *Beginning and Intermediate Algebra, The Language and Symbolism of Mathematics, Third Edition* by James W. Hall and Brian A. Mercer.

Solutions are worked out using the same methods presented in the text, and graphs and TI-84 calculator screens are shown where appropriate. It is my hope that the solutions in this manual will increase your understanding of the material and enable you to develop a structured approach to solving the problems presented in the text. This manual is a text supplement. It is intended to be read along with the text itself.

I would like to thank my family for their patience and support during this project.

Mark W. Smith
College of Lake County

Section 1.2: The Real Number Line

Quick Review 1.2

1. The digit in the hundreds place of 9876.54321 is 8.
2. The digit in the tens place of 9876.54321 is 7.
3. The digit in the tenths place of 9876.54321 is 5.
4. The digit in the hundredths place of 9876.54321 is 4.
5. 9876.54321 rounded to the nearest hundred is 9900.

Exercises 1.2

1.
  a. The additive inverse of 9 is -9
  b. The additive inverse of -13 is $-(-13) = 13$
  c. The additive inverse of $-\dfrac{3}{5}$ is $-\left(-\dfrac{3}{5}\right) = \dfrac{3}{5}$
  d. The additive inverse of 7.23 is -7.23
  e. The additive inverse
     of $-\sqrt{13}$ is $-\left(-\sqrt{13}\right) = \sqrt{13}$
  f. The additive inverse of 0 is 0

3.
  a. $-(-7) = 7$
  b. $-\left[-(-7)\right] = -7$
  c. $0 + 7 = 7$

5.
  a. $17 + (-17) = 0$
  b. $-17 + 17 = 0$
  c. $-\pi + \pi = 0$
  d. $x + (-x) = 0$

7.
  a. $-6x + 6x = 0$
  b. $6x + 0 = 6x$
  c. $6x + (-6x) = 0$
  d. $-6x + 0 = -6x$

9.
  a. $|29| = 29$
  b. $|-29| = 29$
  c. $-|29| = -29$
  d. $-|-29| = -29$

11.
  a. $83 > 38$
  b. $-83 < -38$

13.
  a. $0 < \dfrac{1}{3}$
  b. $0 > -\dfrac{1}{3}$

15.
  a. $|-5| > -|5|$
  b. $|-5| > -|-5|$

	Inequality Notation	Verbally	Graphically	Interval Notation
Example:	$x > 2$	x is greater than 2.		$(2, +\infty)$
17.	$x > 1$	x is greater than 1.		$(1, +\infty)$
19.	$x \ge -3$	x is greater than or equal to -3.		$[-3, +\infty)$
21.	$-3 < x \le 3$	x is greater than -3 and less than or equal to 3.		$(-3, 3]$
23.	$x \le 4$	x is less than or equal to 4.		$(-\infty, 4]$

25. **a.** $\sqrt{25} = 5$

   b. $-\sqrt{25} = -5$

   c. $\sqrt{0.25} = 0.5$

   d. $\sqrt{2,500} = 50$

27. $\sqrt{17} \approx \sqrt{16} = 4$. Since $17 > 16$, we know that $\sqrt{17} > 4$. Thus, we choose the answer **B.** 4.12

29. $\sqrt{62.41} \approx \sqrt{64} = 8$. Since $62.41 < 64$, we know that $\sqrt{63.41} < 8$. Thus, we choose the answer **C.** 7.9

	Integer Estimate	Inequality	Approximation
Example $\sqrt{5}$	2	$2 < \sqrt{5}$	2.236
31. $\sqrt{50.6}$	7 (since $50.6 \approx 49$)	$7 < \sqrt{50.6}$ (since $50.6 > 49$)	7.113
33. $\sqrt{0.976}$	1 (since $0.976 \approx 1$)	$1 > \sqrt{0.976}$ (since $0.976 < 1$)	0.988

35. **a.** Natural numbers: 15

   b. Whole numbers: 0, 15

   c. Integers: $-11, -\sqrt{9}, 0, 15$

   d. Rational numbers: $-11, -4.8, -\sqrt{9}, 0, 1\frac{3}{5}, 15$

   e. Irrational numbers: $\sqrt{5}$

37. **a.** Natural numbers: $\sqrt{1}, \sqrt{16}$

   b. Whole numbers: $0, \sqrt{1}, \sqrt{16}$

   c. Integers: $-\sqrt{4}, 0, \sqrt{1}, \sqrt{16}$

   d. Rational numbers: $-\sqrt{\dfrac{9}{25}}, -\sqrt{4}, 0, \sqrt{1}, \sqrt{16}$

   e. Irrational numbers: $-\sqrt{5}, \sqrt{6}$

39. -18 belongs to the integers and the rational numbers.

41. 81 belongs to the natural numbers, the whole numbers, the integers, and the rational numbers.

43. $\sqrt{8}$ belongs to the irrational numbers.

45. $5\frac{3}{7}$ belongs to the rational numbers.

47.

49. **a.** $\sqrt{9} = 3$ is a rational number since it has a decimal representation that terminates.

   b. $\sqrt{10} \approx 3.162278$ is an irrational number since it has a decimal representation that does not repeat of terminate.

51. **a.** $0.171717\ldots$ is a rational number since it has a decimal representation that repeats.

   b. $0.171771777\ldots$ is an irrational number since it has a decimal representation that does not repeat or terminate.

53. $\underbrace{\text{Twenty percent}}\underbrace{\text{is equal to}}\underbrace{\text{one-fifth}}$

$$20\% \qquad = \qquad \frac{1}{5}$$

Answer: $|x| = y$

55. $\underbrace{\text{The absolute value of } x}\underbrace{\text{is equal to}}\underbrace{y}$

$$|x| \qquad = \qquad y$$

Answer: $|x| = y$

57. $\underbrace{\text{The square root of } x}\underbrace{\text{is}}\underbrace{\text{equal to}}\underbrace{y}$

$$\sqrt{x} \qquad = \qquad y$$

Answer: $\sqrt{x} = y$

59. "π is greater than 3.14 and less than 3.15," means π is between 3.14 and 3.15.
Answer: $3.14 < \pi < 3.15$

61. **a.** **b.**

c.

63. The only number that is less than or equal to 7 but not less than 7 must be equal to 7.

65. The only number that is greater than or equal to 3 and less than or equal to 3 simultaneously is 3 itself.

67. **a.** The only number that is a whole number but not a natural number is 0.
b. Any integer that is negative is not a natural number. For example, -4 or -12.

c. Any negative fraction that can not be reduced to an integer will work. For example, $-\dfrac{4}{7}$ or $-\dfrac{12}{13}$.

d. $\dfrac{3}{2}$ and $\dfrac{7}{5}$ are examples of rational numbers between 1 and 2.

69.

x	$\sqrt{x}$
2	1.41
3	1.73
4	2
5	2.24

Section 1.3: Operations with Positive Fractions

Quick Review 1.3

1. The next prime number after 17 is 19.

2. $35 = 5 \cdot 7$

3. $36 = 4 \cdot 9 = 2 \cdot 2 \cdot 3 \cdot 3$

4. $45 = 9 \cdot 5 = 3 \cdot 3 \cdot 5$

5. $88 = 8 \cdot 11 = 2 \cdot 2 \cdot 2 \cdot 11$

Exercises 1.3

1. $\dfrac{3}{7}$

3. $\dfrac{2}{8} = \dfrac{\cancel{2}^{1}}{\cancel{2} \cdot 4_{1}} = \dfrac{1}{4}$

5. $\dfrac{4}{18} = \dfrac{\cancel{2}^{1} \cdot 2}{\cancel{2} \cdot 9_{1}} = \dfrac{2}{9}$

7. $\dfrac{10}{15} = \dfrac{2 \cdot \cancel{5}^{1}}{3 \cdot \cancel{5}_{1}} = \dfrac{2}{3}$

9. $\dfrac{35}{7} = \dfrac{5 \cdot \cancel{7}^{1}}{\cancel{7}_{1}} = 5$

11. $\dfrac{11}{99} = \dfrac{\cancel{11}^{1}}{9 \cdot \cancel{11}_{1}} = \dfrac{1}{9}$

13. **a.** The multiplicative inverse of $\dfrac{5}{11}$ is $\dfrac{11}{5}$.

    b. The multiplicative inverse of $\dfrac{11}{5}$ is $\dfrac{5}{11}$.

15. **a.** The multiplicative inverse of 6 is $\dfrac{1}{6}$.

    b. The multiplicative inverse of $\dfrac{1}{6}$ is 6.

17. $\dfrac{3}{8} \cdot \dfrac{5}{7} = \dfrac{3 \cdot 5}{8 \cdot 7} = \dfrac{15}{56}$

19. $\dfrac{3}{8} \cdot \dfrac{4}{7} = \dfrac{3}{\cancel{8}_{2}} \cdot \dfrac{\cancel{4}^{1}}{7} = \dfrac{3 \cdot 1}{2 \cdot 7} = \dfrac{3}{14}$

21. $\dfrac{18}{15} \cdot \dfrac{4}{27} = \dfrac{\cancel{18}^{6}}{\cancel{15}_{5}} \cdot \dfrac{4}{\cancel{27}_{9}} = \dfrac{\cancel{6}^{2}}{5} \cdot \dfrac{4}{\cancel{27}_{9}} = \dfrac{2 \cdot 4}{5 \cdot 9} = \dfrac{8}{45}$

23. $6 \cdot \dfrac{3}{2} = \dfrac{\cancel{6}^{3}}{1} \cdot \dfrac{3}{\cancel{2}_{1}} = \dfrac{3 \cdot 3}{1 \cdot 1} = 9$

25. $\dfrac{2}{5} \cdot \dfrac{2}{5} \cdot \dfrac{2}{5} = \dfrac{2 \cdot 2 \cdot 2}{5 \cdot 5 \cdot 5} = \dfrac{8}{125}$

27. $\dfrac{2}{15} \cdot \dfrac{5}{12} \cdot \dfrac{36}{11} = \dfrac{2}{\cancel{15}_{3}} \cdot \dfrac{\cancel{5}^{1}}{\cancel{12}_{1}} \cdot \dfrac{\cancel{36}^{3}}{11} = \dfrac{2 \cdot 1 \cdot \cancel{3}}{\cancel{3} \cdot 1 \cdot 11}$

$$= \dfrac{2 \cdot 1 \cdot 1}{1 \cdot 1 \cdot 11} = \dfrac{2}{11}$$

29. $\dfrac{3}{8} \div \dfrac{5}{7} = \dfrac{3}{8} \cdot \dfrac{7}{5} = \dfrac{3 \cdot 7}{8 \cdot 5} = \dfrac{21}{40}$

31. $\dfrac{3}{8} \div 6 = \dfrac{3}{8} \cdot \dfrac{1}{\cancel{6}_{2}} = \dfrac{1 \cdot 1}{8 \cdot 2} = \dfrac{1}{16}$

33. $\dfrac{16}{27} \div \dfrac{18}{24} = \dfrac{\cancel{16}^{8}}{\cancel{27}_{9}} \cdot \dfrac{\cancel{24}^{8}}{\cancel{18}_{9}} = \dfrac{8 \cdot 8}{9 \cdot 9} = \dfrac{64}{81}$

35. $\dfrac{3}{5} \cdot 360 = \dfrac{3}{\cancel{5}_{1}} \cdot \dfrac{\cancel{360}^{72}}{1} = \dfrac{3 \cdot 72}{1} = 216$

37. $42 \div \dfrac{3}{7} = \dfrac{\cancel{42}^{14}}{1} \cdot \dfrac{7}{\cancel{3}_{1}} = \dfrac{14 \cdot 7}{1 \cdot 1} = 98$

39. $\dfrac{10}{21} \cdot 35 = \dfrac{10}{\cancel{21}_{3}} \cdot \dfrac{\cancel{35}^{5}}{1} = \dfrac{10 \cdot 5}{3 \cdot 1} = \dfrac{50}{3}$

41. $\dfrac{2}{7} + \dfrac{3}{7} = \dfrac{2+3}{7} = \dfrac{5}{7}$

43. $\dfrac{5}{8} - \dfrac{1}{8} = \dfrac{5-1}{8} = \dfrac{\cancel{4}^{1}}{\cancel{8}_{2}} = \dfrac{1}{2}$

45. $\dfrac{21}{48}+\dfrac{19}{48}=\dfrac{21+19}{48}=\dfrac{\overset{5}{\cancel{40}}}{\underset{6}{\cancel{48}}}=\dfrac{5}{6}$

47. $\dfrac{91}{126}-\dfrac{27}{126}=\dfrac{91-27}{126}=\dfrac{\overset{32}{\cancel{64}}}{\underset{63}{\cancel{126}}}=\dfrac{32}{63}$

49. $\dfrac{5}{36}+\dfrac{11}{36}+\dfrac{17}{36}=\dfrac{5+11+17}{36}=\dfrac{\overset{11}{\cancel{33}}}{\underset{12}{\cancel{36}}}=\dfrac{11}{12}$

51. $\dfrac{5}{11}=\dfrac{5}{11}\cdot\dfrac{3}{3}=\dfrac{15}{33}$; Answer: 15

53. $\dfrac{4}{15}=\dfrac{4}{15}\cdot\dfrac{4}{4}=\dfrac{16}{60}$; Answer: 16

55. $\dfrac{9}{26}=\dfrac{9}{26}\cdot\dfrac{5}{5}=\dfrac{45}{130}$; Answer: 45

57. $\dfrac{1}{4}+\dfrac{3}{8}=\dfrac{1}{4}\cdot\dfrac{2}{2}+\dfrac{3}{8}=\dfrac{2}{8}+\dfrac{3}{8}=\dfrac{2+3}{8}=\dfrac{5}{8}$

59. $\dfrac{5}{12}+\dfrac{7}{20}=\dfrac{5}{12}\cdot\dfrac{5}{5}+\dfrac{7}{20}\cdot\dfrac{3}{3}$

$=\dfrac{25}{60}+\dfrac{21}{60}=\dfrac{25+21}{60}=\dfrac{\overset{23}{\cancel{46}}}{\underset{30}{\cancel{60}}}=\dfrac{23}{30}$

61. $\dfrac{5}{7}-\dfrac{3}{14}=\dfrac{5}{7}\cdot\dfrac{2}{2}-\dfrac{3}{14}=\dfrac{10}{14}-\dfrac{3}{14}=\dfrac{10-3}{14}$

$=\dfrac{\overset{1}{\cancel{7}}}{\underset{2}{\cancel{14}}}=\dfrac{1}{2}$

63. $\dfrac{13}{18}-\dfrac{3}{14}=\dfrac{13}{18}\cdot\dfrac{7}{7}-\dfrac{3}{14}\cdot\dfrac{9}{9}=\dfrac{91}{126}-\dfrac{27}{126}$

$=\dfrac{91-27}{126}=\dfrac{\overset{32}{\cancel{64}}}{\underset{63}{\cancel{126}}}=\dfrac{32}{63}$

65. $\dfrac{5}{6}+\dfrac{3}{10}+\dfrac{7}{15}=\dfrac{5}{6}\cdot\dfrac{5}{5}+\dfrac{3}{10}\cdot\dfrac{3}{3}+\dfrac{7}{15}\cdot\dfrac{2}{2}$

$=\dfrac{25}{30}+\dfrac{9}{30}+\dfrac{14}{30}=\dfrac{25+9+14}{30}$

$=\dfrac{\overset{8}{\cancel{48}}}{\underset{5}{\cancel{30}}}=\dfrac{8}{5}$

67. $4\dfrac{1}{2}+2\dfrac{1}{3}=4\dfrac{1}{2}\cdot\dfrac{3}{3}+2\dfrac{1}{3}\cdot\dfrac{2}{2}=4\dfrac{3}{6}+2\dfrac{2}{6}$

$=6\dfrac{3+2}{6}=6\dfrac{5}{6}$

69. $7\dfrac{2}{3}-5\dfrac{3}{4}=6\dfrac{5}{3}-5\dfrac{3}{4}=6\dfrac{5}{3}\cdot\dfrac{4}{4}-5\dfrac{3}{4}\cdot\dfrac{3}{3}$

$=6\dfrac{20}{12}-5\dfrac{9}{12}=1\dfrac{20-9}{12}=1\dfrac{11}{12}$

71. $5\dfrac{1}{2}+2\dfrac{2}{3}+7\dfrac{5}{6}=5\dfrac{1}{2}\cdot\dfrac{3}{3}+2\dfrac{2}{3}\cdot\dfrac{2}{2}+7\dfrac{5}{6}$

$=5\dfrac{3}{6}+2\dfrac{4}{6}+7\dfrac{5}{6}=14\dfrac{3+4+5}{6}$

$=14\dfrac{\overset{2}{\cancel{12}}}{\underset{1}{\cancel{6}}}=14+2=16$

73. $7\dfrac{1}{2}\times1\dfrac{2}{3}=\left(7+\dfrac{1}{2}\right)\left(1+\dfrac{2}{3}\right)=\left(\dfrac{14}{2}+\dfrac{1}{2}\right)\left(\dfrac{3}{3}+\dfrac{2}{3}\right)$

$=\left(\dfrac{\overset{5}{\cancel{15}}}{2}\right)\left(\dfrac{5}{\underset{1}{\cancel{3}}}\right)=\dfrac{25}{2}=12\dfrac{1}{2}$

75. $1\dfrac{7}{8}\div1\dfrac{5}{7}=\left(1+\dfrac{7}{8}\right)\div\left(1+\dfrac{5}{7}\right)=\left(\dfrac{8}{8}+\dfrac{7}{8}\right)\div\left(\dfrac{7}{7}+\dfrac{5}{7}\right)$

$=\left(\dfrac{8+7}{8}\right)\div\left(\dfrac{7+5}{7}\right)=\left(\dfrac{15}{8}\right)\div\left(\dfrac{12}{7}\right)$

$=\left(\dfrac{\overset{5}{\cancel{15}}}{8}\right)\cdot\left(\dfrac{7}{\underset{4}{\cancel{12}}}\right)=\dfrac{35}{32}=1\dfrac{3}{32}$

77. $\dfrac{360}{960}=\dfrac{\overset{1}{\cancel{2}}\cdot\overset{1}{\cancel{2}}\cdot\overset{1}{\cancel{2}}\cdot\overset{1}{\cancel{3}}\cdot3\cdot\overset{1}{\cancel{5}}}{\underset{1}{\cancel{2}}\cdot\underset{1}{\cancel{2}}\cdot\underset{1}{\cancel{2}}\cdot2\cdot2\cdot2\cdot\underset{1}{\cancel{3}}\cdot\underset{1}{\cancel{5}}}=\dfrac{3}{2\cdot2\cdot2}=\dfrac{3}{8}$

79. $\dfrac{2}{5}$ of 155 is $\dfrac{2}{5}\cdot155=\dfrac{2}{\cancel{5}}\cdot\dfrac{\overset{31}{\cancel{155}}}{1}=\dfrac{2\cdot31}{1\cdot1}=62$; A person weighing 155 lb has approximately 62 lb of muscle.

81. 12 divided by $\dfrac{1}{4}$ is $12 \div \dfrac{1}{4} = \dfrac{12}{1} \cdot \dfrac{4}{1} = 48$; She can fertilize 48 rose bushes.

83. $\dfrac{3}{8} + \dfrac{1}{3} + \dfrac{1}{4} = \dfrac{3}{8} \cdot \dfrac{3}{3} + \dfrac{1}{3} \cdot \dfrac{8}{8} + \dfrac{1}{4} \cdot \dfrac{6}{6} = \dfrac{9}{24} + \dfrac{8}{24} + \dfrac{6}{24} = \dfrac{9+8+6}{24} = \dfrac{23}{24}$;

The fraction of the barrel that would be filled is $\dfrac{23}{24}$.

85. The fraction of the circle that is not shaded is $1 - \dfrac{9}{40} = \dfrac{40}{40} - \dfrac{9}{40} = \dfrac{40-9}{40} = \dfrac{31}{40}$.

87. $19\dfrac{1}{4}$ divided by $1\dfrac{3}{4}$ is

$$\left(19\dfrac{1}{4}\right) \div \left(1\dfrac{3}{4}\right) = \left(19 + \dfrac{1}{4}\right) \div \left(1 + \dfrac{3}{4}\right) = \left(\dfrac{76}{4} + \dfrac{1}{4}\right) \div \left(\dfrac{4}{4} + \dfrac{3}{4}\right) = \left(\dfrac{77}{4}\right) \div \left(\dfrac{7}{4}\right) = \left(\dfrac{\overset{11}{\cancel{77}}}{\cancel{4}}\right)\left(\dfrac{\overset{1}{\cancel{4}}}{\underset{1}{\cancel{7}}}\right) = 11.$$

Thus, the welder can cut 11 pieces from the pipe.

Cumulative Review

1. The additive inverse of $-\dfrac{5}{8}$ is $\dfrac{5}{8}$.

2. The integers between -5 and 5 are $-4, -3, -2, -1, 0, 1, 2, 3, 4$.

3. The natural numbers between -5 and 5 are $1, 2, 3, 4$.

4. The inequality $-2 < x \le 3$ is equivalent to $(-2, 3]$.

5. The only natural number n such that $n < \sqrt{7} < n+1$ is 2.

Section 1.4: Addition and Subtraction of Real Numbers

Quick Review 1.4

1. When rounded to the nearest integer, 19.85 is approximately 20.

2. When rounded to the nearest integer, 6.23 is approximately 6.

3. $|-15.12| = 15.12 > 12.15$; Thus, -15.12 has the greater absolute value.

4. $|-5.73| = 5.73$; $|-7.35| = 7.35$; $7.35 > 5.73$; Thus, -7.35 has the greater absolute value.

5. $\dfrac{2}{5} + \dfrac{2}{7} = \dfrac{2}{5} \cdot \dfrac{7}{7} + \dfrac{2}{7} \cdot \dfrac{5}{5} = \dfrac{14}{35} + \dfrac{10}{35} = \dfrac{14+10}{35} = \dfrac{24}{35}$

Exercises 1.4

1.   **a.** $8 + (+5) = 13$

     b. $-8 + (+5) = -3$

     c. $8 + (-5) = 3$

     d. $-8 + (-5) = -13$

3.   **a.** $-45 + 45 = 0$

     b. $45 + (-45) = 0$

5. $-8 + (-7) + (-6) = -15 + (-6) = -21$

7. $-17 + [(-11) + 9] = -17 + (-2) = -19$

9. $-4.8 + 0 + 6.09 = 1.29$

11. $\dfrac{7}{11} + \left(-\dfrac{3}{11}\right) = \dfrac{7+(-3)}{11} = \dfrac{4}{11}$

13.
$$-\frac{1}{2}+\left(-\frac{1}{3}\right)+\left(-\frac{1}{4}\right)=-\frac{1}{2}\left(\frac{6}{6}\right)+\left(-\frac{1}{3}\right)\left(\frac{4}{4}\right)+\left(-\frac{1}{4}\right)\left(\frac{3}{3}\right)$$
$$=-\frac{6}{12}+\left(-\frac{4}{12}\right)+\left(-\frac{3}{12}\right)=\frac{(-6)+(-4)+(-3)}{12}=\frac{-13}{12}=-\frac{13}{12}$$

15.
$$-3\frac{2}{5}+7\frac{3}{4}=-\left(3+\frac{2}{5}\right)+7+\frac{3}{4}=-3-\frac{2}{5}+7+\frac{3}{4}=-3-\frac{2}{5}\cdot\frac{4}{4}+7+\frac{3}{4}\cdot\frac{5}{5}=-3-\frac{8}{20}+7+\frac{15}{20}=4+\frac{-8+15}{20}$$
$$=4+\frac{7}{20}=4\frac{7}{20}\quad\text{or}\quad\frac{87}{20}$$

17. $\left[11+(-17)\right]+\left[(-8)+(-4)\right]=\left[-6\right]+\left[-12\right]=-18$

19. $\left[-5+(-6)+(-7)\right]+\left[8+4+3\right]=(-18)+15=-3$

21. The property that says $(5+7)+9=(7+5)+9$ is the commutative property of addition since the order of the addends has changed.

23. To use the associative property of addition to rewrite $11+(12+13)$ we regroup the addends. Thus,
$$11+(12+13)=(11+12)+13.$$

25.   **a.** $7-13=7+(-13)=-6$
  b. $7-(-13)=7+13=20$
  c. $-7-13=-7+(-13)=-20$
  d. $-7-(-13)=-7+13=6$

27.   **a.** $9-9=0$
  b. $-9-(-9)=-9+9=0$

29. $-18-18=-18+(-18)=-36$

31. $-18-(-21)=-18+21=3$

33. $-\frac{2}{3}-\frac{5}{3}=-\frac{2}{3}+\left(-\frac{5}{3}\right)=\frac{-2+(-5)}{3}=-\frac{7}{3}$

35. $\frac{3}{5}-\left(-\frac{5}{6}\right)=\frac{3}{5}+\frac{5}{6}=\frac{3}{5}\left(\frac{6}{6}\right)+\frac{5}{6}\left(\frac{5}{5}\right)=\frac{18}{30}+\frac{25}{30}=\frac{18+25}{30}=\frac{43}{30}$

37. $-14.8-(-21.9)=7.1$

39.
$$-3\frac{2}{5}-7\frac{3}{4}=-\left(3+\frac{2}{5}\right)-\left(7+\frac{3}{4}\right)=-3-\frac{2}{5}\cdot\frac{4}{4}-7-\frac{3}{4}\cdot\frac{5}{5}=-3-\frac{8}{20}-7-\frac{15}{20}=-10+\frac{-8-15}{20}=-10+\frac{-23}{20}$$
$$=-\left(10+\frac{23}{20}\right)=-10\frac{23}{20}\quad\text{or}\quad-\frac{223}{20}$$

41.

Quarterly Profit/Loss Statement for Emmett's Barbeque				
	Quarter 1	Quarter 2	Quarter 3	Quarter 4
Springfield Store	+$7000	+$7000	−$7000	−$7000
Washington Store	+$5000	−$5000	+$5000	−$5000
Total	$7000+5000$ $=$$12000$	$7000+(-5000)$ $=$$2000$	$(-7000)+5000$ $=-$$2000$	$(-7000)+(-5000)$ $=-$$12000$

43. The temperature is $-12+21=9$ degrees Fahrenheit.

45. To find the change in temperature we take the difference of the most recent reading minus the early reading. Answer: $(-12)-(-5)=-12+5=-7$ (The temperature dropped 7 degrees Fahrenheit)

47. **a.** $8-2=8+(-2)=6$ (The temperature rose 6 degrees.)

    b. $2-8=2+(-8)=-6$ (The temperature dropped 6 degrees.)

    c. $8-(-2)=8+2=10$ (The temperature rose 10 degrees.)

    d. $-8-(-2)=-8+2=-6$ (The temperature dropped 6 degrees.)

49. The total sales of iPods for 2005 is $5.3+6.2+6.5+14.0=32$ million units.

51. The net income for the 3-year period is $1.4+(-12.6)+(-2.7)=-13.9$ billion dollars. Therefore the company lost approximately $14,000,000,000 over that period.

53. The total number of semester hours taken is $12+14+6=32$ hours.

55. To find the net yards for the three plays we evaluate the following $-7+10+2.5=5.5$. The net gain was 5.5 yards.

57. **a.** $0+0+0+0+4+0=4$

    b. $4\cdot3=12$

    c. $3+0+0+6+3=12$

    d. $12+12=24$

    e. The number that must be added to 24 to produce the next multiple of 10 is 6.

    f. Yes, the result from part **e.** matches the check digit of 6.

59. The sum of the lengths of all sides is $20+21+29=70$. The perimeter is 70 cm.

61.

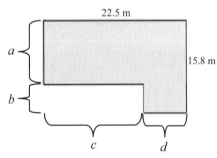

The perimeter of the room is
$$22.5+15.8+(a+b)+(c+d)=$$
$$=22.5+15.8+(15.8)+(22.5)=76.6\text{ meters.}$$

63. $-35.764+66.056\approx-36+66=30$; The most appropriate answer is **D.**

65. $\dfrac{1}{3}-0.3333=0.33333-0.3333=0.00003$; The most appropriate answer is **C.**

Problem	Sign of Sum	Sum
67. $-47.6+53.4$	+	5.8
69. $-\dfrac{5}{4}+\left(-\dfrac{3}{8}\right)$	−	$-\dfrac{5}{4}+\left(-\dfrac{3}{8}\right)=-\dfrac{5}{4}\cdot\dfrac{2}{2}-\dfrac{3}{8}=-\dfrac{10}{8}-\dfrac{3}{8}=\dfrac{-10-3}{8}=-\dfrac{13}{8}$

71. The subtraction fact $a-b=c$ can be written as the following addition fact: $b+c=a$.

73. The subtraction fact $-17-(-25)=8$ can be written as the following addition fact: $8+(-25)=-17$.

75.   **a.** $\underbrace{a}\text{ plus }\underbrace{b}\text{ equals }\underbrace{c}$
$$a+b \quad = \quad c$$

Answer: $a+b=c$

b. $\underbrace{a}\text{ minus }\underbrace{b}\text{ equals }\underbrace{c}$
$$a-b \quad = \quad c$$

Answer: $a-b=c$

77.   **a.** $\underbrace{\text{The change from }y\text{ to }z}\text{ equals }\underbrace{x}$
$$z-y \qquad = \quad x$$

Answer: $z-y=x$

b. $\underbrace{\text{The difference of }a\text{ from }b}\text{ equals }\underbrace{c}$
$$b-a \qquad = \quad c$$

Answer: $b-a=c$

79.   **a.** $\underbrace{m}\text{ is }\underbrace{11\text{ more than n}}$
$$m \quad = \quad n+11$$

Answer: $m=n+11$

b. $\underbrace{m}\text{ is more than }\underbrace{n}$
$$m \quad > \quad n$$

Answer: $m>n$

Cumulative Review

1. $|-17|+|17|=17+17=34$

2. $\sqrt{16}-\sqrt{25}=4-5=-1$

3.   The additive inverses of the first three natural numbers are -1, -2, and -3. The sum of these additive inverses is $(-1)+(-2)+(-3)=-6$.

4. $-\dfrac{35}{49}=-\dfrac{5\cdot\cancel{7}}{7\cdot\cancel{7}}=-\dfrac{5}{7}$

5. $(-2,3]$

Section 1.5: Multiplication and Division of Real Numbers

Quick Review 1.5

1. $\dfrac{8}{20}=\dfrac{2\cdot\cancel{4}}{\cancel{4}\cdot 5}=\dfrac{2}{5}$

2. $\dfrac{75}{60}=\dfrac{\cancel{15}\cdot 5}{\cancel{15}\cdot 4}=\dfrac{5}{4}$

3. $\dfrac{2}{5}\cdot\dfrac{2}{7}=\dfrac{2\cdot 2}{5\cdot 7}=\dfrac{4}{35}$

4. $\dfrac{2}{5}\div\dfrac{3}{4}=\dfrac{2}{5}\cdot\dfrac{4}{3}=\dfrac{2\cdot 4}{5\cdot 3}=\dfrac{8}{15}$

5. $\dfrac{6}{35}\div\dfrac{10}{21}=\dfrac{\overset{3}{\cancel{6}}}{\underset{5}{\cancel{35}}}\cdot\dfrac{\overset{3}{\cancel{21}}}{\underset{5}{\cancel{10}}}=\dfrac{3\cdot 3}{5\cdot 5}=\dfrac{9}{25}$

Exercises 1.5

1. $6\times 7=7\times 6$ is an example of the commutative property of multiplication since the order of the factors has changed.

3.   **a.** The proper choice is **B** since the order of the factors has changed.
  b. The proper choice is **A** since the factors has changed.

5.   **a.** The proper choice is **A** since the order of the addends has changed.

b. The proper choice is **B** since the order of the factors has changed.

7. **a.** $7(-11) = -77$

b. $-7(11) = -77$

c. $(-7)(-11) = 77$

d. $-(-7)(-11) = -(77) = -77$

9. **a.** $2(-3)(10) = (-6)(10) = -60$

b. $2(-3)(-10) = (-6)(-10) = 60$

c. $(-2)(-3)(-10) = (6)(-10) = -60$

d. $-(-2)(-3)(0) = 0$

11. **a.** $-0.1(1234) = -123.4$

b. $-100(1234) = -123400$

c. $-0.001(1234) = -1.234$

d. $-1000(1234) = -1234000$

13. **a.** $\dfrac{1}{2} \cdot \dfrac{3}{5} = \dfrac{(1)(3)}{(2)(5)} = \dfrac{3}{10}$

b. $-\dfrac{1}{2} \cdot \dfrac{3}{5} = -\dfrac{(1)(3)}{(2)(5)} = -\dfrac{3}{10}$

15. **a.** $\left(\dfrac{1}{5}\right)(5) = 1$

b. $\left(\dfrac{1}{5}\right)(-5) = -1$

17. **a.** $48 \div (-6) = -8$

b. $-48 \div (-6) = 8$

c. $-48 \div 6 = -8$

d. $0 \div 6 = 0$

19. **a.** $-48 \div \left(\dfrac{1}{2}\right) = -48 \cdot \left(\dfrac{2}{1}\right) = -96$

b. $-48 \div 2 = -24$

c. $-48 \div \left(-\dfrac{1}{2}\right) = -48 \cdot \left(-\dfrac{2}{1}\right) = 96$

d. $-48 \div (-2) = 24$

21. **a.** $123 \div (0.1) = 1,230$

b. $123 \div (-0.01) = -12,300$

c. $123 \div (-1000) = -0.123$

d. $-123 \div (-10) = 12.3$

23. **a.** $\dfrac{2}{3} \div \left(\dfrac{1}{6}\right) = \dfrac{2}{3} \cdot \dfrac{6}{1} = \dfrac{2 \cdot \overset{2}{\cancel{6}}}{\cancel{3} \cdot 1} = \dfrac{2 \cdot 2}{1 \cdot 1} = 4$

b. $-\dfrac{2}{3} \div \left(\dfrac{1}{6}\right) = -\dfrac{2}{3} \cdot \dfrac{6}{1} = -\dfrac{2 \cdot \overset{2}{\cancel{6}}}{\cancel{3} \cdot 1} = -\dfrac{2 \cdot 2}{1 \cdot 1} = -4$

c. $-\dfrac{2}{3} \div (-6) = \dfrac{2}{3} \cdot \dfrac{1}{6} = \dfrac{\overset{1}{\cancel{2}} \cdot 1}{3 \cdot \underset{3}{\cancel{6}}} = \dfrac{1 \cdot 1}{3 \cdot 3} = \dfrac{1}{9}$

d. $\dfrac{2}{3} \div (-1) = -\dfrac{2}{3}$

25. **a.** $0 \div (-7) = 0$

b. $-7 \div 0$ is undefined.

c. $7 \div 0$ is undefined.

d. $0 \div 0$ is undefined.

27. The ratio $8 : 20$ is equivalent to $\dfrac{8}{20} = \dfrac{2 \cdot \cancel{4}}{\cancel{4} \cdot 5} = \dfrac{2}{5}$ or $2 : 5$.

29. The ratio $24 : 36$ is equivalent to $\dfrac{24}{36} = \dfrac{2 \cdot \cancel{12}}{3 \cdot \cancel{12}} = \dfrac{2}{3}$ or $2 : 3$.

31. Thirteen of 52 cards in a deck of cards are diamonds. The ratio of diamonds to all cards in the deck is

$\dfrac{13}{52} = \dfrac{\overset{1}{\cancel{13}}}{4 \cdot \cancel{13}} = \dfrac{1}{4}$ or 1:4.

33.   A tree 24 meters tall casts an 8-meter shadow. The ratio of the height of the tree to the length of its shadow is $\dfrac{24}{8} = \dfrac{3 \cdot \cancel{8}}{\cancel{8}} = \dfrac{3}{1}$ or 3:1.

35.   A wildlife study involved banding ducks and then studying those birds when they were recaptured. Of the 85 captured ducks, 17 had already been banded.

   a. The ratio of banded ducks to the total captured is $\dfrac{17}{85} = \dfrac{\cancel{17}}{5 \cdot \cancel{17}} = \dfrac{1}{5}$ or 1:5.

   a. The ratio of banded ducks to those not banded is $\dfrac{17}{85-17} = \dfrac{17}{68} = \dfrac{\cancel{17}}{4 \cdot \cancel{17}} = \dfrac{1}{4}$ or 1:4.

37.   The radius of one pulley is 24 centimeters, and the radius of a second pulley is 15 centimeters. The ratio of the radius of the larger pulley to that of the smaller pulley is $\dfrac{24}{15} = \dfrac{\cancel{3} \cdot 8}{\cancel{3} \cdot 5} = \dfrac{8}{5}$ or 8:5.

39.   8% of \$180 is $(0.08)(\$180) = \$14.40$

41.   **a.** The price increase is $\$250 - \$200 = \$50$.

   b. The percent of increase is $\dfrac{50}{200} = 0.25$ or 25%.

43.

Game	Number of Tickets	Price Per Ticket	Cost Per Game
1	4	\$16	$4(16) = \$64$
2	2	\$16	$2(16) = \$32$
3	3	\$25	$3(25) = \$75$
4	6	\$25	$6(25) = \$150$

Total cost for all tickets:
$64 + 32 + 75 + 150 = \$321$

45.   A student scored 75, 88, 82, and 80 on exams. The student's average for these four exams is found by dividing the sum of these scores by four (the number of exams). Thus, the average is $\dfrac{75 + 88 + 94 + 78 + 91}{4} = \dfrac{426}{4} = 85.2$.

47.   The distance traveled is $D = R \cdot T = (420)(3) = 1260$ miles.

49.   The rate of travel is $R = \dfrac{D}{T} = \dfrac{870}{3} = 290$ miles per hour.

51.   The rate of work is $R = \dfrac{W}{T} = \dfrac{2400}{8} = 300$ light bulbs per hour.

53.   The area is $(2\,\text{cm})(8\,\text{cm}) = 16\,\text{cm}^2$.

55. $V = l \cdot w \cdot h = (14)(15)(16) = 3360$. The volume is 3,360 cubic inches.

57. $(-9.9)(15.12) \approx (-10)(15) = -150$; Thus, the most appropriate answer is **A**.

59. $45.1 \div (-0.11) \approx 45 \div \left(-\dfrac{1}{10}\right) = 45 \cdot (-10) = -450$; Thus, the most appropriate choice is **C**.

61. $x + x + x + x$ is equivalent to $4x$.

63. $5(-4)$ is equivalent to $(-4) + (-4) + (-4) + (-4) + (-4)$.

65. $\underbrace{\text{The product of } a \text{ and } b}_{a \cdot b} \underbrace{\text{equals}}_{=} \underbrace{\text{the product of } b \text{ and } a.}_{b \cdot a}$

Answer: $a \cdot b = b \cdot a$

67. $\underbrace{\text{The product of three and } x}_{3x} \underbrace{\text{is less than}}_{<} \underbrace{\text{nine.}}_{9}$

Answer: $3x < 9$

69. $\underbrace{\text{The quotient of } a \text{ and } b}_{\dfrac{a}{b}} \underbrace{\text{is greater than or equal to}}_{\geq} \underbrace{c.}_{c}$

Answer: $\dfrac{a}{b} \geq c$

71. If n represents an integer, then the expression that represents twice this integer is $2n$.

73.

x	y	$x + y$	xy
5	8	$5 + 8 = 13$	$(5)(8) = 40$
-5	8	$-5 + 8 = 3$	$(-5)(8) = -40$
5	-8	$5 + (-8) = -3$	$(5)(-8) = -40$
-5	-8	$-5 + (-8) = -13$	$(-5)(-8) = 40$

Cumulative Review

1. **a.** $x + y = y + x$

b. The commutative property of addition states that the order of the addends can be changed.

2. $4\dfrac{2}{5} + 3\dfrac{2}{7} = 4 + \dfrac{2}{5} \cdot \dfrac{7}{7} + 3 + \dfrac{2}{7} \cdot \dfrac{5}{5} = 4 + \dfrac{14}{35} + 3 + \dfrac{10}{35} = 7 + \dfrac{14 + 10}{35} = 7 + \dfrac{24}{35} = 7\dfrac{24}{35}$

3. The only number listed that is not a natural number is zero.

4. Choice **B** is unacceptable, since $3 > 2$.

5. **a.** The additive inverse of 4 is -4. **b.** The multiplicative inverse of 4 is $\dfrac{1}{4}$.

Section 1.6: Natural Number Exponents and Order of Operations

Quick Review 1.6

1. $3 \cdot 3 \cdot 3 \cdot 3 = 81$

2. $-1 \cdot 3 \cdot 3 \cdot 3 \cdot 3 = -81$

3. $(-4)(-4) = 16$

4. $-1 \cdot 4 \cdot 4 = -4$

5. $\sqrt{64} = 8$

Exercises 1.6

1.   a. $5 \cdot 5 \cdot 5 \cdot 5 = 5^4$

     b. $(-4)(-4)(-4) = (-4)^3$

     c. $y \cdot y \cdot y \cdot y \cdot y = y^5$

     d. $(3z)(3z)(3z)(3z)(3z)(3z) = (3z)^6$

3.   a. $4^3 = 4 \cdot 4 \cdot 4$

     b. $(-3)^4 = (-3)(-3)(-3)(-3)$

     c. $(-x)^3 = (-x)(-x)(-x)$

     d. $(2y)^3 = (2y)(2y)(2y)$

5.   a. In the exponential expression 3^4 the base is 3, the exponent is 4 and the expanded form is $3 \cdot 3 \cdot 3 \cdot 3$.

     b. In the exponential expression 4^3 the base is 4, the exponent is 3 and the expanded form is $4 \cdot 4 \cdot 4$.

7.   a. In the exponential expression $-3x^2$ the base is x, the exponent is 2 and the expanded form is $-3 \cdot x \cdot x$.

     b. In the exponential expression $(-3x)^2$ the base is $(-3x)$, the exponent is 2 and the expanded form is

       $(-3x)(-3x)$.

9.   a. $(-3)^2 = (-3)(-3) = 9$

     b. $-3^2 = -3 \cdot 3 = -9$

11.   a. $0^4 = 0 \cdot 0 \cdot 0 \cdot 0 = 0$

     b. $(-1)^4 = (-1)(-1)(-1)(-1) = 1$

13.   a. $(0.1)^3 = (0.1)(0.1)(0.1) = 0.001$

     b. $(-10)^3 = (-10)(-10)(-10) = -1000$

15.   a. $\left(\dfrac{1}{2}\right)^3 = \dfrac{1}{2} \cdot \dfrac{1}{2} \cdot \dfrac{1}{2} = \dfrac{1}{8}$

     b. $\left(-\dfrac{1}{2}\right)^3 = \left(-\dfrac{1}{2}\right)\left(-\dfrac{1}{2}\right)\left(-\dfrac{1}{2}\right) = -\dfrac{1}{8}$

17.   a. $5 + 2 \cdot 8 = 5 + 16 = 21$

     b. $(5 + 2) \cdot 8 = (7) \cdot 8 = 56$

19.   a. $17 - 3 \cdot 5 = 17 - 15 = 2$

     b. $(17 - 3)(5) = (14)(5) = 70$

21.   a. $(6 + 4)^2 = (10)^2 = 100$

     b. $6^2 + 4^2 = 36 + 16 = 52$

23.   a. $25 \div 5 \cdot 5 = (25 \div 5) \cdot 5 = (5) \cdot 5 = 25$

     b. $25 \div (5 \cdot 5) = 25 \div (25) = 1$

25.   a. $19 - 19 \cdot 2 = 19 - 38 = -19$

     b. $(19 - 19) \cdot 2 = (0) \cdot 2 = 0$

27.   a. $4 - 7^2 = 4 - 49 = -45$

     b. $(4 - 7)^2 = (-3)^2 = 9$

29.   a. $(3 + 4)^2 = (7)^2 = 49$

     b. $3^2 + 4^2 = 9 + 16 = 25$

31.   a. $3 \cdot 5 - 6 \cdot 7 = 15 - 42 = -27$

     b. $3 \cdot (5 - 6) \cdot 7 = 3 \cdot (-1) \cdot 7 = -21$

33.   a. $15 - 3^2 - 6 = 15 - 9 - 6 = 6 - 6 = 0$

     b. $15 - (3^2 - 6) = 15 - (9 - 6) = 15 - 3 = 12$

35.   a. $5^3 - 2^3 = 125 - 8 = 117$

     b. $(5 - 2)^3 = (3)^3 = 27$

37.   a. $36 - 24 \div 3 + 5 = 36 - (24 \div 3) + 5$

       $= 36 - 8 + 5$

       $= 28 + 5 = 33$

     b. $36 - (24 \div 3 + 5) = 36 - ((24 \div 3) + 5)$

       $= 36 - (8 + 5)$

       $= 36 - 13 = 23$

39.   a. $\dfrac{15 - 3(4)}{(15 - 3)(4)} = \dfrac{15 - 12}{(12)(4)} = \dfrac{3}{48} = \dfrac{\cancel{3}}{\cancel{3} \cdot 16} = \dfrac{1}{16}$

     b. $\dfrac{15 \div 3(4)}{(15 - 3)(4)} = \dfrac{(15 \div 3)(4)}{(12)(4)} = \dfrac{(5)\,\cancel{(4)}}{(12)\,\cancel{(4)}} = \dfrac{5}{12}$

41. **a.** $\sqrt{9}+\sqrt{16}=3+4=7$
    b. $\sqrt{9+16}=\sqrt{25}=5$

43. **a.** $\sqrt{169}-\sqrt{144}-\sqrt{16}=13-12-4=-3$
    b. $\sqrt{169-144-16}=\sqrt{169-144-16}=\sqrt{9}=3$

45. **a.** $|-23|+|17|=23+17=40$
    b. $|-23+17|=|-6|=6$

47. $12+2\big[8-3(7-5)\big]=12+2\big[8-3(2)\big]$
$$=12+2\big[8-6\big]$$
$$=12+2\big[2\big]$$
$$=12+4=16$$

49. $113+5\big[8+2\big(13-3^2\big)-7\big]$
$$=113+5\big[8+2(13-9)-7\big]$$
$$=113+5\big[8+2(4)-7\big]$$
$$=113+5\big[8+8-7\big]$$
$$=113+5\big[16-7\big]$$
$$=113+5\big[9\big]$$
$$=113+45=158$$

51. $\dfrac{5}{16}+\dfrac{1}{2}\cdot\dfrac{3}{8}=\dfrac{5}{16}+\dfrac{3}{16}$
$$=\dfrac{5+3}{16}=\dfrac{8}{16}$$
$$=\dfrac{\cancel{8}}{2\cdot\cancel{8}}=\dfrac{1}{2}$$

53. **a.** $7(x+5)=7(x)+7(5)=7x+35$
    b. $-7(x+5)=(-7)(x)+(-7)(5)=-7x-35$

55. **a.** $-1(2x-3y)=(-1)(2x)-(-1)(3y)=-2x+3y$
    b. $-(2x-3y)=(-1)(2x)-(-1)(3y)=-2x+3y$

57. **a.** $2x+5x=(2+5)x=7x$
    b. $2x-5x=(2-5)x=-3x$

59. **a.** $(2a+3b)+(4a-5b)=2a+3b+4a-5b=2a+4a+3b-5b=(2+4)a+(3-5)b=6a-2b$
    b. $(2a+3b)-(4a-5b)=2a+3b-4a+5b=2a-4a+3b+5b=(2-4)a+(3+5)b=-2a+8b$

61. **a.** $z^4=z\cdot z\cdot z\cdot z$ **b.** $z+z+z+z=4z$

63. **a.** The term **quantity** refers to the use of parenthesis to group the sum or difference that follows. In this way, the statement, "5 times the quantity x plus $3y$," refers to $5(x+3y)$.
    b. "$5x$ plus $3y$" refers to $5x+3y$.

65. **a.** The term **quantity** refers to the use of parenthesis to group the sum or difference that follows. In this way, the statement, "the quantity $2xy$ raised to the 5th power," refers to $(2xy)^5$.
    b. "$2x$ times y to the 5th power" refers to $2x\cdot y^5=2xy^5$.

67. **a.** The verbal expression equivalent to x^2+y^2 is "x squared plus y squared."
    b. The verbal expression equivalent to $(x+y)^2$ is "the quantity of x plus y squared."

69. $2\big[5-(8-3)\big]$ is equivalent to $2\big(5-(8-3)\big)$.

71. $\dfrac{5-7}{11-7}$ is equivalent to $(5-7)/(11-7)$.

73. $(x+5y\text{^}3)/(x\text{^}2+9y)$ is equivalent to $\dfrac{x+5y^3}{x^2+9y}$.

75. $(w+x)/(y-z)$ is equivalent to $\dfrac{w+x}{y-z}$.

77. $(6.07 + 3.98)^2 \approx (6 + 4)^2 = 10^2 = 100$; The most appropriate answer is **D**.

79. $7(x-1) - 4(2x+3) = 7(x) - 7(1) - 4(2x) - 4(3) = 7x - 7 - 8x - 12 = 7x - 8x - 7 - 12 = -x - 19$

81. $5(2x-1) + 3(x-3) = 5(2x) - 5(1) + 3(x) - 3(3) = 10x - 5 + 3x - 9 = 10x + 3x - 5 - 9 = 13x - 14$

Cumulative Review

1. $\dfrac{30}{75} = \dfrac{2 \cdot \cancel{15}}{5 \cdot \cancel{15}} = \dfrac{2}{5}$

2. $3\dfrac{2}{7} - 1\dfrac{2}{5} = \left(3 + \dfrac{2}{7}\right) - \left(1 + \dfrac{2}{5}\right) = \left(2 + \dfrac{7}{7} + \dfrac{2}{7}\right) - \left(1 + \dfrac{2}{5}\right) = \left(2 + \dfrac{7+2}{7}\right) - \left(1 + \dfrac{2}{5}\right)$

$= 2 + \dfrac{9}{7} - 1 - \dfrac{2}{5} = 1 + \dfrac{9}{7} \cdot \dfrac{5}{5} - \dfrac{2}{5} \cdot \dfrac{7}{7} = 1 + \dfrac{45}{35} - \dfrac{14}{35} = 1 + \dfrac{45-14}{35} = 1 + \dfrac{31}{35} = 1\dfrac{31}{35}$

3. Division and subtraction are not commutative. $\left(\dfrac{2}{3} \neq \dfrac{3}{2}\right)$, $(5 - 3 \neq 3 - 5)$

4.   **a.** $2^3 = 8$, $3^2 = 9$; Thus, $2^3 < 3^2$.   **b.** $2^5 = 32$, $5^2 = 25$; Thus, $2^5 > 5^2$.

5. $\dfrac{2}{3}$ is equal to $0.\overline{6}$. These expressions are only equal to each other if it is noted that the 6 is repeating. In this way, if it is not indicated that the 6 is repeating, then each of the following statement are accurate:

$\dfrac{2}{3} \neq 0.666$, $\dfrac{2}{3} > 0.666$, $\dfrac{2}{3} \geq 0.666$ $\dfrac{2}{3} \approx 0.666$

Section 1.7: Using Variables and Formulas

Quick Review 1.7

1. $23\% = 0.23$

2. $1.4\% = 0.014$

3. $0.04\% = 0.0004$

4. $0.125 = 12.5\%$

5. $1.4 = 140\%$

Exercises 1.7

1. $x^2 - 5x + 3 = (6)^2 - 5(6) + 3 = 36 - 30 + 3 = 9$

3. $x^2 - 5x + 3 = (-10)^2 - 5(-10) + 3$
$= 100 + 50 + 3 = 153$

5. $2x - 7y = 2(3) - 7(-5) = 6 + 35 = 41$

7. $x^2 - y^2 = (3)^2 - (-5)^2 = 9 - 25 = -16$

9. $w + x + y = (7) + (-3) + (-6) = -2$

11. $-w + (-x) + y = -(7) + (-(-3)) + (-6)$
$= -7 + 3 - 6 = -10$

13. $\sqrt{x} + \sqrt{y} = \sqrt{9} + \sqrt{16} = 3 + 4 = 7$

15. $\sqrt{25 - x} = \sqrt{25 - 9} = \sqrt{16} = 4$

17. $\dfrac{x + 3y}{x - 2y} = \dfrac{(-4) + 3(-6)}{(-4) - 2(-6)} = \dfrac{-4 - 18}{-4 + 12} = \dfrac{-22}{8}$

$= -\dfrac{\cancel{2} \cdot 11}{\cancel{2} \cdot 4} = -\dfrac{11}{4}$

19. $\dfrac{x^2 - xy - y^2}{x^2 + 3xy + 2y^2} = \dfrac{(-4)^2 - (-4)(-6) - (-6)^2}{(-4)^2 + 3(-4)(-6) + 2(-6)^2}$

$= \dfrac{16 - 24 - 36}{16 + 72 + 72} = \dfrac{-44}{160} = -\dfrac{\cancel{4} \cdot 11}{\cancel{4} \cdot 40} = -\dfrac{11}{40}$

21. $I = PRT = (4000)(0.07)(1) = 280$; The interest is \$280.

23. $I = PRT = (7000)(0.085)(1) = 595$; The interest is \$595.

25. $D = RT = (450)(4) = 1800$; The plane flew 1,800 miles.

27. $D = RT = (5)(4.4) = 22$; The ant crawled 22 meters.

29. $A = RB = (0.15)(500) = 75$; There is 75 milliliters of juice in the solution.

31. $A = RB = (0.225)(3) = 0.675$; There is 0.675 liters of hydrochloric acid in the solution.

33. $m = \dfrac{y_2 - y_1}{x_2 - x_1} = \dfrac{17-8}{6-3} = \dfrac{9}{3} = 3$

35. $m = \dfrac{y_2 - y_1}{x_2 - x_1} = \dfrac{-5-1}{4-(-3)} = \dfrac{-6}{7} = -\dfrac{6}{7}$

37.

n	$a_n = 2n - 4$
1	$2(1) - 4 = -2$
2	$2(2) - 4 = 0$
3	$2(3) - 4 = 2$

Answer: $-2, 0, 2$

39.

n	$a_n = 400n + 1000$
1	$400(1) + 1000 = 1400$
2	$400(2) + 1000 = 1800$
3	$400(3) + 1000 = 2200$

The total paid after each of the first 3 months is \$1,400, \$1,800, \$2,200.

41. To determine if $x = 4$ is a solution of $x + 7 = 12$ we replace x with 4 then simplify.

$$x + 7 = 12$$
$$(4) + 7 = 12$$
$$11 \neq 12$$

Thus, $x = 4$ is not a solution of $x + 7 = 12$.

To determine if $x = 5$ is a solution of $x + 7 = 12$ we replace x with 5 then simplify.

$$x + 7 = 12$$
$$(5) + 7 = 12$$
$$12 = 12$$

Thus, $x = 5$ is a solution of $x + 7 = 12$.

43. To determine if $x = 4$ is a solution of $3(x-1) = 2(x+1) - 1$ we replace x with 4 then simplify.

$$3(x-1) = 2(x+1) - 1$$
$$3(4-1) = 2(4+1) - 1$$
$$3(3) = 2(5) - 1$$
$$9 = 9$$

Thus, $x = 4$ is a solution of $3(x-1) = 2(x+1) - 1$.

To determine if $x = 5$ is a solution of $3(x-1) = 2(x+1) - 1$ we replace x with 5 then simplify.

$$3(x-1) = 2(x+1) - 1$$
$$3(5-1) = 2(5+1) - 1$$
$$3(4) = 2(6) - 1$$
$$12 \neq 11$$

Thus, $x = 5$ is not a solution of $3(x-1) = 2(x+1) - 1$.

45. To determine if $x = 4$ is a solution of $\dfrac{2x+1}{x-1} = 3$ we replace x with 4 then simplify.

$$\frac{2x+1}{x-1} = 3$$
$$\frac{2(4)+1}{(4)-1} = 3$$
$$\frac{9}{3} = 3$$
$$3 = 3$$

Thus, $x = 4$ is a solution of $\dfrac{2x+1}{x-1} = 3$.

To determine if $x = 5$ is a solution of $\dfrac{2x+1}{x-1} = 3$ we replace x with 5 then simplify.

$$\frac{2x+1}{x-1} = 3$$
$$\frac{2(5)+1}{(5)-1} = 3$$
$$\frac{11}{4} \neq 3$$

Thus, $x = 5$ is not a solution of $\dfrac{2x+1}{x-1} = 3$.

47. To determine if $x = -2$ is a solution of $2x+1 = 3(x+1)$ we replace x with -2 then simplify.

$$2x+1 = 3(x+1)$$
$$2(-2)+1 = 3(-2+1)$$
$$-4+1 = 3(-1)$$
$$-3 = -3$$

Thus, $x = -2$ is a solution of $2x+1 = 3(x+1)$.

To determine if $x = 8$ is a solution of $2x+1 = 3(x+1)$ we replace x with 8 then simplify.

$$2x+1 = 3(x+1)$$
$$2(8)+1 = 3(8+1)$$
$$16+1 = 3(9)$$
$$17 \neq 27$$

Thus, $x = 8$ is not a solution of $2x+1 = 3(x+1)$.

49. To determine if $x = -2$ is a solution of $(x+2)(x-8) = 0$ we replace x with -2 then simplify.

$$(x+2)(x-8) = 0$$
$$(-2+2)(-2-8) = 0$$
$$(0)(-10) = 0$$
$$0 = 0$$

Thus, $x = -2$ is a solution of $(x+2)(x-8) = 0$.

To determine if $x = 8$ is a solution of $(x+2)(x-8) = 0$ we replace x with 8 then simplify.

$$(x+2)(x-8) = 0$$
$$(8+2)(8-8) = 0$$
$$(10)(0) = 0$$
$$0 = 0$$

Thus, $x = 8$ is a solution of $(x+2)(x-8) = 0$.

51. To determine if $x = -2$ is a solution of $\dfrac{2x-7}{x-5} = 3$ we replace x with -2 then simplify.

$$\frac{2x-7}{x-5} = 3$$
$$\frac{2(-2)-7}{-2-5} = 3$$
$$\frac{-4-7}{-7} = 3$$
$$\frac{-11}{-7} \neq 3$$

Thus, $x = -2$ is not a solution of $\dfrac{2x-7}{x-5} = 3$.

To determine if $x = 8$ is a solution of $\dfrac{2x-7}{x-5} = 3$ we replace x with 8 then simplify.

$$\frac{2x-7}{x-5} = 3$$
$$\frac{2(8)-7}{8-5} = 3$$
$$\frac{16-7}{3} = 3$$
$$\frac{9}{3} = 3$$

Thus, $x = 8$ is a solution of $\dfrac{2x-7}{x-5} = 3$.

53. To determine if $x = 1/2$ is a solution of $4x+3 = 2(x+2)$ we replace x with $1/2$ then simplify.

$$4x+3 = 2(x+2)$$
$$4\left(\frac{1}{2}\right)+3 = 2\left(\frac{1}{2}+2\right)$$
$$2+3 = 1+4$$
$$5 = 5$$

Thus, $x = 1/2$ is a solution of $4x+3 = 2(x+2)$.

To determine if $x = 3/5$ is a solution of $4x+3 = 2(x+2)$ we replace x with $3/5$ then simplify.

$$4x+3 = 2(x+2)$$
$$4\left(\frac{3}{5}\right)+3 = 2\left(\frac{3}{5}+2\right)$$
$$\frac{12}{5}+3 = \frac{6}{5}+4$$
$$\frac{12}{5}+\frac{15}{5} = \frac{6}{5}+\frac{20}{5}$$
$$\frac{27}{5} \neq \frac{26}{5}$$

Thus, $x = 3/5$ is not a solution of $4x+3 = 2(x+2)$.

55. To determine if $x = 1/2$ is a solution of $10x^2 - 11x + 3 = 0$ we replace x with $1/2$ then simplify.

$$10x^2 - 11x + 3 = 0$$

$$10\left(\frac{1}{2}\right)^2 - 11\left(\frac{1}{2}\right) + 3 = 0$$

$$10\left(\frac{1}{4}\right) - 11\left(\frac{1}{2}\right) + 3 = 0$$

$$\frac{10}{4} - \frac{11}{2} + 3 = 0$$

$$\frac{10}{4} - \frac{22}{4} + \frac{12}{4} = 0$$

$$\frac{10 - 22 + 12}{4} = 0$$

$$\frac{0}{4} = 0$$

$$0 = 0$$

Thus, $x = 1/2$ is a solution of $10x^2 - 11x + 3 = 0$.

To determine if $x = 3/5$ is a solution of $10x^2 - 11x + 3 = 0$ we replace x with $3/5$ then simplify.

$$10x^2 - 11x + 3 = 0$$

$$10\left(\frac{3}{5}\right)^2 - 11\left(\frac{3}{5}\right) + 3 = 0$$

$$10\left(\frac{9}{25}\right) - 11\left(\frac{3}{5}\right) + 3 = 0$$

$$\frac{90}{25} - \frac{33}{5} + 3 = 0$$

$$\frac{90}{25} - \frac{165}{25} + \frac{75}{25} = 0$$

$$\frac{90 - 165 + 75}{25} = 0$$

$$\frac{0}{25} = 0$$

Thus, $x = 3/5$ is a solution of $10x^2 - 11x + 3 = 0$.

57. $C = 2\pi r = 2\pi(6.7) = 13.4\pi \text{ cm} \approx 42.1 \text{ cm}$

59. Approximation: $A = LW \approx (9)(6) = 54 \text{ cm}^2$

Exact Value: $A = LW = (8.8)(6.1) = 53.68 \text{ cm}^2$

61.
```
12.45→X
            12.45
(2.5X-3.3)(3.4X+
7.1)
        1375.38975
```

63.
```
12.45→X
            12.45
400X²-70X-30
          61099.5
```

65. **a.** The price decrease is $\$400 - \$300 = \$100$.

    b. The percent decrease is $\dfrac{100}{400} = 0.25 = 25\%$.

Cumulative Review

1.   **a.** $1.25 = \dfrac{125}{100} = \dfrac{5 \cdot 25}{4 \cdot 25} = \dfrac{5}{4}$ **b.** $1.25 = \dfrac{5}{4} = 1\dfrac{1}{4}$ **c.** $1.25 = 125\%$

2. $|-6.35| = 6.63 > 5.63$; Thus, $|-6.35|$ is farther to the right on a number line.

3. $\dfrac{12}{35} \div \dfrac{18}{14} = \dfrac{\overset{2}{\cancel{12}}}{\underset{5}{\cancel{35}}} \cdot \dfrac{\overset{2}{\cancel{14}}}{\underset{3}{\cancel{18}}} = \dfrac{2 \cdot 2}{5 \cdot 3} = \dfrac{4}{15}$

4. $5 - 4(7 - 2) = 5 - 4(5) = 5 - 20 = -15$

5. $\left(5^2 - 4^2\right)^2 = (25 - 16)^2 = (9)^2 = 81$

Section 1.8: Geometry Review

Quick Review 1.8

1. The irrational number π can be defined as the ratio of the circumference of a circle to its diameter.
2. In decimal form π is an infinite non-repeating decimal.
3. $A = LW = (15)(4) = 60$
4. $V = s^3 = 5^3 = 125$
5. $C = \pi d = \pi(11) = 11\pi \approx 34.56$

Exercises 1.8

1. A three-sided polygon is a triangle. The proper choice is **J**.
3. A five-sided polygon is a pentagon. The proper choice is **D**.
5. An eight-sided polygon is an octagon. The proper choice is **B**.
7. A quadrilateral with two opposite sides parallel is a trapezoid. The proper choice is **I**.
9. A parallelogram with four equal sides is a rhombus. The proper choice is **G**.
11. The perimeter is $5(9.4) = 47\,\text{cm}$.
13. The perimeter is $2(3.9) + 2(11.2) = 30.2\,\text{cm}$
15. **a.** The exact circumference of the circle is $2\pi(3.4) = 6.8\pi\,\text{cm}$.

    b. $6.8\pi \approx 21.4\,\text{cm}$
17. The area of the soccer field is $(75)(110) = 8,250\,\text{m}^2$.
19. The area of the base of the tank is $\pi(3)^2 = 9\pi \approx 28.3\,\text{m}^2$.
21. The area of the semicircle is $\dfrac{1}{2}\pi(6)^2 = 18\pi\,\text{m}^2$.
23. The volume of the pool is $(20)(40)(8) = 6,400\,\text{ft}^3$.
25. **a.** The volume of the tank is $V = \dfrac{4}{3}\pi(15)^3 = \dfrac{4}{3}\pi(3375) \approx 14,137\,\text{ft}^3$.

    b. If each cubic foot contains approximately 7.48 gallons of water, then the capacity of the tank is approximately $(7.48)(14,137) = 105,700$ gallons.
27. An angle that measures between $0°$ and $90°$ is an acute angle. The proper choice is **C**.
29. An angle that measures $180°$ is a straight angle. The proper choice is **I**.
31. Two angles are supplementary if the sum of their measure is $180°$. The proper choice is **B**.
33. The angles w and y are vertical angles. The proper choice is **J**.
35. The angles b and z are alternate exterior angles. The proper choice is **E**.
37. The angles a and b are supplementary. Thus, $m\angle b = 180° - 36° = 144°$.
39. The angles a and b are supplementary. Thus, $m\angle d = 180° - 36° = 144°$.
41. The angles a and y are alternate exterior angles. Thus, $m\angle y = m\angle a = 36°$.
43. The angles a and d are supplementary. Thus, $m\angle d = 180° - 40° = 140°$.
45. $m\angle B = 180° - m\angle A = 180° - 21° = 159°$
47. Area is measured in square units. The proper choice is **D**.
49. Volume is measured in cubic units. The proper choice is **C**.

Cumulative Review

1. **a.** This is an example of the distributive property of multiplication over addition. The proper choice is **D**.
   b. This is an example of the commutative property of multiplication (the order of the factors has changed). The proper choice is **C**.
   c. This is an example of the commutative property of addition (the order of the addends has changed). The proper choice is **B**.
   d. This is an example of the associative property of addition (the addends have been regrouped). The proper choice is **A**.

2. $\quad (x+y)^2 = (-3+8)^2 = (5)^2 = 25$

3. $\quad x^2 + y^2 = (-3)^2 + (8)^2 = 9 + 64 + 73$

4. $\quad xy^2 = (-3)(8)^2 = (-3)(64) = -192$

5. $\quad x^2 y^2 = (-3)^2 (8)^2 = (9)(64) = 576$

Review Exercises for Chapter 1

1.
 a. $-16 + 4 = -12$
 b. $-16 + (-4) = -20$
 c. $-16 - 4 = -16 + (-4) = -20$
 d. $-16 - (-4) = -16 + 4 = -12$

2.
 a. $-16(4) = -64$
 b. $-16(-4) = 64$
 c. $-16 \div 4 = -4$
 d. $-16 \div (-4) = 4$

3.
 a. $-7 + 0 = -7$
 b. $-7(0) = 0$
 c. $\dfrac{0}{-7} = 0$
 d. $\dfrac{-7}{0}$ is undefined

4.
 a. $24 + (-6) = 18$
 b. $24 - (-6) = 24 + 6 = 30$
 c. $24(-6) = -144$
 d. $24 \div (-6) = -4$

5.
 a. $9 + 0.01 = 9.01$
 b. $9 - 0.01 = 8.99$
 c. $9(0.01) = 0.09$
 d. $9 \div 0.01 = 900$

6.
 a. $-4.5 + 1000 = 995.5$
 b. $-4.5 - 1000 = -4.5 + (-1000) = -1004.5$
 c. $-4.5(1000) = -4500$
 d. $-4.5 \div 1000 = -0.0045$

7.
 a. $\dfrac{2}{3} + \dfrac{3}{4} = \dfrac{2}{3}\left(\dfrac{4}{4}\right) + \dfrac{3}{4}\left(\dfrac{3}{3}\right) = \dfrac{8}{12} + \dfrac{9}{12} = \dfrac{8+9}{12} = \dfrac{17}{12}$

 b. $\dfrac{2}{3} - \dfrac{3}{4} = \dfrac{2}{3}\left(\dfrac{4}{4}\right) + \left(-\dfrac{3}{4}\right)\left(\dfrac{3}{3}\right) = \dfrac{8}{12} + \left(-\dfrac{9}{12}\right) = \dfrac{8+(-9)}{12} = \dfrac{-1}{12} = -\dfrac{1}{12}$

 c. $\left(\dfrac{2}{3}\right)\left(\dfrac{3}{4}\right) = \dfrac{\cancel{2}^{\,1} \cdot \cancel{3}^{\,1}}{\cancel{3}_{\,1} \cdot \cancel{4}_{\,2}} = \dfrac{1}{2}$

 d. $\left(\dfrac{2}{3}\right) \div \left(\dfrac{3}{4}\right) = \left(\dfrac{2}{3}\right) \times \left(\dfrac{4}{3}\right) = \dfrac{2 \cdot 4}{3 \cdot 3} = \dfrac{8}{9}$

8.
 a. $-\dfrac{14}{15} + \dfrac{21}{25} = -\dfrac{14}{15}\left(\dfrac{5}{5}\right) + \dfrac{21}{25}\left(\dfrac{3}{3}\right) = -\dfrac{70}{75} + \dfrac{63}{75} = \dfrac{-70+63}{75} = \dfrac{-7}{75} = -\dfrac{7}{75}$

 b. $-\dfrac{14}{15} - \dfrac{21}{25} = -\dfrac{14}{15}\left(\dfrac{5}{5}\right) + \left(-\dfrac{21}{25}\right)\left(\dfrac{3}{3}\right) = -\dfrac{70}{75} + \left(-\dfrac{63}{75}\right) = \dfrac{-70+(-63)}{75} = \dfrac{-133}{75} = -\dfrac{133}{75}$

 c. $-\dfrac{14}{15} \cdot \dfrac{21}{25} = -\dfrac{14}{\cancel{15}_{\,5}} \cdot \dfrac{\cancel{21}^{\,7}}{25} = -\dfrac{14 \cdot 7}{5 \cdot 25} = -\dfrac{98}{125}$

 d. $-\dfrac{14}{15} \div \dfrac{21}{25} = -\dfrac{14}{15} \times \dfrac{25}{21} = -\dfrac{\cancel{14}^{\,2} \cdot \cancel{25}^{\,5}}{\cancel{15}_{\,3} \cdot \cancel{21}_{\,3}} = -\dfrac{10}{9}$

9.   **a.** $0^{37} = 0$

         b. $0^{38} = 0$

         c. $(-1)^{37} = -1$; Since the exponent is odd.

         d. $(-1)^{38} = 1$; Since the exponent is even.

10.   **a.** $-7 - 8 + 9 = -7 + (-8) + 9 = -15 + 9 = -6$

         b. $-7 - (8 + 9) = -7 - (17) = -7 + (-17) = -24$

11.   **a.** $-6 + 8 - 11 - 15 = (-6 + 8) + ((-11) + (-15))$

                 $= 2 + (-26) = -24$

         b. $(-6 + 8) - (11 - 15) = (2) - (11 + (-15))$

                 $= 2 - (-4) = 2 + 4 = 6$

12.   **a.** $(15 - 6)(9 - 11) = (15 + (-6))(9 + (-11))$

                 $= (9)(-2) = -18$

         b. $15 - 6(9 - 11) = 15 - 6(9 + (-11))$

                 $= 15 - 6(-2) = 15 + (-6(-2))$

                 $= 15 + 12 = 27$

13.   **a.** $-36 \div 4 \cdot 3 = (-36 \div 4) \cdot 3 = (-9) \cdot 3 = -27$

         b. $-36 \div (4 \cdot 3) = -36 \div (12) = -3$

14.   **a.** $(-10)^2 = (-10)(-10) = 100$

         b. $-10^2 = -(10)(10) = -100$

15.   **a.** $(3 + 4)^2 = (7)^2 = 49$

         b. $3^2 + 4^2 = 9 + 16 = 25$

16.   **a.** $5^2 = (5)(5) = 25$

         b. $2^5 = (2)(2)(2)(2)(2) = 32$

17.   **a.** $|3 - 11| = |3 + (-11)| = |-8| = 8$

         b. $|3| - |11| = 3 - 11 = 3 + (-11) = -8$

18.   **a.** $\sqrt{64} + \sqrt{36} = 8 + 6 = 14$

         b. $\sqrt{64 + 36} = \sqrt{100} = 10$

19.   **a.** $(-1)(-2)(-3)(-4) = ((-1)(-2))((-3)(-4)) = (2)(12) = 24$

         b. $(-1)(-2)(-3)(-4)(-5) = ((-1)(-2)(-3)(-4))(-5) = (24)(-5) = -120$

20. $-48 + 12 \div 6 + 3 - 1 = -48 + (12 \div 6) + 3 - 1 = -48 + (2) + 3 - 1 = -44$

21. $14 - 2[11 - 5(13 - 10)] = 14 - 2[11 - 5(3)] = 14 - 2(11 - 15) = 14 - 2(-4) = 14 + 8 = 22$

22. $19 + 3[(40 - 7) - (4 + 3^2)] = 19 + 3[(33) - (4 + 9)] = 19 + 3[(33) - (13)] = 19 + 3(20) = 19 + 60 = 79$

23. $\dfrac{-3 + 7}{8 - 10} = \dfrac{4}{8 + (-10)} = \dfrac{4}{-2} = -\dfrac{\overset{2}{\cancel{4}}}{\underset{1}{\cancel{2}}} = -2$

24. $\dfrac{14 - 7(-5)}{-3(9) - 2(-10)} = \dfrac{14 + 35}{-27 + 20} = \dfrac{49}{-7} = -\dfrac{\overset{7}{\cancel{49}}}{\underset{1}{\cancel{7}}} = -7$

25.   The fraction that represents the shaded part is $\dfrac{9}{15} = \dfrac{\overset{3}{\cancel{9}}}{\underset{5}{\cancel{15}}} = \dfrac{3}{5}$.

26.   The fraction that represents the shaded part is $\dfrac{5}{15} = \dfrac{\overset{1}{\cancel{5}}}{\underset{3}{\cancel{15}}} = \dfrac{1}{3}$.

27.   The equation is an example of the associative property of multiplication (the factors have been regrouped). The proper choice is **B**.

28.   The equation is an example of the associative property of addition (the addends have been regrouped). The proper choice is **A**.

29.   The equation is an example of the commutative property of multiplication (the factors have been rearranged). The proper choice is **D**.

30.   The equation is an example of the distributive property of multiplication over addition. The proper choice is **E**.

31. The equation is an example of the commutative property of addition (the addends have been rearranged). The proper choice is **C**.

32. The additive identity is 0. The proper choice is **B**.

33. The multiplicative identity is 1. The proper choice is **C**.

34. The multiplicative inverse of $0.2 = \dfrac{1}{5}$ is 5. The proper choice is **D**.

35. The additive inverse of 0.2 is -0.2. The proper choice is **A**.

36. $\sqrt{4}$ is an example of a natural number. The proper choice is **C**.

37. 0 is an integer that is not a natural number. The proper choice is **A**.

38. $\sqrt{5}$ is an example of an irrational number. The proper choice is **D**.

39. 3/4 is an example of a rational number that is not an integer. The proper choice is **B**.

40. **a.** $\left\{\sqrt{9}, 15\right\}$ **b.** $\left\{0, \sqrt{9}, 15\right\}$ **c.** $\left\{-7, 0, \sqrt{9}, 15\right\}$ **d.** $\left\{-8.1, -7, 0, \sqrt{9}, \dfrac{15}{2}, 15\right\}$ **e.** $\left\{\pi\right\}$

41. $\underbrace{\text{The opposite of } x}_{-x} \underbrace{\text{is}}_{=} \underbrace{\text{eleven.}}_{11}$

    Answer: $-x = 11$

42. $\underbrace{\text{The absolute value of } x}_{|x|} \underbrace{\text{is less than or equal to}}_{\leq} \underbrace{\text{seven.}}_{7}$

    Answer: $|x| \leq 7$

43. $\underbrace{\text{The square root of twenty-six}}_{\sqrt{26}} \underbrace{\text{is greater than}}_{>} \underbrace{\text{five.}}_{5}$

    Answer: $\sqrt{26} > 5$

44. $\underbrace{\text{The sum of } x \text{ and five}}_{x + 5} \underbrace{\text{is equal to}}_{=} \underbrace{\text{four.}}_{4}$

    Answer: $x + 5 = 4$

45. $\underbrace{\text{The product of negative three and } y}_{-3y} \underbrace{\text{is}}_{=} \underbrace{\text{negative one.}}_{-1}$

    Answer: $-3y = -1$

46. $\underbrace{\text{The quotient of } x \text{ and three}}_{\frac{x}{3}} \underbrace{\text{is}}_{=} \underbrace{12.}_{12}$

    Answer: $\dfrac{x}{3} = 12$

47. $\underbrace{\text{The ratio of } x \text{ to } y}_{\frac{x}{y}} \underbrace{\text{equals}}_{=} \underbrace{\text{three fourths.}}_{\frac{3}{4}}$

    Answer: $\dfrac{x}{y} = \dfrac{3}{4}$

48. $\underbrace{\text{Five times the quantity three } x \text{ minus four}}_{5(3x-4)} \underbrace{\text{equals}}_{=} \underbrace{\text{thirteen.}}_{13}$

Answer: $5(3x-4)=13$

49. The change from x_1 to x_2 is $x_2 - x_1$.

50. $x^2 - y^2$ is the difference of x squared minus y squared.

51. $(x-y)^2$ is the square of the difference of x minus y.

52. $7(x-5)$ is seven times the quantity of x minus five.

53. $7x-5$ is seven x minus five.

54.
  a. $4\cdot 3 = 3+3+3+3$; The proper choice is **G**.
  b. $4^3 = 4\cdot 4\cdot 4$; The proper choice is **F**.
  c. $3^4 = 3\cdot 3\cdot 3\cdot 3$; The proper choice is **J**.
  d. $-3^4 = -3\cdot 3\cdot 3\cdot 3$; The proper choice is **I**.
  e. $(-3)^4 = (-3)(-3)(-3)(-3)$; The proper choice is **H**.
  f. $15\div 5 = 3$ is equivalent to $3\cdot 5 = 15$; The proper choice is **E**.
  g. $7-4=3$ is equivalent to $3+4=7$; The proper choice is **D**.
  h. $\dfrac{3}{4} = 0.75$; The proper choice is **B**.
  i. $\dfrac{1}{3} = 0.333\cdots$; The proper choice is **A**.
  j. $\dfrac{1}{2} = 0.5 = 50\%$; The proper choice is **C**.

55. $\dfrac{17+7^2}{20-9} = (17+7\text{^}2)/(20-9)$

56. $13-4\big[(2-8)-3(7-2)\big] = 13-4\big((2-8)-3(7-2)\big)$

Inequality Symbols	Verbally	Graphically	Interval Notation
57. $x<3$	x is less than 3.		$(-\infty,\,3)$
58. $x\geq -1$	x is greater than or equal to -1.		$[-1,\,\infty)$
59. $-4\leq x<10$	x is greater than or equal to -4 and less than 10.		$[4,\,10)$
60. $-2<x\leq 3$	x is greater than -2 and less than or equal to 3.		$(-2,\,3]$

Problem	Sign of the result
61. $-312+(-221)$	$-$
62. $-41-(-72)$	$+$
63. $(53)(-37)(-21)$	$+$
64. $(-123.3)(0)(-893.8)+1$	Neither; 0
65. $(-3)^2 \cdot 5 \cdot (-7)$	$-$
66. $\sqrt{196} - \sqrt{361}$	$-$
67. $(-7.2)^{12}$	$+$

68. $-5.96+2.01 \approx -6+2 = -4$; The proper choice is **C**.

69. $-5.96-2.01 \approx -6-2 = -8$; The proper choice is **B**.

70. $-5.96(2.01) \approx -6(2) = -12$; The proper choice is **A**.

71. $-5.96 \div 2.01 \approx -6 \div 2 = -3$; The proper choice is **D**.

72. $\dfrac{1}{2}-\dfrac{1}{8}$ is between 0 and 1; The proper choice is **C**.

73. $0.6666 - \dfrac{2}{3} = 0.6666 - 0.66666\overline{6} = -0.00006\overline{6}$; The proper choice is **B**.

74. $2x-5y+7x = 2x+7x-5y = (2+7)x-5y = 9x-5y$

75. $5a-(3a-b) = 5a-3a+b = (5-3)a+b = 2a+b$

76. $5(3a+2)-4(2a-3) = 15a+10-8a+12 = 15a-8a+10+12 = (15-8)a+22 = 7a+22$

77. $8(2x-1)-3(3x-5) = 16x-8-9x+15 = 16x-9x-8+15 = (16-9)x+7 = 7x+7$

78. $x^2 - 2xy - y^2 = (-8)^2 - 2(-8)(7) - (7)^2 = 64+112-49 = 127$

79. $\dfrac{(x-y)(x+y)}{2x-3y} = \dfrac{(-8-7)(-8+7)}{2(-8)-3(7)} = \dfrac{(-15)(-1)}{-16-21} = \dfrac{15}{-37} = -\dfrac{15}{37}$

80. $\dfrac{y_2 - y_1}{x_2 - x_1} = \dfrac{2-(-4)}{2-5} = \dfrac{2+4}{2-5} = \dfrac{6}{-3} = -2$

81.
n	$a_n = 10n-3$
1	$10(1)-3 = 7$
2	$10(2)-3 = 17$
3	$10(3)-3 = 27$

Answer: $7, 17, 27$

82. To determine if $x = -7$ is a solution of $5x - 17 = x - 1$ we replace x with -7 then simplify.

$$5x - 17 = x - 1$$
$$5(-7) - 17 = (-7) - 1$$
$$-35 - 17 = -8$$
$$-52 \neq -8$$

Thus, $x = -7$ is not a solution of $5x - 17 = x - 1$.

To determine if $x = 4$ is a solution of $5x - 17 = x - 1$ we replace x with 4 then simplify.

$$5x - 17 = x - 1$$
$$5(4) - 17 = (4) - 1$$
$$20 - 17 = 3$$
$$3 = 3$$

Thus, $x = 4$ is a solution of $5x - 17 = x - 1$.

83. To determine if $x = -7$ is a solution of $4x + 29 = x + 8$ we replace x with -7 then simplify.

$$4x + 29 = x + 8$$
$$4(-7) + 29 = (-7) + 8$$
$$-28 + 29 = 1$$
$$1 = 1$$

Thus, $x = -7$ is a solution of $4x + 29 = x + 8$.

To determine if $x = 4$ is a solution of $4x + 29 = x + 8$ we replace x with 4 then simplify.

$$4x + 29 = x + 8$$
$$4(4) + 29 = (4) + 8$$
$$16 + 29 = 12$$
$$45 \neq 12$$

Thus, $x = 4$ is not a solution of $4x + 29 = x + 8$.

84. To determine if $x = -7$ is a solution of $(x + 7)(x - 4) = 0$ we replace x with -7 then simplify.

$$(x + 7)(x - 4) = 0$$
$$(-7 + 7)(-7 - 4) = 0$$
$$(0)(-11) = 0$$
$$0 = 0$$

Thus, $x = -7$ is a solution of $(x + 7)(x - 4) = 0$.

To determine if $x = 4$ is a solution of $(x + 7)(x - 4) = 0$ we replace x with 4 then simplify.

$$(x + 7)(x - 4) = 0$$
$$(4 + 7)(4 - 4) = 0$$
$$(11)(0) = 0$$
$$0 = 0$$

Thus, $x = 4$ is a solution of $(x + 7)(x - 4) = 0$.

85. To determine if $x = -7$ is a solution of $\dfrac{4x - 1}{2x - 3} = 3$ we replace x with -7 then simplify.

$$\frac{4x - 1}{2x - 3} = 3$$
$$\frac{4(-7) - 1}{2(-7) - 3} = 3$$
$$\frac{-28 - 1}{-14 - 3} = 3$$
$$\frac{-29}{-11} \neq 3$$

Thus, $x = -7$ is not a solution of $\dfrac{4x - 1}{2x - 3} = 3$.

To determine if $x = 4$ is a solution of $\dfrac{4x - 1}{2x - 3} = 3$ we replace x with 4 then simplify.

$$\frac{4x - 1}{2x - 3} = 3$$
$$\frac{4(4) - 1}{2(4) - 3} = 3$$
$$\frac{16 - 1}{8 - 3} = 3$$
$$\frac{15}{5} = 3$$
$$3 = 3$$

Thus, $x = 4$ is a solution of $\dfrac{4x - 1}{2x - 3} = 3$.

86. The total cost of the three items is $\$45 + \$35 + \$58 = \$138$.

87. The change in temperature from $-6°$ to $5°$ is $5° - (-6°) = 5° + 6° = 11°$.

88. 40% of $\$65$ is $(0.40)(\$65) = \$26$.

89. **a.** The price increase is $\$630 - \$600 = \$30$.

b. The percent increase is $\dfrac{30}{600} = 0.05 = 5\%$.

90. The ratio of the radius of the larger pulley to that of the smaller pulley is $\dfrac{32}{20} = \dfrac{\cancel{4} \cdot 8}{\cancel{4} \cdot 5} = \dfrac{8}{5}$ or $8:5$.

91. **a.** $(400)(0.10) = 40$ liters of active ingredient **b.** $(600)(0.05) = 30$ gallons of active ingredient.

92. **a.** $R = \dfrac{W}{T} = \dfrac{1600}{8} = 200$ golf balls per hour **b.** $R = \dfrac{W}{T} = \dfrac{1}{4}$ of one brewery vat per hour

93. **a.** Perimeter: $P = 2l + 2w = 2(18) + 2(9) = 36 + 18 = 54$ m

b. Area: $A = l \cdot w = (18)(9) = 162$ m^2

94. **a.** Volume: $V = l \cdot w \cdot h = 6 \cdot 5 \cdot 4.5 = 135$ ft^3

b. Surface Area: $S = 2lw + 2hl + 2hw = 2(6)(5) + 2(4.5)(6) + 2(4.5)(5) = 159$ ft^2

95. **a.** Circumference: $C = 2\pi r = 2\pi(95) = 190\pi$ cm

b. Area: $A = \pi r^2 = \pi(95)^2 = 9025\pi$ cm^2

96. The other angle must measure $90° - 63° = 27°$.

Mastery Test for Chapter 1

1. **a.-c.** Answers will vary. **d.** odd

2. **a.** The additive inverse of -2 is 2.
b. The additive inverse of 1.5 is -1.5.

c. The additive inverse of $\dfrac{1}{5}$ is $-\dfrac{1}{5}$.

d. The additive inverse of 0 is 0.

3. **a.** $|23| = 23$

b. $|-23| = 23$

c. $|23 - 23| = |0| = 0$

d. $|23| + |-23| = 23 + 23 = 46$

4. **a.** $(-2, 3]$

b. $[-1, \infty)$

c. $(-\infty, 4)$

d. $[5, 9)$

5. **a.** $\sqrt{26} \approx \sqrt{25} = 5$; $\sqrt{26} \approx 5.10$

b. $\sqrt{99} \approx \sqrt{100} = 10$; $\sqrt{99} \approx 9.95$

c. $\sqrt{4+4} = \sqrt{8} \approx \sqrt{9} = 3$; $\sqrt{4+4} = \sqrt{8} \approx 2.83$

d. $\sqrt{4} + \sqrt{4} = 2 + 2 = 4$; $\sqrt{4} + \sqrt{4} = 2 + 2 = 4$

6. **a.** The number -5 is an integer that is not a whole number. Answer: **B**.

b. The number $-\dfrac{2}{3}$ is a rational number that is not an integer. Answer: **C**.

c. The number 0 is a whole number that is not a natural number. Answer: **A**.

d. The number $\sqrt{9} = 3$ is a natural number. Answer: **E**.

e. The number $\sqrt{11}$ is a positive number that is not rational. Answer: **D**.

7.   **a.** The fraction that represents the shaded part is $\dfrac{6}{18}=\dfrac{\cancel{6}\cdot 1}{\cancel{6}\cdot 3}=\dfrac{1}{3}$.

       b. The fraction that represents the shaded part is $\dfrac{10}{16}=\dfrac{\cancel{2}\cdot 5}{\cancel{2}\cdot 8}=\dfrac{5}{8}$.

8.   **a.** $\dfrac{66}{99}=\dfrac{2\cdot\cancel{33}}{3\cdot\cancel{33}}=\dfrac{2}{3}$ **b.** $\dfrac{75}{120}=\dfrac{5\cdot\cancel{15}}{8\cdot\cancel{15}}=\dfrac{5}{8}$

9.   **a.** $\dfrac{1}{3}\cdot\dfrac{1}{5}=\dfrac{1\cdot 1}{3\cdot 5}=\dfrac{1}{15}$

       b. $\dfrac{3}{7}\cdot\dfrac{7}{9}=\dfrac{\overset{1}{\cancel{3}}}{\cancel{7}}\cdot\dfrac{\overset{1}{\cancel{7}}}{\underset{3}{\cancel{9}}}=\dfrac{1\cdot 1}{1\cdot 3}=\dfrac{1}{3}$

       c. $\dfrac{2}{5}\div\dfrac{14}{15}=\dfrac{2}{5}\cdot\dfrac{15}{14}=\dfrac{\cancel{2}}{\underset{1}{\cancel{5}}}\cdot\dfrac{\overset{3}{\cancel{15}}}{\underset{7}{\cancel{14}}}=\dfrac{1\cdot 3}{1\cdot 7}=\dfrac{3}{7}$

       d. $\dfrac{12}{35}\div\dfrac{14}{45}=\dfrac{\overset{6}{\cancel{12}}}{\underset{7}{\cancel{35}}}\cdot\dfrac{\overset{9}{\cancel{45}}}{\underset{7}{\cancel{14}}}=\dfrac{6\cdot 9}{7\cdot 7}=\dfrac{54}{49}$

10.   **a.** $\dfrac{3}{8}+\dfrac{1}{8}=\dfrac{3+1}{8}=\dfrac{\overset{1}{\cancel{4}}}{\underset{2}{\cancel{8}}}=\dfrac{1}{2}$

       b. $\dfrac{5}{6}-\dfrac{1}{6}=\dfrac{5-1}{6}=\dfrac{\overset{2}{\cancel{4}}}{\underset{3}{\cancel{6}}}=\dfrac{2}{3}$

       c. $\dfrac{1}{42}+\dfrac{13}{42}=\dfrac{1+13}{42}=\dfrac{\overset{1}{\cancel{14}}}{\underset{3}{\cancel{42}}}=\dfrac{1}{3}$

       d. $\dfrac{13}{42}-\dfrac{1}{42}=\dfrac{13-1}{42}=\dfrac{\overset{2}{\cancel{12}}}{\underset{7}{\cancel{42}}}=\dfrac{2}{7}$

11.   **a.** $\dfrac{2}{5}+\dfrac{3}{8}=\dfrac{2}{5}\cdot\dfrac{8}{8}+\dfrac{3}{8}\cdot\dfrac{5}{5}=\dfrac{16}{40}+\dfrac{15}{40}=\dfrac{16+15}{40}=\dfrac{31}{40}$

       b. $\dfrac{5}{6}-\dfrac{3}{5}=\dfrac{5}{6}\cdot\dfrac{5}{5}-\dfrac{3}{5}\cdot\dfrac{6}{6}=\dfrac{25}{30}-\dfrac{18}{30}=\dfrac{25-18}{30}=\dfrac{7}{30}$

       c. $\dfrac{2}{7}+\dfrac{5}{6}=\dfrac{2}{7}\cdot\dfrac{6}{6}+\dfrac{5}{6}\cdot\dfrac{7}{7}=\dfrac{12}{42}+\dfrac{35}{42}=\dfrac{12+35}{42}=\dfrac{47}{42}$

       d. $\dfrac{7}{15}-\dfrac{3}{35}=\dfrac{7}{15}\cdot\dfrac{7}{7}-\dfrac{3}{35}\cdot\dfrac{3}{3}=\dfrac{49}{105}-\dfrac{9}{105}=\dfrac{49-9}{105}=\dfrac{\overset{8}{\cancel{40}}}{\underset{21}{\cancel{105}}}=\dfrac{8}{21}$

12.   **a.** $11\dfrac{1}{8}+5\dfrac{3}{8}=16\dfrac{1+3}{8}=16\dfrac{\overset{1}{\cancel{4}}}{\underset{2}{\cancel{8}}}=16\dfrac{1}{2}$

       b. $11\dfrac{1}{8}-5\dfrac{3}{8}=11+\dfrac{1}{8}-\left(5+\dfrac{3}{8}\right)=10+\dfrac{9}{8}-5-\dfrac{3}{8}=5+\dfrac{\overset{3}{\cancel{6}}}{\underset{4}{\cancel{8}}}=5\dfrac{3}{4}$

       c. $\left(2\dfrac{1}{7}\right)\left(4\dfrac{2}{3}\right)=\dfrac{\overset{5}{\cancel{15}}}{\underset{1}{\cancel{7}}}\cdot\dfrac{\overset{2}{\cancel{14}}}{\underset{1}{\cancel{3}}}=\dfrac{5\cdot 2}{1\cdot 1}=10$

       d. $\left(2\dfrac{1}{7}\right)\div\left(1\dfrac{2}{3}\right)=\dfrac{15}{7}\div\dfrac{5}{3}=\dfrac{\overset{3}{\cancel{15}}}{7}\cdot\dfrac{3}{\underset{1}{\cancel{5}}}=\dfrac{9}{7}=1\dfrac{2}{7}$

13. **a.** $17 + (-11) = 17 - 11 = 6$

  b. $-17 + (-11) = -17 - 11 = -28$

  c. $-\dfrac{3}{8} + \dfrac{1}{8} = \dfrac{-3}{8} + \dfrac{1}{8} = \dfrac{-3+1}{8} = \dfrac{-\overset{1}{\cancel{2}}}{\underset{4}{\cancel{8}}} = \dfrac{-1}{4} = -\dfrac{1}{4}$

  d. $57.3 + (-57.3) = 57.3 - 57.3 = 0$

14. **a.** The property that says that $5(6+7) = 5(7+6)$ is the Commutative Property of Addition.

  b. The property that says that $5 + (6+7) = (5+6) + 7$ is the Associative Property of Addition.

  c. $(x+y) + 5 = x + (y+5)$

  d. $5(x+y) = 5(y+x)$.

15. **a.** $15 - 8 = 15 + (-8) = 7$

  b. $-15 - 8 = -15 + (-8) = -23$

  c. $\dfrac{1}{2} - \left(-\dfrac{1}{3}\right) = \dfrac{1}{2} + \dfrac{1}{3} = \dfrac{1}{2} \cdot \dfrac{3}{3} + \dfrac{1}{3} \cdot \dfrac{2}{2} = \dfrac{3}{6} + \dfrac{2}{6} = \dfrac{3+2}{6} = \dfrac{5}{6}$

  d. $-7.35 - (-3.75) = -7.35 + 3.75 = -3.6$

16. **a.** The property that says that $5 \cdot (6+7) = (6+7) \cdot 5$ is the Commutative Property of Multiplication.

  b. The property that says that $5(6 \cdot 7) = (5 \cdot 6) \cdot 7$ is the Associative Property of Multiplication.

  c. $(5x)(y) = (5)(xy) = 5(xy)$.

  d. $x(a+b) = (a+b)x$.

17. **a.** $5(-6) = -30$

  b. $-5(-6) = 30$

  c. $-5(0) = 0$

  d. $\left(-\dfrac{6}{35}\right)\left(-\dfrac{14}{15}\right) = \dfrac{\overset{2}{\cancel{6}}}{\underset{5}{\cancel{35}}} \cdot \dfrac{\overset{2}{\cancel{14}}}{\underset{5}{\cancel{15}}} = \dfrac{2 \cdot 2}{5 \cdot 5} = \dfrac{4}{25}$

18. **a.** $-12 \div 4 = -3$

  b. $-12 \div (-4) = 3$

  c. $0 \div 4 = 0$

  d. $-4578.91 \div (-0.001) = -4,578,910$

19. **a.** $16:12$ is equivalent to $\dfrac{\overset{4}{\cancel{16}}}{\underset{3}{\cancel{12}}} = \dfrac{4}{3}$ or $4:3$

  b. $\dfrac{4}{52} = \dfrac{\overset{1}{\cancel{4}}}{\underset{13}{\cancel{52}}} = \dfrac{1}{13}$ or $1:13$

  c. $\dfrac{52}{24} = \dfrac{\overset{13}{\cancel{52}}}{\underset{6}{\cancel{24}}} = \dfrac{13}{6}$ or $13:6$

  d. $\dfrac{21}{105} = \dfrac{21}{5 \cdot 21} = \dfrac{1}{5}$ or $1:5$

20.
  a. $2^5 = 2 \cdot 2 \cdot 2 \cdot 2 \cdot 2 = 32$

  b. $(-5)^2 = (-5)(-5) = 25$

  c. $-5^2 = -25$

  d. $(-1)^{219} = -1$

21.
  a. $15 - 2(8-5) = 15 - 2(3) = 15 - 6 = 9$

  b. $4 \cdot 7 - 2 \cdot 3 + 5 = 28 - 6 + 5 = 27$

  c. $15 - 63 \div 3^2 + 11 = 15 - 63 \div 9 + 11$
$$= 15 - 7 + 11 = 19$$

  d. $\dfrac{14 - 3 \cdot 6}{(14-3) \cdot 6} = \dfrac{14-18}{(11) \cdot 6} = \dfrac{-4}{(11) \cdot 6}$
$$= -\dfrac{4}{66} = -\dfrac{2}{33}$$

  e. $(3+5)^2 = (8)^2 = 64$

  f. $3^2 + 5^2 = 9 + 25 = 34$

  g. $-8 - 3\big[5 - 4(6-9)\big] = -8 - 3\big[5 - 4(-3)\big]$
$$= -8 - 3(5 + 12) = -8 - 3(17)$$
$$= -8 - 51 = -59$$

  h. $\sqrt{25-16} - \left(\sqrt{25} - \sqrt{16}\right) = \sqrt{9} - (5-4)$
$$= 3 - (1) = 2$$

22.
  a. $3(5x+9) = 3 \cdot 5x + 3 \cdot 9 = 15x + 27$

  b. $-4(8x-5) = (-4)8x - (-4)5 = -32x + 20$

  c. $\dfrac{1}{2}(4x - 6y) = \dfrac{1}{2} \cdot 4x - \dfrac{1}{2} \cdot 6y = 2x - 3y$

  d. $-(11x - 13y) = (-1)(11x - 13y) = -11x + 13y$

23.
  a. $20x - 11x + 3x = (20 - 11 + 3)x = 12x$

  b. $20x - 11(x+3) = 20x - 11x - 33 = (20-11)x - 33 = 9x - 33$

  c. $(-5x - 9) - (4x - 3) = -5x - 9 - 4x + 3 = -5x - 4x - 9 + 3 = (-5-4)x - 6 = -9x - 6$

  d. $3(x-1) - 2(x+2) = 3x - 3 - 2x - 4 = 3x - 2x - 3 - 4 = (3-2)x - 7 = x - 7$

24.
  a. $x + y + z = (-1) + (-2) + (-3) = -6$

  b. $-x + yz = -(-1) + (-2)(-3) = 1 + 6 = 7$

  c. $-2x - 3(2y - z - 1) = -2(-1) - 3\big[2(-2) - (-3) - 1\big] = 2 - 3(-4 + 3 - 1) = 2 - 3(-2) = 2 + 6 = 8$

  d. $\dfrac{2x - y}{2x + z} = \dfrac{2(-1) - (-2)}{2(-1) + (-3)} = \dfrac{-2 + 2}{-2 - 3} = \dfrac{0}{-5} = 0$

25.
  a. $A = l \cdot w = (12)(5) = 60 \text{ m}^2$

  b. $P = 2l + 2w = 2(12) + 2(5) = 24 + 10 = 34 \text{ m}$

  c. $A = RB = (0.015)(500) = 7.5 \text{ gallons}$

  d. $A = P(1+r)^2 = 1200(1+0.06)^2 = \$1,348.32$

26.
$$m = \dfrac{y_2 - y_1}{x_2 - x_1} = \dfrac{-7 - 7}{3 - (-1)} = \dfrac{-\overset{7}{\cancel{14}}}{\underset{2}{\cancel{4}}} = -\dfrac{7}{2}$$

27.

n	$a_n = -2n + 11$
1	$-2(1) + 11 = 9$
2	$-2(2) + 11 = 7$
3	$-2(3) + 11 = 5$

Answer: 9, 7, 5

28. **a.** To determine if $x = -5$ is a solution of $3x + 2 = 2x - 3$ we replace x with -5 then simplify. $3x + 2 = 2x - 3$

$$3(-5) + 2 = 2(-5) - 3$$
$$-15 + 2 = -10 - 3$$
$$-13 = -13$$

Thus, $x = -5$ is a solution of $3x + 2 = 2x - 3$.

b. To determine if $x = -5$ is a solution of $2(x + 1) = x + 4$ we replace x with -5 then simplify. $2(x + 1) = x + 4$

$$2((-5) + 1) = (-5) + 4$$
$$2(-4) = -1$$
$$-8 \ne -1$$

Thus, $x = -5$ is not a solution of $2(x + 1) = x + 4$.

c. To determine if $x = -5$ is a solution of $(x - 3)(x + 5) = 0$ we replace x with -5 then simplify.

$$(x - 3)(x + 5) = 0$$
$$((-5) - 3)((-5) + 5) = 0$$
$$(-8)(0) = 0$$
$$0 = 0$$

Thus, $x = -5$ is a solution of $(x - 3)(x + 5) = 0$.

d. To determine if $x = -5$ is a solution of $\dfrac{2x + 13}{1 - x} = \dfrac{1}{2}$ we replace x with -5 then simplify.

$$\frac{2x + 13}{1 - x} = \frac{1}{2}$$
$$\frac{2(-5) + 13}{1 - (-5)} = \frac{1}{2}$$
$$\frac{-10 + 13}{1 + 5} = \frac{1}{2}$$
$$\frac{3}{6} = \frac{1}{2}$$

Thus, $x = -5$ is a solution of $\dfrac{2x + 13}{1 - x} = \dfrac{1}{2}$.

29. **a.** A polygon with four sides is called a quadrilateral.
b. A parallelogram with adjacent sides perpendicular is called a rectangle.
c. A polygon with six sides is called a hexagon.
d. A regular pentagon has five sides that are all equal in length.

30. **a.** The perimeter is $4(5.25) = 21$ cm .

b. The circumference is $C = 2\pi r = 2\pi(9) = 18\pi$ cm ≈ 56.5 cm .

31. **a.** The area is $A = \dfrac{1}{2} bh = \dfrac{1}{2}(7)(4) = 14\,\text{cm}^2$.

b. The area is $A = \pi r^2 = \pi(9)^2 = 81\pi\,\text{cm}^2 \approx 254.5\,\text{cm}^2$.

32. The volume of the freezer is $(25)(20)(15) = 7500\,\text{in}^3$.

33. **a.** A $90°$ angle is called a right angle.
b. A straight angle measures $180°$.
c. If the sum of the measures of two angles is $90°$, then these angles are complementary.
d. Adjacent angles are distinct angles that share a common vertex and one common side.
e. If two parallel lines are cut by a transversal, then two angles that lie on opposite sides of the transversal and outside the parallel lines are called alternate external angles.

Section 2.1: The Rectangular Coordinate System

Quick Review 2.1

1.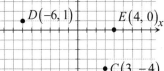

2.

3.

4.

5. $(2, \infty)$

Exercises 2.1

1. A: $(-1, 5)$ is in quadrant II

   B: $(5, -2)$ is in quadrant IV

   C: $(3, 2)$ is in quadrant I

   D: $(-4, -1)$ is in quadrant III

3.

5. **a.** $(-1.3, 3.7)$ is in quadrant II

   b. $(-5.8, -9.3)$ is in quadrant III

   c. $(6.7, -2.1)$ is in quadrant IV

   d. $(0.4, 0.1)$ is in quadrant I

7. **a.** $(0, 8)$ is on the y-axis.

   b. $(-8, 0)$ is on the x-axis.

   c. $\left(-\sqrt{3}, 0\right)$ is on the x-axis.

   d. $\left(0, \sqrt{2}\right)$ is on the y-axis.

9.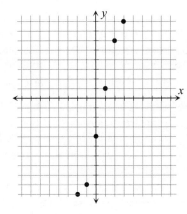

11.

n	a_n
1	−4
2	−3
3	−2
4	−1
5	0
6	1
7	2

13. **a.** $a_1 = 5$

   $a_2 = 13$

   $a_3 = 19$

   $a_4 = 8$

   $a_5 = 6$

 b.

x	y
1	5
2	13
3	19
4	8
5	6

15. **a.** $(1, 8), (2, 5), (3, 2), (4, -1), (5, -4)$ **b.**

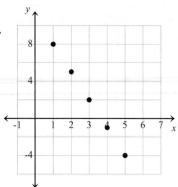

17. **a.** $(1, -2), (2, 4), (3, 1), (4, 1), (5, 3)$ **b.**

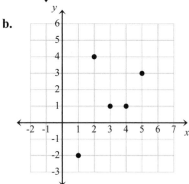

19. The points given in the graph can be written as the set of ordered pairs: $\{(1, 4),(2, 1),(3, -2),(4, -5),(5, -8)\}$. The x-value is the term number and the y-value is the sequence value. Therefore, the first five terms of the sequence are: $4, 1, -2, -5, -8$.

21. Numerical difference between terms
$$1-(-3) = 4$$
$$5-1 = 4$$
$$9-5 = 4$$
The sequence is arithmetic since the difference between terms is constant. The graph forms a linear pattern.

23. Numerical difference between terms
$$30-40 = -10$$
$$20-30 = -10$$
$$10-20 = -10$$
$$0-10 = -10$$
The sequence is arithmetic since the difference between terms is constant. The graph forms a linear pattern.

25. Numerical difference between terms
$$5-3 = 2$$
$$8-5 = 3$$
$$12-8 = 4$$
$$17-12 = 5$$
This is not an arithmetic sequence because the change from term to term is not constant. The graph does not form a linear pattern.

27. The points form a linear pattern with the points rising 2 units from one term to the next. Therefore, the sequence is arithmetic with a common difference of 2.

29. The sequence is not arithmetic because the change from term to term is not constant. The points do not form a linear pattern. The height change between consecutive terms is not constant.

31. **a.** 30 ft
b. 15 ft
c. After 2 months
d. 10 ft

33. **a.** The description best describes graph **D**.
b. The description best describes graph **A**.
c. The description best describes graph **B**.
d. The description best describes graph **C**.

35. If the point (x, y) is in quadrant I, then each of x and y are positive. Therefore, $x > 0$ and $y > 0$.

37. If the point (x, y) is in quadrant III, then each of x and y are negative. Therefore, $x < 0$ and $y < 0$.

39. If $xy > 0$ then x and y must have the same sign. If both variables are positive then the point (x, y) is in quadrant I. If both variables are negative then the point (x, y) is in quadrant III.

41. An arithmetic sequence that has a positive common difference will have terms that increase in value from one term to the next. Such a sequence will correspond to a graph that increases from left to right. Thus, the graph will go up as the points move to the right.

43. The even integers: 0, 2, 4, 6, 8,... is an arithmetic sequence. The common difference between consecutive terms is 2. (Assuming these integers are listed in increasing order.)

45.   **a.** $a_1 = 450(1) + 2400 = 2850$; The total amount paid after one month is $2,850.

   b. $a_{18} = 450(18) + 2400 = 10500$; The total amount paid after eighteen months is $10,500

   c. $a_{24} = 450(24) + 2400 = 13200$; The total amount paid after twenty four months is $13,200.

47. The area of the rectangle is found by multiplying the length times the width ($A = lw$). The length is 5 units. The width is 4 units. Thus, the Area is $A = (5)(4) = 20$ square units. The perimeter of the rectangle is found by taking the sum of twice the length and twice the width ($P = 2l + 2w$). Thus the perimeter is $P = 2(5) + 2(4) = 18$ units.

49. 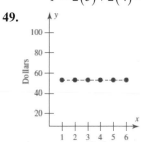   **51.** 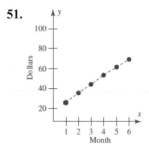   **53.** 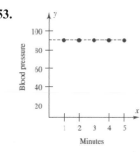   **55.**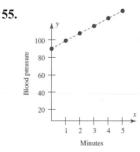

Cumulative Review

1. $5x + 7x = (5 + 7)x = 12x$

2. $12v - 7v + 2v = (12 - 7 + 2)v = 7v$

3. $5a + 3 - 2(2a - 4) = 5a + 3 - 4a + 8 = 5a - 4a + 3 + 8 = (5 - 4)a + 11 = (1)a + 11 = a + 11$

4. The angle A is supplementary to $68°$. Thus, $m\angle A = 180° - 68° = 112°$.

5. The angle B is congruent to the given angle. Thus, $m\angle B = 68°$.

Section 2.2: Function Notation and Linear Functions

Quick Review 2.2

1. $-\dfrac{1}{2}(-6) + 3 = 3 + 3 = 6$

2. $-\dfrac{1}{2}(4) + 3 = -2 + 3 = 1$

3. $4 + 2(3x - 8) = 4 + 2[3(-2) - 8] = 4 + 2(-6 - 8) = 4 + 2(-14) = 4 + (-28) = 4 - 28 = -24$

4. $(4x - 7) - 2(3x - 8) = [4(-2) - 7] - 2[3(-2) - 8] = (-8 - 7) - 2(-6 - 8) = (-15) - 2(-14) = -15 + 28 = 13$

5. $\dfrac{x + 4}{2} = (x + 4)/2$

Exercises 2.2

1. $f(0) = 3(0) + 7 = 7$ **3.** $f(-1) = 3(-1) + 7 = 4$

5. $f(2) = 5(2) - 6 = 4$ **7.** $f(-10) = 5(-10) - 6 = -56$

9. $\quad f(-4) = -6(-4) + 4 = 28$

11. $\quad f(-4) = -6\left(\dfrac{1}{6}\right) + 4 = 3$

13. $\quad f\left(\dfrac{1}{4}\right) = -8\left(\dfrac{1}{4}\right) + 5 = 3$

15. $\quad f\left(-\dfrac{1}{8}\right) = -8\left(-\dfrac{1}{8}\right) + 5 = 6$

17.

x	$f(x)$
-2	$-2(-2) + 4 = 8$
-1	$-2(-1) + 4 = 6$
0	$-2(0) + 4 = 4$
1	$-2(1) + 4 = 2$
2	$-2(2) + 4 = 0$

19.

x	$f(x)$
0	$\dfrac{(0)+3}{2} = \dfrac{3}{2} = 1.5$
1	$\dfrac{(1)+3}{2} = \dfrac{4}{2} = 2$
2	$\dfrac{(2)+3}{2} = \dfrac{5}{2} = 2.5$
3	$\dfrac{(3)+3}{2} = \dfrac{6}{2} = 3$

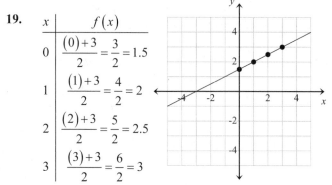

21.

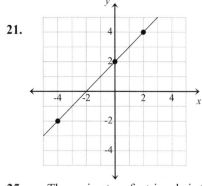

23. If a board has an initial length of 18 ft and three pieces each of length x ft are cut off, then the length of the remaining piece is given by the function $f(x) = 18 - 3x$.

25. The perimeter of a triangle is the sum of the lengths of the sides. Thus, the perimeter is given by the function $f(x) = x + x + 17 = 2x + 17$.

27. **a.** The perimeter of a rectangle is found by adding twice the length and twice the width. Thus, the perimeter is given by the function $f(x) = 2x + 2(32) = 2x + 64$.

    b. The area of a rectangle is found by multiplying the length and the width. Thus, the area is given by the function $f(x) = 32x$.

29. **a.** To find the speed of the boat traveling downstream we add the rate of the boat, x mi/hr, to the rate of the current, 5mi/hr. Thus, $f(x) = x + 5$.

    b. To find the speed of the boat traveling upstream we subtract the speed of the current, 5 mi/hr, from the speed of the boat, x mi/hr. Thus, $f(x) = x - 5$.

    c. Using $D = r \cdot t$ with $t = 2$ and the answer in part **a.** for the rate we obtain the following function for the distance traveled $f(x) = (x + 5) \cdot 2 = 2x + 10$.

31. Use the y-values from following points in the graph to complete the table:
$(-2, -3), (-1, -1), (0, 1),$
$(1, 3), (2, 5)$

x	$f(x)$
-2	-3
-1	-1
0	1
1	3
2	5

33. Use the x-values from following points in the graph to complete the table:
$(-2, -5), (0, -3),$
$(3, 0), (5, 2)$

x	$f(x)$
-2	-5
0	-3
3	0
5	2

35.   **a.** From the table we can see that $f(x) = -8$ when $x = 1$, thus $f(1) = -8$.

       b. From the table we can see that $f(x) = 2$ when $x = 6$, thus $f(6) = 2$.

       c. From the table we can see that $x = 8$ when $f(x) = 6$.

       d. From the table we can see that $x = 0$ when $f(x) = -10$.

37.   **a.** From the graph we can see that $y = 3$ when $x = -2$, thus $f(-2) = 3$.

       b. From the graph we can see that $y = 1$ when $x = 2$, thus $f(2) = 1$.

       c. From the table we can see that $x = 0$ when $y = f(x) = 2$.

       d. From the table we can see that $x = 4$ when $y = f(x) = 0$.

39.   **a.**   **b.**

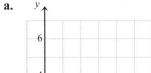

       c. The line in part **b.** passes through the points found in part **a.**

41.   Let $y_1 = -\dfrac{x}{2}$ in your calculator, use the following settings to generate the given table and sketch the given graph.

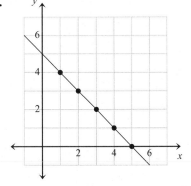

$$[-10, 10, 1] \text{ by } [-10, 10, 1]$$

Note: These window settings are established by using ZStandard under the Zoom Menu.

43.   Let $y_1 = 2.7x + 4.5$ in your calculator, use the following settings to generate the given tables.

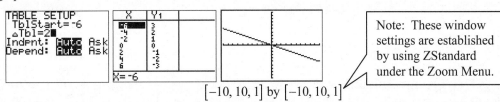

45.   Let $y_1 = 2.7x + 4.5$ in your calculator, use the following settings to generate the given tables.

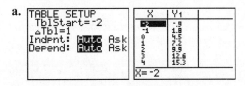

47.   **a.** If the entrée is priced at x dollars and the discount is 20%, then the function for the amount of the discount is $f(x) = 0.20x$.

b. $f(25) = 0.20(25) = 5$; There is a discount of $5 discount on an entrée priced at $25.

49.   **a.** To find the new price on an item that is reduced by 15% we multiply the original price by 0.85 since the new price will be 85% of the original price. If the original price is x dollars, then the function $f(x) = 0.85x$ can be used to determine the new price.

b.

x	$f(x) = 0.85x$
20	$0.85(20) = \$17.00$
44	$0.85(44) = \$37.50$
60	$0.85(60) = \$51.00$
68	$0.85(68) = \$57.80$
90	$0.85(90) = \$76.50$

51.   **a.** The total cost of producing x units per day is the sum of the variable cost and the overhead cost. The variable cost is the product of x, the number of units, and $15, the cost per unit. The overhead is $500. Thus, the total cost is given by the function $f(x) = 15x + 500$.

b.

x	0	100	200	300	400	500
$f(x) = 15x + 500$	500	2000	3500	5000	6500	8000

c. $f(250) = 15(250) + 500 = 4250$. The cost of producing 250 units per day is $4,250.

53.   **a.** $f(x) = 180 - 2x$

b.

x	$f(x) = 180 - 2x$
10	$180 - 2(10) = 160$
20	$180 - 2(20) = 140$
30	$180 - 2(30) = 120$
40	$180 - 2(40) = 100$
50	$180 - 2(50) = 80$
60	$180 - 2(60) = 60$
70	$180 - 2(70) = 40$

c. $f(40) = 100$; When $x = 40°$ the remaining angle is $100°$.

d. From the table we can see that when $f(x) = 40$, $x = 70$; When $x = 70°$ the remaining angle is $40°$.

e. 100 is not a practical input for x. The sum of all angles must not exceed $180°$ $(x < 90°)$

Cumulative Review

1. $I = PRT = (5000)(0.07)(1) = \$350$

2. $D = RT = (60)(3.5) = 210 \text{ miles}$

3. $2^4 - 4^2 = 16 - 16 = 0$

4. $2^5 - 5^2 = 32 - 25 = 7$

5. $(2 - 5)^2 = (-3)^2 = 9$

Section 2.3: Graphs of Linear Equations in Two Variables

Quick Review 2.3

1. Point **A** is $(-4, -4)$.

2. Point **B** is $(0, -2)$.

3. Point **C** is $(4, 0)$.

4. From the table we can see that $f(17) = 2$.

5. From the table we can see that $x = 5$ when $f(x) = 11$

Exercises 2.3

1. To determine if $(1, 5)$ is a solution of $y = 6x - 1$ we replace x with 1 and y with 5 and then simplify.

$$y = 6x - 1$$
$$5 = 6(1) - 1$$
$$5 = 6 - 1$$
$$5 = 5 \text{ checks.}$$

Thus, $(1, 5)$ is a solution of $y = 6x - 1$.

3. To determine if $\left(\dfrac{1}{6}, 6\right)$ is a solution of $y = 6x - 1$ we replace x with $\dfrac{1}{6}$ and y with 6 and then simplify.

$$y = 6x - 1$$
$$6 = 6\left(\dfrac{1}{6}\right) - 1$$
$$6 = 1 - 1$$
$$6 \neq 0$$

Thus, $\left(\dfrac{1}{6}, 6\right)$ is a not solution of $y = 6x - 1$.

5. To determine if $(2, 11)$ is a solution of $y = 6x - 1$ we replace x with 2 and y with 11 and then simplify.

$$y = 6x - 1$$
$$11 = 6(2) - 1$$
$$11 = 12 - 1$$
$$11 = 11 \text{ checks.}$$

Thus, $(2, 11)$ is a solution of $y = 6x - 1$.

7. To determine if $\left(\dfrac{1}{6}, 0\right)$ is a solution of $y = 6x - 1$ we replace x with $\dfrac{1}{6}$ and y with 0 and then simplify.

$$y = 6x - 1$$
$$0 = 6\left(\dfrac{1}{6}\right) - 1$$
$$0 = 1 - 1$$
$$0 = 0 \text{ checks.}$$

Thus, $\left(\dfrac{1}{6}, 0\right)$ is a solution of $y = 6x - 1$.

9. To determine if $(0, 6)$ is a solution of $y = -\dfrac{x}{2} + 5$ we replace x with 0 and y with 6 and then simplify.

$$y = -\dfrac{x}{2} + 5$$
$$6 = -\dfrac{0}{2} + 5$$
$$6 = 0 + 5$$
$$6 \neq 5$$

Thus, $(0, 6)$ is not on the graph.

11. To determine if $(-6, -8)$ is a solution of $y = -\dfrac{x}{2} + 5$ we replace x with -6 and y with -8 and then simplify.

$$y = -\dfrac{x}{2} + 5$$
$$-8 = -\dfrac{-6}{2} + 5$$
$$-8 = 3 + 5$$
$$-8 \neq 8$$

Thus, $(-6, -8)$ is not on the graph.

13. To determine if $(0, 5)$ is a solution of

$y = -\dfrac{x}{2} + 5$ we replace x with 0 and y with 5

and then simplify.

$$y = -\frac{x}{2} + 5$$
$$5 = -\frac{0}{2} + 5$$
$$5 = 0 + 5$$
$$5 = 5$$

Thus, $(0, 5)$ is on the graph

15. To determine if $(12, -1)$ is a solution of

$y = -\dfrac{x}{2} + 5$ we replace x with 12 and y with

-1 and then simplify.

$$y = -\frac{x}{2} + 5$$
$$-1 = -\frac{12}{2} + 5$$
$$-1 = -6 + 5$$
$$-1 = -1$$

Thus, $(12, -1)$ is a on the graph.

17. Check the point $C(-4, 3)$:

$$y = \frac{x}{4} + 1$$
$$3 = \frac{-4}{4} + 1$$
$$3 = -1 + 1$$
$$3 \neq 0$$

Thus, the point $C(-4, 3)$ is not a solution.

Check the point $D(4, 2)$:

$$y = \frac{x}{4} + 1$$
$$2 = \frac{4}{4} + 1$$
$$2 = 1 + 1$$
$$2 = 2$$

Thus, the point $D(4, 2)$ is a solution.

Check the point $A(0, 1)$:

$$y = \frac{x}{4} + 1$$
$$1 = \frac{0}{4} + 1$$
$$1 = 0 + 1$$
$$1 = 1$$

Thus, the point $A(0, 1)$ is a solution.

Check the point $B(5, 0)$:

$$y = \frac{x}{4} + 1$$
$$0 = \frac{-5}{4} + 1$$
$$0 \neq -\frac{1}{4}$$

Thus, the point $B(5, 0)$ is not a solution.

19. Only the point $C(-4, 3)$ has a y coordinate that is equal to 3. Thus, $C(-4, 3)$ is the only solution to the equation $y = 3$.

21. The x-intercept is the point on the graph that has a y coordinate of 0. Thus, the x-intercept is $(3, 0)$.

The y-intercept is the point on the graph that has a x coordinate of 0. Thus, the y-intercept is $(0, 3)$.

23. The x-intercept is $(80, 0)$. When 80 units are produced the profit is \$0.

The y-intercept is $(0, -500)$. When 0 units are produced there is a loss of \$500. \$500 is the overhead cost.

25. The x-intercept is the point on the graph that has a y coordinate of 0. Thus, the x-intercept is $(-3, 0)$.

The y-intercept is the point on the graph that has a x coordinate of 0. Thus, the y-intercept is $(0, -3)$.

27.   The point of intersection is $(-2, 3)$.   **29.**   The point of intersection is $(-1, -2)$.

31.   The point of intersection is $(3, 2)$.

33. 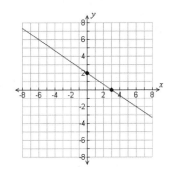   **35.** 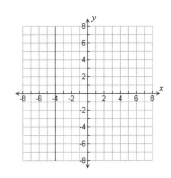   **37.**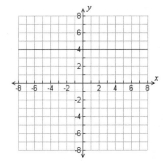

39.   **_y_-intercept**
To find the y-intercept, substitute 0 for x.
$$y = x + 2$$
$$y = 0 + 2$$
$$y = 2$$
$(0, 2)$ is the y-intercept.

Second Point
To find a second point, find y when x is any other value. For example, substitute 3 for x.
$$y = x + 2$$
$$y = 3 + 2$$
$$y = 5$$
$(3, 5)$ is another point on the line.

Third Point
To find a third point, find y when x is any other value. For example, substitute -2 for x.
$$y = x + 2$$
$$y = -2 + 2$$
$$y = 0$$
$(-2, 0)$ is another point on the line.

Graph

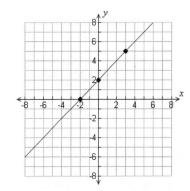

41.   **_y_-intercept**
To find the y-intercept, substitute 0 for x.
$$y = \frac{x}{3} - 1$$
$$y = \frac{0}{3} - 1$$
$$y = -1$$
$(0, -1)$ is the y-intercept

Second Point
To find a second point, find y when x is any other value. For example, substitute 3 for x.
$$y = \frac{x}{3} - 1$$
$$y = \frac{3}{3} - 1$$
$$y = 0$$
$(3, 0)$ is another point on the line.

Third Point

To find a third point, find y when x is any other value. For example, substitute -6 for x.

$$y = \frac{x}{3} - 1$$

$$y = \frac{-6}{3} - 1$$

$$y = -2 - 1$$

$$y = -3$$

$(-6, -3)$ is another point on the line.

Graph

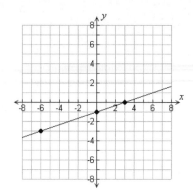

43. **_y-intercept_**

To find the y-intercept, substitute 0 for x.

$$f(x) = -x + 4$$

$$f(0) = -0 + 4$$

$$f(0) = 4$$

$(0, 4)$ is the y-intercept

Second Point

To find a second point, find y when x is any other value. For example, substitute 2 for x.

$$f(x) = -x + 4$$

$$f(2) = -2 + 4$$

$$f(2) = 2$$

$(2, 2)$ is another point on the line.

Third Point

To find a third point, find y when x is any other value. For example, substitute -3 for x.

$$f(x) = -x + 4$$

$$f(-3) = -(-3) + 4$$

$$f(-3) = 7$$

$(-3, 7)$ is another point on the line.

Graph

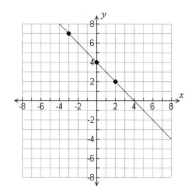

45. **_y-intercept_**

To find the y-intercept, substitute 0 for x.

$$f(x) = 2x + 3$$

$$f(0) = 2(0) + 3$$

$$f(0) = 3$$

$(0, 3)$ is the y-intercept

Second Point

To find a second point, find y when x is any other value. For example, substitute 2 for x.

$$f(x) = 2x + 3$$

$$f(2) = 2(2) + 3$$

$$f(2) = 4 + 3$$

$$f(2) = 7$$

$(2, 7)$ is another point on the line.

Third Point

To find a third point, find y when x is any other value. For example, substitute -1 for x.

$$f(x) = 2x + 3$$
$$f(-1) = 2(-1) + 3$$
$$f(-1) = -2 + 3$$
$$f(-1) = 1$$

$(-1, 1)$ is another point on the line.

Graph

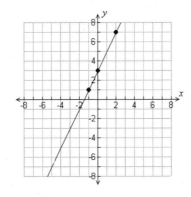

47.

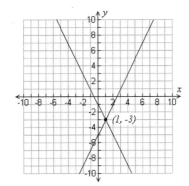

To check the solution, replace x with 1 and y with -3 in each equation.

$$y = 2x - 5$$
$$(-3) = 2(1) - 5$$
$$-3 = 2 - 5$$
$$-3 = -3 \text{ checks.}$$

$$y = -2x - 1$$
$$(-3) = -2(1) - 1$$
$$-3 = -2 - 1$$
$$-3 = -3 \text{ checks.}$$

49.

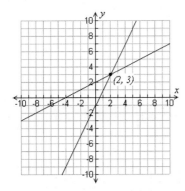

To check the solution, replace x with 2 and y with 3 in each equation.

$$y = 2x - 1$$
$$(3) = 2(2) - 1$$
$$3 = 4 - 1$$
$$3 = 3 \text{ checks.}$$

$$y = \frac{x}{2} + 2$$
$$(3) = \frac{(2)}{2} + 2$$
$$3 = 1 + 2$$
$$3 = 3 \text{ checks.}$$

51.

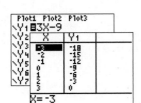

The y-intercept is the point that has an x value of 0. Thus, $(0, -9)$ is the y-intercept.

The x-intercept is the point that has an y value of 0. Thus, the next point in the table, $(3, 0)$, is the x-intercept.

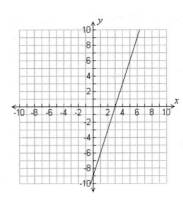

53.

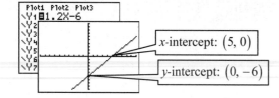

x-intercept: $(5, 0)$

y-intercept: $(0, -6)$

55.

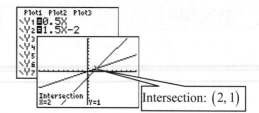

Intersection: $(2, 1)$

57.

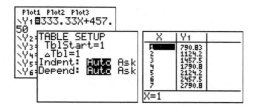

59.

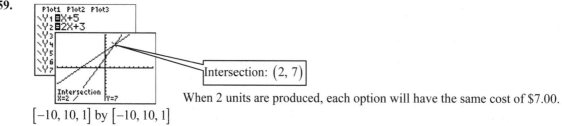

Intersection: $(2, 7)$

When 2 units are produced, each option will have the same cost of $7.00.

$[-10, 10, 1]$ by $[-10, 10, 1]$

61.

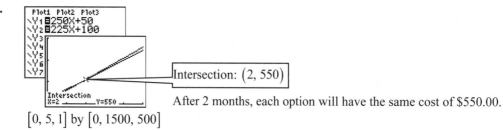

Intersection: $(2, 550)$

After 2 months, each option will have the same cost of $550.00.

$[0, 5, 1]$ by $[0, 1500, 500]$

Cumulative Review

1. $5 - 2(6 - 2^2) = 5 - 2(6 - 4) = 5 - 2(2) = 5 - 4 = 1$

2. $5 - 2(6 - 2)^2 = 5 - 2(4)^2 = 5 - 2(16) = 5 - 32 = -27$

3. $(1 - 2)^3 = (-1)^3 = -1$

4. $1^3 - 2^3 = 1 - 8 = -7$

5. $\dfrac{3 - (4 - 10)}{6 - 3(4)} = \dfrac{3 - (-6)}{6 - 12} = \dfrac{3 + 6}{-6} = -\dfrac{\overset{3}{\cancel{9}}}{\underset{2}{\cancel{6}}} = -\dfrac{3}{2}$

Section 2.4: Solving Linear Equations in One Variable Using the Addition-Subtraction Principle

Quick Review 2.4

1. To determine if $x = 1$ is a solution of $4(3x + 2) = 11x + 4$ we replace x with 1 then simplify.

$$4(3x + 2) = 11x + 4$$
$$4(3(1) + 2) = 11(1) + 4$$
$$4(5) = 11 + 4$$
$$20 \neq 15$$

Thus, $x = 1$ is not a solution of $4(3x + 2) = 11x + 4$.

To determine if $x = -4$ is a solution of $4(3x + 2) = 11x + 4$ we replace x with -4 then simplify.

$$4(3x + 2) = 11x + 4$$
$$4(3(-4) + 2) = 11(-4) + 4$$
$$4(-12 + 2) = -44 + 4$$
$$4(-10) = -40$$
$$-40 = -40$$

Thus, $x = -4$ is a solution of $4(3x + 2) = 11x + 4$

2. For the expression $3x^2$, the exponent on x is 2.
3. For the expression $3x$, the exponent on x is 1.
4. For the expression $3x$, the coefficient of x is 3.
5. The verbal statement, "Five less than three times x equals thirteen" is equivalent to $3x - 5 = 13$.

Exercises 2.4

1.   **a.** $5x + 7$ is not an *equation* since it does not contain an "$=$" sign. It is a linear expression in one variable.
     b. $5x + 7 = 4x$ is a linear equation in one variable.
     c. $y = 5x + 7$ is not a linear equation in *one* variable. It is a linear equation in two variables.
     d. $x^2 = 25$ is not a *linear* equation in one variable since it contains the non linear term x^2

3.

Solution:
$$x - 11 = 13$$
$$x - 11 + 11 = 13 + 11$$
$$x = 24$$

Check:
$$x - 11 = 13$$
$$24 - 11 = 13$$
$$13 = 13$$

Answer: $x = 24$

5.

Solution:
$$v + 6 = 2$$
$$v + 6 - 6 = 2 - 6$$
$$v = -4$$

Check:
$$v + 6 = 2$$
$$-4 + 6 = 2$$
$$2 = 2$$

Answer: $v = -4$

7.

Solution:
$$2y = y - 1$$
$$2y - y = y - y - 1$$
$$y = -1$$

Check:
$$2y = y - 1$$
$$2(-1) = -1 - 1$$
$$-2 = -2$$

Answer: $y = -1$

9.

Solution:
$$3z + 7 = 2z - 4$$
$$3z - 2z + 7 = 2z - 2z - 4$$
$$z + 7 = -4$$
$$z + 7 - 7 = -4 - 7$$
$$z = -11$$

Check:
$$3z + 7 = 2z - 4$$
$$3(-11) + 7 = 2(-11) - 4$$
$$-33 + 7 = -22 - 4$$
$$-26 = -26$$

Answer: $z = -11$

11.

Solution:

$$10y + 17 = 9y + 21$$
$$10y - 9y + 17 = 9y - 9y + 21$$
$$y + 17 = 21$$
$$y + 17 - 17 = 21 - 17$$
$$y = 4$$

Check:

$$10y + 17 = 9y + 21$$
$$10(4) + 17 = 9(4) + 21$$
$$40 + 17 = 36 + 21$$
$$57 = 57$$

Answer: $y = 4$

13.

$$6x + 2 = 5x + 18$$
$$6x - 5x + 2 = 5x - 5x + 18$$
$$x + 2 = 18$$
$$x + 2 - 2 = 18 - 2$$
$$x = 16$$

15.

$$9y - 11 = 8y + 52$$
$$9y - 8y - 11 = 8y - 8y + 52$$
$$y - 11 = 52$$
$$y - 11 + 11 = 52 + 11$$
$$y = 63$$

17.

$$5v + 7 = 4v + 9$$
$$5v - 4v + 7 = 4v - 4v + 9$$
$$v + 7 = 9$$
$$v + 7 - 7 = 9 - 7$$
$$v = 2$$

19.

$$12y + 2 = 11y + 2$$
$$12y - 11y + 2 = 11y - 11y + 2$$
$$y + 2 = 2$$
$$y + 2 - 2 = 2 - 2$$
$$y = 0$$

21.

$$5m - 7 + 3m = 19 + 7m$$
$$8m - 7 = 19 + 7m$$
$$8m - 7m - 7 = 19 + 7m - 7m$$
$$m - 7 = 19$$
$$m - 7 + 7 = 19 + 7$$
$$m = 26$$

23.

$$12n - 103 = 9n - 4 + 2n$$
$$12n - 103 = 11n - 4$$
$$12n - 11n - 103 = 11n - 11n - 4$$
$$n - 103 = -4$$
$$n - 103 + 103 = -4 + 103$$
$$n = 99$$

25.

$$3t + 3t + 3t = 4t + 4t$$
$$9t = 8t$$
$$9t - 8t = 8t - 8t$$
$$t = 0$$

27.

$$10v - 8v = 9v - 8v$$
$$2v = v$$
$$2v - v = v - v$$
$$v = 0$$

29.

$$3x - 4 + 5x = 6x + 3 + x$$
$$8x - 4 = 7x + 3$$
$$8x - 7x - 4 = 7x - 7x + 3$$
$$x - 4 = 3$$
$$x - 4 + 4 = 3 + 4$$
$$x = 7$$

31.

$$3(v - 5) = 2(v + 5)$$
$$3v - 15 = 2v + 10$$
$$3v - 2v - 15 = 2v - 2v + 10$$
$$v - 15 = 10$$
$$v - 15 + 15 = 10 + 15$$
$$v = 25$$

33.

$$5(w - 2) = 4(w + 3)$$
$$5w - 10 = 4w + 12$$
$$5w - 4w - 10 = 4w - 4w + 12$$
$$w - 10 = 12$$
$$w - 10 + 10 = 12 + 10$$
$$w = 22$$

35.
$$8(m-2) = 7(m-3)$$
$$8m-16 = 7m-21$$
$$8m-7m-16 = 7m-7m-21$$
$$m-16 = -21$$
$$m-16+16 = -21+16$$
$$m = -5$$

37.
$$4(n-6) = 3(n-5)$$
$$4n-24 = 3n-15$$
$$4n-3n-24 = 3n-3n-15$$
$$n-24 = -15$$
$$n-24+24 = -15+24$$
$$n = 9$$

39.
$$3(5y+2) = 2(7y-3)$$
$$15y+6 = 14y-6$$
$$15y-14y+6 = 14y-14y-6$$
$$y+6 = -6$$
$$y+6-6 = -6-6$$
$$y = -12$$

41. From the graph we can see that the lines intersect at $x = 1$.
Check: $1.5x - 2 = 0.5x - 1$
$$1.5(1)-2 = 0.5(1)-1$$
$$1.5-2 = 0.5-1$$
$$-0.5 = -0.5$$
Solution: $x = 1$

43. From the graph we can see that the lines intersect at $x = 2$.
Check: $1.5x - 2 = 1$
$$1.5(2)-2 = 1$$
$$3-2 = 1$$
$$1 = 1$$
Solution: $x = 2$

45. From the table we can see that the last two columns are equal when $x = 2$. Therefore, the solution is $x = 2$.

47. From the table we can see that the last two columns are equal when $x = 1$. Therefore, the solution is $x = 1$.

49. Let $y_1 = 2x - 2$, $y_2 = x - 3$ and sketch the graphs. The solution is the value of x in the point of intersection.

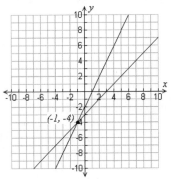

Solution: $x = -1$

51. Let $y_1 = 1.8x - 4.6$, $y_2 = 0.8x - 2.6$ and sketch the graphs. The solution is the value of x in the point of intersection.

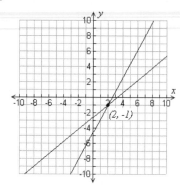

Solution: $x = 2$

53. Let $y_1 = \dfrac{1}{3}x - \dfrac{2}{3}$, $y_2 = \dfrac{7}{3} - \dfrac{2}{3}x$ and sketch the graphs. The solution is the value of x in the point of intersection.

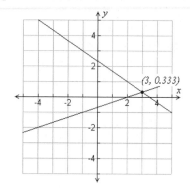

Solution: $x = 3$

55. a.
$$2x = x$$
$$2x - x = x - x$$
$$x = 0$$
The equation is a conditional equation. The solution is $x = 0$

b.
$$x = x + 2$$
$$x - x = x - x + 2$$
$$0 = 2 \text{ is a false statement.}$$
The equation is a contradiction. There is no solution.

c.
$$x + 2 = x + 2$$
$$x - x + 2 = x - x + 2$$
$$2 = 2 \text{ is a true statement.}$$
The equation is an identity. Every real number is a solution.

57. a.
$$v = v + 4$$
$$v - v = v - v + 4$$
$$0 = 4 \text{ is a false statement.}$$
The equation is a contradiction. There is no solution.

b.
$$4 + v = v + 4$$
$$4 + v - v = v - v + 4$$
$$4 = 4 \text{ is a true statement.}$$
The equation is an identity. Every real number is a solution

c.
$$4v = 3v + 4$$
$$4v - 3v = 3v - 3v + 4$$
$$v = 4$$
The equation is a conditional equation. The solution is $v = 4$.

59. **a.** $5x + 1 + 4x - 6 = 5x + 4x + 1 - 6$
$$= 9x - 5$$

b. $\quad 5x + 1 = 4x - 6$
$$5x - 4x + 1 = 4x - 4x - 6$$
$$x + 1 = -6$$
$$x + 1 - 1 = -6 - 1$$
$$x = -7$$

61. **a.** $6x - 4 - (5x + 3) = 6x - 4 - 5x - 3$
$$= 6x - 5x - 4 - 3$$
$$= x - 7$$

b. $\quad 6x - 4 = 5x + 3$
$$6x - 5x - 4 = 5x - 5x + 3$$
$$x - 4 = 3$$
$$x - 4 + 4 = 3 + 4$$
$$x = 7$$

63. **a.** $3.4x - 1.7 + 2.4x + 2.3 = 3.4x + 2.4x - 1.7 + 2.3$
$$= 5.8x + 0.6$$

b. $\quad 3.4x - 1.7 = 2.4x + 2.3$
$$3.4x - 2.4x - 1.7 = 2.4x - 2.4x + 2.3$$
$$x - 1.7 = 2.3$$
$$x - 1.7 + 1.7 = 2.3 + 1.7$$
$$x = 4$$

65. **Mental Estimate:** $x - 1 \approx 1$

$$x - 1 + 1 \approx 1 + 1$$
$$x \approx 2$$

Calculator Solution: $x - 0.918 = 0.987$

$$x - 0.918 + 0.918 = 0.987$$
$$x = 1.905$$

67. **Mental Estimate:**

$$2x + 354 \approx x + 855$$
$$2x - x + 354 \approx x - x + 855$$
$$x + 354 \approx 855$$
$$x + 354 - 354 \approx 855 - 354$$
$$x \approx 501$$

Calculator Solution:

$$2x + 354.916 = x + 855.193$$
$$2x - x + 354.916 = x - x + 855.193$$
$$x + 354.916 = 855.193$$
$$x + 354.016 - 354.916 = 855.193 - 354.916$$
$$x = 501.277$$

69. Seven more than three times a number equals eight less than twice the number.

$$3m + 7 \quad = \quad 2m - 8$$
$$3m - 2m + 7 = 2m - 2m - 8$$
$$m + 7 = -8$$
$$m + 7 - 7 = -8 - 7$$
$$m = -15$$

The number is -15.

71. Twelve minus nine times a number is the same as two minus ten times the number.

$$12 - 9m \quad = \quad 2 - 10m$$
$$12 - 9m + 10m = 2 - 10m + 10m$$
$$12 + m = 2$$
$$12 - 12 + m = 2 - 12$$
$$m = -10$$

The number is -10.

73. Twice the quantity three times a number minus nine is the same as five times the sum of the number and thirteen.

$$2(3m - 9) \quad = \quad 5(m + 13)$$
$$6m - 18 = 5m + 65$$
$$6m - 5m - 18 = 5m - 5m + 65$$
$$m - 18 = 65$$
$$m - 18 + 18 = 65 + 18$$
$$m = 83$$

The number is 83.

75. The perimeter of the triangle shown in the figure is 28 centimeters.

$$10 + 7 + (a + 4) \quad = \quad 28$$
$$10 + 7 + a + 4 = 28$$
$$21 + a = 28$$
$$21 - 21 + a = 28 - 21$$
$$a = 7$$

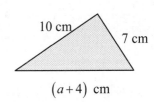

77. The perimeter of the basketball court shown in the figure is $x + 35$ feet.

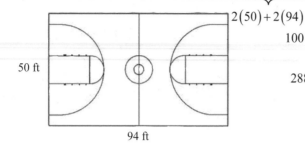

50 ft

94 ft

$$2(50) + 2(94) = x + 35$$
$$100 + 188 = x + 35$$
$$288 = x + 35$$
$$288 - 35 = x + 35 - 35$$
$$253 = x \text{ or } x = 253$$

Cumulative Review

1. $f(10) = 25(10) - 100 = 250 - 100 = 150$

2. From the table we can see that $f(x) = -0.5$, when $x = 1$. Therefore, $f(1) = -0.5$.

3. From the table we can see that $f(x) = 1$, when $x = 2$. Therefore, $f(2) = 1$.

4. From the graph we can see that $y = 3$, when $x = -1$. Therefore, $f(-1) = 3$.

5. From the graph we can see that $y = 0$, when $x = 2$. Therefore, $f(2) = 0$.

Section 2.5: Solving Linear Equations in One Variable Using the Multiplication-Division Principle

Quick Review 2.5

1. The LCD for the fractions $\dfrac{5}{12}$ and $\dfrac{4}{15}$ is 60.

2. $5x - 2 - (5x + 2) = 5x - 2 - 5x - 2 = 5x - 5x - 2 - 2 = 5x - 5x - 2 - 2 = -4$

3. $5x - 2(5x + 2) = 5x - 2(5x) - 2(2) = 5x - 10x - 4 = (5 - 10)x - 4 = -5x - 4$

4. $12\left(5 - \dfrac{3-x}{6}\right) = \dfrac{12}{1}\left(\dfrac{5}{1} - \dfrac{3-x}{6}\right) = \dfrac{12}{1} \cdot \dfrac{5}{1} - \dfrac{\overset{2}{\cancel{12}}}{1} \cdot \dfrac{3-x}{\underset{1}{\cancel{6}}} = 12 \cdot 5 - 2(3 - x) = 60 - 6 + 2x = 54 + 2x$

5. The formula for the perimeter of a rectangle is $P = 2w + 2l$

Exercises 2.5

1. a.

Solution:	Check:
$7x = 42$	$7x = 42$
$\dfrac{7x}{7} = \dfrac{42}{7}$	$7(6) = 42$
$x = 6$	$42 = 42$

Answer: $x = 6$

b.

Solution:	Check:
$x + 7 = 42$	$x + 7 = 42$
$x + 7 - 7 = 42 - 7$	$35 + 7 = 42$
$x = 35$	$42 = 42$

Answer: $x = 35$

3. a.

Solution:	Check:
$-v = 8$	$-v = 8$
$(-1)(-v) = (-1)8$	$-(-8) = 8$
$v = -8$	$8 = 8$

Answer: $v = -8$

b.

Solution:	Check:
$v - 1 = 8$	$v - 1 = 8$
$v - 1 + 1 = 8 + 1$	$(9) - 1 = 8$
$v = 9$	$8 = 8$

Answer: $v = 9$

5. a.

Solution:

$$\frac{3}{4}t = -36$$

$$\left(\frac{4}{3}\right)\frac{3}{4}t = \left(\frac{4}{3}\right)\frac{-36}{1}$$

$$t = \left(\frac{4}{1}\right)\frac{-12}{1}$$

$$t = -48$$

Check:

$$\frac{3}{4}t = -36$$

$$\frac{3}{4}(-48) = -36$$

$$-36 = -36$$

Answer: $t = -48$

b.

Solution:

$$\frac{4}{3}t = -36$$

$$\left(\frac{3}{4}\right)\frac{4}{3}t = \left(\frac{3}{4}\right)\frac{-36}{1}$$

$$t = \left(\frac{3}{1}\right)\frac{-9}{1}$$

$$t = -27$$

Check:

$$\frac{4}{3}t = -36$$

$$\frac{4}{3}(-27) = -36$$

$$-36 = -36$$

Answer: $t = -27$

7.
$$3(2t-1) = 7t+1$$
$$6t-3 = 7t+1$$
$$6t-6t-3 = 7t-6t+1$$
$$-3 = t+1$$
$$-3-1 = t+1-1$$
$$-4 = t \text{ or } t = -4$$

9.
$$4(2-3x) = 3-13x$$
$$8-12x = 3-13x$$
$$8-12x+13x = 3-13x+13x$$
$$8+x = 3$$
$$8-8+x = 3-8$$
$$x = -5$$

11.
$$\frac{y}{3}+\frac{2}{3} = \frac{y}{2}+\frac{3}{2}$$
$$6\left(\frac{y}{3}+\frac{2}{3}\right) = 6\left(\frac{y}{2}+\frac{3}{2}\right)$$
$$2y+2(2) = 3y+3(3)$$
$$2y+4 = 3y+9$$
$$2y-2y+4 = 3y-2y+9$$
$$4 = y+9$$
$$4-9 = y+9-9$$
$$-5 = y \text{ or } y = -5$$

13.
$$2-6(y+1) = 4(2-3y)+6$$
$$2-6y-6 = 8-12y+6$$
$$-4-6y = 14-12y$$
$$-4-6y+12y = 14-12y+12y$$
$$-4+6y = 14$$
$$-4+4+6y = 14+4$$
$$6y = 18$$
$$\frac{6y}{6} = \frac{18}{6}$$
$$y = 3$$

15.
$$24 = -8z$$
$$\frac{24}{-8} = \frac{-8z}{-8}$$
$$-3 = z \text{ or } z = -3$$

17.
$$-1 = 9m$$
$$\frac{-1}{9} = \frac{9m}{9}$$
$$-\frac{1}{9} = m \text{ or } m = -\frac{1}{9}$$

19.
$$-47w = 0$$
$$\frac{-47w}{-47} = \frac{0}{-47}$$
$$w = 0$$

21.
$$\frac{-5v}{3} = 25$$
$$\left(-\frac{3}{5}\right)\left(\frac{-5v}{3}\right) = \left(-\frac{3}{5}\right)25$$
$$v = -15$$

23.
$$8x - 1 = 13x - 1$$
$$8x - 13x - 1 = 13x - 13x - 1$$
$$-5x - 1 = -1$$
$$-5x - 1 + 1 = -1 + 1$$
$$-5x = 0$$
$$\frac{-5x}{-5} = \frac{0}{-5}$$
$$x = 0$$

25.
$$4(3y - 5) = 5(4y + 4)$$
$$12y - 20 = 20y + 20$$
$$12y - 20y - 20 = 20y - 20y + 20$$
$$-8y - 20 = 20$$
$$-8y - 20 + 20 = 20 + 20$$
$$-8y = 40$$
$$\frac{-8y}{-8} = \frac{40}{-8}$$
$$y = -5$$

27.
$$0.12a = 13.2$$
$$\frac{0.12a}{0.12} = \frac{13.2}{0.12}$$
$$a = 110$$

29.
$$2.3x + 29.3 = 1.2(4 - x)$$
$$2.3x + 29.3 = 4.8 - 1.2x$$
$$2.3x + 1.2x + 29.3 = 4.8 - 1.2x + 1.2x$$
$$3.5x + 29.3 = 4.8$$
$$3.5x + 29.3 - 29.3 = 4.8 - 29.3$$
$$3.5x = -24.5$$
$$\frac{3.5x}{3.5} = \frac{-24.5}{3.5}$$
$$x = -7$$

31.
$$6 - 3(2v + 2) = 4(8 - v)$$
$$6 - 6v - 6 = 32 - 4v$$
$$6 - 6v - 6 = 32 - 4v$$
$$-6v = 32 - 4v$$
$$-6v + 4v = 32 - 4v + 4v$$
$$-2v = 32$$
$$\frac{-2v}{-2} = \frac{32}{-2}$$
$$v = -16$$

33.
$$4(x + 1) + 3(x + 2) = 9(x + 1) - 5$$
$$4x + 4 + 3x + 6 = 9x + 9 - 5$$
$$7x + 10 = 9x + 4$$
$$7x - 7x + 10 = 9x - 7x + 4$$
$$10 = 2x + 4$$
$$10 - 4 = 2x + 4 - 4$$
$$6 = 2x$$
$$\frac{6}{2} = \frac{2x}{2}$$
$$x = 3$$

35.

$$\frac{w+1}{3} = \frac{w-5}{5}$$

$$15\left(\frac{w+1}{3}\right) = 15\left(\frac{w-5}{5}\right)$$

$$\frac{15}{3}(w+1) = \frac{15}{5}(w-5)$$

$$5(w+1) = 3(w-5)$$

$$5w+5 = 3w-15$$

$$5w-3w+5 = 3w-3w-15$$

$$2w+5-5 = -15-5$$

$$2w = -20$$

$$\frac{2w}{2} = \frac{-20}{2}$$

$$w = -10$$

37.

$$4 - \frac{x+2}{3} = \frac{x}{2}$$

$$6\left(4 - \frac{x+2}{3}\right) = 6\left(\frac{x}{2}\right)$$

$$6(4) - 6\left(\frac{x+2}{3}\right) = \frac{6}{2}(x)$$

$$24 - \frac{6}{3}(x+2) = 3x$$

$$24 - 2(x+2) = 3x$$

$$24 - 2x - 4 = 3x$$

$$20 - 2x = 3x$$

$$20 - 2x + 2x = 3x + 2x$$

$$20 = 5x$$

$$\frac{20}{5} = \frac{5x}{5}$$

$$4 = x \text{ or } x = 4$$

39.

$$7(x-1) - 4(2x+3) = 2(x+1) - 3(4-x)$$

$$7x - 7 - 8x - 12 = 2x + 2 - 12 + 3x$$

$$-x - 19 = 5x - 10$$

$$-x - 5x - 19 = 5x - 5x - 10$$

$$-6x - 19 = -10$$

$$-6x - 19 + 19 = -10 + 19$$

$$-6x = 9$$

$$\frac{-6x}{-6} = \frac{9}{-6}$$

$$x = -\frac{3}{2}$$

41. **a.**

$$3(x+1) = 3x$$

$$3x + 3 = 3x$$

$$3x - 3x + 3 = 3x - 3x$$

$$3 = 0 \text{ is a false statement.}$$

The equation is a contradiction.

There is no solution.

b.

$$3(x+1) = 3x + 3$$

$$3x + 3 = 3x + 3$$

$$3x - 3x + 3 = 3x - 3x + 3$$

$$3 = 3 \text{ is a true statement.}$$

The equation is an identity.

Every real number is a solution.

c.

$$3(x+2) = 2(x+3)$$

$$3x + 6 = 2x + 6$$

$$3x - 2x + 6 = 2x - 2x + 6$$

$$x + 6 = 6$$

$$x + 6 - 6 = 6 - 6$$

$$x = 0$$

The equation is a conditional equation.

The solution is 0.

43.   **a.** $3(2x-4)-5(x-2) = 6x-12-5x+10$
$$= x-2$$

b. $3(2x-4) = 5(x-2)$
$$6x-12 = 5x-10$$
$$6x-5x-12 = 5x-5x-10$$
$$x-12 = -10$$
$$x-12+12 = -10+12$$
$$x = 2$$

45.   **a.** $1.5(4x-6)+2.5(6x-4) = 6x-9+15x-10$
$$= 21x-19$$

b. $1.5(4x-6) = -2.5(6x-4)$
$$6x-9 = -15x+10$$
$$6x+15x-9 = -15x+15x+10$$
$$21x-9 = 10$$
$$21x-9+9 = 10+9$$
$$21x = 19$$
$$\frac{21x}{21} = \frac{19}{21}$$
$$x = \frac{19}{21}$$

47.   To find the adult dosage when the child dosage is 5 mg we set $y = 5$ and solve for x.
$$0.8x = 5$$
$$\frac{0.8x}{0.8} = \frac{5}{0.8}$$
$$x = 6.25 \text{ mg}$$

49.   The perimeter of a square is given by the formula $P = 4s$. With a perimeter of 99.837 cm ≈ 100 cm we can approximate the length of each side by solving the equation $100 \approx 4s$
$$\frac{100}{4} \approx \frac{4s}{4}$$
$$25 \approx s \text{ or } s \approx 25 \text{ cm}$$

51.   To estimate the pretax room charges for a room with a tax charge of $7.58 we solve the equation
$$7.58 = 0.10C$$
$$\frac{7.58}{0.10} = \frac{0.10C}{0.10}$$
$$75.80 = C \text{ or } C = \$75.80$$

53.   **Mental Estimate:** $-2x \approx 8$
$$\frac{-2x}{-2} \approx \frac{8}{-2}$$
$$x \approx -4$$

Calculator solution: $-2.1x = 8.82$
$$\frac{-2.1x}{-2.1} = \frac{8.82}{-2.1}$$
$$x = -4.2$$

55. **Mental Estimate:**

$$-0.5x \approx -2$$

$$-\frac{1}{2}x \approx -2$$

$$(-2)\left(-\frac{1}{2}x\right) \approx (-2)(-2)$$

$$x \approx 4$$

Calculator solution: $-0.49x = -2.009$

$$\frac{-0.49x}{-0.49} = \frac{-2.009}{-0.49}$$

$$x = 4.1$$

57. To solve the equation using the table. We find the x value for which the y values are the same. Thus, the solution is $x = 1.5$.

59.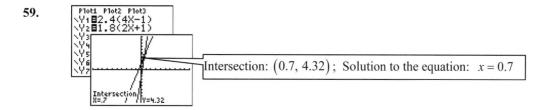

Intersection: $(0.7, 4.32)$; Solution to the equation: $x = 0.7$

61. Five times the sum of x and 2 is the same as seven times the quantity x minus 3.

$$5(x+2) = 7(x-3)$$

$$5x+10 = 7x-21$$

$$5x-7x+10 = 7x-7x-21$$

$$-2x+10 = -21$$

$$-2x+10-10 = -21-10$$

$$-2x = -31$$

$$\frac{-2x}{-2} = \frac{-31}{-2}$$

$$x = \frac{31}{2}$$

The number is $\dfrac{31}{2}$.

63. Twice the quantity three v minus 2 equals four times the quantity v plus 9.

$$2(3v-2) = 4(v+9)$$

$$6v-4 = 4v+36$$

$$6v-4v-4 = 4v-4v+36$$

$$2v-4 = 36$$

$$2v-4+4 = 36+4$$

$$2v = 40$$

$$\frac{2v}{2} = \frac{40}{2}$$

$$v = 20$$

The number is 20.

65. Twice the difference of three m minus five is four less than three times the sum of m and six.

$$2(3m-5) \quad = \quad 3(m+6)-4$$
$$6m-10 = 3m+18-4$$
$$6m-10 = 3m+14$$
$$6m-3m-10 = 3m-3m+14$$
$$3m-10 = 14$$
$$3m-10+10 = 14+10$$
$$3m = 24$$
$$\frac{3m}{3} = \frac{24}{3}$$
$$m = 8$$

The number is 8.

67. One-third of the quantity two x plus five is the same as the quantity four x plus two.

$$\frac{1}{3}(2x+5) \quad = \quad 4x+2$$
$$3\left(\frac{1}{3}(2x+5)\right) = 3(4x+2)$$
$$2x+5 = 12x+6$$
$$2x-12x+5 = 12x-12x+6$$
$$-10x+5 = 6$$
$$-10x+5-5 = 6-5$$
$$-10x = 1$$
$$\frac{-10x}{-10} = \frac{1}{-10}$$
$$x = -\frac{1}{10}$$

The number is $-\dfrac{1}{10}$.

69. The perimeter of a square is 4 times the length of the square. Thus, if the perimeter is 108 ft, to find the value of x we solve the equation

$$4(4x+3) = 108$$
$$16x+12 = 108$$
$$16x+12-12 = 108-12$$
$$16x = 96$$
$$\frac{16x}{16} = \frac{96}{16}$$
$$x = 6$$

The value of x is 6.

71. The perimeter of a rectangle is the sum of twice the width and twice the length. Thus, if the perimeter is 17 ft, to find the value of a we solve the equation

$$2(2a+1)+2(3a+5) = 17$$
$$4a+2+6a+10 = 17$$
$$10a+12 = 17$$
$$10a+12-12 = 17-12$$
$$10a = 5$$
$$\frac{10a}{10} = \frac{5}{10}$$
$$a = \frac{1}{2}$$

The value of a is $\dfrac{1}{2}$.

73. The area of a triangle is one half the base times the height. Thus, if the area is 51 square centimeters, to find the value of x we solve the equation

$$\frac{1}{2}(6)(5x+7)=51$$
$$3(5x+7)=51$$
$$15x+21=51$$
$$15x+21-21=51-21$$
$$15x=30$$
$$\frac{15x}{15}=\frac{30}{15}$$
$$x=2$$

The value of x is 2.

Cumulative Review

1. From the graph we can see that the company had 125 employees in 2004.
2. From the graph we can see that the company had 175 employees in 2006.
3. From the graph we can see that the company first had 150 employees in 2005.
4. From the graph we can see that the company had the most employees (250) in 2007.
5. From the graph we can see that the company had 200 employees in 2008 and 100 employees in 2009. Therefore, the company lost 100 employees from 2008 to 2009.

Section 2.6: Calculating Intercepts and Rearranging Formulas

Quick Review 2.6

1. $I = PRT = (5000)(0.06)(1) = \$300$

2. To determine if $(3, 0)$ is a solution of $5x-3y=15$ we replace x with 3 and y with 0 and then simplify.
$$5x-3y=15$$
$$5(3)-3(0)=15$$
$$15=15$$
Thus, $(3, 0)$ is a solution of $5x-3y=15$.

3. To determine if $(0, 5)$ is a solution of $5x-3y=15$ we replace x with 0 and y with 5 and then simplify.
$$5x-3y=15$$
$$5(0)-3(5)=15$$
$$-15 \neq 15$$
Thus, $(0, 5)$ is not a solution of $5x-3y=15$.

4. $$3x-(2x-5)+3=5x$$
$$3x-2x+5+3=5x$$
$$x+8=5x$$
$$x-x+8=5x-x$$
$$8=4x$$
$$\frac{8}{4}=\frac{4x}{4}$$
$$2=x \text{ or } x=2$$

5. $$\frac{x}{5}-\frac{3x}{2}=13$$
$$10\left(\frac{x}{5}-\frac{3x}{2}\right)=10(13)$$
$$\frac{10 \cdot x}{5}-\frac{10 \cdot 3x}{2}=130$$
$$\frac{\overset{2}{\cancel{10}} \cdot x}{\cancel{5}}-\frac{\overset{5}{\cancel{10}} \cdot 3x}{\cancel{2}}=130$$
$$2x-15x=130$$
$$\frac{-13x}{-13}=\frac{130}{-13}$$
$$x=-10$$

Exercises 2.6

1.
$$2x + y = 7$$
$$2x - 2x + y = 7 - 2x$$
$$y = 7 - 2x$$
$$y = -2x + 7$$

3.
$$3x - y = 2$$
$$3x - 3x - y = 2 - 3x$$
$$-y = 2 - 3x$$
$$-1(-y) = -1(2 - 3x)$$
$$y = -2 + 3x$$
$$y = 3x - 2$$

5.
$$-6x + 3y = -9$$
$$-6x + 6x + 3y = -9 + 6x$$
$$3y = -9 + 6x$$
$$\frac{3y}{3} = \frac{-9}{3} + \frac{6x}{3}$$
$$y = -3 + 2x$$
$$y = 2x - 3$$

7.
$$\frac{x}{2} - \frac{y}{4} = -1$$
$$4\left(\frac{x}{2} - \frac{y}{4}\right) = 4(-1)$$
$$2x - y = -4$$
$$2x - 2x - y = -4 - 2x$$
$$-y = -4 - 2x$$
$$-1(-y) = -1(-4 - 2x)$$
$$y = 4 + 2x$$
$$y = 2x + 4$$

9.
$$-0.3x - 0.1y = 0.2$$
$$-0.3x + 0.3x - 0.1y = 0.2 + 0.3x$$
$$-0.1y = 0.2 + 0.3x$$
$$\frac{-0.1y}{-0.1} = \frac{0.2}{-0.1} + \frac{0.3x}{-0.1}$$
$$y = -2 - 3x$$
$$y = -3x - 2$$

11.
$$5x - 2y = x - 3y + 4$$
$$5x - 2y + 3y = x - 3y + 3y + 4$$
$$5x + y = x + 4$$
$$5x - 5x + y = x - 5x + 4$$
$$y = -4x + 4$$

13.
$$2(3x - y + 1) = 3(4x - y - 2)$$
$$6x - 2y + 2 = 12x - 3y - 6$$
$$6x - 2y + 3y + 2 = 12x - 3y + 3y - 6$$
$$6x - 6x + y + 2 - 2 = 12x - 6x - 6 - 2$$
$$y = 6x - 8$$

15.
$$2x + 3y = 4x + 2y - 3$$
$$2x + 3y - 2y = 4x + 2y - 2y - 3$$
$$2x - 2x + y = 4x - 2x - 3$$
$$y = 2x - 3$$

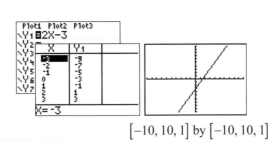

$$[-10, 10, 1] \text{ by } [-10, 10, 1]$$

17.

$$-5x + 4y = -2(2x - 3y) + 4$$
$$-5x + 4y = -4x + 6y + 4$$
$$-5x + 4y - 6y = -4x + 6y - 6y + 4$$
$$-5x + 5x - 2y = -4x + 5x + 4$$
$$-2y = x + 4$$
$$\frac{-2y}{-2} = \frac{x + 4}{-2}$$
$$y = -\frac{1}{2}x - 2$$

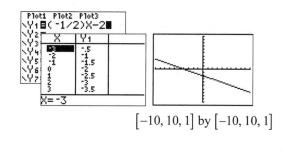

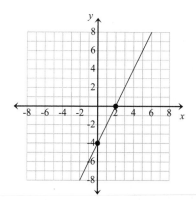

$[-10, 10, 1]$ by $[-10, 10, 1]$

19.

To find the x-intercept, set $y = 0$ and solve for x.
$$6x - 3y = 12$$
$$6x - 3(0) = 12$$
$$6x = 12$$
$$\frac{6x}{6} = \frac{12}{6}$$
$$x = 2$$
$(2, 0)$ is the x-intercept.

To find the y-intercept, set $x = 0$ and solve for y.
$$6x - 3y = 12$$
$$6(0) - 3y = 12$$
$$-3y = 12$$
$$\frac{-3y}{-3} = \frac{12}{-3}$$
$$y = -4$$
$(0, -4)$ is the y-intercept.

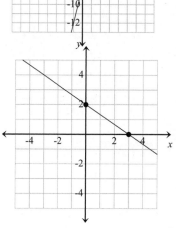

21.

To find the x-intercept, set $y = 0$ and solve for x.
$$\frac{x}{2} - \frac{y}{8} = 1$$
$$\frac{x}{2} - \frac{0}{8} = 1$$
$$2\left(\frac{x}{2}\right) = 2(1)$$
$$x = 2$$
$(2, 0)$ is the x-intercept.

To find the y-intercept, set $x = 0$ and solve for y.
$$\frac{x}{2} - \frac{y}{8} = 1$$
$$\frac{0}{2} - \frac{y}{8} = 1$$
$$-8\left(-\frac{y}{8}\right) = -8(1)$$
$$y = -8$$
$(0, -8)$ is the y-intercept.

23.

To find the x-intercept, set $y = 0$ and solve for x.
$$0.2x + 0.3y = 0.6$$
$$0.2x + 0.3(0) = 0.6$$
$$\frac{0.2x}{0.2} = \frac{0.6}{0.2}$$
$$x = 3$$
$(3, 0)$ is the x-intercept.

To find the y-intercept, set $x = 0$ and solve for y.
$$0.2x + 0.3y = 0.6$$
$$0.2(0) + 0.3y = 0.6$$
$$\frac{0.3y}{0.3} = \frac{0.6}{0.3}$$
$$y = 2$$
$(0, 2)$ is the y-intercept.

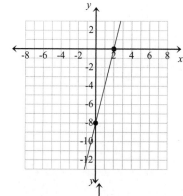

25.
$$A = lw$$
$$\frac{A}{w} = \frac{lw}{w}$$
$$\frac{A}{w} = l$$
$$l = \frac{A}{w}$$

27.
$$C = 2\pi r$$
$$\frac{C}{2\pi} = \frac{2\pi r}{2\pi}$$
$$\frac{C}{2\pi} = r$$
$$r = \frac{C}{2\pi}$$

29.
$$V_1 T_2 = V_2 T_1$$
$$\frac{V_1 T_2}{T_2} = \frac{V_2 T_1}{T_2}$$
$$V_1 = \frac{V_2 T_1}{T_2}$$

31.
$$V = \frac{1}{3}\pi r^2 h$$
$$3V = 3\left(\frac{1}{3}\pi r^2 h\right)$$
$$3V = \pi r^2 h$$
$$\frac{3V}{\pi r^2} = \frac{\pi r^2 h}{\pi r^2}$$
$$h = \frac{3V}{\pi r^2}$$

33.
$$P = a + b + c$$
$$P - b - c = a + b - b + c - c$$
$$P - b - c = a$$
$$a = P - b - c$$

35.
$$F = \frac{9}{5}C + 32$$
$$F - 32 = \frac{9}{5}C + 32 - 32$$
$$F - 32 = \frac{9}{5}C$$
$$\frac{5}{9}(F - 32) = \frac{5}{9}\left(\frac{9}{5}C\right)$$
$$\frac{5}{9}(F - 32) = C$$
$$C = \frac{5}{9}(F - 32)$$

37.
$$A = \frac{1}{2}h(a + b)$$
$$\frac{2}{h}(A) = \frac{2}{h}\left(\frac{1}{2}h(a + b)\right)$$
$$\frac{2A}{h} = a + b$$
$$\frac{2A}{h} - a = a - a + b$$
$$\frac{2A}{h} - a = b$$
$$b = \frac{2A}{h} - a$$

39.
$$\frac{9}{5}(C) = \frac{9}{5}\left(\frac{5}{9}(F - 32)\right)$$
$$\frac{9C}{5} = F - 32$$
$$\frac{9C}{5} + 32 = F - 32 + 32$$
$$\frac{9C}{5} + 32 = F$$
$$F = \frac{9}{5}C + 32$$

41.
$$l = a + (n - 1)d$$
$$l - (n - 1)d = a + (n - 1)d - (n - 1)d$$
$$l - (n - 1)d = a$$
$$a = l - (n - 1)d$$

43.
$$l = a + (n - 1)d$$
$$l - a = a - a + (n - 1)d$$
$$l - a = (n - 1)d$$
$$\frac{l - a}{d} = \frac{(n - 1)d}{d}$$
$$\frac{l - a}{d} = n - 1$$
$$\frac{l - a}{d} + 1 = n - 1 + 1$$
$$\frac{l - a}{d} + 1 = n$$
$$n = \frac{l - a}{d} + 1$$

45.

$$y = mx + b$$
$$y - b = mx + b - b$$
$$y - b = mx$$
$$\frac{y-b}{x} = \frac{mx}{x}$$
$$\frac{y-b}{x} = m$$
$$m = \frac{y-b}{x}$$

47.

$$P = 2l + 2w$$
$$P - 2l = 2l - 2l + 2w$$
$$P - 2l = 2w$$
$$\frac{P-2l}{2} = \frac{2w}{2}$$
$$\frac{P-2l}{2} = w$$
$$w = \frac{P-2l}{2}$$

49. **a.**

$$T = PR$$
$$\frac{T}{R} = \frac{PR}{R}$$
$$\frac{T}{R} = P$$
$$P = \frac{T}{R}$$

b. $P = \dfrac{T}{0.08}$

c.

T	$P = T/0.08$
100	1250
200	2500
300	3750
400	5000
500	6250
600	7500

51. **a.**

$$P = 2W + 2L$$
$$P - 2L = 2W + 2L - 2L$$
$$P - 2L = 2W$$
$$\frac{P-2L}{2} = \frac{2W}{2}$$
$$\frac{P-2L}{2} = W$$
$$W = \frac{P-2L}{2}$$

b. $W = \dfrac{800 - 2L}{2} = 400 - L$

c.

L	$W = 400 - L$
100	300
120	280
140	260
160	240
180	220
200	200
220	180

53. **a.** If the x is number of orders and the shop makes $0.75 on each order, then the revenue is $0.75x$. We subtract the overhead costs from the revenue to find the profit. Thus, the profit is $y = 0.75x - 120$.

b. If $y = 0$ then $x = \dfrac{(0) + 120}{0.75} = 160$. Thus, the ice cream shop will break even when 160 ice cream products are sold each day.

c. If $x = 0$ then $y = 0.75(0) - 120 = -120$. Thus, the ice cream shop loses $120 daily if no ice cream products are sold.

55. With $t = \dfrac{1}{12}$, we have

$$I = PR\left(\frac{1}{12}\right)$$
$$I = \frac{PR}{12}$$
$$I\left(\frac{12}{P}\right) = \frac{PR}{12}\left(\frac{12}{P}\right)$$
$$\frac{12I}{P} = R$$
$$R = \frac{12I}{P}$$

P	$R = \dfrac{12(50)}{P}$
10000	0.06
12000	0.05
14000	0.0429
16000	0.0375
18000	0.0333
20000	0.03
22000	0.0273

Cumulative Review

1. If six equal pieces each of length x is cut from a 50 foot cable, then the length of the remaining piece is $f(x) = 50 - 6x$.

2. $\quad 45:60 = \dfrac{45}{60} = \dfrac{3 \cdot \cancel{15}}{4 \cdot \cancel{15}} = \dfrac{3}{4} \quad \text{or} \quad 3:4$

3. $\quad 3\dfrac{1}{3} + 4\dfrac{1}{5} = 3 + \dfrac{1}{3} \cdot \dfrac{5}{5} + 4 + \dfrac{1}{5} \cdot \dfrac{3}{3} = 3 + 4 + \dfrac{5}{15} + \dfrac{3}{15} = 7 + \dfrac{5+3}{15} = 7 + \dfrac{8}{15} = 7\dfrac{8}{15}$

4. $\quad \left(3\dfrac{1}{3}\right)\left(4\dfrac{1}{5}\right) = \dfrac{10}{3} \cdot \dfrac{21}{5} = \dfrac{\overset{2}{\cancel{10}}}{\underset{1}{\cancel{3}}} \cdot \dfrac{\overset{7}{\cancel{21}}}{\underset{1}{\cancel{5}}} = \dfrac{2 \cdot 7}{1 \cdot 1} = 14$

5. $\quad 7x - 14y = 7 \cdot x - 7 \cdot 2y = 7(x - 2y); \quad \text{(answer: } x - 2y\text{)}$

Section 2.7: Proportions and Direct Variation

Quick Review 2.7

1. $\quad \dfrac{1}{2} + \dfrac{2}{3} - \dfrac{3}{4} = \dfrac{1}{2} \cdot \dfrac{6}{6} + \dfrac{2}{3} \cdot \dfrac{4}{4} - \dfrac{3}{4} \cdot \dfrac{3}{3} = \dfrac{6}{12} + \dfrac{8}{12} - \dfrac{9}{12} = \dfrac{6+8-9}{12} = \dfrac{5}{12}$

2. $\quad \dfrac{2}{3}x = 12$

$\quad \dfrac{3}{2}\left(\dfrac{2}{3}x\right) = \dfrac{3}{2}\left(\dfrac{12}{1}\right)$

$\quad x = \dfrac{3}{\underset{1}{\cancel{2}}} \cdot \dfrac{\overset{6}{\cancel{12}}}{1}$

$\quad x = \dfrac{3 \cdot 6}{1 \cdot 1} = 18$

3. $\quad 0.45x = 0.54$

$\quad \dfrac{0.45x}{0.45} = \dfrac{0.54}{0.45}$

$\quad x = 1.2$

4.

Let $y = 0$
$0 = 2.5x - 10$
$\dfrac{10}{2.5} = \dfrac{2.5x}{2.5}$
$x = 4$

Let $y = 15$
$15 = 2.5x - 10$
$\dfrac{25}{2.5} = \dfrac{2.5x}{2.5}$
$x = 10$

x	0	4	20	10
y	-10	0	40	15

Let $x = 0$
$y = 2.5(0) - 10 = -10$

Let $x = 20$
$y = 2.5(20) - 10 = 40$

5. $\quad$ Division by <u>zero</u> is undefined.

Exercises 2.7

1. $\quad 20\left(\dfrac{x}{20}\right) = 20\left(\dfrac{3}{5}\right)$

$\quad x = 4(3)$

$\quad x = 12$

3. $\quad 5x\left(\dfrac{3}{5}\right) = 5x\left(\dfrac{6}{x}\right)$

$\quad x(3) = 5(6)$

$\quad 3x = 30$

$\quad \dfrac{3x}{3} = \dfrac{30}{3}$

$\quad x = 10$

5. $\quad 12\left(\dfrac{5x}{2}\right) = 12\left(\dfrac{45}{6}\right)$

$\quad 6(5x) = 2(45)$

$\quad \dfrac{30x}{30} = \dfrac{90}{30}$

$\quad x = 3$

7. $\quad 66y\left(\dfrac{9}{2y}\right) = 66y\left(\dfrac{27}{66}\right)$

$\quad 33(9) = y(27)$

$\quad 297 = 27y$

$\quad \dfrac{297}{27} = \dfrac{27y}{27}$

$\quad 11 = y \quad \text{or} \quad y = 11$

9.
$$\frac{5}{6} = \frac{40}{3y}$$
$$6y\left(\frac{5}{6}\right) = 6y\left(\frac{40}{3y}\right)$$
$$y(5) = 2(40)$$
$$5y = 80$$
$$\frac{5y}{5} = \frac{80}{5}$$
$$y = 16$$

11. $a:3 = 4:6$ is equivalent to the proportion
$$\frac{a}{3} = \frac{4}{6}$$
$$6\left(\frac{a}{3}\right) = 6\left(\frac{4}{6}\right)$$
$$2(a) = 4$$
$$\frac{2a}{2} = \frac{4}{2}$$
$$a = 2$$

13. $5:2v = 3:4$ is equivalent to the proportion
$$\frac{5}{2v} = \frac{3}{4}$$
$$8v\left(\frac{5}{2v}\right) = 8v\left(\frac{3}{4}\right)$$
$$4(5) = 2v(3)$$
$$20 = 6v$$
$$\frac{20}{6} = \frac{6v}{6}$$
$$\frac{10}{3} = v \ \text{ or } \ v = \frac{10}{3}$$

15.
$$\frac{x+1}{5} = \frac{8}{10}$$
$$10\left(\frac{x+1}{5}\right) = 10\left(\frac{8}{10}\right)$$
$$2(x+1) = 8$$
$$2x + 2 = 8$$
$$2x + 2 - 2 = 8 - 2$$
$$2x = 6$$
$$\frac{2x}{2} = \frac{6}{2}$$
$$x = 3$$

17.
$$\frac{z+2}{3} = \frac{z}{4}$$
$$12\left(\frac{z+2}{3}\right) = 12\left(\frac{z}{4}\right)$$
$$4(z+2) = 3(z)$$
$$4z + 8 = 3z$$
$$4z - 3z + 8 = 3z - 3z$$
$$z + 8 = 0$$
$$z + 8 - 8 = 0 - 8$$
$$z = -8$$

19.
$$\frac{x}{3} = \frac{2x-3}{5}$$
$$15\left(\frac{x}{3}\right) = 15\left(\frac{2x-3}{5}\right)$$
$$5(x) = 3(2x-3)$$
$$5x = 6x - 9$$
$$5x - 6x = 6x - 6x - 9$$
$$-x = -9$$
$$-1(-x) = -1(-9)$$
$$x = 9$$

21.

$$\frac{2v-1}{5} = \frac{2v-5}{1}$$

$$5\left(\frac{2v-1}{5}\right) = 5\left(\frac{2v-5}{1}\right)$$

$$2v-1 = 5(2v-5)$$

$$2v-1 = 10v-25$$

$$2v-10v-1 = 10v-10v-25$$

$$-8v-1 = -25$$

$$-8v-1+1 = -25+1$$

$$-8v = -24$$

$$\frac{-8v}{-8} = \frac{-24}{-8}$$

$$v = 3$$

23. At a fixed speed, the distance d that a car travels varies directly as the time t it travels.

$$d = kt$$

25. $v = kw$ means v varies directly as w.

27.

$$\frac{v_1}{w_1} = \frac{v_2}{w_2}$$

$$\frac{22}{77} = \frac{v_2}{35}$$

$$\frac{2}{7} = \frac{v_2}{35}$$

$$35\left(\frac{2}{7}\right) = 35\left(\frac{v_2}{35}\right)$$

$$5(2) = v_2$$

$$10 = v_2$$

Thus, $v = 10$ when $w = 35$

29.

$$\frac{p_1}{g_1} = \frac{p_2}{g_2}$$

$$\frac{0.375}{1} = \frac{1.5}{g_2}$$

$$g_2(0.375) = g_2\left(\frac{1.5}{g_2}\right)$$

$$0.375g_2 = 1.5$$

$$\frac{0.375g_2}{0.375} = \frac{1.5}{0.375}$$

$$g_2 = 4$$

Thus, $g = 4$ when $p = 1.5$

31. If v varies directly as w then $v = kw$ for some constant of variation k. Replacing v with 12 and w with 15 gives us the equation

$$12 = k(15)$$

$$\frac{12}{15} = \frac{k(15)}{15}$$

$$\frac{4}{5} = k$$

Thus, the constant of variation is $\frac{4}{5}$.

33. Set up a verbal equation.

$$\frac{\text{cups of sugar}}{\text{number of people}} = \frac{\text{cups of sugar}}{\text{number of people}}$$

Substitute the given values to translate the word equation into an algebraic one then solve the equation.

$$\frac{3}{50} = \frac{x}{75}$$

$$150\left(\frac{3}{50}\right) = 150\left(\frac{x}{75}\right)$$

$$3(3) = 2(x)$$

$$9 = 2x$$

$$\frac{9}{2} = \frac{2x}{2}$$

$$\frac{9}{2} = x$$

$\frac{9}{2}$ or $4\frac{1}{2}$ cups of sugar are needed for 75 people.

35. Set up a verbal equation.

$$\frac{\text{apparent length}}{\text{actual length}} = \frac{\text{apparent length}}{\text{actual length}}$$

Substitute the given values to translate the word equation into an algebraic one then solve the equation.

$$\frac{7.5}{1.5} = \frac{x}{2}$$

$$\frac{7.5}{1.5} = \frac{x}{2}$$

$$5 = \frac{x}{2}$$

$$2(5) = 2\left(\frac{x}{2}\right)$$

$$10 = x$$

An object that is 2 millimeters long appears to be 10 millimeters long.

39. Set up a verbal equation.

$$\frac{\text{number of bricks}}{\text{length of wall}} = \frac{\text{number of bricks}}{\text{length of wall}}$$

Substitute the given values to translate the word equation into an algebraic one then solve the equation.

$$\frac{118}{2} = \frac{x}{24}$$

$$59 = \frac{x}{24}$$

$$24(59) = 24\left(\frac{x}{24}\right)$$

$$1416 = x$$

A 24 foot section of a wall requires 1,416 bricks.

43. Set up a verbal equation.

$$\frac{\text{pounds of seed}}{\text{area in square feet}} = \frac{\text{pounds of seed}}{\text{area in square feet}}$$

Substitute the given values to translate the word equation into an algebraic one then solve the equation.

37. Set up a verbal equation.

$$\frac{\text{number of defective bulbs}}{\text{total number of bulbs}} = \frac{\text{number of defective bulbs}}{\text{total number of bulbs}}$$

Substitute the given values to translate the word equation into an algebraic one then solve the equation.

$$\frac{2.5}{500} = \frac{x}{10000}$$

$$0.005 = \frac{x}{10000}$$

$$10000(0.005) = 10000\left(\frac{x}{10000}\right)$$

$$50 = x$$

Out of 10,000 bulbs, one should expect to find 50 defective ones.

41. To find the actual dimensions of the room we can use the fact that the actual size of the room is directly proportional to the drawing size with the constant of variation, $k = 2.5$. Thus, the length of the room is $l = 2.5(3.5) = 8.75$ meters and the width of the room is $w = 2.5(3) = 7.5$ meters.

$$\frac{3}{100} = \frac{x}{450}$$

$$450\left(\frac{3}{100}\right) = 450\left(\frac{x}{450}\right)$$

$$13.5 = x$$

450 square feet would require 13.5 pounds of seed.

45. Set up a verbal equation.

$$\frac{\text{number of face cards}}{\text{total number of cards}} = \frac{\text{number of face cards}}{\text{total number of cards}}$$

Substitute the given values to translate the word equation into an algebraic one then solve the equation.

$$\frac{12}{52} = \frac{x}{39}$$

$$39\left(\frac{12}{52}\right) = 39\left(\frac{x}{39}\right)$$

$$9 = x$$

One should expect 9 face cards out of 39 cards dealt.

47. **a.** Let c represent the commission made off of s gross sales. If c varies directly as s then $c = ks$ for some constant of variation k. Replacing c with 2,700 and s with 18,000 gives us the equation

$$2700 = k(18000)$$

$$\frac{2700}{18000} = \frac{k(18000)}{18000}$$

$$0.15 = k$$

Thus, the commission rate is $k = 0.15$ (or 15%).

b. The equation relating the commission and sales is $c = 0.15s$

c.

Gross Sales	Commission
16,000	2,400
18,000	2,700
20,000	3,000
22,000	3,300
24,000	3,600
26,000	3,900
28,000	4,200

49. Let U = Number of U.S. dollars

E = Number of Euros

k = Constant of variation

a. If the number of Euros varies directly as the number of U.S. dollars then $E = kU$. We can find the constant of variation by replacing U with 500 and E with 390 then solving the equation

$$390 = k(500)$$

$$\frac{390}{500} = \frac{k(500)}{500}$$

$$0.78 = k$$

0.78 Euros for one U.S. dollar.

b. $E = 0.78U$

c.

51. **a.** $W = (6.7)(11.4)t$

$W = 76.38t$

b. 76.38 is the number of pounds of fuel consumed per minute.

53. Using similar triangles, we can find the width, w, by solving the equation

$$\frac{w}{40} = \frac{28}{50}$$

$$40\left(\frac{w}{40}\right) = 40\left(\frac{28}{50}\right)$$

$$w = 22.4$$

The width of the river is 22.4 feet.

55. Set up a verbal equation.

$$\frac{\text{width}}{\text{length}} = \frac{\text{width}}{\text{length}}$$

Substitute the given values to translate the word equation into an algebraic one then solve the equation. $\dfrac{7}{10} = \dfrac{x}{25}$

$$25\left(\frac{7}{10}\right) = 25\left(\frac{x}{25}\right)$$
$$17.5 = x$$

The width of the enlargement is 17.5 centimeters.

57. Set up a verbal equation.

$$\frac{\text{height of the object}}{\text{length of the shadow}} = \frac{\text{height of the object}}{\text{length of the shadow}}$$

Substitute the given values to translate the word equation into an algebraic one then solve the equation. $\dfrac{x}{21} = \dfrac{5}{6}$

$$21\left(\frac{x}{21}\right) = 21\left(\frac{5}{6}\right)$$
$$x = 17.5$$

The height of the flagpole is 17.5 feet.

59. Set up a verbal equation.

$$\frac{\text{rise}}{\text{run}} = \frac{\text{rise}}{\text{run}}$$

Substitute the given values to translate the word equation into an algebraic one then solve the equation.

$$\frac{x}{40} = \frac{8}{6}$$
$$40\left(\frac{x}{40}\right) = 40\left(\frac{8}{6}\right)$$
$$x = 53.\overline{33}$$

The height of the tower is $53\dfrac{1}{3}$ feet (53 feet 4 inches) tall.

61. Set up a verbal equation.

$$\frac{\text{runs}}{\text{outs}} = \frac{\text{runs}}{\text{outs}}$$

Substitute the given values to translate the word equation into an algebraic one then solve the equation.

$$\frac{x}{27} = \frac{2}{6}$$
$$27\left(\frac{x}{27}\right) = 27\left(\frac{2}{6}\right)$$
$$x = 9$$

The pitcher has an ERA of 9.

63.
a. The truck will travel a distance that is equal to the circumference of the tire. The circumference is $C = 2\pi r$. If the radius is 50 cm, then the distance traveled is $2\pi(50) = 100\pi \approx 314.2\,\text{cm}$ per revolution.

b. To the nearest thousandth of a km, the truck will travel
$$\frac{100\pi}{100000} \approx 0.00314\,\text{km per revolution.}$$

c. If x is the number of revolutions, then the distance traveled is $0.00314x$ km

d. If $x = 500$, then the distance traveled is $0.00314(500) = 1.57\,\text{km}$.

e.
$$0.00314x = 1$$
$$\left(\frac{1}{0.00314}\right)0.00314x = \left(\frac{1}{0.00314}\right)1$$
$$x \approx 318\,\text{revolutions}$$

65.
a. $C = 0.80x$
b. $C = 0.80(500) = \$400$
c. $0.80x = 500$
$$x = \$625$$

67.   Since y varies directly as x we know that $y = kx$ for some constant k. We can find the constant of variation by substituting a pair of given values for x and y and solving for k. For example, substitute 5 for x and 4 for y.

$$4 = k(5)$$

$$\frac{4}{5} = \frac{k(5)}{5}$$

$$\frac{4}{5} = k$$

The constant of variation is $\dfrac{4}{5} = 0.80$.

69.

Algebraically	**Numerically**	**Graphically**	**Verbally**

Algebraically
$$y = \frac{-x}{2}$$

Numerically

x	y
1	$-1/2$
2	-1
3	$-3/2$
4	-2
5	$-5/2$

Graphically

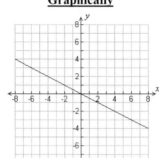

Verbally

y varies directly as x with constant of variation $-1/2$

71.

Algebraically
$$y = -x$$

Numerically

x	y
1	-1
2	-2
3	-3
4	-4
5	-5

Graphically

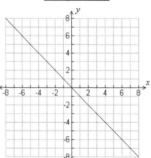

Verbally

y varies directly as x with constant of variation -1

73.   Since the corresponding sides of similar rectangles are proportional, to find w, we can solve the following equation.

$$\frac{w}{5} = \frac{24}{32}$$

$$\frac{w}{5} = \frac{3}{4}$$

$$20\left(\frac{w}{5}\right) = 20\left(\frac{3}{4}\right)$$

$$4(w) = 5(3)$$

$$4w = 15$$

$$w = \frac{15}{4}$$

The length of the missing side is $\dfrac{15}{4}$ or 3.75 cm.

75. Since the corresponding lengths of similar triangles are proportional, to find a, we can solve the following equation.

$$\frac{9}{4} = \frac{x+9}{x}$$

$$4x\left(\frac{9}{4}\right) = 4x\left(\frac{x+9}{x}\right)$$

$$9x = 4(x+9)$$

$$9x = 4x + 36$$

$$5x = 36$$

$$x = 7.2$$

The value of x is 7.2

Cumulative Review

1.

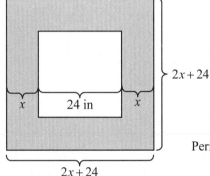

Perimeter: $4(2x+24) = 4 \cdot 2x + 4 \cdot 24 = 8x + 96$ in

2. $\sqrt{4} + \sqrt{4} + \sqrt{4} + \sqrt{4} = 2 + 2 + 2 + 2 = 8$

3. $\sqrt{4 + 4 + 4 + 4} = \sqrt{16} = 4$

4. The new price is $P + 0.10P = (1 + 0.10)P = 1.10P$.

5. The new price is $P - 0.10P = (1 - 0.10)P = 0.90P$.

Section 2.8: More Applications of Linear Equations

Quick Review 2.8

1. $D = RT = (250)(3) = 750$: The plane will fly 750 miles.

2.
$$1.50x + 3.25x = 323$$
$$4.75x = 323$$
$$\frac{4.75x}{4.75} = \frac{323}{4.75}$$
$$x \approx 68$$

3.
$$3x - 6 = 2x + 7$$
$$3x - 2x - 6 = 2x - 2x + 7$$
$$x - 6 + 6 = 7 + 6$$
$$x = 13$$
The equation is a conditional equation. The solution is $x = 13$.

5.
$$3x - 6 = 3(x - 2)$$
$$3x - 6 = 3x - 6$$
$$3x - 3x - 6 = 3x - 3x - 6$$
$$-6 = -6$$
The equation is an identity.

4.
$$3x - 6 = 3(x - 4)$$
$$3x - 6 = 3x - 12$$
$$3x - 3x - 6 = 3x - 3x - 12$$
$$-6 \neq -12$$
The equation is a contradiction.

Exercises 2.8

1.   You can only remove an integer number of pieces each 50 ft long. The least number of pieces removed is zero. The greatest number of pieces is 10 (only 500 total ft is available). Therefore the practical domain is **B.** $\{0, 1, 2, 3, \ldots, 10\}$.

3.   Since the tank has a capacity of 100 gallons and there is already 70 gallons of a 5% solution present, then the amount of 8% solution that can be added to the tank can be any real number between zero and thirty. Therefore the practical domain is **D.** $[0, 30]$.

5.   The number of trips on the toll road must be an integer between zero and fifty (only $100 is available). Therefore the practical domain is $\{0, 1, 2, 3, \ldots, 49, 50\}$.

7.   Since the tank has a capacity of 400 gallons and there is already 175 gallons of a 7% solution present, then the amount of the stronger solution that can be added to the tank can be any real number between 0 and 225. Therefore the practical domain is $[0, 225]$.

9.   **a.** Let x represent the number of months the truck is used.
      b. $\boxed{\text{Current Thickness}} - \boxed{\text{Wear}} = 4.0$
      c. $11.2 - 0.2x = 4.0$
      d. $11.2 - 0.2x = 4.0$
      $$-0.2x = -7.2$$
      $$x = 36$$
      e. This solution seems reasonable.
      f. The truck can be used for 36 months before the brake pad is reduced to 4.0 mm.

11.   **Define the Variable:** Let x represent the number of minutes of long distance billed.
      Verbal Equation: $\boxed{\text{Total Charge}} = \boxed{\text{Variable Charge}} + \boxed{\text{Fixed Charge}}$
      Algebraic Equation: $42.20 = 0.05x + 24.95$
      $$0.05x = 17.25$$
      $$x = 345$$
      Answer: The bill was for 345 minutes of long distance.

13.   **Define the Variable:** Let x represent the number of cushions manufactured.
      Verbal Equation: $\boxed{\text{Total Cost}} = \left(\boxed{\text{Average Cost Per Cushion}}\right)\left(\boxed{\text{Number of Cushions}}\right)$
      Algebraic Equation: $(150 + 6x) = (9)(x)$
      $$3x = 150$$
      $$x = 50$$
      Answer: The manufacturer should make 50 cushions per day to have an average cost of $9.00 per cushion.

15.   **Define the Variable:** Let x represent the rate of return on the second investment.
      Verbal Equation: $\boxed{\begin{array}{c}\text{Interest From}\\ \text{Treasury Bond}\end{array}} + \boxed{\begin{array}{c}\text{Interest From}\\ \text{Second Inverstment}\end{array}} = \boxed{\begin{array}{c}\text{Total Interest}\\ \text{Earned}\end{array}}$
      Algebraic Equation: $(0.05)(60000) + x(90000) = 10200$
      $$90000x = 7200$$
      $$x = 0.08$$
      Answer: The rate of return on the second investment must be 8%.

17. **Define the Variable:** Let x represent the principal that is invested in the corporate bond.

    Verbal Equation: $\boxed{\begin{array}{c}\text{Interest From}\\\text{Treasury Bond}\end{array}} + \boxed{\begin{array}{c}\text{Interest From}\\\text{the Corporate Bond}\end{array}} = \boxed{\begin{array}{c}\text{Total Interest}\\\text{Earned}\end{array}}$

    Algebraic Equation: $(0.055)(10000) + (0.06)(x) = 4000$

    $$0.06x = 3450$$
    $$x = 57500$$

    Answer: The principal that is invested in the corporate bond is \$57,500.

19. **Define the Variable:** Let x represent the number of hours that the boats have been traveling.

    Verbal Equation: $\boxed{\begin{array}{c}\text{Distance Traveled}\\\text{by the First Boat}\end{array}} + \boxed{\begin{array}{c}\text{Distance Traveled}\\\text{by the Second Boat}\end{array}} = \boxed{\begin{array}{c}\text{Total Distance}\\\text{Between Boats}\end{array}}$

    Algebraic Equation: $12x + 8x = 64$

    $$20x = 64$$
    $$x = 3.2$$

    Answer: The boats have been traveling for 3.2 hours (3 hours and 12 minutes).

21. **Define the Variable:** Let x represent the number of hours that it takes for the vehicles to meet.

    Verbal Equation: $\boxed{\begin{array}{c}\text{Distance Traveled}\\\text{by the Car}\end{array}} + \boxed{\begin{array}{c}\text{Distance Traveled}\\\text{by the Truck}\end{array}} = \boxed{\begin{array}{c}\text{Total Distance Traveled}\\\text{by the Vehicles}\end{array}}$

    Algebraic Equation: $70x + 60x = 364$

    $$130x = 364$$
    $$x = 2.8$$

    Answer: It takes 2.8 hours (2 hours and 48 minutes) for the vehicles to meet.

23. **Define the Variable:** Let x represent the number of gallons of the 1% solution added.

    Verbal Equation: $\boxed{\begin{array}{c}\text{Pesticide in}\\\text{Existing Mixture}\end{array}} + \boxed{\begin{array}{c}\text{Pesticide in}\\\text{Mixture Added}\end{array}} = \boxed{\begin{array}{c}\text{Total Pesticide}\\\text{in Desired Mixture}\end{array}}$

    Algebraic Equation: $0.005(100) + 0.01x = 0.008(100 + x)$

    $$0.5 + 0.01x = 0.8 + 0.008x$$
    $$0.002x = 0.3$$
    $$x = 150$$

    Answer: The crop dusting service should add 150 gallons of the 1% solution.

25. **Define the Variable:** Let x represent the number of gallons of ethanol added.

    Verbal Equation: $\boxed{\begin{array}{c}\text{Ethanol in}\\\text{Existing Mixture}\end{array}} + \boxed{\begin{array}{c}\text{Ethanol in}\\\text{Added Mixture}\end{array}} = \boxed{\begin{array}{c}\text{Total Ethanol}\\\text{in Desired Mixture}\end{array}}$

    Algebraic Equation: $0.04(12000) + 1.00x = 0.10(12000 + x)$

    $$480 + x = 1200 + 0.10x$$
    $$0.9x = 720$$
    $$x = 800$$

    Answer: The gasoline distributor should add 800 gallons of pure ethanol.

27. **Define the Variable:** Let x represent the number of gallons of water added.

    Verbal Equation:
Pesticide in Existing Mixture	+	Pesticide in Water Added	=	Total Pesticide in Desired Mixture

    Algebraic Equation: $0.01(75) + (0.00)x = 0.004(75 + x)$

    $$0.75 = 0.3 + 0.004x$$
    $$0.004x = 0.45$$
    $$x = 112.5$$

    Answer: The crop dusting service should add 112.5 gallons of water.

29. **Define the Variable:** Let x represent the amount of sand added.

    Verbal Equation:
Sand in Existing Mixture	+	Sand in Mixture Added	=	Total Sand in Desired Mixture

    Algebraic Equation: $0.15(360000) + 1.00x = 0.20(360000 + x)$

    $$54000 + x = 72000 + 0.20x$$
    $$0.80x = 18000$$
    $$x = 22500$$

    Answer: The company should add 22,500 lb of sand to the pile.

31. **Define the Variable:** Let x represent the number of MW of windmill generation capacity added.

    Verbal Equation:
MW of Windmill Generation	=	20% of Total Electricity

    Algebraic Equation: $x = 0.20(2 + x)$

    $$x = 0.4 + 0.20x$$
    $$0.8x = 0.4$$
    $$x = 0.5$$

    Answer: The city should add 0.5 MW of windmill generation capacity.

33. a. **Define the Variable:** Let x represent the number of tiles produced.

    Verbal Equation:
Fixed Cost	+	Variable Cost	=	Total Cost

    Algebraic Equation: $2000 + 0.50x = 5750$

    $$0.50x = 3750$$
    $$x = 7500$$

    Answer: The manufacturer produced 7,500 tiles.

    b. **Define the Variable:** Let x represent the number of tiles produced.

    Verbal Equation:
Total Cost	=	Average Cost Per Tile		Number of Tiles

    Algebraic Equation: $2000 + 0.50x = (0.70)(x)$

    $$2000 = 0.20x$$
    $$x = 10000$$

    Answer: The manufacturer must produce 10,000 tiles. (Since the capacity is 8000 tiles, the company can not manufacture the tiles at an average cost of $0.70 per tile.)

35. **a.** **<u>Define the Variable:</u>** Let x represent the number of gallons of ethanol added.

<u>Verbal Equation:</u> $\boxed{\begin{array}{c}\text{Ethanol in}\\\text{Existing Mixture}\end{array}} + \boxed{\begin{array}{c}\text{Ethanol in}\\\text{Added Mixture}\end{array}} = \boxed{\begin{array}{c}\text{Total Ethanol}\\\text{in Desired Mixture}\end{array}}$

<u>Algebraic Equation:</u> $0.04(19000) + 1.00x = 0.08(19000 + x)$

$$760 + x = 1520 + 0.08x$$
$$0.92x = 760$$
$$x \approx 826$$

<u>Answer:</u> The gasoline distributor must add approximately 826 gallons of ethanol.

b. **<u>Define the Variable:</u>** Let x represent the number of gallons of ethanol added.

<u>Verbal Equation:</u> $\boxed{\begin{array}{c}\text{Ethanol in}\\\text{Existing Mixture}\end{array}} + \boxed{\begin{array}{c}\text{Ethanol in}\\\text{Added Mixture}\end{array}} = \boxed{\begin{array}{c}\text{Total Ethanol}\\\text{in Desired Mixture}\end{array}}$

<u>Algebraic Equation:</u> $0.04(19000) + 1.00x = 0.10(19000 + x)$

$$760 + x = 1900 + 0.10x$$
$$0.90x = 1140$$
$$x \approx 1267$$

<u>Answer:</u> The gasoline distributor must add approximately 1,267 gallons of ethanol. (Since the capacity is 20,000 gallons, the company can not produce a 10% mixture from the existing mixture.)

37. **a.** **<u>Define the Variable:</u>** Let x represent the number of gallons of 1% pesticide added.

<u>Verbal Equation:</u> $\boxed{\begin{array}{c}\text{Pesticide in}\\\text{Existing Mixture}\end{array}} + \boxed{\begin{array}{c}\text{Pesticide in}\\\text{Added Mixture}\end{array}} = \boxed{\begin{array}{c}\text{Total Pesticide}\\\text{in Desired Mixture}\end{array}}$

<u>Algebraic Equation:</u> $0.005(80) + 0.01x = 0.009(80 + x)$

$$0.4 + 0.01x = 0.72 + 0.009x$$
$$0.001x = 0.32$$
$$x = 320$$

<u>Answer:</u> The crop dusting service should add 320 gallons of the 1% solution. (Since the tank capacity is 350 gallons, the company can not produce a 0.9% mixture from the existing mixture.)

b. **<u>Define the Variable:</u>** Let x represent the number of gallons of 1% pesticide added.

<u>Verbal Equation:</u> $\boxed{\begin{array}{c}\text{Pesticide in}\\\text{Existing Mixture}\end{array}} + \boxed{\begin{array}{c}\text{Pesticide in}\\\text{Added Mixture}\end{array}} = \boxed{\begin{array}{c}\text{Total Pesticide}\\\text{in Desired Mixture}\end{array}}$

<u>Algebraic Equation:</u> $0.005(80) + 0.01x = 0.008(80 + x)$

$$0.4 + 0.01x = 0.64 + 0.008x$$
$$0.002x = 0.24$$
$$x = 120$$

<u>Answer:</u> The crop dusting service should add 120 gallons of the 1% solution.

39. **a.** **<u>Verbal Equation:</u>** $\boxed{\text{Cost of Premium Mix}} + \boxed{\text{Cost of Standard Mix}} = \boxed{\text{Total Cost}}$

<u>Algebraic Equation:</u> $1.25(20) + 0.95(20) = 44$

<u>Answer:</u> The total cost of the mixture is $44.00

b. The mix should be sold for $\dfrac{\$44.00}{40\,\text{lb}} = \$1.10\,\text{per lb}$

c. **Define the Variable:** Let x represent the number of pounds of standard mix added.

Verbal Equation:

Cost of Premium Mix	+	Cost of Standard Mix	=	Total Cost of Desired Mixture

Algebraic Equation: $1.25(20) + 0.95x = 1.00(20 + x)$

$$25 + 0.95x = 20 + x$$
$$0.05x = 5$$
$$x = 100$$

The company should add 100 pounds of the standard mix.

d. The barrel must hold a total of $20 + 100 = 120$ pounds.

e. **Define the Variable:** Let x represent the number of pounds of standard mix added.

Verbal Equation:

Cost of Premium Mix	+	Cost of Standard Mix	=	Total Cost of Desired Mixture

Algebraic Equation: $1.25(20) + 0.95x = 1.05(20 + x)$

$$25 + 0.95x = 21 + 1.05x$$
$$0.10x = 4$$
$$x = 40$$

The company should add 40 pounds of the standard mix.

Cumulative Review

1. A polygon with equal sides is called a <u>regular</u> polygon.
2. A hexagon has <u>six</u> sides.
3. A trapezoid has <u>four</u> sides.
4. If the sum of the measures of two angles is $90°$, the angles are <u>complementary</u>.
5. If two parallel lines are cut by a transversal, then two angles that are on opposite sides of the transversal and between the parallel lines are called <u>alternate interior</u> angles.

Review Exercises for Chapter 2

1. A: $(4, 0)$ is on the x axis

        B: $(2, 4)$ is in quadrant I

        C: $(-6, 2)$ is in quadrant II

        D: $(0, -2)$ is on the y axis

2.

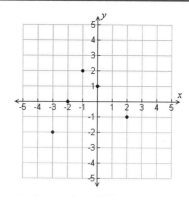

3.　　**a.** $\{(1, 1), (2, -1), (3, -3), (4, -5), (5, -7)\}$

b.

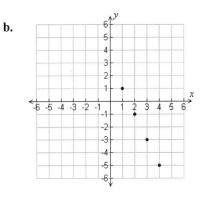

4.

Numerical difference
Between terms
$7 - 4 = 3$
$10 - 7 = 3$
$13 - 10 = 3$
$16 - 13 = 3$

This is an arithmetic sequence because there is a common difference of 3. The sequence forms a linear pattern.

5.

Numerical difference
Between terms
$1 - 0 = 1$
$3 - 1 = 2$
$6 - 3 = 3$
$10 - 6 = 4$

This is not an arithmetic sequence because the change from term to term is not constant. The sequence does not form linear pattern.

6. The sequence is not arithmetic because the points do not lie along the same line. The sequence does not form linear pattern.

7. The sequence is arithmetic because the points lie along the same line. $d = 2$. The sequence forms a linear pattern.

8.　　**a.** We can see from the graph that the elevation of the water in 2009 was 3,610 ft.
　　b. We can see from the graph that the water level was increasing from 2004 to 2006.
　　c. We can see from the graph that the water level was at its lowest in 2004.

9. To determine if $(3, -2)$ is a solution of $y - 3 = 4(x + 2)$ we replace x with 3 and y with -2 and then simplify.

$$y - 3 = 4(x + 2)$$
$$(-2) - 3 = 4((3) + 2)$$
$$-5 = 4(5)$$
$$-5 \neq 20$$

Thus, $(3, -2)$ is not a solution of $y - 3 = 4(x + 2)$.

To determine if $(-3, 2)$ is a solution of $y - 3 = 4(x + 2)$ we replace x with -3 and y with 2 and then simplify.

$$y - 3 = 4(x + 2)$$
$$(2) - 3 = 4((-3) + 2)$$
$$-1 = 4(-1)$$
$$-1 \neq -4$$

Thus, $(-3, 2)$ is not a solution of $y - 3 = 4(x + 2)$.

10. To determine if $(3, -2)$ is a solution of $y = x + 5$ we replace x with 3 and y with -2 and then simplify.

$$y = x + 5$$
$$(-2) = (3) + 5$$
$$-2 \neq 8$$

Thus, $(3, -2)$ is not a solution of $y = x + 5$.

To determine if $(-3, 2)$ is a solution of $y = x + 5$ we replace x with -3 and y with 2 and then simplify.

$$y = x + 5$$
$$(2) = (-3) + 5$$
$$2 = 2$$

Thus, $(-3, 2)$ is a solution of $y = x + 5$.

11.

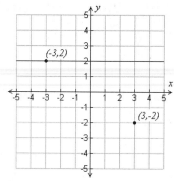

From the graph we see that the line contains the point $(-3, 2)$ but not $(3, -2)$. Thus, $(-3, 2)$ is a solution and $(3, -2)$ is not.

12.

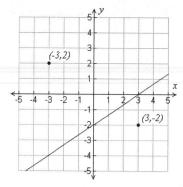

From the graph we can see that the line does not contain either point. Thus, neither point is a solution.

13. **x-intercept**
To find the x-intercept, substitute 0 for y.
$$2x - 3y = 6$$
$$2x - 3(0) = 6$$
$$2x = 6$$
$$\frac{2x}{2} = \frac{6}{2}$$
$$x = 3$$
$(3, 0)$ is the x-intercept.

y-intercept
To find the y-intercept, substitute 0 for x.
$$2x - 3y = 6$$
$$2(0) - 3y = 6$$
$$-3y = 6$$
$$\frac{-3y}{-3} = \frac{6}{-3}$$
$$y = -2$$
$(0, -2)$ is the y-intercept.

14. **_x-intercept_**
To find the _x_-intercept, substitute 0 for _y_.
$$y = x + 5$$
$$(0) = x + 5$$
$$0 - 5 = x + 5 - 5$$
$$-5 = x$$
$(-5, 0)$ is the _x_-intercept.

y-intercept
To find the _y_-intercept, substitute 0 for _x_.
$$y = x + 5$$
$$y = (0) + 5$$
$$y = 5$$
$(0, 5)$ is the _y_-intercept.

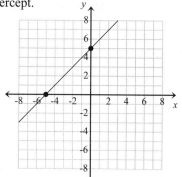

15. **x-intercept**
To find the _x_-intercept, substitute 0 for _y_.
$$y - 3 = 4(x + 2)$$
$$(0) - 3 = 4(x + 2)$$
$$-3 = 4x + 8$$
$$-3 - 8 = 4x + 8 - 8$$
$$-11 = 4x$$
$$\frac{-11}{4} = \frac{4x}{4}$$
$$-\frac{11}{4} = x$$
$\left(-\dfrac{11}{4}, 0\right)$ or $(-2.75, 0)$ is the _x_-intercept.

y-intercept
To find the _y_-intercept, substitute 0 for _x_.
$$y - 3 = 4(x + 2)$$
$$y - 3 = 4((0) + 2)$$
$$y - 3 = 8$$
$$y - 3 + 3 = 8 + 3$$
$$y = 11$$
$(0, 11)$ is the _y_-intercept.

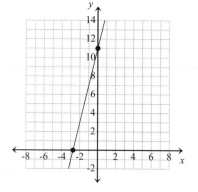

16. $5x + 3 = 2(x + 4)$ is a linear equation in x. Answer: **B**.

17. $5x^2 = 3$ is an equation that is not linear. Answer: **C**.

18. $y = 2x + 4$ is a linear equation in two variables. Answer: **D**.

19. $5x + 3 - 2(x + 4)$ is a first degree expression in x, but not a linear equation. Answer: **A**.

20. From the graph we can determine the point of intersection to be $(1, 2)$.

21. From the graph we can determine the point of intersection to be $(2, -3)$.

22. To determine if $x = 2$ is a solution of $3x + 5 = 4x + 2$ we replace x with 2 then simplify.

$$3x + 5 = 4x + 2$$
$$3(2) + 5 = 4(2) + 2$$
$$6 + 5 = 8 + 2$$
$$11 \neq 10$$

Thus, $x = 2$ is not a solution of $3x + 5 = 4x + 2$.

To determine if $x = 3$ is a solution of $3x + 5 = 4x + 2$ we replace x with 3 then simplify.

$$3x + 5 = 4x + 2$$
$$3(3) + 5 = 4(3) + 2$$
$$9 + 5 = 12 + 2$$
$$14 = 14 \text{ checks.}$$

Thus, $x = 3$ is a solution of $3x + 5 = 4x + 2$.

23. To determine if $x = 2$ is a solution of $3(x + 5) = 4(x + 3) + 1$ we replace x with 2 then simplify.

$$3(x + 5) = 4(x + 3) + 1$$
$$3((2) + 5) = 4((2) + 3) + 1$$
$$3(7) = 4(5) + 1$$
$$21 = 20 + 1$$
$$21 = 21 \text{ checks.}$$

Thus, $x = 2$ is a solution of $3(x + 5) = 4(x + 3) + 1$.

To determine if $x = 3$ is a solution of $3(x + 5) = 4(x + 3) + 1$ we replace x with 3 then simplify.

$$3(x + 5) = 4(x + 3) + 1$$
$$3((3) + 5) = 4((3) + 3) + 1$$
$$3(8) = 4(6) + 1$$
$$24 = 24 + 1$$
$$24 \neq 25$$

Thus, $x = 3$ is not a solution of $3(x + 5) = 4(x + 3) + 1$.

24. From the table we can determine that the y values are the same when x is 2.5. Thus, the solution is $x = 2.5$

25. From the table we can determine that the y values are the same when x is 24. Thus, the solution is $x = 24$.

26. From the graph we can see that the lines intersect at a point where $x = 3$. Therefore, the solution to the equation is $x = 3$.

27. From the graph we can see that the lines intersect at a point where $x = -1$. Therefore, the solution to the equation is $x = -1$.

28.
$$x + 2 = 17$$
$$x + 2 - 2 = 17 - 2$$
$$x = 15$$

29.
$$5v + 7 = 4v + 9$$
$$5v - 4v + 7 = 4v - 4v + 9$$
$$v + 7 = 9$$
$$v + 7 - 7 = 9 - 7$$
$$v = 2$$

30.
$$7m = 6m$$
$$7m - 6m = 6m - 6m$$
$$m = 0$$

31.
$$-x = 3$$
$$(-1)(-x) = (-1)(3)$$
$$x = -3$$

32.
$$-17m = -34$$
$$\frac{-17m}{-17} = \frac{-34}{-17}$$
$$m = 2$$

33.
$$\frac{n}{3} = -12$$
$$3\left(\frac{n}{3}\right) = 3(-12)$$
$$n = -36$$

34.
$$-\frac{2y}{7} = 28$$
$$\left(-\frac{7}{2}\right)\left(-\frac{2y}{7}\right) = (28)\left(-\frac{7}{2}\right)$$
$$y = -\frac{28}{2}(7)$$
$$y = -14(7)$$
$$y = -98$$

35.
$$0.045w = -0.18$$
$$\frac{0.045w}{0.045} = \frac{-0.18}{0.045}$$
$$w = -4$$

36.
$$117 = 0.01t$$
$$\frac{117}{0.01} = \frac{0.01t}{0.01}$$
$$11,700 = t \text{ or } t = 11,700$$

37.
$$0 = -147b$$
$$\frac{0}{-147} = \frac{-147b}{-147}$$
$$0 = b \text{ or } b = 0$$

38.
$$5x - 8 = 27$$
$$5x - 8 + 8 = 27 + 8$$
$$5x = 35$$
$$\frac{5x}{5} = \frac{35}{5}$$
$$x = 7$$

39.
$$-8z + 7 - 2z = 5z + 4 + z$$
$$-8z - 2z + 7 = 5z + z + 4$$
$$-10z + 7 = 6z + 4$$
$$-10z - 6z + 7 = 6z - 6z + 4$$
$$-16z + 7 - 7 = 4 - 7$$
$$-16z = -3$$
$$\frac{-16z}{-16} = \frac{-3}{-16}$$
$$z = \frac{3}{16}$$

40.
$$-r - r - r - r - r = r$$
$$-5r = r$$
$$-5r - r = r - r$$
$$\frac{-6r}{-6} = \frac{0}{-6}$$
$$r = 0$$

41.
$$3(2x + 7) = x + 1$$
$$6x + 21 = x + 1$$
$$6x - x + 21 = x - x + 1$$
$$5x + 21 - 21 = 1 - 21$$
$$\frac{5x}{5} = \frac{-20}{5}$$
$$x = -4$$

42.
$$(6x - 9) - (3x + 8) = 4(x - 11)$$
$$6x - 9 - 3x - 8 = 4x - 44$$
$$6x - 3x - 9 - 8 = 4x - 44$$
$$3x - 17 = 4x - 44$$
$$3x - 3x - 17 = 4x - 3x - 44$$
$$-17 = x - 44$$
$$-17 + 44 = x - 44 + 44$$
$$27 = x \text{ or } x = 27$$

43.
$$7y - 5(2 - y) = 3(2y + 1) + 5$$
$$7y - 10 + 5y = 6y + 3 + 5$$
$$7y + 5y - 10 = 6y + 3 + 5$$
$$12y - 10 = 6y + 8$$
$$12y - 6y - 10 = 6y - 6y + 8$$
$$6y - 10 = 8$$
$$6y - 10 + 10 = 8 + 10$$
$$6y = 18$$
$$\frac{6y}{6} = \frac{18}{6}$$
$$y = 3$$

44.

$$9(2y-3)-13(5y-1)=14(3y-1)$$
$$18y-27-65y+13=42y-14$$
$$18y-65y-27+13=42y-14$$
$$-47y-14=42y-14$$
$$-47y-42y-14=42y-42y-14$$
$$-89y-14=-14$$
$$-89y-14+14=-14+14$$
$$-89y=0$$
$$\frac{-89y}{-89}=\frac{0}{-89}$$
$$y=0$$

45.

$$0.55(w-10)=0.80(w+3)$$
$$0.55w-5.5=0.80w+2.4$$
$$0.55w-0.80w-5.5=0.80w-0.80w+2.4$$
$$-0.25w-5.5=2.4$$
$$-0.25w-5.5+5.5=2.4+5.5$$
$$-0.25w=7.9$$
$$\frac{-0.25w}{-0.25}=\frac{7.9}{-0.25}$$
$$w=-31.6$$

46.

$$\frac{t}{8}-5=\frac{t}{12}-6$$
$$24\left(\frac{t}{8}-5\right)=24\left(\frac{t}{12}-6\right)$$
$$\frac{24}{8}t-24(5)=\frac{24}{12}t-24(6)$$
$$3t-120=2t-144$$
$$3t-2t-120=2t-2t-144$$
$$t-120=-72$$
$$t-120+120=-144+120$$
$$t=-24$$

47.

$$\frac{7m+27}{6}=\frac{4m+6}{5}$$
$$30\left(\frac{7m+27}{6}\right)=30\left(\frac{4m+6}{5}\right)$$
$$\frac{30}{6}(7m+27)=\frac{30}{5}(4m+6)$$
$$5(7m+27)=6(4m+6)$$
$$35m+135=24m+36$$
$$35m-24m+135=24m-24m+36$$
$$11m+135=36$$
$$11m+135-135=36-135$$
$$11m=-99$$
$$\frac{11m}{11}=\frac{-99}{11}$$
$$m=-9$$

48.

$$\frac{167-3n}{10} = 6 - \frac{5n-1}{4}$$

$$20\left(\frac{167-3n}{10}\right) = 20\left(6 - \frac{5n-1}{4}\right)$$

$$\frac{20}{10}(167-3n) = 20(6) - \frac{20}{4}(5n-1)$$

$$2(167-3n) = 120 - 5(5n-1)$$

$$334 - 6n = 120 - 25n + 5$$

$$334 - 6n = 120 + 5 - 25n$$

$$334 - 6n = 125 - 25n$$

$$334 - 6n + 25n = 125 - 25n + 25n$$

$$334 + 19n = 125$$

$$334 - 334 + 19n = 125 - 334$$

$$19n = -209$$

$$\frac{19n}{19} = \frac{-209}{19}$$

$$n = -11$$

49.

$$1293y = 1294y + 1295$$

$$1293y - 1294y = 1294y - 1294y + 1295$$

$$-y = 1295$$

$$(-1)(-y) = (-1)(1295)$$

$$y = -1,295$$

50.

$$0.289x - 5 = 0.488 - 0.78(2-x)$$

$$0.289x - 5 = 0.488 - 1.56 + 0.78x$$

$$0.289x - 5 = -1.072 + 0.78x$$

$$0.289x - 0.78x - 5 = -1.072 + 0.78x - 0.78x$$

$$-0.491x - 5 = -1.072$$

$$-0.491x - 5 + 5 = -1.072 + 5$$

$$-0.491x = 3.928$$

$$\frac{-0.491x}{-0.491} = \frac{3.928}{-0.491}$$

$$x \approx -8$$

51.

$$\frac{3v}{10} - \frac{5v}{6} = -\frac{8v}{15}$$

$$30\left(\frac{3v}{10} - \frac{5v}{6}\right) = 30\left(-\frac{8v}{15}\right)$$

$$\frac{30}{10}(3v) - \frac{30}{6}(5v) = -\frac{30}{15}(8v)$$

$$3(3v) - 5(5v) = -2(8v)$$

$$9v - 25v = -16v$$

$$-16v = -16v$$

$$-16v + 16v = -16v + 16v$$

$$0 = 0$$

The equation is an identity. All real numbers are solutions.

52.

$$1.8a - 7.8a + 1.97a - 8.3a = 0$$

$$1.8a - 7.8a + 1.97a - 8.3a = 0$$

$$-12.33a = 0$$

$$\frac{-12.33a}{-12.33} = \frac{0}{-12.33}$$

$$a = 0$$

53. Let $y_1 = 1.5x - 1.2$, $y_2 = 2.7x - 3.0$ and sketch the graphs. The solution is the value of x in the point of intersection.

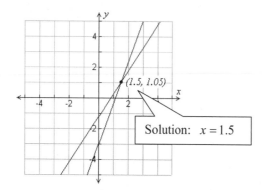

54. Let $y_1 = 8.5x - 24$, $y_2 = 12.5x - 33.6$ and sketch the graphs. The solution is the value of x in the point of intersection.

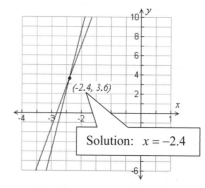

55.
$$7(y-3)-4(y+2)=3(y-7)$$
$$7y-21-4y-8=3y-21$$
$$7y-4y-21-8=3y-21$$
$$3y-39=3y-21$$
$$3y-3y-39=3y-3y-21$$
$$-39 \neq -21$$
The equation is a contradiction. There is no solution.

57.
$$4(w-1)+(7-2w)=2(w+1)+1$$
$$4w-4+7-2w=2w+2+1$$
$$4w-2w-4+7=2w+3$$
$$2w+3=2w+3$$
$$2w-2w+3=2w-2w+3$$
$$3=3 \text{ is a true statement.}$$
The equation is an identity. Every real number is a solution.

59.
 a. $f(-10)=7(-10)-11=-70-11=-81$
 b. $f(0)=7(0)-11=0-11=-11$
 c. $f(9)=7(9)-11=63-11=52$
 d. $f(\pi)=7(\pi)-11\approx 10.991$

56.
$$3(2v+1)=2(3v+1)$$
$$6v+3=6v+2$$
$$6v-6v+3=6v-6v+2$$
$$3 \neq 2$$
The equation is a contradiction. There is no solution.

58.
$$2v+2v+2v=5v$$
$$6v=5v$$
$$6v-5v=5v-5v$$
$$v=0$$
The equation is a conditional equation. The solution is 0.

60.
 a. $f(-3)=5(4(-3)-3)+1=5(-12-3)+1$
 $$=5(-15)+1=-75+1=-74$$
 b. $f(0)=5(4(0)-3)+1=5(0-3)+1$
 $$=5(-3)+1=-15+1=-14$$
 c. $f(6)=5(4(6)-3)+1=5(24-3)+1$
 $$=5(21)+1=105+1=106$$
 d. $f(100)=5(4(100)-3)+1=5(400-3)+1$
 $$=5(397)+1=1985+1=1,986$$

61.
$$v+w=x+y$$
$$v+w-y=x+y-y$$
$$v+w-y=x$$
$$\text{or } x=v+w-y$$

62.
$$vw=xy$$
$$\frac{vw}{y}=\frac{xy}{y}$$
$$\frac{vw}{y}=x$$
$$\text{or } x=\frac{vw}{y}$$

63.
$$3x-5y=7z$$
$$3x-5y+5y=7z+5y$$
$$3x=7z+5y$$
$$\frac{3x}{3}=\frac{7z+5y}{3}$$
$$x=\frac{7z+5y}{3}$$

64.
$$2(x-y)+3(2x+y)=38$$
$$2x-2y+6x+3y=38$$
$$2x+6x-2y+3y=38$$
$$8x+y=38$$
$$8x+y-y=38-y$$
$$8x=38-y$$
$$\frac{8x}{8}=\frac{38-y}{8}$$
$$x=\frac{38-y}{8}=-\frac{1}{8}y+\frac{19}{4}$$

65.
 a. $3x+4+5x+6=3x+5x+4+6$
 $$=8x+10$$

 b.
 $$3x+4=5x+6$$
 $$3x-5x+4=5x-5x+6$$
 $$-2x+4=6$$
 $$-2x+4-4=6-4$$
 $$-2x=2$$
 $$\frac{-2x}{-2}=\frac{2}{-2}$$
 $$x=-1$$

66.   **a.** $3x + 4 - (5x + 6) = 3x + 4 - 5x - 6$
$$= 3x - 5x + 4 - 6$$
$$= -2x - 2$$

67.   **a.** $-2x + 3 + 4(x - 1) = -2x + 3 + 4x - 4$
$$= -2x + 4x + 3 - 4$$
$$= 2x - 1$$

b. $3x + 4 = -5x + 6$
$$3x + 5x + 4 = -5x + 5x + 6$$
$$8x + 4 = 6$$
$$8x + 4 - 4 = 6 - 4$$
$$8x = 2$$
$$\frac{8x}{8} = \frac{2}{8}$$
$$x = \frac{1}{4}$$

b. $-2x + 3 = -4(x - 1)$
$$-2x + 3 = -4x + 4$$
$$-2x + 4x + 3 = -4x + 4x + 4$$
$$2x + 3 = 4$$
$$2x + 3 - 3 = 4 - 3$$
$$2x = 1$$
$$\frac{2x}{2} = \frac{1}{2}$$
$$x = \frac{1}{2}$$

68.   **a.** $5(x + 1) - 6(x + 2) = 5x + 5 - 6x - 12$
$$= 5x - 6x + 5 - 12$$
$$= -x - 7$$

b. $5(x + 1) = 6(x + 2)$
$$5x + 5 = 6x + 12$$
$$5x - 5x + 5 = 6x - 5x + 12$$
$$5 = x + 12$$
$$5 - 12 = x + 12 - 12$$
$$-7 = x \text{ or } x = -7$$

Problem	Mental Estimate	Calculator Solution
69. $0.99x - 5.1 = 4.8495$	$0.99x - 5.1 = 4.8495$ $x - 5 \approx 5$ $x - 5 + 5 \approx 5 + 5$ $x \approx 10$	$x = 10.05$
70. $11x - 20 = 9x + 19.9$	$11x - 20 = 9x + 19.9$ $11x - 20 \approx 9x + 20$ $11x - 9x - 20 \approx 9x - 9x + 20$ $2x - 20 \approx 20$ $2x - 20 + 20 \approx 20 + 20$ $2x \approx 40$ $\frac{2x}{2} \approx \frac{40}{2}$ $x \approx 20$	$x = 19.95$

71. $\underbrace{\text{Four more than five times a number}}\ \underbrace{\text{is}}\ \underbrace{\text{forty-nine.}}$

$$5m + 4 \qquad = \qquad 49$$
$$5m + 4 - 4 = 49 - 4$$
$$5m = 45$$
$$\frac{5m}{5} = \frac{45}{5}$$
$$m = 9$$

The number is 9.

72. One-third of the sum of a number and seven equals twelve.

$$\frac{1}{3}(m+7) \qquad = \qquad 12$$

$$\frac{1}{3}(m+7) = 12$$

$$3\left(\frac{1}{3}(m+7)\right) = 3(12)$$

$$\frac{\cancel{3}}{\cancel{3}}(m+7) = 36$$

$$m+7 = 36$$

$$m+7-7 = 36-7$$

$$m = 29$$

The number is 29.

73. Twice the quantity of two more than a number is the opposite of the quantity of three less than the number.

$$2(m+2) \qquad = \qquad -(m-3)$$

$$2m+4 = -m+3$$

$$2m+m+4 = -m+m+3$$

$$3m+4 = 3$$

$$3m+4-4 = 3-4$$

$$3m = -1$$

$$\frac{3m}{3} = \frac{-1}{3}$$

$$m = -\frac{1}{3}$$

The number is $-\frac{1}{3}$.

74. The sum of a number, one more than the number, and two more than the number is ninety-three.

$$m+(m+1)+(m+2) \qquad = \qquad 93$$

$$m+(m+1)+(m+2) = 93$$

$$m+m+1+m+2 = 93$$

$$m+m+m+1+2 = 93$$

$$3m+3 = 93$$

$$3m+3-3 = 93-3$$

$$3m = 90$$

$$\frac{3m}{3} = \frac{90}{3}$$

$$m = 30$$

The number is 30.

75. If v varies directly as w then we can set up and solve the following proportion.

$$\frac{v}{35} = \frac{22}{77}$$

$$35\left(\frac{v}{35}\right) = 35\left(\frac{22}{77}\right)$$

$$v = 10$$

Thus $v = 10$ when $w = 35$.

76. If v varies directly as w then $v = kw$ for some constant of variation k to find the value of k we can substitute w with 15 and v with 12 and solve the equation.

$$v = kw$$

$$12 = k(15)$$

$$\frac{12}{15} = \frac{k(15)}{15}$$

$$\frac{\cancel{3} \cdot 4}{\cancel{3} \cdot 5} = k \ \text{ or } \ k = \frac{4}{5}$$

77. If x and y are directly proportional and y is 20 when x is 6 then we can set up and solve the following proportion.

$$\frac{y}{15} = \frac{20}{6}$$

$$30\left(\frac{y}{15}\right) = 30\left(\frac{20}{6}\right)$$

$$2y = 5 \cdot 20$$

$$2y = 100$$

$$y = 50$$

Thus $v = 50$ when $x = 15$.

78.   **a.** The perimeter of the rectangle is found by adding twice the width with twice the length. Thus the perimeter is $2w + 2(3w + 4) = 2w + 6w + 8 = 8w + 8$.

b. If $w = 12$ then the perimeter is $8w + 8 = 8(12) + 8$

$$= 104 \text{ cm}$$

c. $8w + 8 = 48$

d. $\quad 8w + 8 = 48$

$$8w + 8 - 8 = 48 - 8$$

$$8w = 40$$

$$w = 5$$

79.   **a.** The cost of making x pieces of pottery per week is the sum of the fixed cost and variable cost. Thus, the cost is $C = 160 + 26x$

b. If $x = 60$ then the cost is $C = 160 + 26x = 160 + 26(60) = \$1,720$

c. $160 + 26x = 1200$

d.
$$160 + 26x = 1200$$
$$160 - 160 + 26x = 1200 - 160$$
$$26x = 1040$$
$$\frac{26x}{26} = \frac{1040}{26}$$
$$x = 40$$

80.   Set up a verbal equation.

$$\frac{\text{actual distance}}{\text{distance on the map}} = \frac{\text{actual distance}}{\text{distance on the map}}$$

Substitute the given values to translate the word equation into an algebraic one then solve the equation.
$$\frac{x}{10.5} = \frac{20}{1}$$
$$10.5\left(\frac{x}{10.5}\right) = 10.5\left(\frac{20}{1}\right)$$
$$x = 210$$

The distance between the cities is 210 miles.

81.   Since corresponding parts of the polygons are proportional we can solve each of the following equations to find a, b, and c.

$$\frac{a}{3} = \frac{7.5}{5} \qquad\qquad \frac{b}{9} = \frac{7.5}{5} \qquad\qquad \frac{c}{5} = \frac{7.5}{5}$$
$$3\left(\frac{a}{3}\right) = 3\left(\frac{7.5}{5}\right) \qquad 9\left(\frac{b}{9}\right) = 9\left(\frac{7.5}{5}\right) \qquad 5\left(\frac{c}{5}\right) = 5\left(\frac{7.5}{5}\right)$$
$$a = 4.5 \text{ cm} \qquad\qquad b = 13.5 \text{ cm} \qquad\qquad c = 7.5 \text{ cm}$$

82.   Set up a verbal equation.

$$\frac{\text{height of the object}}{\text{length of the shadow}} = \frac{\text{height of the object}}{\text{length of the shadow}}$$

Substitute the given values to translate the word equation into an algebraic one then solve the equation.
$$\frac{x}{46.2} = \frac{.64}{6.72}$$
$$46.2\left(\frac{x}{46.2}\right) = 46.2\left(\frac{.64}{6.72}\right)$$
$$x = 4.4$$

The height of the tree is 4.4 meters.

83. Let x be the airspeed of the plane. If there is a 50 mi/hr headwind and the airplane travels 20 miles in 5 minutes ($\frac{5}{60} = \frac{1}{12}$ of an hour), then using $\text{Distance} = \text{Rate} \cdot \text{Time}$ we have $20 = (x - 50)\left(\frac{1}{12}\right)$. Solving the equation gives us the following:

$$20 = (x - 50)\left(\frac{1}{12}\right)$$
$$20(12) = (x - 50)\left(\frac{1}{12}\right)(12)$$
$$240 = x - 50$$
$$240 + 50 = x - 50 + 50$$
$$290 = x$$

Thus, the airplane has an airspeed of 290 mi/hr.

84. Set up a verbal equation.

$$\frac{\text{defective panels}}{\text{devices tested}} = \frac{\text{defective panels}}{\text{devices tested}}$$

Substitute the given values to translate the word equation into an algebraic one then solve the equation.

$$\frac{x}{500} = \frac{3}{75}$$
$$500\left(\frac{x}{500}\right) = 500\left(\frac{3}{75}\right)$$
$$x = 20$$

One should expect 20 defective panels.

85. You can only remove an integer number of pieces each 50 ft long. The least number of pieces removed is zero. The greatest number of pieces is 20 (only 1000 total ft is available). Therefore the practical domain is **B.** $\{0, 1, 2, 3, \ldots, 20\}$.

86. You can remove 50 pieces of any length between 0 ft and 20 ft (only 1000 total ft is available). Therefore the practical domain is **C.** $[0, 20]$.

87. Since the tank has a capacity of 1000 gallons and there is already 635 gallons of a 8% solution present, then the amount of 12% solution that can be added to the tank can be any real number between 0 gallons and 365 gallons. Therefore the practical domain is **D.** $[0, 365]$

88. Since you can only rent the sign for an whole number of days and there are only 365 days in 2007, then the practical domain is **A.** $\{0, 1, 2, 3, \ldots, 365\}$.

89. Let t be the time it takes for the airplanes to be 2,975 miles apart. Using $\text{Distance} = \text{Rate} \cdot \text{Time}$ and the sum of the distances traveled by each plane is 2,975 miles we can solve the following equation:

$$400t + 450t = 2975$$
$$850t = 2975$$
$$\frac{850t}{850} = \frac{2975}{850}$$
$$t = 3.5$$

Thus, it takes 3.5 hours for the planes to be 2,975 miles apart.

90.   <u>**Define the Variable:**</u> Let x represent the number of gallons of water added.

<u>**Verbal Equation:**</u> $\boxed{\begin{array}{c}\text{Pesticide in}\\\text{Existing Mixture}\end{array}} + \boxed{\begin{array}{c}\text{Pesticide in}\\\text{Water Added}\end{array}} = \boxed{\begin{array}{c}\text{Total Pesticide}\\\text{in Desired Mixture}\end{array}}$

<u>**Algebraic Equation:**</u> $0.003(300) + (0.00)x = 0.002(300 + x)$

$$0.9 = 0.6 + 0.002x$$

$$0.002x = 0.3$$

$$x = 150$$

<u>**Answer:**</u> The crop dusting service should add 150 gallons of water. There is enough room in the tank.

Mastery Test for Chapter 2

1.   The point A is $(-3, 1)$ and is in quadrant II.

The point B is $(1, -3)$ and is in quadrant IV.

The point C is $(4, 2)$ and is in quadrant I.

The point D is $(-2, -2)$ and is in quadrant III.

2.

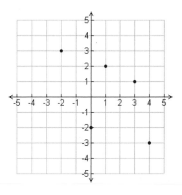

3.   **a.**

Numerical difference Between terms	This is an arithmetic sequence because there is a common difference of 2. The sequence forms a linear pattern.
$2 - 0 = 2$	
$4 - 2 = 2$	
$6 - 4 = 2$	
$8 - 6 = 2$	

b.

Numerical difference Between terms	This is not an arithmetic sequence because the difference between terms is not constant. The sequence does not form a linear pattern.
$2 - 1 = 1$	
$4 - 2 = 2$	
$8 - 4 = 4$	
$16 - 8 = 8$	

c.

Numerical difference Between terms	This is an arithmetic sequence because there is a common difference of 0. The sequence forms a linear pattern.
$4 - 4 = 0$	
$4 - 4 = 0$	
$4 - 4 = 0$	
$4 - 4 = 0$	

4.   **a.** From the graph we can see that the highest blood pressure that was recorded was 145.
b. From the graph we can see that the lowest blood pressure that was recorded was 130.
c. From the graph we can see that the lowest blood pressure was recorded in the third week.

Chapter 2: Linear Equations and Patterns

5. **a.** $f(0)=11(0)-7=0-7=-7$ **b.** $f(0)=11(-1)-7=-11-7=-18$

c. $f(7)=11(7)-7=77-7=70$ **d.** $f(0)=11(10)-7=110-7=103$

6. **a.**

x	$y=x+1$
1	$(1)+1=2$
2	$(2)+1=3$
3	$(3)+1=4$
4	$(4)+1=5$
5	$(5)+1=6$

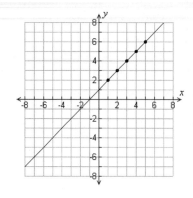

b.

x	$y=-x+2$
1	$-(1)+2=1$
2	$-(2)+2=0$
3	$-(3)+2=-1$
4	$-(4)+2=-2$
5	$-(5)+2=-3$

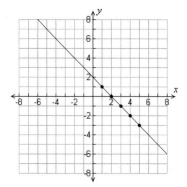

c.

x	$y=2x-5$
1	$2(1)-5=2-5=-3$
2	$2(2)-5=4-5=-1$
3	$2(3)-5=6-5=1$
4	$2(4)-5=8-5=3$
5	$2(5)-5=10-5=5$

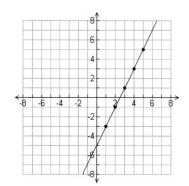

d.

x	$y=-2x+4$
1	$-2(1)+4=-2+4=2$
2	$-2(2)+4=-4+4=0$
3	$-2(3)+4=-6+4=-2$
4	$-2(4)+4=-8+4=-4$
5	$-2(5)+4=-10+4=-6$

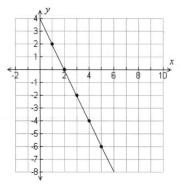

7. **a.** The total amount paid is the sum of the down payment ($800) and the total of the monthly payments ($375 for each of the x months paid). Thus the function for the total paid after x months is
$f(x) = 375x + 800$.

b.

x	$f(x) = 375x + 800$
0	$375(0) + 800 = 800$
6	$375(6) + 800 = 3,050$
12	$375(12) + 800 = 5,300$
18	$375(18) + 800 = 7,550$
24	$375(24) + 800 = 9,800$
30	$375(30) + 800 = 12,050$

c. $f(25) = 375(25) + 800 = 10175$. After 25 months the total amount paid is $10,175.

8. **a.** To determine if $(-2, 3)$ is a solution of
$y = 2x + 7$ we replace x with -2 and y with 3 and then simplify.
$$y = 2x + 7$$
$$(3) = 2(-2) + 7$$
$$3 = -4 + 7$$
$$3 = 3 \text{ checks.}$$
Thus, $(-2, 3)$ is a solution of $y = 2x + 7$.

b. To determine if $(-2, 3)$ is a solution of
$y = -x - 1$ we replace x with -2 and y with 3 and then simplify.
$$y = -x - 1$$
$$(3) = -(-2) - 1$$
$$3 = 2 - 1$$
$$3 \neq 1$$
Thus, $(-2, 3)$ is not a solution of $y = -x - 1$.

c. To determine if $(-2, 3)$ is a solution of $y = 3$ we replace y with 3 and then simplify.
$$y = 3$$
$$(3) = 3$$
$$3 = 3 \text{ checks.}$$
Thus, $(-2, 3)$ is a solution of $y = 3$.

d. To determine if $(-2, 3)$ is a solution of $x = -2$ we replace x with -2 and then simplify.
$$x = -2$$
$$(-2) = -2$$
$$-2 = -2 \text{ checks.}$$
Thus, $(-2, 3)$ is a solution of $x = -2$.

9. **a.** The x- and y- intercepts are the points where the line crosses the x- and y-axis respectfully. Thus, from the graph, we see that $(-2, 0)$ is the x-intercept and $(0, 3)$ is the y-intercept.

b. The x- and y- intercepts are the points where the line crosses the x- and y-axis respectfully. Thus, from the graph, we see that $(-3, 0)$ is the x-intercept and $(0, -1)$ is the y-intercept.

c. The x- and y- intercepts are the points where the line crosses the x- and y-axis respectfully. Thus, from the graph, we see that $(0, 2)$ is the y-intercept and since the graph never crosses the x-axis there is no x-intercept.

d. The x- and y- intercepts are the points where the line crosses the x- and y-axis respectfully. Thus, from the graph, we see that $(-1, 0)$ is the x-intercept and since the graph never crosses the y-axis there is no y-intercept.

10. **a.** From the graph we can see that the point of intersection is $(2, 1)$.

b. From the graph we can see that the point of intersection is $(-1, 3)$.

11. **a.** $x + 7 = 11$

$x + 7 - 7 = 11 - 7$

$x = 4$

b. $2x + 7 = x + 21$

$2x - x + 7 = x - x + 21$

$x + 7 = 21$

$x + 7 - 7 = 21 - 7$

$x = 14$

c. $7x + 1 = 6x + 1$

$7x - 6x + 1 = 6x - 6x + 1$

$x + 1 = 1$

$x + 1 - 1 = 1 - 1$

$x = 0$

d. $x + 2(x + 1) = 4x - 4$

$x + 2x + 2 = 4x - 4$

$3x + 2 = 4x - 4$

$3x - 3x + 2 = 4x - 3x - 4$

$2 = x - 4$

$2 + 4 = x - 4 + 4$

$x = 6$

12. **a.** Let $y_1 = \dfrac{x-4}{2}$, $y_2 = \dfrac{-3x+4}{2}$ and sketch the graphs. The solution is the value of x in the point of intersection.

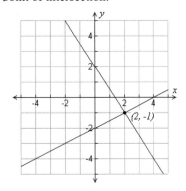

Solution: $x = 2$

b. Let $y_1 = 2.3x + 1.6$, $y_2 = 1.7x + 0.4$ and sketch the graphs. The solution is the value of x in the point of intersection.

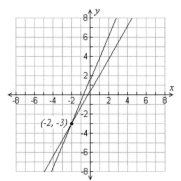

Solution: $x = -2$

13. **a.** $4(x + 2) = 4x + 8$

$4x + 8 = 4x + 8$

$4x - 4x + 8 = 4x - 4x + 8$

$8 = 8$ is a true statement.

The equation is an identity. Every real number is a solution.

b. $4(x + 2) = 4x + 2$

$4x + 8 = 4x + 2$

$4x - 4x + 8 = 4x - 4x + 2$

$8 \neq 2$

The equation is a contradiction. There is no solution.

c. $4(x + 2) = 2(x + 4)$

$4x + 8 = 2x + 8$

$4x - 2x + 8 = 2x - 2x + 8$

$2x + 8 = 8$

$2x + 8 - 8 = 8 - 8$

$2x = 0$

$\dfrac{2x}{2} = \dfrac{0}{2}$

$x = 0$

The equation is a conditional equation. The solution is 0.

14.   **a.**

$$-x = 3x - 12$$
$$-x - 3x = 3x - 3x - 12$$
$$-4x = -12$$
$$\frac{-4x}{-4} = \frac{-12}{-4}$$
$$x = 3$$

b.

$$-\frac{5}{21} = \frac{3y}{7}$$
$$21\left(-\frac{5}{21}\right) = 21\left(\frac{3y}{7}\right)$$
$$-\frac{21}{21}(5) = \frac{21}{7}(3v)$$
$$-5 = 3(3v)$$
$$-5 = 9v$$
$$\frac{-5}{9} = \frac{9v}{9}$$
$$-\frac{5}{9} = v \ \text{ or } \ v = -\frac{5}{9}$$

c.

$$3(2v + 4) = 4(v + 3) + 3$$
$$6v + 12 = 4v + 12 + 3$$
$$6v + 12 = 4v + 15$$
$$6v - 4v + 12 = 4v - 4v + 15$$
$$2v + 12 = 15$$
$$2v + 12 - 12 = 15 - 12$$
$$2v = 3$$
$$\frac{2v}{2} = \frac{3}{2}$$
$$v = \frac{3}{2}$$

d.

$$\frac{w-1}{6} = \frac{w-3}{5}$$
$$30\left(\frac{w-1}{6}\right) = 30\left(\frac{w-3}{5}\right)$$
$$\frac{30}{6}(w-1) = \frac{30}{5}(w-3)$$
$$5(w-1) = 6(w-3)$$
$$5w - 5 = 6w - 18$$
$$5w - 5w - 5 = 6w - 5w - 18$$
$$-5 = w - 18$$
$$-5 + 18 = w - 18 + 18$$
$$w = 13$$

15.

$$2x - y = 2(3x - y - 1) + 1$$
$$2x - y = 6x - 2y - 2 + 1$$
$$2x - y = 6x - 2y - 1$$
$$2x - y + 2y = 6x - 2y + 2y - 1$$
$$2x + y = 6x - 1$$
$$2x - 2x + y = 6x - 2x - 1$$
$$y = 4x - 1$$

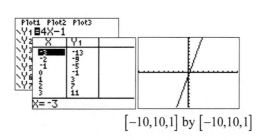

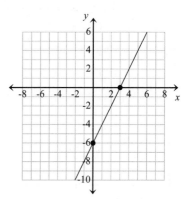

$$[-10, 10, 1] \text{ by } [-10, 10, 1]$$

16.   **a.** <u>**x-intercept**</u>

To find the *x*-intercept, substitute 0 for *y*.

$$y = 2x - 6$$
$$(0) = 2x - 6$$
$$0 - 2x = 2x - 2x - 6$$
$$-2x = -6$$
$$\frac{-2x}{-2} = \frac{-6}{-2}$$
$$x = 3$$

$(3, 0)$ is the *x*-intercept.

<u>**y-intercept**</u>

To find the *y*-intercept, substitute 0 for *x*.

$$y = 2x - 6$$
$$y = 2(0) - 6$$
$$y = -6$$

$(0, -6)$ is the *y*-intercept.

b. <u>*x*-intercept</u>

To find the *x*-intercept, substitute 0 for *y*.

$$y = 4$$

$$(0) = 4$$

$$0 \neq 4$$

The result is a contradiction. Thus there is no *x*-intercept. The line $y = 4$ is a horizontal line never intersecting with the *x*-axis.

<u>*y*-intercept</u>

To find the *y*-intercept, substitute 0 for *x*.

$$y = 4$$

Since the equation $y = 4$ is independent of *x*. $y = 4$ for all values of *x* (including zero). Thus, $(0, 4)$ is the *y*-intercept.

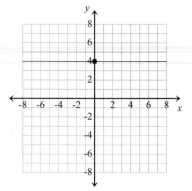

c. <u>*x*-intercept</u>

To find the *x*-intercept, substitute 0 for *y*.

$$2x - 5y = 10$$

$$2x - 5(0) = 10$$

$$2x = 10$$

$$\frac{2x}{2} = \frac{10}{2}$$

$$x = 5$$

$(5, 0)$ is the *x*-intercept.

<u>*y*-intercept</u>

To find the *y*-intercept, substitute 0 for *x*.

$$2x - 5y = 10$$

$$2(0) - 5y = 10$$

$$-5y = 10$$

$$\frac{-5y}{-5} = \frac{10}{-5}$$

$$y = -2$$

$(0, -2)$ is the *y*-intercept.

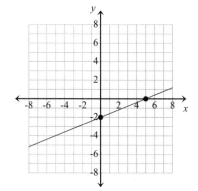

d. <u>*x*-intercept</u>

To find the *x*-intercept, substitute 0 for *y*.

$$3(2x - 1) = 4(3y - 2) - 7$$

$$6x - 3 = 4(3(0) - 2) - 7$$

$$6x - 3 = 4(-2) - 7$$

$$6x - 3 = -8 - 7$$

$$6x - 3 = -15$$

$$6x - 3 + 3 = -15 + 3$$

$$6x = -12$$

$$\frac{6x}{6} = \frac{-12}{6}$$

$$x = -2$$

$(-2, 0)$ is the *x*-intercept.

<u>*y*-intercept</u>

To find the *y*-intercept, substitute 0 for *x*.

$$3(2x - 1) = 4(3y - 2) - 7$$

$$3(2(0) - 1) = 12y - 8 - 7$$

$$3(-1) = 12y - 15$$

$$-3 + 15 = 12y - 15 + 15$$

$$12 = 12y$$

$$\frac{12}{12} = \frac{12y}{12}$$

$$1 = y$$

$(0, 1)$ is the *y*-intercept.

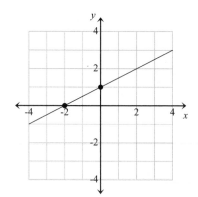

17.   **a.**
$$A = \frac{1}{2}h(a+b)$$
$$2 \cdot A = 2 \cdot \frac{1}{2}h(a+b)$$
$$\frac{2A}{h} = \frac{h(a+b)}{h}$$
$$\frac{2A}{h} - b = a + b - b$$
$$a = \frac{2A}{h} - b$$

b.
$$y = mx + b$$
$$\frac{y-b}{m} = \frac{mx}{m}$$
$$x = \frac{y-b}{m}$$

18.   **a.**
$$\frac{m-1}{m-7} = \frac{2}{5}$$
$$5(m-7)\left(\frac{m-1}{m-7}\right) = 5(m-7)\left(\frac{2}{5}\right)$$
$$5\frac{(m-7)}{(m-7)}(m-1) = \frac{5}{5}(m-7)(2)$$
$$5(1)(m-1) = (1)(m-7)(2)$$
$$5m - 5 = 2m - 14$$
$$5m - 2m - 5 = 2m - 2m - 14$$
$$3m - 5 = -14$$
$$3m - 5 + 5 = -14 + 5$$
$$3m = -9$$
$$\frac{3m}{3} = \frac{-9}{3}$$
$$m = -3$$

b.
$$\frac{2x-1}{7} = \frac{x+1}{4}$$
$$28\left(\frac{2x-1}{7}\right) = 28\left(\frac{x+1}{4}\right)$$
$$\frac{28}{7}(2x-1) = \frac{28}{4}(x+1)$$
$$4(2x-1) = 7(x+1)$$
$$8x - 4 = 7x + 7$$
$$8x - 7x - 4 = 7x - 7x + 7$$
$$x - 4 = 7$$
$$x - 4 + 4 = 7 + 4$$
$$x = 11$$

c. Set up a verbal equation.

$$\frac{\text{actual distance}}{\text{distance on the map}} = \frac{\text{actual distance}}{\text{distance on the map}}$$

Substitute the given values to translate the word equation into an algebraic one then solve the equation.
$$\frac{x}{5} = \frac{75}{2}$$
$$5\left(\frac{x}{5}\right) = 5\left(\frac{75}{2}\right)$$
$$x = 187.5$$
The distance between the cities is 187.5 kilometers.

19.   **a.** If y varies directly as x then we can set up and solve the following proportion.

$$\frac{y}{8} = \frac{33}{22}$$

$$8\left(\frac{y}{8}\right) = 8\left(\frac{33}{22}\right)$$

$$y = 12$$

Thus $y = 12$ when $x = 8$.

b. Let U = Number of U.S. dollars

M = Number Mexican Pesos

k = Constant of variation

If the number of Mexican Pesos varies directly as the number of U.S. dollars then $M = kU$. We can find the constant of variation by replacing U with 50 and M with 475 then solving the equation

$$475 = k(50)$$

$$\frac{475}{50} = \frac{k(50)}{50}$$

$$9.5 = k$$

The constant of variation is 9.5.

20.   **a.** The amount of pesticide can be any real number between 0 gallons and 30 gallons. Therefore the practical domain is $[0, 30]$.

b. The number of days that one can rent a paint sprayer in June can be any whole number between 0 and 30. Thus the practical domain is $\{0, 1, 2, 3, ..., 29, 30\}$.

c. Since the tank has a capacity of 500 gallons and there is already 200 gallons of a 6% solution present, then the amount of stronger solution that can be added to the tank can be any real number between 0 gallons and 300 gallons. Therefore the practical domain $[0, 300]$.

d. You can only remove an integer number of pieces each 25 ft long. The least number of pieces removed is zero. The greatest number of pieces is 10 (only 250 total ft is available). Therefore the practical domain is $\{0, 1, 2, 3, ..., 10\}$.

21.   **a.** Of the 5000 gallons already in the tank $(0.05)(5000) = 250$ gallons is pure ethanol. If 1000 additional gallons of pure ethanol is added, then the resulting 6000 gallon mixture will have an alcohol percentage of $\frac{1250}{6000} \approx 0.208$ or 20.8%.

b. Let x be the number of gallons of pure ethanol to add. If we already have 5000 gallons of a 5% solution and we want the resultant solution to be an 8% solution, then

$$1.00x + 0.05(5000) = 0.08(x + 5000)$$

$$x + 250 = 0.08x + 400$$

$$0.92x = 150$$

$$x \approx 163.04$$

Thus, approximately 163 gallons of pure ethanol must be added.

c. Let x be the number of gallons of pure ethanol to add. If we already have 5000 gallons of a 5% solution and we want the resultant solution to be an 10% solution, then

$$1.00x + 0.05(5000) = 0.10(x + 5000)$$

$$x + 250 = 0.10x + 500$$

$$0.90x = 250$$

$$x \approx 277.78$$

Thus, approximately 278 gallons of pure ethanol must be added.

Section 3.1: Slope of a Line and Applications of Slope

Quick Review 3.1

1. $\dfrac{6}{8} = \dfrac{\cancel{2} \cdot 3}{\cancel{2} \cdot 4} = \dfrac{3}{4}$

2. $\dfrac{2}{-8} = -\dfrac{\cancel{2}}{\cancel{2} \cdot 4} = -\dfrac{1}{4}$

3. $\dfrac{-9}{12} = -\dfrac{\cancel{3} \cdot 3}{\cancel{3} \cdot 4} = -\dfrac{3}{4}$

4. $\dfrac{5}{4} = 1.25$

5. -0.875

Exercises 3.1

1. **a.** Use $x_1 = 4$, $y_1 = 3$, $x_2 = 3$, $y_2 = 1$

$$m = \frac{y_2 - y_1}{x_2 - x_1} = \frac{1-3}{3-4} = \frac{-2}{-1} = 2$$

b. The points are the same as found in part **a**. Therefore the slope is the same. $m = 2$

3. Use $x_1 = 2$, $y_1 = -7$, $x_2 = -7$, $y_2 = 4$

$$m = \frac{y_2 - y_1}{x_2 - x_1} = \frac{4-(-7)}{-7-2} = \frac{11}{-9} = -\frac{11}{9}$$

5. Use $x_1 = 2$, $y_1 = -7$, $x_2 = 4$, $y_2 = -7$

$$m = \frac{y_2 - y_1}{x_2 - x_1} = 4\frac{-7-(-7)}{4-2} = \frac{0}{2} = 0$$

7. Use $x_1 = 2$, $y_1 = -7$, $x_2 = 2$, $y_2 = -10$

$$m = \frac{y_2 - y_1}{x_2 - x_1} = \frac{-10-(-7)}{2-2} = \frac{-3}{0}$$

m is undefined.

9. Use $x_1 = 0$, $y_1 = 0$, $x_2 = 1.40$, $y_2 = 0.56$

$$m = \frac{y_2 - y_1}{x_2 - x_1} = \frac{0.56-0}{1.40-0} = \frac{0.56}{1.40} = 0.40 = \frac{2}{5}$$

11. Use $x_1 = 0$, $y_1 = 0$, $x_2 = \dfrac{1}{3}$, $y_2 = \dfrac{1}{5}$

$$m = \frac{y_2 - y_1}{x_2 - x_1} = \frac{\frac{1}{5}-0}{\frac{1}{3}-0} = \frac{\frac{1}{5}}{\frac{1}{3}} = \frac{1}{5} \cdot \frac{3}{1} = \frac{3}{5}$$

13. **a.** Use $x_1 = 0$, $y_1 = -1$, $x_2 = 3$, $y_2 = 0$

$$m = \frac{y_2 - y_1}{x_2 - x_1} = \frac{0-(-1)}{3-0} = \frac{1}{3}$$

b. Use $x_1 = 0$, $y_1 = -2$, $x_2 = -1$, $y_2 = 0$

$$m = \frac{y_2 - y_1}{x_2 - x_1} = \frac{0-(-2)}{-1-0} = \frac{2}{-1} = -2$$

c. The line is vertical, and its slope is undefined.

d. The line is horizontal, and its slope is $m = 0$.

15. The slope of the line can be determined by using any two points in the table. For example, substitute $(0, 1)$ for (x_1, y_1) and $(2, 4)$ for (x_2, y_2).

$$m = \frac{y_2 - y_1}{x_2 - x_1} = \frac{4-1}{2-0} = \frac{3}{2}$$

17. First determine the intercepts so we have two points on the line.

x-intercept	y-intercept	Slope
$3x+5y=15$	$3x+5y=15$	Substitute $(5,0)$ for (x_1, y_1) and $(0,3)$
$3x+5(0)=15$	$3(0)+5y=15$	for (x_2, y_2)
$3x=15$	$5x=15$	
$x=5$	$x=3$	$m=\dfrac{y_2-y_1}{x_2-x_1}=\dfrac{3-0}{0-5}=\dfrac{3}{-5}=-\dfrac{3}{5}$
The x-intercept is $(5,0)$	The y-intercept is $(0,3)$	

19. The slope of the wheelchair ramp is
$$m=\frac{\text{rise}}{\text{run}}=\frac{3}{21}=\frac{1}{7}.$$

	m_1	$m_2=m_1$	$m_3=-\dfrac{1}{m_1}$
21.	$\dfrac{3}{7}$	$\dfrac{3}{7}$	$-\dfrac{7}{3}$
23.	0	0	Undefined

25. Calculate the slope of each line by substituting in the given points.

$(-3,5)$ and $(-6,3)$

$m=\dfrac{y_2-y_1}{x_2-x_1}$

$m=\dfrac{3-5}{-6-(-3)}$

$m=\dfrac{-2}{-3}$

$m=\dfrac{2}{3}$

$(3,-3)$ and $(6,-1)$

$m=\dfrac{y_2-y_1}{x_2-x_1}$

$m=\dfrac{-1-(-3)}{6-3}$

$m=\dfrac{2}{3}$

The slopes are equal. Thus the two lines are parallel.

27. Calculate the slope of each line by substituting in the given points.

$(5,4)$ and $(10,1)$

$m=\dfrac{y_2-y_1}{x_2-x_1}$

$m=\dfrac{1-4}{10-5}$

$m=\dfrac{-3}{5}$

$m=-\dfrac{3}{5}$

$(6,8)$ and $(3,3)$

$m=\dfrac{y_2-y_1}{x_2-x_1}$

$m=\dfrac{3-8}{3-6}$

$m=\dfrac{-5}{-3}$

$m=\dfrac{5}{3}$

Since $\left(-\dfrac{3}{5}\right)\left(\dfrac{5}{3}\right)=-1$, the two lines are perpendicular.

29. Calculate the slope of each line by substituting in the given points.

$(0,6)$ and $(8,0)$

$m = \dfrac{y_2 - y_1}{x_2 - x_1}$

$m = \dfrac{0-6}{8-0}$

$m = \dfrac{-6}{8}$

$m = -\dfrac{3}{4}$

$(-5,0)$ and $(0,-7)$

$m = \dfrac{y_2 - y_1}{x_2 - x_1}$

$m = \dfrac{-7-0}{0-(-5)}$

$m = \dfrac{-7}{5}$

$m = -\dfrac{7}{5}$

The two lines are neither perpendicular nor parallel.

31. Calculate the slope of each line by substituting in the given points.

$(0,6)$ and $(4,6)$ $\qquad$ $(0,6)$ and $(0,0)$

$m = \dfrac{y_2 - y_1}{x_2 - x_1}$ $\qquad$ $m = \dfrac{y_2 - y_1}{x_2 - x_1}$

$m = \dfrac{6-6}{4-0}$ $\qquad$ $m = \dfrac{0-6}{0-0}$

$m = \dfrac{0}{4}$ $\qquad$ $m = \dfrac{-6}{0}$

$m = 0$ $\qquad$ m is undefined.

The First line is horizontal and the second line is vertical. Thus, the lines are perpendicular.

33. Calculate the slope of each line by substituting in the given points.

$(5,3)$ and $(5,-3)$ $\qquad$ $(7,6)$ and $(7,-6)$

The two lines are both vertical lines. Thus they are

$m = \dfrac{y_2 - y_1}{x_2 - x_1}$ $\qquad$ $m = \dfrac{y_2 - y_1}{x_2 - x_1}$

$m = \dfrac{-3-3}{5-5}$ $\qquad$ $m = \dfrac{-6-6}{7-7}$

$m = \dfrac{-6}{0}$ $\qquad$ $m = \dfrac{-12}{0}$

m is undefined $\qquad$ m is undefined.

The lines are parallel.

35. To find the elevation permitted we can solve the following proportion.

$$\frac{y}{1800} = \frac{5}{100}$$

$$1800\left(\frac{y}{1800}\right) = 1800\left(\frac{5}{100}\right)$$

$$y = 90$$

The maximum elevation permitted over 1800 feet is 90 m.

37. The slope represents the change in y (cost) divided by the change in x (units produced). Therefore, the slope, indicates a production cost of $35 per unit produced.

39. The slope of the line can be determined by using any two points in he graph. For example, substitute $(1, 65)$ for (x_1, y_1) and $(2, 130)$ for (x_2, y_2).

$$m = \frac{y_2 - y_1}{x_2 - x_1} = \frac{130-65}{2-1} = \frac{65}{1} = 65$$

The speed of the car is 65 miles per hour.

	Change in x	Change in y	Slope $= \dfrac{\text{Change in } y}{\text{Change in } x}$
41.	-5	8	$\dfrac{8}{-5} = -\dfrac{8}{5}$
43.	3	2	$\dfrac{2}{3}$
45.	3	2	$\dfrac{2}{3}$
47.	6	0	$0 = \dfrac{0}{6}$

49. To find the height of the brace we can solve the following proportion.

$$\frac{h}{3} = \frac{14}{12}$$

$$3\left(\frac{h}{3}\right) = 3\left(\frac{14}{12}\right)$$

$$h = \frac{7}{2}$$

The brace has a height of 3.5 feet.

51. **a.** The rate at which the volume changes with respect to time is equivalent to the slope of the line passing through the points in the table. Use

$$x_1 = 0, \ y_1 = 500, \ x_2 = 20, \ y_2 = 440;$$

$$m = \frac{y_2 - y_1}{x_2 - x_1} = \frac{440 - 500}{20 - 0} = \frac{-60}{20} = -3.$$

Thus, the rate of change in the volume is -3 gallons per second.

b. The water is being used at a rate of 3 gallons per second.

c. At this rate the water will run out in

$$\frac{500}{3} \approx 166.7 \text{ seconds}$$

or 2 minutes and 47 seconds.

53. The line through P and Q is the same as the line through Q and P. Therefore, the lines have the same slope of $\frac{3}{7}$.

55. The slope of a line represents the change in y divided by the change in x. If the slope is

$m = -\frac{2}{3} = \frac{-2}{3}$, then for every 3 unit change in

x there will be a -2 unit change in y. Thus, table **a.** can be completed as described at the right. In tables b. and c. we adjust the change in y accordingly.

a.

x	y
0	5
3	$5 - 2 = 3$
6	$3 - 2 = 1$
9	$1 - 2 = -1$
12	$-1 - 2 = -3$

b.

x	y
0	5
6	$5 - 2(2) = 1$
12	$1 - 2(2) = -3$
18	$-3 - 2(2) = -7$
24	$-7 - 2(2) = -11$

57. **a.**

b. $\Delta x = 3$

c. $\Delta y = 5$

d. slope: $m = \dfrac{\Delta y}{\Delta x} = \dfrac{5}{3}$

59.

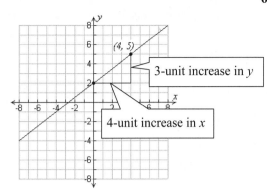

61.

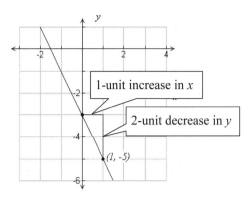

63. The line through the point $(1, 3)$ with a slope $m = 0$ is a horizontal line.

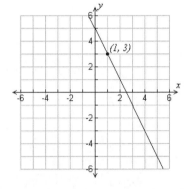

65.

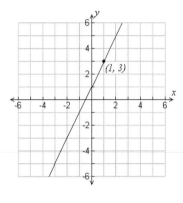

67.

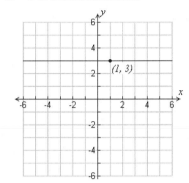

69.

  a. The x-intercept is $(2, 0)$.

  b. The y-intercept is $(0, 4)$.

  c. $m = \dfrac{y_2 - y_1}{x_2 - x_1} = \dfrac{4 - 0}{0 - 2} = \dfrac{4}{-2} = -2$

71. The x-axis is a horizontal line. It has a slope of $m = 0$.

73. If a line passes through quadrants I, II, and III but not quadrant IV, then it must slope upward to the right. Thus it has a positive slope.

75. If a line passes through quadrants II, III, and IV but not quadrant I, then it must slope downward to the right. Thus it has a negative slope.

77. If a line passes through quadrants I and III but not quadrants II and IV, then it must slope upward to the right. Thus it has a positive slope.

79. If y varies directly as x with a constant of variation 2, then $y = 2x$ and y will increase by 2 units for every one-unit change in x. Thus the slope of the line containing the data points is $m = 2$.

Cumulative Review

1. $(ab)c = a(bc)$ is an example of the associative property of multiplication since the factors have been regrouped. The proper choice is **B**.

2. $(a+b)+c = a+(b+c)$ is an example of the associative property of addition since the terms have been regrouped. The proper choice is **A**.

3. $a(bc+d) = a(cb+d)$ is an example of the commutative property of multiplication since the factors have been reordered. The proper choice is **D**.

4. $a(bc+d) = abc+ad$ is an example of the distributive property of multiplication over addition. The proper choice is **E**.

5. $a(bc+d) = a(d+bc)$ is an example of the commutative property of addition since the terms have been reordered. The proper choice is **C**.

Section 3.2: Special Forms of Linear Equations in Two Variables

Quick Review 3.2

1. **a.** Vertical lines have undefined slopes. The proper choice is **C**.
   b. Lines with negative slopes decrease from left to right. The proper choice is **D**.
   c. Horizontal lines have a slope of zero. The proper choice is **A**.
   d. Lines with positive slopes increase from left to right. The proper choice is **B**.

2.
$$2x+5y+20 = 0$$
$$2x-2x+5y+20-20 = 0-2x-20$$
$$5y = -2x-20$$
$$\frac{5y}{5} = \frac{-2x-20}{5}$$
$$y = \frac{-2x-20}{5} \text{ or } -\frac{2}{5}x-4$$

3.
x-intercept	**y-intercept**
To find the x-intercept, substitute 0 for y.	To find the y-intercept, substitute 0 for x.

x-intercept:
$$2x+5y+20 = 0$$
$$2x+5(0)+20 = 0$$
$$2x+20 = 0$$
$$2x+20-20 = -20$$
$$2x = -20$$
$$\frac{2x}{2} = \frac{-20}{2}$$
$$x = -10$$
The x-intercept is $(-10, 0)$

y-intercept:
$$2x+5y+20 = 0$$
$$2(0)+5y+20 = 0$$
$$5y+20 = 0$$
$$5y+20-20 = 0-20$$
$$5y = -20$$
$$\frac{5y}{5} = \frac{-20}{5}$$
$$y = -4$$
The y-intercept is $(0, -4)$

4. The least common denominator of the fractions $\frac{5}{6}$ and $\frac{2}{15}$ is 30.

5. The multiplicative inverse of $\frac{2}{15}$ is $\frac{15}{2}$.

Exercises 3.2

1. **a.** The equation $f(x) = 2x + 5$ is in the slope intercept form, $f(x) = mx + b$, with $m = 2$ and $b = 5$. Thus the slope is $m = 2$ and the y-intercept is $(0, 5)$.

b. The equation $f(x) = -\dfrac{3}{11}x - \dfrac{4}{5}$ is in the slope intercept form, $f(x) = mx + b$, with $m = -\dfrac{3}{11}$ and $b = -\dfrac{4}{5}$. Thus the slope is $m = -\dfrac{3}{11}$ and the y-intercept is $\left(0, -\dfrac{4}{5}\right)$.

c. The equation $f(x) = 6x$ is in the slope intercept form, $f(x) = mx + b$, with $m = 6$ and $b = 0$. Thus the slope is $m = 6$ and the y-intercept is $(0, 0)$.

3. Use the slope-intercept form. Substitute 4 for m and 7 for b.
$$y = mx + b$$
$$y = 4x + 7$$

5. Use the slope-intercept form. Substitute $-\dfrac{2}{11}$ for m and 5 for b.
$$y = mx + b$$
$$y = -\dfrac{2}{11}x + 5$$

7. Use the slope-intercept form. Substitute 0 for m and -6 for b.
$$y = mx + b$$
$$y = (0)x + (-6)$$
$$y = -6$$

9. Use the slope-intercept form to determine the slope and the y-intercept. To produce a second point, start with the y-intercept and adjust the x and y coordinates using the change in x and y from the slope.

Slope: $m = \dfrac{2}{3}$

y-intercept: $(0, -4)$

Second Point: $(0 + 3, -4 + 2) = (3, -2)$

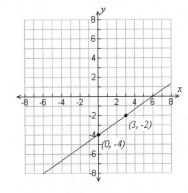

11. Use the slope-intercept form to determine the slope and the y-intercept. To produce a second point, start with the y-intercept and adjust the x and y coordinates using the change in x and y from the slope.

Slope: $m = \dfrac{-5}{3}$

y-intercept: $(0, 2)$

Second Point: $(0+3, 2-5) = (3, -3)$

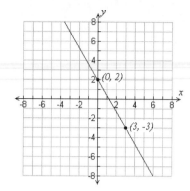

13. The line $f(x) = 2$ is a horizontal line with a y-intercept $(0, 2)$.

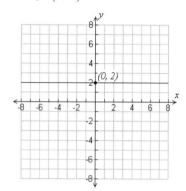

15. **a.** We can see the change in x is 5 and the change in y is 2 when obtaining a second point on the line. Thus the slope is $m = \dfrac{2}{5}$.

b. From the graph we can see that the y-intercept is $(0, 1)$.

c. The slope-intercept form of the line is $f(x) = \dfrac{2}{5}x + 1$.

17. **a.** We can the change in x is 4 and the change in y is -1 when obtaining a second point on the line. Thus the slope is $m = \dfrac{-1}{4}$.

b. From the graph we can see that the y-intercept is $(0, -1)$.

c. The slope-intercept form of the line is $f(x) = -\dfrac{1}{4}x - 1$.

19. **a.** From the table, we can see that $\Delta x = 1$.

b. From the table, we can see that $\Delta y = 7$.

c. The slope of the line is $m = \dfrac{\Delta y}{\Delta x} = \dfrac{7}{1} = 7$

d. From the table, we can see that the y-intercept is $(0, 1)$.

e. The slope-intercept form of the line is $f(x) = 7x + 1$.

21. **a.** From the table we can see that $\Delta x = 2$.

b. From the table we can see that $\Delta y = -1$.

c. The slope of the line is $m = \dfrac{\Delta y}{\Delta x} = \dfrac{-1}{2} = -\dfrac{1}{2}$

d. From the table we can see that the y-intercept is $(0, 8)$.

e. The slope-intercept form of the line is $f(x) = -\dfrac{1}{2}x + 8$.

23.   The point-slope form of the equation of a line is $y - y_1 = m(x - x_1)$.
Let $(x_1, y_1) = (2, 3)$ and $m = -4$. Thus the point-slope form
equation of the line is $y - 3 = -4(x - 2)$.

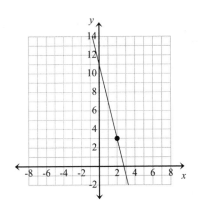

25.   The point-slope form of the equation of a line is $y - y_1 = m(x - x_1)$.
Let $(x_1, y_1) = (-1, 4)$ and $m = \dfrac{3}{5}$. Thus the point-slope form

equation of the line is $y - 4 = \dfrac{3}{5}(x - (-1))$.

$$y - 4 = \frac{3}{5}(x + 1)$$

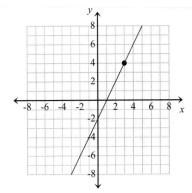

27.   The point-slope form of the equation of a line is $y - y_1 = m(x - x_1)$.
If we are given the equation $y - 4 = 2(x - 3)$, then we can conclude
$(x_1, y_1) = (3, 4)$ and $m = 2$.

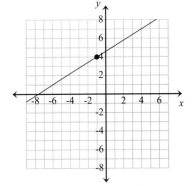

29.   The point-slope form of the equation of a line is $y - y_1 = m(x - x_1)$.
If we are given the equation $y + 5 = -\dfrac{3}{2}(x - 2)$, then we can

conclude $(x_1, y_1) = (2, -5)$ and $m = -\dfrac{3}{2}$.

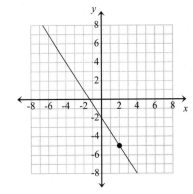

31. Determine the slope of the line passing through the given points

$$m = \frac{y_2 - y_1}{x_2 - x_1} = \frac{4-6}{-3-0} = \frac{-2}{-3} = \frac{2}{3}$$

Use the point-slope form with either point.

Substitute $(0, 6)$ for (x_1, y_1) and $\frac{2}{3}$ for m.

Then write the equation in slope intercept form by solving for y.

$$y - y_1 = m(x - x_1)$$

$$y - 6 = \frac{2}{3}(x - 0)$$

$$y - 6 = \frac{2}{3}x$$

$$y = \frac{2}{3}x + 6$$

33. Determine the slope of the line passing through the given points

$$m = \frac{y_2 - y_1}{x_2 - x_1} = \frac{4-2}{4-(-4)} = \frac{2}{8} = \frac{1}{4}$$

Use the point-slope form with either point.

Substitute $(4, 4)$ for (x_1, y_1) and $\frac{1}{4}$ for m.

Then write the equation in slope intercept form by solving for y.

$$y - y_1 = m(x - x_1)$$

$$y - 4 = \frac{1}{4}(x - 4)$$

$$y - 4 = \frac{1}{4}x - 1$$

$$y = \frac{1}{4}x + 3$$

35. Determine the slope of the line passing through the given points

$$m = \frac{y_2 - y_1}{x_2 - x_1} = \frac{2-1}{3-(-2)} = \frac{1}{5}$$

Use the point-slope form with either point.

Substitute $(3, 2)$ for (x_1, y_1) and $\frac{1}{5}$ for m.

Then write the equation in slope intercept form by solving for y.

$$y - y_1 = m(x - x_1)$$

$$y - 2 = \frac{1}{5}(x - 3)$$

$$y - 2 = \frac{1}{5}x - \frac{3}{5}$$

$$y = \frac{1}{5}x + \frac{7}{5}$$

37. Determine the slope of the line passing through the given points

$$m = \frac{y_2 - y_1}{x_2 - x_1} = \frac{3-(-2)}{-1-(-4)} = \frac{5}{3}$$

Use the point-slope form with either point.

Substitute $(-1, 3)$ for (x_1, y_1) and $\frac{5}{3}$ for m.

Then write the equation in slope intercept form by solving for y.

$$y - y_1 = m(x - x_1)$$

$$y - 3 = \frac{5}{3}(x - (-1))$$

$$y - 3 = \frac{5}{3}x + \frac{5}{3}$$

$$y = \frac{5}{3}x + \frac{5}{3} + 3$$

$$y = \frac{5}{3}x + \frac{5}{3} + \frac{9}{3}$$

$$y = \frac{5}{3}x + \frac{14}{3}$$

39. Use the point slope form. Substitute $(1, 3)$ for (x_1, y_1) and $\dfrac{1}{3}$ for m. Then write the equation in slope intercept form by solving for y.

$$y - y_1 = m(x - x_1)$$
$$y - 3 = \frac{1}{3}(x - 1)$$
$$y - 3 = \frac{1}{3}x - \frac{1}{3}$$
$$y = \frac{1}{3}x + \frac{8}{3}$$

41. Determine the slope of the line passing through the given points

$$m = \frac{y_2 - y_1}{x_2 - x_1} = \frac{1 - 3}{3 - (-4)} = \frac{-2}{7} = -\frac{2}{7}$$

Use the point-slope form with either point.

Substitute $(3, 1)$ for (x_1, y_1) and $-\dfrac{2}{7}$ for m.

Then write the equation in slope intercept form by solving for y.

$$y - y_1 = m(x - x_1)$$
$$y - 1 = -\frac{2}{7}(x - 3)$$
$$y - 1 = -\frac{2}{7}x + \frac{6}{7}$$
$$y = -\frac{2}{7}x + \frac{13}{7}$$

43. The line that passes through the points $(2, 7)$ and $(2, 4)$ is the vertical line $x = 2$.

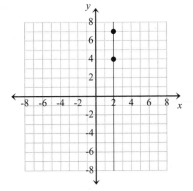

45. The line that passes through the points $(3, -5)$ and $(5, -5)$ is the horizontal line $y = -5$.

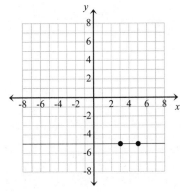

47. The equation of a horizontal line is determined by the y-coordinates. Thus the equation is $y = 5$.

49. The equation of a vertical line is determined by the x-coordinates. Thus the equation is $x = -4$.

51. A line that is parallel to the x-axis is a horizontal line. The equation of a horizontal line is determined by the y-coordinate. Thus the equation is $y = -8$.

53. The slopes of the lines are $m_1 = 5$ and $m_2 = -5$. The slopes are not equal to each other and their product is not -1. Thus the lines are neither parallel nor perpendicular.

55. The slopes of the lines are $m_1 = \dfrac{2}{3}$ and $m_2 = -\dfrac{3}{2}$. Since $\left(\dfrac{2}{3}\right)\left(-\dfrac{3}{2}\right) = -1$, the lines are perpendicular.

57. Write each equation in slope-intercept form so the slope can be determined by inspection.

First Equation	**Second Equation**
$2x + 5y = 8$	$6x + 15y - 7 = 0$
$5y = -2x + 8$	$15y = -6x + 7$
$y = -\dfrac{2}{5}x + \dfrac{8}{5}$	$y = -\dfrac{6}{15}x + \dfrac{7}{15}$
Slope: $m = -\dfrac{2}{5}$	$y = -\dfrac{2}{5}x + \dfrac{7}{15}$
	Slope: $m = -\dfrac{2}{5}$

Since the slopes are equal, the lines are parallel.

59. Each of the equations are in point-slope form. The slopes of the lines are $m_1 = 4$ and $m_2 = 5$. The slopes are not equal to each other and their product is not -1. Thus the lines are neither parallel nor perpendicular.

61. Use the point slope form. Substitute $(2, 3)$ for (x_1, y_1) and $\dfrac{3}{7}$ for m. Then write the equation in slope intercept form by solving for y.

$$y - y_1 = m(x - x_1)$$
$$y - 3 = \frac{3}{7}(x - 2)$$
$$y - 3 = \frac{3}{7}x - \frac{6}{7}$$
$$y = \frac{3}{7}x + \frac{15}{7}$$

63. Use the point slope form. Substitute $(-5, 1)$ for (x_1, y_1) and $\dfrac{3}{4}$ for m (This is the slope of a line perpendicular to one with a slope of $-\dfrac{4}{3}$). Then write the equation in slope intercept form by solving for y. $y - y_1 = m(x - x_1)$

$$y - 1 = \frac{3}{4}\big(x - (-5)\big)$$
$$y - 1 = \frac{3}{4}(x + 5)$$
$$y - 1 = \frac{3}{4}x + \frac{15}{4}$$
$$y = \frac{3}{4}x + \frac{19}{4}$$

65.

x	y
0	-2
4	$-2 + 3 = 1$
8	$1 + 3 = 4$
12	$4 + 3 = 7$
16	$7 + 3 = 10$

This is the y-intercept.

Since the slope is $m = \dfrac{3}{4}$, for each 4 unit increase in x there is a 3 unit increase in y.

Point-Slope Form	**Slope-Intercept Form** $(y = mx + b)$	**General Form** $(Ax + By = C)$
67. $y - 3 = 4(x + 1)$	$y - 3 = 4(x + 1)$ $y - 3 = 4x + 4$ $y = 4x + 7$	$y - 3 = 4(x + 1)$ $y - 3 = 4x + 4$ $-7 = 4x - y$ or $4x - y = -7$

	Point-Slope Form	**Slope-Intercept Form** $(y = mx + b)$	**General Form** $(Ax + By = C)$
69.	$y + 4 = -\dfrac{2}{3}(x - 5)$	$y + 4 = -\dfrac{2}{3}(x - 5)$ $3(y + 4) = 3\left(-\dfrac{2}{3}(x - 5)\right)$ $3y + 12 = -2(x - 5)$ $3y + 12 = -2x + 10$ $3y = -2x - 2$ $y = -\dfrac{2}{3}x - \dfrac{2}{3}$	$y + 4 = -\dfrac{2}{3}(x - 5)$ $3(y + 4) = 3\left(-\dfrac{2}{3}(x - 5)\right)$ $3y + 12 = -2(x - 5)$ $3y + 12 = -2x + 10$ $2x + 3y = -2$

71. From the graph we can see that the y-intercept is $(0, 500)$. To find the slope of the line we can use any two points on the line. For example, using the points $(4, 300)$ and $(0, 500)$, we find that the slope is $m = \dfrac{500 - 300}{0 - 4} = \dfrac{200}{-4} = -50$. Thus the slope-intercept form of the line is $f(x) = -50x + 500$. The intercept is the initial distance that the truck is from the dispatcher (500 miles). The slope is the rate at which the distance between the truck and the dispatcher is changing (-50 miles per hour).

73.　**a.** From the table we can see that $\Delta x = 15 - 0 = 15$ and $\Delta y = 3320 - 3500 = -180$. Thus the slope is
$$m = \frac{\Delta y}{\Delta x} = \frac{-180}{15} = -12$$

b. The slope of the line is the rate at which the volume of water is changing with respect to time. The Jet is using 12 gallons of fuel per minute from the main tank.

c. Using the y-intercept of $(0, 3500)$ and the slope from part **a.** we can determine that the slope-intercept form of the line is $f(x) = -12x + 3500$.

d. If $x = 300$ we will have a negative volume of fuel left in the tank. Therefore 300 is not a practical input value.

75. From the table we can see that the y-intercept is $(0, 75)$. To find the slope of the line we can use any two points on the line. For example, using the points $(0, 75)$ and $(1, 125)$, we find that the slope is $m = \dfrac{125 - 75}{1 - 0} = \dfrac{50}{1} = 50$. Thus the slope-intercept form of the line is $f(x) = 50x + 75$. The y-intercept is the flat fee for making a service call ($75.00). The slope is the hourly charge for the service ($50.00 per hour).

77.   Determine the slope of the line passing through the any pair of points

$$m = \frac{y_2 - y_1}{x_2 - x_1} = \frac{8.85 - 6.45}{7 - 4} = \frac{2.4}{3} = 0.80$$

Use the point-slope form with any of the points. Substitute $(1.5, 4.45)$ for (x_1, y_1) and 0.80 for m. Then write the equation in slope intercept form by solving for y.

$$y - y_1 = m(x - x_1)$$
$$y - 4.45 = 0.80(x - 1.5)$$
$$y - 4.45 = 0.80x - 1.2$$
$$y = 0.80x + 3.25$$
$$\text{or } f(x) = 0.80x + 3.25$$

The slope is the variable cost for riding the taxi ($0.80 per mile). The y-intercept gives us the fixed cost for riding the taxi ($3.25).

79.   If the length of the spring stretches 2 cm for each of the x kilograms attached then the distance the spring has streched is $2x$. Along with the original length of the spring the total length of the spring can be represented by $y = 2x + 8$. The slope represents the rate at which the spring stretches (in cm/kg) and the y-intercept represents the original length of the spring.

81.   **a.** Using x for the number of years after 2000 and y for the annual dividend, we determine that the equation of the line must pass through the points $(2, 1.10)$ and $(5, 1.17)$. Determine the slope of the line passing through these points

$$m = \frac{y_2 - y_1}{x_2 - x_1} = \frac{1.17 - 1.10}{5 - 2} = \frac{0.07}{3} = \frac{7}{300}$$

Use the point-slope form with either of the points. Substitute $(2, 1.10)$ for (x_1, y_1) and $\frac{7}{300}$ for m. Then write the equation in slope intercept form by solving for y.

$$y - y_1 = m(x - x_1)$$
$$y - 1.10 = \frac{7}{300}(x - 2)$$
$$y - 1.10 = \frac{7}{300}x - \frac{7}{150}$$
$$y = \frac{7}{300}x - \frac{7}{150} + \frac{11}{10}$$
$$\text{or } \quad y = \frac{7}{300}x + \frac{79}{75}$$

b. To estimate the dividend for 2006 let $x = 6$. $y = \frac{7}{300}(6) + \frac{79}{75} = 1.19\overline{3} \approx \$1.19$ per share.

Cumulative Review

1. $\sqrt{16} = 4$ is a natural number. The proper choice is **E**.
2.   Zero is a whole number that is not a natural number. The proper choice is **A**.
3. $\sqrt{3}$ is an example of an irrational number. The proper choice is **D**.
4.   0.25 is a rational number that is not an integer. The proper choice is **B**.
5. $-\sqrt{9} = -3$ is an integer that is not a whole number. The proper choice is **C**.

Section 3.3: Solving Systems of Linear Equations in Two Variables Graphically and Numerically

Quick Review 3.3

1. Since the equation is in slope intercept form $(y = mx + b)$, we can see that the slope is $m = \dfrac{2}{3}$.

2. Since the equation is in slope intercept form $(y = mx + b)$, we can see that the y-intersection is $(0, -3)$.

3.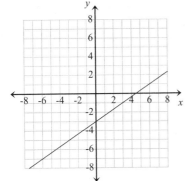

4.

x	$y = \dfrac{2}{3}x - 3$
-3	$\dfrac{2}{3}(-3) - 3 = -5$
0	$\dfrac{2}{3}(0) - 3 = -3$
3	$\dfrac{2}{3}(3) - 3 = -1$
6	$\dfrac{2}{3}(6) - 3 = 1$

5.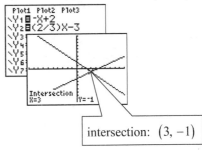

intersection: $(3, -1)$

Exercises 3.3

1. Check the point $(-1, -2)$ in both equations.

First Equation	**Second Equation**
$7x - 3y + 1 = 0$	$5x - 4y - 3 = 0$
$7(-1) - 3(-2) + 1 = 0$	$5(-1) - 4(-2) - 3 = 0$
$-7 + 6 + 1 = 0$	$-5 + 8 - 3 = 0$
$0 = 0$	$0 = 0$

The point $(-1, -2)$ is a solution to the system of linear equations.

3. Check the point $\left(\dfrac{1}{2}, \dfrac{1}{3}\right)$ in both equations.

First Equation	**Second Equation**
$4x - 3y = 1$	$6x - 6y = 1$
$4\left(\dfrac{1}{2}\right) - 3\left(\dfrac{1}{3}\right) = 1$	$6\left(\dfrac{1}{2}\right) - 6\left(\dfrac{1}{3}\right) = 1$
$2 - 1 = 1$	$3 - 2 = 1$
$1 = 1$	$1 = 1$

The point $\left(\dfrac{1}{2}, \dfrac{1}{3}\right)$ is a solution to the system of linear equations.

5. Check the point $(0.1, -0.2)$ in both equations.

First Equation	**Second Equation**
$4x - 3y = 1$	$2x + y = 0$
$4(0.1) - 3(-0.2) = 1$	$2(0.1) + (-0.2) = 0$
$0.4 + 0.6 = 1$	$0.2 - 0.2 = 0$
$1 = 1$	$0 = 0$

The point $(0.1, -0.2)$ is a solution to the system of linear equations.

7. Check the point $(0, 6)$ in both equations.

First Equation	**Second Equation**
$2x - y = -6$	$3x + y = 3$
$2(0) - (6) = -6$	$3(0) + (6) = 3$
$-6 = -6$	$6 \neq 3$

The point $(0, 6)$ is a not a solution to the system of linear equations since it does not satisfy both equations.

9. By inspection, we can see that the point of intersection is $(-2, 3)$.

11. By inspection, we can see that the point of intersection is $(3, 2)$.

13. By inspection, we can see that the point of intersection is $(2, 2)$.

15. By inspection, we can see that the point of intersection is $(2, -6)$.

17. From the table we can determine that the y coordinates are equal $(y = -8)$ when the x coordinate is 5. Thus the solution is $(5, -8)$.

19. From the table we can determine that the y coordinates are equal $(y = 4)$ when the x coordinate is $-.5$. Thus the solution is $(-0.5, 4)$.

21.

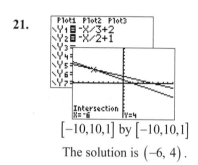

$[-10,10,1]$ by $[-10,10,1]$

The solution is $(-6, 4)$.

23. The equation $x + 3 = 0$ is a vertical line $(x = -3)$ and the equation $y - 2 = 0$ is a horizontal line $(y = 2)$. Thus the intersection of these two lines is the point $(-3, 2)$.

25. The equation $x = 6$ is a vertical line. This line must intersect the line $y = -2x + 10$ where $x = 6$. Thus $y = -2(6) + 10 = -2$ and the point of intersection must be $(6, -2)$.

27.

First Equation	**Second Equation**
$y = \dfrac{3}{7}x - 17$	$y = -\dfrac{7}{8}x + 8$
$m_1 = \dfrac{3}{7}$	$m_2 = -\dfrac{7}{8}$

Since $m_1 \neq m_2$, the lines are not parallel and must intersect. The system has exactly one solution. This is consistent system of independent equations.

29.

First Equation	**Second Equation**
$y = \dfrac{3}{8}x + 11$	$y = \dfrac{3}{8}x - 5$
$m_1 = \dfrac{3}{8}, \ b_1 = 11$	$m_2 = \dfrac{3}{8}, \ b_2 = -5$

Since $m_1 = m_2$, and $b_1 \neq b_2$, the lines are parallel and do not coincide. Thus the system has no solutions. This is an inconsistent system of independent equations.

31.

First Equation	**Second Equation**
$6x + 2y = 4$	$9x = 6 - 3y$
$2y = -6x + 4$	$3y = -9x + 6$
$y = -3x + 2$	$y = -3x + 2$
$m_1 = -3, \ b_1 = 2$	$m_2 = -3, \ b_2 = 2$

Since $m_1 = m_2$, and $b_1 = b_2$, both equations represent the same line. Thus the system has an infinite number of solutions. This is a consistent system of dependent equations.

33.

First Equation	**Second Equation**
$2x + 3y = 3$	$4x - 3y = -3$
$3y = -2x + 3$	$-3y = -4x - 3$
$y = -\dfrac{2}{3}x + 1$	$y = \dfrac{4}{3}x + 1$
$m_1 = -\dfrac{2}{3}$	$m_2 = \dfrac{4}{3}$

Since $m_1 \neq m_2$, the lines are not parallel and must intersect. The system has exactly one solution. This is consistent system of independent equations.

35. The table describes a consistent system of independent equations since there is exactly one solution, $(1.4, 0.4)$.

37. The table describes an inconsistent system since, for every value of x, the y coordinates are always 2 units apart. The two lines are parallel and distinct.

39.

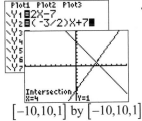

$[-10,10,1]$ by $[-10,10,1]$

The solution is $(4, 1)$.

41. Before we use the graphics calculator, we must write each equation in slope-intercept form.

$$2x - 3y - 6 = 0 \qquad 4x - 3y + 3 = 0$$

$$-3y = -2x + 6 \qquad -3y = -4x - 3$$

$$y = \frac{2}{3}x - 2 \qquad y = \frac{4}{3}x + 1$$

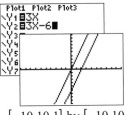

$[-10,10,1]$ by $[-10,10,1]$

The solution is
$(-4.5, -5)$ or $\left(-\frac{9}{2}, -5\right)$.

43.

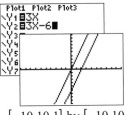

$[-10,10,1]$ by $[-10,10,1]$

The two lines are parallel. The system is inconsistent and has no solution.

45. Before we use the graphics calculator, we must write each equation in slope-intercept form.

$$x - 2y - 2 = 0 \qquad 2x - 4y - 4 = 0$$

$$-2y = -x + 2 \qquad -4y = -2x + 4$$

$$y = \frac{1}{2}x - 1 \qquad y = \frac{1}{2}x - 1$$

$[-10,10,1]$ by $[-10,10,1]$

The equations produce the same line. There are infinitely many solutions.

47.

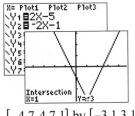

$[-4.7, 4.7, 1]$ by $[-3.1, 3.1, 1]$

Check the point $(1, -3)$ in both equations.

First Equation	**Second Equation**
$y = 2x - 5$	$y = -2x - 1$
$-3 = 2(1) - 5$	$-3 = -2(1) - 1$
$-3 = -3$	$-3 = -3$

Solution: $(1, -3)$

49.

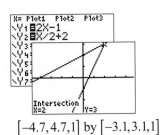

$[-4.7, 4.7, 1]$ by $[-3.1, 3.1, 1]$

Check the point $(2, 3)$ in both equations.

First Equation	**Second Equation**
$y = 2x - 1$	$y = \dfrac{x}{2} + 2$
$3 = 2(2) - 1$	
$3 = 3$	$3 = \dfrac{2}{2} + 2$
	$3 = 3$

Solution: $(2, 3)$

51. Before we use the graphics calculator, we must write each equation in slope-intercept form.

$$14x - 7y = -5 \qquad 7x + 21y = 29$$

$$-7y = -14x - 5 \qquad 21y = -7x + 29$$

$$y = 2x + \frac{5}{7} \qquad y = -\frac{1}{3}x + \frac{29}{21}$$

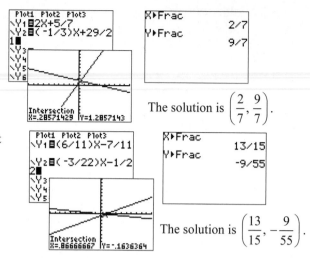

The solution is $\left(\dfrac{2}{7}, \dfrac{9}{7} \right)$.

53. Before we use the graphics calculator, we must write each equation in slope-intercept form.

$$6x - 11y = 7 \qquad 3x + 22y = -1$$

$$-11y = -6x + 7 \qquad 22y = -3x - 1$$

$$y = \frac{6}{11}x - \frac{7}{11} \qquad y = -\frac{3}{22}x - \frac{1}{22}$$

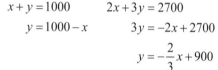

The solution is $\left(\dfrac{13}{15}, -\dfrac{9}{55} \right)$.

55. Before we use the graphics calculator, we must write each equation in slope-intercept form.

$$x + y = 1000 \qquad 2x + 3y = 2700$$

$$y = 1000 - x \qquad 3y = -2x + 2700$$

$$y = -\frac{2}{3}x + 900$$

$[0,1000,100]$ by $[0,1000,100]$

The solution is $(300,\ 700)$.

57. Before we use the graphics calculator, we must write each equation in slope-intercept form.

$$x + y = 1 \qquad 8x + 11y = 10.1$$

$$y = 1 - x \qquad 11y = -8x + 10.1$$

$$y = \frac{-8x + 10.1}{11}$$

$[0,1,.1]$ by $[0,1,.1]$

The solution is $(0.3,\ 0.7)$.

59.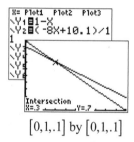

From the table we can see that the solution is $(1,\ -3)$.

61.

From the table we can see that the solution is $(0,\ 3)$.

63.

From the table we can see that the solution is $(30, 40)$.

65. By inspection, we see that the point $(300, 90)$ is the solution to the system. From this point of intersection we determine that each company has a rental charge of $90.00 when 300 miles are driven.

67. The point of intersection is $(2006, 8000)$. The European Union and the rest of the world each had a wind power capacity of 8000 megawatts in 2006.

69. From the tables we can determine that the y coordinates are equal $(y = 450)$ when the x coordinate is 1.0. Thus the solution to the system is $(1, 450)$. By 3:00 PM (one hour past 2:00), each of the two planes has traveled 450 miles from O'Hare Airport

71. Let x be the number of degrees in the smaller angle.
Let y be the number of degrees in the larger angle.

If the angles are supplementary then the total of their measures is $180°$.
Thus $x + y = 180$
or $y = 180 - x$

If the larger angle is 5 more than three times the smaller angle then
$y = 3x + 5$

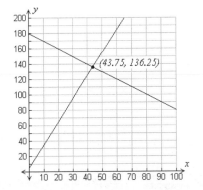

Upon sketching the graph of the equations and finding the intersection point, we determine that the smaller angle is $43.75°$ and the larger angle is $136.25°$.

73. Let y be the total cost for producing x units.

Machine One
$y = 3x + 75$

Machine Two
$y = 4.50x + 60$

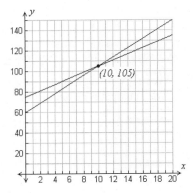

Upon sketching the graphs of the equations and finding the intersection point, we determine that each machine will have a cost of $105.00 when 10 units are produced.

75.

x	$y_1 = 2x + 7$	$y_2 = 13 - x$
-3	1	16
-2	3	15
-1	5	14
0	7	13
1	9	12
2	11	11
3	13	10

The two numbers are 2 and 11.

77. The horizontal and vertical lines that pass through the point $(3, 5)$ are $y = 5$ and $x = 3$ respectfully. Thus the system is
$$y = 5$$
$$x = 3$$

79. Each of the lines has a y-intercept of $(0, 3)$ thus by using the given slopes we determine that system of equations is
$$y = \frac{1}{2}x + 3$$
$$y = -4x + 3$$

Cumulative Review

1. $-24 \div 4 \cdot 2 = (-24 \div 4) \cdot 2 = (-6) \cdot 2 = -12$

2. $-24 \div (4 \cdot 2) = -24 \div (8) = -3$

3. $x > 5$ is equivalent to $(5, \infty)$.

4. $x \leq -2$ is equivalent to $(-\infty, -2]$.

5. $-4 \leq x < 10$ is equivalent to $[-4, 10)$.

Section 3.4: Solving Systems of Linear Equations in Two Variables by the Substitution Method

Quick Review 3.4

1. If we solve the equation: $x + x = 2$
$$2x = 2$$
$$\frac{2x}{2} = \frac{2}{2}$$
$$x = 1$$
We see that there is exactly one solution. Thus the equation is a conditional equation. The proper choice is **A**.

2. If we solve the equation: $x + x = 2x$
$$2x = 2x$$
$$\frac{2x}{2} = \frac{2x}{2}$$
$$x = x$$
We see that the equation is true for all values of x. Thus the equation is an identity. The proper choice is **C**.

3. If we solve the equation: $2x = 2(x + 1)$
$$2x = 2x + 2$$
$$2x - 2x = 2x - 2x + 2$$
$$0 \neq 2$$
We see that the equation is a contradiction. The proper choice is **B**.

4. Two angles are complementary if the sum of their measure is $90°$.

5. Determine the slope of the line passing through the given points

$$m = \frac{y_2 - y_1}{x_2 - x_1} = \frac{0-4}{-5-5} = \frac{-4}{-10} = \frac{2}{5}$$

Use the point-slope form with either point. Substitute $(-5, 0)$ for (x_1, y_1) and $\frac{2}{5}$ for m. Then write the equation in slope intercept form by solving for y.

$$y - y_1 = m(x - x_1)$$

$$y - 0 = \frac{2}{5}\left(x - (-5)\right)$$

$$y = \frac{2}{5}x + 2$$

Exercises 3.4

1.

Step 1

Solve one of the equations for one variable in terms of the other.

$$y = 2x - 3$$

$$x + y = 9$$

(y is currently written in terms of x in the first equation.)

Step 2

Substitute $2x - 3$ for y in the second equation and then solve for x.

$$x + y = 9$$

$$x + (2x - 3) = 9$$

$$3x - 3 = 9$$

$$3x = 12$$

$$x = 4$$

Step 3

Back-substitute 4 for x in the first equation.

$$y = 2x - 3$$

$$y = 2(4) - 3$$

$$y = 5$$

Solution: $(4, 5)$

3.

Step 1

Solve one of the equations for one variable in terms of the other.

$$y = 5x - 10$$

$$2x + 3y = 4$$

(y is currently written in terms of x in the first equation.)

Step 2

Substitute $5x - 10$ for y in the second equation and then solve for x.

$$2x + 3y = 4$$

$$2x + 3(5x - 10) = 4$$

$$2x + 15x - 30 = 4$$

$$17x = 34$$

$$x = 2$$

Step 3

Back-substitute 2 for x in the first equation.

$$y = 5x - 10$$

$$y = 5(2) - 10$$

$$y = 0$$

Solution: $(2, 0)$

5.

Step 1

Solve one of the equations for one variable in terms of the other.

$$x = 6 - 5y$$

$$2x + 9y = 4$$

(x is currently written in terms of y in the first equation.)

Step 2

Substitute $6 - 5y$ for x in the second equation and then solve for y.

$$2x + 9y = 4$$

$$2(6 - 5y) + 9y = 4$$

$$12 - 10y + 9y = 4$$

$$-y = -8$$

$$y = 8$$

Step 3

Back-substitute 8 for y in the first equation.

$$x = 6 - 5y$$

$$x = 6 - 5(8)$$

$$x = -34$$

Solution: $(-34, 8)$

7.

Step 1
Solve the second equation for x.

$$3x - y = 1$$
$$x + 2y = 2$$

Second equation: $x = 2 - 2y$

Step 2
Substitute $2 - 2y$ for x in the first equation and then solve for y.

$$3x - y = 1$$
$$3(2 - 2y) - y = 1$$
$$6 - 6y - y = 1$$
$$-7y = -5$$
$$y = \frac{5}{7}$$

Step 3
Back-substitute $\frac{5}{7}$ for y in the equation obtained in step 1.

$$x = 2 - 2y$$
$$x = 2 - 2\left(\frac{5}{7}\right)$$
$$x = \frac{4}{7}$$

Solution: $\left(\frac{4}{7}, \frac{5}{7}\right)$

9.

Step 1
Solve the second equation for x.

$$2x - y - 6 = 0$$
$$x - y - 6 = 0$$

Second equation: $x = y + 6$

Step 2
Substitute $y + 6$ for x in the first equation and then solve for y.

$$2x - y - 6 = 0$$
$$2(y + 6) - y - 6 = 0$$
$$2y + 12 - y - 6 = 0$$
$$y = -6$$

Step 3
Back-substitute -6 for y in the equation obtained in step 1.

$$x = y + 6$$
$$x = (-6) + 6$$
$$x = 0$$

Solution: $(0, -6)$

11.

Step 1
Solve the second equation for x.

$$2x + 3y = -7$$
$$x + 4y = -6$$

Second equation:
$x = -4y - 6$

Step 2
Substitute $-4y - 6$ for x in the first equation and then solve for y.

$$2x + 3y = -7$$
$$2(-4y - 6) + 3y = -7$$
$$-8y - 12 + 3y = -7$$
$$-5y = 5$$
$$y = -1$$

Step 3
Back-substitute -1 for y in the equation obtained in step 1.

$$x = -4y - 6$$
$$x = -4(-1) - 6$$
$$x = -2$$

Solution: $(-2, -1)$

13.

Step 1
Solve the second equation for x.

$$2x - 5y = 9$$
$$x - 3 = 0$$

Second equation: $x = 3$

Step 2
Substitute 3 for x in the first equation and then solve for y.

$$2x - 5y = 9$$
$$2(3) - 5y = 9$$
$$6 - 5y = 9$$
$$-5y = 3$$
$$y = -\frac{3}{5}$$

Step 3
Back-substitute is not necessary.

Solution: $\left(3, -\frac{3}{5}\right)$

15.

Step 1
Solve the second equation for y.

$$3x - 2y = 1$$
$$y + 7 = 0$$

Second equation: $y = -7$

Step 2
Substitute -2 for y in the first equation and then solve for x.

$$3x - 2y = 1$$
$$3x - 2(-7) = 1$$
$$3x + 14 = 1$$
$$3x = -13$$
$$x = -\frac{13}{3}$$

Step 3
Back-substitute is not necessary.

Solution: $\left(-\frac{13}{3}, -7\right)$

17.

Step 1	**Step 2**	**Step 3**

Step 1

Solve one of the equations for one variable in terms of the other.

$$y = -2x$$
$$5x - y = -7$$

(y is currently written in terms of x in the first equation.)

Step 2

Substitute $-2x$ for y in the second equation and then solve for x.

$$5x - y = -7$$
$$5x - (-2x) = -7$$
$$7x = -7$$
$$x = -1$$

Step 3

Back-substitute -1 for x in the first equation.

$$y = -2x$$
$$y = -2(-1)$$
$$y = 2$$

Solution: $(-1, 2)$

19.

Step 1

Solve the first equation for x.

$$3x - 2y = 0$$
$$11x - 9y = 5$$

First equation: $3x - 2y = 0$

$$3x = 2y$$
$$x = \frac{2}{3}y$$

Step 2

Substitute $\frac{2}{3}y$ for x in the second equation and then solve for y.

$$11x - 9y = 5$$
$$11\left(\frac{2}{3}y\right) - 9y = 5$$
$$\frac{22}{3}y - 9y = 5$$
$$3\left(\frac{22}{3}y - 9y\right) = 3(5)$$
$$22y - 27y = 15$$
$$-5y = 15$$
$$y = -3$$

Step 3

Back-substitute -3 for y in the equation obtained in step 1.

$$x = \frac{2}{3}y$$
$$x = \frac{2}{3}(-3)$$
$$x = -2$$

Solution: $(-2, -3)$

21.

Step 1

Solve the first equation for x.

$$x + y = 21$$
$$x - y = 3$$

First equation: $x = 21 - y$

Step 2

Substitute $21 - y$ for x in the second equation and then solve for y.

$$x - y = 3$$
$$(21 - y) - y = 3$$
$$21 - 2y = 3$$
$$-2y = -18$$
$$y = 9$$

Step 3

Back-substitute 9 for y in the equation obtained in step 1.

$$x = 21 - y$$
$$x = 21 - (9)$$
$$x = 12$$

Solution: $(12, 9)$

23. We know from the second equation that $x = 0$. We need only substitute 0 for x in the first equation to solve for y.

$$2x - 7y = 42$$
$$2(0) - 7y = 42$$
$$-7y = 42$$
$$y = -6$$

Solution: $(0, -6)$

25.

Step 1	**Step 2**	**Step 3**
Solve the second equation for x.	Substitute $-y+5$ for x in the first equation and then solve for y.	Back-substitute 2 for y in the equation obtained in step 1.

Step 1

Solve the second equation for x.

$$5x - 2y = 11$$
$$3x + 3y = 15$$

Second equation:
$$3x + 3y = 15$$
$$3x = -3y + 15$$
$$x = -y + 5$$

Step 2

Substitute $-y+5$ for x in the first equation and then solve for y.

$$5x - 2y = 11$$
$$5(-y+5) - 2y = 11$$
$$-5y + 25 - 2y = 11$$
$$-7y = -14$$
$$y = 2$$

Step 3

Back-substitute 2 for y in the equation obtained in step 1.

$$x = -y + 5$$
$$x = -(2) + 5$$
$$x = 3$$

Solution: $(3, 2)$

27.

Step 1

Solve the second equation for x.

$$5x - 4y + 12 = 0$$
$$2x - 3y + 2 = 0$$

Second equation:
$$2x - 3y + 2 = 0$$
$$2x = 3y - 2$$
$$x = \frac{3}{2}y - 1$$

Step 2

Substitute $\frac{3}{2}y - 1$ for x in the first equation and then solve for y.

$$5x - 4y + 12 = 0$$
$$5\left(\frac{3}{2}y - 1\right) - 4y + 12 = 0$$
$$\frac{15}{2}y - 5 - 4y + 12 = 0$$
$$\frac{15}{2}y - 4y = -7$$
$$2\left(\frac{15}{2}y - 4y\right) = 2(-7)$$
$$15y - 8y = -14$$
$$7y = -14$$
$$y = -2$$

Step 3

Back-substitute -2 for y in the equation obtained in step 1.

$$x = \frac{3}{2}y - 1$$
$$x = \frac{3}{2}(-2) - 1$$
$$x = -4$$

Solution: $(-4, -2)$

29.

Step 1

Solve one of the equations for one variable in terms of the other.

$$y = x + 3$$
$$\frac{x}{2} - \frac{y}{5} = 3$$

(y is currently written in terms of x in the first equation.)

Step 2

Substitute $x+3$ for y in the second equation and then solve for x.

$$\frac{x}{2} - \frac{(x+3)}{5} = 3$$
$$10\left(\frac{x}{2} - \frac{(x+3)}{5}\right) = 10(3)$$
$$5x - 2(x+3) = 30$$
$$5x - 2x - 6 = 30$$
$$3x = 36$$
$$x = 12$$

Step 3

Back-substitute 8 for x in the first equation.

$$y = x + 3$$
$$y = (12) + 3$$
$$y = 15$$

Solution: $(12, 15)$

31.

Step 1

Solve one of the equations for one variable in terms of the other.

$$x = 2y + 4$$
$$3x - 6y = 12$$

(x is currently written in terms of y in the first equation.)

Step 2

Substitute $2y+4$ for x in the second equation and then solve for y.

$$3x - 6y = 12$$
$$3(2y+4) - 6y = 12$$
$$6y + 12 - 6y = 12$$
$$12 = 12 \ \text{(an identity)}$$

The system has an infinite number of solutions.

33.

Step 1

Solve one of the equations for one variable in terms of the other.

$$y = 5x + 3$$

$$10x - 2y = 6$$

(y is currently written in terms of x in the first equation.)

Step 2

Substitute $5x + 3$ for y in the second equation and then solve for x.

$$10x - 2y = 6$$

$$10x - 2(5x + 3) = 6$$

$$10x - 10x - 6 = 6$$

$$-6 = 6 \ \left(\text{a contradiction}\right)$$

The system does not have a solution.

35.

Step 1

Solve the first equation for x.

$$4x + 7y = 0$$

$$7x - 4y = 0$$

First equation:

$$4x + 7y = 0$$

$$4x = -7y$$

$$x = -\frac{7}{4}y$$

Step 2

Substitute $-\dfrac{7}{4}y$ for x in the second equation and then solve for y.

$$7x - 4y = 0$$

$$7\left(-\frac{7}{4}y\right) - 4y = 0$$

$$-\frac{49}{4}y - 4y = 0$$

$$-4\left(-\frac{49}{4}y - 4y\right) = -4(0)$$

$$49y + 16y = 0$$

$$65y = 0$$

$$y = 0$$

Step 3

Back-substitute 0 for y in the equation obtained in step 1.

$$x = -\frac{7}{4}y$$

$$x = -\frac{7}{4}(0)$$

$$x = 0$$

Solution: $(0, 0)$

37.

Step 1

Solve one of the equations for one variable in terms of the other.

$$x = 2y - 5$$

$$\frac{x}{6} + \frac{y}{8} = 1$$

(x is currently written in terms of y in the first equation.)

Step 2

Substitute $2y - 5$ for x in the second equation and then solve for y.

$$\frac{x}{6} + \frac{y}{8} = 1$$

$$\frac{(2y - 5)}{6} + \frac{y}{8} = 1$$

$$48\left(\frac{(2y - 5)}{6} + \frac{y}{8}\right) = 48(1)$$

$$8(2y - 5) + 6y = 48$$

$$16y - 40 + 6y = 48$$

$$22y = 88$$

$$y = 4$$

Step 3

Back-substitute 4 for y in the first equation.

$$x = 2y - 5$$

$$x = 2(4) - 5$$

$$x = 3$$

Solution: $(3, 4)$

39.

Step 1	**Step 2**	**Step 3**
Solve the second equation for x.	Substitute $3y+5$ for x in the first equation and then solve for y.	Back-substitute -1 for y in the equation obtained in step 1.

Step 1

Solve the second equation for x.

$$\frac{x}{2}+\frac{y}{5}=\frac{4}{5}$$

$$\frac{x}{6}-\frac{y}{2}=\frac{5}{6}$$

Second equation:
$$\frac{x}{6}-\frac{y}{2}=\frac{5}{6}$$

$$6\left(\frac{x}{6}-\frac{y}{2}\right)=6\left(\frac{5}{6}\right)$$

$$x-3y=5$$

$$x=3y+5$$

Step 2

Substitute $3y+5$ for x in the first equation and then solve for y.

$$\frac{x}{2}+\frac{y}{5}=\frac{4}{5}$$

$$\frac{(3y+5)}{2}+\frac{y}{5}=\frac{4}{5}$$

$$10\left(\frac{(3y+5)}{2}+\frac{y}{5}\right)=10\left(\frac{4}{5}\right)$$

$$5(3y+5)+2y=8$$

$$15y+25+2y=8$$

$$17y=-17$$

$$y=-1$$

Step 3

Back-substitute -1 for y in the equation obtained in step 1.

$$x=3y+5$$

$$x=3(-1)+5$$

$$x=2$$

Solution: $(2,-1)$

41.

Step 1

Solve the second equation for x.

$$\frac{x}{4}-\frac{y}{2}=\frac{7}{24}$$

$$\frac{x}{3}+\frac{y}{2}=0$$

Second equation:
$$\frac{x}{3}+\frac{y}{2}=0$$

$$\frac{x}{3}=-\frac{y}{2}$$

$$x=-\frac{3}{2}y$$

Step 2

Before we substitute $-\frac{3}{2}y$ for x in the first equation and solve for y, we write the first equation in a simpler form by multiplying both sides by 24.

$$\frac{x}{4}-\frac{y}{2}=\frac{7}{24}$$

$$24\left(\frac{x}{4}-\frac{y}{2}\right)=24\left(\frac{7}{24}\right)$$

$$6x-12y=7$$

$$6\left(-\frac{3}{2}y\right)-12y=7$$

$$-9y-12y=7$$

$$-21y=7$$

$$y=-\frac{1}{3}$$

Step 3

Back-substitute $-\frac{1}{3}$ for y in the equation obtained in step 1.

$$x=-\frac{3}{2}y$$

$$x=-\frac{3}{2}\left(-\frac{1}{3}\right)$$

$$x=\frac{1}{2}$$

Solution: $\left(\frac{1}{2},-\frac{1}{3}\right)$

43. **a.** Determine the slope of the line passing through the given points

$$m = \frac{y_2 - y_1}{x_2 - x_1} = \frac{4-(-2)}{-1-2} = \frac{6}{-3} = -2$$

Use the point-slope form with either point. Substitute $(-1, 4)$ for (x_1, y_1) and -2 for m. Then write the equation in slope intercept form by solving for y.

$$y - y_1 = m(x - x_1)$$
$$y - 4 = -2(x - (-1))$$
$$y - 4 = -2x - 2$$
$$y = -2x + 2$$

b. Determine the slope of the line passing through the given points

$$m = \frac{y_2 - y_1}{x_2 - x_1} = \frac{-2-1}{5-(-1)} = \frac{-3}{6} = -\frac{1}{2}$$

Use the point-slope form with either point. Substitute $(-1, 1)$ for (x_1, y_1) and $-\frac{1}{2}$ for m. Then write the equation in slope intercept form by solving for y.

$$y - y_1 = m(x - x_1)$$
$$y - 1 = -\frac{1}{2}(x - (-1))$$
$$y - 1 = -\frac{1}{2}x - \frac{1}{2}$$
$$y = -\frac{1}{2}x + \frac{1}{2}$$

c.

Step 1	**Step 2**	**Step 3**

Step 1

Solve one of the equations for one variable in terms of the other.

$$y = -2x + 2$$
$$y = -\frac{1}{2}x + \frac{1}{2}$$

(*y* is currently written in terms of *x* in each equation.)

Step 2

Substitute $-2x + 2$ for y in the second equation and then solve for x.

$$-2x + 2 = -\frac{1}{2}x + \frac{1}{2}$$
$$-2(-2x + 2) = -2\left(-\frac{1}{2}x + \frac{1}{2}\right)$$
$$4x - 4 = x - 1$$
$$3x = 3$$
$$x = 1$$

Step 3

Back-substitute 1 for x in the first equation.

$$y = -2x + 2$$
$$y = -2(1) + 2$$
$$y = 0$$

Solution: $(1, 0)$

45. **B**

47. **C**

49.

x	$y_1 = 8 - x$	$y_2 = x - 2$
2	6	0
3	5	1
4	4	2
5	3	3
6	2	4
7	1	5
8	0	6

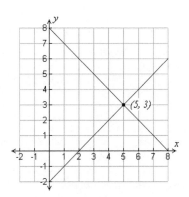

The two numbers are 5 and 3.

51.   Let x be the number of degrees in the smaller angle.
Let y be the number of degrees in the larger angle.

If theangles are supplementary then the total of their measures is $90°$. Thus $x + y = 90$	If the larger angle is $18°$ more than the smaller angle then $y = x + 18$

Now solve the system of equations.

Substitute $x + 18$ for y in the first equation.

$$x + y = 90$$
$$x + (x + 18) = 90$$
$$2x + 18 = 90$$
$$2x = 72$$
$$x = 36$$

Back-substitute to find y.

$$y = x + 18$$
$$y = 36 + 18$$
$$y = 54$$

The angles are $36°$ and $54°$.

---

53.   Let x be the score on the first exam.
Let y be the score on the second exam.

If the mean of these exam scores is 76 then $\dfrac{x+y}{2} = 76$	If the range of the exam scores is 28 then $x - y = 28$

Now solve the system of equations. Solve the second equation for x.

$$x - y = 28$$
$$x = y + 28$$

Substitute $y + 28$ for x in the first equation.

$$\frac{x+y}{2} = 76$$
$$\frac{(y+28)+y}{2} = 76$$
$$\frac{2y+28}{2} = 76$$
$$y + 14 = 76$$
$$y = 62$$

Back-substitute to find x.

$$x = y + 28$$
$$x = (62) + 28$$
$$x = 90$$

The exam scores are 62 and 90.

---

55.   Let x be Tiger's score on each of the first three rounds.
Let y be Tiger's score on the final round.

If the mean of these scores is 66 then $\dfrac{3x+y}{4} = 66$	If the range of the scores is 8 then $x - y = 8$

Now solve the system of equations. Solve the second equation for x.

$$x - y = 8$$
$$x = y + 8$$

Substitute $y + 8$ for x in the first equation.

$$\frac{3x+y}{4} = 66$$
$$\frac{3(y+8)+y}{4} = 66$$
$$\frac{3y+24+y}{4} = 66$$
$$\frac{4y+24}{4} = 66$$
$$y + 6 = 66$$
$$y = 60$$

Back-substitute to find x.

$$x = y + 8$$
$$x = (60) + 8$$
$$x = 68$$

Tiger scored 68 on each of the first three rounds and 60 on the final round.

---

57.   **a.** Yes, the two formulas will give the same dosage. To find the age at which this occurs, we solve the system of equations.

$$y = 3.84x$$
$$y = 2x + 2$$

Substitute $2x + 2$ for y in the first equation.

$$2x + 2 = 3.84x$$
$$2 = 1.84x$$
$$x \approx 1.09$$

b. The two formulas will require the same dosage when the child is about 1.1 years old.

59.   **a., b.** We can determine the equations of the lines by finding the slopes and intercepts.

$$\underline{\textbf{Company A}}$$

Slope: $m = \dfrac{2-1}{2-0} = \dfrac{1}{2}$;

$b = 1$

Equation of line: $y = \dfrac{1}{2}x + 1$

$$\underline{\textbf{Company B}}$$

Slope: $m = \dfrac{3-2}{5-0} = \dfrac{1}{5}$;

$b = 2$

Equation of line: $y = \dfrac{1}{5}x + 2$

c. Now solve the system of equations.

Substitute $\dfrac{1}{5}x + 2$ for y in the first equation.

$$\dfrac{1}{5}x + 2 = \dfrac{1}{2}x + 1$$

$$10\left(\dfrac{1}{5}x + 2\right) = 10\left(\dfrac{1}{2}x + 1\right)$$

$$2x + 20 = 5x + 10$$

$$-3x = -10$$

$$x = \dfrac{10}{3} \approx 3.33$$

Back-substitute to find y.

$$y = \dfrac{1}{2}x + 1$$

$$y = \dfrac{1}{2}\left(\dfrac{10}{3}\right) + 1$$

$$y = \dfrac{8}{3} \approx 2.67$$

d. Yes, The solution seems consistent with the graph.

e. Each company will have a charge of $2.67 when 3.33 miles are driven.

61.   **a., b.** We can determine the equations of the lines by finding the slopes and intercepts.

$$\underline{\textbf{Investment A}}$$

Slope: $m = \dfrac{2400 - 1500}{5 - 0} = \dfrac{900}{5} = 180$

$b = 1500$

Equation of line: $y = 180x + 1500$

$$\underline{\textbf{Investment B}}$$

Slope: $m = \dfrac{2700 - 2000}{5 - 0} = \dfrac{700}{5} = 140$

$b = 2000$

Equation of line: $y = 140x + 2000$

c. Now solve the system of equations.
Substitute $140x + 2000$ for y in the first equation.

$$140x + 2000 = 180x + 1500$$

$$-40x = -500$$

$$x = 12.5$$

Back-substitute to find y.

$$y = 180x + 1500$$

$$y = 180(12.5) + 1500$$

$$y = 3750$$

d. Yes, The solution seems consistent with the graph.

e. Each investment had a value of $3750 half way through 1997 (12.5 years since 1985).

63. The table illustrates that the x-coordinate of the solution to the system is between the integers 1 and 2.

We solve the system of equations using the substitution method.

$$x + 2y = 9$$
$$x - y = -2$$

Solve the second equation for x.

$$x - y = -2$$
$$x = y - 2$$

Substitute $y - 2$ for x in the first equation and then solve for y.

$$x + 2y = 9$$
$$(y - 2) + 2y = 9$$
$$3y = 11$$
$$y = \frac{11}{3}$$

Now, back substitute to find x.

$$x = y - 2$$
$$x = \left(\frac{11}{3}\right) - 2 = \frac{5}{3}$$

Solution: $\left(\frac{5}{3}, \frac{11}{3}\right)$

65. Substitute $1.05x - 2.1325$ for y in the second equation and solve for x:

$$7.14x - 8.37(1.05x - 2.1325) = 10.1835$$
$$7.14x - 8.7885x + 17.849025 = 10.1835$$
$$-1.6485x = -7.665525$$
$$x = 4.65$$

Back-substitute to find y.

$$y = 1.05x - 2.1325$$
$$y = 1.05(4.65) - 2.1325$$
$$y = 2.75$$

Solution: $(4.65, 2.75)$

67. Substitute $4.91y - 5.899$ for x in the second equation and solve for y:

$$2.1(4.91y - 5.899) - 9.9y = -12.84$$
$$10.311y - 12.3879 - 9.9y = -12.84$$
$$0.411y = -0.4521$$
$$y = -1.1$$

Back-substitute to find x.

$$x = 4.91y - 5.899$$
$$x = 4.91(-1.1) - 5.899$$
$$x = -11.3$$

Solution: $(-11.3, -1.1)$

Cumulative Review

1. To determine if $x = -2$ is a solution of $3x - 4 = 5x - 8$ we replace x with -2 then simplify.

$$3x - 4 = 5x - 8$$
$$3(-2) - 4 = 5(-2) - 8$$
$$-6 - 4 = -10 - 8$$
$$-10 \neq -18$$

Thus, $x = -2$ is not a solution of $3x - 4 = 5x - 8$.

To determine if $x = 2$ is a solution of $3x - 4 = 5x - 8$ we replace x with 2 then simplify.

$$3x - 4 = 5x - 8$$
$$3(2) - 4 = 5(2) - 8$$
$$6 - 4 = 10 - 8$$
$$2 = 2$$

Thus, $x = 2$ is a solution of $3x - 4 = 5x - 8$.

2. To determine if $x = -2$ is a solution of $-4(2x + 7) = 3x - 6$ we replace x with -2 then simplify.

$$-4(2x + 7) = 3x - 6$$
$$-4(2(-2) + 7) = 3(-2) - 6$$
$$-4(-4 + 7) = -6 - 6$$
$$-4(3) = -12$$
$$-12 = -12$$

Thus, $x = -2$ is a solution of $-4(2x + 7) = 3x - 6$.

To determine if $x = 2$ is a solution of $-4(2x + 7) = 3x - 6$ we replace x with 2 then simplify.

$$-4(2x + 7) = 3x - 6$$
$$-4(2(2) + 7) = 3(2) - 6$$
$$-4(4 + 7) = 3(2) - 6$$
$$-4(11) = 6 - 6$$
$$-44 \neq 0$$

Thus, $x = 2$ is not a solution of $-4(2x + 7) = 3x - 6$

3.
$$1-4(x+3)=-5(x-1)$$
$$1-4x-12=-5x+5$$
$$-4x+5x-11=-5x+5x+5$$
$$x-11=5$$
$$x=16$$

4.
$$\frac{x}{2}=4-\frac{x-3}{3}$$
$$6\left(\frac{x}{2}\right)=6\left(4-\frac{x-3}{3}\right)$$
$$3x=24-2(x-3)$$
$$3x+2x=24-2x+2x+6$$
$$5x=30$$
$$\frac{5x}{5}=\frac{30}{5}$$
$$x=6$$

5.
$$3.4x-36.17=-2.3(x-4.1)$$
$$3.4x-36.17=-2.3x+9.43$$
$$3.4x+2.3x-36.17=-2.3x+2.3x+9.43$$
$$5.7x-36.17+36.17=9.43+36.17$$
$$5.7x=45.6$$
$$\frac{5.7x}{5.7}=\frac{45.6}{5.7}$$
$$x=8$$

Section 3.5: Solving Systems of Linear Equations in Two Variables by the Addition Method

Quick Review 3.5

1. The LCD of $\dfrac{7}{15}$ and $\dfrac{6}{35}$ is 105.

2. $4(x-2y-3)-5(3x+y-2)=4x-8y-12-15x-5y+10=4x-15x-8y-5y-12+10=-11x-13y-2$

3. If n is an even integer, then
a. the next 3 consecutive integers are $n+1$, $n+2$, $n+3$.
b. the next 3 consecutive even integers are $n+2$, $n+4$, $n+6$.
c. the next 3 consecutive odd integers are $n+1$, $n+3$, $n+5$.

4. The mean score is $\dfrac{84+76+93+87}{4}=\dfrac{340}{4}=85$.

5. If the average weight has been trending higher, then the line will have a **positive** slope.

Exercises 3.5

1. Add the two equations to eliminate x. Solve this equation for y.
$$\begin{aligned} x+2y&=6 \\ -x+3y&=4 \\ \hline 5y&=10 \\ y&=2 \end{aligned}$$

Back substitute 2 for y in the first equation to find x.
$$x+2y=6$$
$$x+2(2)=6$$
$$x+4=6$$
$$x=2 \quad \text{Solution: } (2,\,2)$$

3. Add the two equations to eliminate y. Solve this equation for x.
$$\begin{aligned} 5x+2y&=-26 \\ 3x-2y&=-38 \\ \hline 8x\phantom{{}+2y}&=-64 \\ x&=-8 \end{aligned}$$

Back substitute -8 for x in the first equation to find y.
$$5x+2y=-26$$
$$5(-8)+2y=-26$$
$$-40+2y=-26$$
$$2y=14$$
$$y=7 \quad \text{Solution: } (-8,\,7)$$

5. To eliminate y, multiply both sides of the second equation by 2 and add the two equations. Solve this equation for x.

$$6x + 2y = -1 \qquad 6x + 2y = -1$$
$$12x - y = 3 \qquad \underline{24x - 2y = 6}$$
$$30x \quad = 5$$
$$x = \frac{1}{6}$$

Back substitute $\dfrac{1}{6}$ for x in the first equation to find y.

$$6x + 2y = -1$$
$$6\left(\frac{1}{6}\right) + 2y = -1$$
$$1 + 2y = -1$$
$$2y = -2$$
$$y = -1$$

Solution: $\left(\dfrac{1}{6}, -1\right)$

7. To eliminate y, multiply both sides of the first equation by -2 and add the two equations. Solve this equation for x.

$$x + 2y = 1 \qquad -2x - 4y = -2$$
$$3x + 4y = 0 \qquad \underline{3x + 4y = 0}$$
$$x = -2$$

Back substitute -2 for x in the first equation to find y.

$$x + 2y = 1$$
$$(-2) + 2y = 1$$
$$2y = 3$$
$$y = \frac{3}{2}$$

Solution: $\left(-2, \dfrac{3}{2}\right)$

9. To eliminate x, multiply both sides of the first equation by 2 and add the two equations. Solve this equation for y.

$$2x + 3y = -9 \qquad 4x + 6y = -18$$
$$-4x + 5y = -37 \qquad \underline{-4x + 5y = -37}$$
$$11y = -55$$
$$y = -5$$

Back substitute -5 for y in the first equation to find x.

$$2x + 3y = -9$$
$$2x + 3(-5) = -9$$
$$2x - 15 = -9$$
$$2x = 6$$
$$x = 3$$

Solution: $(3, -5)$

11. To eliminate y, multiply both sides of the first equation by 2 and add the two equations. Solve this equation for x.

$$5x - 3y = 5 \qquad 10x - 6y = 10$$
$$4x + 6y = 46 \qquad \underline{4x + 6y = 46}$$
$$14x \quad = 56$$
$$x = 4$$

Back substitute 4 for x in the first equation to find y.

$$5x - 3y = 5$$
$$5(4) - 3y = 5$$
$$20 - 3y = 5$$
$$-3y = -15$$
$$y = 5$$

Solution: $(4, 5)$

13. To eliminate x, multiply both sides of the first equation by 3, then multiply the second equation by -2 and add the two equations. Solve this equation for y.

$$2x + 5y = -3 \qquad 6x + 15y = -9$$
$$3x + 8y = -5 \qquad \underline{-6x - 16y = 10}$$
$$-y = 1$$
$$y = -1$$

Back substitute -1 for y in the first equation to find x.

$$2x + 5y = -3$$
$$2x + 5(-1) = -3$$
$$2x - 5 = -3$$
$$2x = 2$$
$$x = 1$$

Solution: $(1, -1)$

15. To eliminate x, multiply both sides of the first equation by 5, then multiply the second equation by -2 and add the two equations. Solve this equation for y.

$$2x + 3y = 15 \qquad 10x + 15y = 75$$
$$5x + 4y = -1 \qquad \underline{-10x - 8y = 2}$$
$$7y = 77$$
$$y = 11$$

Back substitute 11 for y in the first equation to find x.
$$2x + 3y = 15$$
$$2x + 3(11) = 15$$
$$2x + 33 = 15$$
$$2x = -18$$
$$x = -9$$

Solution: $(-9, 11)$

17. To eliminate x, multiply both sides of the first equation by 5, then multiply the second equation by -2 and add the two equations. Solve this equation for y.

$$2x - 13y = 38 \qquad 10x - 65y = 190$$
$$5x + 27y = 95 \qquad \underline{-10x - 54y = -190}$$
$$-119y = 0$$
$$y = 0$$

Back substitute 0 for y in the first equation to find x.
$$2x - 13y = 38$$
$$2x - 13(0) = 38$$
$$2x = 38$$
$$x = 19$$

Solution: $(19, 0)$

19. Write the equations in general form. To eliminate x, multiply both sides of the first equation by 5, then multiply the second equation by -2 and add the two equations. Solve this equation for y.

$$2x - 11y = 0 \qquad 10x - 55y = 0$$
$$5x - 19y = 0 \qquad \underline{-10x + 38y = 0}$$
$$-17y = 0$$
$$y = 0$$

Back substitute 0 for y in the first equation to find x.
$$2x - 11y = 0$$
$$2x - 11(0) = 0$$
$$2x = 0$$
$$x = 0$$

Solution: $(0, 0)$

21. Solve the first equation for x.
$$2x + 6 = 0$$
$$2x = -6$$
$$x = -3$$

Back substitute -3 for x in the second equation to find y.
$$3x + 2y = 1$$
$$3(-3) + 2y = 1$$
$$-9 + 2y = 1$$
$$2y = 10$$
$$y = 5$$

Solution: $(-3, 5)$

23. Multiply each equation by the least common denominator to write with integer coefficients.

$$6\left(\frac{x}{2} + \frac{y}{3}\right) = 6(5) \qquad 3x + 2y = 30$$
$$\qquad\qquad\qquad\qquad 2x - 3y = -6$$
$$6\left(\frac{x}{3} - \frac{y}{2}\right) = 6(-1)$$

To eliminate x, multiply both sides of the first equation by 2, then multiply the second equation by -3 and add the two equations. Solve this equation for y.

$$3x + 2y = 30 \qquad 6x + 4y = 60$$
$$2x - 3y = -6 \qquad \underline{-6x + 9y = 18}$$
$$13y = 78$$
$$y = 6$$

Back substitute 6 for y in the first equation to find x.
$$3x + 2y = 30$$
$$3x + 2(6) = 30$$
$$3x + 12 = 30$$
$$3x = 18$$
$$x = 6$$

Solution: $(6, 6)$

25. To eliminate x, multiply both sides of the first equation by $1/2$, then multiply the second equation by $1/5$ and add the two equations.

$$6x - 8y = 10 \qquad\qquad 3x - 4y = 5$$
$$-15x + 20y = -20 \qquad \underline{-3x + 4y = -4}$$
$$0 = -9$$

Since the resulting equation is a contradiction, there is no solution.

27. Write the equations in general form. To eliminate x, multiply both sides of the first equation by $1/3$, then multiply the second equation by $-1/4$ and add the two equations. Solve this equation for y.

$$6x + 3y = 9 \qquad\qquad 2x + y = 3$$
$$8x + 4y = 12 \qquad \underline{-2x - y = -3}$$
$$0 = 0$$

Since the resulting equation is an identity, there is an infinite number of solutions.

29. To eliminate y, multiply both sides of the first equation by 2, then multiply the second equation by 4 and add the two equations. Solve this equation for x.

$$\frac{x}{2} - \frac{y}{2} = \frac{3}{4} \qquad\qquad x - y = \frac{3}{2}$$
$$\frac{x}{2} + \frac{y}{4} = \frac{5}{8} \qquad \underline{2x + y = \frac{5}{2}}$$
$$3x \qquad = 4$$
$$x = \frac{4}{3}$$

Back substitute $\dfrac{4}{3}$ for x in the first equation to find y.

$$x - y = \frac{3}{2}$$
$$\frac{4}{3} - y = \frac{3}{2}$$
$$-y = \frac{1}{6}$$
$$y = -\frac{1}{6}$$

Solution: $\left(\dfrac{4}{3}, -\dfrac{1}{6}\right)$

31. Use the Substitution method. Substitute $2x - 1$ for y in the second equation and then solve for x.

$$7x - 4y = -1$$
$$7x - 4(2x - 1) = -1$$
$$7x - 8x + 4 = -1$$
$$-x = -5$$
$$x = 5$$

Back substitute 6 for x in the first equation.

$$y = 2x - 1$$
$$y = 2(5) - 1$$
$$y = 10 - 1$$
$$y = 9$$

Solution: $(5, 9)$

33. Use the addition method. Add the two equations to eliminate y. Solve this equation for x.

$$3x + 7y = 20$$
$$\underline{5x - 7y = -4}$$
$$8x \quad = 16$$
$$x = 2$$

Back substitute 2 for x in the first equation to find y.

$$3x + 7y = 20$$
$$3(2) + 7y = 20$$
$$6 + 7y = 20$$
$$7y = 14$$
$$y = 2$$

Solution: $(2, 2)$

35. Use the Substitution method. Substitute $-x$ for y in the second equation and then solve for x.

$$5x - 7y = 6$$
$$5x - 7(-x) = 6$$
$$5x + 7x = 6$$
$$12x = 6$$
$$x = \frac{1}{2}$$

Back substitute $\dfrac{1}{2}$ for x in the first equation.

$$y = -x$$
$$y = -\left(\frac{1}{2}\right)$$

Solution: $\left(\dfrac{1}{2}, -\dfrac{1}{2}\right)$

37. Use the addition method. To eliminate y, multiply both sides of the first equation by -2, then add the two equations.

$$\dfrac{x}{4} - \dfrac{y}{3} = \dfrac{5}{12} \qquad\qquad -\dfrac{x}{2} + \dfrac{2y}{3} = -\dfrac{5}{6}$$

$$\dfrac{x}{2} - \dfrac{2y}{3} = 1 \qquad\qquad \dfrac{x}{2} - \dfrac{2y}{3} = 1$$

$$\overline{\phantom{\dfrac{x}{2} - \dfrac{2y}{3} = 1}}$$

$$0 = \dfrac{1}{6}$$

Since the resulting equation is a contradiction, there is no solution.

39. Write the equations in general form. To eliminate x, multiply both sides of the first equation by -3, then add the two equations. Solve this equation for y.

$$-2x - 2y = -6 \qquad\qquad 6x + 6y = 18$$

$$-6x - 7y = -21 \qquad\qquad -6x - 7y = -21$$

$$\overline{}$$

$$-y = -3$$

$$y = 3$$

Back substitute -15 for y in the first equation to find x.

$$-2x - 2y = -6$$

$$-2x - 2(3) = -6$$

$$-2x - 6 = -6$$

$$-2x = 0$$

$$x = 0$$

Solution: $(0,\ 3)$

41. To eliminate x multiply both sides of the first equation by 40 and the second equation by -50 then add the two equations. Solve this equation for y.

$$0.5x + 1.2y = 0.3 \qquad\qquad 20x + 48y = 12$$

$$0.4x + 0.9y = 0.3 \qquad\qquad -20x - 45y = -15$$

$$\overline{}$$

$$3y = -3$$

$$y = -1$$

Back substitute -1 for y in the second equation to find x.

$$0.4x + 0.9(-1) = 0.3$$

$$0.4x - 0.9 = 0.3$$

$$0.4x = 1.2$$

$$x = 3$$

Solution: $(3,\ -1)$

43. **a.** Determine the slope of the line passing through the given points

$$m = \dfrac{y_2 - y_1}{x_2 - x_1} = \dfrac{1.0 - (-3.0)}{0.5 - 11.5} = \dfrac{4.0}{-11.0} = -\dfrac{4}{11}$$

Use the point-slope form with either point.

Substitute $\left(\dfrac{1}{2}, 1\right)$ for $(x_1,\ y_1)$ and $-\dfrac{4}{11}$ for m.

Then write the equation in slope intercept form by solving for y.

$$y - y_1 = m(x - x_1)$$

$$y - (1) = -\dfrac{4}{11}\left(x - \dfrac{1}{2}\right)$$

$$y - 1 = -\dfrac{4}{11}x + \dfrac{2}{11}$$

$$y = -\dfrac{4}{11}x + \dfrac{13}{11}$$

b. Determine the slope of the line passing through the given points

$$m = \dfrac{y_2 - y_1}{x_2 - x_1} = \dfrac{2 - (-7)}{-11 - 40} = \dfrac{\overset{3}{\cancel{9}}}{\underset{17}{\cancel{51}}} = -\dfrac{3}{17}$$

Use the point-slope form with either point.

Substitute $(-11, 2)$ for $(x_1,\ y_1)$ and $-\dfrac{3}{17}$ for m.

Then write the equation in slope intercept form by solving for y.

$$y - y_1 = m(x - x_1)$$

$$y - 2 = -\dfrac{3}{17}(x - (-11))$$

$$y - 2 = -\dfrac{3}{17}x - \dfrac{33}{17}$$

$$y = -\dfrac{3}{17}x + \dfrac{1}{17}$$

(Continued on the next page.)

c.

<u>Step 1</u>	<u>Step 2</u>	<u>Step 3</u>

Step 1

Solve one of the equations for one variable in terms of the other.

$$y = -\frac{4}{11}x + \frac{13}{11}$$

$$y = -\frac{3}{17}x + \frac{1}{17}$$

(y is currently written in terms of x in each equation.)

Step 2

Substitute $-\frac{4}{11}x + \frac{13}{11}$ for y in the second equation and then solve for x.

$$-\frac{4}{11}x + \frac{13}{11} = -\frac{3}{17}x + \frac{1}{17}$$

$$187\left(-\frac{4}{11}x + \frac{13}{11}\right) = 187\left(-\frac{3}{17}x + \frac{1}{17}\right)$$

$$-68x + 221 = -33x + 11$$

$$-35x = -210$$

$$x = 6$$

Step 3

Back-substitute 6 for x in the second equation.

$$y = -\frac{3}{17}x + \frac{1}{17}$$

$$y = -\frac{3}{17}(6) + \frac{1}{17}$$

$$y = -\frac{18}{17} + \frac{1}{17}$$

$$y = -\frac{17}{17} = -1$$

Solution: $(6, -1)$

45. The system of equations is **C**. Add the two equations to eliminate y. Solve this equation for x.

$$3x + y = 1$$
$$\underline{x - y = 7}$$
$$4x \quad = 8$$
$$x = 2$$

Back substitute 2 for x in the first equation to find y.

$$3x + y = 1$$
$$3(2) + y = 1$$
$$6 + y = 1$$
$$y = -5$$

The two numbers are 2 and -5.

47. The system of equations is **D**. To eliminate x, multiply both sides of the first equation by 2, then multiply the second equation by -5 and add the two equations. Solve this equation for y.

$$5x + 2y = 2 \qquad\qquad 10x + 4y = 4$$
$$2x + 5y = 26 \qquad\quad \underline{-10x - 25y = -130}$$
$$\qquad\qquad\qquad\qquad -21y = -126$$
$$\qquad\qquad\qquad\qquad y = 6$$

Back substitute 6 for y in the first equation to find x.

$$5x + 2y = 2$$
$$5x + 2(6) = 2$$
$$5x + 12 = 2$$
$$5x = -10$$
$$x = -2$$

The two numbers are -2 and 6.

49. Let x and y be the two numbers.

If the sum of the numbers is 88 then

$$x + y = 88$$

If the difference of the two numbers is 28 then

$$x - y = 28$$

Add the two equations to eliminate y. Solve the equation for x.

$$x + y = 88$$
$$\underline{x - y = 28}$$
$$2x \quad = 116$$
$$x = 58$$

Back substitute 58 for x in the first equation to find y.

$$x + y = 88$$
$$(58) + y = 88$$
$$y = 30$$

The two numbers are 58 and 30.

51. Let x and y be the two numbers.

If the sum of the numbers is 102 then	If one number is twice the other then
$x + y = 102$	$y = 2x$

Substitute $2x$ for y in the first equation and solve for x.

$$x + y = 102$$
$$x + 2x = 102$$
$$3x = 102$$
$$x = 34$$

Back substitute 34 for x in the first equation to find y.

$$x + y = 102$$
$$(34) + y = 102$$
$$y = 68$$

The two numbers are 34 and 68.

53. Let x be the score on each of the first four games.
Let y be the score on the fifth game.

If the mean score for the five games was 25 then	If the range of the scores was 15 then
$\dfrac{4x + y}{5} = 25$	$y - x = 15$
or $4x + y = 125$	or $y = x + 15$

Substitute $x + 15$ for y in the first equation and solve for x.

$$4x + (x + 15) = 125$$
$$5x = 110$$
$$x = 22$$

Back substitute 22 for x in the first equation to find y.

$$4x + y = 125$$
$$4(22) + y = 125$$
$$88 + y = 125$$
$$y = 37$$

The basketball player scored 22 points in each of the first four games and 37 points in the fifth game.

55. **a., b.** We can determine the equations of the lines by finding the slopes and using the point-slope form of the line.

Community College

Slope: $m = \dfrac{42 - 18}{2011 - 1995}$

$= \dfrac{24}{16} = 1.5$

$y - y_1 = m(x - x_1)$

$y - (18) = 1.5(x - (1995))$

$y = 1.5x - 2974.5$

4-Year College

Slope: $m = \dfrac{30 - 38}{2011 - 1995}$

$= \dfrac{-8}{16} = -0.5$

$y - y_1 = m(x - x_1)$

$y - (38) = -0.5(x - (1995))$

$y = -0.5x + 1035.5$

Now solve the system of equations.

c. Substitute $-0.5x + 1035.5$ for y in the first equation.

$$-0.5x + 1035.5 = 1.5x - 2974.5$$
$$-2x = -4010$$
$$x = 2005$$

Back-substitute to find y.

$$y = -0.5x + 1035.5$$
$$y = -0.5(2005) + 1035.5$$
$$y = 33$$

d. In 2005, 33% of all graduates of Mason High School attended a four-year college and 33% of all graduates attended a community college.

57. The table illustrates that the *x*-coordinate of the solution of the system is between the integers 0 and 1.

To eliminate *y*, multiply both sides of the first equation by −1 and add the two equations. Solve this equation for *y*.

$$11x - 2y = 1 \qquad -11 + 2y = -1$$
$$11x + 3y = 11 \qquad \underline{11x + 3y = 11}$$
$$5y = 10$$
$$y = 2$$

Back substitute 2 for *y* in the first equation to find *y*.

$$11x - 2y = 1$$
$$11x - 2(2) = 1$$
$$11x - 4 = 1$$
$$11x = 5$$
$$x = \frac{5}{11}$$

Solution: $\left(\dfrac{5}{11}, 2\right)$

59. Solve each equation for *y*. Sketch the graphs of the equations and find the point of intersection.

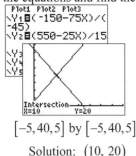

$[-5, 40, 5]$ by $[-5, 40, 5]$

Solution: $(10, 20)$

61. Solve each equation for *y*. Sketch the graphs of the equations and find the point of intersection.

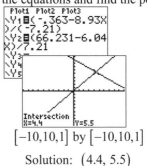

$[-10, 10, 1]$ by $[-10, 10, 1]$

Solution: $(4.4, 5.5)$

Cumulative Review

1. $[-3, \infty)$ is equivalent to $x \geq -3$.

2. $(-\infty, -2)$ is equivalent to $x < -2$.

3. $(-2, 6]$ is equivalent to $-2 < x \leq 6$.

4. The inequality is equivalent to $-1 < x \leq 2$.

5. The inequality is equivalent to $x \leq 4$.

Section 3.6: More Applications of Linear Systems

Quick Review 3.6

1. The cost that does not change with the number of items produced is called the **fixed** cost.

2. The cost of making each unit that can change with the number of items produced is called the **variable** cost.

3. The phrase "**restrictions** on the variable" refers to the values of the variable that are permissible in an equation.

4. **Equivalent** equations have the same solution set.

5. Two angles are **supplementary** if the sum of their measure is $180°$.

Exercises 3.6

---

1.   Let x be the width of the poster.
Let y be the length of the poster.

b, c.

If the perimeter of the poster is 204, then $2x + 2y = 204$	If the length of the poster is 6 more than the width, then $y = x + 6$

Substitute $x + 6$ for y in the first equation.

$$2x + 2y = 204$$
$$2x + 2(x + 6) = 204$$
$$2x + 2x + 12 = 204$$
$$4x = 192$$
$$x = 48$$

Back substitute 48 for x in the second equation

$$y = x + 6$$
$$y = (48) + 6$$
$$y = 54$$

e. yes

f. The dimensions of the poster are 48 cm by 54 cm.

---

3.   Let x and y be the two numbers

If the sum of the numbers is 100, then $x + y = 100$	If one number is 16 more than twice the smaller number, then $y = 2x + 16$

Substitute $2x + 16$ for y in the first equation.

$$x + 2x + 16 = 100$$
$$3x + 16 = 100$$
$$3x = 84$$
$$x = 28$$

Back substitute 28 for x in the first equation

$$x + y = 100$$
$$28 + y = 100$$
$$y = 72$$

The two numbers are 28 and 72.

5.

If the perimeter of the triangle is 72, then $2x + y = 72$	If the base is 12 cm longer than the two sides, then $y = x + 12$

Substitute $x + 12$ for y in the first equation.

$$2x + y = 72$$
$$2x + (x + 12) = 72$$
$$3x = 60$$
$$x = 20$$

Back substitute 20 for x in the second equation

$$y = x + 12$$
$$y = (20) + 12$$
$$y = 32$$

The base of the triangle is 32 cm. The other two sides measure 20 cm.

---

7.   Let the two numbers be x and y.

If the sum of the 7 times the first number plus 4 times the second number is 294, then $7x + 4y = 294$	If 6 times the first number minus the second number is 97, then $6x - y = 97$

Use the addition method to solve the equations. Multiply both sides of the second equation by 4 and add the equations.

$$7x + 4y = 294$$
$$\underline{24x - 4y = 388}$$
$$31x \quad\;\; = 682$$
$$x = 22$$

Back substitute 22 for x in the second equation.

$$6x - y = 97$$
$$6(22) - y = 97$$
$$132 - y = 97$$
$$-y = -35$$
$$y = 35$$

The numbers are 22 and 35.

---

9.   Let x be score of the four equivalent rounds.
Let y be the score of the fifth round.

If the mean score was 83, then $\dfrac{4x + y}{5} = 83$ or $4x + y = 415$	If the fifth round was 10 strokes higher than the others, then $y = x + 10$

Substitute $x + 10$ for y in the first equation.

$$4x + y = 415$$
$$4x + (x + 10) = 415$$
$$5x + 10 = 415$$
$$5x = 405$$
$$x = 81$$

Back substitute 81 for x in the second equation.

$$y = x + 10$$
$$y = 81 + 10$$
$$y = 91$$

The scores were 81 for each of the four equivalent rounds and 91 for the fifth round.

11.   **a.** Grade points are computed by multiplying the number of academic hours by the numeric grade (4 for A, 3 for B, 2 for C, 1 for D, and 0 for F).
   In this case the *total* grade point earned for the semester is $3 \cdot 2 + 4 \cdot 3 + 3 \cdot 2 + 3 \cdot 2 = 30$.

   b. We determine the grade point average by dividing the total grade points(found in part **a.**)for the semester by the total number of semester hours.
   In this case the grade point average is $\dfrac{30}{13} \approx 2.31$.

   c. Let x be the required number of semester hours with a grade of A to raise the GPA to 3.00. To find x we solve the following equation.

$$\frac{\boxed{\text{Previous Grade Points} + \text{New Grade Points}}}{\boxed{\text{Total Semester Hours}}} = 3.00$$

$$\frac{30 + 4x}{13 + x} = 3.00$$

$$30 + 4x = 3(13 + x)$$

$$30 + 4x = 39 + 3x$$

$$x = 9$$

The student would need 9 semester hours with a grade of A to meet the goal of a GPA of 3.00.

13.   Let x be the required number of semester hours with a grade of A to raise the GPA to 2.75. To find x we solve the following equation.

$$\frac{\boxed{\text{Previous Grade Points} + \text{New Grade Points}}}{\boxed{\text{Total Semester Hours}}} = 2.75$$

$$\frac{(30)(2.50) + 4x}{30 + x} = 2.75$$

$$75 + 4x = 2.75(30 + x)$$

$$75 + 4x = 82.5 + 2.75x$$

$$1.25x = 7.5$$

$$x = 6$$

The student would need 6 semester hours with a grade of A to meet the goal of a GPA of 2.75. The total grade points would be $(30)(2.50) + (6)(4) = 99$.

15.   Let x be the fixed monthly charge. Let y be the charge for each pay per view movie.

If a $44 bill included four pay-per-view movies, then
$$x + 4y = 44$$
or $x = 44 - 4y$

If a $54.50 bill included seven pay-per-view movies, then
$$x + 7y = 54.50$$

Substitute $44 - 4y$ for y in the second equation.
$$x + 7y = 54.50$$
$$(44 - 4y) + 7y = 54.50$$
$$3y = 10.5$$
$$y = 3.5$$

Back substitute 3.5 for y in the first equation.
$$x = 44 - 4y$$
$$x = 44 - 4(3.5)$$
$$x = 30$$

The fixed monthly charge is $30.00 and the charge for each pay per view movie is $3.50.

17. Let x be the number of union employees. Let y be the number of union stewards.

| If the total number of employees is 50, then $x + y = 50$ or $y = 50 - x$ | If the budget for the daily payroll is 6072, then $120x + 144y = 6072$ |

Substitute $50 - x$ for y in the second equation.
$$120x + 144(50 - x) = 6072$$
$$120x + 7200 - 144x = 6072$$
$$-24x = -1128$$
$$x = 47$$

Back substitute 332 for x in the second equation.
$$y = 50 - x$$
$$y = 50 - (47)$$
$$y = 3$$
Hire 47 union employees and 3 union stewards.

19. Let x be the number of adult tickets sold. Let y be the number of student tickets sold.

| If adults paid \$2.50 for admission and students paid \$1.25 and the total receipts for a basketball game are \$1400, then $2.5x + 1.25y = 1400$ | If a total of 788 tickets were sold, then $x + y = 788$ or $y = 788 - x$ |

Substitute $788 - x$ for y in the first equation.
$$2.5x + 1.25y = 1400$$
$$2.5x + 1.25(788 - x) = 1400$$
$$2.5x + 985 - 1.25x = 1400$$
$$1.25x = 415$$
$$x = 332$$

Back substitute 332 for x in the second equation.
$$y = 788 - x$$
$$y = 788 - (332)$$
$$y = 456$$
There were 332 adult tickets and 456 student tickets sold.

21.

| If the angles are complementary, then $x + y = 90$ | If one angle is $28°$ larger than the other, then $y = x + 28$ |

Substitute $x + 28$ for y in the first equation.
$$x + y = 90$$
$$x + (x + 28) = 90$$
$$2x = 62$$
$$x = 31$$

Back substitute 31 for x in the second equation.
$$y = x + 28$$
$$y = (31) + 28$$
$$y = 59$$
The two angles are $31°$ and $59°$.

23.

| If the angles are supplementary, then $x + y = 180$ | If one angle is $5°$ more than four times the other angle, then $y = 4x + 5$ |

Substitute $4x + 5$ for y in the first equation.
$$x + y = 180$$
$$x + (4x + 5) = 180$$
$$5x = 175$$
$$x = 35$$
Back substitute 35 for x in the second equation.
$$y = 4x + 5$$
$$y = 4(35) + 5$$
$$y = 145$$
The two angles are $35°$ and $145°$.

25. Let x be the number of left-handed desks needed.
Let y be the number of right-handed desks needed.

If a total of 600 desks are needed, then $x + y = 600$	If there are nine times as many right-handed people than left-handed people, then $y = 9x$

Substitute $9x$ for y in the first equation.
$$x + y = 600$$
$$x + (9x) = 600$$
$$10x = 600$$
$$x = 60$$

Back substitute 60 for x in the second equation.
$$y = 9x$$
$$y = 9(60)$$
$$y = 540$$

The manager should order 60 left-handed desks and 540 right-handed desks.

27. Let x be the number of days of usage for each bulb.
Let y be the cost of buying and using the bulbs.

If an incandescent bulb costs $0.50 to buy and $0.12 per day to use, then the total cost for using the bulb is $y = 0.12x + 0.50$	If a CFL costs $2.50 to buy and $0.02 per day to use, then the total cost for using the CFL is $y = 0.02x + 2.50$

Substitute $0.02x + 2.50$ for y in the first equation.
$$0.02x + 2.50 = 0.12x + 0.50$$
$$0.10x = 2.00$$
$$x = 20$$

Back substitute 20 for x in the second equation.
$$y = 0.02x + 2.50$$
$$y = 0.02(20) + 2.50$$
$$y = 2.90$$

After 20 days the total cost for using either bulb is $2.90

29. Let x be the amount invested at 7%.
Let y be the amount invested at 9%.

If the total amount invested is $12,000, then $x + y = 12000$ or $x = 12000 - y$	If the combined interest earned at the end of one year was $890, then $0.07x + 0.09y = 890$

Substitute $12000 - y$ for x in the second equation.
$$0.07x + 0.09y = 890$$
$$0.07(12000 - y) + 0.09y = 890$$
$$840 - 0.07y + 0.09y = 890$$
$$0.02y = 50$$
$$y = 2500$$

Back substitute 2500 for y in the first equation.
$$x = 12000 - y$$
$$x = 12000 - 2500$$
$$x = 9500$$

$2500 was invested at 9% and $9500 was invested at 7%.

31. Let x be the amount in the first investment.
Let y be the amount in the second investment.

According to the first scenario we have	According to the second scenario we have
$0.08x + 0.05y = 600$	$0.04x + 0.07y = 480$

Use the addition method to solve the equations. Multiply both sides of the second equation by -2 then add the equations to eliminate x.

$$0.08x + 0.05y = 600$$
$$-0.08x - 0.14y = -960$$
$$\overline{\ -0.09y = -360}$$
$$y = 4000$$

Back substitute 4000 for y in the first equation.
$$0.08x + 0.05y = 600$$
$$0.08x + 0.05(4000) = 600$$
$$0.08x + 200 = 600$$
$$0.08x = 400$$
$$x = 5000$$

$5000 was in the first investment and $4000 was in the second investment.

33. Let x and y be the speeds of the two trains.

If one averages 10 kilometers per hour more than the other, then $x - y = 10$	If after ½ hour they are 89 kilometers apart, then $\frac{1}{2}x + \frac{1}{2}y = 89$ or $x + y = 178$

Use the addition method to solve the equations. Add the equations to eliminate y.

$$x - y = 10$$
$$x + y = 178$$
$$\overline{2x = 188}$$
$$x = 94$$

Back substitute 94 for x in the first equation.
$$x - y = 10$$
$$94 - y = 10$$
$$-y = -84$$
$$y = 84$$

The trains are traveling at speeds of 94 km/hr and 84 km/hr.

35. Let x be the speed of the train that leaves at 6:30.
Let y be the speed of the train that leaves at 6:00.

If the 6:30 train travels 15 km faster than the 6:00 train, then $x = y + 15$	If, at 7:00, the trains are 135 km apart, then $\frac{1}{2}x + (1)y = 135$ or $x + 2y = 270$

Substitute $y + 15$ for x in the second equation.
$$x + 2y = 270$$
$$(y + 15) + 2y = 270$$
$$3y + 15 = 270$$
$$3y = 255$$
$$y = 85$$

Back substitute 85 for y in the first equation.
$$x = y + 15$$
$$x = 85 + 15$$
$$x = 100$$

The 6:30 train has a speed of 100 km/hr.
The 6:00 train has a speed of 85 km/hr.

37. Let x be the speed of the riverboat.
Let y be the speed of the current.

If riverboat takes one hour to go 24 kilometers downstream, then $1(x+y)=24$ or $x+y=24$	If riverboat takes one hours hour to go 24 kilometers upstream, then $4(x-y)=24$ or $4x-4y=24$

Use the addition method to solve the equations.
Multiply both sides of the first equation by 4 then add the equations to eliminate y.

$$4x+4y=96$$
$$\underline{4x-4y=24}$$
$$8x \quad\quad =120$$
$$x=15$$

Back substitute 15 for x in the first equation.
$$x+y=24$$
$$15+y=24$$
$$y=9$$

The speed of the riverboat is 15 km/hr and the speed of the current is 9 km/hr.

39. Let x be the number of liters of the 33% solution.
Let y be the number of liters of the 5% solution.

If the total amount of the new mixture is 80 liters, then $x+y=80$	If new mixture is to be a 12% solution, then $0.33x+0.05y=0.12(80)$ or $0.33x+0.05y=9.6$

Use the addition method to solve the equations.
Multiply both sides of the first equation by -0.05 then add the equations to eliminate y.
$$-0.05x-0.05y=-4$$
$$\underline{0.33x+0.05y=9.6}$$
$$0.28x \quad\quad =5.6$$
$$x=20$$

Back substitute 20 for x in the first equation.
$$x+y=80$$
$$20+y=80$$
$$y=60$$

Use 20 liters of the 33% solution and 60 liters of the 5% solution.

41. Let x be the number of grams of the 80% alloy.

If x grams of the 80% alloy is to be mixed with 80 grams of a 50% alloy to make a 72% alloy, then the total ammout of the new alloy will be $x+80$ and
$$0.80x+0.50(80)=0.72(x+80)$$
$$0.80x+40=0.72x+57.6$$
$$0.08x=17.6$$
$$x=220$$
Thus, the goldsmith should use 220 grams of the 80% pure gold alloy.

43. Let x be the number of liters of pure water (100% water).

If x liters of pure water is to be added to 12 liters of 15% water to make a 50% mixture, then the total ammout of the new mixture will be $x+12$ and
$$1.00x+0.15(12)=0.50(x+12)$$
$$x+1.8=0.50x+6$$
$$0.50x=4.2$$
$$x=8.4$$
Thus, we should use 8.4 liters of pure water.

45. Let x be the rate for the older bricklayer. Let y be the rate for the younger bricklayer.

If each worked 8 hours and laid a total of 4000 bricks, then
$$8x + 8y = 4000$$
or
$$x + y = 500$$

If the older bricklayer worked 6 hours and the younger worked 7 hours and they laid a total of 3220 bricks, then
$$6x + 7y = 3220$$

Use the addition method to solve the equations. Multiply both sides of the first equation by -7 then add the equations to eliminate y.

$$-7x - 7y = -3500$$
$$6x + 7y = 3220$$
$$\overline{-x = -280}$$
$$x = 280$$

Back substitute 280 for x in the first equation.
$$x + y = 500$$
$$280 + y = 500$$
$$y = 220$$

The older bricklayer can lay 280 bricks per hour and the younger bricklayer can lay 220 bricks per hour.

47. **a.** Solve the system.
$$y = 200$$
$$y = 6.8x + 160$$

Substitute 200 for y in the second equation and solve for x.
$$y = 6.8x + 160$$
$$200 = 6.8x + 160$$
$$40 = 6.8x$$
$$x = 5.88$$

The corresponding value for y is 200.

b. In 1995 (5.88 years after 1990), the United States and Europe were producing 200,000 publications.

49. We can determine the equations of the lines by finding the slopes and intercepts.

a, b.

Option A

Slope: $m = \dfrac{2900 - 500}{12 - 0} = \dfrac{2400}{12} = 200$

$b = 500$

Equation of line: $y = 200x + 500$

Option B

Slope: $m = \dfrac{2200 - 1000}{12 - 0} = \dfrac{1200}{12} = 100$

$b = 1000$

Equation of line: $y = 100x + 1000$

c. Now solve the system of equations.
Substitute $100x + 1000$ for y in the first equation.
$$y = 200x + 500$$
$$100x + 1000 = 200x + 500$$
$$-100x = -500$$
$$x = 5$$

Back-substitute to find y.
$$y = 200x + 500$$
$$y = 200(5) + 500$$
$$y = 1500$$

d. yes

e. Each option costs $1500 after 5 years.

51.   **a.**   Let x be the fixed cost.

Let y be the variable cost per pair of shoes

If the company produced 400 pairs of shoes at a cost of $5700, then	If the company produced 525 pairs of shoes at a cost of $6700, then
$x + 400y = 5700$	$x + 525y = 6700$

Use the addition method to solve the equations. Multiply both sides of the first equation by -1 then add the equations to eliminate x.

$$-x - 400y = -5700$$
$$x + 525y = 6700$$
$$\overline{125y = 1000}$$
$$y = 8$$

Back substitute 8 for y in the first equation.

$$x + 400y = 5700$$
$$x + 400(8) = 5700$$
$$x = 2500$$

The fixed cost is $2500 a day and the variable cost is $8.00 per pair of shoes.

b.   Let x be the fixed cost.

Let y be the variable cost per pair of shoes

If the company produced 400 pairs of shoes at a cost of $9100, then	If the company produced 525 pairs of shoes at a cost of $12,100, then
$x + 400y = 9100$	$x + 525y = 12100$

Use the addition method to solve the equations. Multiply both sides of the first equation by -1 then add the equations to eliminate x.

$$-x - 400y = -9100$$
$$x + 525y = 12100$$
$$\overline{125y = 3000}$$
$$y = 375$$

Back substitute 375 for y in the first equation.

$$x + 400y = 9100$$
$$x + 400(375) = 9100$$
$$x = -140900$$

This is not possible.

53.   **a.**   The total time to fly to Pearl Harbor is $t = \dfrac{\text{Distance}}{\text{Rate against the wind}} = \dfrac{350}{175 - 25} = \dfrac{350}{150} = 2.\overline{3}$ hours or 2 hours and 20 minutes.

b.   Let d = distance from the point of no return to Pearl Harbor.

Let t = time to complete the trip from the point of no return (in either direction).

En route to Pearl Harbor we know:
$$d = 150t$$

En route back to the aircraft carrier we know:
$$350 - d = 200t$$

Adding these equations together will yield the equation: $350 = 350t$ Which implies the time to complete the trip is 1 hour.

c.   The time it take for the aircraft to reach the point of no return is $2.\overline{3} - 1 = 1.\overline{3}$ hours or 1 hour and 20 minutes.

Cumulative Review

1.
$$2(x-3)+4(x-3) = 2x-6+4x-12$$
$$= 2x+4x-6-12$$
$$= 6x-18$$

2.
$$2(x-3)+4(x-3) = 0$$
$$2x-6+4x-12 = 0$$
$$2x+4x-6-12 = 0$$
$$6x-18 = 0$$
$$6x = 18$$
$$x = 3$$

3. To determine if $(-1, 2)$ is a solution of $3x+y=-1$ we replace x with -1 and y with 2 and then simplify.
$$3x+y = -1$$
$$3(-1)+(2) = -1$$
$$-3+2 = -1$$
$$-1 = -1$$
Thus, $(-1, 2)$ is a solution of $3x+y=-1$.

4. To determine if $(-1, 2)$ is a solution of $y=-2x+4$ we replace x with -1 and y with 2 and then simplify.
$$y = -2x+4$$
$$(2) = -2(-1)+4$$
$$2 = 2+4$$
$$2 \neq 6$$
Thus, $(-1, 2)$ is not a solution of $y=-2x+4$.

5. To find the x-intercept, set $y=0$ and solve for x.
$$3x-4y = 12$$
$$3x-4(0) = 12$$
$$3x = 12$$
$$x = 4$$
$(4, 0)$ is the x-intercept.

To find the y-intercept, set $x=0$ and solve for y.
$$3x-4y = 12$$
$$3(0)-4y = 12$$
$$-4y = 12$$
$$y = -3$$
$(0, -3)$ is the y-intercept.

Review Exercises for Chapter 3

1. Use $x_1 = 1$, $y_1 = -3$, $x_2 = 4$, $y_2 = 3$
$$m = \frac{y_2-y_1}{x_2-x_1} = \frac{3-(-3)}{4-1} = \frac{6}{3} = 2$$

2. Use $x_1 = 1$, $y_1 = 4$, $x_2 = 6$, $y_2 = 1$
$$m = \frac{y_2-y_1}{x_2-x_1} = \frac{1-4}{6-1} = \frac{-3}{5} = -\frac{3}{5}$$

3. The equation is in slope intercept form $y = mx+b$. Thus $m = \frac{4}{7}$.

4. The equation is in point-slope form
$$y-y_1 = m(x-x_1)$$
Thus $m = -1$.

5. The line $y = -7$ is a horizontal line and has a slope $m = 0$.

6. Use $x_1 = 5$, $y_1 = 0$, $x_2 = 0$, $y_2 = -2$
$$m = \frac{y_2-y_1}{x_2-x_1} = \frac{-2-0}{0-5} = \frac{-2}{-5} = \frac{2}{5}$$

7. The line $x = 2$ is a vertical line and has an undefined slope.

8. Using any pair of points in the table we can see that the *change* in y is always zero. Thus the slope is $m = 0$.

9. Using any pair of points in the table we can see that the *change* in x is always zero. Thus the slope is undefined.

10. We can find the slope by using any two points from the table. For example:

Use $x_1 = -3$, $y_1 = -.5$, $x_2 = 0$, $y_2 = 1$

$$m = \frac{y_2 - y_1}{x_2 - x_1} = \frac{1 - (-0.5)}{0 - (-3)} = \frac{1.5}{3} = 0.5$$

11.

	Change in x	Change in y	Slope
a.	5	4	$\dfrac{4}{5}$
b.	5	4	$\dfrac{4}{5}$
c.	-5	-4	$\dfrac{4}{5}$
d.	1	$\dfrac{4}{5}$	$\dfrac{4}{5}$
e.	-1	$-\dfrac{4}{5}$	$\dfrac{4}{5}$

12. If the slope is $m = \dfrac{3}{5}$ then $\Delta x = 5$ and $\Delta y = 3$.

a.

x	y
0	6
5	9
10	12
15	15
20	18

The change in the x-values is 5, thus we use 3 for the change in the y-values.

b.

x	y
0	6
10	12
20	18
30	24
40	30

The change in the x-values is $10 = 2(5)$, thus we use $6 = 2(3)$ for the change in the y-values.

c.

x	y
0	6
-5	3
-10	0
-15	-3
-20	-6

The change in the x-values is $-5 = -(5)$, thus we use $-3 = -(3)$ for the change in the y-values.

13. The slope of the wheelchair ramp is $m = \dfrac{\text{rise}}{\text{run}} = \dfrac{2}{12} = \dfrac{1}{6}$.

14. a. Calculate the slope of each line by substituting in the given points.

$(4, -2)$ and $(6, 2)$

$$m = \frac{y_2 - y_1}{x_2 - x_1}$$

$$m = \frac{2 - (-2)}{6 - 4}$$

$$m = \frac{4}{2}$$

$$m = 2$$

$(5, 3)$ and $(9, 11)$

$$m = \frac{y_2 - y_1}{x_2 - x_1}$$

$$m = \frac{11 - 3}{9 - 5}$$

$$m = \frac{8}{4}$$

$$m = 2$$

The two lines are parallel.

b. The First line is horizontal and the second line is vertical. Thus, the lines are perpendicular.

c. The slope of the first line is $m = 5$ and the slope of the second line is $m = -5$. The two lines are neither perpendicular nor parallel.

15. Mental estimate: $m = \dfrac{\text{Change in } y}{\text{Change in } x} \approx \dfrac{2}{2} = 1$ **16.** Mental estimate: $m = \dfrac{\text{Change in } y}{\text{Change in } x} \approx \dfrac{-3}{3} = -1$

Actual slope: $m = \dfrac{\text{Change in } y}{\text{Change in } x} \approx \dfrac{1.71}{1.9} = 0.9$ Actual slope: $m = \dfrac{\text{Change in } y}{\text{Change in } x} \approx \dfrac{-3.63}{3.3} = -1.1$

17.

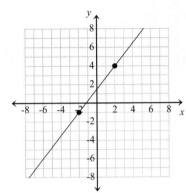

18.

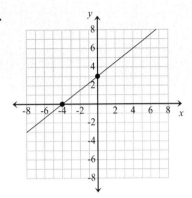

19.

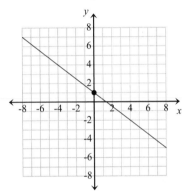

20.

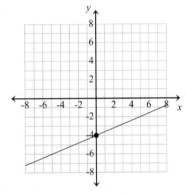

21.

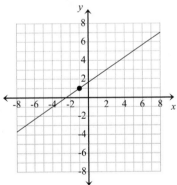

22.

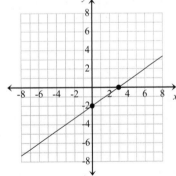

23. Use the slope-intercept form with $-\dfrac{1}{2}$ for m and 6 for b. $y = mx + b \Rightarrow y = -\dfrac{1}{2}x + 6$

24. Determine the slope of the line passing through the given points

$$m = \frac{y_2 - y_1}{x_2 - x_1} = \frac{-2 - 0}{0 - 3} = \frac{-2}{-3} = \frac{2}{3}$$

Use the slope-intercept form with $\frac{2}{3}$ for m and -2 for b.

$$y = mx + b$$
$$y = \frac{2}{3}x - 2$$

25. Determine the slope of the line passing through the given points

$$m = \frac{y_2 - y_1}{x_2 - x_1} = \frac{5 - (-1)}{2 - 4} = \frac{6}{-2} = -3$$

Use the point-slope form with either point. Substitute $(2, 5)$ for (x_1, y_1) and -3 for m. Then write the equation in slope-intercept form.

$$y - y_1 = m(x - x_1)$$
$$y - 5 = -3(x - 2)$$
$$y - 5 = -3x + 6$$
$$y = -3x + 11$$

26. The slope of this line must be $m = \frac{3}{2}$.

Use the slope-intercept form with $\frac{3}{2}$ for m and -4 for b.

$$y = mx + b$$
$$y = \frac{3}{2}x - 4$$

27. Use the slope-intercept form with 5 for m and 0 for b.

$$y = mx + b$$
$$y = 5x + 0$$
$$y = 5x$$

28. Use the point-slope form with either point. Substitute $(2, 5)$ for (x_1, y_1) and $\frac{1}{2}$ for m. Then write the equation in slope-intercept form.

$$y - y_1 = m(x - x_1)$$
$$y - 5 = \frac{1}{2}(x - 2)$$
$$y - 5 = \frac{1}{2}x - 1$$
$$y = \frac{1}{2}x + 4$$

29. The equation of a horizontal line is determined by the y-coordinates. Thus the equation is $y = 9$.

30. The equation of a vertical line is determined by the x-coordinates. Thus the equation is $x = 4$.

31. **a.** The y-intercept is $(0, -4)$.

b. The value of Δx in the table is 2.
c. The value of Δy in the table is 3.

d. The slope of the line is $m = \frac{\Delta y}{\Delta x} = \frac{3}{2}$

e. To find the equation of the line we use the slope intercept form where $m = \frac{3}{2}$ and $b = -4$. Thus the equation is $y = \frac{3}{2}x - 4$.

32.

a. To determine if $(5, 0)$ is a solution of
$2x - 5y = 10$ we replace x with 5 and y
with 0 and then simplify.
$$2x - 5y = 10$$
$$2(5) - 5(0) = 10$$
$$10 = 10$$
Thus, $(5, 0)$ is a solution of $2x - 5y = 10$.

b. To determine if $(10, 2)$ is a solution of
$2x - 5y = 10$ we replace x with 0 and y with -1
and then simplify.
$$2x - 5y = 10$$
$$2(10) - 5(2) = 10$$
$$10 = 10$$
Thus, $(10, 2)$ is a solution of $2x - 5y = 10$.

c. To determine if $(2, 10)$ is a solution of
$2x - 5y = 10$ we replace x with 1 and y
with 5 and then simplify.
$$2x - 5y = 10$$
$$2(2) - 5(10) = 10$$
$$-46 \neq 10$$
Thus, $(2, 10)$ is not a solution of
$2x - 5y = 10$.

d. To determine if $(0, -2)$ is a solution of
$2x - 5y = 10$ we replace x with 0 and y with -1
and then simplify.
$$2x - 5y = 10$$
$$2(0) - 5(-2) = 10$$
$$10 = 10$$
Thus, $(0, -2)$ is a solution of $2x - 5y = 10$.

33.

a. Check the point $(1, -5)$ in both equations.

First Equation	Second Equation
$3x + y = -2$	$x + 2y = 6$
$3(1) + (-5) = -2$	$(1) + 2(-5) = 6$
$-2 = -2$	$-9 \neq 6$

The point $(1, -5)$ is not a solution to the system of linear equations.

b. Check the point $(2, 2)$ in both equations.

First Equation	Second Equation
$3x + y = -2$	$x + 2y = 6$
$3(2) + (2) = -2$	$(2) + 2(2) = 6$
$8 \neq -2$	$6 = 6$

The point $(2, 2)$ is not a solution to the system of linear equations.

c. Check the point $(0, 1)$ in both equations.

First Equation	Second Equation
$3x + y = -2$	$x + 2y = 6$
$3(0) + (1) = -2$	$(0) + 2(1) = 6$
$1 \neq -2$	$2 \neq 6$

The point $(0, 1)$ is not a solution to the system of linear equations.

d. Check the point $(-2, 4)$ in both equations.

First Equation	Second Equation
$3x + y = -2$	$x + 2y = 6$
$3(-2) + 4 = -2$	$(-2) + 2(4) = 6$
$-2 = -2$	$6 = 6$

The point $(-2, 4)$ is a solution to the system of linear equations.

34. The solution of the system of equations is the point of intersection. Thus the solution is $(2, 3)$.

35. The solution of the system of equations is the point of intersection. Thus the solution is $(3, -1)$.

36. The solution of the system of equations is the point of intersection. Thus the solution is $(-5, 15)$.

37. The two lines are coincident. Thus there are an infinite number of solutions. It is a consistent system of dependent equations.

38. The solution of the system of equations is the point of intersection. Since the lines are parallel, there is no point of intersection and the system of equations does not have a solution. It is an inconsistent system.

39. From the table we can determine that the y coordinates are equal $(y = 5)$ when the x coordinate is 6. Thus the solution is $(6, 5)$.

40.   The table describes a consistent system of dependent solutions since the two lines are coincident and there are an infinite number of solutions.

41.   The table describes an inconsistent system since, for every value of x, the y coordinates are always 2 units apart. The two lines are parallel and distinct. No solution.

42.   From the table we can determine that the y coordinates are equal $(y = 0.25)$ when the x coordinate is -0.5.
Thus the solution is $(-0.5, 0.25)$.

43.

Step 1	**Step 2**	**Step 3**
Solve the first equation for y.	Substitute $15 - 2x$ for y in the second equation and then solve for x.	Back-substitute 11 for x in the equation obtained in step 1.

$$2x + y = 15$$
$$3x + 5y = -2$$

First equation: $y = 15 - 2x$

$$3x + 5y = -2$$
$$3x + 5(15 - 2x) = -2$$
$$3x + 75 - 10x = -2$$
$$-7x = -77$$
$$x = 11$$

$$y = 15 - 2(11)$$
$$y = -7$$

Solution: $(11, -7)$

44.

Step 1	**Step 2**
Solve the second equation for x.	Substitute $11 - 3y$ for x in the first equation and then solve for y.

$$5x + 15y = 11$$
$$x + 3y = 11$$

Second equation: $x = 11 - 3y$

$$5x + 15y = 11$$
$$5(11 - 3y) + 15y = 11$$
$$55 - 15y + 15y = 11$$
$$55 = 11$$

This is a contradiction. Therefore there is no solution. The system is inconsistent.

45.

Step 1	**Step 2**	**Step 3**
Solve one of the equations for one variable in terms of the other.	Substitute $3y - 4$ for x in the second equation and then solve for y.	Back-substitute $\dfrac{4}{3}$ for y in the first equation.

$$x = 3y - 4$$
$$0.8x + 2.4y = 3.2$$

(x is currently written in terms of y in the first equation.)

$$0.8x + 2.4y = 3.2$$
$$0.8(3y - 4) + 2.4y = 3.2$$
$$2.4y - 3.2 + 2.4y = 3.2$$
$$4.8y = 6.4$$
$$y = \frac{6.4}{4.8} = \frac{4}{3}$$

$$x = 3\left(\frac{4}{3}\right) - 4$$
$$x = 0$$

Solution: $\left(0, \dfrac{4}{3}\right)$

46.

Step 1	**Step 2**	**Step 3**
Solve one of the equations for one variable in terms of the other.	Substitute $4y + 3$ for x in the second equation and then solve for y.	Back-substitute -1 for y in the first equation.

$$x = 4y + 3$$
$$0.8x + 3.2y = -4.0$$

(x is currently written in terms of y in the first equation.)

$$0.8x + 3.2y = -4.0$$
$$0.8(4y + 3) + 3.2y = -4.0$$
$$3.2y + 2.4 + 3.2y = -4.0$$
$$6.4y = -6.4$$
$$y = -1$$

$$x = 4(-1) + 3$$
$$x = -1$$

Solution: $(-1, -1)$

47. To eliminate y, multiply both sides of the first equation by -2 and add the two equations. Solve this equation for x.

$$2x - y = -1$$
$$3x - 2y = -7$$

$$\begin{array}{l} -4x + 2y = 2 \\ \underline{3x - 2y = -7} \\ -x = -5 \\ x = 5 \end{array}$$

Back substitute 5 for x in the first equation to find y.

$$2x - y = -1$$
$$2(5) - y = -1$$
$$10 - y = -1$$
$$-y = -11$$
$$y = 11$$

Solution: $(5, 11)$

48. To eliminate y, multiply both sides of the first equation by 2 and add the two equations. Solve this equation for x.

$$3x + 2y = 5$$
$$5x - 4y = 8$$

$$\begin{array}{l} 6x + 4y = 10 \\ \underline{5x - 4y = 8} \\ 11x = 18 \\ x = \dfrac{18}{11} \end{array}$$

Back substitute $\dfrac{11}{18}$ for x in the first equation to find y.

$$3x + 2y = 5$$
$$3\left(\frac{18}{11}\right) + 2y = 5$$
$$3\left(\frac{18}{11}\right) + 2y = 5$$
$$\frac{54}{11} + 2y = 5$$
$$2y = \frac{1}{11}$$
$$y = \frac{1}{22}$$

Solution: $\left(\dfrac{18}{11}, \dfrac{1}{22}\right)$

49. To eliminate x, multiply both sides of the second equation by -2 and add the two equations. Solve this equation for y.

$$\frac{x}{2} + \frac{y}{3} = 1$$
$$\frac{x}{4} + \frac{y}{5} = 8$$

$$\begin{array}{l} \dfrac{x}{2} + \dfrac{y}{3} = 1 \\ \underline{-\dfrac{x}{2} - \dfrac{2}{5}y = -16} \\ -\dfrac{1}{15}y = -15 \\ y = 225 \end{array}$$

Back substitute 225 for y in the first equation to find x.

$$\frac{x}{2} + \frac{y}{3} = 1$$
$$\frac{x}{2} + \frac{225}{3} = 1$$
$$\frac{x}{2} + 75 = 1$$
$$\frac{x}{2} = -74$$
$$x = -148$$

Solution: $(-148, 225)$

50.

Step 1	**Step 2**	**Step 3**

Step 1

Solve the second equation for x.

$$1.2x + 2.3y = 168$$
$$2.5x - 3.1y = -123.5$$

Second equation:

$$2.5x - 3.1y = -123.5$$
$$2.5x = -123.5 + 3.1y$$
$$x = -49.4 + 1.24y$$

Step 2

We substitute $-49.4 + 1.24y$ for x in the first equation and solve for y.

$$1.2x + 2.3y = 168$$
$$1.2(-49.4 + 1.24y) + 2.3y = 168$$
$$-59.28 + 1.488 + 2.3y = 168$$
$$3.788y = 227.28$$
$$y = 60$$

Step 3

Back-substitute 60 for y in the equation obtained in step 1.

$$x = -49.4 + 1.24y$$
$$x = -49.4 + 1.24(60)$$
$$x = 25$$

Solution: $(25, 60)$

51. To eliminate y, multiply both sides of the first equation by -1 and add the two equations. Solve this equation for x.

$$4x - 7y = 3 \qquad -4x + 7y = -3$$
$$\underline{4x - 7y = 8} \qquad \underline{4x - 7y = 8}$$
$$0 = 5 \text{ is false.}$$

Since the result is a contradiction, the system is inconsistent and does not have a solution.

52. To eliminate x, multiply both sides of the first equation by -2 and add the two equations. Solve this equation for y.

$$7x + 10y = 4 \qquad -14x - 20y = -8$$
$$14x - 5y = -7 \qquad \underline{14x - 5y = -7}$$
$$-25y = -15$$
$$y = \frac{3}{5}$$

Back substitute $\dfrac{3}{5}$ for y in the first equation to find x.

$$7x + 10y = 4$$
$$7x + 10\left(\frac{3}{5}\right) = 4$$
$$7x + 6 = 4$$
$$7x = -2$$
$$x = -\frac{2}{7}$$

Solution: $\left(-\dfrac{2}{7}, \dfrac{3}{5}\right)$

53.

First Equation	**Second Equation**
$y = \dfrac{2}{9}x - 7$	$y = -\dfrac{2}{9}x + 7$
$m_1 = \dfrac{2}{9}$	$m_2 = -\dfrac{2}{9}$

Since $m_1 \neq m_2$, the lines are not parallel and must intersect. The system has exactly one solution. This is consistent system of independent equations.

54.

First Equation	**Second Equation**
$y = \dfrac{2}{9}x - 7$	$y = \dfrac{2}{9}x + 7$
$m_1 = \dfrac{2}{9}$	$m_2 = \dfrac{2}{9}$

Since $m_1 = m_2$, and $b_1 \neq b_2$, the lines are parallel and do not coincide. Thus the system has no solutions. This is an inconsistent system of independent equations.

55.

First Equation	**Second Equation**
$6x + 2y = 4$	$15x = 10 - 5y$
$2y = -6x + 4$	$5y = -15x + 10$
$y = -3x + 2$	$y = -3x + 2$
$m_1 = -3$	$m_2 = -3$

Since $m_1 = m_2$, and $b_1 = b_2$, both equations represent the same line. Thus the system has an infinite number of solutions. This is a consistent system of dependent equations.

56.

First Equation	**Second Equation**
$\dfrac{x}{6} + \dfrac{y}{4} = \dfrac{1}{3}$	$\dfrac{x}{3} + \dfrac{y}{2} = \dfrac{1}{4}$
$\dfrac{y}{4} = -\dfrac{x}{6} + \dfrac{1}{3}$	$\dfrac{y}{2} = -\dfrac{x}{3} + \dfrac{1}{4}$
$y = -\dfrac{2}{3}x + \dfrac{4}{3}$	$y = -\dfrac{2}{3}x + \dfrac{1}{2}$
$m_1 = -\dfrac{2}{3}, \; b_1 = \dfrac{4}{3}$	$m_2 = -\dfrac{2}{3}, \; b_2 = \dfrac{1}{2}$

Since $m_1 = m_2$, and $b_1 \neq b_2$, the lines are parallel and do not coincide. Thus the system has no solutions. This is an inconsistent system of independent equations.

57. The word equation matches **B**.

$$x + y = 100$$
$$x - y = 20$$

Add the two equations to eliminate y then solve the equation for x.

$$2x = 120$$
$$x = 60$$

Back substitute $x = 60$ in the first equation to find y.

$$x + y = 100$$
$$60 + y = 100$$
$$y = 40$$

The two numbers are 60 and 40.

58. The word equation matches **D**.

$$x + y = 20$$
$$x - y = 100$$

Add the two equations to eliminate y then solve the equation for x.

$$2x = 120$$
$$x = 60$$

Back substitute $x = 60$ in the first equation to find y.

$$x + y = 20$$
$$60 + y = 20$$
$$y = -40$$

The two numbers are 60 and -40.

59. The word equation matches **C**.

$$x + y = 20$$
$$x - y = 20$$

Add the two equations to eliminate y then solve the equation for x.

$$2x = 40$$
$$x = 20$$

Back substitute $x = 20$ in the first equation to find y.

$$x + y = 20$$
$$20 + y = 20$$
$$y = 0$$

The two numbers are 20 and 0.

60. The word equation matches **A**.

$$x + y = 120$$
$$x - y = 20$$

Add the two equations to eliminate y then solve the equation for x.

$$2x = 140$$
$$x = 70$$

Back substitute $x = 70$ in the first equation to find y.

$$x + y = 120$$
$$70 + y = 120$$
$$y = 50$$

The two numbers are 70 and 50.

61. Let x be the required number of semester hours with a grade of A to raise the GPA to 3.00. To find x we solve the following equation.

$$\frac{\boxed{\text{Previous Grade Points} + \text{New Grade Points}}}{\boxed{\text{Total Semester Hours}}} = 3.00$$

$$\frac{(45)(2.80) + 4x}{45 + x} = 3.00$$

$$126 + 4x = 3(45 + x)$$

$$126 + 4x = 135 + 3x$$

$$x = 9$$

The student would need 9 semester hours with a grade of A to meet the goal of a GPA of 3.00. The total grade points would be $(45)(2.80) + 4(9) = 162$.

62. Let y be the cost of printing x pages.
The cost for using the local printer is $y = 0.35x$
.

The cost of buying the printer and printing the pages in the department is $y = 0.13x + 2200$.

To determine the page count that produces the same cost we solve the following equation.

$$0.35x = 0.13x + 2200$$
$$0.22x = 2200$$
$$x = 10000$$

Thus the options have the same cost when 10,000 pages are printed.

63. Let x and y be the angles. To determine the number of degrees in each angle we solve the following system.

$$x + y = 180$$
$$y = 2x + 42$$

Substitute $2x + 42$ for y in the first equation and solve for x.

$$x + y = 180$$
$$x + (2x + 42) = 180$$
$$3x = 138$$
$$x = 46$$

The angles are $46°$ and $180° - 46° = 134°$

64. Let x be score of the nine equivalent diameters.
Let y be the score of the tenth diameter.

If the mean score was 25.05, then	If the tenth diameter was 0.75 cm greater than the others, then
$\dfrac{9x + y}{10} = 25.05$ or $9x + y = 250.5$	$y = x + 0.75$

Substitute $x + 0.75$ for y in the first equation.

$$9x + y = 250.5$$
$$9x + (x + 0.75) = 250.5$$
$$10x + 0.75 = 250.5$$
$$10x = 249.75$$
$$x = 24.975$$

Back substitute 24.975 for x in the second equation.

$$y = x + 0.75$$
$$y = 24.975 + 0.75$$
$$y = 25.725$$

The diameters were 24.975 cm for each of the nine equivalent wheels and 25.725 cm for the tenth wheel.

65. Let x be the amount borrowed at 8%.
Let y be the amount borrowed at 5%.

If the total amount borrowed is $9,000, then	If the combined interest after one *month* $45, then
$x + y = 9000$ or $x = 9000 - y$	$\dfrac{0.08}{12}x + \dfrac{0.05}{12}y = 45$ or $0.08x + 0.05y = 540$

Substitute $9000 - y$ for x in the second equation.

$$0.08x + 0.05y = 540$$
$$0.08(9000 - y) + 0.05y = 540$$
$$720 - 0.08y + 0.05y = 540$$
$$-0.03y = -180$$
$$y = 6000$$

Back substitute 6000 for y in the first equation.

$$x = 9000 - y$$
$$x = 9000 - 6000$$
$$x = 3000$$

The amount of the car loan is $3000 and the amount of the educational loan is $6000.

66. To find the values of x and y we solve the following system.

$$2x + y = 37$$
$$y = x - 5$$

Substitute $x - 5$ for y in the first equation and solve for x.

$$2x + y = 37$$
$$2x + (x - 5) = 37$$
$$3x = 42$$
$$x = 14$$

Back substitute $x = 14$ in the second equation to find y.

$$y = x - 5$$
$$y = 14 - 5$$
$$y = 9$$

The base is 9 centimeters.

67. **a.** <u>**Define the Variable:**</u> Let x represent the number of hours that it takes the trains to be 450 km apart.

<u>**Verbal Equation:**</u> $\boxed{\begin{array}{c}\text{Distance Traveled}\\ \text{by the First Train}\end{array}} + \boxed{\begin{array}{c}\text{Distance Traveled}\\ \text{by the Second Train}\end{array}} = \boxed{\begin{array}{c}\text{Total Distance}\\ \text{Between Trains}\end{array}}$

<u>**Algebraic Equation:**</u> $80x + 100x = 450$

$$180x = 450$$
$$x = 2.5$$

<u>**Answer:**</u> It takes 2.5 hours for the trains to be 450 km apart.

b. Let x be the speed of the first train.
Let y be the speed of the second train.

Substitute $x+8$ for y in the second equation and solve for x.

If one train averages 8 km/hr more than the other, then
$$y = x + 8$$

If after 1/2 hour the trains are 100 km apart, then
$$\frac{1}{2}x + \frac{1}{2}y = 100$$
or $x + y = 200$

$$x + y = 200$$
$$x + (x+8) = 200$$
$$2x + 8 = 200$$
$$2x = 192$$
$$x = 96$$

The speeds of the trains are 96 km/hr and $96 + 8 = 104$ km/hr.

68. **a.** <u>**Define the Variable:**</u> Let x represent the number of hours that it takes the workers to lay 1170 bricks.

<u>**Verbal Equation:**</u> $\boxed{\begin{array}{c}\text{Bricks laid by the}\\ \text{Younger Worker}\end{array}} + \boxed{\begin{array}{c}\text{Bricks laid by the}\\ \text{Older Worker}\end{array}} = \boxed{\begin{array}{c}\text{Total number}\\ \text{of Bricks Laid}\end{array}}$

<u>**Algebraic Equation:**</u> $20x + 25x = 1170$

$$45x = 1170$$
$$x = 26$$

<u>**Answer:**</u> It takes 26 hours for the workers to lay 1170 bricks together.

b. Let x be the rate for the younger worker.
Let y be the rate for the older worker.

Substitute $48 - x$ for y in the second equation and solve for x.

On Monday it was observed that
$$8x + 8y = 384$$
$$\frac{8x}{8} + \frac{8y}{8} = \frac{384}{8}$$
$$x + y = 48$$
or $y = 48 - x$

On Tuesday it was observed that
$$5x + 7y = 292$$

$$5x + 7y = 292$$
$$5x + 7(48 - x) = 292$$
$$5x + 336 - 7x = 292$$
$$-2x = -44$$
$$x = 22$$

The younger bricklayer works at a rate of 22 bricks per hour and the older bricklayer works at a rate of $48 - 22 = 26$ bricks per hour.

69. **a.** <u>**Define the Variable:**</u> Let x represent the number of liters of petrochemicals added.

<u>**Verbal Equation:**</u> $\boxed{\begin{array}{c}\text{Total Cost of the}\\ \text{Petrochemicals}\end{array}} + \boxed{\begin{array}{c}\text{Total Cost of the}\\ \text{Other Chemicals}\end{array}} = \boxed{\begin{array}{c}\text{Total cost of the}\\ \text{Desired Mixture}\end{array}}$

<u>**Algebraic Equation:**</u> $6 \cdot x + 9 \cdot 40 = 7.20(x + 40)$

$$6x + 360 = 7.20x + 288$$
$$72 = 1.2x$$
$$60 = x$$

<u>**Answer:**</u> 60 liters of the petrochemicals should be added.

b. Let x be the number of liters of petrochemicals added. Let y be the number of liters of the other chemicals.

If the desired mixture is worth \$7.65 a liter, then	If the total number of liters in the desired mixture is 100, then
$6 \cdot x + 9 \cdot y = 100 \cdot 7.65$	$x + y = 100$
or $6x + 9y = 765$	or $y = 100 - x$

Substitute $100 - x$ for y in the first equation and solve for x.

$$6x + 9y = 765$$
$$6x + 9(100 - x) = 765$$
$$6x + 900 - 9x = 765$$
$$-3x = -135$$
$$x = 45$$

45 liters of the petrochemicals and $100 - 45 = 55$ liters of the other chemicals should be added.

70.

a. Let x be the number of CD's purchased the total cost for Club A is $y = 0.95x + 6$.

b. The slope is the cost per CD. The y-intercept is the initial fee.

c. Let x be the number of CD's purchased the total cost for Club B is $y = 1.95x$.

d. The slope is the cost per CD. The y-intercept is the initial fee.

e. From the graph we can deterimine that the intersection has an x value of 6. The corresponding value of y (using either equation) is 11.70.

f. Each plan costs \$11.70 when 6 CD's are purchased.

71.

a. Use any two points to find the slope of the line.

$$m = \frac{80 - 50}{2 - 1} = \frac{30}{1} = 30$$

Now use any of the given points and the point slope form to find the equation of the line.

$$y - y_1 = m(x - x_1)$$
$$y - 110 = 30(x - 3)$$
$$y - 110 = 30x - 90$$
$$y = 30x + 20$$

b. The slope (\$30) represents the charge per hour. The y-intercept (\$20) represents the flat fee for all repairs.

c. Use any two points to find the slope of the line.

$$m = \frac{82 - 56}{2 - 1} = \frac{26}{1} = 26$$

Now use any of the given points and the point slope form to find the equation of the line.

$$y - y_1 = m(x - x_1)$$
$$y - 108 = 26(x - 3)$$
$$y - 108 = 26x - 78$$
$$y = 26x + 30$$

d. The slope (\$26) represents the charge per hour. The y-intercept (\$30) represents the flat fee for all repairs.

e. To solve the system we substitute $26x + 30$ for y in the first equation and solve for x.

$$y = 30x + 20$$
$$26x + 30 = 30x + 20$$
$$-4x = -10$$
$$x = 2.5$$

Back substitute $x = 2.5$ in the first equation to find y.

$$y = 30x + 20$$
$$y = 30(2.5) + 20$$
$$y = 95$$

Solution: $(2.5, 95)$

f. The total charge for each shop is \$95.00 when the repairs require 2.5 hours.

1.

a. Use $x_1 = 3$, $y_1 = -1$, $x_2 = 5$, $y_2 = 3$

$$m = \frac{y_2 - y_1}{x_2 - x_1} = \frac{3 - (-1)}{5 - 3} = \frac{4}{2} = 2$$

b. Use $x_1 = 3$, $y_1 = -1$, $x_2 = 1$, $y_2 = 5$

$$m = \frac{y_2 - y_1}{x_2 - x_1} = \frac{5 - (-1)}{1 - 3} = \frac{6}{-2} = -3$$

c. Use any two points on the line. For example:

$x_1 = 0$, $y_1 = 2$, $x_2 = 2$, $y_2 = -1$

$$m = \frac{y_2 - y_1}{x_2 - x_1} = \frac{-1 - 2}{2 - 0} = \frac{-3}{2} = -\frac{3}{2}$$

d. Use any two points on the line. For example:

$x_1 = -5$, $y_1 = 1$, $x_2 = 10$, $y_2 = 7$

$$m = \frac{y_2 - y_1}{x_2 - x_1} = \frac{7 - 1}{10 - (-5)} = \frac{6}{15} = \frac{2}{5}$$

e. The line is in slope-intercept form $y = mx + b$. Thus the slope must be $m = -3$

f. The line is in point-slope form $y - y_1 = m(x - x_1)$. Thus the slope must be $m = 7$

2.

a. The slopes of the two lines are $m_1 = \frac{1}{2}$ and $m_2 = -2$. The two lines are perpendicular since $m_1 m_2 = -1$.

b. The slopes of the two lines are $m_1 = \frac{1}{2}$ and $m_2 = \frac{1}{2}$. The two lines are parallel since $m_1 = m_2$.

c. The first line is a horizontal line and the second line is a vertical line. Thus the lines are perpendicular.

d. The slopes of the two lines are $m_1 = 2$ and $m_2 = -2$. The two lines are neither parallel nor perpendicular.

3.

a. The value of Δx is 5.
b. The value of Δy is 20.
c. The slope of the line is

$$m = \frac{\Delta y}{\Delta x} = \frac{20}{5} = 4$$

d. The slope represents the rate at which the altitude changes per second.

e. Solve the equation: $4x = 1200$

$$\frac{4x}{4} = \frac{1200}{4}$$

$$x = 300$$

Therefore it will take 300 seconds (5 minutes) for the altitude to reach 1200 ft.

4.

a. Use the slope-intercept form with $\frac{2}{3}$ for m and 5 for b.

$$y = mx + b$$

$$y = \frac{2}{3}x + 5$$

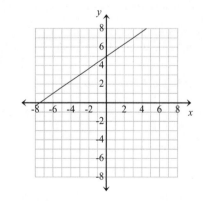

b. Use the slope-intercept form with $-\dfrac{5}{3}$ for m and -2 for b.

$$y = mx + b$$

$$y = -\frac{5}{3}x - 2$$

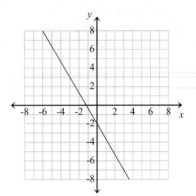

5.   **a.** Use the point-slope form with either point. Substitute $(-1, 3)$ for (x_1, y_1) and 4 for m. Then write the equation in slope intercept form by solving for y.

$$y - y_1 = m(x - x_1)$$

$$y - (3) = 4(x - (-1))$$

$$y - 3 = 4x + 4$$

$$y = 4x + 7$$

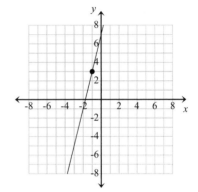

b. Determine the slope of the line passing through the given points

$$m = \frac{y_2 - y_1}{x_2 - x_1} = \frac{-2 - (-1)}{1 - 4} = \frac{-1}{-3} = \frac{1}{3}$$

Use the point-slope form with either point. Substitute $(4, -1)$ for (x_1, y_1) and $\dfrac{1}{3}$ for m. Then write the equation in slope intercept form by solving for y.

$$y - y_1 = m(x - x_1)$$

$$y - (-1) = \frac{1}{3}(x - 4)$$

$$y + 1 = \frac{1}{3}x - \frac{4}{3}$$

$$y = \frac{1}{3}x - \frac{7}{3}$$

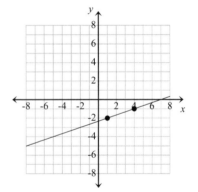

6.   **a.** The horizontal line is defined by the y value of the point: $y = 3$.

b. The vertical line is defined by the x value of the point: $x = -4$.

c. If the line is parallel to $x = 5$ then it must be a vertical line and the equation is $x = -4$.

d. If the line is perpendicular to $x = 5$ then it must be a horizontal line and the equation is $y = 3$.

7. **a.** Check the point $(2, 1)$ in both equations.

First Equation	**Second Equation**
$x + 2y = 4$	$3x - 5y = 1$
$(2) + 2(1) = 4$	$3(2) - 5(1) = 1$
$4 = 4$	$6 - 5 = 1$

The point $(2, 1)$ is a solution to the system of linear equations.

b. Check the point $(-3, -2)$ in both equations.

First Equation	**Second Equation**
$x + 2y = 4$	$3x - 5y = 1$
$(-3) + 2(-2) = 4$	$3(-3) - 5(-2) = 1$
$-3 - 4 \neq 4$	$-9 + 10 = 1$

The point $(-3, -2)$ is not a solution to the system of linear equations.

c. Check the point $(-2, 3)$ in both equations.

First Equation	**Second Equation**
$x + 2y = 4$	$3x - 5y = 1$
$(-2) + 2(3) = 4$	$3(-2) - 5(3) = 1$
$-2 + 6 = 4$	$-6 - 15 \neq 1$

The point $(-2, 3)$ is not a solution to the system of linear equations.

8. **a.** The solution to the system of equations is the point of intersection $(0, 2)$

b.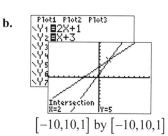

$[-10, 10, 1]$ by $[-10, 10, 1]$ Solution: $(2, 5)$.

c. From the table we can determine that the y coordinates are equal $(y = -1)$ when the x coordinate is -2. Thus the solution is $(-2, -1)$.

d.

Solution: $(12, 5)$.

9. **a.** The slopes of the lines are different. Therefore there is exactly one solution and we have a consistent system of independent equations. Answer: **B**.

b. The slopes of the lines are the same and the y-intercepts are different. Therefore the lines are parallel and never intersect and we have an inconsistent system of equations. Answer: **C**.

c. The two lines are identical. Therefore the system has infinitely many solutions. Answer: **A**.

10. **a.**

Step 1	**Step 2**	**Step 3**
Solve one of the equations for one variable in terms of the other.	Substitute $-4x - 1$ for y in the second equation and then solve for x.	Back-substitute -2 for x in the first equation.

Step 1

$$y = -4x - 1$$
$$2x + y = 3$$

(y is currently written in terms of x in the first equation.)

Step 2

$$2x + y = 3$$
$$2x + (-4x - 1) = 3$$
$$-2x - 1 = 3$$
$$-2x = 4$$
$$x = -2$$

Step 3

$$y = -4x - 1$$
$$y = -4(-2) - 1$$
$$y = 7$$

Solution: $(-2, 7)$

b.   <u>**Step 1**</u>

Solve one of the equations for one variable in terms of the other.

$$y = 4x - 1$$
$$2x + 3y = -2$$

(*y* is currently written in terms of *x* in the first equation.)

<u>**Step 2**</u>

Substitute $4x - 1$ for *y* in the second equation and then solve for *x*.

$$2x + 3y = -2$$
$$2x + 3(4x - 1) = -2$$
$$2x + 12x - 3 = -2$$
$$14x = 1$$
$$x = \frac{1}{14}$$

<u>**Step 3**</u>

Back-substitute $\frac{1}{14}$ for *x* in the first equation.

$$y = 4x - 1$$
$$y = 4\left(\frac{1}{14}\right) - 1$$
$$y = \frac{2}{7} - 1$$
$$y = -\frac{5}{7}$$

Solution: $\left(\dfrac{1}{14}, -\dfrac{5}{7}\right)$

c.   <u>**Step 1**</u>

Solve the first equation for *x*.
$$x + 3y = 1$$
$$\frac{x}{3} - \frac{y}{2} = \frac{5}{6}$$

First equation: $x = 1 - 3y$

<u>**Step 2**</u>

Substitute $1 - 3y$ for *x* in the second equation and then solve for *y*.

$$6\left(\frac{x}{3} - \frac{y}{2}\right) = 6\left(\frac{5}{6}\right)$$
$$2x - 3y = 5$$
$$2(1 - 3y) - 3y = 5$$
$$2 - 6y - 3y = 5$$
$$-9y = 3$$
$$y = -\frac{1}{3}$$

<u>**Step 3**</u>

Back-substitute $-\frac{1}{3}$ for *y* in the equation obtained in step 1.

$$x = 1 - 3\left(-\frac{1}{3}\right)$$
$$x = 1 + 1$$
$$x = 2$$

Solution: $\left(2, -\dfrac{1}{3}\right)$

d.   <u>**Step 1**</u>

Solve the first equation for *x*.
$$x - 2y = 5$$
$$5x + 10y = 12$$

First equation: $x = 5 + 2y$

<u>**Step 2**</u>

Substitute $5 + 2y$ for *x* in the second equation and then solve for *y*.

$$5x + 10y = 12$$
$$5(5 + 2y) + 10y = 12$$
$$25 + 10y + 10y = 12$$
$$20y = -13$$
$$y = -\frac{13}{20}$$

<u>**Step 3**</u>

Back-substitute $-\frac{13}{20}$ for *y* in the equation obtained in step 1.

$$x = 5 + 2\left(-\frac{13}{20}\right)$$
$$x = 5 - \frac{13}{10}$$
$$x = \frac{37}{10}$$

Solution: $\left(\dfrac{37}{10}, -\dfrac{13}{20}\right)$

11.   **a.**   Add the two equations to eliminate *y*. Solve this equation for *x*.

$$3x - 7y = -13$$
$$\underline{2x + 7y = 3}$$
$$5x \quad\quad = -10$$
$$x = -2$$

Back substitute -2 for *x* in the first equation to find *y*.

$$3x - 7y = -13$$
$$3(-2) - 7y = -13$$
$$-6 - 7y = -13$$
$$-6 - 7y = -13$$
$$-7y = -7$$
$$y = 1$$

Solution: $(-2, 1)$

b. To eliminate y, multiply both sides of the first equation by -20, the second equation by 10 and add the two equations. Solve this equation for x.

$$0.3x + 1.9y = 1.6 \qquad -6x - 38y = -32$$
$$0.6x - 1.1y = -1.7 \qquad \underline{6x - 11y = -17}$$
$$-49y = -49$$
$$y = 1$$

Back substitute 1 for x in the first equation to find y.

$$0.3x + 1.9y = 1.6$$
$$0.3x + 1.9(1) = 1.6$$
$$0.3x = -0.3$$
$$x = -1$$

Solution: $(-1, 1)$

c. To eliminate x, multiply both sides of the first equation by -2 and add the two equations.

$$3x - 2y = 6 \qquad -6x + 4y = -12$$
$$-6x + 4y = -12 \qquad \underline{-6x + 4y = -12}$$
$$0 = 0$$

Since the resulting equation is an identity, there is an infinite number of solutions.

d. Write the equations in general form. To eliminate x, multiply both sides of the first equation by 3 and add the two equations.

$$-3x + 5y = 10 \qquad -9x + 15y = 30$$
$$9x - 15y = 20 \qquad \underline{9x - 15y = 20}$$
$$0 = 50 \text{ is false.}$$

Since the resulting equation is a contradiction, there is no solution.

12. a. Let x and y be the angles. To determine the number of degrees in each angle we solve the following system.

$$x + y = 90$$
$$y = 5x + 12$$

Substitute $2x + 42$ for y in the first equation and solve for x.

$$x + y = 90$$
$$x + (5x + 12) = 90$$
$$6x + 12 = 90$$
$$6x = 78$$
$$x = 13$$

Back substitute $x = 13$ in the first equation to find y.

$$x + y = 90$$
$$13 + y = 90$$
$$y = 77$$

The angles are $13°$ and $77°$.

b. Let x be the amount invested at 7%.
Let y be the amount invested at 4%.

If the total amount invested is 10,000, then
$$x + y = 10000$$
or $x = 10000 - y$

If the combined interest earned at the end of one year was $625, then
$$0.07x + 0.04y = 625$$

Substitute $10000 - y$ for x in the second equation.

$$0.07x + 0.04y = 625$$
$$0.07(10000 - y) + 0.04y = 625$$
$$700 - 0.07y + 0.04y = 625$$
$$-0.03y = -75$$
$$y = 2500$$

Back substitute 2500 for y in the first equation.

$$x = 10000 - y$$
$$x = 10000 - 2500$$
$$x = 7500$$

$7500 was invested in bonds and $2500 was invested in the savings account.

c. Let x be the number of milliliters of the 30% solution.

Let y be the number of milliliters of the 80% solution.

If the total amount of the new mixture is 25 milliliters, then	If new mixture is to be a 50% solution, then
$x + y = 25$	$0.30x + 0.80y = 0.50(25)$
or $y = 25 - x$	or $0.30x + 0.80y = 12.5$

Substitute $25 - x$ for y in the second equation and solve for x.

$$0.30x + 0.80(25 - x) = 12.5$$
$$0.30x + 20 - 0.80x = 12.5$$
$$-0.50x = -7.5$$
$$x = 15$$

Back substitute 15 for x in the first equation.

$$y = 25 - x$$
$$y = 25 - (15)$$
$$y = 10$$

Use 15 milliliters of the 30% solution and 10 milliliters of the 80% solution.

d. Let x be the speed of the jet.

Let y be the speed of the tanker.

If the jet flies 250 miles per hour faster than the tanker, then	If the total distance traveled after 1/2 of an hour is 350 miles, then
$x - y = 250$	$\dfrac{1}{2}x + \dfrac{1}{2}y = 350$
	or $x + y = 700$

Use the addition method to solve the equations.
Multiply both sides of the first equation by 3 then add the equations to eliminate y.

$$x - y = 250$$
$$\underline{x + y = 700}$$
$$2x \quad\;\; = 950$$
$$x = 475$$

Back substitute 475 for x in the first equation.

$$x - y = 250$$
$$475 - y = 250$$
$$-y = -225$$
$$y = 225$$

The jet has a speed of 475 mi/hr and the tanker has a speed of 225 mi/hr.

Section 4.1: Solving Linear Inequalities Using the Addition-Subtraction Principle

Quick Review 4.1

1. The only number that is a solution of $[-2, 5)$ but on a solution of $(-2, 5)$ is -2.

2. In interval notation, a **parenthesis** indicates that an endpoint is not included in the interval.

3. $4(2x-7)+8=11-3(x-8)$

    $8x-28+8=11-3x+24$

    $8x-20=35-3x$

    $11x=55$

    $x=5$

4. The solution to the equation is the x value of the point on intersection. Thus, the solution is $x=4$.

5. The solution to the equation is the value of x where the y values in the table are equal.
    Thus, the solution is $x=-5$.

Exercises 4.1

1. **a.** $6x-3$ is not a linear inequality in one variable. It is a linear expression in one variable.
    b. $6x-3 \le 4x$ is a linear inequality in one variable.
    c. $y=6x-3$ is not a linear inequality in one variable. It is a linear equation in two variables.
    d. $x^2 \ge 36$ is not a linear inequality in one variable. It is a non-linear inequality in one variable.

3. **a.** $(-\infty, -4]$ **b.** $(5, \infty)$

    c. $(-\infty, 3)$ **d.** $[-1, \infty)$

5. **a.** Substitute 3 for x and determine if the inequality is a true statement.

    $x < 3$

    $3 < 3$ is a false statement.
    Thus $x = 3$ is not a solution to the inequality.

    b. Substitute 3 for x and determine if the inequality is a true statement.

    $x \le 3$

    $3 \le 3$ is a true statement.
    Thus $x = 3$ is a solution to the inequality.

    c. Substitute 3 for x and determine if the inequality is a true statement.

    $x > 3$

    $3 > 3$ is a false statement.
    Thus $x = 3$ is not a solution to the inequality.

    d. Substitute 3 for x and determine if the inequality is a true statement.

    $x \ge 3$

    $3 \ge 3$ is a true statement.
    Thus $x = 3$ is a solution to the inequality.

7. **a.** Substitute 3 for x and determine if the inequality is a true statement.

    $x > -3$

    $3 > -3$ is a true statement.
    Thus $x = 3$ is a solution to the inequality.

    b. Substitute 3 for x and determine if the inequality is a true statement.

    $x > 5$

    $3 > 5$ is a false statement.
    Thus $x = 3$ is not a solution to the inequality.

    c. Substitute 3 for x and determine if the inequality is a true statement.

    $3x-5 \ge 2(x-1)$

    $3(3)-5 \ge 2((3)-1)$

    $9-5 \ge 2(2)$

    $4 \ge 4$ is a true statement.
    Thus $x = 3$ is a solution to the inequality

    b. Substitute 3 for x and determine if the inequality is a true statement.

    $5x-3 \le 2x+3$

    $5(3)-3 \le 2(3)+3$

    $15-3 \le 6+3$

    $12 \le 9$ is a false statement.
    Thus $x = 3$ is not a solution to the inequality.

9.
$$x + 7 > 11$$
$$x + 7 - 7 > 11 - 7$$
$$x > 4$$
Answer: $(4, \infty)$

11.
$$2x + 3 \le x + 4$$
$$2x - x + 3 \le x - x + 4$$
$$x + 3 \le 4$$
$$x + 3 - 3 \le 4 - 3$$
$$x \le 1$$
Answer: $(-\infty, 1]$

13.
$$x - 7 \ge -3$$
$$x - 7 + 7 \ge -3 + 7$$
$$x \ge 4$$
Answer: $[4, \infty)$

15.
$$5x - 8 < 4x - 8$$
$$5x - 4x - 8 < 4x - 4x - 8$$
$$x - 8 < -8$$
$$x - 8 + 8 < -8 + 8$$
$$x < 0$$
Answer: $(-\infty, 0)$

17.
$$7 \le x$$
or $x \ge 7$
Answer: $[7, \infty)$

19.
$$x - 4 > 2x - 3$$
$$x - x - 4 > 2x - x - 3$$
$$-4 > x - 3$$
$$-4 + 3 > x - 3 + 3$$
$$-1 > x$$
or $x < -1$
Answer: $(-\infty, -1)$

21.
$$5 - 9x < 6 - 10x$$
$$5 - 9x + 10x < 6 - 10x + 10x$$
$$5 + x < 6$$
$$5 - 5 + x < 6 - 5$$
$$x < 1$$
Answer: $(-\infty, 1)$

23.
$$5(x - 2) \ge 4(x - 2)$$
$$5x - 10 \ge 4x - 8$$
$$5x - 4x - 10 \ge 4x - 4x - 8$$
$$x - 10 \ge -8$$
$$x - 10 + 10 \ge -8 + 10$$
$$x \ge 2$$
Answer: $[2, \infty)$

25.
$$5(2 - x) > 4(3 - x)$$
$$10 - 5x > 12 - 4x$$
$$10 - 5x + 5x > 12 - 4x + 5x$$
$$10 > 12 + x$$
$$10 - 12 > 12 - 12 + x$$
$$-2 > x$$
or $x < -2$
Answer: $(-\infty, -2)$

27.
$$9(x - 5) \ge 4(2x - 2) + 3$$
$$9x - 45 \ge 8x - 8 + 3$$
$$9x - 45 \ge 8x - 5$$
$$9x - 8x - 45 \ge 8x - 8x - 5$$
$$x - 45 \ge -5$$
$$x - 45 + 45 \ge -5 + 45$$
$$x \ge 40$$
Answer: $[40, \infty)$

29. **a.** The solution to $y_1 = y_2$ is the x value in the point of intersection. Thus the solution is $x = 1$.

  b. The solution to $y_1 < y_2$ is the set of x-values for which the graph of y_1 is below that of y_2. Thus the solution is $(-\infty, 1)$.

  c. The solution to $y_1 > y_2$ is the set of x-values for which the graph of y_1 is above that of y_2. Thus the solution is $(1, \infty)$.

31. **a.** The solution to $y_1 = y_2$ is the x value in the point of intersection. Thus the solution is $x = -3$.

  b. The solution to $y_1 \le y_2$ is the set of x-values for which the graph of y_1 is below or equal to that of y_2. Thus the solution is $(-\infty, -3]$.

  c. The solution to $y_1 \ge y_2$ is the set of x-values for which the graph of y_1 is above or equal to that of y_2. Thus the solution is $[-3, \infty)$.

33. **a.** The solution to $y_1 = y_2$ is the x value in the point of intersection. Thus the solution is $x = 500$.

  b. The solution to $y_1 < y_2$ is the set of x-values for which the graph of y_1 is below that of y_2. Thus the solution is $(500, 800]$.   (The maximum possible number of hours worked by all the foreman is 800 hours.)

  c. The solution to $y_1 > y_2$ is the set of x-values for which the graph of y_1 is above that of y_2. Thus the solution is $[0, 500)$.

  d. When 500 hours of overtime are worked, the spending limit is met.
  When more than 500 hours of overtime are worked, the spending limit is exceeded.
  When less than 500 hours of overtime are worked, the spending limit is not met.

35. **a.** The solution to $y_1 = y_2$ is the x value for which the y_1 column equals the y_2 column. Thus the solution is $x = 5$.

  b. The solution to $y_1 \le y_2$ is the set of x-values for which the y_1 column is less than or equal to the y_2 column. Thus the solution is $(-\infty, 5]$.

  c. The solution to $y_1 \ge y_2$ is the set of x-values for which the y_1 column is greater than or equal to the y_2 column. Thus the solution is $[5, \infty)$.

37. **a.** The solution to $y_1 = y_2$ is the x value for which the y_1 column equals the y_2 column. Thus the solution is $x = -5$.

  b. The solution to $y_1 < y_2$ is the set of x-values for which the y_1 column is less than the y_2 column. Thus the solution is $(-5, \infty)$.

  c. The solution to $y_1 > y_2$ is the set of x-values for which the y_1 column is greater than the y_2 column. Thus the solution is $(-\infty, -5)$.

39. **a.** The solution to $y_1 = y_2$ is the x value for which the y_1 column equals the y_2 column. Thus the solution is $x = 8$.

  b. The solution to $y_1 < y_2$ is the set of x-values for which the y_1 column is less than the y_2 column. Thus the solution is $[0, 8)$.

  c. The solution to $y_1 > y_2$ is the set of x-values for which the y_1 column is greater than the y_2 column. Thus the solution is $(8, 24]$. Ace Office Supply charges less when more than 8 boxes are ordered.

d. The two office supply companies charge the the same amount when 8 boxes of paper are ordered.
Ace Office Supply charges less when less than 8 boxes are ordered.
Ace Office Supply charges less when more than 8 boxes are ordered.

	Problem	Mental Estimate	Calculator Solution
41.	$x - 0.727 > 0.385$	$x - 1 > 0$ $x - 1 + 1 > 0 + 1$ $x > 1$ Answer: $(1, +\infty)$	$x - 0.727 > 0.385$ $x - 0.727 + 0.727 > 0.385 + 0.727$ $x > 1.112$ Answer: $(1.112, +\infty)$
43.	$2x + 25.87 < x + 3.94$	$2x + 26 < x + 4$ $2x - x + 26 < x - x + 4$ $x + 26 < 4$ $x + 26 - 26 < 4 - 26$ $x < -22$ Answer: $(-\infty, -22)$	$2x + 25.87 < x + 3.94$ $2x - x + 25.87 < x - x + 3.94$ $x + 25.87 < 3.94$ $x + 25.87 < 3.94$ $x < -21.93$ Answer: $(-\infty, -21.93)$

45.

Algebraically	Graphically	Numerically	Verbally
$2x - 1 \geq x + 2$ $2x - x - 1 \geq x - x + 2$ $x - 1 \geq 2$ $x - 1 + 1 \geq 2 + 1$ $x \geq 3$	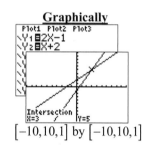 $[-10, 10, 1]$ by $[-10, 10, 1]$	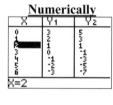	All values of x greater than or equal to 3 satisfy the inequality. Answer: $[3, +\infty)$

47.

Algebraically	Graphically	Numerically	Verbally
$-x + 3 < -2x + 5$ $-x + 2x + 3 < -2x + 2x + 5$ $x + 3 < 5$ $x + 3 - 3 < 5 - 3$ $x < 2$	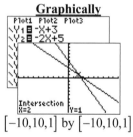 $[-10, 10, 1]$ by $[-10, 10, 1]$		All values of x less than 2 satisfy the inequality. Answer: $(-\infty, 2)$

49. $\underbrace{\text{Five minus two times } x}$ is less than or equal to $\underbrace{\text{seven minus three times } x.}$

$$5 - 2x \qquad \leq \qquad 7 - 3x$$
$$5 - 2x + 3x \leq 7 - 3x + 3x$$
$$5 + x \leq 7$$
$$5 - 5 + x \leq 7 - 5$$
$$x \leq 2$$

Answer: $(-\infty, 2]$

51. Twice w plus three results in a minimum of eleven more than w.

$$2w+3 \qquad \geq \qquad w+11$$
$$2w+3-3 \geq w+11-3$$
$$2w \geq w+8$$
$$2w-w \geq w-w+8$$
$$w \geq 8$$

Answer: $[8, \infty)$

53. Three times the quantity m plus five exceeds twelve more than twice m.

$$3(m+5) \qquad > \qquad 2m+12$$
$$3m+15 > 2m+12$$
$$3m-2m+15 > 2m-2m+12$$
$$m+15 > 12$$
$$m+15-15 > 12-15$$
$$m > -3$$

Answer: $(-3, \infty)$

55.
$$5(w-2)+14 > 4(w+3)$$
$$5w-10+14 > 4w+12$$
$$5w+4 > 4w+12$$
$$5w-4w+4 > 4w-4w+12$$
$$w+4 > 12$$
$$w+4-4 > 12-4$$
$$w > 8$$
Answer: $(8, \infty)$

57.
$$3(5n-2) \leq 7(2n-1)$$
$$15n-6 \leq 14n-7$$
$$15n-14n-6 \leq 14n-14n-7$$
$$n-6 \leq -7$$
$$n-6+6 \leq -7+6$$
$$n \leq -1$$
Answer: $(-\infty, -1]$

59.
$$4(6m+7)-2m \geq 7(3m+1)+1$$
$$24m+28-2m \geq 21m+7+1$$
$$22m+28 \geq 21m+8$$
$$22m-21m+28 \geq 21m-21m+8$$
$$m+28 \geq 8$$
$$m+28-28 \geq 8-28$$
$$m \geq -20$$
Answer: $[-20, \infty)$

61.
$$-3(2-m) < -4(3-m)+4.5$$
$$-6+3m < -12+4m+4.5$$
$$-6+3m < 4m-7.5$$
$$-6+3m-3m < 4m-3m-7.5$$
$$-6 < m-7.5$$
$$-6+7.5 < m-7.5+7.5$$
$$1.5 < m$$
$$\text{or } m > 1.5$$
Answer: $(1.5, \infty)$

63.
$$4y - 4(5 + 2y) > y - 6(3 + y)$$
$$4y - 20 - 8y > y - 18 - 6y$$
$$-4y - 20 > -5y - 18$$
$$-4y + 5y - 20 > -5y + 5y - 18$$
$$y - 20 > -18$$
$$y - 20 + 20 > -18 + 20$$
$$y > 2$$
Answer: $(2, \infty)$

65.
$$\frac{1}{2}x - \frac{1}{3} \geq \frac{5}{3} - \frac{1}{2}x$$
$$\frac{1}{2}x + \frac{1}{2}x - \frac{1}{3} \geq \frac{5}{3} - \frac{1}{2}x + \frac{1}{2}x$$
$$x - \frac{1}{3} \geq \frac{5}{3}$$
$$x - \frac{1}{3} + \frac{1}{3} \geq \frac{5}{3} + \frac{1}{3}$$
$$x \geq 2$$
Answer: $[2, +\infty)$

67. Let x be the score on the last exam. If he has 535 points so far and he needs at least 630 points after the last exam then
$$x + 535 \geq 630$$
$$x + 535 - 535 \geq 630 - 535$$
$$x \geq 95$$
He needs to score at least 95 on the last exam to earn an A for the class.

69. If the farmer has 84 feet of woven wire fence available, then the perimeter of the pen must not exceed 84 feet. Thus,
$$x + 2(12) \leq 84$$
$$x + 24 \leq 84$$
$$x \leq 60$$

Therefore, x must be between 0 ft and 60 ft.

71. Let y_1 be the income. If x represents the number of computer mice sold at $5 per unit, then $y_1 = 5x$. Let y_2 be the cost. If each unit costs $4 to produce, then including the fixed cost of $450 per day, we have $y_2 = 4x + 450$. To find the loss interval we solve the inequality at right.

$$y_1 < y_2$$
$$5x < 4x + 450$$
$$5x - 4x < 4x - 3x + 450$$
$$x < 450$$
Thus, the company will have a loss if fewer than 450 mice are produced and sold. The company will have a profit if more than 450 mice are produced and sold.

Cumulative Review

1. The numerical coefficient of $-7x^2$ is -7.
2. The numerical coefficient of $-x^3$ is -1.
3. The exponent on x in $-x^3$ is 3.
4. The exponent on x in $-9x$ is 1.
5. $|2x - 3| = \left|2\left(\frac{1}{2}\right) - 3\right| = |1 - 3| = |-2| = 2$

Section 4.2: Solving Linear Inequalities Using the Multiplication-Division Principle

Quick Review 4.2

1. $1.5x + 1.2 = 1.3(x-1)$
    $1.5x + 1.2 = 1.3x - 1.3$
    $0.2x = -2.5$
    $x = -12.5$

2. $\dfrac{x-3}{2} = \dfrac{2x+3}{5}$
    $10\left(\dfrac{x-3}{2}\right) = 10\left(\dfrac{2x+3}{5}\right)$
    $5(x-3) = 2(2x+3)$
    $5x - 15 = 4x + 6$
    $x = 21$

3. $5(4x-1) + 3 = 3(6x-5) - 7$
    $20x - 5 + 3 = 18x - 15 - 7$
    $20x - 2 = 18x - 22$
    $2x = -20$
    $x = -10$

4. Two equations are equivalent if they have the **same** solution set.

5. The equation $2x - 6 = 0$ is equivalent to: $2x = 6$ and $-2x + 6 = 0$. Thus the proper choice is **D**.

Exercises 4.2

1. **a.** If $x > y$ then $x + 2 > y + 2$
    b. If $x > y$ then $x - 2 > y - 2$
    c. If $x > y$ then $\dfrac{x}{2} > \dfrac{y}{2}$

    d. If $x > y$ then $\dfrac{x}{-2} < \dfrac{y}{-2}$ $\longleftarrow$ Dividing by a *negative* number reverses the order of the inequality.

3. $-2x < 4$
    $\dfrac{-2x}{-2} > \dfrac{4}{-2}$ $\longleftarrow$ Dividing by a *negative* number reverses the order of the inequality.
    $x > -2$
    Answer: $(-2, \infty)$

5. $-3x + 4 \geq 7$
    $-3x + 4 - 4 \geq 7 - 4$
    $\dfrac{-3x}{-3} \leq \dfrac{3}{-3}$ $\longleftarrow$ Dividing by a *negative* number reverses the order of the inequality.
    $x \leq -1$
    Answer: $(-\infty, -1]$

7. $2x \geq 4$
    $\dfrac{2x}{2} \geq \dfrac{4}{2}$
    $x \geq 2$
    Answer: $[2, \infty)$

9. $\dfrac{1}{2}v < -4$
    $2\left(\dfrac{1}{2}v\right) < 2(-4)$
    $v < -8$
    Answer: $(-\infty, -8)$

11.
$$-\frac{3}{4}w < -12$$
$$-\frac{4}{3}\left(-\frac{3}{4}w\right) > -\frac{4}{3}(-12)$$

Multiplying by a *negative* number reverses the order of the inequality.

$$w > 16$$
Answer: $(16, \infty)$

13.
$$-x \geq 0$$
$$-1(-x) \leq -1(0)$$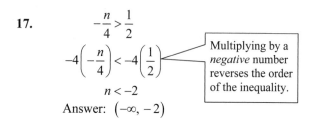

Multiplying by a *negative* number reverses the order of the inequality.

$$x \leq 0$$
Answer: $(-\infty, 0]$

15.
$$1.1m < 2.53$$
$$\frac{1.1m}{1.1} < \frac{2.53}{1.1}$$
$$m < 2.3$$
Answer: $(-\infty, 2.3)$

17.
$$-\frac{n}{4} > \frac{1}{2}$$
$$-4\left(-\frac{n}{4}\right) < -4\left(\frac{1}{2}\right)$$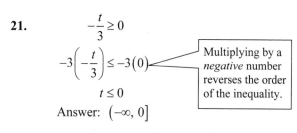

Multiplying by a *negative* number reverses the order of the inequality.

$$n < -2$$
Answer: $(-\infty, -2)$

19.
$$-8z \geq 40$$
$$\frac{-8z}{-8} \leq \frac{40}{-8}$$

Dividing by a *negative* number reverses the order of the inequality.

$$z \leq -5$$
Answer: $(-\infty, -5]$

21.
$$-\frac{t}{3} \geq 0$$
$$-3\left(-\frac{t}{3}\right) \leq -3(0)$$

Multiplying by a *negative* number reverses the order of the inequality.

$$t \leq 0$$
Answer: $(-\infty, 0]$

23.
$$-10 > -5x$$
$$\frac{-10}{-5} < \frac{-5x}{-5}$$

Dividing by a *negative* number reverses the order of the inequality.

$$2 < x$$
or $x > 2$
Answer: $(2, \infty)$

25.
$$5t \leq 21 - 2t$$
$$5t + 2t \leq 21 - 2t + 2t$$
$$7t \leq 21$$
$$\frac{7t}{7} \leq \frac{21}{7}$$
$$t \leq 3$$
Answer: $(-\infty, 3]$

27.
$$9x + 7 > 5x - 13$$
$$9x - 5x + 7 > 5x - 5x - 13$$
$$4x + 7 > -13$$
$$4x + 7 - 7 > -13 - 7$$
$$4x > -20$$
$$\frac{4x}{4} > \frac{-20}{4}$$
$$x > -5$$
Answer: $(-5, \infty)$

29.
$$11y - 8 > 14y + 7$$
$$11y - 14y - 8 > 14y - 14y + 7$$
$$-3y - 8 > 7$$
$$-3y - 8 + 8 > 7 + 8$$
$$-3y > 15$$
$$\frac{-3y}{-3} < \frac{15}{-3}$$

Dividing by a *negative* number reverses the order of the inequality.

$$y < -5$$
Answer: $(-\infty, -5)$

31.

$$5 - 9y \leq 19 - 2y$$
$$5 - 9y + 2y \leq 19 - 2y + 2y$$
$$5 - 7y \leq 19$$
$$5 - 5 - 7y \leq 19 - 5$$
$$-7y \leq 14$$
$$\frac{-7y}{-7} \geq \frac{14}{-7}$$

Dividing by a *negative* number reverses the order of the inequality.

$$y \geq -2$$

Answer: $[-2, \infty)$

33.

$$2(3t - 4) > 2(t - 2)$$
$$6t - 8 > 2t - 4$$
$$6t - 2t - 8 > 2t - 2t - 4$$
$$4t - 8 > -4$$
$$4t - 8 + 8 > -4 + 8$$
$$4t > 4$$
$$\frac{4t}{4} > \frac{4}{4}$$
$$t > 1$$

Answer: $(1, \infty)$

35.

$$4(3 - x) \geq 7(2 - x)$$
$$12 - 4x \geq 14 - 7x$$
$$12 - 4x + 7x \geq 14 - 7x + 7x$$
$$12 + 3x \geq 14$$
$$12 - 12 + 3x \geq 14 - 12$$
$$3x \geq 2$$
$$\frac{3x}{3} \geq \frac{2}{3}$$
$$x \geq \frac{2}{3}$$

Answer: $\left[\frac{2}{3}, \infty\right)$

37.

$$\frac{x}{6} + \frac{1}{2} \leq \frac{x}{4} + \frac{1}{3}$$
$$12\left(\frac{x}{6} + \frac{1}{2}\right) \leq 12\left(\frac{x}{4} + \frac{1}{3}\right)$$
$$2x + 6 \leq 3x + 4$$
$$2x - 2x + 6 \leq 3x - 2x + 4$$
$$6 - 4 \leq x + 4 - 4$$
$$2 \leq x \quad \text{or} \quad x \geq 2$$

Answer: $[2, \infty)$

39.

$$-2(3w + 7) < 3(5 - w) + 2$$
$$-6w - 14 < 15 - 3w + 2$$
$$-6w - 14 < 17 - 3w$$
$$-6w + 3w - 14 < 17 - 3w + 3w$$
$$-3w - 14 < 17$$
$$-3w - 14 + 14 < 17 + 14$$
$$\frac{-3w}{-3} > \frac{31}{-3}$$

Dividing by a *negative* number reverses the order of the inequality.

$$w > -\frac{31}{3}$$

Answer: $\left(-\frac{31}{3}, \infty\right)$

41.

$$-3(5 - 2x) > -2(5x + 1) + 3$$
$$-15 + 6x > -10x - 2 + 3$$
$$-15 + 6x > -10x + 1$$
$$-15 + 6x + 10x > -10x + 10x + 1$$
$$-15 + 16x > 1$$
$$-15 + 15 + 16x > 1 + 15$$
$$16x > 16$$
$$\frac{16x}{16} > \frac{16}{16}$$
$$x > 1$$

Answer: $(1, \infty)$

43. $6(7x-8)-4(3x+2) \le 8(5x+3)$

$$42x-48-12x-8 \le 40x+24$$
$$30x-56 \le 40x+24$$
$$30x-40x-56 \le 40x-40x+24$$
$$-10x-56 \le 24$$
$$-10x-56+56 \le 24+56$$
$$-10x \le 80$$
$$\frac{-10x}{-10} \ge \frac{80}{-10}$$
$$x \ge -8$$

Answer: $[-8, \infty)$

45. **a.** The solution to $y_1 = y_2$ is the x value in the point of intersection. Thus the solution is $x = -1$.

  b. The solution to $y_1 < y_2$ is the set of x-values for which the graph of y_1 is below that of y_2. Thus the solution is $(-\infty, -1)$.

  c. The solution to $y_1 > y_2$ is the set of x-values for which the graph of y_1 is above that of y_2. Thus the solution is $(-1, \infty)$.

47. **a.** The solution to $y_1 = y_2$ is the x value in the point of intersection. Thus the solution is $x = -2$.

  b. The solution to $y_1 \le y_2$ is the set of x-values for which the graph of y_1 is below or equal to that of y_2. Thus the solution is $[-2, \infty)$.

  c. The solution to $y_1 \ge y_2$ is the set of x-values for which the graph of y_1 is above or equal to that of y_2. Thus the solution is $(-\infty, -2]$.

49. **a.** The solution to $y_1 = y_2$ is the x value for which the y_1 column equals the y_2 column. Thus the solution is $x = 3$.

  b. The solution to $y_1 < y_2$ is the set of x-values for which the y_1 column is less than the y_2 column. Thus the solution is $(-\infty, 3)$.

  c. The solution to $y_1 > y_2$ is the set of x-values for which the y_1 column is greater than the y_2 column. Thus the solution is $(3, \infty)$.

51. **a.** The solution to $y_1 = y_2$ is the x value for which the y_1 column equals the y_2 column. Thus the solution is $x = -5$.

  b. The solution to $y_1 \le y_2$ is the set of x-values for which the y_1 column is less than or equal to the y_2 column. Thus the solution is $[-5, +\infty)$.

  c. The solution to $y_1 > y_2$ is the set of x-values for which the y_1 column is greater than or equal to the y_2 column. Thus the solution is $(-\infty, -5]$.

Problem	Mental Estimate	Calculator Solution
61. $5.02x \le 35.642$	$5x \le 35$	$5.02x \le 35.642$
	$\dfrac{5x}{5} \le \dfrac{35}{5}$	$\dfrac{5.02x}{5.02} \le \dfrac{35.642}{5.02}$
	$x \le 7$	$x \le 7.1$
	Answer: $(-\infty, 7]$	Answer: $(-\infty, 7.1]$

Problem	Mental Estimate	Calculator Solution
63. $-0.47x > -4.183$	$-\dfrac{1}{2}x > -4$	$-0.47x > -4.183$
		$\dfrac{-0.47x}{-0.47} < \dfrac{-4.183}{-0.47}$
		$x < 8.9$
		Answer: $(-\infty, 8.9)$

Multiplying by a *negative* number reverses the order of the inequality.

$-2\left(-\dfrac{1}{2}x\right) < -2(-4)$

$x < 8$

Answer: $(-\infty, 8)$

Dividing by a *negative* number reverses the order of the inequality.

65. **a.** The solution to $y_1 = y_2$ is the x value in the point of intersection. Thus the solution is $x = 2$. The two rental companies charge the the same amount when the machines are rented for two hours.

  b. The solution to $y_1 < y_2$ is the set of x-values for which the graph of y_1 is below that of y_2. Thus the solution is $(2, \infty)$. The Dependable Rental Company charges less when the machines are rented for more than two hours.

  c. The solution to $y_1 > y_2$ is the set of x-values for which the graph of y_1 is above that of y_2. Thus the solution is $(0, 2)$. The Dependable Rental Company charges more when the machines are rented for less than two hours.

67. **a.** The solution to $y_1 = y_2$ is the x value for which the y_1 column equals the y_2 column. Thus the solution is $x = 30$. The two stores charge the same amount when 30 sweatshirts are ordered.

  b. The solution to $y_1 < y_2$ is the set of x-values for which the y_1 column is less than the y_2 column. Thus the solution is $(0, 30)$. Mel's Sports charges less than Micheal's Sporting Goods when the order is for less than 30 sweatshirts.

  c. The solution to $y_1 > y_2$ is the set of x-values for which the y_1 column is greater than the y_2 column. Thus the solution is $(30, 60]$. Mel's Sports charges more than Micheal's Sporting Goods when the order is for more than 30 sweatshirts.

69. If the temperature in a computer room must be at least $41°$ Fahrenheit and $F = \dfrac{9}{5}C + 32$, then

$$\dfrac{9}{5}C + 32 \geq 41$$

$$\dfrac{9}{5}C + 32 - 32 \geq 41 - 32$$

$$\dfrac{9}{5}C \geq 9$$

$$\dfrac{5}{9}\left(\dfrac{9}{5}C\right) \geq \dfrac{5}{9}(9)$$

$$C \geq 5$$

Thus, the temperature must be at least $5°$ Celsius.

71. Let x be the amount that the family borrows. If the amount that the family can budget each month for an interest payment is $450 and interest payment for one month will be approximately 0.75% of the amount they can borrow, then

$$0.0075x \le 450$$
$$\frac{0.0075x}{0.0075} \le \frac{450}{0.0075}$$
$$x \le 60000$$

Thus, the family can borrow at most $60,000.

73. Let y_1 represent the income received from an order for x bricks. If all bricks are custom ordered and the charge for manufacturing these bricks includes a set-up fee of $150 plus a charge of $1 per brick, then $y_1 = (1)x + 150$. Let y_2 represent the cost of producing x bricks. If the cost of producing an order of bricks includes a fixed cost of $250 and a variable cost of $0.50 per brick, then $y_2 = 0.50x + 250$.

a. To determine the loss interval for this order we solve the following inequality:

$$y_1 < y_2$$
$$x + 150 < 0.50x + 250$$
$$x - 0.50x + 150 < 0.50x - 0.50x + 250$$
$$0.50x + 150 < 250$$
$$0.50x + 150 - 150 < 250 - 150$$
$$0.50x < 100$$
$$\frac{0.50x}{0.50} < \frac{100}{0.50}$$
$$x < 200$$

Thus, the company will have a loss if fewer than 200 bricks are ordered. Loss interval: $[0,\, 200)$

b. The company will have a profit if more than 200 bricks are ordered. Profit interval: $(200,\, \infty)$

Cumulative Review

1. From the table we can see that $f(-2) = 1$

2. From the table we can see that if $f(x) = -2$, then $x = 3$.

3. $f(x) = 16 - 2x$

4. Since the function $f(x) = 16 - 2x$ represents the length of the board remaining, then it must satisfy the following inequality: $\quad 0 < 16 - 2x < 16$

$$-16 < -2x < 0$$
$$\frac{-16}{-2} > \frac{-2x}{-2} > \frac{0}{-2}$$
$$8 > x > 0$$
$$0 < x < 8 \quad \text{or} \quad (0,\, 8)$$

5. $f(3) = 16 - 2(3) = 10$; If two pieces of length 3 ft are cut from a 16 foot board, then the remaining piece will be 10 ft long.

Section 4.3: Solving Compound Inequalities

Quick Review 4.3

1.
$$2(x-2)+3=3(x-2)-(x-5)$$
$$2x-4+3=3x-6-x+5$$
$$2x-1=2x-1$$
The equation is an identity, since both sides of the equation are exactly the same..

2.
$$3(x-2)+1=2(x-2)+x$$
$$3x-6+1=2x-4+x$$
$$3x-5=3x-4$$
$$-5\neq-4$$
The equation is a contradiction.

3.
$$2(x-2)+3=3(x-2)$$
$$2x-4+3=3x-6$$
$$2x-1=3x-6$$
$$-x=-5$$
$$x=5$$
The equation is satisfied only when $x=5$. It is a conditional equation.

4.
$$\frac{2}{5}(x+3)+2=\frac{4}{7}(x+2)$$
$$35\left[\frac{2}{5}(x+3)+2\right]=35\left[\frac{4}{7}(x+2)\right]$$
$$14(x+3)+70=20(x+2)$$
$$14x+42+70=20x+40$$
$$14x+112=20x+40$$
$$-6x=-72$$
$$x=12$$

5.
$$0.24(x+10)+1.2=0.76x-1.6$$
$$0.24x+2.4+1.2=0.76x-1.6$$
$$0.24x+3.6=0.76x-1.6$$
$$-0.52x=-5.2$$
$$x=10$$

Exercises 4.3

1. The inequality $x>x+5$ is a contradiction since it is false for all values of x. Answer: **C**.

3. The inequality $x<x+5$ is an unconditional inequality since it is true for all values of x. Answer: **B**.

5.
$$2(x+3)\geq3(x-2)$$
$$2x+6\geq3x-6$$
$$2x-2x+6\geq3x-2x-6$$
$$6\geq x-6$$
$$6+6\geq x-6+6$$
$$12\geq x$$
or $x\leq12$
The inequality is a conditional inequality and the solution is $(-\infty,12]$.

7.
$$2(x+3)<2(x-2)$$
$$2x+6<2x-4$$
$$2x-2x+6<2x-2x-4$$
$$6<-4$$ is a false statement.
Thus the inequality is a contradiction and there is no solution.

9.
$$2(x+3)<2(x+4)$$
$$2x+6<2x+8$$
$$2x-2x+6<2x-2x+8$$
$$6<8$$ is a true statement.
Thus the inequality is an unconditional inequality. The soluiton is all real numbers: $\mathbb{R}$.

11. $x>2$ and $x\leq8$

13. $5x+2>-13$ and $5x+2<7$

15. The intersection of $x \geq 0$ and $x \leq 4$ is $0 \leq x \leq 4$.

17. $A \cap B = \{0, 1\}$

$A \cup B = \{-5, -4, 0, 1, 2, 3\}$

19. $x \leq 5$ or $x > 7$

21. $-2 < x \leq 5$ or $7 < x < 10$

23. $A \cap B = (-4, 7] \cap [5, 11) = [5, 7]$

$A \cup B = (-4, 7] \cup [5, 11) = (-4, 11)$

25. $A \cap B = (-4, \infty) \cap [5, 11) = [5, 11)$

$A \cup B = (-4, \infty) \cup [5, 11) = (-4, \infty)$

27. $A \cap B = (-\infty, -2] \cap [-4, \infty) = [-4, -2]$

$A \cup B = (-\infty, -2] \cup [-4, \infty) = (-\infty, \infty)$ or $\mathbb{R}$

29.

Inequality Notation	**Interval Notation**	**Graph**	**Verbally**
$-1 \leq x < 6$	$[-1, 6)$		x is greater than or equal to -1 and less than 6.

Graph: number line from -1 to 6.

31.
a. $1 \leq x < 3$
b. $x < 1$ or $x > 3$

33.
a. $x \geq 4$ or $x \leq -2$
b. $-2 < x < 4$

35. $-30 < 5x < -20$

$\dfrac{-30}{5} < \dfrac{5x}{5} < \dfrac{-20}{5}$

$-6 < x < -4$

Answer: $(-6, -4)$

37. $-4 < -4x \leq 8$

$\dfrac{-4}{-4} > \dfrac{-4x}{-4} \geq \dfrac{8}{-4}$

$1 > x \geq -2$

or $-2 \leq x < 1$

Answer: $[-2, 1)$

Dividing by a *negative* number reverses the order of the inequalities.

39. $-14 \leq -\dfrac{7v}{2} \leq 0$

$-\dfrac{2}{7}(-14) \geq -\dfrac{2}{7}\left(-\dfrac{7v}{2}\right) \geq -\dfrac{2}{7}(0)$

$4 \geq v \geq 0$

or $0 \leq v \leq 4$

Answer: $[0, 4]$

Multiplying by a *negative* number reverses the order of the inequalities.

41. $3 \leq 2w + 3 < 11$

$3 - 3 \leq 2w + 3 - 3 < 11 - 3$

$0 \leq 2w < 8$

$\dfrac{0}{2} \leq \dfrac{2w}{2} < \dfrac{8}{2}$

$0 \leq w < 4$

Answer: $[0, 4)$

43. $-4 < 6 - 5t < 11$

$-4 - 6 < 6 - 6 - 5t < 11 - 6$

$-10 < -5t < 5$

$\dfrac{-10}{-5} > \dfrac{-5t}{-5} > \dfrac{5}{-5}$

$2 > t > -1$

or $-1 < t < 2$

Answer: $(-1, 2)$

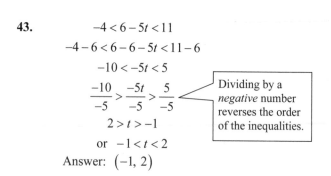

Dividing by a *negative* number reverses the order of the inequalities.

45.
$$-2 \leq \frac{m}{2} - 3 \leq -1$$
$$-2 + 3 \leq \frac{m}{2} - 3 + 3 \leq -1 + 3$$
$$1 \leq \frac{m}{2} \leq 2$$
$$2(1) \leq 2\left(\frac{m}{2}\right) \leq 2(2)$$
$$2 \leq m \leq 4$$
Answer: $[2, 4]$

47.
$$-2 < \frac{m-3}{2} \leq -1$$
$$2(-2) < 2\left(\frac{m-3}{2}\right) \leq 2(-1)$$
$$-4 < m - 3 \leq -2$$
$$-4 + 3 < m - 3 + 3 \leq -2 + 3$$
$$-1 < m \leq 1$$
Answer: $(-1, 1]$

49.
$$\frac{x-3}{10} \geq \frac{x-2}{3}$$
$$30\left(\frac{x-3}{10}\right) \geq 30\left(\frac{x-2}{3}\right)$$
$$3(x-3) \geq 10(x-2)$$
$$3x - 9 \geq 10x - 20$$
$$3x - 10x - 9 \geq 10x - 10x - 20$$
$$-7x - 9 \geq -20$$
$$-7x - 9 + 9 \geq -20 + 9$$
$$-7x \geq -11$$
$$\frac{-7x}{-7} \leq \frac{-11}{-7}$$
$$x \leq \frac{11}{7}$$
Answer: $\left(-\infty, \dfrac{11}{7}\right]$

Multiplying by a *negative* number reverses the order of the inequalities.

51.
$$x - 1 < 2x < x + 2$$
$$x - x - 1 < 2x - x < x - x + 2$$
$$-1 < x < 2$$
Answer: $(-1, 2)$

53.
$$3x - 4 \leq 4x + 1 \leq 3x + 2$$
$$3x - 3x - 4 \leq 4x - 3x + 1 \leq 3x - 3x + 2$$
$$-4 \leq x + 1 \leq 2$$
$$-4 - 1 \leq x + 1 - 1 \leq 2 - 1$$
$$-5 \leq x \leq 1$$
Answer: $[-5, 1]$

55.

$5(x + 4) < 28$	and	$3(x - 4) > -11$
$5x + 20 < 28$		$3x - 12 > -11$
$5x + 20 - 20 < 28 - 20$		$3x - 12 + 12 > -11 + 12$
$5x < 8$		$3x > 1$
$\dfrac{5x}{5} < \dfrac{8}{5}$		$\dfrac{3x}{3} > \dfrac{1}{3}$
$x < \dfrac{8}{5}$		$x > \dfrac{1}{3}$

The intersection of $x < \dfrac{8}{5}$ and $x > \dfrac{1}{3}$ is $\left(\dfrac{1}{3}, \dfrac{8}{5}\right)$.

57.

$2x - 1 < -5$	or	$3x + 1 > 4$
$2x - 1 + 1 < -5 + 1$		$3x + 1 - 1 > 4 - 1$
$2x < -4$		$3x > 3$
$x < -2$		$x > 1$

Answer: $(-\infty, -2) \cup (1, +\infty)$

59.

$$2x - 1 < 3x + 1 \qquad \text{or} \qquad 5x - 6 < 3x - 12$$
$$2x - 2x - 1 < 3x - 2x + 1 \qquad 5x - 3x - 6 < 3x - 3x - 12$$
$$-1 < x + 1 \qquad\qquad 2x - 6 < -12$$
$$-1 - 1 < x + 1 - 1 \qquad 2x - 6 + 6 < -12 + 6$$
$$-1 - 1 < x \qquad\qquad 2x < -6$$
$$-2 < x \qquad\qquad \frac{2x}{2} < \frac{-6}{2}$$
$$x > -2 \qquad\qquad x < -3$$

Answer: $(-\infty, -3) \cup (-2, +\infty)$

61. In the graph, y_2 is between y_1 and y_3 for the x values: $-1 \le x < 2$. Thus, the solution is $[-1, 2)$.

63. In the graph, y_2 is between y_1 and y_3 for the x values: $-1 < x < 4$. Thus, the solution is $(-1, 4)$.

65. The solution to the inequality is the set of x values in the table such that the y values are greater than -1 and less than 3. Thus the solution is $(1, 5)$.

67. The solution to the inequality is the set of x values in the table such that the y values are greater than -3 and less or equal to 7. Thus the solution is $(-2, 3]$.

69.

Algebraically	**Graphically**	**Numerically**	**Verbally**
$0 \le x + 5 < 6$			All values of x greater than or equal to -5 and less than 1 satisfy the inequality.
$0 - 5 \le x + 5 - 5 < 6 - 5$			
$-5 \le x < 1$			

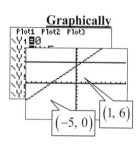 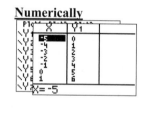

$(-5, 0)$ $(1, 6)$

Answer: $[-5, 1)$

71.

Algebraically	**Graphically**	**Numerically**	**Verbally**
$-7 \le x - 8 \le -6$			All values of x greater than or equal to 1 and less than or equal to 2 satisfy the inequality.
$-7 + 8 \le x - 8 + 8 \le -6 + 8$			
$1 \le x \le 2$			

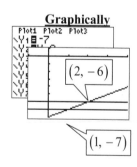

$(2, -6)$

$(1, -7)$

Answer: $[1, 2]$

	Problem	**Mental Estimate**	**Calculator Solution**
73.	$5.719 < 3.01x < 9.331$	$6 < 3x < 9$	$5.719 < 3.01x < 9.331$
		$\dfrac{6}{3} < \dfrac{3x}{3} < \dfrac{9}{3}$	$\dfrac{5.719}{3.01} < \dfrac{3.01x}{3.01} < \dfrac{9.331}{3.01}$
		$2 < x < 3$	$1.9 < x < 3.1$
		Answer: $(2, 3)$	Answer: $(1.9, 3.1)$

	Problem	Mental Estimate	Calculator Solution
75.	$-4.179 \le -1.99x < 5.771$	$-4 \le -2x < 6$	$-4.179 \le -1.99x < 5.771$

For 75:

Mental Estimate:

$\dfrac{-4}{-2} \ge \dfrac{-2x}{-2} > \dfrac{6}{-2}$

$2 \ge x > -3$

or $-3 < x \le 2$

Answer: $(-3, 2]$

Dividing by a negative number reverses the order of the inequalities.

Calculator Solution:

$\dfrac{-4.179}{-1.99} \ge \dfrac{-1.99x}{-1.99} > \dfrac{5.771}{-1.99}$

$2.1 \ge x > -2.9$

or $-2.9 < x \le 2.1$

Answer: $(-2.9, 2.1]$

Dividing by a negative number reverses the order of the inequalities.

77.   Let x be the length of the tee shot. x must be at greater than 155 yards, but less than 190 yards. Thus, $155 < x < 190$.

79.   Let x be the length of the golf shot. If the shot is to not to land in the lake then $x \le 150$ or $220 \le x \le 270$. In other words x must lie in the interval: $[0, 150] \cup [220, 270]$

81.   **a.** $4000 \le 250x \le 6000$

      b. $\dfrac{4000}{250} \le \dfrac{250x}{250} \le \dfrac{6000}{250}$

        $16 \le x \le 24$

      Solution: $[16, 24]$

      Use between 16 and 24 steel wires to have a safety factor from 2 to 3.

83.   In the graph, y_3 is between y_1 and y_2 for the x values: $50 \le x \le 100$. Thus, the solution to the inequality is $[50, 100]$. A belt with at least 50 cable strands but no more than 100 strands will satisfy the requirement for the belt.

85.

$41 < \dfrac{9}{5}C + 32 < 95$

$41 - 32 < \dfrac{9}{5}C + 32 - 32 < 95 - 32$

$9 < \dfrac{9}{5}C < 63$

$\dfrac{5}{9}(9) < \dfrac{5}{9}\left(\dfrac{9}{5}C\right) < \dfrac{5}{9}(63)$

$5 < C < 35$

The acceptable range of temperature is between $5°$ and $35°$ Celsius.

87.   Let x be the length of the third side of the triangle. If the other two sides of the triangle measure 8 meters and 12 meters and the perimeter must be at least 24 meters and at most 40 meters, then

$24 \le 8 + 12 + x \le 40$

$24 \le 20 + x \le 40$

$24 - 20 \le 20 - 20 + x \le 40 - 20$

$4 \le x \le 20$

Thus x must be at least 4 meters and at most 20 meters.

Cumulative Review

1. $5|2x - 11| - 8 = 5|2(-4) - 11| - 8 = 5|-8 - 11| - 8 = 5|-19| - 8 = 5(19) - 8 = 95 - 8 = 87$

2. $|-5| + |3| + |-5 + 3| = 5 + 3 + |-2| = 8 + 2 = 10$

3. $2^3 < 3^2 \ (8 < 9)$

4. $2^4 = 4^2 \ (16 = 16)$

5. $2^5 > 5^2 \ (32 > 25)$

Section 4.4: Solving Absolute Value Equations and Inequalities

Quick Review 4.4

1. $|34| = 34$

2. $|-34| = 34$

3. $|-3+4| = |1| = 1$

4. $|-3|+|4| = 3+4 = 7$

5. $|-3|-|4| = 3-4 = -1$

Exercises 4.4

1. The set given in the graph is the interval of points less than 5 units from the origin (0). Thus, in absolute-value notation, the set is the solution to $|x-0| < 5$ or $|x| < 5$.

3. The set given in the graph is the interval of points greater than or equal to 2 units from the origin (0). Thus, in absolute-value notation, the set is the solution to $|x-0| \geq 2$ or $|x| \geq 2$.

5. The set of points between -4 and 4 is the interval of points less than 4 units from the origin (0). Thus, in absolute-value notation, the set is the solution to $|x-0| < 4$ or $|x| < 4$.

7. The set of numbers that are at least -5 and at most 5 is the interval of points that are less than or equal to 5 units from the origin (0). Thus, in absolute-value notation, the set is the solution to $|x-0| \leq 5$ or $|x| \leq 5$.

9. The set given in the graph is the set of points that are three units from 1. Thus, in absolute-value notation, the set is the solution to $|x-1| = 3$.

11. The set given in the graph is the set of points that are less than 3 units from -7. Thus, in absolute-value notation, the set is the solution to $|x-(-7)| < 3$ or $|x+7| < 3$.

13. The set given in the graph is the interval of points less than or equal to 2 units from 4. Thus, in absolute-value notation, the set is the solution to $|x-4| \leq 2$.

15. The set given in the graph is the interval of points greater than or equal to 2 units from 1. Thus, in absolute-value notation, the set is the solution to $|x-1| \geq 2$.

17. The interval given is the set of points less than or equal to 3 units from the origin (0). Thus, in absolute-value notation, the set is the solution to $|x-0| \leq 3$ or $|x| \leq 3$.

19. The interval given is the set of points greater than 3 units from the origin (0). Thus, in absolute-value notation, the set is the solution to $|x-0| > 3$ or $|x| > 3$.

21. The interval given is the set of points less than 7 units from the origin (0). Thus, in absolute-value notation, the set is the solution to $|x-0| < 7$ or $|x| < 7$.

23. **a.** $|x| < 3$ is equivalent to $-3 < x < 3$. Answer: $(-3, 3)$.

b. $|x| \le 3$ is equivalent to $-3 \le x \le 3$. Answer: $[-3, 3]$.

c. $|x| \ge 3$ is equivalent to $x \le -3$ or $x \ge 3$. Answer: $(-\infty, -3] \cup [3, \infty)$.

25.
$$|x| = 6$$
is equivalent to
$$x = 6 \text{ or } x = -6$$
Answer: $x = 6$ or $x = -6$

27.
$$|x| = 0$$
is equlivalent to
$$x = 0 \text{ or } x = -0$$
Answer: $x = 0$

29.
$$|x - 2| = 5$$
is equivalent to
$$x - 2 = 5 \quad \text{or} \quad x - 2 = -5$$
$$x - 2 + 2 = 5 + 2 \quad x - 2 + 2 = -5 + 2$$
$$x = 7 \qquad x = -3$$
Answer: $x = 7$ or $x = -3$

31.
$$|x + 2| = 5$$
is equlivalent to
$$x + 2 = 5 \quad \text{or} \quad x + 2 = -5$$
$$x + 2 - 2 = 5 - 2 \quad x + 2 - 2 = -5 - 2$$
$$x = 3 \qquad x = -7$$
Answer: $x = 3$ or $x = -7$

33.
$$|3x + 4| \ge 2 \text{ is equivalent to}$$
$$3x + 4 \ge 2 \quad \text{or } 3x + 4 \le -2$$
$$3x \ge -2 \qquad 3x \le -6$$
$$x \ge -\frac{2}{3} \qquad x \le -2$$
Answer: $\left(-\infty, -2\right] \cup \left[-\frac{2}{3}, +\infty\right)$

35.
$$\left|\frac{-7x}{2}\right| \le 14 \text{ is equivalent to}$$
$$-14 \le \frac{-7x}{2} \le 14$$

Multiplying by a *negative* number reverses the order of the inequalities.

$$-\frac{2}{7}(-14) \ge -\frac{2}{7}\left(\frac{-7x}{2}\right) \ge -\frac{2}{7}(14)$$
$$4 \ge x \ge -4$$
Answer: $[-4, 4]$

37.
$$|2x + 3| - 4 < 1$$
$$|2x + 3| < 5$$
is equivalent to
$$-5 < 2x + 3 < 5$$
$$-8 < 2x < 2$$
$$-4 < x < 1$$
Answer: $(-4, 1)$

39.
$$|2(x + 3) - 4| < 1 \text{ is equivalent to}$$
$$-1 < 2(x + 3) - 4 < 1$$
$$-1 < 2x + 6 - 4 < 1$$
$$-1 < 2x + 2 < 1$$
$$-3 < 2x < -1$$
$$-\frac{3}{2} < x < -\frac{1}{2}$$
Answer: $\left(-\frac{3}{2}, -\frac{1}{2}\right)$

41.
$$|2x + 1| + 4 > 11$$
$$|2x + 1| > 7$$
is equivalent to
$$2x + 1 > 7 \text{ or } 2x + 1 < -7$$
$$2x > 6 \qquad 2x < -8$$
$$x > 3 \qquad x < -4$$
Answer: $(-\infty, -4) \cup (3, +\infty)$

43.
$$\left|\frac{x - 1}{7}\right| \ge 14$$
is equivalent to
$$\frac{x - 1}{7} \ge 14 \text{ or } \frac{x - 1}{7} \le -14$$
$$x - 1 \ge 98 \qquad x - 1 \le -98$$
$$x \ge 99 \qquad x \le -97$$
Answer: $(-\infty, -97] \cup [99, +\infty)$

45.

$$|2(2x-1)-(x-3)|<11$$
$$|4x-2-x+3|<11$$
$$|3x+1|<11$$

is equivalent to
$$-11<3x+1<11$$
$$-12<3x<10$$
$$-4<x<\frac{10}{3}$$

Answer: $\left(-4,\dfrac{10}{3}\right)$

47.

$|2x|=|x-1|$ is equivalent to
$$2x=x-1 \text{ or } 2x=-(x-1)$$
$$x=-1 \qquad 2x=-x+1$$
$$3x=1$$
$$x=\frac{1}{3}$$

Answer: $x=-1$ or $x=\dfrac{1}{3}$

49.

$\left|x-1\right|=\left|\dfrac{x+1}{2}\right|$ is equivalent to

$$x-1=\frac{x+1}{2} \text{ or } \qquad x-1=-\frac{x+1}{2}$$
$$2(x-1)=x+1 \qquad -2(x-1)=x+1$$
$$2x-2=x+1 \qquad -2x+2=x+1$$
$$x=3 \qquad\qquad -3x=-1$$
$$x=\frac{1}{3}$$

Answer: $x=3$ or $x=\dfrac{1}{3}$

51.

$$|2x+3|=|3x-1|$$

is equivalent to
$$2x+3=3x-1 \text{ or } 2x+3=-(3x-1)$$
$$4=x \qquad\qquad 2x+3=-3x+1$$
$$5x=-2$$
$$x=-\frac{2}{5}$$

Answer: $x=4$ or $x=-\dfrac{2}{5}$

53.
  a. The solution to $|x-2|=4$ is the set x values in the points of intersection. Thus the solution is $x=-2$ or $x=6$.

  b. The solution to $|x-2|<4$ is the set x values such that the graph of $y=|x-4|$ is below the horizontal line $y=4$. Thus the solution is the interval $(-2,6)$.

  c. The solution to $|x-2|>4$ is the set x values such that the graph of $y=|x-4|$ is above the horizontal line $y=4$. Thus the solution is $(-\infty,-2)\cup(6,+\infty)$.

55.
  a. The solution to $\left|\dfrac{x-4}{2}\right|=1$ is the set x values in the points of intersection. Thus the solution is $x=2$ or $x=6$.

  b. The solution to $\left|\dfrac{x-4}{2}\right|<1$ is the set x values such that the graph of $y=\left|\dfrac{x-4}{2}\right|$ is below the horizontal line $y=1$. Thus the solution is the interval $(2,6)$.

  c. The solution to $\left|\dfrac{x-4}{2}\right|\geq1$ is the set x values such that the graph of $y=\left|\dfrac{x-4}{2}\right|$ is above or equal to the horizontal line $y=1$. Thus the solution is $(-\infty,2]\cup[6,+\infty)$.

57. **a.** The solution to $|x+2| = 2$ is the set x values in the table such that $y_1 = 2$. Thus the solution is $x = -4$ or $x = 0$.

b. The solution to $|x+2| \leq 2$ is the set x values in the table such that $y_1 \leq 2$. Thus the solution is the interval $[-4, 0]$.

c. The solution to $|x+2| \geq 2$ is the set x values in the table such that $y_1 \geq 2$. Thus the solution is the interval $(-\infty, -4] \cup [0, +\infty)$.

59. **a.** The solution to $|x-5| = 10$ is the set x values in the table such that $y_1 = 10$. Thus the solution is $x = -5$ or $x = 15$.

b. The solution to $|x-5| < 10$ is the set x values in the table such that $y_1 < 10$. Thus the solution is the interval $(-5, 15)$.

c. The solution to $|x-5| \geq 10$ is the set x values in the table such that $y_1 \geq 10$. Thus the solution is the interval $(-\infty, -5] \cup [15, +\infty)$.

61.

Algebraically	**Graphically**	**Numerically**	**Verbally**
$|x+1| < 1$ is equivalent to $-1 < x+1 < 1$ $-2 < x < 0$	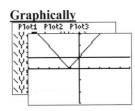	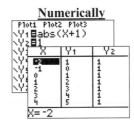	From the table, $y_1 < y_2$ for $-2 < x < 0$ and from the graph y_1 is below y_2 for these same x values. Answer: $(-2, 0)$

63.

Algebraically	**Graphically**	**Numerically**	**Verbally**
$|2x-1| < 3$ is equivalent to $-3 < 2x-1 < 3$ $-2 < 2x < 4$ $-1 < x < 2$	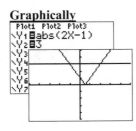	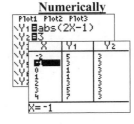	From the table, $y_1 < y_2$ for $-1 < x < 2$ and from the graph y_1 is below y_2 for these same x values. Answer: $(-1, 2)$

65. The distance from one end of this interval to the other is $|6-(-12)| = |18| = 18$. Thus the midpoint is 9 units to the right of -12 and 9 units to the left of 6. This midpoint is -3 since $-12+9 = -3$ and $6-9 = -3$. $(-12, 6)$ is the interval of points less than 9 units from -3. In absolute-value notation, $|x-(-3)| < 9$ or $|x+3| < 9$.

67. The distance from one end of this interval to the other is $|26-(-4)| = |30| = 30$. Thus the midpoint is 15 units to the right of -4 and 15 units to the left of 26. This midpoint is 11 since $-4+15 = 11$ and $26-15 = 11$. $[-4, 26]$ is the interval of points less than or equal to 15 units from 11. In absolute-value notation, $|x-11| \leq 15$.

69. The distance between these intervals $\left|6-(-2)\right|=\left|8\right|=8$. Thus the midpoint is 4 units to the right of -2 and 4 units to the left of 6. This midpoint is 2 since $-2+4=2$ and $6-4=2$. $(-\infty,\,-2)\cup(6\,,+\infty)$ is the set of points greater than 4 units from 2. In absolute-value notation, $\left|x-2\right|>4$.

Problem	Mental Estimate	Calculator Solution
71. $\left|2.01x\right|=9.849$	$\left|2x\right|\approx10$ is equivalent to $2x\approx10$ or $2x\approx-10$ $x\approx5\qquad x\approx-5$	$\left|2.01x\right|=9.849$ is equivalent to $2.01x=9.849\quad$ or $\ 2.01x=-9.849$ $x=4.9245\qquad x=-4.9245$
73. $\left|x+7.93\right|=15.03$	$\left|x+8\right|\approx15$ is equivalent to $x+8\approx15$ or $x+8\approx-15$ $x\approx7\qquad x\approx-23$	$\left|x+7.93\right|=15.03$ is equivalent to $x+7.93=15.03$ or $x+7.93=-15.03$ $x=7.1\qquad\quad x=-22.96$

75. $\left|x-22\right|<6$

is equivalent to
$-6<x-22<6$
$16<x<28$
Solution: $(16,\,28)$

77. The tolerance interval is the set of lengths less than or equal to 0.001 cm from 15 cm. Thus the tolerance interval is expressed by $\left|x-15\right|\le0.001$. The lower limit is 14.999 cm and the upper limit is 15.001 cm.

79. The tolerance interval is the set of values less than or equal to 0.25 ounces from 16 ounces. Thus the tolerance interval is expressed by $\left|x-16\right|\le0.25$. The lower limit is 15.75 ounces and the upper limit is 16.25 ounces.

81. The tolerance interval is the set of values less than or equal to $2°$ from $25°$. Thus the tolerance interval is expressed by $\left|x-25\right|\le2$. The lower limit is $23°$ and the upper limit is $27°$.

83.   **a.** $3000\le500x+250\le9000$
      b. $3000\le500x+250\le9000$
          $2750\le500x\le8750$
            $5.5\le x\le17.5$
    Therefore between 6 and 17 strands should be used.

85.   **a.** $100<250x-150<250$

    b. $\qquad\quad100<250x-150<250$
$$100+150<250x-150+150<250+150$$
$$250<250x<400$$
$$\frac{250}{250}<\frac{250x}{250}<\frac{400}{250}$$
$$1.0<x<1.6$$
Use a strand diameter from 1.0 in to 1.6 in to produce a cable that can support a load with a safety factor between 2 and 5 (from 100,000 to 250,000 lb) for this bridge.

Cumulative Review

1.

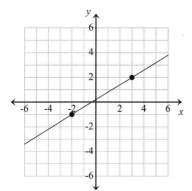

2.

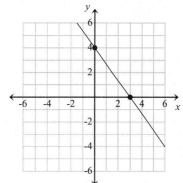

3.

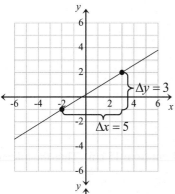

$\Delta y = 3$

$\Delta x = 5$

4.

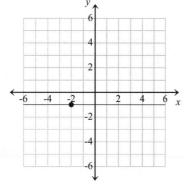

5.

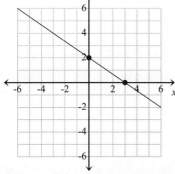

Section 4.5: Graphing Systems of Linear Inequalities in Two Variables

Quick Review 4.5

1.

_x_-intercept

To find the *x*-intercept, substitute 0 for *y*.

$$2x + 5y = 10$$

$$2x + 5(0) = 10$$

$$2x = 10$$

$$x = 5$$

The *x*-intercept is $(5, 0)$

_y_-intercept

To find the *y*-intercept, substitute 0 for *x*.

$$2x + 5y = 10$$

$$2(0) + 5y = 10$$

$$5y = 10$$

$$y = 2$$

The *y*-intercept is $(0, 2)$

2.
$$2x + 5y = 10$$
$$5y = -2x + 10$$
$$\frac{5y}{5} = \frac{-2x}{5} + \frac{10}{5}$$
$$y = -\frac{2}{5}x + 2$$

3.

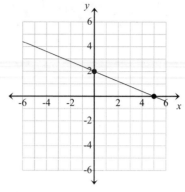

4.

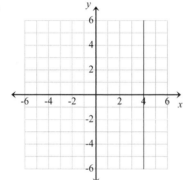

5.

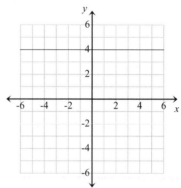

Exercises 4.5

1.   Substitute the coordinates of the point $(0, 0)$ into the inequalities, and determine whether a true statement results.

a. $2x + 3y < 1$
$$2(0) + 3(0) < 1$$
$$0 < 1 \text{ is true.}$$
$(0, 0)$ is a solution.

b. $2x + 3y \le 1$
$$2(0) + 3(0) \le 1$$
$$0 \le 1 \text{ is true.}$$
$(0, 0)$ is a solution.

c. $2x + 3y > 1$
$$2(0) + 3(0) > 1$$
$$0 > 1 \text{ is false.}$$
$(0, 0)$ is not a solution.

d. $2x + 3y \ge 1$
$$2(0) + 3(0) \ge 1$$
$$0 \ge 1 \text{ is false.}$$
$(0, 0)$ is not a solution.

3. Substitute the coordinates of the point $(2, -3)$ into the inequalities, and determine whether a true statement results.

a.
$$3x - y < 9$$
$$3(2) - (-3) < 9$$
$$9 < 9 \text{ is false.}$$
$(2, -3)$ is not a solution.

b.
$$3x - y \le 9$$
$$3(2) - (-3) \le 9$$
$$9 \le 9 \text{ is true.}$$
$(2, -3)$ is a solution.

c.
$$3x - y > 9$$
$$3(2) - (-3) > 9$$
$$9 > 9 \text{ is false.}$$
$(2, -3)$ is not a solution.

d.
$$3x - y \ge 9$$
$$3(2) - (-3) \ge 9$$
$$9 \ge 9 \text{ is true.}$$
$(2, -3)$ is a solution.

5. For a point to be a solution to the inequality it must lie in the shaded region (including the solid line). Thus the points A and B are solutions.

7. For a point to be a solution to the inequality it must lie in the shaded region (not including the dashed line). Thus the points B and C are solutions.

9. The inequality that corresponds to the graph must be either $\ge$ or $\le$ since it uses a solid line. Also, the inequality must be satisfied by the origin $(0, 0)$, which is in the shaded area. Thus the inequality that corresponds to the graph must be **A.** $x - 3y \le 3$.

11. **Step 1:** Draw a solid line for $x - y = 5$ because the equality is part of the solution. The line passes through the intercepts $(5, 0)$ and $(0, -5)$.

Step 2: Test the origin:
$$x - y \ge 5$$
$$(0) - (0) \ge 5$$
$$0 \ge 5 \text{ is false.}$$

Step 3: Shade the half-plane that does *not* include the test point $(0, 0)$.

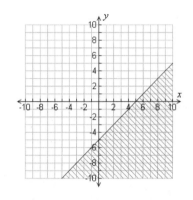

13. **Step 1:** Draw a dashed line for $3x - 2y - 12 = 0$ because the equality is not part of the solution. The line passes through the intercepts $(4, 0)$ and $(0, -6)$.

Step 2: Test the origin:
$$3x - 2y - 12 < 0$$
$$3(0) - 2(0) - 12 < 0$$
$$-12 < 0 \text{ is true.}$$

Step 3: Shade the half-plane that includes the test point $(0, 0)$.

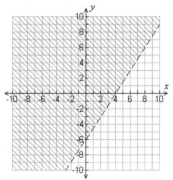

15. **Step 1:** Draw a dashed line for $x = 3y$ because the equality is not part of the solution. The line passes through the points $(0, 0)$ and $(6, 2)$.

Step 2: Test the point $(3, 0)$. (Do not test the origin, since it lies on the line):

$$x > 3y$$
$$(3) > 3(0)$$
$$3 > 0 \text{ is true.}$$

Step 3: Shade the half-plane that includes the test point $(3, 0)$.

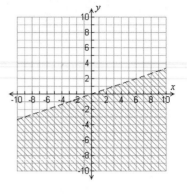

17. **Step 1:** Draw a solid line for $\dfrac{1}{2}x + \dfrac{1}{3}y = 1$ because the equality is part of the solution. The line passes through the intercepts $(2, 0)$ and $(0, 3)$.

Step 2: Test the origin:

$$\frac{1}{2}x + \frac{1}{3}y \le 1$$
$$\frac{1}{2}(0) + \frac{1}{3}(0) \le 1$$
$$0 \le 1 \text{ is true.}$$

Step 3: Shade the half-plane that includes the test point $(0, 0)$.

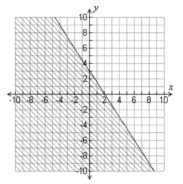

19. To determine which of the points satisfy the system, we must test the points in each of the inequalities. Only the points that satisfy *both* inequalities simultaneously are solutions to the system.

Test the point $A(4, 5)$: $\left. \begin{matrix} -x + 2y > 4 \\ 2x - y \ge -2 \end{matrix} \right\} \Rightarrow \left. \begin{matrix} -(4) + 2(5) > 4 \\ 2(4) - (5) \ge -2 \end{matrix} \right\} \Rightarrow \left. \begin{matrix} 6 > 4 \\ 3 \ge -2 \end{matrix} \right\}$ Since both inequalities are

true, the point $A(4, 5)$ is a solution to the system of inequalities.

To determine which of the points satisfy the system, we must test the points in each of the inequalities. Only the points that satisfy *both* inequalities simultaneously are solutions to the system.

Test the point $B(0, 2)$: $\left. \begin{matrix} -x + 2y > 4 \\ 2x - y \ge -2 \end{matrix} \right\} \Rightarrow \left. \begin{matrix} -(0) + 2(2) > 4 \\ 2(0) - (2) \ge -2 \end{matrix} \right\} \Rightarrow \left. \begin{matrix} 4 > 4 \\ -2 \ge -2 \end{matrix} \right\}$ Since the first

inequality is false, the point $B(0, 2)$ is not a solution to the system of inequalities.

Test the point $C(2, 6)$: $\left. \begin{matrix} -x + 2y > 4 \\ 2x - y \ge -2 \end{matrix} \right\} \Rightarrow \left. \begin{matrix} -(2) + 2(6) > 4 \\ 2(2) - (6) \ge -2 \end{matrix} \right\} \Rightarrow \left. \begin{matrix} 10 > 4 \\ -2 \ge -2 \end{matrix} \right\}$ Since both

inequalities are true, the point $C(2, 6)$ is a solution to the system of inequalities.

Test the point $D(-3, -2)$: $\left. \begin{matrix} -x + 2y > 4 \\ 2x - y \ge -2 \end{matrix} \right\} \Rightarrow \left. \begin{matrix} -(-3) + 2(-2) > 4 \\ 2(-3) - (-2) \ge -2 \end{matrix} \right\} \Rightarrow \left. \begin{matrix} -1 > 4 \\ -4 \ge -2 \end{matrix} \right\}$ Since both

inequalities are false, the point $D(-3, -2)$ is not a solution to the system of inequalities.

For exercises **21** and **23**, the solution corresponds to the region in which the shaded portions overlap.

21.

a.

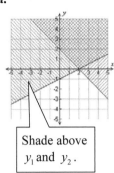

Shade above y_1 and y_2.

b.

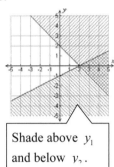

Shade above y_1 and below y_2.

c.

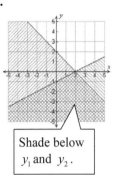

Shade below y_1 and y_2.

d.

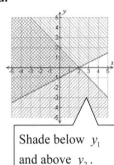

Shade below y_1 and above y_2.

23.

a.

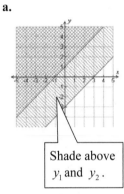

Shade above y_1 and y_2.

b.

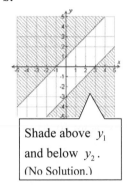

Shade above y_1 and below y_2. (No Solution.)

c.

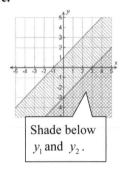

Shade below y_1 and y_2.

d.

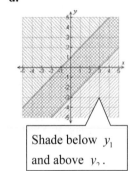

Shade below y_1 and above y_2.

25. Using the process described in problems **11-17**, we sketch the graphs of the solutions to each of the inequalities in the system.

With each of the inequalities sketched on the same coordinate system, the solution to the *system* is the intersection of the two regions.

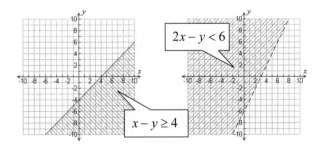

$2x - y < 6$

$x - y \geq 4$

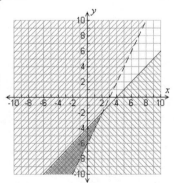

183

27. Using the process described in problems 17-23, we sketch the graphs of the solutions to each of the inequalities in the system.

With each of the inequalities sketched on the same coordinate system, the solution to the *system* is the intersection of the two regions.

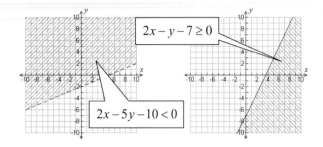 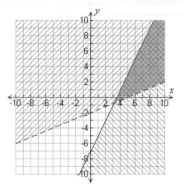

29. Using the process described in problems 17-23, we sketch the graphs of the solutions to each of the inequalities in the system.

With each of the inequalities sketched on the same coordinate system, the solution to the *system* is the intersection of the two regions.

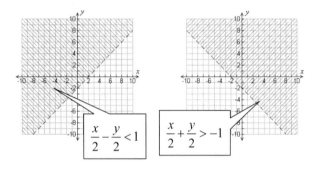 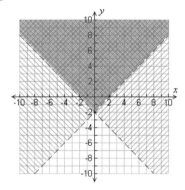

31. Using the process described in problems 17-23, we sketch the graphs of the solutions to each of the inequalities in the system.

With each of the inequalities sketched on the same coordinate system, the solution to the *system* is the intersection of the two regions.

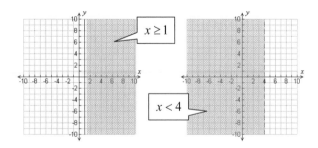 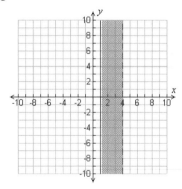

33. Using the process described in problems 17-23, we sketch the graphs of the solutions to each of the inequalities in the system.

With each of the inequalities sketched on the same coordinate system, the solution to the *system* is the intersection of the two regions.

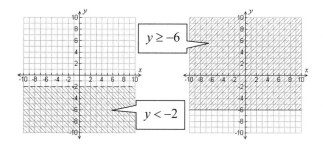

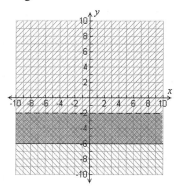

35. Using the process described in problems 17-23, we sketch the graphs of the solutions to each of the inequalities in the system.

With each of the inequalities sketched on the same coordinate system, the solution to the *system* is the intersection of the two regions.

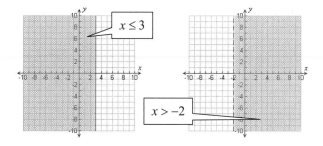

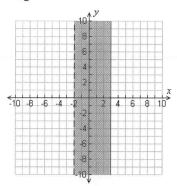

37. Using the process described in problems 17-23, we sketch the graphs of the solutions to each of the inequalities in the system.

With each of the inequalities sketched on the same coordinate system, the solution to the *system* is the intersection of the two regions. Since the regions do not intersect, there is no solution.

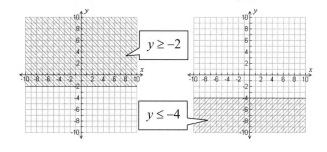

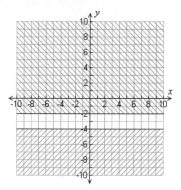

39. We sketch the graph of $2x + 3y < 6$ using the process described in previous problems. The inequalities $x \ge 0$ and $y \ge 0$ require that the shaded area is contained to the first quadrant.

41.

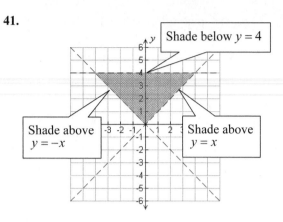

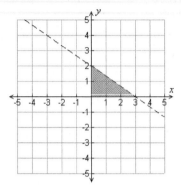

43.

45.

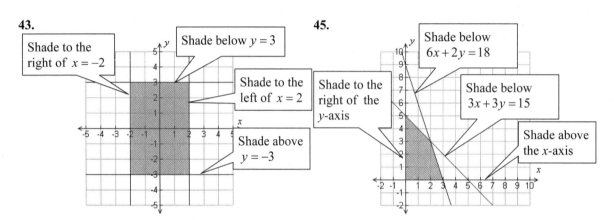

47. Neither inequality contains the origin $(0, 0)$.

Thus the system is

$$\begin{cases} y \le x - 4 \\ y \le \dfrac{x}{2} - 3 \end{cases}.$$

49. "The x-coordinate is at most one more than the y-coordinate" is equivalent to $x \ge y + 2$.

51. "The y-coordinate is at most four more than the x-coordinate" is equivalent to $y \le x + 4$.

53. "Both the x and y coordinates are positive and the sum of the two coordinates does not exceed 10" is equivalent to the system

$$\begin{cases} x > 0 \\ y > 0 \\ x + y \le 10 \end{cases}.$$

55. "Both the x and y coordinates are nonnegative and the sum of x and twice y is at most 5" is equivalent to the system

$$\begin{cases} x \geq 0 \\ y \geq 0 \\ x + 2y \leq 5 \end{cases}.$$

57. If neither length x nor length y can be negative and their total is at most 150 meters, then

$$\begin{cases} x \geq 0 \\ y \geq 0 \\ x + y \leq 150 \end{cases}$$

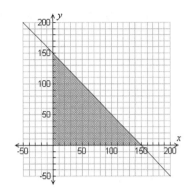

59. If the number of units of each item shipped is nonnegative and the profit per day for the factory has never exceeded \$4400, then

$$\begin{cases} x \geq 0 \\ y \geq 0 \\ 40x + 50y \leq 4400 \end{cases}$$

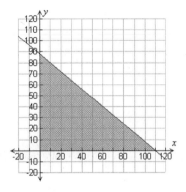

Cumulative Review

1. $\left(1+2+3\right)^2 = \left(6\right)^2 = 36$

2. $1^2 + 2^2 + 3^2 = 1+4+9 = 14$

3. $\left(7-4\right)^2 = \left(3\right)^2 = 9$

4. $7^2 - 4^2 = 49 - 16 = 33$

5. $\dfrac{3^2}{5} - \left(\dfrac{3}{5}\right)^2 = \dfrac{3^2}{5} - \dfrac{3^2}{5^2} = \dfrac{9}{5} - \dfrac{9}{25} = \dfrac{9}{5} \cdot \dfrac{5}{5} - \dfrac{9}{25} = \dfrac{45}{25} - \dfrac{9}{25} = \dfrac{36}{25}$

Review Exercises for Chapter 4

1. Substitute 4 for x in the inequalities, and determine whether a true statement results.

   a. $2x > -8$

   $2(-4) > -8$

   $-8 > -8$ is false.

   $x = -4$ is not a solution.

   b. $x + 3 \le -1$

   $(-4) + 3 \le -1$

   $-1 \le -1$ is true.

   $x = -4$ is a solution.

   c. $5x + 3 < 2x - 3$

   $5(-4) + 3 < 2(-4) - 3$

   $-17 < -11$ is true.

   $x = -4$ is a solution.

   d. $5(x - 2) \ge 3(2x - 4) + 7$

   $5((-4) - 2) \ge 3(2(-4) - 4) + 7$

   $-30 \ge -29$ is false.

   $x = -4$ is not a solution.

2. To graph the solution to the inequality $y \le \dfrac{x}{3} - 2$ we shade below the line. The only solutions are **C** and **D**.

3. From the graph we can see that the only points that lie in the shaded region are **B** and **D**. Thus, these points are the only solutions.

4. Substitute the coordinates of the point $(-2, 5)$ into the inequalities, and determine whether a true statement results.

   a. $y \le 2x - 12$

   $(5) \le 2(-2) - 12$

   $5 \le -16$ is false.

   $(-2, 5)$ is not a solution.

   b. $y \ge 3x - 12$

   $(5) \ge 3(-2) - 12$

   $5 \ge -18$ is true.

   $(-2, 5)$ is a solution.

   c. $3x + 5y < 15$

   $3(-2) + 5(5) < 15$

   $19 < 15$ is false.

   $(-2, 5)$ is not a solution.

   d. $-2x + 4y > 22$

   $-2(-2) + 4(5) > 22$

   $24 > 22$ is true.

   $(-2, 5)$ is a solution.

5. **a.** The solution to $y_1 = y_2$ is the x value in the point of intersection. Thus the solution is $x = 3$.

   b. The solution to $y_1 > y_2$ is the set of x-values for which the graph of y_1 is above that of y_2. Thus the solution is $(3, \infty)$.

   c. The solution to $y_1 < y_2$ is the set of x-values for which the graph of y_1 is below that of y_2. Thus the solution is $(-\infty, 3)$.

6.

x	y_1	$<, =, or >$	y_2
-3	-5	$<$	1
-2	0	$<$	3
-1	5	$=$	5
0	10	$>$	7
1	15	$>$	9
2	20	$>$	11
3	25	$>$	13

   a. The solution to $y_1 = y_2$ is the x value for which the y_1 column equals the y_2 column. Thus the solution is $x = -1$.

   b. The solution to $y_1 < y_2$ is the set of x-values for which the y_1 column is less than the y_2 column. Thus the solution is $(-\infty, -1)$.

   c. The solution to $y_1 > y_2$ is the set of x-values for which the y_1 column is greater than the y_2 column. Thus the solution is $(-1, \infty)$.

7. $\quad x + 7 < 5$

$\quad\quad\quad x < -2$

$\quad$ Answer: $(-\infty, -2)$

8. $\quad x - 11 > -10$

$\quad\quad\quad x > 1$

$\quad$ Answer: $(1, +\infty)$

9. $\quad -10 \geq 2x$

$\quad\quad -5 \geq x \;$ or $\; x \leq -5$

$\quad$ Answer: $(-\infty, -5]$

10. $\quad -3x \leq 12$

$\quad\quad\quad x \geq -4$

$\quad$ Answer: $[-4, \infty)$

> Dividing by a *negative* number reverses the order of the inequality.

11. $\quad 3x + 7 > 5x + 13$

$\quad\quad -2x + 7 > 13$

$\quad\quad\quad -2x > 6$

$\quad\quad\quad\quad x < -3$

$\quad$ Answer: $(-\infty, -3)$

> Dividing by a *negative* number reverses the order of the inequality.

12. $\quad 7 \geq 7 - 9y$

$\quad\quad 0 \geq -9y$

$\quad\quad 0 \leq y \;$ or $\; y \geq 0$

$\quad$ Answer: $[0, \infty)$

> Dividing by a *negative* number reverses the order of the inequality.

13. $\quad -\dfrac{x}{2} < \dfrac{1}{4}$

$\quad\quad\quad x > -\dfrac{1}{2}$

$\quad$ Answer: $\left(-\dfrac{1}{2}, \infty\right)$

> Multiplying by a *negative* number reverses the order of the inequality.

14. $\quad \dfrac{3x}{7} + \dfrac{4}{5} > \dfrac{3x}{5} + \dfrac{2}{7}$

$\quad\quad 35\left(\dfrac{3x}{7} + \dfrac{4}{5}\right) > 35\left(\dfrac{3x}{5} + \dfrac{2}{7}\right)$

$\quad\quad\quad 15x + 28 > 21x + 10$

$\quad\quad\quad -6x + 28 > 10$

$\quad\quad\quad\quad -6x > -18$

$\quad\quad\quad\quad\quad x < 3$

$\quad$ Answer: $(-\infty, 3)$

> Dividing by a *negative* number reverses the order of the inequality.

15. $\quad 7y + 14 \geq 2(3y + 8)$

$\quad\quad 7y + 14 \geq 6y + 16$

$\quad\quad\quad y + 14 \geq 16$

$\quad\quad\quad\quad y \geq 2$

$\quad$ Answer: $[2, \infty)$

16. $\quad -5(2y - 2) \leq 7 - 11y$

$\quad\quad -10x + 10 \leq 7 - 11y$

$\quad\quad\quad x + 10 \leq 7$

$\quad\quad\quad\quad x \leq -3$

$\quad$ Answer: $(-\infty, -3]$

17. $\quad 2(3t - 4) > 3(t - 6) + 1$

$\quad\quad 6t - 8 > 3t - 18 + 1$

$\quad\quad 3t - 8 > -17$

$\quad\quad\quad 3t > -9$

$\quad\quad\quad\quad t > -3$

$\quad$ Answer: $(-3, \infty)$

18. $\quad 2(11t - 3) < 5(3t + 2) - 20$

$\quad\quad 22t - 6 < 15t + 10 - 20$

$\quad\quad 7t - 6 < -10$

$\quad\quad\quad 7t < -4$

$\quad\quad\quad\quad t < -\dfrac{4}{7}$

$\quad$ Answer: $\left(-\infty, -\dfrac{4}{7}\right)$

19. $\quad 5(x - 4) + 6 < (x + 4) - 30$

$\quad\quad 5x - 20 + 6 < x + 4 - 30$

$\quad\quad 4x - 14 < -26$

$\quad\quad\quad 4x < -12$

$\quad\quad\quad\quad x < -3$

$\quad$ Answer: $(-\infty, -3)$

20. $\quad 7(x - 3) + 6 \geq 12(x + 4) + 2$

$\quad\quad 7x - 21 + 6 \geq 12x + 48 + 2$

$\quad\quad -5x - 15 \geq 50$

$\quad\quad\quad -5x \geq 65$

$\quad\quad\quad\quad x \leq -13$

$\quad$ Answer: $(-\infty, -13]$

> Dividing by a *negative* number reverses the order of the inequality.

21. $4(y-1)-7(y+1) \le -3(y+2)-5$
$4y-4-7y-7 \le -3y-6-5$
$-3y-11 \le -3y-11$
$-11 \le -11$ is true.
Answer: $(-\infty, \infty)$ or $\mathbb{R}$

22. $1-4(y-2) \ge 3(y-7)-5(4-y)$
$1-4y+8 \ge 3y-21-20+5y$
$-4y+9 \ge 8y-41$
$-12y+9 \ge -41$
$-12y \ge -50$
$y \le \dfrac{25}{6}$

> Dividing by a *negative* number reverses the order of the inequality.

Answer: $\left(-\infty, \dfrac{25}{6}\right]$

23. $\dfrac{v}{2} - \dfrac{3v+4}{4} > \dfrac{v+40}{4}$
$4\left(\dfrac{v}{2} - \dfrac{3v+4}{4}\right) > 4\left(\dfrac{v+40}{4}\right)$
$2v-3v-4 > v+40$
$-v-4 > v+40$
$-4 > 2v+40$
$-44 > 2v$
$-22 > v$
Answer: $(-\infty, -22)$

24. $\dfrac{v}{8} + 6 > \dfrac{v}{12} + 5$
$24\left(\dfrac{v}{8}+6\right) > 24\left(\dfrac{v}{12}+5\right)$
$3v+144 > 2v+120$
$v+144 > 120$
$v > -24$
Answer: $(-24, \infty)$

25. $9 < x+7 \le 13$
$2 < x \le 6$
Answer: $(2, 6]$

26. $0 \le \dfrac{4}{5}x < 20$
$0 \le x < 25$
Answer: $[0, 25)$

27. $42 \le \dfrac{-3m}{7} < 60$
$-98 \ge m > -140$

> Dividing by a *negative* number reverses the order of the inequality.

or $-140 < m \le -98$
Answer: $(-140, -98]$

28. $-5 \le 9-x \le 5$
$-14 \le -x \le -4$
$14 \ge x \ge 4$

> Dividing by a *negative* number reverses the order of the inequality.

or $4 \le x \le 14$
Answer: $[4, 14]$

29. $-7 \le 5x+3 \le 13$
$-10 \le 5x \le 10$
$-2 \le x \le 2$
Answer: $[-2, 2]$

30. $-10 < 5-3x < 8$
$-15 < -3x < 3$
$5 > x > -1$

> Dividing by a *negative* number reverses the order of the inequality.

or $-1 < x < 5$
Answer: $(-1, 5)$

31. $3v+3v > 5v$
$6v > 5v$
$v > 0$

The inequality is a conditional inequality. The solution is $(0, \infty)$.

32. $3v+3v \le 5v$
$6v \le 5v$
$v \le 0$

The inequality is a conditional inequality. The solution is $(-\infty, 0]$.

33. $3(v+1) < 3v+4$
$3v+3 < 3v+4$
$3 < 4$ is true.

The inequality is an unconditional inequality. The solution is all real numbers.

34. $5(3v-1) > 3(5v-1)$
$15v-5 > 15v-3$
$-5 > -3$ is false.

The inequality is a contradiction. There is no solution.

35. In the graph, y_2 is between y_1 and y_3 for the x values: $-1 \le x \le 5$. Thus, the solution to the inequality is $[-1, 5]$.

36. The solution to the inequality is the set of x values in the table such that the y values are greater than or equal to -1 and less than 1. Thus the solution is $[-1, 3)$.

37.

Shade to the left of $x = 3$

Shade to the right of $x = -1$

38.

Shade below $y = 4$

Shade above $y = 1$

39.

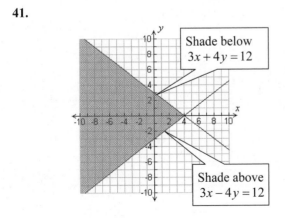

Shade above $2x + 5y = 10$

Shade above $2x - 3y = 6$

40.

Shade below $2x + y = 4$

Shade above $2x + y = 1$

41.

Shade below $3x + 4y = 12$

Shade above $3x - 4y = 12$

42.

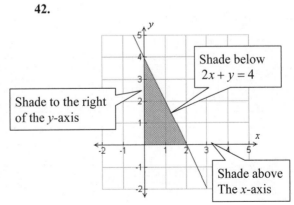

Shade to the right of the y-axis

Shade below $2x + y = 4$

Shade above The x-axis

43. $|x-3| = 4$ is equivalent to
$$x - 3 = 4 \quad \text{or} \quad x - 3 = -4$$
$$x = 7 \qquad\qquad x = -1$$
Answer: $x = 7$ or $x = -1$

44. $|2x-5| + 6 = 9$ is equivalent to
$$|2x-5| = 3$$
$$2x - 5 = 3 \quad \text{or} \quad 2x - 5 = -3$$
$$2x = 8 \qquad\qquad 2x = 2$$
$$x = 4 \qquad\qquad x = 1$$
Answer: $x = 4$ or $x = 1$

45. $|5x-2| > 8$ is equivalent to
$$5x - 2 > 8 \quad \text{or} \quad 5x - 2 < -8$$
$$5x > 10 \qquad\qquad 5x < -6$$
$$x > 2 \qquad\qquad x < -\frac{6}{5}$$
Answer: $\left(-\infty, -\dfrac{6}{5}\right) \cup \left(2, +\infty\right)$

46. $|x-5| < 3$ is equivalent to
$$-3 < x - 5 < 3$$
$$2 < x < 8$$
Answer: $\left(2, 8\right)$

47. The interval $\left(-5, 5\right)$ is the set of points less than 5 units from the origin (0). Thus the absolute value inequality is $|x-0| < 5$ or $|x| < 5$.

48. The interval $\left[-4, 4\right]$ is the set of points less than or equal to 4 units from the origin (0). Thus the absolute value inequality is $|x-0| \leq 4$ or $|x| \leq 4$.

49. The interval $\left(-2, 10\right)$ is the set of points less than 6 units from 4. Thus the absolute value inequality is $|x-4| < 6$.

50. The interval $\left[-4, 20\right]$ is the set of points less than or equal to 12 units from 8. Thus the absolute value inequality is $|x-8| \leq 12$.

51.

Verbally	Inequality Notation	Interval Notation	Graph
a. x exceeds 3	$x > 3$	$\left(3, +\infty\right)$	
b. x is at most 4	$x \leq 4$	$\left(-\infty, 4\right]$	
c. x is at least 2	$x \geq 2$	$\left[2, +\infty\right)$	
d. x does not exceed 5	$x < 5$	$\left(-\infty, 5\right)$	

52.

Verbally	Inequality Notation	Interval Notation	Graph
a. x is greater than 2 and less than 6	$2 < x < 6$	$\left(2, 6\right)$	
b. x is greater than -3 and less than or equal to 4	$-3 < x \leq 4$	$\left(-3, 4\right]$	
c. x is at least -2	$-2 \leq x < 0$	$\left[-2, 0\right)$	
d. x is greater than or equal to -1 and less than or equal to 3	$-1 \leq x \leq 3$	$\left[-1, 3\right]$	

53.
  a. "$x + 7$ is at most 11" is equivalent to $x + 7 \le 11$.
  b. "Twice the quantity x minus 1 exceeds 13" is equivalent to $2(x-1) > 13$.
  c. "Three x minus 5 is at least 7" is equivalent to $3x - 5 \ge 7$.
  d. "Four x plus 9 never exceeds 21" is equivalent to $4x + 9 \le 21$.

54. "Four times the quantity x plus three is greater than eight" is equivalent to
$$4(x+3) > 8$$
$$4x + 12 > 8$$
$$4x > -4$$
$$x > -1$$
The values of x are greater than -1 or $(-1, \infty)$.

55. "Three times the quantity x minus seventeen is less than or equal to twice the quantity x plus eleven" is equivalent to
$$3(x-17) \le 2(x+11)$$
$$3x - 51 \le 2x + 22$$
$$x - 51 \le 22$$
$$x \le 73$$
The values of x are less than or equal to 73 or $(-\infty, 73]$.

56. "Three x minus two is greater than or equal to seven and is less than nineteen" is equivalent to
$$7 \le 3x - 2 < 19$$
$$9 \le 3x < 21$$
$$3 \le x < 7$$
The values of x are greater than or equal to 3 and less than 7 or $[3, 7)$.

57. $x > -3$ and $x \le 4$ is equivalent to $-3 < x \le 4$.

58. $x \ge 0$ and $x < \pi$ is equivalent to $0 \le x < \pi$.

59.
Algebraically
$$x + 3 > 1$$
$$x + 3 - 3 > 1 - 3$$
$$x > -2$$

Graphically

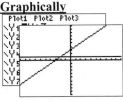

Numerically

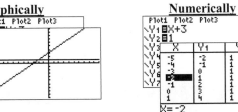

Verbally
All values of x greater than -2 satisfy the inequality.

Answer: $(-2, \infty)$

60.
Algebraically
$$\frac{x}{2} - 1 \le 1$$
$$\frac{x}{2} - 1 + 1 \le 1 + 1$$
$$\frac{x}{2} \le 2$$
$$x \le 4$$

Graphically

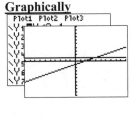

Numerically

Verbally
All values of x less than or equal to 4 satisfy the inequality.

Answer: $(-\infty, 4]$

61.
Algebraically
$$\frac{x}{2} + 4 \ge 1 - \frac{x}{2}$$
$$\frac{x}{2} + \frac{x}{2} + 4 \ge 1 - \frac{x}{2} + \frac{x}{2}$$
$$x + 4 \ge 1$$
$$x + 4 - 4 \ge 1 - 4$$
$$x \ge -3$$

Graphically

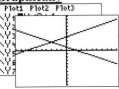

Numerically

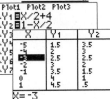

Verbally
All values of x greater than or equal to -3 satisfy the inequality.

Answer: $[-3, \infty)$

62.

Algebraically

$2x - 1 < x + 2$

$2x - x - 1 < x - x + 2$

$x - 1 < 2$

$x - 1 + 1 < 2 + 1$

$x < 3$

Graphically

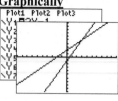

Numerically

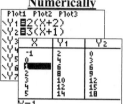

Verbally

All values of x less than 3 satisfy the inequality.

Answer: $(-\infty, 3)$

63.

Algebraically

$2(x + 2) \le 3(x + 1)$

$2x + 4 \le 3x + 3$

$2x - 2x + 4 \le 3x - 2x + 3$

$4 \le x + 3$

$4 - 3 \le x + 3 - 3$

$1 \le x$

Graphically

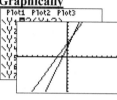

Numerically

Verbally

All values of x greater than or equal to 1 satisfy the inequality.

Answer: $[1, \infty)$

64.

Algebraically

$|x - 2| < 2$ is equivalent to

$-2 < x - 2 < 2$

$-2 + 2 < x - 2 + 2 < 2 + 2$

$0 < x < 4$

Graphically

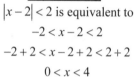

Numerically

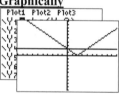

Verbally

All values of x greater than 0 and less than 4 satisfy the inequality.

Answer: $(0, 4)$

65.
$(1, 4) \cap (2, 7) = (2, 4)$

$(1, 4) \cup (2, 7) = (1, 7)$

66.
$[2, 5) \cap [3, 6] = [3, 5)$

$[2, 5) \cup [3, 6] = [2, 6]$

67.
$(-\infty, 2] \cap [-3, +\infty) = [-3, 2]$

$(-\infty, 2] \cap [-3, +\infty) = (-\infty, +\infty)$ or $\mathbb{R}$

68.
$(-\infty, 5) \cap [-2, 6) = [-2, 5)$

$(-\infty, 5) \cup [-2, 6) = (-\infty, 6)$

69.
$x - 2 < 3$ and $3 > x + 2$

$\quad x < 5 \qquad 1 > x$ or $x < 1$

Answer: $(-\infty, 5) \cap (-\infty, 1) = (-\infty, 1)$

70.
$x - 2 < 4x + 2 \qquad$ or $6x - 6 < 4x - 12$

$\quad -2 < 3x + 2 \qquad\qquad 2x - 6 < -12$

$\quad -4 < 3x \qquad\qquad\qquad 2x < -6$

$\quad -\dfrac{4}{3} < x$ or $x > -\dfrac{4}{3} \qquad x < -3$

Answer: $(-\infty, -3) \cup \left(-\dfrac{4}{3}, +\infty\right)$

71.

a. The solution to $y_1 = y_2$ is the x value in the point of intersection. Thus the solution is $x = 1998$.

b. The solution to $y_1 < y_2$ is the set of x-values for which the graph of y_1 is below that of y_2. Thus the solution is $[1990, 1998)$.

c. The solution to $y_1 > y_2$ is the set of x-values for which the graph of y_1 is above that of y_2. Thus the solution is $(1998, 2000]$.

d. In 1998 the community generated the same amount of electricity from coal as it did from wind. Before 1998 the community generated less electricity from wind. Since 1998 the community has generated more electricity from wind.

72.

    a. The solution to $y_1 = y_2$ is the x value for which the y_1 column equals the y_2 column. Thus the solution is $x = 2$.

    b. The solution to $y_1 < y_2$ is the set of x-values for which the y_1 column is less than the y_2 column. Thus the solution is $(0,\ 2)$.

    c. The solution to $y_1 > y_2$ is the set of x-values for which the y_1 column is greater than the y_2 column. Thus the solution is $(2,\ 4]$.

    d. The two repair shops charge the same amount if 2 hours is required.
Shop A charges less for jobs requiring less than 2 hours of labor.
Shop A charges more for jobs requiring more than 2 hours of labor.

73. Let x be the score in the fourth game. If the average is to be at least 20 points, then

$$\frac{x + 17 + 27 + 18}{4} \geq 20$$

$$x + 62 \geq 80$$

$$x \geq 18$$

The basketball player must score at least 18 points in the fourth game.

74. Let x be the amount of money made in the fourth week. If the average is to be at least $500, then

$$\frac{x + 560 + 450 + 480}{4} \geq 500$$

$$x + 1490 \geq 2000$$

$$x \geq 510$$

The amount made in the fourth week must be at least $510.

75. If the width of a rectangle must be exactly 12 centimeters and the perimeter must be between 44 centimeters and 64 centimeters, then

$$44 \leq 2(L) + 2(12) \leq 64$$

$$44 \leq 2L + 24 \leq 64$$

$$20 \leq 2L \leq 40$$

$$10 \leq L \leq 20$$

The length must be between 10 cm and 20 cm.

76. Let x be the length of the tee shot. x must be greater than 160 yards, but less than 200 yards. Thus, $160 < x < 200$.

77. The tolerance interval is the set of values less than or equal to 0.25 grams from 7.2 grams. Thus the tolerance interval is expressed by $|x - 7.2| \leq 0.25$. The lower limit is 6.95 grams and the upper limit is 7.45 grams. The tolerance interval is $[6.95,\ 7.45]$.

78. Let y_1 represent the income received from an order for x posters. If all posters are custom ordered and the charge for printing these posters includes a set-up fee of $50 plus a charge of $1 per poster, then $y_1 = (1)x + 50$. Let y_2 represent the cost of printing x posters. If the cost of printing an order of posters includes a fixed cost of $75 and a variable cost of $0.50 per poster, then $y_2 = 0.50x + 75$. To determine the loss interval for this order we solve the following inequality:

$$y_1 < y_2$$

$$x + 50 < 0.50x + 75$$

$$0.50x < 25$$

$$x < 50$$

Thus, the company will have a loss if fewer than 50 posters are ordered. The company will have a profit if more than 50 posters are ordered.

Problem	Mental Estimate	Exact Solution
79. $x - 2.53 < 7.52$	$x - 2.5 < 7.5$ $x < 10$ Answer: $(-\infty, 10)$	$x - 2.53 < 7.52$ $x < 10.05$ Answer: $(-\infty, 10.05)$
80. $-2.53x \geq 5.0853$	$-\dfrac{5}{2}x \geq 5$ $x \leq -2$ Answer: $(-\infty, -2]$	$-2.53x \geq 5.0853$ $x \leq -2.01$ Answer: $(-\infty, -2.01]$
81. $10.89 < 9.9x \leq 29.601$	$10 < 10x \leq 30$ $1 < x \leq 3$ Answer: $(1, 3]$	$10.89 < 9.9x \leq 29.601$ $1.1 < x \leq 2.99$ Answer: $(1.1, 2.99]$

Mastery Exam for Chapter 4

1. Substitute 10 for x in the inequalities, and determine whether a true statement results.

   a. $4x - 1 \geq x + 29$

   $4(10) - 1 \geq (10) + 29$

   $39 \geq 39$ is true.

   $x = 10$ is a solution.

   b. $2(x + 15) > -2(x + 5)$

   $2((10) + 15) > -2((10) + 5)$

   $2(25) > -2(15)$

   $50 > -30$ is true.

   $x = 10$ is a solution.

   c. $5(x + 2) < 2(x + 20)$

   $5((10) + 2) < 2((10) + 20)$

   $5(12) < 2(30)$

   $60 < 60$ is false.

   $x = 10$ is not a solution.

   d. $5(x - 2) \leq 3(x - 10)$

   $5((10) - 2) \leq 3((10) - 10)$

   $5(8) \leq 3(0)$

   $40 \leq 0$ is false.

   $x = 10$ is not a solution.

2. a. $x + 12 \leq 17$

   $x \leq 5$

   Answer: $(-\infty, 5]$

   b. $x - 9 < -11$

   $x < -2$

   Answer: $(-\infty, -2)$

   c. $4x + 3 > 3x - 8$

   $x + 3 > -8$

   $x > -11$

   Answer: $(-11, \infty)$

   d. $-2x - 5 \geq -3x - 1$

   $x - 5 \geq -1$

   $x \geq 4$

   Answer: $[4, \infty)$

3. a. The solution to $\dfrac{x}{3} - 2 < -\dfrac{1}{2}(x - 1)$ is the set of x-values for which the graph of y_1 is below that of y_2. Thus the solution is $(-\infty, 3)$.

   b. The solution to $\dfrac{x}{3} - 2 \geq -\dfrac{1}{2}(x - 1)$ is the set of x-values for which the graph of y_1 is above or equal to that of y_2. Thus the solution is $[3, \infty)$.

   c. The solution to $4(x + 1) \leq 2(x + 6)$ is the set of x-values for which the y_1 column is less than or equal to the y_2 column. Thus the solution is $(-\infty, 4]$.

d. The solution to $4(x+1) > 2(x+6)$ is the set of x-values for which the y_1 column is greater than the y_2 column. Thus the solution is $(4, \infty)$.

4. **a.** $-11x \le 165$

$\dfrac{-11x}{-11} \ge \dfrac{165}{-11}$ — Dividing by a *negative* number reverses the order of the inequality.

$x \ge -15$

Answer: $[-15, +\infty)$

b. $\dfrac{3x}{7} > 105$

$\dfrac{7}{3}\left(\dfrac{3x}{7}\right) > \dfrac{7}{3}(105)$

$x > 245$

Answer: $(245, \infty)$

c. $8(x+3) < 4(x+4)-(10-2x)$

$8x+24 < 4x+16-10+2x$

$8x+24 < 6x+6$

$2x < -18$

$x < -9$

Answer: $(-\infty, -9)$

d. $-5 \le \dfrac{4x-9}{3}$

$3(-5) \le 3\left(\dfrac{4x-9}{3}\right)$

$-15 \le 4x-9$

$-6 \le 4x$

$-\dfrac{3}{2} \le x$ or $x \ge -\dfrac{3}{2}$

Answer: $\left[-\dfrac{3}{2}, \infty\right)$

5. **a.** $x+x < x$

$x+x-x < x-x$

$x < 0$

The inequality is a conditional inequality. The solution is $(-\infty, 0)$.

b. $2(3x+5) \ge 3(2x-6)$

$6x+10 \ge 6x-18$

$10 \ge -18$ is true.

The inequality is an unconditional inequality. The solution set is all real numbers.

c.
$3(8x+1) > 4(6x+5)$

$24x+3 > 24x+20$

$3 > 20$ is false.

The inequality is a contradiction. There is no solution.

d. $2x+3 \le 3x+3$

$3 \le x+3$

$0 \le x$

The inequality is a conditional inequality. The solution is $[0, +\infty)$.

6. **a.** $[-3, 7) \cup [2, 9] = [-3, 9]$

b. $[-3, 7) \cap [2, 9] = [2, 7)$

c. $(-3, 3) \cup (-1, 5) = (-3, 5)$

d. $(-\infty, 5] \cap (-2, \infty) = (-2, 5]$

7. **a.** $-30 < -6x \le 48$

$5 > x \ge -8$ — Dividing by a *negative* number reverses the order of the inequality.

or $-8 \le x < 5$

Answer: $[-8, 5)$

b. $-30 \le x-6 < 48$

$-24 \le x < 54$

Answer: $[-24, 54)$

c. $-1 \le 4x+3 \le 19$

$-4 \le 4x \le 16$

$-1 \le x \le 4$

Answer: $[-1, 4]$

d. $2x+1 \le -7$ or $3x-2 \ge 7$

$2x \le -8 \qquad 3x \ge 9$

$x \le -4 \qquad x \ge 3$

Answer: $(-\infty, -4] \cup [3, \infty)$

8.   **a.** The points -2 and 2 are two units from the origin (0). Thus the absolute value equation is $|x-0|=2$ or $|x|=2$.

   b. The interval $(-2,\ 2)$ is the set of points less than 2 units from the origin (0). Thus the absolute value inequality is $|x-0|<2$ or $|x|<2$.

   c. The interval $(-\infty,\ -2]\cup[2,\ \infty)$ is the set of points greater than or equal to 2 units from the origin (0). Thus the absolute value inequality is $|x-0|\geq 2$ or $|x|\geq 2$.

9.   **a.** $|x|=8$ is equivalent to

   $\qquad x=8 \quad$ or $\quad x=-8$

   Answer: $x=8$ or $x=-8$

   b. $|2x+5|=49$ is equivalent to

   $\qquad 2x+5=49 \quad$ or $\quad 2x+5=-49$

   $\qquad\quad 2x=44 \qquad\qquad 2x=-54$

   $\qquad\qquad x=22 \qquad\qquad\ x=-27$

   Answer: $x=22$ or $x=-27$

   c. $|x-5|>4$ is equivalent to

   $\qquad x-5>4 \quad$ or $\quad x-5<-4$

   $\qquad\quad x>9 \qquad\qquad x<1$

   Answer: $(-\infty,\ 1)\cup(9,\ \infty)$

   d. $|5x-3|+2\leq 10$

   $\qquad |5x-3|\leq 8$

   is equivalent to

   $\qquad -8\leq 5x-3\leq 8$

   $\qquad -5\leq 5x\leq 11$

   $\qquad -1\leq x\leq \dfrac{11}{5}$

   Answer: $\left[-1,\ \dfrac{11}{5}\right]$

   e. The solution to $|2x-3|<3$ is the set of x values such that the graph of $y=|2x-3|$ is below the graph of $y=3$. Thus the solution is $(0,\ 3)$.

   f. The solution to $|2x-3|<3$ is the set of x values such that the graph of $y=|2x-3|$ is above the graph of $y=3$. Thus the solution is $(-\infty,\ 0)\cup(3,\ \infty)$.

   g. The solution to $\left|\dfrac{x}{2}+1\right|\leq 1$ is the set of x values such that the y_1 column in the table is less than or equal to 1. Thus the solution is $[-4,\ 0]$.

   h. The solution to $\left|\dfrac{x}{2}+1\right|\geq 1$ is the set of x values such that the y_1 column in the table is greater than or equal to 1. Thus the solution is $(-\infty,\ -4]\cup[0,\infty)$.

10. Substitute the coordinates of the point $(3, -5)$ into the inequality, and determine whether a true statement results.

$$6x - 5y \le 40$$
$$6(3) - 5(-5) \le 40$$
$$18 + 25 \le 40$$
$$43 \le 40 \text{ is false.}$$
$$(3, -5) \text{ is not a solution.}$$

Substitute the coordinates of the point $\left(\dfrac{2}{3}, -\dfrac{4}{5}\right)$ into the inequality, and determine whether a true statement results.

$$6x - 5y \le 40$$
$$6\left(\dfrac{2}{3}\right) - 5\left(-\dfrac{4}{5}\right) \le 40$$
$$4 + 4 \le 40$$
$$8 \le 40 \text{ is true.}$$
$$\left(\dfrac{2}{3}, -\dfrac{4}{5}\right) \text{ is a solution.}$$

11.   **a.**

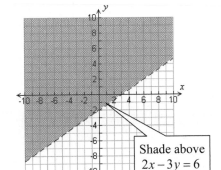

b.

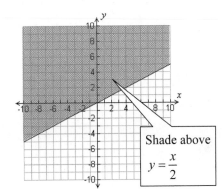

c.

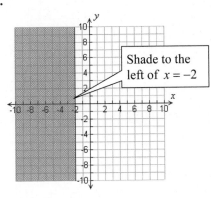

d.

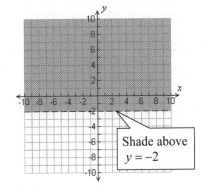

12. **a.**

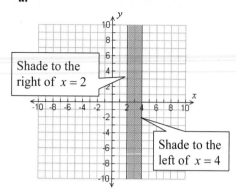

Shade to the right of $x = 2$

Shade to the left of $x = 4$

b.

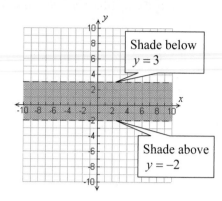

Shade below $y = 3$

Shade above $y = -2$

c.

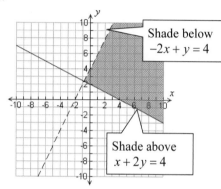

Shade below $-2x + y = 4$

Shade above $x + 2y = 4$

d.

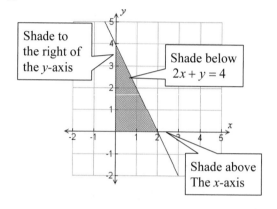

Shade to the right of the y-axis

Shade below $2x + y = 4$

Shade above The x-axis

Section 5.1: Product and Power Rules for Exponents

Quick Review 5.1

1. $-5^2 = -5 \cdot 5 = -25$

2. $(-5)^2 = (-5)(-5) = 25$

3. $2(3+4) = 2 \cdot 7 = 14$

4. $(3+4)^2 = (7)^2 = 49$

5. $3^2 + 4^2 = 9 + 16 = 25$

Exercises 5.1

1. **a.** $x \cdot x \cdot x \cdot x \cdot x = x^5$ **b.** $x \cdot y \cdot y \cdot y \cdot y = xy^4$ **c.** $(x \cdot y)(x \cdot y)(x \cdot y) = (xy)^3$

3. **a.** $(a+b)(a+b)(a+b)$ **b.** $a \cdot a \cdot a + b \cdot b \cdot b = a^3 + b^3$ **c.** $a + b \cdot b \cdot b = a + b^3$
$= (a+b)^3$

5. **a.** $m^6 = m \cdot m \cdot m \cdot m \cdot m \cdot m$ **b.** $(-m)^6 = (-m)(-m)(-m)(-m)(-m)(-m)$ **c.** $-m^6 = -m \cdot m \cdot m \cdot m \cdot m \cdot m$

7. **a.** $(m+n)^2 = (m+n)(m+n)$ **b.** $m^2 + n^2 = m \cdot m + n \cdot n$ **c.** $m + n^2 = m + n \cdot n$

9. **a.** $\dfrac{a^2}{b^3} = \dfrac{a \cdot a}{b \cdot b \cdot b}$ **b.** $\left(\dfrac{a}{b}\right)^4 = \left(\dfrac{a}{b}\right)\left(\dfrac{a}{b}\right)\left(\dfrac{a}{b}\right)\left(\dfrac{a}{b}\right)$ **c.** $\dfrac{a}{b^4} = \dfrac{a}{b \cdot b \cdot b \cdot b}$

11. $x^5 x^3 = (x \cdot x \cdot x \cdot x \cdot x)(x \cdot x \cdot x) = x \cdot x \cdot x \cdot x \cdot x \cdot x \cdot x \cdot x = x^8$

13. $x^9 x^{11} = x^{9+11} = x^{20}$

15. $(3m^4)(5m^6) = (3)(5)m^{4+6} = 15m^{10}$

17. $-x(2x^2)(3x^3) = -(2)(3)x^{1+2+3} = -6x^6$

19. $(x^3)^2 = (x^3)(x^3) = (x \cdot x \cdot x)(x \cdot x \cdot x) = x \cdot x \cdot x \cdot x \cdot x \cdot x = x^6$

21. $(x^5)^2 = x^{5 \cdot 2} = x^{10}$

23. $(3xy)^2 = 3^2 x^2 y^2 = 9x^2 y^2$

25. $(-n^2)^6 = n^{2 \cdot 6} = n^{12}$

27. $5(abc)^2 = 5a^2 b^2 c^2 = 5a^2 b^2 c^2$

29. $(xy^2)^3 = x^3(y^2)^3 = x^3 y^{2 \cdot 3} = x^3 y^6$

31. $\left(\dfrac{3}{4}\right)^2 = \dfrac{3^2}{4^2} = \dfrac{9}{16}$

33. $\left(\dfrac{4}{w}\right)^3 = \dfrac{4^3}{w^3} = \dfrac{64}{w^3}$

35. $\left(\dfrac{x^2}{y^3}\right)^{11} = \dfrac{(x^2)^{11}}{(y^3)^{11}} = \dfrac{x^{2 \cdot 11}}{y^{3 \cdot 11}} = \dfrac{x^{22}}{y^{33}}$

37. **a.** $-1^{10} = -(1^{10}) = -1$
    b. $(-1)^{10} = 1$

39. **a.** $(-1)^{11} = -1$
    b. $-1^{11} = -1$

41. $\left(-5x^2y^4\right)^3 = \left(-5\right)^3\left(x^2\right)^3\left(y^4\right)^3 = -125x^{2\cdot3}y^{4\cdot3} = -125x^6y^{12}$

43. $\left(-2xy^2\right)\left(-3x^2y^4\right) = \left(-2\right)\left(-3\right)x^{1+2}y^{2+4} = 6x^3y^6$

45. $\left(5x^2\right)^2\left(2x^3\right)^3 = 5^2 2^3 x^{2\cdot2}x^{3\cdot3} = 25\cdot8\cdot x^{4+9} = 200x^{13}$

47. $\left(\dfrac{3x}{2y^2}\right)^3 = \dfrac{3^3x^3}{2^3\left(y^2\right)^3} = \dfrac{27x^3}{8y^{2\cdot3}} = \dfrac{27x^3}{8y^6}$

49. $\left(-\dfrac{2x^2}{3y^3}\right)^4 = \left(-1\right)^4\dfrac{2^4\left(x^2\right)^4}{3^4\left(y^3\right)^4} = \dfrac{16x^{2\cdot4}}{81y^{3\cdot4}} = \dfrac{16x^8}{81y^{12}}$

51.
  a. $-x^2 = -\left(2\right)^2 = -4$
  b. $\left(-x\right)^2 = \left(-\left(2\right)\right)^2 = 4$

53.
  a. $\left(xy\right)^2 = \left(\left(2\right)\left(3\right)\right)^2 = \left(6\right)^2 = 36$
  b. $xy^2 = \left(2\right)\left(3\right)^2 = 2\left(9\right) = 18$

55.
  a. $x^3 + y^3 = \left(2\right)^3 + \left(3\right)^3 = 8 + 27 = 35$
  b. $\left(x+y\right)^3 = \left(\left(2\right)+\left(3\right)\right)^3 = \left(5\right)^3 = 125$

57.
  a. $5x^2y^2 = 5\left(2\right)^2\left(3\right)^2 = 5\left(4\right)\left(9\right) = 180$
  b. $\left(5xy\right)^2 = \left(5\left(2\right)\left(3\right)\right)^2 = \left(30\right)^2 = 900$

59.
  a. $\left(-\dfrac{x^2}{y}\right) = -\dfrac{\left(2\right)^2}{3} = -\dfrac{4}{3}$
  b. $\left(-\dfrac{x}{y}\right)^2 = \left(-\dfrac{2}{3}\right)^2 = \left(-1\right)^2\dfrac{2^2}{3^2} = \dfrac{4}{9}$

61.
  a. $v + v + v = 3v$
  b. $v\cdot v\cdot v = v^3$

63.
  a. $4m^3 + 6m^3 = 10m^3$
  b. $\left(4m^3\right)\left(6m^3\right) = \left(4\right)\left(6\right)m^{3+3} = 24m^6$

65.
  a. $3x^2 + 2x$ is simplified.
  b. $\left(3x^2\right)\left(2x\right) = 3\cdot2x^{2+1} = 6x^3$

	Problem	Mental Estimate	Calculator Value
67.	-6.98^2	$-7^2 = -49$	$-6.98^2 = -48.7204$
69.	$\left(1.01+1.01\right)^2$	$\left(1+1\right)^2 = \left(2\right)^2 = 4$	$\left(1.01+1.01\right)^2 = 4.0804$
71.	$7.99^2 - 5.9^2$	$8^2 - 6^2 = 64 - 36 = 28$	$7.99^2 - 5.9^2 = 29.0301$

73. $A = P\left(1+r\right)^t = 1\left(1+.08\right)^{10} \approx \$2.16$

75.
  a. $P\left(20\right) = 0.01\left(20\right)^3 = 80$; A wind speed of 20 mi/hr will produce 80 kilowatts of energy.
  b. $P\left(27\right) = 0.01\left(27\right)^3 = 196.83$; A wind speed of 27 mi/hr will produce 196.83 kilowatts of energy.

77. $P\left(10\right) = 10$; A wind speed of 10 mi/hr will produce 10 kilowatts of energy.

  $P\left(20\right) = 80$; A wind speed of 20 mi/hr will produce 80 kilowatts of energy.

  Thus a wind speed of 20 mi/hr will produce 8 times as much energy as a wind speed of 10 mi/hr.

79.
  a. x^2
  b. y^2
  c. $x^2 - y^2$

81. Volume of smaller cube: x^3

  Volume of larger cube: $\left(2x\right)^3 = 8x^3$

  (The volume of the larger cube is 8 times the volume of the smaller cube.)

83.

x	Y_1	Y_2	Y_3
-3	729	-243	729
-2	64	-32	64
-1	1	.1	1
0	0	0	0
1	1	1	1
2	64	32	64
3	729	243	729

Conclusion: $Y_1 = Y_3$

Cumulative Review

1. $\dfrac{3(4)-6\div 2}{3(4)} = \dfrac{12-3}{12} = \dfrac{9}{12} = \dfrac{3}{4}$

2.
a. $9+0=9$
b. $9-0=9$
c. $9\cdot 0=0$
d. $0\cdot 9=0$
e. $0\div 9=0$
f. $9\div 0$ is undefined.

3.
$$5x-3(2x+1)=5-2(x-5)$$
$$5x-6x-3=5-2x+10$$
$$-x-3=-2x+15$$
$$-x+2x-3+3=-2x+2x+15+3$$
$$x=18$$

4.
$$3x-4\le 3-5(x-2)$$
$$3x-4\le 3-5x+10$$
$$3x-4\le -5x+13$$
$$3x+5x-4+4\le -5x+5x+13+4$$
$$8x\le 17$$
$$x\le \frac{17}{8}$$
Solution: $\left(-\infty, \dfrac{17}{8}\right]$

5.
$|2x-1|\ge 9$ is equivalent to
$2x-1\le -9$ or $2x-1\ge 9$
$2x\le -8$ $2x\ge 10$
$x\le -4$ $x\ge 5$
Solution: $(-\infty, -4]\cup[5, \infty)$

Section 5.2: Quotient Rule and Zero Exponents

Quick Review 5.2

1. $-3x^2 = -3(-2)^2 = -3\cdot 4 = -12$

2. $(-3x)^2 = (-3(-2))^2 = (6)^2 = 36$

3. $6^2 = 36$

4. $2^6 = 64$

5. $\dfrac{45}{60} = \dfrac{3\cdot \cancel{15}}{4\cdot \cancel{15}} = \dfrac{3}{4}$

Exercises 5.2

1. $\dfrac{x^6}{x^3} = \dfrac{x\cdot x\cdot x\cdot \cancel{x}\cdot \cancel{x}\cdot \cancel{x}}{\cancel{x}\cdot \cancel{x}\cdot \cancel{x}} = x\cdot x\cdot x = x^3$

3. $\dfrac{x^{15}}{x^5} = x^{15-5} = x^{10}$

5. $\dfrac{m^{42}}{m^{18}} = m^{42-18} = m^{24}$

7. $\dfrac{-x^{11}}{x^7} = -x^{11-7} = -x^4$

9. $\dfrac{t^8}{t^{12}} = \dfrac{1}{t^{12-8}} = \dfrac{1}{t^4}$

11. $\dfrac{v^{10}}{v^{15}} = \dfrac{1}{v^{15-10}} = \dfrac{1}{v^5}$

13. $-\dfrac{a^6}{a^9} = -\dfrac{1}{a^{9-6}} = -\dfrac{1}{a^3}$

15. $\dfrac{a^3}{b^4} = \dfrac{a^3}{b^4}$

17. $\dfrac{14m^5}{21m^2} = \dfrac{2m^{5-2}}{3} = \dfrac{2m^3}{3}$

19. $\dfrac{36v^5}{66v^8} = \dfrac{6}{11v^{8-5}} = \dfrac{6}{11v^3}$

21. $\dfrac{15a^2b^3}{20a^2b^2} = \dfrac{3a^{2-2}b^{3-2}}{4}$

$= \dfrac{3a^0b^1}{4} = \dfrac{3b}{4}$

23. $\dfrac{8m^7n^7}{6m^9n^2} = \dfrac{4n^{7-2}}{3m^{9-7}} = \dfrac{4n^5}{3m^2}$

25. $-\dfrac{27v^4w^9}{45v^6w^6} = -\dfrac{3w^{9-6}}{5v^{6-4}}$

$= -\dfrac{3w^3}{5v^2}$

27.
  a. $7^0 = 1$
  b. $-7^0 = -1$
  c. $(-7)^0 = 1$

29.
  a. $2^0 + 8^0 = 1 + 1 = 2$
  b. $(2+8)^0 = 10^0 = 1$
  c. $2^0 - 8^0 = 1 - 1 = 0$

31.
  a. $3^0 = 1$
  b. $0^3 = 0$
  c. $-3^0 = -1$

33.
  a. $x^0 = 1$ for $x \neq 0$
  b. x^0 is undefined for $x = 0$

35.
  a. $-3x^0 = -3(1) = -3$ for $x \neq 0$
  b. $(-3x)^0$ is undefined for $x = 0$

37.
  a. $(4x)^0 = 1$
  b. $4x^0 = 4(1) = 4$
  c. $4 + x^0 = 4 + 1 = 5$

39.
  a. $(4x - 3y)^0 = 1$ (provided $4x \neq 3y$)
  b. $(4x)^0 - (3y)^0 = 1 - 1 = 0$
  c. $4x^0 - 3y^0 = 4(1) - 3(1) = 1$

41. $(5a + 3b)^0 + (5a)^0 + (3b)^0 + 5a^0 + 3b^0 = 1 + 1 + 1 + 5(1) + 3(1) = 11$

43. $\dfrac{y^{48}}{y^{48}} = y^{48-48} = y^0 = 1$

45. $\left(\dfrac{x^5}{x^2}\right)^2 = \left(x^{5-2}\right)^2$

$= \left(x^3\right)^2 = x^{3\cdot2} = x^6$

47. $\left(\dfrac{m^3}{m^9}\right)^2 = \left(\dfrac{1}{m^{9-3}}\right)^2 = \left(\dfrac{1}{m^6}\right)^2$

$= \dfrac{1^2}{\left(m^6\right)^2} = \dfrac{1}{m^{6\cdot2}} = \dfrac{1}{m^{12}}$

49. $\left[\left(2x^5\right)\left(3x^4\right)\right]^2 = \left[(2)(3)x^{5+4}\right]^2 = \left(6x^9\right)^2$

$= 6^2\left(x^9\right)^2 = 36x^{9\cdot2} = 36x^{18}$

51. $\left[\left(3x^2\right)\left(2x^3\right)\right]^2 = \left[(3)(2)x^2x^3\right]^2 = \left[6x^{2+3}\right]^2$

$= \left[6x^5\right]^2 = 6^2x^{5\cdot2} = 36x^{10}$

53. $\left(\dfrac{10x^7}{5x^4}\right)^5 = \left(2x^{7-4}\right)^5 = \left(2x^3\right)^5 = 2^5x^{3\cdot5} = 32x^{15}$

55. $\left[\left(6m^4\right)\left(2m^5\right)\right]^2 = \left[(6)(2)m^4m^5\right]^2 = \left[12m^{4+5}\right]^2$

$= \left[12m^9\right]^2 = 12^2m^{9\cdot2} = 144m^{18}$

57. $\left(5x^3\right)^2\left(2x^5\right)^3 = \left(5x^3\right)^2\left(2x^5\right)^3 = \left(5^2 x^{3\cdot2}\right)\left(2^3 x^{5\cdot3}\right)$
$$= \left(25x^6\right)\left(8x^{15}\right) = 200x^{6+15} = 200x^{21}$$

59. $\left(\dfrac{12x^5}{6x^3}\right)\left(\dfrac{15x^7}{5x^3}\right) = \left(2x^{5-3}\right)\left(3x^{7-3}\right) = \left(2x^2\right)\left(3x^4\right)$
$$= 6x^{2+4} = 6x^6$$

61. $\dfrac{36a^7b^8}{12a^3b^3} = 3a^{7-3}b^{8-3} = 3a^4b^5$

63. $\dfrac{\left(4x^2y\right)^3}{\left(8xy^2\right)^2} = \dfrac{4^3 x^{2\cdot3} y^3}{8^2 x^2 y^{2\cdot2}} = \dfrac{64x^6 y^3}{64x^2 y^4} = \dfrac{x^{6-2}}{y^{4-3}} = \dfrac{x^4}{y}$

65.
  a. $\dfrac{2^{45}}{2^{43}} = 2^{45-43} = 2^2 = 4$

  b. $\dfrac{2^{43}}{2^{45}} = \dfrac{1}{2^{45-43}} = \dfrac{1}{2^2} = \dfrac{1}{4}$

  c. $\dfrac{2^{43}}{2^{43}} = 2^{43-43} = 2^0 = 1$

67.
  a. $0-5 = -5$
  b. $0\cdot5 = 0$
  c. $5^0 = 1$
  d. $0^5 = 0$
  e. $5\div0$ is undefined.

69.
  a. $\dfrac{10^8}{10^5} = 10^{8-5} = 10^3 = 1000$

  b. $\dfrac{10^5}{10^5} = 10^{5-5} = 10^0 = 1$

  c. $\dfrac{10^5}{10^8} = \dfrac{1}{10^{8-5}} = \dfrac{1}{10^3} = \dfrac{1}{1000}$

71.
  a. $38x - 2x = 36x$
  b. $\dfrac{38x}{2x} = 19$

73.
  a. $3x^2 - 3x = 3x^2 - 3x$
  b. $\dfrac{3x^2}{3x} = x$

Problem	Mental Estimate	Calculator Value
75. $\dfrac{8.014^2}{7.99}$	$\dfrac{8^2}{8} = 8^{2-1} = 8$	$\dfrac{8.014^2}{7.99} \approx 8.04$
77. $(1.99)^3(5.02)^2$	$(2)^3(5)^2 = 8\cdot25 = 200$	$(1.99)^3(5.02)^2 \approx 198.59$

79. $A = P\left(1+r\right)^t = 8500\left(1+0.055\right)^{10} \approx \$14,519.23$

81.

x	Y_1	Y_2	Y_3
-3	81	81	-27
-2	16	16	-8
-1	1	1	-1
0	*ERROR*	0	0
1	1	1	1
2	16	16	8
3	81	81	27

Conclusion: $Y_1 = Y_2$ $\left(x \neq 0\right)$

Chapter 5: Exponents and Operations with Polynomials

Cumulative Review

1. $\dfrac{2}{15}+\dfrac{5}{12}=\dfrac{2}{15}\cdot\dfrac{4}{4}+\dfrac{5}{12}\cdot\dfrac{5}{5}=\dfrac{8}{60}+\dfrac{25}{60}$

$=\dfrac{33}{60}=\dfrac{\cancel{3}\cdot 11}{\cancel{3}\cdot 20}=\dfrac{11}{20}$

2. Determine the slope of the line passing through the given points

$$m=\dfrac{y_2-y_1}{x_2-x_1}=\dfrac{5-(-3)}{-2-4}=\dfrac{8}{-6}=-\dfrac{4}{3}$$

Use the point-slope form with either point.

Substitute $(-2, 5)$ for (x_1, y_1) and $-\dfrac{4}{3}$ for m.

Then write the equation in slope intercept form by solving for y.

$$y-y_1=m(x-x_1)$$

$$y-5=-\dfrac{4}{3}\left(x-(-2)\right)$$

$$y-5=-\dfrac{4}{3}x-\dfrac{8}{3}$$

$$y=-\dfrac{4}{3}x+\dfrac{7}{3}$$

3. To eliminate y, multiply both sides of the first equation by 4 and add the two equations. Solve this equation for x.

$$2x-y=1 \qquad\qquad 8x-4y=4$$
$$3x+4y=18 \qquad\qquad \underline{3x+4y=18}$$
$$\qquad\qquad\qquad\qquad 11x\quad=22$$
$$\qquad\qquad\qquad\qquad x=2$$

Back substitute 2 for x in the first equation to find y.

$$2x-y=1$$
$$2(2)-y=1$$
$$4-y=1$$
$$-y=-3$$
$$y=3$$

Solution: $(2, 3)$

4.

5. $$-3<2x+7\le 11$$
$$-3-7<2x+7-7\le 11-7$$
$$-10<2x\le 4$$
$$\dfrac{-10}{2}<\dfrac{2x}{2}\le\dfrac{4}{2}$$
$$-5<x\le 2$$

Solution: $(-5, 2]$

Section 5.3: Negative Exponents and Scientific Notation

Quick Review 5.3

1. $10^4=10\cdot 10\cdot 10\cdot 10=10000$

2. $\left(\dfrac{1}{10}\right)^3=\left(\dfrac{1}{10}\right)\left(\dfrac{1}{10}\right)\left(\dfrac{1}{10}\right)=\dfrac{1}{1000}$

3. $10^3+10^2+10^1=1000+100+10=1110$

4. $\left(-2x^3\right)\left(3x^2\right)=-6x^{3+2}=-6x^5$

5. $\left(\dfrac{-2x^3}{y^5}\right)^2=\dfrac{(-2)^2\left(x^3\right)^2}{\left(y^5\right)^2}=\dfrac{4x^{3\cdot 2}}{y^{5\cdot 2}}=\dfrac{4x^6}{y^{10}}$

Exercises 5.3

1.   **a.** $2^{-5} = \dfrac{1}{2^5} = \dfrac{1}{32}$

     b. $-2^5 = -32$

     c. $\dfrac{1}{5^{-2}} = 5^2 = 25$

3.   **a.** $\left(\dfrac{6}{5}\right)^{-1} = \dfrac{5}{6}$

     b. $\left(\dfrac{6}{5}\right)^{-2} = \left(\dfrac{5}{6}\right)^2 = \dfrac{5^2}{6^2} = \dfrac{25}{36}$

     c. $\left(\dfrac{6}{5}\right)^0 = 1$

5.   **a.** $10^{-2} = \dfrac{1}{10^2} = \dfrac{1}{100}$

     b. $10^{-3} = \dfrac{1}{10^3} = \dfrac{1}{1,000}$

     c. $-10^{-2} = -\dfrac{1}{10^2} = -\dfrac{1}{100}$

7.   **a.** $(2+5)^{-1} = (7)^{-1} = \dfrac{1}{7}$

     b. $2^{-1} + 5^{-1} = \dfrac{1}{2} + \dfrac{1}{5} = \dfrac{5}{10} + \dfrac{2}{10} = \dfrac{7}{10}$

     c. $-2 + 5^{-1} = -2 + \dfrac{1}{5} = \dfrac{-10}{5} + \dfrac{1}{5} = \dfrac{-9}{5}$

9.   **a.** $\left(\dfrac{1}{2} + \dfrac{1}{5}\right)^{-1} = \left(\dfrac{5}{10} + \dfrac{2}{10}\right)^{-1} = \left(\dfrac{7}{10}\right)^{-1} = \dfrac{10}{7}$

     b. $\left(\dfrac{1}{2}\right)^{-1} + \left(\dfrac{1}{5}\right)^{-1} = 2 + 5 = 7$

     c. $\left(\dfrac{1}{2}\right)^0 + \left(\dfrac{1}{5}\right)^0 = 1 + 1 = 2$

11.   **a.** $\left(\dfrac{x}{y}\right)^{-1} = \dfrac{y}{x}$

     b. $\left(\dfrac{x}{y}\right)^{-2} = \left(\dfrac{y}{x}\right)^2 = \dfrac{y^2}{x^2}$

     c. $\dfrac{x^{-2}}{y} = \dfrac{1}{x^2 y}$

13.   **a.** $(3x)^{-2} = \dfrac{1}{(3x)^2} = \dfrac{1}{9x^2}$

     b. $3x^{-2} = \dfrac{3}{x^2}$

     c. $\dfrac{-3}{x^{-2}} = -3x^2$

15.   **a.** $(m+n)^{-1} = \dfrac{1}{m+n}$

     b. $m^{-1} + n^{-1} = \dfrac{1}{m} + \dfrac{1}{n}$

     c. $m + n^{-1} = m + \dfrac{1}{n}$

17.   **a.** $v^{-3}v^{12} = v^{-3+12} = v^9$

     b. $\dfrac{v^{12}}{v^{-3}} = v^{12-(-3)} = v^{15}$

     c. $\dfrac{v^{-12}}{v^3} = \dfrac{1}{v^{3-(-12)}} = \dfrac{1}{v^{15}}$

19.   **a.** $x^3 x^0 x^{-7} = x^{3+(-7)} = x^{-4} = \dfrac{1}{x^4}$

     b. $(x^3 x^{-7})^0 = 1$

     c. $x^0 x^{-3} x^{-7} = x^{-3-7} = x^{-10} = \dfrac{1}{x^{10}}$

21.   **a.** $\dfrac{6x^{-4}}{2x^{-3}} = \dfrac{3}{x^{-3-(-4)}} = \dfrac{3}{x}$

     b. $(2x^{-3})(6x^4) = (2)(6)x^{-3}x^4$
         $= 12x^{-3+4} = 12x$

     c. $(2x^{-3})(6x^{-4}) = (2)(6)x^{-3}x^{-4}$
         $= 12x^{-3-4} = 12x^{-7} = \dfrac{12}{x^7}$

23.   **a.** $\left(\dfrac{3x}{5y}\right)^2 = \dfrac{3^2 x^2}{5^2 y^2} = \dfrac{9x^2}{25y^2}$

     b. $\left(\dfrac{3x}{5y}\right)^{-2} = \left(\dfrac{5y}{3x}\right)^2 = \dfrac{5^2 y^2}{3^2 x^2} = \dfrac{25y^2}{9x^2}$

     c. $\left[(3x)(5y)\right]^2 \left[(3)(5)xy\right]^2 = (15xy)^2$
         $= 15^2 x^2 y^2 = 225x^2 y^2$

25. $\left[(5x^3)(-4x^{-2})\right]^{-1} = \left[(5)(-4)x^3 x^{-2}\right]^{-1} = \left[-20x^1\right]^{-1} = -\dfrac{1}{20x}$

27. $(2x^{-3}y^4)^3(3x^4 y^{-2})^2 = 2^3(x^{-3})^3(y^4)^3 3^2(x^4)^2(y^{-2})^2 = 8x^{-9}y^{12}9x^8 y^{-4} = 72x^{-9+8}y^{12+(-4)} = 72x^{-1}y^8 = \dfrac{72y^8}{x}$

29. $\dfrac{-6x^6}{4x^{-4}} = -\dfrac{3x^{6+4}}{2} = -\dfrac{3x^{10}}{2}$

31. $\dfrac{24x^3 y^{-8}}{-6x^{-12}y^{24}} = -\dfrac{4x^{3+12}}{y^{24+8}} = -\dfrac{4x^{15}}{y^{32}}$

Chapter 5: Exponents and Operations with Polynomials

33. $\left(\dfrac{12x^3}{6x^{-2}}\right)^2 = \left(2x^{3-(-2)}\right)^2 = \left(2x^5\right)^2$

$= 2^2\left(x^5\right)^2 = 4x^{10}$

35. $\left(\dfrac{m^3 n^{-7}}{m^7 n^{-11}}\right)^{-3} = \left(\dfrac{n^{-7-(-11)}}{m^{7-3}}\right)^{-3} = \left(\dfrac{n^4}{m^4}\right)^{-3}$

$= \left(\dfrac{m^4}{n^4}\right)^{3} = \dfrac{\left(m^4\right)^3}{\left(n^4\right)^3} = \dfrac{m^{12}}{n^{12}}$

37. $\dfrac{\left(2x^{-1}y^2\right)\left(4x^2y^{-3}\right)^{-2}}{\left(12x^{-2}y^{-2}\right)^{-1}} = \dfrac{2x^{-1}y^2\,4^{-2}\left(x^2\right)^{-2}\left(y^{-3}\right)^{-2}}{12^{-1}\left(x^{-2}\right)^{-1}\left(y^{-2}\right)^{-1}} = \dfrac{2x^{-1}y^2\,4^{-2}x^{-4}y^6}{12^{-1}x^2y^2} = \dfrac{2\cdot 12x^{-1-4}y^{2+6}}{4^2x^2y^2}$

$= \dfrac{24x^{-5}y^8}{16x^2y^2} = \dfrac{3y^{8-2}}{2x^{2-(-5)}} = \dfrac{3y^{8-2}}{2x^{2-(-5)}} = \dfrac{3y^6}{2x^7}$

39.   **a.** $4.58\times10^4 = 45,800$

     b. $4.58\times10^{-4} = 0.000458$

     c. $4.58\times10^6 = 4,580,000$

     d. $4.58\times10^{-6} = 0.00000458$

41.   **a.** $8.1\times10^3 = 8,100$

     b. $8.1\times10^{-3} = 0.0081$

     c. $-8.1\times10^3 = -8,100$

     d. $-8.1\times10^{-7} = -0.00000081$

43.   **a.** $9,700 = 9.7\times10^3$

     b. $97,000,000 = 9.7\times10^7$

     c. $0.97 = 9.7\times10^{-1}$

     d. $0.00097 = 9.7\times10^{-4}$

45.   **a.** $35,000,000,000 = 3.5\times10^{10}$

     b. $0.0000000035 = 3.5\times10^{-9}$

     c. $-3500 = -3.5\times10^3$

     d. $-0.035 = -3.5\times10^{-2}$

47. $4.493\times10^9 = 4,493,000,000$

49. $1.0\times10^{-12} = 0.000000000001$

51. $14,000,000 = 1.4\times10^7$

53. $0.0000568 = 5.68\times10^{-5}$

55.   **a.** $2.3\times10^3 = 2,300$ transistors.

     b. $2.2\times10^8 = 220,000,000$ transistors.

     c. The claim is accurate. $(2,300)(100,000) = 230,000,000$.

57.   Using $t = \dfrac{D}{r}$. The time it takes for the signal to reach earth is $\dfrac{2.85\times10^{11}}{2.998\times10^8} \approx 950$ seconds (≈ 16 minutes)

	Problem	Pencil and Paper Estimate	Calculator Approximation
59.	$(10,013)(0.00007943)$	$\left(1.0\times10^4\right)\left(8.0\times10^{-5}\right) = 8\times10^{-1} = 0.8$	0.7953
61.	$\dfrac{0.000005034}{0.00009893}$	$\dfrac{5.0\times10^{-6}}{1.0\times10^{-4}} = 5\times10^{-2} = 0.05$	0.05088
63.	$(0.02973)^3$	$\left(3.0\times10^{-2}\right)^3 = 27.0\times10^{-6} = 2.7\times10^{-5}$	0.00002628

65. $x^{-3} = \dfrac{1}{x^3} = \dfrac{1}{3^3} = \dfrac{1}{27}$; $-x^3 = -(3)^3 = -27$

	$x^2 + y^2$	$(x+y)^2$	$x^{-1} + y^{-1}$	$(x+y)^{-1}$
67. $x=-3, \; y=4$	$(-3)^2 + (4)^2 = 9 + 16$ $= 25$	$(-3+(4))^2 = (1)^2$ $= 1$	$(-3)^{-1} + (4)^{-1}$ $= -\dfrac{1}{3} + \dfrac{1}{4}$ $= -\dfrac{4}{12} + \dfrac{3}{12} = -\dfrac{1}{12}$	$(-3+(4))^{-1} = (1)^{-1}$ $= \dfrac{1}{1} = 1$

69. $1.764 \times 10^{-4} = 0.0001764$

71. $3.51 \times 10^{-3} = 0.00351$

73. **a.**
```
(4.32E15)(8.49E-
17)
              .366768
```
≈ 0.367

   b.
```
(7.16E3)²
        51265600
```
$\approx 51,300,000$

75.

x	Y_1	Y_2	Y_3
-3	0.111	0.111	-0.667
-2	0.25	0.25	-1
-1	1	1	-2
0	*ERROR*	*ERROR*	*ERROR*
1	1	1	2
2	0.25	0.25	1
3	0.111	0.111	0.667

Conclusion: $Y_1 = Y_2 \qquad (x \neq 0)$

Cumulative Review

1. **a.** $y + y + y + y = 4y$

   b. $y^4 = y \cdot y \cdot y \cdot y$

2. $8x + 5 - 2(x - (3x+5)) = 8x + 5 - 2(x - 3x - 5)$
$= 8x + 5 - 2(-2x - 5)$
$= 8x + 5 + 4x + 10$
$= 8x + 4x + 5 + 10$
$= 12x + 15$

3. Let x be the number of milliliters of the 20% solution.
Let y be the number of milliliters of the 4% solution.

If the total amount of the new mixture is 40 milliliters, then $x + y = 40$	If new mixture is to be a 16% solution, then $0.20x + 0.04y = 0.16(40)$ or $0.20x + 0.04y = 6.4$

Use the addition method to solve the equations. Multiply both sides of the first equation by -0.04 then add the equations to eliminate y.

$$-0.04x - 0.04y = -1.6$$
$$\underline{0.20x + 0.04y = 6.4}$$
$$0.16x \qquad\quad = 4.8$$
$$x = 30$$

Back substitute 30 for x in the first equation.
$$x + y = 40$$
$$30 + y = 40$$
$$y = 10$$

Use 30 milliliters of the 20% solution and 10 milliliters of the 4% solution.

4. First, find the slope of $4x - 3y = 24$ by writing it in slope-intercept form.

$$4x - 3y = 24$$

$$-3y = -4x + 24$$

$$\frac{-3y}{-3} = \frac{-4x}{-3} + \frac{24}{-3}$$

$$y = \frac{4}{3}x - 8$$

The slope of the given line is $m = \frac{4}{3}$. Thus the slope of the line perpendicular to this line is

$$m = -\frac{3}{4}$$

5. $A \cup B = (-\infty, 8)$

$A \cap B = [-3, 6]$

Section 5.4: Adding and Subtracting Polynomials

Quick Review 5.4

1. The result of the addtion of two numbers is called their sum.
2. The result of the subtraction of two numbers is called their difference.
3. The additive inverse of 15 is -15.
4. $f(-4) = 3(-4) - 7 = -12 - 7 = -19$
5. $f(0) = 3(0) - 7 = -7$

Exercises 5.4

1.
   a. -12 is a monomial of degree zero. The coefficient is -12.
   b. $-12x$ is a first degree monomial. The coefficient is -12.
   c. $-x^{12}$ is a 12th degree monomial. The coefficient is -1.
   d. x^{-12} is not a monomial. The exponent must be a whole number.

3.
   a. $\frac{2}{5}x^4$ is a 4th degree monomial. The coefficient is $\frac{2}{5}$.
   b. $\frac{5x^4}{2}$ is a 4th degree monomial. The coefficient is $\frac{5}{2}$.
   c. $-\frac{5x^4}{2}$ is a 4th degree monomial. The coefficient is $-\frac{5}{2}$.
   d. $\frac{2}{5x^4}$ is not a monomial. The exponent must be a whole number.

5.
   a. $5x^2y^2$ is a monomial of degree $2 + 2 = 4$. The coefficient is 5.
   b. $-5x^2y^2$ is a monomial of degree $2 + 2 = 4$. The coefficient is -5.
   c. $\frac{5x^2}{y^2} = 5x^2y^{-2}$ is not a monomial. The exponents must be whole numbers.
   d. $5x^2 + y^2$ is not a monomial. It is a binomial.

7.   **a.** $3x^2 - 7x$ is a second degree binomial.

     b. $x^3 - 8x^2 + 9$ is a third degree trinomial.

     c. $-9x^4$ is a fourth degree monomial.

     d. -9 is a monomial of degree zero.

9.   **a.** $11xy$ is a second degree monomial.

     b. $11x + y$ is a first degree binomial.

     c. $\dfrac{11x}{y} = 11xy^{-1}$ is not a polynomial.

     d. $x^3 + y^2 - 11$ is a third degree trinomial.

11.   **a.** $8yx^2z^3 = 8x^2yz^3$

     b. $-9 + x^2 - 5x = x^2 - 5x - 9$

     c. $-2x^2 + 7 - 4x^3 + 9x = -4x^3 - 2x^2 + 9x + 7$

13.   **a.** $7xy$ and $-xy$ are like terms.

     b. $-4x^3y^2$ and $6x^2y^3$ are not like terms.

     c. $5xy^2z^3$ and $5xy^2z^2$ are not like terms.

15.   **a.** The additive inverse of $7xy$ is $-7xy$.

     b. The additive inverse of $7x - y$ is $-(7x - y) = -7x + y$.

     c. The additive inverse of $-2x^2 + 3xy - 7y^2$ is $-(-2x^2 + 3xy - 7y^2) = 2x^2 - 3xy + 7y^2$.

17.   **a.** $7x + (5x + 9x) = 7x + 5x + 9x$
$$= (7 + 5 + 9)x = 21x$$

     b. $7x - (5x + 9x) = 7x - 5x - 9x$
$$= (7 - 5 - 9)x = -7x$$

19.   **a.** $(3x^2 - 7x) + (4x^2 - 5x)$
$$= 3x^2 - 7x + 4x^2 - 5x$$
$$= 3x^2 + 4x^2 - 7x - 5x$$
$$= (3 + 4)x^2 + (-7 - 5)x$$
$$= 7x^2 - 12x$$

     b. $(3x^2 - 7x) - (4x^2 - 5x)$
$$= 3x^2 - 7x - 4x^2 + 5x$$
$$= 3x^2 - 4x^2 - 7x + 5x$$
$$= (3 - 4)x^2 + (-7 + 5)x$$
$$= -x^2 - 2x$$

21.   **a.** $(5x^2 - 7x + 9) + (4x^2 + 6x - 3)$
$$= 5x^2 - 7x + 9 + 4x^2 + 6x - 3$$
$$= 5x^2 + 4x^2 + 6x - 7x + 9 - 3$$
$$= (5 + 4)x^2 + (6 - 7)x + 6$$
$$= 9x^2 - x + 6$$

     b. $(5x^2 - 7x + 9) - (4x^2 + 6x - 3)$
$$= 5x^2 - 7x + 9 - 4x^2 - 6x + 3$$
$$= 5x^2 - 4x^2 - 7x - 6x + 9 + 3$$
$$= (5 - 4)x^2 + (-7 - 6)x + 12$$
$$= x^2 - 13x + 12$$

23. $(6x + 5) + 2(8x - 7)$
$$= 6x + 5 + 16x - 14$$
$$= 6x + 16x + 5 - 14$$
$$= (6 + 16)x - 9$$
$$= 22x - 9$$

25. $(-7v + 3) - 5(2v - 11)$
$$= -7v + 3 - 10v + 55$$
$$= -7v - 10v + 3 + 55$$
$$= (-7 - 10)v + 58$$
$$= -17v + 58$$

27. $(5a^2 - 7a + 9) + (4a^2 + 6a - 3)$
$$= 5a^2 - 7a + 9 + 4a^2 + 6a - 3$$
$$= 5a^2 + 4a^2 + 6a - 7a + 9 - 3$$
$$= (5 + 4)a^2 + (6 - 7)a + 6$$
$$= 9a^2 - a + 6$$

29. $(8x^2 - 3x - 4) - (2x^2 - 2x - 9)$
$$= 8x^2 - 3x - 4 - 2x^2 + 2x + 9$$
$$= 8x^2 - 2x^2 + 2x - 3x - 4 + 9$$
$$= (8 - 2)x^2 + (2 - 3)x + 5$$
$$= 6x^2 - x + 5$$

31. $(-w^2 + 4) - (-4w^2 + 7w - 6)$
$= -w^2 + 4 + 4w^2 - 7w + 6$
$= 4w^2 - w^2 - 7w + 4 + 6$
$= (4 - 1)w^2 - 7w + 10$
$= 3w^2 - 7w + 10$

33. $(-2m^4 + 3m^3 + m^2 - 1) + (m^4 - m^2 - 2m + 5)$
$= -2m^4 + 3m^3 + m^2 - 1 + m^4 - m^2 - 2m + 5$
$= -2m^4 + m^4 + 3m^3 + m^2 - m^2 - 2m + 5 - 1$
$= (-2 + 1)m^4 + 3m^3 - 2m + 4$
$= -m^4 + 3m^3 - 2m + 4$

35. $(-3n^4 + 7n^3 + n - 8) - (n^4 - 2n^3 - n^2 + 4)$
$= -3n^4 + 7n^3 + n - 8 - n^4 + 2n^3 + n^2 - 4$
$= -3n^4 - n^4 + 2n^3 + 7n^3 + n^2 + n - 8 - 4$
$= (-3 - 1)n^4 + (2 + 7)n^3 + n^2 + n - 12$
$= -4n^4 + 9n^3 + n^2 + n - 12$

37. $(-7y^4 + 3y^6 - y + 4y^5 - 11 + 2y^2) - 2(3y^5 - 5y + 7y^6 - 9y^2 + 7 - y^4)$
$= -7y^4 + 3y^6 - y + 4y^5 - 11 + 2y^2 - 6y^5 + 10y - 14y^6 + 18y^2 - 14 + 2y^4$
$= 3y^6 - 14y^6 + 4y^5 - 6y^5 - 7y^4 + 2y^4 + 2y^2 + 18y^2 - y + 10y - 11 - 14$
$= (3 - 14)y^6 + (4 - 6)y^5 + (-7 + 2)y^4 + (2 + 18)y^2 + (-1 + 10)y - 25$
$= -11y^6 - 2y^5 - 5y^4 + 20y^2 + 9y - 25$

39. $2(x^2 - 3x - 5) - 7(x^2 + 2x - 1)$
$= 2x^2 - 6x - 10 - 7x^2 - 14x + 7$
$= 2x^2 - 7x^2 - 6x - 14x - 10 + 7$
$= (2 - 7)x^2 + (-6 - 14)x - 10 + 7$
$= -5x^2 - 20x - 3$

41. $3(2a^2 - 5a + 1) - 2(3a^2 - a - 5)$
$= 6a^2 - 15a + 3 - 6a^2 + 2a + 10$
$= 6a^2 - 6a^2 + 2a - 15a + 3 + 10$
$= (2 - 15)a + 13$
$= -13a + 13$

43. $(5x + 7) + (4x - 8) + (3x - 11)$
$= 5x + 7 + 4x - 8 + 3x - 11$
$= (5 + 4 + 3)x + 7 - 8 - 11$
$= 12x - 12$

45. $(13x - 8) - 4(7x - 9)$
$= 13x - 8 - 28x + 36$
$= 13x - 28x - 8 + 36$
$= (13 - 28)x + 28$
$= -15x + 28$

47. $(5x^2 + 7xy - 9y^2) + (6x^2 - 3xy + y^2)$
$= 5x^2 + 7xy - 9y^2 + 6x^2 - 3xy + y^2$
$= 5x^2 + 6x^2 + 7xy - 3xy + y^2 - 9y^2$
$= (5 + 6)x^2 + (7 - 3)xy + (1 - 9)y^2$
$= 11x^2 + 4xy - 8y^2$

49. $(-7x^2 + 6xy + 8y^2) - (13x^2 - xy - 3y^2)$
$= -7x^2 + 6xy + 8y^2 - 13x^2 + xy + 3y^2$
$= -7x^2 - 13x^2 + 6xy + xy + 8y^2 + 3y^2$
$= (-7 - 13)x^2 + (6 + 1)xy + (8 + 3)y^2$
$= -20x^2 + 7xy + 11y^2$

51. $(5x^3 - 7x + 9 + 5x^2) + (2x^2 + 13 + x^3 - x) - (4x - 3x^3 + x^2 - 8)$
$= 5x^3 - 7x + 9 + 5x^2 + 2x^2 + 13 + x^3 - x - 4x + 3x^3 - x^2 + 8$
$= 5x^3 + x^3 + 3x^3 + 5x^2 + 2x^2 - x^2 - 7x - x - 4x + 9 + 13 + 8$
$= (5 + 1 + 3)x^3 + (5 + 2 - 1)x^2 + (-7 - 1 - 4)x + 30$
$= 9x^3 + 6x^2 - 12x + 30$

53.
$$\left(x^4 - 2x^3y + x^2y^2 + xy^3 - 3y^4\right) - \left(2x^4 + x^3y - 5x^2y^2 - 7y^4\right) - \left(7x^4 + 3x^2y^2 + 2y^4\right)$$
$$= x^4 - 2x^3y + x^2y^2 + xy^3 - 3y^4 - 2x^4 - x^3y + 5x^2y^2 + 7y^4 - 7x^4 - 3x^2y^2 - 2y^4$$
$$= x^4 - 2x^4 - 7x^4 - 2x^3y - x^3y + x^2y^2 + 5x^2y^2 - 3x^2y^2 + xy^3 - 3y^4 + 7y^4 - 2y^4$$
$$= (1 - 2 - 7)x^4 + (-2 - 1)x^3y + (1 + 5 - 3)x^2y^2 + xy^3 + (-3 + 7 - 2)y^4$$
$$= -8x^4 - 3x^3y + 3x^2y^2 + xy^3 + 2y^4$$

55.
    a. $P(0) = 5(0)^2 + 3(0) - 2 = -2$

    b. $P(2) = 5(2)^2 + 3(2) - 2$
$$= 5(4) + 6 - 2 = 24$$

    c. $P(10) = 5(10)^2 + 3(10) - 2$
$$= 5(100) + 30 - 2 = 528$$

    d. $P(8) = 5(8)^2 + 3(8) - 2$
$$= 5(64) + 24 - 2 = 342$$

57. $P(0) = -40$; When 0 units are produced and sold the company has a loss of $40.00.

59. $P(4) = 32$; When 4 units are produced and sold the profit is $32.00.

61. $P(9) = 77$; When 9 units are produced and sold the profit is $77.00.

    Also, $P(13) = 77$; When 13 units are produced and sold the profit is $77.00.

63.   The perimeter is the sum of the lengths of the sides.

Perimeter: $\left(x^2 + x + 2\right) + (x + 2) + \left(x^2 + x + 1\right) + (x + 3)$
$$= x^2 + x + 2 + x + 2 + x^2 + x + 1 + x + 3$$
$$= x^2 + x^2 + x + x + x + x + 2 + 2 + 1 + 3$$
$$= 2x^2 + 4x + 8$$

65.   The perimeter is the sum of the lengths of the sides.

Perimeter: $\left(2x^2 + x + 5\right) + (7) + \left(x^2 + 3x + 4\right) + (3x + 2) + (3x + 3)$
$$= 2x^2 + x + 5 + 7 + x^2 + 3x + 4 + 3x + 2 + 3x + 3$$
$$= 2x^2 + x^2 + x + 3x + 3x + 3x + 5 + 7 + 4 + 2 + 3$$
$$= 3x^2 + 10x + 21$$

67.   Two times x cubed minus five x plus eleven is equivalent to $2x^3 - 5x + 11$.

69.   Three times the sixth power of w plus five times the fourth power of w is equivalent to $3w^6 + 5w^4$.

71. x squared minus y squared is equivalent to $x^2 - y^2$.

73.   Seven more than twice w is equivalent to $2w + 7$.

75.   1965 is 15 years after 1950. The production of CFC in 1965 is approximately
$$C(15) = -0.05(15)^3 + 3.0x^2 - 13.5x + 47.7 \approx 540 \text{ thousand tons. (350,000 tons).}$$

77.

x	Y_1	Y_2	Y_3
-3	18	38	18
-2	3	23	3
-1	-8	12	-8
0	-15	5	-15
1	-18	2	-18
2	-17	3	-17
3	-12	8	-12

Conclusion: $Y_1 = Y_3$

Cumulative Review

1. The equation of a vertical line is determined by the x-coordinates. Thus the equation is $x = -3$.

2. The equation of a horizontal line is determined by the y-coordinates. Thus the equation is $y = 4$.

3. $f(4) = 1$ **4.** $f(2) = 0$ **5.** $f(2) = 0;\ (x = 2)$

Section 5.5: Multiplying Polynomials

Quick Review 5.5

1. $-3(4x - 7) = -12x + 21$

2. $5(2x + 9) = 10x + 45$

3. $-6(3x - 5y + 8) = -18x + 30y - 48$

4.   **a.** $(3x^2)(4x) = 12x^3$

     b. $3x^2 + 4x$ cannot be simplified. The terms are not like terms.

5.   **a.** $(-2x^2)(5x^2) = -10x^4$

     b. $-2x^2 + 5x^2 = 3x^2$

Exercises 5.5

1. $(-9v^2)(-7v^3) = (-9)(-7)(v^2 v^3) = 63v^{2+3} = 63v^5$

3. $(a^3 b^4)(4a^6 b) = 4(a^3 a^6)(b^4 b) = 4(a^{3+6})(b^{4+1}) = 4(a^{3+6})(b^{4+1}) = 4a^9 b^5$

5. $4x^2(6x - 5) = (4x^2)(6x) - (4x^2)(5) = (4)(6)(xx^2) - (4)(5)(x^2) = 24x^3 - 20x^2$

7. $-4v^2(8v + 3) = (-4v^2)(8v) + (-4v^2)(3) = (-4)(8)(v^2 v) + (-4)(3)(v^2) = -32v^3 - 12v^2$

9. $2x(7x^2 - 9x - 4) = (2x)(7x^2) - (2x)(9x) - (2x)(4) = (2)(7)(xx^2) - (2)(9)(xx) - (2)(4)(x) = 14x^3 - 18x^2 - 8x$

11. $-11x^2(4x^2 - 5x - 8)$

$= (-11x^2)(4x^2) - (-11x^2)(5x) - (-11x^2)(8)$

$= -44x^4 + 55x^3 + 88x^2$

13. $(2x^2 - xy - y^2)(5xy)$

$= (2x^2)(5xy) - (xy)(5xy) - (y^2)(5xy)$

$= 10x^3 y - 5x^2 y^2 - 5xy^3$

15. $3a^2b(2a^2 + 4ab - b^2)$

$= (3a^2b)(2a^2) + (3a^2b)(4ab) - (3a^2b)(b^2)$

$= 6a^4b + 12a^3b^2 - 3a^2b^3$

17. $(y+2)(y+3)$

$= (y+2)(y) + (y+2)(3)$

$= [(y)(y) + (2)(y)] + [(y)(3) + (2)(3)]$

$= (y^2 + 2y) + (3y + 6)$

$= y^2 + 5y + 6$

19. $(2v+5)(3v-4)$

$= (2v+5)(3v) - (2v+5)(4)$

$= [(2v)(3v) + (5)(3v)] - [(2v)(4) + (5)(4)]$

$= (6v^2 + 15v) - (8v + 20)$

$= 6v^2 + 15v - 8v - 20$

$= 6v^2 + 7v - 20$

21. $(6x+5)(9x+3)$

$= (6x+5)(9x) + (6x+5)(3)$

$= [(6x)(9x) + (5)(9x)] + [(6x)(3) + (5)(3)]$

$= (54x^2 + 45x) + (18x + 15)$

$= 54x^2 + 63x + 15$

23. $(x+y)(2x-y)$

$= (x+y)(2x) - (x+y)(y)$

$= [(x)(2x) + (y)(2x)] - [(x)(y) + (y)(y)]$

$= (2x^2 + 2xy) - (xy + y^2)$

$= 2x^2 + 2xy - xy - y^2$

$= 2x^2 + xy - y^2$

25. $(2x+4y)(5x-7y)$

$= (2x+4y)(5x) - (2x+4y)(7y)$

$= [(2x)(5x) + (4y)(5x)] - [(2x)(7y) + (4y)(7y)]$

$= (10x^2 + 20xy) - (14xy + 28y^2)$

$= 10x^2 + 20xy - 14xy - 28y^2$

$= 10x^2 + 6xy - 28y^2$

27. $(x+2)(x^2 - 3x - 4)$

$= (x+2)(x^2) - (x+2)(3x) - (x+2)(4)$

$= [(x)(x^2) + (2)(x^2)] - [(x)(3x) + (2)(3x)] - [(x)(4) + (2)(4)]$

$= (x^3 + 2x^2) - (3x^2 + 6x) - (4x + 8)$

$= x^3 + 2x^2 - 3x^2 - 6x - 4x - 8$

$= x^3 - x^2 - 10x - 8$

29.
$$
\begin{array}{r}
m^2 + 3m + 2 \\
\times \quad 2m - 5 \\
\hline
-5m^2 - 15m - 10 \\
2m^3 + 6m^2 + 4m \\
\hline
2m^3 + m^2 - 11m - 10
\end{array}
$$

31.
$$
\begin{array}{r}
x^2 - xy + y^2 \\
\times \quad x + y \\
\hline
x^2y - xy^2 + y^3 \\
x^3 - x^2y + xy^2 \\
\hline
x^3 \qquad\quad + y^3
\end{array}
$$

33.
$$
\begin{array}{r}
2x^2 - 5x + 11 \\
\times \ 3x^2 + 4x - 9 \\
\hline
-18x^2 + 45x - 99 \\
8x^3 - 20x^2 + 44x \\
6x^4 - 15x^3 + 33x^2 \\
\hline
6x^4 - 7x^3 - 5x^2 + 89x - 99
\end{array}
$$

35. $5x(x+3)(x-2)$

$$=\big[(5x)(x)+(5x)(3)\big](x-2)$$
$$=(5x^2+15x)(x-2)$$
$$=(5x^2+15x)(x)-(5x^2+15x)(2)$$
$$=\big[(5x^2)(x)+(15x)(x)\big]-\big[(5x^2)(2)+(15x)(2)\big]$$
$$=(5x^3+15x^2)-(10x^2+30x)$$
$$=5x^3+15x^2-10x^2-30x$$
$$=5x^3+5x^2-30x$$

37. $(2x-1)(x+3)(x+4)$

$$=\big[(2x-1)(x)+(2x-1)(3)\big](x+4)$$
$$=\Big[\big[(2x)(x)-(1)(x)\big]+\big[(2x)(3)-(1)(3)\big]\Big](x+4)$$
$$=\big[(2x^2-x)+(6x-3)\big](x+4)$$
$$=(2x^2+5x-3)(x+4)$$
$$=(2x^2)(x+4)+(5x)(x+4)-(3)(x+4)$$
$$=\big[(2x^2)(x)+(2x^2)(4)\big]+\big[(5x)(x)+(5x)(4)\big]-\big[(3)x+(3)(4)\big]$$
$$=(2x^3+8x^2)+(5x^2+20x)-(3x+12)$$
$$=2x^3+8x^2+5x^2+20x-3x-12$$
$$=2x^3+13x^2+17x-12$$

39. $(m+3)(m+4)=m^2+4m+3m+12$
$$=m^2+7m+12$$

41. $(n-5)(n+8)=n^2+8n-5n-40$
$$=n^2+3n-40$$

43. $(5x+7)(4x-3)=20x^2-15x+28x-21$
$$=20x^2+13x-21$$

45. $(9y-1)(y-7)=9y^2-63y-y+7$
$$=9y^2-64y+7$$

47. $(3a-2b)(4a+7b)=12a^2+21ab-8ab-14b^2$
$$=12a^2+13ab-14b^2$$

49. $(9x-7y)(10x+3y)=90x^2+27xy-70xy-21y^2$
$$=90x^2-43xy-21y^2$$

51. The area of the rectangle is

$A = l \cdot w$

$A = (2x+3)(4x-1)$

$A = (2x+3)(4x)-(2x+3)(1)$

$A = \left[(2x)(4x)+(3)(4x)\right]-(2x+3)$

$A = (8x^2+12x)-(2x+3)$

$A = 8x^2+12x-2x-3$

$A = (8x^2+10x-3)\ \text{cm}^2$

53. The area of the figure is the sum of the area of the rectangle and the square described below.

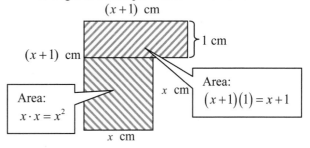

$(x+1)$ cm

1 cm

$(x+1)$ cm

Area:
$(x+1)(1) = x+1$

x cm

Area:
$x \cdot x = x^2$

x cm

The total area of the figure is

$x^2+(x+1) = (x^2+x+1)\ \text{cm}^2$

55. The area of the triangle is

$A = \dfrac{1}{2}b \cdot h$

$A = \dfrac{1}{2}(4x-2)(2x-1)$

$A = \left(\left(\dfrac{1}{2}\right)(4x)-\left(\dfrac{1}{2}\right)(2)\right)(2x-1)$

$A = (2x-1)(2x-1)$

$A = (2x-1)(2x)-(2x-1)(1)$

$A = \left[(2x)(2x)-(1)(2x)\right]-(2x-1)$

$A = (4x^2-2x)-(2x-1)$

$A = 4x^2-2x-2x+1$

$A = (4x^2-4x+1)\ \text{cm}^2$

57. The area of the shaded region is equivalent to the area of the rectangle minus the area of the triangle.

$A = (2x+1)(x+1)-\dfrac{1}{2}(x)(x+1)$

$= \left[(2x+1)(x)+(2x+1)(1)\right]-\dfrac{1}{2}x^2-\dfrac{1}{2}x$

$= (2x^2+x+2x+1)-\dfrac{1}{2}x^2-\dfrac{1}{2}x$

$= \left(\dfrac{3}{2}x^2+\dfrac{5}{2}x+1\right)\text{cm}^2$

59. Since the areas of the semicircles are the same, the area of the figure is equal to the length times the width. Thus the area is

$A = (2x+3)(2x-1)$

$A = (2x+3)(2x)-(2x+3)(1)$

$A = \left[(2x)(2x)+(3)(2x)\right]-(2x+3)$

$A = \left[(2x)(2x)+(3)(2x)\right]-(2x+3)$

$A = (4x^2+6x)-(2x+3)$

$A = 4x^2+6x-2x-3$

$A = (4x^2+4x-3)\ \text{cm}^2$

61. The volume of the box is

$V = x(x+1)(x+5)$

$= x\left[(x+1)(x+5)\right]$

$= x\left[(x+1)x+(x+1)5\right]$

$= x\left[(x^2+x)+(5x+5)\right]$

$= x(x^2+x+5x+5)$

$= x(x^2+6x+5)$

$= (x^3+6x^2+5x)\text{cm}^3$

63.

x	Y_1	Y_2
-3	117	96
-2	50	36
-1	7	0
0	-12	-12
1	-7	0
2	22	36
3	75	96

Conclusion: $Y_1 \neq Y_2$

65.

x	Y_1	Y_2
-3	5	5
-2	0	0
-1	-3	-3
0	-4	-4
1	-3	-3
2	0	0
3	5	5

Conclusion: $Y_1 = Y_2$

67. **a.** $5v(8v-7) = (5v)(8v) - (5v)(7) = 40v^2 - 35v$

b. $(5v)(8v) - (5v)(7) = 5v(8v-7)$

69. **a.** $2mn(m^2 - mn + 5n^2)$

$= (2mn)(m^2) - (2mn)(mn) + (2mn)(5n^2)$

$= 2m^3n - 2m^2n^2 + 10mn^3$

b. $(2mn)(m^2) - (2mn)(mn) + (2mn)(5n^2)$

$= 2mn(m^2 - mn + 5n^2)$

71. **a.** $x(x-3) + 2(x-3)$

$= \left[(x)(x) - (x)(3)\right] + \left[(2)(x) - (2)(3)\right]$

$= x^2 - 3x + 2x - 6$

$= x^2 - x - 6$

b. $x(x-3) + 2(x-3) = (x-3)(x+2)$

73. **a.** $3x(5x-2) - 4(5x-2)$

$= \left[(3x)(5x) - (3x)(2)\right] - \left[(4)(5x) - (4)(2)\right]$

$= (15x^2 - 6x) - (20x - 8)$

$= 15x^2 - 6x - 20x + 8$

$= 15x^2 - 26x + 8$

b. $3x(5x-2) - 4(5x-2) = (5x-2)(3x-4)$

75. $(5 - 2x^2)(3x^2 + 4)$

$= (5 - 2x^2)(3x^2) + (5 - 2x^2)(4)$

$= \left[(5)(3x^2) - (2x^2)(3x^2)\right] + \left[(5)(4) - (2x^2)(4)\right]$

$= (15x^2 - 6x^4) + (20 - 8x^2)$

$= -6x^4 + 15x^2 - 8x^2 + 20$

$= -6x^4 + 7x^2 + 20$

77. $(x + 4 - x^2)(5 - x + x^2)$

$= (x + 4 - x^2)(5) - (x + 4 - x^2)(x) + (x + 4 - x^2)(x^2)$

$= \left[x(5) + 4(5) - x^2(5)\right] - \left[x(x) + 4(x) - x^2(x)\right] + \left[x(x^2) + 4(x^2) - x^2(x^2)\right]$

$= (5x + 20 - 5x^2) - (x^2 + 4x - x^3) + (x^3 + 4x^2 - x^4)$

$= 5x + 20 - 5x^2 - x^2 - 4x + x^3 + x^3 + 4x^2 - x^4$

$= -x^4 + x^3 + x^3 - 5x^2 - x^2 + 4x^2 + 5x - 4x + 20$

$= -x^4 + 2x^3 - 2x^2 + x + 20$

79. $(v+5)^2$

$= (v+5)(v+5)$

$= (v+5)(v)+(v+5)(5)$

$= [v(v)+5(v)]+[v(5)+5(5)]$

$= (v^2+5v)+(5v+25)$

$= v^2+10v+25$

81 $(x+2)^3$

$= (x+2)(x+2)(x+2)$

$= [(x+2)(x)+(x+2)(2)](x+2)$

$= [(x(x)+2(x))+(x(2)+2(2))](x+2)$

$= [(x^2+2x)+(2x+4)](x+2)$

$= (x^2+4x+4)(x+2)$

$= (x^2)(x+2)+(4x)(x+2)+(4)(x+2)$

$= [(x^2)x+(x^2)2]+[(4x)x+(4x)2]+[(4)x+(4)2]$

$= (x^3+2x^2)+(4x^2+8x)+(4x+8)$

$= x^3+2x^2+4x^2+8x+4x+8$

$= x^3+6x^2+12x+8$

83. $V = (24-2x)(12-2x)(x)$

$= (288-48x-24x+4x^2)(x)$

$= (288-72x+4x^2)(x)$

$= 288x-72x^2+4x^3$

$= 4x^3-72x^2+288x$

85. $A = \pi(x+15)^2 - \pi(15)^2$

$= \pi(x+15)(x+15) - \pi(15)^2$

$= \pi(x^2+15x+15x+225) - \pi(225)$

$= \pi(x^2+30x+225) - \pi(225)$

$= \pi x^2+30\pi x+225\pi - 225\pi$

$= \pi x^2+30\pi x$

87. **a.** The revenue is the product of the number of units and the price per unit. Thus

$$R(x) = x(280-2x)$$
$$= 280x-2x^2$$
$$= -2x^2+280x$$

b.

x	$R(x) = -2x^2 + 280x$
40	$-2(40)^2 + 280(40) = 8000$
45	$-2(45)^2 + 280(45) = 8550$
50	$-2(50)^2 + 280(50) = 9000$
55	$-2(55)^2 + 280(55) = 9350$
60	$-2(60)^2 + 280(60) = 9600$
65	$-2(65)^2 + 280(65) = 9750$
70	$-2(70)^2 + 280(70) = 9800$

c. $R(50) = -2(50)^2 + 280(50) = \$9,000$; When the price is \$50 per unit the revenue will be \$9000.

Cumulative Review

1. $\dfrac{5}{12} + \dfrac{3}{10} = \dfrac{5}{12} \cdot \dfrac{5}{5} + \dfrac{3}{10} \cdot \dfrac{6}{6} = \dfrac{25}{60} + \dfrac{18}{60} = \dfrac{43}{60}$

2. $\dfrac{5}{12} \cdot \dfrac{3}{10} = \dfrac{\overset{1}{\cancel{5}}}{\underset{4}{\cancel{12}}} \cdot \dfrac{\overset{1}{\cancel{3}}}{\underset{2}{\cancel{10}}} = \dfrac{1 \cdot 1}{4 \cdot 2} = \dfrac{1}{8}$

3. Using the points: $(0, -1)$ and $(4, 1)$ we can determine that the slope of the line is

$$m = \frac{1-(-1)}{4-0} = \frac{2}{4} = \frac{1}{2}$$

Also, we know that the y-intercept is $(0, -1)$. Thus using the slope-intercept form of a line we can write the equation of the line as $y = \frac{1}{2}x - 1$

4. **a.** $|x-5| = 9$ is equivalent to

$x - 5 = 9$ or $x - 5 = -9$

$x = 14$ $x = -4$

Solution: $x = 14$ or $x = -4$

b. $|x-5| \le 9$ is equivalent to

$-9 \le x - 5 \le 9$

$-4 \le x \le 14$

Solution: $[-4, 14]$

c. $|x-5| > 9$ is equivalent to

$x - 5 < -9$ or $x - 5 > 9$

$x < -4$ $x > 14$

Solution: $(-\infty, -4) \cup (14, \infty)$

5. $\left(\dfrac{-12x^8 y^{-3}}{20x^{-2}y^6}\right)^{-2} = \left(\dfrac{-\overset{3}{\cancel{12}} x^8 x^2}{\underset{5}{\cancel{20}} y^6 y^3}\right)^{-2} = \left(\dfrac{-3x^{8+2}}{5y^{6+3}}\right)^{-2} = \left(\dfrac{-3x^{10}}{5y^9}\right)^{-2} = \left(\dfrac{5y^9}{-3x^{10}}\right)^2 = \dfrac{5^2\left(y^9\right)^2}{(-3)^2\left(x^{10}\right)^2} = \dfrac{25y^{9\cdot2}}{9x^{10\cdot2}} = \dfrac{25y^{18}}{9x^{20}}$

Section 5.6: Special Products of Binomials

Quick Review 5.6

1. $(3+7)^2 = 10^2 = 100$

2. $3^2 + 7^2 = 9 + 49 = 58$

3. $5^2 - 3^2 + (5-3)^2 = 25 - 9 + 2^2 = 25 - 9 + 4 = 20$

4. $(x+4)(x-5) = x^2 - x - 20$

5. $(2x+3)(2x+5) = 4x^2 + 16x + 15$

Exercises 5.6

1. $(7a+1)(7a-1) = (7a)^2 - (1)^2 = 49a^2 - 1$

3. $(z-10)(z+10) = (z)^2 - (10)^2 = z^2 - 100$

5. $(2w-3)(2w+3) = (2w)^2 - (3)^2 = 4w^2 - 9$

7. $(9a+4b)(9a-4b) = (9a)^2 - (4b)^2 = 81a^2 - 16b^2$

9 $(4x-11y)(4x+11y) = (4x)^2 - (11y)^2$
$= 16x^2 - 121y^2$

11. $(x^2-2)(x^2+2) = (x^2)^2 - (2)^2 = x^4 - 4$

13 $(4m+1)^2 = (4m)^2 + 2(4m)(1) + (1)^2$
$= 16m^2 + 8m + 1$

15. $(n-9)^2 = (n)^2 - 2(n)(9) + (9)^2$
$= n^2 - 18n + 81$

17. $(3t+2)^2 = (3t)^2 + 2(3t)(2) + (2)^2$
$= 9t^2 + 12t + 4$

19. $(5v-8)^2 = (5v)^2 - 2(5v)(8) + (8)^2$
$= 25v^2 - 80v + 64$

21. $\left(4x+5y\right)^2 = \left(4x\right)^2 + 2\left(4x\right)\left(5y\right)+\left(5y\right)^2$
$= 16x^2 + 40xy + 25y^2$

23. $\left(6a-11b\right)^2 = \left(6a\right)^2 - 2\left(6a\right)\left(11b\right)+\left(11b\right)^2$
$= 36a^2 - 132ab + 121b^2$

25. $\left(a+bc\right)^2 = \left(a\right)^2 + 2\left(a\right)\left(bc\right)+\left(bc\right)^2$
$= a^2 + 2abc + b^2c^2$

27. $\left(x^2-3\right)^2 = \left(x^2\right)^2 - 2\left(x^2\right)\left(3\right)+\left(3\right)^2$
$= x^4 - 6x^2 + 9$

29. $\left(x^2+y\right)^2 = \left(x^2\right)^2 + 2\left(x^2\right)\left(y\right)+\left(y\right)^2$
$= x^4 + 2x^2y + y^2$

31. **a.** $5x-6\left(5x+6\right) = 5x - 6\left(5x\right)-6\left(6\right)$
$= 5x - 30x - 36 = -25x - 36$

b. $\left(5x-6\right)\left(5x+6\right) = \left(5x\right)^2 - \left(6\right)^2 = 25x^2 - 36$

33. **a.** $\left(4x-9\right)^2 = \left(4x\right)^2 - 2\left(4x\right)\left(9\right)+\left(9\right)^2$
$= 16x^2 - 72x + 81$

b. $\left(4x\right)^2 - \left(9\right)^2 = 16x^2 - 81$

35. $\left(v+7\right)^2 - \left(v^2-7^2\right) = \left(v^2+14v+49\right)-\left(v^2-49\right)$
$= v^2 + 14v + 49 - v^2 + 49$
$= 14v + 98$

37. $\left(2x+y\right)^2 - \left[\left(2x\right)^2 + y^2\right]$
$= \left(4x^2 + 4xy + y^2\right) - 4x^2 - y^2$
$= 4x^2 + 4xy + y^2 - 4x^2 - y^2$
$= 4xy$

39. $\left(v+w\right)\left(v-w\right)-\left(v-w\right)^2$
$= \left(v^2 - w^2\right) - \left(v^2 - 2vw + w^2\right)$
$= v^2 - w^2 - v^2 + 2vw - w^2$
$= -2w^2 + 2vw = 2vw - 2w^2$

41. $\left(a-b\right)^2 - \left(b-a\right)^2 = \left(a^2 - 2ab + b^2\right) - \left(b^2 - 2ab + a^2\right) = a^2 - 2ab + b^2 - b^2 + 2ab - a^2 = 0$

43. $2\left(3x-2y\right)^2 - \left(3x+2y\right)^2 = 2\left[\left(3x\right)^2 - 2\left(3x\right)\left(2y\right)+\left(2y\right)^2\right]-\left[\left(3x\right)^2 + 2\left(3x\right)\left(2y\right)+\left(2y\right)^2\right]$
$= 2\left(9x^2 - 12xy + 4y^2\right) - \left(9x^2 + 12xy + 4y^2\right)$
$= 18x^2 - 24xy + 8y^2 - 9x^2 - 12xy - 4y^2$
$= 18x^2 - 9x^2 - 24xy - 12xy + 8y^2 - 4y^2$
$= 9x^2 - 36xy + 4y^2$

45. $\left(3x+7y\right)^2 = \left(3x\right)^2 + 2\left(3x\right)\left(7y\right)+\left(7y\right)^2$
$= 9x^2 + 42xy + 49y^2$

47. $\left(x+8\right)^2 - \left(x-6\right)^2$
$= \left(x^2 + 16x + 64\right) - \left(x^2 - 12x + 36\right)$
$= x^2 + 16x + 64 - x^2 + 12x - 36$
$= 28x + 28$

49. $\left(a^2+1\right)\left[\left(a+1\right)\left(a-1\right)\right]$
$= \left(a^2+1\right)\left(a^2-1\right)$
$= a^4 - 1$

51.

x	Y_1	Y_2
-3	35	35
-2	15	15
-1	3	3
0	-1	-1
1	3	3
2	15	15
3	35	35

Conclusion: $Y_1 = Y_2$

53.

x	Y_1	Y_2
-3	9	45
-2	1	25
-1	1	13
0	9	9
1	25	13
2	49	25
3	81	45

Conclusion: $Y_1 \neq Y_2$

55. **Expand:** $(9x-1)(9x+1) = (9x)^2 - (1)^2 = 81x^2 - 1$

Factor: $81x^2 - 1 = (9x)^2 - (1)^2 = (9x-1)(9x+1)$

57. **Expand:** $(10w-3x)^2 = (10w)^2 - 2(10w)(3x) + (3x)^2 = 100w^2 - 60wx + 9x^2$

Factor: $100w^2 - 60wx + 9x^2 = (10w)^2 - 2(10w)(3x) + (3x)^2 = (10w-3x)^2$

Cumulative Review

1. A   **2.** C   **3.** B

4. If the line is parallel to $y = -\dfrac{2}{5}x + 7$ then the slope must be $m = -\dfrac{2}{5}$. using the point-slope form of a line with the given point we obtain:

$$y - y_1 = m(x - x_1)$$
$$y - 3 = -\frac{2}{5}(x - (-2))$$
$$y - 3 = -\frac{2}{5}(x + 2)$$
$$y - 3 = -\frac{2}{5}x - \frac{4}{5}$$
$$y = -\frac{2}{5}x + \frac{11}{5}$$

5. If the line is parallel to $y = -\dfrac{2}{5}x + 7$ then the slope must be $m = \dfrac{5}{2}$. using the point-slope form of a line with the given point we obtain:

$$y - y_1 = m(x - x_1)$$
$$y - 3 = \frac{5}{2}(x - (-2))$$
$$y - 3 = \frac{5}{2}(x + 2)$$
$$y - 3 = \frac{5}{2}x + 5$$
$$y = \frac{5}{2}x + 8$$

Section 5.7: Dividing Polynomials

Quick Review 5.7

1. $\dfrac{56}{24} = \dfrac{\cancel{8} \cdot 7}{\cancel{8} \cdot 3} = \dfrac{7}{3}$

2. $\dfrac{25x^{10}}{10x^5} = \dfrac{\overset{5}{\cancel{25}}\, x^{10-5}}{\underset{2}{\cancel{10}}} = \dfrac{5x^5}{2}$

3. $-3x^2 y^5 (4x^2 - 5xy + 7y^2)$

$= \left(-3x^2 y^5\right)4x^2 - \left(-3x^2 y^5\right)5xy + \left(-3x^2 y^5\right)7y^2$

$= -12x^4 y^5 + 15x^3 y^6 - 21x^2 y^7$

4. $(4x+3)(2x-7) - 9 = 8x^2 - 22x - 21 - 9$

$= 8x^2 - 22x - 30$

5. $\dfrac{621}{57} = \dfrac{\cancel{3} \cdot 207}{\cancel{3} \cdot 19} = \dfrac{207}{19} = \dfrac{190}{19} + \dfrac{17}{19} = 10 + \dfrac{17}{19} = 10\dfrac{17}{19}$

Exercises 5.7

1. $\dfrac{18x^3}{6x} = 3x^{3-1} = 3x^2$

3. $\dfrac{35a^3b^2}{-7ab} = -5a^{3-1}b^{2-1} = -5a^2b$

5. $\dfrac{15a^2 - 20a}{5a} = \dfrac{15a^2}{5a} - \dfrac{20a}{5a} = 3a - 4$

7. $\dfrac{9a^3 - 15a^2 + 6a}{3a^2} = \dfrac{9a^3}{3a^2} - \dfrac{15a^2}{3a^2} + \dfrac{6a}{3a^2}$

   $\quad = 3a - 5 + \dfrac{2}{a}$

9. $\dfrac{16m^4 - 8m^3 + 10m^2 + 6m}{2m} = \dfrac{16m^4}{2m} - \dfrac{8m^3}{2m} + \dfrac{10m^2}{2m} + \dfrac{6m}{2m} = 8m^3 - 4m^2 + 5m + 3$

11. $\dfrac{45x^5y^2 - 54x^4y^5 + 99x^2y^4}{9x^2y^2} = \dfrac{45x^5y^2}{9x^2y^2} - \dfrac{54x^4y^5}{9x^2y^2} + \dfrac{99x^2y^4}{9x^2y^2} = 5x^3 - 6x^2y^3 + 11y^2$

13. $\dfrac{54v^2 - 36v^4 + 12v - 18v^3}{-6v} = \dfrac{54v^2}{-6v} + \dfrac{-36v^4}{-6v} + \dfrac{12}{-6v} + \dfrac{-18v^3}{-6v} = -9v + 6v^3 - \dfrac{2}{v} + 3v^2 = 6v^3 + 3v^2 - 9v - \dfrac{2}{v}$

15. $\left(35v^3w - 7v^2w - 28vw^2\right) \div 7vw = \dfrac{35v^3w - 7v^2w - 28vw^2}{7vw} = \dfrac{35v^3w}{7vw} - \dfrac{7v^2w}{7vw} - \dfrac{28vw^2}{7vw} = 5v^2 - v - 4w$

17. $\left(100x^{20} - 50x^{12} + 30x^9\right) \div 10x^9 = \dfrac{100x^{20} - 50x^{12} + 30x^9}{10x^9} = \dfrac{100x^{20}}{10x^9} - \dfrac{50x^{12}}{10x^9} + \dfrac{30x^9}{10x^9} = 10x^{11} - 5x^3 + 3$

19.
$$
\begin{array}{r}
x + 7 \\
x+2{\overline{\smash{\big)}\,x^2 + 9x + 14}} \\
\underline{x^2 + 2x} \\
7x + 14 \\
\underline{7x + 14} \\
0
\end{array}
$$
quotient

   Check: $(x+2)(x+7) = x^2 + 7x + 2x + 14$
   $\qquad\qquad\quad = x^2 + 9x + 14$

21. $\dfrac{v^2 + 2v - 24}{v - 4};$
$$
\begin{array}{r}
v + 6 \\
v-4{\overline{\smash{\big)}\,v^2 + 2v - 24}} \\
\underline{v^2 - 4v} \\
6v - 24 \\
\underline{6v - 24} \\
0
\end{array}
$$
quotient

   Check: $(v-4)(v+6) = v^2 + 6v - 4v - 24$
   $\qquad\qquad\quad = v^2 + 2v - 24$

23. $\dfrac{4m^3 - 9m^2 + 10m + 7}{m-3}$;

quotient

$$\begin{array}{r} 4m^2 \;\;+3m+19 \\ m-3\overline{)4m^3 - 9m^2 + 10m + 7} \\ \underline{4m^3 - 12m^2} \\ 3m^2 + 10m \\ \underline{3m^2 \;\;-9m} \\ 19m + 7 \\ \underline{19m - 57} \\ 64 \end{array}$$

$$\dfrac{4m^3 - 9m^2 + 10m + 7}{m-3} = 4m^2 \;\;+3m+19+\dfrac{64}{m-3}$$

25. $\dfrac{6w^2 + w - 12}{2w+3}$;

quotient

$$\begin{array}{r} 3w \;\;-4 \\ 2w+3\overline{)6w^2 + w - 12} \\ \underline{6w^2 + 9w} \\ -8v - 12 \\ \underline{-8v - 12} \\ 0 \end{array}$$

27. $\dfrac{20m^2 - 43m + 14}{5m-2}$;

quotient

$$\begin{array}{r} 4m \;\;-7 \\ 5m-2\overline{)20m^2 - 43m + 14} \\ \underline{20m^2 \;\;-8m} \\ -35m + 14 \\ \underline{-35m + 14} \\ 0 \end{array}$$

29. $\dfrac{63y^2 - 130y + 63}{7y-9}$;

quotient

$$\begin{array}{r} 9y \;\;-7 \\ 7y-9\overline{)63y^2 - 130y + 63} \\ \underline{63y^2 \;\;-81y} \\ -49y + 63 \\ \underline{-49y + 63} \\ 0 \end{array}$$

31. $\dfrac{30x^2 - 45x^3 + 10x + 35x^4}{5x} = \dfrac{30x^2}{5x} - \dfrac{45x^3}{5x} + \dfrac{10x}{5x} + \dfrac{35x^4}{5x} = 6x - 9x^2 + 2 + 7x^3 = 7x^3 - 9x^2 + 6x + 2$

33.
quotient
$$\begin{array}{r} x-7 \\ x-5\overline{)x^2 - 12x + 35} \\ \underline{x^2 \;\;-5x} \\ -7x + 35 \\ \underline{-7x + 35} \\ 0 \end{array}$$

35.
quotient
$$\begin{array}{r} 3a \;\;+2 \\ 2a-5\overline{)6a^2 - 11a - 10} \\ \underline{6a^2 - 15a} \\ 4a - 10 \\ \underline{4a - 10} \\ 0 \end{array}$$

37.
quotient
$$\begin{array}{r} 3v^2 + 2v + 4 \\ v-2\overline{)3v^3 - 4v^2 + 0v - 8} \\ \underline{3v^2 - 6v^2} \\ 2v^2 + 0v \\ \underline{2v^2 - 4v} \\ 4v - 8 \\ \underline{4v - 8} \\ 0 \end{array}$$

39.
quotient
$$\begin{array}{r} x^2 + 2x + 4 \\ x-2\overline{)x^3 + 0x^2 + 0x - 8} \\ \underline{x^3 - 2x^2} \\ 2x^2 + 0x \\ \underline{2x^2 - 4x} \\ 4x - 8 \\ \underline{4x - 8} \\ 0 \end{array}$$

41.

$$\begin{array}{r} 4y^2 + 8y \ \ +9 \\ 5y-6\overline{)20y^3 + 16y^2 - 3y - 54} \\ \underline{20y^3 - 24y^2} \\ 40y^2 - 3y \\ \underline{40y^2 - 48y} \\ 45y - 54 \\ \underline{45y - 54} \\ 0 \end{array}$$

quotient

43.

quotient

$$\begin{array}{r} 7x^2 \ \ \ \ -9 \\ 3x^2 - x - 5\overline{)21x^4 - 7x^3 - 62x^2 + 9x + 45} \\ \underline{21x^4 - 7x^3 - 35x^2} \\ -27x^2 + 9x + 45 \\ \underline{-27x^2 + 9x + 45} \\ 0 \end{array}$$

45. The area of a rectangle is $A = l \cdot w$. Thus
$$w = \frac{A}{l} = \frac{4x^2 + 4x - 3}{2x + 3} = (2x - 1) \text{ cm}. \text{ Since}$$

$$\begin{array}{r} 2x - 1 \\ 2x + 3\overline{)4x^2 + 4x - 3} \\ \underline{4x^2 + 6x} \\ -2x - 3 \\ \underline{-2x - 3} \\ 0 \end{array}$$

47. The area of a triangle is $A = \frac{1}{2}b \cdot h$. Thus
$$h = 2\left(\frac{A}{b}\right) = 2\left(\frac{12x^2 - 17x - 7}{4x - 7}\right).$$
$$= 2(3x + 1) = (6x + 2) \text{ cm}$$

Since
$$\begin{array}{r} 3x + 1 \\ 4x - 7\overline{)12x^2 - 17x - 7} \\ \underline{12x^2 - 21x} \\ 4x - 7 \\ \underline{4x - 7} \\ 0 \end{array}$$

49. The volume of a box is $V = l \cdot w \cdot h$. Thus
$$h = \frac{V}{w \cdot l} = \frac{8x^3 + 14x^2 + 3x}{x(4x + 1)} = \frac{8x^2 + 14x + 3}{4x + 1}.$$
$$= (2x + 3) \text{ cm}$$

Since
$$\begin{array}{r} 2x + 3 \\ 4x + 1\overline{)8x^2 + 14x + 3} \\ \underline{8x^2 \ + 2x} \\ 12x + 3 \\ \underline{12x + 3} \\ 0 \end{array}$$

51.

x	Y_1	Y_2
-3	11	11
-2	9	9
-1	7	7
0	5	5
1	3	3
2	1	1
3	*ERROR*	-1

Conclusion:
$$Y_1 = Y_2 \ (x \neq 3)$$

53.

x	Y_1	Y_2
-3	0	-6
-2	1	-5
-1	2	-4
0	3	-3
1	4	-2
2	5	-1
3	*ERROR*	0

Conclusion: $Y_1 \neq Y_2$

55. Let $P(x)$ be the polynomial. If $\dfrac{P(x)}{x + 3} = x^2 - 3x - 5$, then
$$P(x) = (x^2 - 3x - 5)(x + 3)$$
$$= (x^2)(x + 3) - (3x)(x + 3) - (5)(x + 3)$$
$$= [(x^2)x + (x^2)3] - [(3x)x + (3x)3] - [(5)x + (5)3]$$
$$= (x^3 + 3x^2) - (3x^2 + 9x) - (5x + 15)$$
$$= x^3 + 3x^2 - 3x^2 - 9x - 5x - 15$$
$$= x^3 - 14x - 15$$

57. Let $P(x)$ be the polynomial.

$$\frac{6x^2 - 2x - 20}{P(x)} = 2x - 4$$

$$P(x)\left(\frac{6x^2 - 2x - 20}{P(x)}\right) = P(x)(2x - 4)$$

$$6x^2 - 2x - 20 = P(x)(2x - 4)$$

$$P(x) = \frac{6x^2 - 2x - 20}{2x - 4}$$

To find $P(x)$, use long division.

$$
\begin{array}{r}
3x + 5 \\
2x - 4 \overline{)6x^2 - 2x - 20} \\
\underline{6x^2 - 12x} \\
10x - 20 \\
\underline{10x - 20} \\
0
\end{array}
$$

$\boxed{P(x) = 3x + 5}$

59. **a.** If a fourth degree trinomial in x is added to a second degree binomial in x the degree of the sum is fourth degree polynomial.
 b. If a fourth degree trinomial in x is multiplied by a second degree binomial in x the degree of the product is sixth degree polynomial.
 c. If a fourth degree trinomial in x is divided by a second degree binomial in x the degree of the quotient is a second degree polynomial.

61. Let $P(x)$ be the polynomial.

$$\frac{P(x)}{2x + 3} = x + 2 + \frac{4}{2x + 3}$$

$$(2x + 3)\left(\frac{P(x)}{2x + 3}\right) = \left(x + 2 + \frac{4}{2x + 3}\right)(2x + 3)$$

$$P(x) = \left[(x)(2x + 3) + (2)(2x + 3) + 4\right]$$

$$P(x) = \left[(x)(2x) + (x)(3)\right] + \left[(2)(2x) + (2)(3)\right] + 4$$

$$P(x) = \left(2x^2 + 3x\right) + (4x + 6) + 4$$

$$P(x) = 2x^2 + 7x + 10$$

63. Use long division to determine the remaining factor.

$$
\begin{array}{r}
4x + 5 \\
7x - 6 \overline{)28x^2 + 11x - 30} \\
\underline{28x^2 - 24x} \\
35x - 30 \\
\underline{35x - 30} \\
0
\end{array}
$$

Remaining factor.

65. a. Use long division to determine the remaining factor.

$$2x+3\overline{)3x^2-19x+20 \atop 6x^3-29x^2-17x+60}$$

Remaining factor.

$$\underline{6x^3+\ 9x^2}$$
$$-38x^2-17x$$
$$\underline{-38x^2-57x}$$
$$40x+60$$
$$\underline{40x+60}$$
$$0$$

b. To complete the equation we must use long division again. This time use the factor found in part **a.** as the dividend and the additional factor that was given as the divisor.

$$3x-4\overline{)x\ -\ 5 \atop 3x^2-19x+20}$$

This is the last factor in the equation.

$$\underline{3x^2-\ 4x}$$
$$-15x+20$$
$$\underline{-15x+20}$$
$$0$$

Finally we can write:
$$6x^3-29x^2-17x+60=(2x+3)(3x-4)(x-5)$$

67. The total number of entries in an array is the product of the number of rows and the number of columns. Thus the number of columns is determined by dividing the total number of entries by the number of rows.

Number of Columns: $\dfrac{30k^2+39k+12}{6k+3}=5k+4$.

Since

$$6k+3\overline{)5k\ +4 \atop 30k^2+39k+12}$$
$$\underline{30k\ +15k}$$
$$24k+12$$
$$\underline{24k+12}$$
$$0$$

69. a. $A(x)=\dfrac{C(x)}{x}=\dfrac{125x+960}{x}=\dfrac{125x}{x}+\dfrac{960}{x}=125+\dfrac{960}{x}$

b. $A(50)=125+\dfrac{960}{50}=144.20$; The average cost of producing 50 units is \$144.20 per unit.

71. a. $A(x)=\dfrac{C(x)}{x}=\dfrac{8x+1200}{x}=\dfrac{8x}{x}+\dfrac{1200}{x}=8+\dfrac{1200}{x}$

b. $C(200)=8(200)+1200=2800$; The cost of producing 200 chairs is \$2,800.

c. $A(200)=8+\dfrac{1200}{200}=14$; The average cost of producing 200 chairs is \$14.00 per chair.

d. $C(250)=8(250)+1200=3200$; The cost of producing 250 chairs is \$3,200.

e. $A(250)=8+\dfrac{1200}{250}=12.80$; The average cost of producing 250 chairs is \$12.80 per chair.

f. The cost increased by \$400.

g. The average cost decreased by \$1.20 per chair.

Cumulative Review

1. The systems is a consistent system of independent equations since the slopes of the lines are different and there will be exactly one intersection point. Answer: **A**

2. The system is an inconsistent system since the lines are parallel and do not intersect. Answer: **C**

3. The system is a consistent system of dependent equations since the lines are identical and intersect at infinitely many points. Answer: **B**

4.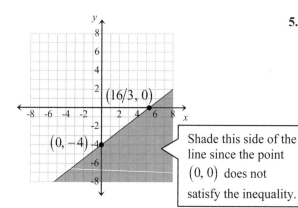

5. $(2x-5)^2 = (2x)^2 - 2(2x)(5) + (5)^2$
$$= 4x^2 - 20x + 25$$

Review Exercises for Chapter 5

1. a. $xyyy = xy^3$

    b. $(xy)(xy)(xy) = (xy)^3$

    c. $xx + yy = x^2 + y^2$

    d. $(x+y)(x+y) = (x+y)^2$

2. a. $x^2 + y^2 = xx + yy$

    b. $(x+y)^2 = (x+y)(x+y)$

    c. $-x^4 = -xxxx$

    d. $(-x)^4 = (-x)(-x)(-x)(-x)$

3. a. $3^2 = 9$

    b. $3^{-2} = \dfrac{1}{3^2} = \dfrac{1}{9}$

    c. $-3^2 = -9$

    d. $(-3)^{-2} = \dfrac{1}{(-3)^2} = \dfrac{1}{9}$

4. a. $3^0 = 1$

    b. $0^3 = 0$

    c. $3^0 + 4^0 = 1 + 1 = 2$

    d. $(3+4)^0 = 7^0 = 1$

5. a. $\left(\dfrac{1}{2}\right)^{-1} + \left(\dfrac{1}{3}\right)^{-1} = \dfrac{2}{1} + \dfrac{3}{1} = 5$

    b. $\left(\dfrac{1}{2} + \dfrac{1}{3}\right)^{-1} = \left(\dfrac{3}{6} + \dfrac{2}{6}\right)^{-1} = \left(\dfrac{5}{6}\right)^{-1} = \dfrac{6}{5}$

    c. $\left(\dfrac{2}{3}\right)^{-1} = \dfrac{3}{2}$

    d. $\dfrac{2^{-1}}{3} = \dfrac{1}{3 \cdot 2^1} = \dfrac{1}{6}$

6. a. $-1^6 = -1$

    b. $(-1)^6 = 1$

    c. $6^{-1} = \dfrac{1}{6}$

    d. $-6^{-1} = -\dfrac{1}{6}$

7.   **a.** $x^3 + x^3 = 2x^3$

　　b. $x^3 x^3 = x^{3+3} = x^6$

　　c. $\dfrac{x^3}{x^3} = x^{3-3} = x^0 = 1$

　　d. $x^3 - x^3 = 0$

8.   **a.** $10^2 = 100$

　　b. $(-10)^2 = 100$

　　c. $10^{-2} = \dfrac{1}{10^2} = \dfrac{1}{100}$

　　d. $-10^{-2} = -\dfrac{1}{10^2} = -\dfrac{1}{100}$

9.   **a.** $5^0 + 6^0 + 7^0 = 1 + 1 + 1 = 3$

　　b. $(5+6)^0 + 7^0 = 11^0 + 1 = 1 + 1 = 2$

　　c. $(5+6+7)^0 = 18^0 = 1$

　　d. $0^5 + 0^6 + 0^7 = 0$

10.   **a.** $2x^0 + 3y^0 + 4z^0 = 2(1) + 3(1) + 4(1) = 9$

　　b. $(2x + 3y + 4z)^0 = (9z)^0 = 1$

　　c. $(2x)^0 + (3y)^0 + (4z)^0 = 1 + 1 + 1 = 3$

　　d. $2x^0 + (3y + 5z)^0 = 2(1) + 1 = 3$

11.   **a.** $x^2 x^5 = x^{2+5} = x^7$

　　b. $\dfrac{x^5}{x^2} = x^{5-2} = x^3$

　　c. $\left(x^2\right)^5 = x^{2 \cdot 5} = x^{10}$

　　d. $\left(\dfrac{x^5}{x}\right)^2 = \left(x^{5-1}\right)^2 = \left(x^4\right)^2 = x^{4 \cdot 2} = x^8$

12.   **a.** $\left(4x^3 y^2\right)\left(12x^5 y^4\right) = (4)(12)\left(x^3 x^5\right)\left(y^2 y^4\right)$
$$= 48x^{3+5} y^{2+4} = 48x^8 y^6$$

　　b. $\dfrac{12x^5 y^4}{4x^3 y^2} = 3x^{5-3} y^{4-2} = 3x^2 y^2$

　　c. $\left(4x^3 y^2\right)^2 = 4^2 x^{3 \cdot 2} y^{2 \cdot 2} = 16x^6 y^4$

　　b. $\left(\dfrac{12x^5 y^4}{4x^3 y^2}\right)^3 = \left(3x^{5-3} y^{4-2}\right)^3 = \left(3x^2 y^2\right)^3$
$$= 3^3 x^{2 \cdot 3} y^{2 \cdot 3} = 27x^6 y^6$$

13.   **a.** $-x^2 = -(3)^2 = -9$

　　b. $(-x)^2 = (-3)^2 = 9$

14.   **a.** $xy^2 = (3)(4)^2 = (3)(16) = 48$

　　b. $(xy)^2 = (3 \cdot 4)^2 = (12)^2 = 144$

15.   **a.** $x^2 + y^2 = (3)^2 + (4)^2 = 9 + 16 = 25$

　　b. $(x + y)^2 = (3 + 4)^2 = (7)^2 = 49$

16.   **a.** $x^{-1} + y^{-1} = (3)^{-1} + (4)^{-1} = \dfrac{1}{3} + \dfrac{1}{4} = \dfrac{4}{12} + \dfrac{3}{12} = \dfrac{7}{12}$

　　b. $(x + y)^{-1} = (3 + 4)^{-1} = (7)^{-1} = \dfrac{1}{7}$

17.   **a.** $x^0 + y^0 = 3^0 + 4^0 = 1 + 1 = 2$

　　b. $(x + y)^0 = (3 + 4)^0 = 7^0 = 1$

18.   **a.** $\dfrac{x}{y^{-2}} = xy^2 = (3)(4)^2 = 3 \cdot 16 = 48$

　　b. $\left(\dfrac{x}{y}\right)^{-2} = \left(\dfrac{y}{x}\right)^2 = \left(\dfrac{4}{3}\right)^2 = \dfrac{4^2}{3^2} = \dfrac{16}{9}$

19. $\left(5x^2 y^3 z^4\right)\left(6xy^4 z^7\right) = (5)(6)\left(x^2 x\right)\left(y^3 y^4\right)\left(z^4 z^7\right)$
$$= 30x^{2+1} y^{3+4} z^{4+7} = 30x^3 y^7 z^{11}$$

20. $\left(5x^2 y^3 z^4\right)^2 = 5^2 x^{2 \cdot 2} y^{3 \cdot 2} z^{4 \cdot 2} = 25x^4 y^6 z^8$

21. $\dfrac{24a^2 b^4 c^5}{40ab^7 c^3} = \dfrac{3a^{2-1} c^{5-3}}{5b^{7-4}} = \dfrac{3ac^2}{5b^3}$

22. $\left(\dfrac{12m^3}{4n^2}\right)^{-2} = \left(\dfrac{3m^3}{n^2}\right)^{-2} = \left(\dfrac{n^2}{3m^3}\right)^2$
$$= \left(\dfrac{n^2}{3m^3}\right)^2 = \dfrac{n^{2 \cdot 2}}{3^2 m^{3 \cdot 2}} = \dfrac{n^4}{9m^6}$$

23. $\left(3x^2\right)\left(4x^3\right)\left(5x^{11}\right) = \left(3\cdot4\cdot5\right)\left(x^2x^3x^{11}\right)$
$$= 60x^{2+3+11} = 60x^{16}$$

24. $\dfrac{\left(3x^2\right)^4}{9x^5} = \dfrac{3^4\,x^{2\cdot4}}{9x^5} = \dfrac{81x^8}{9x^5} = 9x^{8-5} = 9x^3$

25. $\left(-2x^5\right)^3\left(-5x^3\right)^2 = \left[\left(-2\right)^3 x^{5\cdot3}\right]\left[\left(-5\right)^2 x^{3\cdot2}\right]$
$$= \left(-8x^{15}\right)\left(25x^6\right) = 200x^{15+6}$$
$$= -200x^{21}$$

26. $\left(7y^8\right)\left(8y^{-6}\right) = \left(7\cdot8\right)\left(y^{8+(-6)}\right) = 56y^2$

27. $\dfrac{16w^{-4}}{8w^{-6}} = 2w^{-4-(-6)} = 2w^2$

28. $\left(5m^{-6}\right)^{-4} = 5^{-4}m^{(-6)(-4)} = \dfrac{m^{24}}{5^4} = \dfrac{m^{24}}{625}$

29. $\left(6x\right)^{-3}\left(\dfrac{x}{6}\right)^{-4} = \dfrac{1}{\left(6x\right)^3}\left(\dfrac{6}{x}\right)^4$
$$= \dfrac{1}{6^3\,x^3}\cdot\dfrac{6^4}{x^4} = \dfrac{6^{4-3}}{x^{3+4}} = \dfrac{6}{x^7}$$

30. $\left(\dfrac{x^{188}}{x^{-439}}\right)^0 = 1$

31. $\dfrac{\left(2a^3b^3\right)\left(8a^2b^5\right)}{\left(4ab^2\right)^2} = \dfrac{\left(2\cdot8\right)\left(a^3a^2\right)\left(b^3b^5\right)}{4^2\,a^2b^{2\cdot2}}$
$$= \dfrac{16a^{3+2}b^{3+5}}{16a^2b^4} = \dfrac{a^5b^8}{a^2b^4}$$
$$= a^{5-2}b^{8-4} = a^3b^4$$

32. $\left(x^2y^{-3}z^{-4}\right)^{-2}\left(x^4y^{-1}z^{-2}\right)^{-1}$
$$= \left(x^{(2)(-2)}y^{(-3)(-2)}z^{(-4)(-2)}\right)\left(x^{(4)(-1)}y^{(-1)(-1)}z^{(-2)(-1)}\right)$$
$$= \left(x^{-4}y^6z^8\right)\left(x^{-4}y^1z^2\right) = \left(x^{-4}x^{-4}\right)\left(y^6y^1\right)\left(z^8z^2\right)$$
$$= \left(x^{-4+(-4)}\right)\left(y^{6+1}\right)\left(z^{8+2}\right) = \left(x^{-8}\right)\left(y^7\right)\left(z^{10}\right)$$
$$= \dfrac{y^7z^{10}}{x^8}$$

33. $1.0\times10^{-12} = 0.000000000001$ liter

34. $2.2\times10^4 = 22,000$ droplets per second

35. $5.23\times10^6 = 5,230,000$

36. $5.23\times10^{-6} = 0.00000523$

37. $t = \dfrac{D}{r} = \dfrac{4.5\times10^{12}}{2.99\times10^8} \approx 15,050$ seconds,

or $\dfrac{15,050}{3,600} \approx 4.181$ hours,

or 4 hours and $\left(0.181\right)\left(60\right) \approx 11$ minutes.

38. $(40,010)(0.0000000001989)$
$$\approx \left(4.0\times10^4\right)\left(2.0\times10^{-10}\right) = 8.0\times10^{-6}$$
Answer: **B.**

39. π is a monomial of degree zero.

40. $3x^6 - 17x^2$ is a sixth degree binomial.

41. $-9x^3 + 7x^2 + 8x - 11$ is a third degree polynomial with four terms.

42. $x^5y - 7x^4y^2 + 23x^3y^3$ is a sixth degree trinomial.

43. $11x^4 - 3x^2 + 9x^3 + 7x^5 + 4 - 8x = 7x^5 + 11x^4 + 9x^3 - 3x^2 - 8x + 4$

44. $-7x^5$

45. $x^2 - 3$

46. $\left(7x^2 - 9x + 13\right) + \left(4x^2 + 6x - 11\right)$

$= 7x^2 - 9x + 13 + 4x^2 + 6x - 11$

$= 7x^2 + 4x^2 - 9x + 6x + 13 - 11$

$= 11x^2 - 3x + 2$

47. $\left(9x^3 - 5x^2 - 7\right) - \left(4x^3 + 8x - 11\right)$

$= 9x^3 - 5x^2 - 7 - 4x^3 - 8x + 11$

$= 9x^3 - 4x^3 - 5x^2 - 8x - 7 + 11$

$= 5x^3 - 5x^2 - 8x + 4$

48. $\left(3x^4 - 8x^3 + 7x^2 + 9x - 4\right) + 2\left(2x^4 + 6x^2 + 9\right)$

$= 3x^4 - 8x^3 + 7x^2 + 9x - 4 + 4x^4 + 12x^2 + 18$

$= 3x^4 + 4x^4 - 8x^3 + 7x^2 + 12x^2 + 9x - 4 + 18$

$= 7x^4 - 8x^3 + 19x^2 + 9x + 14$

49. $7x^5 + 9x^3 + 6x - 3 - 3\left(4x^5 - 3x^4 - 7x^3 - x^2 - x + 8\right)$

$= 7x^5 + 9x^3 + 6x - 3 - 12x^5 + 9x^4 + 21x^3 + 3x^2 + 3x - 24$

$= 7x^5 - 12x^5 + 9x^4 + 9x^3 + 21x^3 + 3x^2 + 6x + 3x - 3 - 24$

$= -5x^5 + 9x^4 + 30x^3 + 3x^2 + 9x - 27$

50. $\left(x^2 - 8x + 7\right) - \left(2x^2 + 7x + 11\right) + \left(3x^2 + 4x - 8\right)$

$= x^2 - 8x + 7 - 2x^2 - 7x - 11 + 3x^2 + 4x - 8$

$= x^2 - 2x^2 + 3x^2 - 8x - 7x + 4x + 7 - 11 - 8$

$= 2x^2 - 11x - 12$

51. $5x^2 \left(7x^3 - 9x^2 + 3x + 1\right)$

$= \left(5x^2\right)\left(7x^3\right) - \left(5x^2\right)\left(9x^2\right) + \left(5x^2\right)\left(3x\right) + \left(5x^2\right)\left(1\right)$

$= 35x^5 - 45x^4 + 15x^3 + 5x^2$

52. $\left(5v + 1\right)\left(7v - 1\right)$

$= \left(5v + 1\right)\left(7v\right) - \left(5v + 1\right)\left(1\right)$

$= \left[\left(5v\right)\left(7v\right) + \left(1\right)\left(7v\right)\right] - \left[\left(5v\right)\left(1\right) + \left(1\right)\left(1\right)\right]$

$= \left(35v^2 + 7v\right) - \left(5v + 1\right)$

$= 35v^2 + 7v - 5v - 1$

$= 35v^2 + 2v - 1$

53. $\left(5y - 7\right)^2 = \left(5y\right)^2 - 2\left(5y\right)\left(7\right) + \left(7\right)^2$

$= 25y^2 - 70y + 49$

54. $\left(9y + 5\right)^2 = \left(9y\right)^2 + 2\left(9y\right)\left(5\right) + \left(5\right)^2$

$= 81y^2 + 90y + 25$

55. $\left(3a + 5b\right)\left(3a - 5b\right) = \left(3a\right)^2 - \left(5b\right)^2 = 9a^2 - 25b^2$

56. $\left(3m + 5\right)\left(2m^2 - 6m + 7\right)$

$= \left(3m + 5\right)\left(2m^2\right) - \left(3m + 5\right)\left(6m\right) + \left(3m + 5\right)\left(7\right)$

$= \left[\left(3m\right)\left(2m^2\right) + \left(5\right)\left(2m^2\right)\right] - \left[\left(3m\right)\left(6m\right) + \left(5\right)\left(6m\right)\right] + \left[\left(3m\right)\left(7\right) + \left(5\right)\left(7\right)\right]$

$= \left(6m^3 + 10m^2\right) - \left(18m^2 + 30m\right) + \left(21m + 35\right)$

$= 6m^3 + 10m^2 - 18m^2 - 30m + 21m + 35$

$= 6m^3 - 8m^2 - 9m + 35$

57. $\dfrac{-36a^3b^7}{9a^4b^4} = \dfrac{-4b^{7-4}}{a^{4-3}} = \dfrac{-4b^3}{a}$

58. $\dfrac{15m^5n^4 - 21m^4n^5 - 3m^3n^6}{3m^2n^3}$

$= \dfrac{15m^5n^4}{3m^2n^3} - \dfrac{21m^4n^5}{3m^2n^3} - \dfrac{3m^3n^6}{3m^2n^3}$

$= 5m^3n - 7m^2n^2 - mn^3$

59. $\dfrac{v^2-6v+8}{v-4}$;

$$v-4\overline{)v^2-6v+8}$$ quotient

$$\underline{v^2-4v}$$
$$-2v+8$$
$$\underline{-2v+8}$$
$$0$$

60. $\dfrac{21w^2-40w-21}{3w-7}$;

quotient

$$3w-7\overline{)21w^2-40w-21} \quad 7w+3$$
$$\underline{21w^2-49w}$$
$$9w-21$$
$$\underline{9w-21}$$
$$0$$

61. $\dfrac{(a+b)^7}{(a+b)^6}=(a+b)^{7-6}=(a+b)^1=a+b$

62.
$$(3x+4y)^2-(3x+4y)(3x-4y)$$
$$=(3x+4y)\left[(3x+4y)-(3x-4y)\right]$$
$$=(3x+4y)(3x+4y-3x+4y)$$
$$=(3x+4y)(8y)$$
$$=(3x)(8y)+(4y)(8y)$$
$$=24xy+32y^2$$

63. $(2x+3y)^2-(2x-3y)^2$
$$=\left[(2x+3y)+(2x-3y)\right]\left[(2x+3y)-(2x-3y)\right]$$
$$=(2x+3y+2x-3y)(2x+3y-2x+3y)$$
$$=(4x)(6y)=24xy$$

64. Use long division to find each of the two quotients:

$$\frac{6x^2+x-2}{2x-1}; \quad 2x-1\overline{)6x^2+x-2} \quad 3x+2$$
$$\underline{6x^2-3x}$$
$$4x-2$$
$$\underline{4x-2}$$
$$0$$

and

$$\frac{8x^2+18x-35}{4x-5}; \quad 4x-5\overline{)8x^2+18x-35} \quad 2x+7$$
$$\underline{8x^2-10x}$$
$$28x-35$$
$$\underline{28x-35}$$
$$0$$

Thus

$$\frac{6x^2+x-2}{2x-1}-\frac{8x^2+18x-35}{4x-5}=(3x+2)-(2x+7)=3x+2-2x-7=x-5$$

65. To check if $\dfrac{x^3+64}{x+4}$ is $x^2-4x+16$, we can establish that $(x+4)(x^2-4x+16)$ is x^3+64:

$$(x+4)(x^2-4x+16)=(x+4)(x^2)-(x+4)(4x)+(x+4)(16)$$
$$=\left[(x)(x^2)+(4)(x^2)\right]-\left[(x)(4x)+(4)(4x)\right]+\left[(x)(16)+(4)(16)\right]$$
$$=(x^3+4x^2)-(4x^2+16x)+(16x+64)$$
$$=x^3+4x^2-4x^2-16x+16x+64$$
$$=x^3+64$$

66. To check if $\dfrac{x^2+4x-5}{x-2}$ is $x+6+\dfrac{7}{x-2}$, we can establish that $(x-2)\left(x+6+\dfrac{7}{x-2}\right)$ is x^2+4x-5:

$$(x-2)\left(x+6+\dfrac{7}{x-2}\right)=(x-2)(x+6)+7$$
$$=(x-2)(x)+(x-2)(6)+7$$
$$=\left[(x)(x)-(2)(x)\right]+\left[(x)(6)-(2)(6)\right]+7$$
$$=\left(x^2-2x\right)+(6x-12)+7$$
$$=x^2-2x+6x-12+7$$
$$=x^2+4x-5$$

67. a. $3x(x-4)=(3x)(x)-(3x)(4)=3x^2-12x$

b. $(3x)(x)-(3x)(4)=3x(x-4)$

68. a. $5x(x+3)-7(x+3)=5x^2+15x-7x-21$
$$=5x^2+8x-21$$

b. $5x(x+3)-7(x+3)=(x+3)(5x-7)$

69. a. $(4x+3)(4x-3)=(4x)^2-(3)^2=16x^2-9$

b. $16x^2-9=(4x)^2-(3)^2=(4x+3)(4x-3)$

70. a. $(6x-7)^2=(6x)^2-2(6x)(7)+(7)^2$
$$=36x^2-84x+49$$

b. $36x^2-84x+49=(6x)^2-2(6x)(7)+(7)^2$
$$=(6x-7)^2$$

71. $(9x-2)(5x+3)=45x^2+27x-10x-6$
$$=45x^2+17x-6$$

72. $(4x-3y)(5x+6y)=20x^2+24xy-15xy-18y^2$
$$=20x^2+9xy-18y^2$$

73. $(5x-6y)(5x+6y)=(5x)^2-(6y)^2$
$$=25x^2-36y^2$$

74. $(5x-6y)^2=(5x)^2-2(5x)(6y)+(6y)^2$
$$=25x^2-60xy+36y^2$$

75. $(7x+2y)^2=(7x)^2+2(7x)(2y)+(2y)^2$
$$=49x^2+28xy+4y^2$$

76. $(x-3)(x+3)(x^2+9)=\left[(x-3)(x+3)\right](x^2+9)$
$$=\left(x^2-9\right)\left(x^2+9\right)$$
$$=\left(x^2\right)^2-(9)^2$$
$$=x^4-81$$

77. a. $3x-7(4x+1)=3x-28x-7=-25x-7$

b. $(3x-7)(4x+1)=12x^2+3x-28x-7$
$$=12x^2-25x-7$$

78. a. $(8x)^2-(5y)^2=64x^2-25y^2$

b. $(8x-5y)^2=(8x)^2-2(8x)(5y)+(5y)^2$
$$=64x^2-80xy+25y^2$$

79. $(7a-2b)^2+(7a+2b)^2=(7a)^2-2(7a)(2b)+(2b)^2+(7a)^2+2(7a)(2b)+(2b)^2$
$$=49a^2-28ab+4b^2+49a^2+28ab+4b^2$$
$$=49a^2+49a^2-28ab+28ab+4b^2+4b^2$$
$$=98a^2+8b^2$$

80. $2(a-3b)^2 + 3(a+3b)^2 + 4a^2 + 5(3b)^2 = 2\left[a^2 - 2(a)(3b) + (3b)^2\right] + 3\left[a^2 + 2(a)(3b) + (3b)^2\right] + 4a^2 + 5 \cdot 9b^2$

$$= 2(a^2 - 6ab + 9b^2) + 3(a^2 + 6ab + 9b^2) + 4a^2 + 45b^2$$

$$= 2a^2 - 12ab + 18b^2 + 3a^2 + 18ab + 27b^2 + 4a^2 + 45b^2$$

$$= 2a^2 + 3a^2 + 4a^2 - 12ab + 18ab + 18b^2 + 27b^2 + 45b^2$$

$$= 9a^2 + 6ab + 90b^2$$

81.
$$\begin{array}{r} 4x - 1 \\ 2x^3 + 0x^2 + 3x - 7 \overline{\smash{\big)}\, 8x^4 - 2x^3 + 12x^2 - 31x + 7} \\ \underline{8x^4 + 0x^3 + 12x^2 - 28x} \\ -2x^3 + 0x^2 - 3x + 7 \\ \underline{-2x^3 + 0x^2 - 3x + 7} \\ 0 \end{array}$$

82.
$$\begin{array}{r} 27x^3 + 18x^2 + 12x + 8 \\ 3x - 2 \overline{\smash{\big)}\, 81x^4 + 0x^3 + 0x^2 + 0x - 16} \\ \underline{81x^4 - 54x^3} \\ 54x^3 + 0x^2 \\ \underline{54x^3 - 36x^2} \\ 36x^2 + 0x \\ \underline{36x^2 - 24x} \\ 24x - 16 \\ \underline{24x - 16} \\ 0 \end{array}$$

83. The area of a rectangle is

$$A = l \cdot w$$
$$A = (2x - 3)(3x + 1)$$
$$A = (2x - 3)(3x) + (2x - 3)(1)$$
$$A = \left[(2x)(3x) - (3)(3x)\right] + 2x - 3$$
$$A = (6x^2 - 9x) + 2x - 3$$
$$A = 6x^2 - 9x + 2x - 3$$
$$A = (6x^2 - 7x - 3) \text{ ft}^2$$

84. The volume of a box is $V = l \cdot w \cdot h$. Thus

$$h = \frac{V}{w \cdot l} = \frac{2x^3 + 2x^2}{x(2x)} = \frac{2x^2(x+1)}{2x^2} = (x+1) \text{ cm}.$$

85. **a.** $R(x) = x(350 - 4x) = 350x - 4x^2 = -4x^2 + 350x$

b. $R(0) = 350(0) - 4(0)^2 = 0$. If the price of the item is $0, then the revenue will be $0.

c. $R(40) = 350(40) - 4(40)^2 = 7600$. If the price of the item is $40, then the revenue will be $7,600.

d. $R(80) = 350(80) - 4(80)^2 = 2400$. If the price of the item is $80, then the revenue will be $2,400.

86. $A = 10000(1 + 0.075)^8 \approx \$17,835.78$

87. **a.** $A(x) = \dfrac{C(x)}{x} = \dfrac{15x + 1000}{x}$

b. $C(100) = 15(100) + 1000 = 2500$; The total cost of producing 100 range finders is $2,500.

c. $A(100) = \dfrac{15(100) + 1000}{100} = 25$; The average cost of producing 100 range finders is $25 per unit.

d. $C(200) = 15(200) + 1000 = 4000$; The total cost of producing 200 range finders is $4,000.

e. $A(200) = \dfrac{15(200)+1000}{200} = 20$; The average cost of producing 200 range finders is $20 per unit.

f. The change in cost when production is increased from 100 to 200 range finders is $1,500.

g. The change in average cost when production is increased from 100 to 200 range finders is –$5 per unit.

88.

x	Y_1	Y_2	Y_3	Y_4
–3	–28	–26	–26	–28
–2	–9	–7	–7	–9
–1	–2	0	0	–2
0	–1	1	1	–1
1	0	2	2	0
2	7	9	9	7
3	26	28	28	26

Conclusion: $Y_1 = Y_4$ and $Y_2 = Y_3$

Mastery Test for Chapter 5

1. **a.** $x \cdot x \cdot x \cdot x = x^4$

b. $x \cdot x \cdot x \cdot y \cdot y \cdot y \cdot y = x^3 y^4$

c. $-2x^3 y^2 - 2 \cdot x \cdot x \cdot x \cdot y \cdot y$

d. $(-2x)^3 y^2 = (-2x)(-2x)(-2x) \cdot y \cdot y$

2. **a.** $x^5 x^8 = x^{5+8} = x^{13}$

b. $(5y^4)(8y^3) = (5 \cdot 8)(y^4 y^3) = 40 y^{4+3} = 40 y^7$

c. $-v^4 v^5 v^6 = -v^{4+5+6} = -v^{15}$

d. $(mn^2)(m^3 n) = (mm^3)(nn^2) = m^{1+3} n^{1+2} = m^4 n^3$

3. **a.** $(w^5)^8 = w^{5 \cdot 8} = w^{40}$

b. $(2y^4)^5 = 2^5 y^{4 \cdot 5} = 32 y^{20}$

c. $(-v^2 w^3)^4 = (-v^2)^4 (w^3)^4 = v^{2 \cdot 4} w^{3 \cdot 4} = v^8 w^{12}$

d. $\left(\dfrac{-3m}{2n}\right)^3 = \dfrac{(-3)^3 m^3}{2^3 n^3} = \dfrac{-27 m^3}{8 n^3}$

4. **a.** $\dfrac{z^8}{z^2} = z^{8-2} = z^6$

b. $\dfrac{4x^9}{2x^3} = 2x^{9-3} = 2x^6$

c. $-\dfrac{v^{23}}{v^{23}} = -v^{23-23} = -v^0 = -1$

d. $\dfrac{-6a^4 b^6}{3a^2 b^2} = -2a^{4-2} b^{6-2} = -2a^2 b^4$

5. **a.** $1^0 = 1$

b. $\left(\dfrac{2}{5}\right)^0 = 1$

c. $(3x + 5y)^0 = 1$

d. $3x^0 + 5y^0 = 3 \cdot 1 + 5 \cdot 1 = 8$

6. **a.** $(x^3 y^5)(x^2 y^6) = (x^3 x^2)(y^5 y^6)$
$$= x^{3+2} y^{5+6} = x^5 y^{11}$$

b. $\left(\dfrac{x^2 y^3}{xy}\right)^3 = (x^{2-1} y^{3-1})^3 = (x^1 y^2)^3$
$$= x^3 y^{2 \cdot 3} = x^3 y^6$$

c. $\dfrac{(6x^2)^2}{(3x^3)^3} = \dfrac{6^2 x^{2 \cdot 2}}{3^3 x^{3 \cdot 3}} = \dfrac{36 x^4}{27 x^9} = \dfrac{4x^4}{3x^9} = \dfrac{4}{3x^{9-4}} = \dfrac{4}{3x^5}$

d. $\left[(2x^2)(3x^4)\right]^2 = \left[(2 \cdot 3)(x^2 x^4)\right]^2$
$$= (6x^6)^2 = 6^2 x^{6 \cdot 2} = 36 x^{12}$$

7. **a.** $3^{-1} = \dfrac{1}{3}$

b. $7^{-2} = \dfrac{1}{7^2} = \dfrac{1}{49}$

c. $\left(\dfrac{2}{3}\right)^{-2} = \left(\dfrac{3}{2}\right)^{2} = \dfrac{3^2}{2^2} = \dfrac{9}{4}$

d. $\left(\dfrac{1}{3}\right)^{-1} + \left(\dfrac{1}{6}\right)^{-1} = \dfrac{3}{1} + \dfrac{6}{1} = 9$

8. **a.** $\dfrac{x^6 y^{-2}}{x^{-3} y^4} = \dfrac{x^6 x^3}{y^4 y^2} = \dfrac{x^{6+3}}{y^{4+2}} = \dfrac{x^9}{y^6}$

b. $\left(\dfrac{-15 x^{10} y^{-12}}{12 x^{15} y^4}\right)^{-2} = \left(\dfrac{-\overset{5}{\cancel{15}}\, x^{10-15} y^{-12-4}}{\underset{4}{\cancel{12}}}\right)^{-2} = \left(\dfrac{-5 x^{-5} y^{-16}}{4}\right)^{-2}$

$= \left(\dfrac{-5}{4 x^5 y^{16}}\right)^{-2} = \left(\dfrac{-4 x^5 y^{16}}{5}\right)^{2}$

$= \dfrac{(-4)^2 \left(x^5\right)^2 \left(y^{16}\right)^2}{(5)^2} = \dfrac{16 x^{10} y^{32}}{25}$

9. **a.** $3.57 \times 10^5 = 357{,}000$

b. $7.35 \times 10^{-5} = 0.0000735$

c. $0.000509 = 5.09 \times 10^{-4}$

d. $93{,}050{,}000 = 9.305 \times 10^7$

10. **a.** $-5y^3 - 13y$ is a third degree binomial.

b. 273 is a monomial of degree zero.

c. $2x^2 - 7x + 1$ is a second degree trinomial

d. $17x^5 - 4x^3 + 9x + 8$ is a fifth degree polynomial with four terms.

11. **a.** $(4x - 9y) + (3x + 8y)$

$= 4x - 9y + 3x + 8y$

$= 4x + 3x - 9y + 8y$

$= 7x - y$

b. $(2x^2 - 3x + 7) - (5x^2 - 9x - 11)$

$= 2x^2 - 3x + 7 - 5x^2 + 9x + 11$

$= 2x^2 - 5x^2 - 3x + 9x + 7 + 11$

$= -3x^2 + 6x + 18$

c. $(5x^4 - 9x^3 + 7x^2 + 13) + (4x^4 + 12x^2 + 9x - 5)$

$= 5x^4 - 9x^3 + 7x^2 + 13 + 4x^4 + 12x^2 + 9x - 5$

$= 5x^4 + 4x^4 - 9x^3 + 7x^2 + 12x^2 + 9x + 13 - 5$

$= 9x^4 - 9x^3 + 19x^2 + 9x + 8$

d. $(3x^3 - 7x + 1) - (12x^2 + 9x - 5)$

$= 3x^3 - 7x + 1 - 12x^2 - 9x + 5$

$= 3x^3 - 12x^2 - 7x - 9x + 1 + 5$

$= 3x^3 - 12x^2 - 16x + 6$

12. **a.**

$(5x^2 y^3)(11x^4 y^7)$

$= (5 \cdot 11)(x^2 x^4)(y^3 y^7)$

$= 55 x^{2+4} y^{3+7} = 55 x^6 y^{10}$

b.

$-3x^2(5x^3 - 2x^2 + 7x - 9)$

$= (-3x^2)(5x^3) - (-3x^2)(2x^2) + (-3x^2)(7x) - (-3x^2)(9)$

$= -15x^5 + 6x^4 - 21x^3 + 27x^2$

c.

$(x + 5)(x^2 + 3x + 1)$

$= (x + 5)(x^2) + (x + 5)(3x) + (x + 5)(1)$

$= \left[x(x^2) + 5(x^2)\right] + \left[x(3x) + 5(3x)\right] + (x + 5)$

$= (x^3 + 5x^2) + (3x^2 + 15x) + (x + 5)$

$= x^3 + 5x^2 + 3x^2 + 15x + x + 5$

$= x^3 + 8x^2 + 16x + 5$

d.

$(x - 3y)(x^2 + xy + y^2)$

$= (x - 3y)(x^2) + (x - 3y)(xy) + (x - 3y)(y^2)$

$= \left[x(x^2) - 3y(x^2)\right] + \left[x(xy) - 3y(xy)\right] + \left[x(y^2) - 3y(y^2)\right]$

$= (x^3 - 3x^2 y) + (x^2 y - 3xy^2) + (xy^2 - 3y^3)$

$= x^3 - 3x^2 y + x^2 y - 3xy^2 + xy^2 - 3y^3$

$= x^3 - 2x^2 y - 2xy^2 - 3y^3$

13. **a.** $(x+8)(x+11) = x^2 + 11x + 8x + 88$

             $= x^2 + 19x + 88$

    b. $(x-9)(x-5) = x^2 - 5x - 9x + 45$

             $= x^2 - 14x + 45$

    c. $(2x+5y)(3x-4y) = 6x^2 - 8xy + 15xy - 20y^2$

             $= 6x^2 + 7xy - 20y^2$

    d. $(5x-3y)(2x+7y) = 10x^2 + 35y - 6xy - 21y^2$

             $= 10x^2 + 29y - 21y^2$

14. **a.** $(6x+1)(6x-1) = (6x)^2 - (1)^2 = 36x^2 - 1$

    b. $(x-9y)(x+9y) = (x)^2 - (9y)^2 = x^2 - 81y^2$

    c. $(5x-11)(5x+11) = (5x)^2 - (11)^2$

             $= 25x^2 - 121$

    d. $(3x-8y)(3x+8y) = (3x)^2 - (8y)^2 = 9x^2 - 64y^2$

15. **a.** $(6x+1)^2 = (6x)^2 + 2(6x)(1) + (1)^2$

             $= 36x^2 + 12x + 1$

    b. $(x-9y)^2 = (x)^2 - 2(x)(9y) + (9y)^2$

             $= x^2 - 18xy + 81y^2$

    c. $(5x-11)^2 = (5x)^2 - 2(5x)(11) + (11)^2$

             $= 25x^2 - 110x + 121$

    d. $(3x+8y)^2 = (3x)^2 + 2(3x)(8y) + (8y)^2$

             $= 9x^2 + 48xy + 64y^2$

16. **a.** $(x-3)^2 - (x^2 - 3^2) = x^2 - 2(3)(x) + (3)^2 - (x^2 - 9) = x^2 - 6x + 9 - x^2 + 9 = -6x + 18$

    b. $(x-5y)^2 - (x+5y)^2 = x^2 - 2(x)(5y) + (5y)^2 - \left[x^2 + 2(x)(5y) + (5y)^2 \right]$

             $= x^2 - 10xy + 25y^2 - \left[x^2 + 10xy + 25y^2 \right]$

             $= x^2 - 10xy + 25y^2 - x^2 - 10xy - 25y^2 = -20xy$

17. **a.** $\dfrac{15a^4 b^2}{5a^2 b^2} = 3a^{4-2}b^{2-2} = 3a^2 b^0 = 3a^2$

    b. $\dfrac{36m^4 n^3 - 48m^2 n^5}{12m^2 n^2} = \dfrac{36m^4 n^3}{12m^2 n^2} - \dfrac{48m^2 n^5}{12m^2 n^2} = 3m^2 n - 4n^3$

18. **a.**
$$
\begin{array}{r}
x + 11 \\
x-2\overline{)x^2 + 9x - 22} \\
\underline{x^2 - 2x} \\
11x - 22 \\
\underline{11x - 22} \\
0
\end{array}
$$

    b. $\dfrac{6x^3 + 10x^2 - 32}{3x - 4}$;
$$
\begin{array}{r}
2x^2 + 6x + 8 \\
3x-4\overline{)6x^3 + 10x^2 + 0x - 32} \\
\underline{6x^3 - 8x^2} \\
18x^2 + 0x \\
\underline{18x^2 + -24x} \\
24x - 32 \\
\underline{24x - 32} \\
0
\end{array}
$$

Comprehensive Review of Beginning Algebra

1.
   a. $15 + (-3) = 12$
   b. $15 - (-3) = 15 + 3 = 18$
   c. $15(-3) = -45$
   d. $15 \div (-3) = -5$

2.
   a. $-0.6 + 0.02 = -0.58$
   b. $-0.6 - 0.02 = -0.62$
   c. $-0.6(0.02) = -0.012$
   d. $-0.6 + 0.02 = -30$

3.
   a. $\dfrac{1}{6} + \dfrac{3}{4} = \dfrac{1}{6} \cdot \dfrac{2}{2} + \dfrac{3}{4} \cdot \dfrac{3}{3} = \dfrac{2}{12} + \dfrac{9}{12} = \dfrac{2+9}{12} = \dfrac{11}{12}$
   b. $\dfrac{1}{6} - \dfrac{3}{4} = \dfrac{1}{6} \cdot \dfrac{2}{2} - \dfrac{3}{4} \cdot \dfrac{3}{3} = \dfrac{2}{12} - \dfrac{9}{12} = \dfrac{2-9}{12} = \dfrac{-7}{12}$
   c. $\dfrac{1}{6}\left(\dfrac{3}{4}\right) = \dfrac{1 \cdot \cancel{3}}{\cancel{6} \cdot 4} = \dfrac{1}{2 \cdot 4} = \dfrac{1}{8}$
   d. $\dfrac{1}{6} \div \dfrac{3}{4} = \dfrac{1}{6} \cdot \dfrac{4}{3} = \dfrac{1}{\cancel{6}} \cdot \dfrac{\cancel{4}}{3} = \dfrac{1 \cdot 2}{3 \cdot 3} = \dfrac{2}{9}$

4.
   a. $3 + 0 = 3$
   b. $3 - 0 = 3$
   c. $3(0) = 0$
   d. $3 \div 0$ is undefined

5.
   a. $6 - 12 \div 3 + 4^2 = 6 - 4 + 16 = 18$
   b. $(6-12) \div 3 + 4^2 = -6 \div 3 + 16 = -2 + 16 = 14$

6.
   a. $\dfrac{2(4) \div 4(-2)}{8 \div 2(-4)} = \dfrac{8 \div 4(-2)}{4(-4)} = \dfrac{2(-2)}{-16} = \dfrac{-4}{-16} = \dfrac{1}{4}$
   b. $\dfrac{5 - 2(3-7)}{(10+3)^2} = \dfrac{5 - 2(-4)}{13^2} = \dfrac{5+8}{13^2} = \dfrac{13}{13^2} = \dfrac{1}{13}$

7.
   a. $\left\{ -5, -3.28, -\dfrac{1}{3}, 0, \sqrt{9}, 11 \right\}$
   b. $\left\{ \sqrt{3} \right\}$
   c. $\left\{ -5, 0, \sqrt{9}, 11 \right\}$
   d. $\left\{ \sqrt{9}, 11 \right\}$

8.
   a. $\dfrac{1}{5} = 0.20 = 20\%$
   b. $0.35 = 35\% = \dfrac{35}{100} = \dfrac{7}{20}$
   c. $60\% = 0.60 = \dfrac{6}{10} = \dfrac{3}{5}$

9.
   a. The statement is an example of the distributive property of multiplication over addition.
   b. The statement is an example of the commutative property of addition.
   c. The statement is an example of the commutative property of multiplication.
   d. The statement is an example of the associative property of addition.

10.
   a. The additive identity is 0.
   b. The additive inverse of 5 is -5.

11.
   a. The multiplicative identity is 1.
   b. The multiplicative inverse of 5 is $\dfrac{1}{5}$.

12.
   a. $(-\infty, 5]$
   b. $(-2, \infty)$
   c. $[-3, 0)$
   d. $(3, 9]$

13. **a.** Area: $A = \pi r^2 = \pi 3^2 = 9\pi$ cm^2 **a.** Area: $A = l \cdot w = 9 \cdot 4 = 36$ in^2

Perimeter: $C = 2\pi r = 2\pi(3) = 6\pi$ cm   Perimeter: $P = 2l + 2w = 2 \cdot 9 + 2 \cdot 4 = 18 + 8 = 26$ in

14. **a.** $m\angle B = 90° - m\angle A = 90° - 28° = 62°$

    b. $m\angle C = 180° - m\angle A = 180° - 28° = 152°$

15. **a.** Replace x with 5   **b.** Replace x with 5

$$2x - 3 = x + 1$$
$$2(5) - 3 = (5) + 1$$
$$10 - 3 = 6$$
$$7 \neq 6$$

Thus, $x = 5$ is not a solution.

$$2(x - 4) = x - 3$$
$$2((5) - 4) = (5) - 3$$
$$2(1) = 2$$
$$2 = 2$$

Thus, $x = 5$ is a solution.

16. **a.**
$$3(x - 2) - 5(x - 4) = 3x - 6 - 5x + 20$$
$$= 3x - 5x - 6 + 20$$
$$= -2x + 14$$

b.
$$3(x - 2) - 5(x - 4) = 0$$
$$3x - 6 - 5x + 20 = 0$$
$$3x - 5x - 6 + 20 = 0$$
$$-2x + 14 = 0$$
$$-2x = -14$$
$$x = 7$$

17. **a.**
$$2(x + 5) - (x + 3) = 2x + 10 - x - 3$$
$$= 2x - x + 10 - 3$$
$$= x + 7$$

b.
$$2(x + 5) - (x + 3) = 0$$
$$2x + 10 - x - 3 = 0$$
$$2x - x + 10 - 3 = 0$$
$$x + 7 = 0$$
$$x = -7$$

18. **a.**
$$3(4x + 1) - 7x = 2x - 21$$
$$12x + 3 - 7x = 2x - 21$$
$$5x + 3 = 2x - 21$$
$$5x - 2x + 3 = 2x - 2x - 21$$
$$3x + 3 - 3 = -21 - 3$$
$$3x = -24$$
$$x = -8$$

b.
$$5(x - 3) = 3(x + 1)$$
$$5x - 15 = 3x + 3$$
$$5x - 3x - 15 + 15 = 3x - 3x + 3 + 15$$
$$2x = 18$$
$$x = 9$$

19. **a.**
$$\frac{x}{4} - 1 = \frac{2x}{5}$$
$$20\left(\frac{x}{4} - 1\right) = 20\left(\frac{2x}{5}\right)$$
$$5x - 20 = 4(2x)$$
$$5x - 20 = 8x$$
$$5x - 8x - 20 + 20 = 8x - 8x + 20$$
$$-3x = 20$$
$$x = -\frac{20}{3}$$

b.
$$2x - \frac{3x + 1}{2} = \frac{1}{3}$$
$$6\left(2x - \frac{3x + 1}{2}\right) = 6\left(\frac{1}{3}\right)$$
$$12x - 3(3x + 1) = 2$$
$$12x - 9x - 3 = 2$$
$$3x - 3 + 3 = 2 + 3$$
$$3x = 5$$
$$x = \frac{5}{3}$$

20. **a.**
$$2x - 3y = 12$$
$$2x - 2x - 3y = 12 - 2x$$
$$-3y = 12 - 2x$$
$$\frac{-3y}{-3} = \frac{12 - 2x}{-3}$$
$$y = \frac{12 - 2x}{-3} = \frac{2x - 12}{3} = \frac{2}{3}x - 4$$

b.
$$\frac{x}{3} - \frac{y}{5} = 1$$
$$15\left(\frac{x}{3} - \frac{y}{5}\right) = 15(1)$$
$$5x - 3y = 15$$
$$5x - 5x - 3y = 15 - 5x$$
$$-3y = 15 - 5x$$
$$\frac{-3y}{-3} = \frac{15 - 5x}{-3}$$
$$y = \frac{15 - 5x}{-3} = \frac{5x - 15}{3} = \frac{5}{3}x - 5$$

21. The solution to the equation is the value of x in the table such that $y_1 = y_2$. Thus the solution is $x = 4$.

22. The solution to the equation is the x value of the point of intersection. Thus the solution is $x = -6$.

23. **a.** By inspection, we can see that the y-intercept is $(0, 4)$ and the x-intercept is $(3, 0)$.

b. To find the x-intercept we set $y = 0$
and solve for x:
$$3x - 2y = 18$$
$$3x - 2(0) = 18$$
$$3x = 18$$
$$x = 6$$
x-intercept: $(6, 0)$

To find the y-intercept we set $x = 0$
And solve for y:
$$3x - 2y = 18$$
$$3(0) - 2y = 18$$
$$-2y = 18$$
$$y = -9$$
y-intercept: $(0, -9)$

24. **a.** Let $y =$ concession sales.
Let $x =$ number of attendees.
We know:
$$\frac{y}{x} = \frac{1000000}{40000} \Rightarrow \frac{y}{x} = 25 \Rightarrow y = 25x.$$

b. The constant of variation represents concession average of $25 per person.

c.

Attendance	Concession Sales ($)
34,000	850,000
38,000	950,000
42,000	1,050,000

25. Since the corresponding lengths of similar triangles are proportional, to find a, we can solve the following equation.
$$\frac{x}{3} = \frac{x + 9}{9}$$
$$9\left(\frac{x}{3}\right) = 9\left(\frac{x + 9}{9}\right)$$
$$3x = x + 9$$
$$2x = 9$$
$$x = \frac{9}{2}$$
The value of x is $\frac{9}{2}$.

26. **a.** The sequence is arithmetic. The common difference is 4.
b. The sequence is arithmetic. The common difference is -3.
c. The sequence is not arithmetic since the difference between any two consecutive terms is not constant.
d. The sequence is arithmetic. The common difference is 0.

27. **a.** $f(0) = 5(0) - 2 = -2$

   b. $f(-3) = 5(-3) - 2 = -17$

   c. $f(4) = 5(4) - 2 = 18$

   d. $f(10) = 5(10) - 2 = 48$

28. **a.** $f(-4) = 3$

   b. $f(0) = 1$

   c. If $f(x) = -1$ then $x = 4$

   d. If $f(x) = 0$ then $x = 2$

29. **a.** To find the new price of the item that is marked down by 20% we multiply the original price by 0.80. If the original price is x dollars then the function $f(x) = 0.80x$ can be used to determine the new price of the item.

   b.

x	$f(x) = 0.80x$
20	$0.80(20) = 16$
48	$0.80(48) = 38.40$
75	$0.80(75) = 60$
90	$0.80(90) = 72$
110	$0.80(110) = 88$

30. Define the Variable: Let x represent the number of hours that the boats have been traveling.

Verbal Equation: $\boxed{\begin{array}{c}\text{Distance Traveled}\\\text{by the First Boat}\end{array}} + \boxed{\begin{array}{c}\text{Distance Traveled}\\\text{by the Second Boat}\end{array}} = \boxed{\begin{array}{c}\text{Total Distance}\\\text{Between Boats}\end{array}}$

Algebraic Equation: $15x + 9x = 72$

$$16x = 72$$

$$x = 3$$

Answer: After 3 hours the boats are 72 miles apart.

31. Define the Variable: Let x represent the number of liters of water added.

Verbal Equation: $\boxed{\begin{array}{c}\text{Acid in}\\\text{Existing Mixture}\end{array}} + \boxed{\begin{array}{c}\text{Acid in}\\\text{Water Added}\end{array}} = \boxed{\begin{array}{c}\text{Total Acid}\\\text{in Desired Mixture}\end{array}}$

Algebraic Equation: $0.25(5) + 0.00x = 0.20(5 + x)$

$$1.25 = 1 + 0.20x$$

$$0.20x = .25$$

$$x = 1.25$$

Answer: She should add 1.25 L of water.

32. **a.** $5x + 2y = -1$

   $5(1) + 2(-3) = -1$

   $5 - 6 = -1$

   $-1 = -1$ is true.

   Thus $(1, -3)$ is a solution.

   b. $y = -2x + 4$

   $(-3) = -2(1) + 4$

   $-3 = -2 + 4$

   $-3 = 2$ is false.

   Thus $(1, -3)$ is not a solution.

   c. $x = 1$

   $(1) = 1$

   $1 = 1$ is true.

   Thus $(1, -3)$ is a solution.

   d. $y = 2$

   $(-3) = 2$

   $-3 = 2$ is false.

   Thus $(1, -3)$ is not a solution.

33. a.

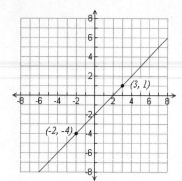

b.

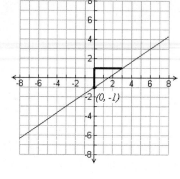

c.

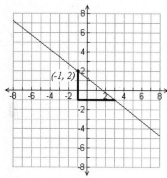

d.

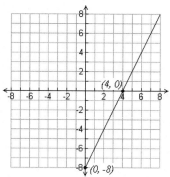

e.

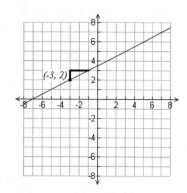

34. a. $y = -\dfrac{3}{2}x + 4$ is parallel to $y = -\dfrac{3}{2}x + 1$. Answer: **C**.

  b. $y = \dfrac{2}{3}x + 7$ is perpendicular to $y = -\dfrac{3}{2}x + 1$. Answer: **D**.

  c. $y = 4$ is a horizontal line. Answer: **A**.

  d. $x = -1$ is a vertical line. Answer: **B**.

35. a. Use $x_1 = 3$, $y_1 = 7$, $x_2 = -2$, $y_2 = 1$

$$m = \frac{y_2 - y_1}{x_2 - x_1} = \frac{1 - 7}{-2 - 3} = \frac{-6}{-5} = \frac{6}{5}$$

  b. The equation is in slope-intercept form $y = mx + b$.

  Thus the slope is $m = \dfrac{3}{4}$.

  c. $y = 2$ is a horizontal line. The slope is $m = 0$

  d. $x = 2$ is a vertical line. The slope is undefined.

36. Use the point-slope form. Substitute $(0, -2)$ for (x_1, y_1) and 3 for m.

$$y - y_1 = m(x - x_1)$$
$$y - (-2) = 3(x - 0)$$
$$y + 2 = 3x$$
$$y = 3x - 2$$

37. Use the point-slope form. Substitute $(3, 1)$ for (x_1, y_1) and -2 for m.

$$y - y_1 = m(x - x_1)$$
$$y - 1 = -2(x - 3)$$
$$y - 1 = -2x + 6$$
$$y = -2x + 7$$

38. Determine the slope of the line passing through the given points

$$m = \frac{y_2 - y_1}{x_2 - x_1} = \frac{3 - 1}{2 - (-1)} = \frac{2}{3}$$

Use the point-slope form with either point.

Substitute $(-1, 1)$ for (x_1, y_1) and $\frac{2}{3}$ for m.

$$y - y_1 = m(x - x_1)$$
$$y - 1 = \frac{2}{3}(x - (-1))$$
$$y - 1 = \frac{2}{3}x + \frac{2}{3}$$
$$y = \frac{2}{3}x + \frac{5}{3}$$

39. The equation of a horizontal line is determined by the y-coordinate. Thus the equation is $y = 4$.

40. The equation of a vertical line is determined by the x-coordinate. Thus the equation is $x = 3$.

41. If the line is parallel to $y = -\frac{2}{5}x + 7$ then is has a slope $m = -\frac{2}{5}$. Use the point-slope form.

Substitute $(0, 2)$ for (x_1, y_1) and $-\frac{2}{5}$ for m.

$$y - y_1 = m(x - x_1)$$
$$y - 2 = -\frac{2}{5}(x - 0)$$
$$y = -\frac{2}{5}x + 2$$

42. **a.** The slopes of the lines are different. Therefore there is exactly one solution and we have a consistent system of independent equations. Answer: **A**.

b. The slopes of the lines are the same and the y-intercepts are different. Therefore the lines are parallel and never intersect and we have an inconsistent system of equations. Answer: **C**.

c. The two lines are identical. Therefore the system has infinitely many solutions. Answer: **B**.

43.

Step 1	**Step 2**	**Step 3**
Solve one of the equations for one variable in terms of the other.	Substitute $3x+5$ for y in the second equation and then solve for x.	Back-substitute 2 for x in the first equation.

$$y = 3x + 5$$

$$3x + 2y = 28$$

(y is currently written in terms of x in the first equation.)

$$3x + 2y = 28$$

$$3x + 2(3x + 5) = 28$$

$$3x + 6x + 10 = 28$$

$$9x = 18$$

$$x = 2$$

$$y = 3x + 5$$

$$y = 3(2) + 5$$

$$y = 11$$

Solution: $(2, 11)$

44. Add the two equations to eliminate y. Solve this equation for x.

$$4x - 7y = 40$$

$$\underline{4x + 7y = -16}$$

$$8x \quad\;\; = 24$$

$$x = 3$$

Back substitute 3 for x in the first equation to find y.

$$4(3) - 7y = 40$$

$$12 - 7y = 40$$

$$-7y = 28$$

$$y = -4$$

Solution: $(3, -4)$

45. Write the equations in general form. To eliminate x, multiply both sides of the first equation by 5, then multiply the second equation by 3 and add the two equations. Solve this equation for y.

$$-3x + 4y = 19 \qquad -15x + 20y = 95$$

$$5x + 7y = -18 \qquad \underline{15x + 21y = -54}$$

$$41y = 41$$

$$y = 1$$

Back substitute 1 for y in the first equation to find x.

$$-3x + 4y = 19$$

$$-3x + 4(1) = 19$$

$$-3x = 15$$

$$x = -5$$

Solution: $(-5, 1)$

46. Let x and y be the speeds of the two trains.

If one averages 8 kilometers per hour less than the other, then

$$x - y = 8$$

If after ½ hour they are 99 kilometers apart, then

$$\frac{1}{2}x + \frac{1}{2}y = 99$$

or $x + y = 198$

Use the addition method to solve the equations. Add the equations to eliminate y.

$$x - y = 8$$

$$\underline{x + y = 198}$$

$$2x \quad\;\; = 206$$

$$x = 103$$

Back substitute 103 for x in the first equation.

$$x - y = 8$$

$$103 - y = 8$$

$$-y = -95$$

$$y = 95$$

The trains are traveling at speeds of 103 km/hr and 95 km/hr.

47. Let x be the number of L of the 10% solution.
Let y be the number of L of the 25% solution.

| If the total amount of the new mixture is 6 L, then $x + y = 6$ | If new mixture is to be a 20% solution, then $0.10x + 0.25y = 0.20(6)$ or $0.10x + 0.25y = 1.2$ |

Use the addition method to solve the equations.
Multiply both sides of the first equation by -0.10 then add the equations to eliminate x.

$$-0.10x - 0.10y = -0.6$$
$$\underline{0.10x + 0.25y = 1.2}$$
$$0.15y = 0.6$$
$$y = 4$$

Back substitute 4 for y in the first equation.
$$x + y = 6$$
$$x + 4 = 6$$
$$x = 2$$

Use 2 L of the 10% solution and 4 L of the 25% solution.

48. Let x be the number of loads of topsoil.
Let y be the number of loads of fill dirt.

| If the total number of truckloads is 24, then $x + y = 24$ | If the total cost is $1090, then $60x + 35y = 1090$ |

Use the addition method to solve the equations.
Multiply both sides of the first equation by -60 then add the equations to eliminate x.

$$-60x - 60y = -1440$$
$$\underline{60x + 35y = 1090}$$
$$-25y = -350$$
$$y = 14$$

Back substitute 14 for y in the first equation.
$$x + y = 24$$
$$x + 14 = 24$$
$$x = 10$$

10 loads of topsoil and 14 loads of fill dirt are planned for the job.

49. **a.** The solution to $y_1 \geq y_2$ is the set of x-values for which the y_1 column is greater than or equal to the y_2 column. Thus the solution is $[2, \infty)$.

  b. The solution to $y_1 \leq y_2$ is the set of x-values for which the y_1 column is less than or equal to the y_2 column. Thus the solution is $(-\infty, 2]$.

50. **a.** The solution to $y_1 > y_2$ is the set of x-values for which the graph of y_1 is above or equal to that of y_2. Thus the solution is $[-1, \infty)$.

  b. The solution to $y_1 < y_2$ is the set of x-values for which the graph of y_1 is below or equal to that of y_2. Thus the solution is $(-\infty, -1]$.

51. **a.**
$$5(x - 3) \geq 2x + 9$$
$$5x - 15 \geq 2x + 9$$
$$5x - 2x - 15 + 15 \geq 2x - 2x + 9 + 15$$
$$2x \geq 16$$
$$x \geq 8$$
Answer: $[8, \infty)$

  b.
$$2(x + 3) < 4(x - 1) - 3(x + 2)$$
$$2x + 6 < 4x - 4 - 3x - 6$$
$$2x + 6 < 4x - 3x - 4 - 6$$
$$2x + 6 < x - 10$$
$$2x - x + 6 - 6 < x - x - 10 - 6$$
$$x < -16$$
Answer: $(-\infty, 16)$

52. **a.** $x + x < 0$

$$2x < 0$$

$$\frac{2x}{2} < \frac{0}{2}$$

$$x < 0$$

The inequality is a conditional inequality. The solution is $(-\infty, 0)$.

b. $x + x < 2x$

$$2x < 2x$$

$$2x - 2x < 2x - 2x$$

$$0 < 0 \text{ is a false statement.}$$

The inequality is a contradiction. There is no solution

c. $x + x \le 2x$

$$2x \le 2x$$

$$2x - 2x \le 2x - 2x$$

$$0 \le 0 \text{ is a true statement.}$$

Thus the inequality is an unconditional inequality. The solution is $(-\infty, +\infty)$ or $\mathbb{R}$.

53. **a.**
$$|2x - 1| = 7$$
is equivalent to
$$2x - 1 = 7 \text{ or } 2x - 1 = -7$$
$$2x = 8 \qquad 2x = -6$$
$$x = 4 \qquad x = -3$$
Answer: $x = 4$ or $x = -3$

b.
$$|2x + 1| < 5$$
is equivalent to
$$-5 < 2x + 1 < 5$$
$$-6 < 2x < 4$$
$$-3 < x < 2$$
Answer: $(-3, 2)$

c.
$$|x - 3| \ge 5$$
is equivalent to
$$x - 3 \le -5 \text{ or } x - 3 \ge 5$$
$$x < -2 \qquad x \ge 8$$
Answer: $(-\infty, -2] \cup [8, \infty)$

54. $2 < 3x - 4 \le 5$

$$6 < 3x \le 9$$

$$2 < x \le 3$$

Answer: $(2, 3]$

55. $2x + 1 \le -5 \quad \text{or} \quad 3x - 2 \ge 4$

$$2x \le -6 \qquad 3x \ge 6$$

$$x \le -3 \qquad x \ge 2$$

Answer: $(-\infty, -3] \cup [2, \infty)$

56. **Step 1:** Draw a solid line for $3x - 4y = 12$ because the equality is part of the solution. The line passes through the intercepts $(4, 0)$ and $(0, -3)$.

Step 2: Test the origin:
$$3x - 4y \le 12$$
$$3(0) - 4(0) \le 12$$
$$0 \le 12 \text{ is true.}$$

Step 3: Shade the half-plane that includes the test point $(0, 0)$.

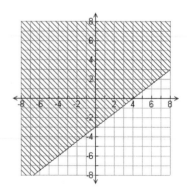

57. Using the process described in problem **56**, we sketch the graphs of the solutions to each of the inequalities in the system.

With each of the inequalities sketched on the same coordinate system, the solution to the *system* is the intersection of the two regions.

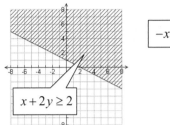 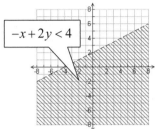

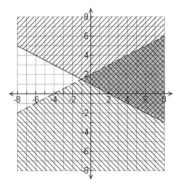

58. We sketch the graph of $3x + y \le 3$ using the process described in previous problems. The inequalities $x \ge 0$ and $y \ge 0$ require that the shaded area is contained to the first quadrant.

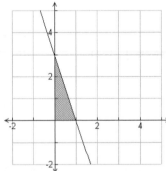

59. **a.** $-5^0 + 3^0 + 4^0 = -1 + 1 + 1 = 1$

 b. $\left(-5\right)^0 + 3^0 + 4^0 = 1 + 1 + 1 = 3$

 c. $\left(-5 + 3 + 4\right)^0 = 1$

 d. $-\left(-5 + 3 + 4\right)^0 = -1$

60. **a.** $\left(\dfrac{1+1}{2+3}\right)^{-1} = \left(\dfrac{2}{5}\right)^{-1} = \dfrac{5}{2}$

 b. $\left(\dfrac{1}{2+3}\right)^{-1} = \left(\dfrac{1}{5}\right)^{-1} = \dfrac{5}{1} = 5$

 c. $\left(\dfrac{1}{2}+\dfrac{1}{3}\right)^{-1} = \left(\dfrac{3}{6}+\dfrac{2}{6}\right)^{-1} = \left(\dfrac{5}{6}\right)^{-1} = \dfrac{6}{5}$

 d. $\left(\dfrac{1}{2}\right)^{-1} + \left(\dfrac{1}{3}\right)^{-1} = \dfrac{2}{1}+\dfrac{3}{1} = 2 + 3 = 5$

61. **a.** $5^0 = 1$

 b. $0^5 = 0$

 c. $6^{-1} = \dfrac{1}{6}$

 d. $\left(-1\right)^6 = 1$

62. **a.** $\left(\dfrac{2}{3}\right)^0 = 1$

 b. $\left(\dfrac{2}{3}\right)^{-2} = \left(\dfrac{3}{2}\right)^2 = \dfrac{3^2}{2^2} = \dfrac{9}{4}$

 c. $\left(\dfrac{2}{3}\right)^{-1} = \left(\dfrac{3}{2}\right)^1 = \dfrac{3}{2}$

 d. $\left(\dfrac{2}{3}\right)^2 = \dfrac{2^2}{3^2} = \dfrac{4}{9}$

63. **a.** $10^2 = 100$

b. $10^4 = 10,000$

c. $10^0 = 1$

d. $10^{-1} = \dfrac{1}{10}$

64. **a.** $(3x + 7y)^0 = 1$

b. $(3x)^0 + (7y)^0 = 1 + 1 = 2$

c. $3(3x + 7y)^0 = 3(1) = 3$

d. $3x^0 + 7y^0 = 3(1) + 7(1) = 10$

65. **a.** $x^3 + x^3 = 2x^3$

b. $x^2 \cdot x^6 = x^{2+6} = x^8$

c. $\dfrac{x^6}{x^2} = x^{6-2} = x^4$

d. $\left(x^2\right)^6 = x^{2 \cdot 6} = x^{12}$

66. **a.** $\left(8x^2 y^3\right)(4xy) = 32x^{2+1} y^{3+1} = 32x^3 y^4$

b. $\dfrac{8x^2 y^3}{4xy} = 2x^{2-1} y^{3-1} = 2x^1 y^2 = 2xy^2$

c. $\dfrac{\left(2x^2\right)^3}{4x^3} = \dfrac{2^3 x^{2+3}}{4x^3} = \dfrac{8x^5}{4x^3} = \dfrac{\overset{2}{\cancel{8}} x^{5-3}}{\underset{1}{\cancel{4}}} = 2x^2$

d. $\left(8x^2 y^3\right)^2 = 8^2 \left(x^2\right)^2 \left(y^3\right)^2 = 16x^{2 \cdot 2} y^{3 \cdot 2} = 16x^4 y^6$

67. **a.** $x^{-2} x^5 = x^{-2+5} = x^3$

b. $\left(\dfrac{x^{-3}}{x^{-4}}\right)^{-2} = \left(x^{-3-(-4)}\right)^{-2} = \left(x^1\right)^{-2} = \dfrac{1}{x^2}$

c. $\left(3x^{-3} y^4\right)^{-2} = \left(\dfrac{3y^4}{x^3}\right)^{-2} = \left(\dfrac{x^3}{3y^4}\right)^2$

$= \dfrac{x^{3 \cdot 2}}{3^2 y^{4 \cdot 2}} = \dfrac{x^6}{9y^8}$

d. $\dfrac{-6x^{-6} y^2}{12x^{12} y^{-8}} = -\dfrac{y^{2+8}}{2x^{12+6}} = -\dfrac{y^{10}}{2x^{18}}$

68. **a.** $1.23 \times 10^{-2} = 0.0123$

b. $1.23 \times 10^4 = 12,300$

69. **a.** $0.0000435 = 4.35 \times 10^{-5}$

b. $1,870,000 = 1.87 \times 10^6$

70. **a.** $(3x + 7y) + (2x - 4y) = 3x + 7y + 2x - 4y$

$= 3x + 2x + 7y - 4y$

$= 5x + 3y$

b. $(3x + 7y) - (2x - 4y) = 3x + 7y - 2x + 4y$

$= 3x - 2x + 7y + 4y$

$= x + 11y$

c. $(3x + 7y) - 2(2x - 4y) = 3x + 7y - 4x + 8y$

$= 3x - 4x + 7y + 8y$

$= -x + 15y$

71. a. $\left(4x^2 - 5x + 3\right) + \left(3x^2 + 4x - 9\right)$

$= 4x^2 - 5x + 3 + 3x^2 + 4x - 9$

$= 4x^2 + 3x^2 - 5x + 4x + 3 - 9$

$= 7x^2 - x - 6$

b. $\left(4x^2 - 5x + 3\right) - \left(3x^2 + 4x - 9\right)$

$= 4x^2 - 5x + 3 - 3x^2 - 4x + 9$

$= 4x^2 - 3x^2 - 5x - 4x + 3 + 9$

$= x^2 - 9x + 12$

c. $3(5x^2 - 4x + 2) - 4(3x^2 + x - 5)$

$= 15x^2 - 12x + 6 - 12x^2 - 4x + 20$

$= 15x^2 - 12x^2 - 12x - 4x + 6 + 20$

$= 3x^2 - 16x + 26$

72. a. $\left(4x + 7\right)\left(4x - 7\right) = \left(4x\right)^2 - \left(7\right)^2$

$= 16x^2 - 49$

b. $\left(2x + 3\right)^2 = \left(2x\right)^2 + 2\left(2x\right)\left(3\right) + \left(3\right)^2$

$= 4x^2 + 12x + 9$

c. $\left(5x - 6\right)^2 = \left(5x\right)^2 - 2\left(5x\right)\left(6\right) + \left(6\right)^2$

$= 25x^2 - 60x + 36$

73. a. $\left(x + 4\right)\left(x^2 - 2x - 3\right)$

$= x^2\left(x + 4\right) - 2x\left(x + 4\right) - 3\left(x + 4\right)$

$= x^3 + 4x^2 - 2x^2 - 8x - 3x - 12$

$= x^3 + 2x^2 - 11x - 12$

b. $\left(x - 3\right)\left(x + 2\right)\left(x - 4\right)$

$= \left(x - 3\right)\left(x^2 - 4x + 2x - 8\right)$

$= \left(x - 3\right)\left(x^2 - 2x - 8\right)$

$= x^2\left(x - 3\right) - 2x\left(x - 3\right) - 8\left(x - 3\right)$

$= x^3 - 3x^2 - 2x^2 + 6x - 8x + 24$

$= x^3 - 5x^2 - 2x + 24$

c. $\left(3x^2 + x - 2\right)\left(2x^2 - 4x - 1\right)$

$$\begin{array}{r} 3x^2 + x - 2 \\ \times\ \ 2x^2 - 4x - 1 \\ \hline -3x^2 - x + 2 \\ -12x^3 - 4x^2 + 8x \\ 6x^4 + 2x^3 + 4x^2 \\ \hline 6x^4 - 10x^3 - 3x^2 + 7x + 2 \end{array}$$

74. a. $\dfrac{6x^3 + 4x^2}{2x} = \dfrac{6x^3}{2x} + \dfrac{4x^2}{2x} = 3x^2 + 2x$

b. $\dfrac{x^2 - x - 12}{x + 3} = \dfrac{\left(x - 4\right)\left(x + 3\right)}{\left(x + 3\right)} = x - 4$

c. $\dfrac{2x^4 - 4x^3 + 2x^2 - 8}{2x - 4} = \dfrac{2\left(x^4 - 2x^3 + x^2 - 4\right)}{2\left(x - 2\right)} = \dfrac{2\left[\left(x^4 - 2x^3\right) + \left(x^2 - 4\right)\right]}{2\left(x - 2\right)} = \dfrac{2\left[x^3\left(x - 2\right) + \left(x - 2\right)\left(x + 2\right)\right]}{2\left(x - 2\right)}$

$= \dfrac{2\left(x - 2\right)\left[x^3 + \left(x + 2\right)\right]}{2\left(x - 2\right)} = \dfrac{2\left(x - 2\right)\left[x^3 + \left(x + 2\right)\right]}{2\left(x - 2\right)} = x^3 + \left(x + 2\right) = x^3 + x + 2$

Review of Technology Perspectives

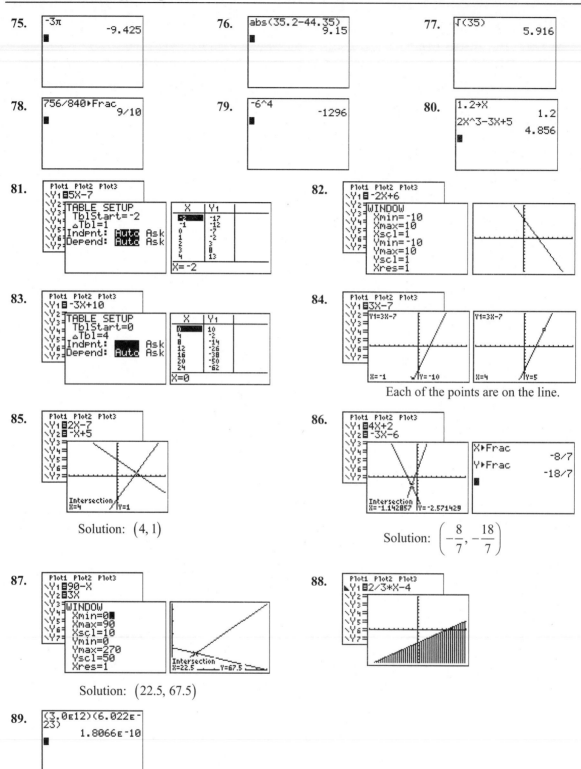

75. -3π -9.425

76. abs(35.2−44.35)   9.15

77. $\sqrt{(35)}$ 5.916

78. 756/840►Frac   9/10

79. -6^4 -1296

80. 1.2→X   1.2
2X^3−3X+5   4.856

81. Y1=5X−7, TABLE SETUP, TblStart=−2, ΔTbl=1, Indpnt: Auto Ask, Depend: Auto Ask

82. Y1=−2X+6, WINDOW, Xmin=−10, Xmax=10, Xscl=1, Ymin=−10, Ymax=10, Yscl=1, Xres=1

83. Y1=−3X+10, TABLE SETUP, TblStart=0, ΔTbl=4, Indpnt: Auto Ask, Depend: Auto Ask

84. Y1=3X−7

Each of the points are on the line.

85. Y1=2X−7, Y2=−X+5

Solution: $(4, 1)$

86. Y1=4X+2, Y2=−3X−6, X►Frac $-8/7$, Y►Frac $-18/7$

Solution: $\left(-\dfrac{8}{7}, -\dfrac{18}{7}\right)$

87. Y1=90−X, Y2=3X, WINDOW, Xmin=0, Xmax=90, Xscl=10, Ymin=0, Ymax=270, Yscl=50, Xres=1

Solution: $(22.5, 67.5)$

88. Y1=2/3*X−4

89. (3.0E12)(6.022E−23)   1.8066E−10

Section 6.1: An Introduction to Factoring Polynomials

Quick Review 6.1

1. $77 = 7 \cdot 11$

2. $90 = 2 \cdot 3^2 \cdot 5$

3. The x-intercept is the point on the line that crosses the x-axis. Thus the x-intercept is $(3, 0)$.

4. The x-intercept is the point on the line such that $y = 0$. Thus the x-intercept is $(2, 0)$.

5. $(x-4)(x+5) = x^2 + 5x - 4x - 20 = x^2 + x - 20$

Exercises 6.1

1. $24 = 2^3 \cdot 3$
$54 = 2 \cdot 3^3$
GCF: $2 \cdot 3 = 6$

3. $20x^2 = 2^2 \cdot 5 \cdot x \cdot x$
$28x = 2^2 \cdot 7 \cdot x$
GCF: $2^2 \cdot x = 4x$

5. $18x^4 y^3 = 2 \cdot 3^2 x \cdot x \cdot x \cdot x \cdot y \cdot y \cdot y$
$45x^2 y = 3^2 \cdot 5 \cdot x \cdot x \cdot y$
GCF: $3^2 x^2 y = 9x^2 y$

7. $12x^3 - 18x^2 = 6x^2 (2x) - 6x^2 (3)$
$\qquad = 6x^2 (2x - 3)$

9. $10a^2 b + 6ab^2 = 2ab(5a) + 2ab(3b)$
$\qquad = 2ab(5a + 3b)$

11. $10x^3 - 15x^2 y + 20xy^2$
$= 5x(2x^2) - 5x(3xy) + 5x(4y^2)$
$= 5x(2x^2 - 3xy + 4y^2)$

13. $2x(x-2y) + y(x-2y) = (2x+y)(x-2y)$

15. $7x(2x-5) - 9(2x-5) = (7x-9)(2x-5)$

17. $14x^2 + 77x = 7x(2x) + 7x(11)$
$\qquad = 7x(2x + 11)$

19. $10x^3 - 15x^2 = 5x^2 (2x) - 5x^2 (3)$
$\qquad = 5x^2 (2x - 3)$

21. $8x^2 y - 20xy^2 = 4xy(2x) - 4xy(5y)$
$\qquad = 4xy(2x - 5y)$

23. $6x^3 - 8x^2 + 10x = 2x(3x^2) - 2x(4x) + 2x(5)$
$\qquad = 2x(3x^2 - 4x + 5)$

25. $(5x-2)(x) + (5x-2)(3) = (5x-2)(x+3)$

27. $(x+2y)(6x) - (x+2y)(7y) = (x+2y)(6x-7y)$

29. $ax + bx + 2a + 2b = x(a+b) + 2(a+b)$
$\qquad = (a+b)(x+2)$

31. $5ax - 2a + 15x - 6 = a(5x-2) + 3(5x-2)$
$\qquad = (5x-2)(a+3)$

33. $2ax - 7a - 2bx + 7b = a(2x-7) - b(2x+7)$
$\qquad = (2x-7)(a-b)$

35. $3x^2 - 5x + 12x - 20 = (3x^2 - 5x) + (12x - 20)$
$\qquad = x(3x-5) + 4(3x-5)$
$\qquad = (3x-5)(x+4)$

37. $12x^2 + 4x - 15x - 5 = (12x^2 + 4x) - (15x + 5)$
$\qquad = 4x(3x+1) - 5(3x+1)$
$\qquad = (3x+1)(4x-5)$

39. **a.** From the table we can see that the zeros of $P(x)$ are $x = 2$ and $x = 5$.

 b. The factored form of $P(x)$ is $P(x) = (x-2)(x-5)$.

41. **a.** From the table we can see that the zeros of $P(x)$ are $x = -4$ and $x = 8$.

    b. The factored form of $P(x)$ is $P(x) = (x+4)(x-8)$.

43. **a.** The x-intercepts are $(2, 0)$ and $(5, 0)$.

    b. The zeros of the $P(x)$ are $x = 2$ and $x = 5$.

    c. $x^2 - 7x + 10 = (x-2)(x-5)$

45. **a.** The x-intercepts are $(-2, 0)$, $(0, 0)$, and $(3, 0)$.

    b. The zeros of the $P(x)$ are $x = -2$, $x = 0$, and $x = 5$.

    c. $x^3 - x^2 - 6x = x(x+2)(x-3)$

47. **a.** If $P(x) = (x+5)(x-9)$ then the zeros of $P(x)$ are $x = -5$ and $x = 9$.

    b. The x-intercepts of $P(x)$ are $(-5, 0)$ and $(9, 0)$.

49. **a.** If $P(x) = (x+3)(x+1)(x-8)$ then the zeros of $P(x)$ are $x = -3$, $x = -1$ and $x = 8$.

    b. The x-intercepts of $P(x)$ are $(-3, 0)$, $(-1, 0)$ and $(8, 0)$.

51. **a.** If $P(x) = (x+3)(x) - (x+3)(17) = (x+3)(x-17)$ then the zeros of $P(x)$ are $x = -3$ and $x = 17$.

    b. The x-intercepts of $P(x)$ are $(-3, 0)$ and $(17, 0)$.

53. **a.**

x	$y = x^2 - 35x + 300$
0	300
5	150
10	50
15	0
20	0
25	50
30	150

    b. The zeros of $P(x)$ are $x = 15$ and $x = 20$.

    c. The factored form of $P(x)$ is $P(x) = (x-15)(x-20)$.

55. **a.**

x	$y = x^3 - 10x^2 + 24x$
0	0
1	15
2	16
3	9
4	0
5	−5
6	0

    b. The zeros of $P(x)$ are $x = 0$, $x = 4$, and $x = 6$.

    c. The factored form of $P(x)$ is $P(x) = x(x-4)(x-6)$.

57.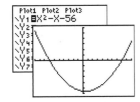

$\left[-10,10,1\right]$ by $\left[-60,60,10\right]$

Answer: $x^2 - x - 56 = (x+7)(x-8)$

59.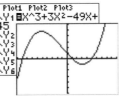

$\left[-10,10,1\right]$ by $\left[-300,300,50\right]$

Answer:

$x^3 + 3x^2 - 49x + 45 = (x+9)(x-1)(x-5)$

61.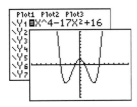

$\left[-10,10,1\right]$ by $\left[-100,100,10\right]$

Answer: $x^4 - 17x^2 + 16 = (x+4)(x+1)(x-1)(x-4)$

Polynomial $P(x)$	Factored Form of $P(x)$	Zeros of $P(x)$	*x*-intercepts of the graph of $y = P(x)$
63. $x^2 + 2x - 63$	$(x-7)(x+9)$	7 and -9	$(7, 0), (-9, 0)$
65. $x^2 - 2x - 80$	$(x+8)(x-10)$	-8 and 10	$(-8, 0), (10, 0)$

67. Factor: $x(x+4) + 2(x+4) = (x+4)(x+2)$

  Expand: $x(x+4) + 2(x+4) = x^2 + 4x + 2x + 8 = x^2 + 6x + 8$

69. Factor: $2x(5x-2) - 7(5x-2) = (5x-2)(2x-7)$

  Expand: $2x(5x-2) - 7(5x-2) = 10x^2 - 4x - 35x + 14 = 10x^2 - 39x + 14$

71. a. $P + P \cdot r = P(1+r)$

  b. $P(1+r) = 2000(1+0.4) = \$2,080$

73. $A = 2\pi r^2 + 2\pi rh = 2\pi r(r+h)$

Cumulative Review

1. using the points: $(0, -2)$ and $(3, 0)$ we can find the slope $m = \dfrac{0-(-2)}{3-0} = \dfrac{2}{3}$. We know that the y-intercept is $(0, -2)$. Thus the equation of the line is

$$y = mx + b$$

$$y = \frac{2}{3}x - 2$$

2.

$$-9 < 2x + 3 \le 11$$

$$-9 - 3 < 2x + 3 - 3 \le 11 - 3$$

$$-12 < 2x \le 8$$

$$\frac{-12}{2} < \frac{2x}{2} \le \frac{8}{2}$$

$$-6 < x \le 4$$

Solution: $(-6, 4]$

3. $\left(\dfrac{6x^{-2}y^8}{2x^{-4}y^{-2}}\right)^{-2} = \left(\dfrac{\overset{3}{\cancel{6}}\, x^{-2-(-4)}y^{8-(-2)}}{\underset{1}{\cancel{2}}}\right)^{-2}$

$= \left(3x^2y^{10}\right)^{-2} = \left(\dfrac{1}{3x^2y^{10}}\right)^2$

$= \dfrac{1^2}{3^2\left(x^2\right)^2\left(y^{10}\right)^2} = \dfrac{1}{9x^{2\cdot2}y^{10\cdot2}} = \dfrac{1}{9x^4y^{20}}$

4.

$$\require{enclose}\begin{array}{r}2x+5\\3x-2\enclose{longdiv}{6x^2+11x-10}\\\underline{6x^2-4x}\\15x-10\\\underline{15x-10}\\0\end{array}$$

5. **a.** The factor pairs of 21 are: $1\cdot21$ and $3\cdot7$.

   b. The factor pairs of 20 are: $1\cdot20$, $2\cdot10$, and $4\cdot5$.

Section 6.2: Factoring Trinomials of the Form x^2+bx+c

Quick Review 6.2

1. $(x+3)(x-5) = x^2-5x+3x-15$

$= x^2-2x-15$

2. $(x+3y)(x-5y) = x^2-5xy+3xy-15y^2$

$= x^2-2xy-15y^2$

3. $x(x-5)(x-2) = x\left(x^2-2x-5x+10\right)$

$= x\left(x^2-7x+10\right)$

$= x^3-7x^2+10x$

4. The factor pairs of 35 are: $1\cdot35$ and $5\cdot7$.

5. The factor pairs of 48 are: $1\cdot48$, $2\cdot24$, $4\cdot12$, $3\cdot16$, and $6\cdot8$.

Exercises 6.2

1. The sign pattern in the factorization of $x^2-10x-11$ must be **B.** $(x+?)(x-?)$ since the product of the last terms is negative.

3. The sign pattern in the factorization of x^2+6x+5 must be **A.** $(x+?)(x+?)$ since the product of the last terms is positive and their sum is positive.

5. $x^2-6x+8 = (x-4)(x-2)$

7. $x^2-11x-12 = (x+1)(x-12)$

9. $x^2+3x+2 = (x+?)(x+?)$

$= (x+1)(x+2)$ — Select factors of 2 with a sum of 3.

11. $x^2-x-2 = (x-?)(x+?)$

$= (x-2)(x+1)$ — Select factors of -2 with a sum of -1.

13. $x^2+x-20 = (x+?)(x-?)$

$= (x+5)(x-4)$ — Select factors of -20 with a sum of 1.

15. $x^2-9x+20 = (x-?)(x-?)$

$= (x-5)(x-4)$ — Select factors of 20 with a sum of -9.

17. $x^2 - 7x - 18 = (x+?)(x-?)$
$\quad = (x+2)(x-9)$ ◁ Select factors of -18 with a sum of -7.

19. $x^2 + 2x - 24 = (x+?)(x-?)$
$\quad = (x+6)(x-4)$ ◁ Select factors of -24 with a sum of 2.

21. $a^2 - 10a - 11 = a^2 + a - 11a - 11$
$\quad = a(a+1) - 11(a+1)$
$\quad = (a-11)(a+1)$

23. $y^2 - 18y + 17 = y^2 - y - 17y + 17$
$\quad = y(y-1) - 17(y-1)$
$\quad = (y-17)(y-1)$

25. $x^2 - 8x + 7 = x^2 - x - 7x + 7$
$\quad = x(x-1) - 7(x-1)$
$\quad = (x-7)(x-1)$

27. $y^2 - 2y - 99 = y^2 - 11y + 9y - 99$
$\quad = y(y-11) + 9(y-11)$
$\quad = (y+9)(y-11)$

29. $p^2 - 29p + 100 = p^2 - 4p - 25p + 100$
$\quad = p(p-4) - 25(p-4)$
$\quad = (p-25)(p-4)$

31. $t^2 + 14t + 48 = t^2 + 6t + 8t + 48$
$\quad = t(t+6) + 8(t+6)$
$\quad = (t+8)(t+6)$

33. $n^2 + 5n - 36 = n^2 - 4n + 9n - 36$
$\quad = n(n-4) + 9(n-4)$
$\quad = (n+9)(n-4)$

35. a. $x^2 + 7x + 12 = x^2 + 3x + 4x + 12$
$\quad = x(x+3) + 4(x+3)$
$\quad = (x+4)(x+3)$

b. $x^2 + 8x + 12 = x^2 + 2x + 6x + 12$
$\quad = x(x+2) + 6(x+2)$
$\quad = (x+6)(x+2)$

c. $x^2 + 10x + 12$ is prime since none of the pairs of factors of 12 have a sum of 10.

d. $x^2 + 13x + 12 = x^2 + x + 12x + 12$
$\quad = x(x+1) + 12(x+1)$
$\quad = (x+12)(x+1)$

37. a. $x^2 - 3x - 28 = x^2 - 7x + 4x - 28$
$\quad = x(x-7) + 4(x-7)$
$\quad = (x+4)(x-7)$

b. $x^2 - 12x - 28 = x^2 - 14x + 2x - 28$
$\quad = x(x-14) + 2(x-14)$
$\quad = (x+2)(x-14)$

c. $x^2 - 15x - 28$ is prime since none of the pairs of factors of -28 have a sum of -15.

d. $x^2 - 27x - 28 = x^2 + x - 28x - 28$
$\quad = x(x+1) - 28(x+1)$
$\quad = (x-28)(x+1)$

39. a. $x^2 - 36 = x^2 - 6x + 6x - 36$
$\quad = x(x-6) + 6(x-6)$
$\quad = (x+6)(x-6)$

b. $x^2 + 9x - 36 = x^2 + 12x - 3x - 36$
$\quad = x(x+12) - 3(x+12)$
$\quad = (x-3)(x+12)$

c. $x^2 + 16x - 36 = x^2 + 18x - 2x - 36$

$\qquad = x(x+18) - 2(x+18)$

$\qquad = (x-2)(x+18)$

d. $x^2 + 18x - 36$ is prime since none of the pairs of factors of -36 have a sum of 18.

41. $x^2 + 5xy + 6y^2 = x^2 + 2xy + 3xy + 6y^2$

$\qquad = x(x+2y) + 3y(x+2y)$

$\qquad = (x+3y)(x+2y)$

43. $x^2 + xy - 6y^2 = x^2 - 2xy + 3xy - 6y^2$

$\qquad = x(x-2y) + 3y(x-2y)$

$\qquad = (x+3y)(x-2y)$

45. $x^2 - 10xy + 25y^2 = x^2 - 5xy - 5xy + 25y^2$

$\qquad = x(x-5y) - 5y(x-5y)$

$\qquad = (x-5y)(x-5y)$

47. $a^2 - 16ab - 36b^2 = a^2 + 2ab - 18ab - 36b^2$

$\qquad = a(a+2b) - 18b(a+2b)$

$\qquad = (a-18b)(a+2b)$

49. $-x^2 + 2x + 35 = -\left(x^2 - 2x - 35\right)$

$\qquad = -\left(x^2 + 5x - 7x - 35\right)$

$\qquad = -\left[x(x+5) - 7(x+5)\right]$

$\qquad = -(x-7)(x+5)$

51. $-m^2 - 3m + 18 = -\left(m^2 + 3m - 18\right)$

$\qquad = -\left(m^2 - 3m + 6m - 18\right)$

$\qquad = -\left[m(m-3) + 6(m-3)\right]$

$\qquad = -(m+6)(m-3)$

53. $-x^2 + 12xy + 45y^2 = -\left(x^2 - 12xy - 45y^2\right) = -\left(x^2 + 3xy - 15xy - 45y^2\right)$

$\qquad = -\left[x(x+3y) - 15y(x+3y)\right] = -(x-15y)(x+3y)$

55. $5x^3 + 15x^2 + 10x = 5x\left(x^2 + 3x + 2\right)$

$\qquad = 5x\left(x^2 + x + 2x + 2\right)$

$\qquad = 5x\left[x(x+1) + 2(x+1)\right]$

$\qquad = 5x(x+2)(x+1)$

57. $4ax^3 - 20ax^2 + 24ax = 4ax\left(x^2 - 5x + 6\right)$

$\qquad = 4ax\left(x^2 - 2x - 3x + 6\right)$

$\qquad = 4ax\left[x(x-2) - 3(x-2)\right]$

$\qquad = 4ax(x-3)(x-2)$

59. $10az^2 + 290az + 1000a = 10a\left(z^2 + 29z + 100\right)$

$\qquad = 10a\left(z^2 + 4z + 25z + 100\right)$

$\qquad = 10a\left[z(z+4) + 25(z+4)\right]$

$\qquad = 10a(z+25)(z+4)$

61. $2abx^2 + 4abx - 96ab = 2ab\left(x^2 + 2x - 48\right)$

$\qquad = 2ab\left(x^2 - 6x + 8x - 48\right)$

$\qquad = 2ab\left[x(x-6) + 8(x-6)\right]$

$\qquad = 2ab(x+8)(x-6)$

63. $x^2(a+b) - 6(a+b)x + 6(a+b)$

$\quad = (a+b)\left(x^2 - 6x + 6\right)$

65. a. $x^2 - 3x - 18 = x^2 - 6x + 3x - 18$

$\qquad = x(x-6) + 3(x-6)$

$\qquad = (x-6)(x+3)$

b. $x^2 - 3x + 18$ is prime.

67. a. $x^2 + 13xy + 12y^2 = x^2 + xy + 12xy + 12y^2$

$\qquad = x(x+y) + 12y(x+y)$

$\qquad = (x+y)(x+12y)$

b. $x^2 + 13xy - 12y^2$ is prime.

69. a. The zeros are $x = -9$ and $x = -5$.

b. $P(x) = (x+9)(x+5)$

71. a. The x-intercepts are $(-10, 0)$ and $(4, 0)$.

b. $P(x) = (x+10)(x-4)$

Polynomial $P(x)$	Factored Form	Zeros of $P(x)$	x-intercepts of the graph of $y = P(x)$
73. $x^2 + 2x - 15$	$\begin{aligned} x^2 + 2x - 15 &= x^2 - 3x + 5x - 15 \\ &= x(x-3) + 5(x-3) \\ &= (x+5)(x-3) \end{aligned}$	$x = -5,\ x = 3$	$(-5, 0),\ (3, 0)$

Expand	Factor

75.

$\begin{aligned} &x(x-3) - 2(x-3) \\ &= x^2 - 3x - 2x + 6 \\ &= x^2 - 5x + 6 \end{aligned}$

$\begin{aligned} &x(x-3) - 2(x-3) \\ &= (x-3)(x-2) \end{aligned}$

Cumulative Review

1.

$$\dfrac{2x-7}{3} = \dfrac{x+4}{2}$$

$$6\left(\dfrac{2x-7}{3}\right) = 6\left(\dfrac{x+4}{2}\right)$$

$$2(2x-7) = 3(x+4)$$

$$4x - 14 = 3x + 12$$

$$4x - 14 + 14 = 3x + 12 + 14$$

$$4x = 3x + 26$$

$$4x - 3x = 3x - 3x + 26$$

$$x = 26$$

2. The slope of the line is $\dfrac{9-5}{-5-(-2)} = \dfrac{4}{-3} = -\dfrac{4}{3}$.

Using the point slope form of a line, we obtain:

$$y - y_1 = m(x - x_1)$$

$$y - 5 = -\dfrac{4}{3}(x - (-2))$$

$$y - 5 = -\dfrac{4}{3}x - \dfrac{8}{3}$$

$$y = -\dfrac{4}{3}x + \dfrac{7}{3}$$

3. $|x+8| \le 9$ is equivalent to

$$-9 \le x + 8 \le 9$$

$$-9 - 8 \le x + 8 - 8 \le 9 - 8$$

$$-17 \le x \le 1$$

Solution: $[-17, 1]$

4.

$$(3x-2)^2 - (2x-3)^2$$

$$= \left[(3x)^2 - 2(3x)(2) + 2^2\right] - \left[(2x)^2 - 2(2x)(3) + 3^2\right]$$

$$= (9x^2 - 12x + 4) - (4x^2 - 12x + 9)$$

$$= 9x^2 - 12x + 4 - 4x^2 + 12x - 9$$

$$= 9x^2 - 4x^2 - 12x + 12x + 4 - 9$$

$$= 5x^2 - 5$$

5.

$$12x^4 y^3 + 9x^3 y^4 + 3x^2 y^2 = (3x^2 y^2)4x^2 y + (3x^2 y^2)3xy^2 + (3x^2 y^2)1$$

$$= (3x^2 y^2)(4x^2 y + 3xy^2 + 1)$$

Section 6.3: Factoring Trinomials of the Form $ax^2 + bx + c$

Quick Review 6.3

1. $(2x+7)(3x-1) = 6x^2 - 2x + 21x - 7$

$= 6x^2 + 19x - 7$

2. $(5x+4y)(2x+7y) = 10x^2 + 35xy + 8xy + 28y^2$

$= 10x^2 + 43xy + 28y^2$

3. $(2x+5)(3x-4) = 6x^2 - 8x + 15x - 20$

$= 6x^2 + 7x - 20$

4. $-3xy(3x+y)(6x-5y) = -3xy(18x^2 - 15xy + 6xy - 5y^2)$

$= -3xy(18x^2 - 9xy - 5y^2)$

$= -54x^3y + 27x^2y^2 + 15xy^3$

5. $2x(3x-5) + 7(3x-5) = (3x-5)(2x+7)$

Exercises 6.3

1. The sign pattern in the factorization of $16x^2 - 50x - 21$ must be **B.** $(?x+?)(?x-?)$ since the product of the last terms is negative.

3. The sign pattern in the factorization of $16x^2 + 38x + 21$ must be **A.** $(?x+?)(?x+?)$ since the product of the last terms is positive and their sum is positive.

5. a. $3x^2 + 4x + 1 = (3x+1)(x+1)$

   b. $3x^2 - 4x + 1 = (3x-1)(x-1)$

7. a. $2x^2 + x - 1 = (2x-1)(x+1)$

   b. $2x^2 - x - 2 = (2x+1)(x-1)$

9. $5x^2 + 9x - 2 = (5x-1)(x+2)$

11. $5x^2 - 7x + 2 = (5x-2)(x-1)$

13. $6v^2 - 5v - 6 = (3v+2)(2v-3)$

15. $6v^2 - 37v + 6 = (6v-1)(v-6)$

17. $5x^2 + 6x + 1 = (5x+1)(x+1)$

19. $7x^2 - 8x + 1 = (7x-?)(x-?)$

$= (7x-1)(x-1)$

21. $7x^2 - 6x - 1 = (7x+1)(x-1)$

23. $11x^2 + 10x - 1 = (11x-1)(x+1)$

25. $2x^2 + 5x + 3 = (2x+?)(x+?)$

$= (2x+3)(x+1)$

27. $3a^2 + 17a + 10 = 3a^2 + 15a + 2a + 10$

$= 3a(a+5) + 2(a+5)$

$= (3a+2)(a+5)$

29. $3m^2 - 10m - 8 = 3m^2 - 12m + 2m - 8$

$= 3m(m-4) + 2(m-4)$

$= (3m+2)(m-4)$

31. a. $3m^2 + 10m + 8 = 3m^2 + 4m + 6m + 8$
$$= m(3m+4) + 2(3m+4)$$
$$= (m+2)(3m+4)$$

b. $3m^2 + 11m + 8 = 3m^2 + 3m + 8m + 8$
$$= 3m(m+1) + 8(m+1)$$
$$= (3m+8)(m+1)$$

c. $3m^2 + 14m + 8 = 3m^2 + 2m + 12m + 8$
$$= m(3m+2) + 4(3m+2)$$
$$= (m+4)(3m+2)$$

d. $3m^2 + 25m + 8 = 3m^2 + m + 24m + 8$
$$= m(3m+1) + 8(3m+1)$$
$$= (m+8)(3m+1)$$

33. $2x^2 + 5x - 7 = 2x^2 + 7x - 2x - 7$
$$= x(2x+7) - (2x+7)$$
$$= (2x+7)(x-1)$$

35. $4w^2 - 9w + 5 = 4w^2 - 4w - 5w + 5$
$$= 4w(w-1) - 5(w-1)$$
$$= (4w-5)(w-1)$$

37. $9z^2 - 9z - 10 = 9z^2 - 15z + 6z - 10$
$$= 3z(3z-5z) + 2(3z-5)$$
$$= (3z+2)(3z-5)$$

39. $10b^2 + 29b + 10 = 10b^2 + 4b + 25b + 10$
$$= 2b(5b+2) + 5(5b+2)$$
$$= (2b+5)(5b+2)$$

41. $12m^2 - mn - 35n^2 = 12m^2 - 21mn + 20mn - 35n^2$
$$= 3m(4m-7n) + 5n(4m-7n)$$
$$= (3m+5n)(4m-7n)$$

43. $18y^2 + 55y - 28 = 18y^2 - 8y + 63y - 28$
$$= 2y(9y-4) + 7(9y-4)$$
$$= (2y+7)(9y-4)$$

45. $55y^2 - 29y - 12 = 55y^2 - 44y + 15y - 12$
$$= 11y(5y-4) + 3(5y-4)$$
$$= (11y+3)(5y-4)$$

47. $20x^2 + 37xy + 15y^2 = 20x^2 + 12xy + 25xy + 15y^2$
$$= 4x(5x+3y) + 5y(5x+3y)$$
$$= (4x+5y)(5x+3y)$$

49. $14x^2 - 39xy + 10y^2 = 14x^2 - 35xy - 4xy + 10y^2$
$$= 7x(2x-5y) - 2y(2x-5y)$$
$$= (7x-2y)(2x-5y)$$

51. $33m^2 + 13mn - 6n^2 = 33m^2 - 9mn + 22mn - 6n^2$
$$= 3m(11m-3n) + 2n(11m-3n)$$
$$= (3m+2n)(11m-3n)$$

53. $6v^2 + 13vw + 6w^2 = 6v^2 + 9vw + 4vw + 6w^2$
$$= 3v(2v+3w) + 2w(2v+3w)$$
$$= (3v+2w)(2v+3w)$$

55. a. $4n^2 + 39n - 10 = 4n^2 - n + 40n - 10$
$$= n(4n-1) + 10(4n-1)$$
$$= (n+10)(4n-1)$$

b. $2n^2 + 3n - 20 = 2n^2 - 5n + 8n - 20$
$$= n(2n-5) + 4(2n-5)$$
$$= (n+4)(2n-5)$$

c. $5n^2 + 6n - 8 = 5n^2 - 4n + 10n - 8$
$$= n(5n-4) + 2(5n-4)$$
$$= (n+2)(5n-4)$$

d. $40n^2 + 8n - 1$ is prime since none of the pairs of factors of -40 have a sum of 8.

57. a. $3x^2 - 25xy + 12y^2$ is prime since none of the pairs of factors of 36 have a sum of -25.

b.
$$4x^2 - 15xy + 9y^2 = 4x^2 - 3xy - 12xy + 9y^2$$
$$= x(4x - 3y) - 3y(4x - 3y)$$
$$= (x - 3y)(4x - 3y)$$

c.
$$2x^2 - 13xy + 18y^2 = 2x^2 - 4xy - 9xy + 18y^2$$
$$= 2x(x - 2y) - 9y(x - 2y)$$
$$= (2x - 9y)(x - 2y)$$

d.
$$6x^2 - 37xy + 6y^2 = 6x^2 - xy - 36xy + 6y^2$$
$$= x(6x - y) - 6y(6x - y)$$
$$= (x - 6y)(6x - y)$$

59. a.
$$4x^2 - 23x + 15 = 4x^2 - 20x - 3x + 15$$
$$= 4x(x - 5) - 3(x - 5)$$
$$= (x - 5)(4x - 3)$$

b. $4x^2 - 18x + 15$ is prime.

61.
$$-12x^2 + 20x - 3 = -(12x^2 - 20x + 3)$$
$$= -(12x^2 - 18x - 2x + 3)$$
$$= -[6x(2x - 3) - (2x - 3)]$$
$$= -(6x - 1)(2x - 3)$$

63.
$$-35y^2 + 4y + 4 = -(35y^2 - 4y - 4)$$
$$= -(35y^2 - 14y + 10y - 4)$$
$$= -[7y(5y - 2) + 5(5y - 2)]$$
$$= -(7y + 5)(5y - 2)$$

65.
$$-12z^2 - 47z - 40 = -(12z^2 + 47z + 40)$$
$$= -(12z^2 + 32z + 15z + 40)$$
$$= -[4z(4z + 8) + 5(3z + 8)]$$
$$= -(4z + 5)(3z + 8)$$

67.
$$-38ax^2 + 32ax + 6a = -2a(19x^2 - 16x - 3)$$
$$= -2a(19x^2 - 19x + 3x - 3)$$
$$= -2a[19x(x - 1) + 3(x - 1)]$$
$$= -2a(19x + 3)(x - 1)$$

69.
$$60x^5 - 145x^4 + 75x^3$$
$$= 5x^3(12x^2 - 29x + 15)$$
$$= 5x^3(12x^2 - 20x - 9x + 15)$$
$$= 5x^3[4x(3x - 5) - 3(3x - 5)]$$
$$= 5x^3(4x - 3)(3x - 5)$$

71.
$$15m^3n - 6m^2n^2 - 21mn^3$$
$$= 3mn(5m^2 - 2mn - 7mn^2)$$
$$= 3mn(5m^2 + 5mn - 7mn - 7n^2)$$
$$= 3mn[5m(m + n) - 7n(m + n)]$$
$$= 3mn(5m - 7n)(m + n)$$

73.
$$210av^3 + 77av^2w - 210avw^2$$
$$= 7av(30v^2 + 11vw - 30w^2)$$
$$= 7av(30v^2 + 36vw - 25vw - 30w^2)$$
$$= 7av[6v(5v + 6w) - 5w(5v + 6w)]$$
$$= 7av(6v - 5w)(5v + 6w)$$

75. $35x^2(a+b)-29x(a+b)+6(a+b)$

$=(a+b)(35x^2-29x+6)$

$=(a+b)(35x^2-15x-14x+6)$

$=(a+b)\left[5x(7x-3)-2(7x-3)\right]$

$=(a+b)(5x-2)(7x-3)$

Polynomial $P(x)$	Factored Form	Zeros of $P(x)$	x-intercepts of the graph of $y=P(x)$
77. $3x^2-16x+5$	$(3x-1)(x-5)$	$\dfrac{1}{3}$ and 5	$\left(\dfrac{1}{3},0\right)$, $(5,0)$
79. $3x^2+10x-8$	$(3x-2)(x+4)$	$\dfrac{2}{3}$ and -4	$\left(\dfrac{2}{3},0\right)$, $(-4,0)$

Cumulative Review

1. $2x-3(y-z)=2(-2)-3\left[(3)-(-5)\right]$
$=-4-3(8)=-4-24=-28$

2. $-3x^2+(2y)^2+2z^2=-3(-2)^2+\left[2(3)\right]^2+2(-5)^2$
$=-3(4)+(6)^2+2(25)$
$=-12+36+50=74$

3. $2x^0+3y^0+(2x)^0+(3y)^0=2(1)+3(1)+1+1$
$=2+3+1+1=7$

4. $|2x+9|-3=11$
$|2x+9|-3+3=11+3$
$|2x+9|=14$ is equivalent to

$2x+9=-14$ or $2x+9=14$
$2x+9-9=-14-9$ $2x+9-9=14-9$
$2x=-23$ $2x=5$
$x=-\dfrac{23}{3}$ $x=\dfrac{5}{2}$

5. $(2x-3)(4x^2+6x+9)=(2x)4x^2+(2x)6x+(2x)9+(-3)4x^2+(-3)6x+(-3)9$
$=8x^3+12x^2+18x-12x^2-18x-27$
$=8x^3+12x^2-12x^2+18x-18x-27$
$=8x^3-27$

Section 6.4: Factoring Special Forms

Quick Review 6.4

1. $(x+7)(x-7)=x^2-7x+7x-49$
$=x^2-49$

2. $(5x+2y)(5x+2y)=25x^2+10xy+10xy-4y^2$
$=25x^2+20xy-4y^2$

3. $(6x-5)(6x-5) = 36x^2 - 30x - 30x + 25$

$\qquad\qquad = 36x^2 - 60x + 25$

4. $(3x-2)(9x^2 + 6x + 4)$

$= (3x)9x^2 + (3x)6x + (3x)4 + (-2)9x^2 + (-2)6x + (-2)4$

$= 27x^3 + 18x^2 + 12x - 18x^2 - 12x - 8$

$= 27x^3 + 18x^2 - 18x^2 + 12x - 12x - 8$

$= 27x^3 - 8$

5.

x	x^2
1	1
2	4
3	9
4	16
5	25
6	36
7	49
8	64
9	81
10	100

x	x^3
1	1
2	8
3	27
4	64
5	125

Exercises 6.4

1. $a^2 + 6a + 9 = a^2 + 2(3)(a) + (3)^2$

$\qquad\qquad\quad = (a+3)^2$

3. $4w^2 - 12w + 9 = (2w)^2 - 2(2w)(3) + 3^2$

$\qquad\qquad\qquad = (2w-3)^2$

5. $m^2 - 2m + 1 = (m)^2 - 2(m)(1) + (1)^2$

$\qquad\qquad\quad = (m-1)^2$

7. $36v^2 + 12v + 1 = (6v)^2 + 2(6v)(1) + (1)^2$

$\qquad\qquad\qquad = (6v+1)^2$

9. $25x^2 - 20xy + 4y^2$

$= (5x)^2 - 2(5x)(2y) + (2y)^2$

$= (5x-2y)^2$

11. $121m^2 + 88mn + 16n^2$

$= (11m)^2 + 2(11m)(4n) + (4n)^2$

$= (11m+4n)^2$

13. $-x^2 + 16xy - 64y^2$

$= -(x^2 - 16xy + 64y^2)$

$= -[(x)^2 - 2(x)(8y) + (8y)^2]$

$= -(x-8y)^2$

15. $9 + 16x^2 - 24x$

$= 16x^2 - 24x + 9$

$= (4x)^2 - 2(4x)(3) + (3)^2$

$= (4x-3)^2$

17. $2x^3 + 16x^2 + 32x$

$= 2x(x^2 + 8x + 16)$

$= 2x[(x)^2 + 2(x)(4) + (4)^2]$

$= 2x(x+4)^2$

19. $w^2 - 49 = (w)^2 - (7)^2$

$\qquad\qquad = (w+7)(w-7)$

21. $9v^2 - 1 = (3v)^2 - (1)^2$
$$= (3v+1)(3v-1)$$

23. $81m^2 - 25 = (9m)^2 - (5)^2$
$$= (9m+5)(9m-5)$$

25. $4a^2 - 9b^2 = (2a)^2 - (3b)^2$
$$= (2a+3b)(2a-3b)$$

27. $16v^2 - 121w^2 = (4v)^2 - (11w)^2$
$$= (4v+11w)(4v-11w)$$

29. $36 - m^2 = (6)^2 - (m)^2$
$$= (6+m)(6-m)$$
$$\text{or} \quad -(m-6)(m+6)$$

31. $20x^2 - 45y^2 = 5(4x^2 - 9y^2)$
$$= 5\left[(2x)^2 - (3y)^2\right]$$
$$= 5(2x+3y)(2x-3y)$$

33. $x^3 + 27 = (x)^3 + (3)^3$
$$= (x+3)\left[(x)^2 - (x)(3) + (3)^2\right]$$
$$= (x+3)(x^2 - 3x + 9)$$

35. $m^3 - 125 = (m)^3 - (5)^3$
$$= (m-5)\left[(m)^2 + (m)(5) + (5)^2\right]$$
$$= (m-5)(m^2 + 5m + 25)$$

37. $64a^3 - b^3 = (4a)^3 - (b)^3$
$$= (4a-b)\left[(4a)^2 + (4a)(b) + (b)^2\right]$$
$$= (4a-b)(16a^2 + 4ab + b^2)$$

39. $125x^3 + 8y^3$
$$= (5x)^3 + (2y)^3$$
$$= (5x+2y)\left[(5x)^2 - (5x)(2y) + (2y)^2\right]$$
$$= (5x+2y)(25x^2 - 10xy + 4y^2)$$

41. a. $x^2 - 6x + 9 = (x)^2 - 2(3)(x) + (3)^2 = (x-3)^2$
b. $x^2 + 9$ is prime
c. $x^2 - 10x + 9 = x^2 - x - 9x + 9$
$$= x(x-1) - 9(x-1)$$
$$= (x-1)(x-9)$$

43. a. $x^2 - 12xy + 36y^2 = (x)^2 - 2(x)(6y) + (6y)^2$
$$= (x-6y)^2$$
b. $x^2 - 36y^2 = (x)^2 - (6y)^2 = (x-6y)(x+6y)$
c. $x^2 - 13xy + 36y^2 = x^2 - 9xy - 4xy + 36y^2$
$$= x(x-9y) - 4y(x-9y)$$
$$= (x-9y)(x-4y)$$

45. a. $x^2 + 9y^2$ is prime
b. $4x^2 - 12xy + 9y^2 = (2x)^2 - 2(2x)(3y) + (3y)^2$
$$= (2x-3y)^2$$
c. $4x^2 + 15xy + 9y^2 = 4x^2 + 12xy + 3xy + 9y^2$
$$= 4x(x+3y) + 3y(x+3y)$$
$$= (x+3y)(4x+3y)$$

47. a. $25x^2 - 64y^2 = (5x)^2 - (8y)^2$
$$= (5x-8y)(5x+8y)$$
b. $25x^2 - 80xy + 64y^2$
$$= (5x)^2 - 2(5x)(8y) + (8y)^2$$
$$= (5x-8y)^2$$
c. $25x^2 - 100xy + 64y^2$
$$= 25x^2 - 80xy - 20xy + 64y^2$$
$$= 5x(5x-16y) - 4y(5x-16y)$$
$$= (5x-16y)(5x-4y)$$

49. **a.** $(x+6)^2 = (x)^2 + 2(x)(6) + (6)^2 = x^2 + 12x + 36$; The missing term is $2(x)(6) = 12x$.

b. $(x+6)^2 = (x)^2 + 2(x)(6) + (6)^2 = x^2 + 12x + 36$; The missing term is $(6)^2 = 36$.

51. **a.** $(x-10)^2 = (x)^2 - 2(x)(10) + (10)^2 = x^2 - 20x + 100$; The missing term is $2(x)(10) = 20x$.

b. $(x-10)^2 = (x)^2 - 2(x)(10) + (10)^2 = x^2 - 20x + 100$; The missing term is $(10)^2 = 100$.

53. $-16t^2 + 96t - 144 = -16(t^2 - 6t + 9)$
$$= -16\left[(t)^2 - 2(t)(3) + (3)^2\right]$$
$$= -16(t-3)^2$$

55. $x^4 - 9 = (x^2)^2 - (3)^2$
$$= (x^2 + 3)(x^2 - 3)$$

57. $25y^4 - 1 = (5y^2)^2 - (1)^2$
$$= (5y^2 + 1)(5y^2 - 1)$$

59. $81y^4 - 1 = (9y^2)^2 - (1)^2$
$$= (9y^2 + 1)(9y^2 - 1)$$
$$= (9y^2 + 1)\left[(3y)^2 - (1)^2\right]$$
$$= (9y^2 + 1)(3y + 1)(3y - 1)$$

61. $(x-5)^2 - 9y^2 = (x-5)^2 - (3y)^2$
$$= ((x-5) + 3y)((x-5) - 3y)$$
$$= (x-5+3y)(x-5-3y)$$

63. $4x^2 - (y-3)^2 = (2x)^2 - (y-3)^2$
$$= (2x + (y-3))(2x - (y-3))$$
$$= (2x + y - 3)(2x - y + 3)$$

65. $(a+2b)^2 - (2a+b)^2$
$$= \left[(a+2b) + (2a+b)\right]\left[(a+2b) - (2a+b)\right]$$
$$= (a+2b+2a+b)(a+2b-2a-b)$$
$$= (3a+3b)(-a+b)$$
$$= 3(a+b)(b-a) \text{ or } -3(a+b)(a-b)$$

67. $(a-5b)x^2 - (a-5b)y^2$
$$= (a-5b)(x^2 - y^2)$$
$$= (a-5b)(x+y)(x-y)$$

69. $(a+b)x^2 + 6(a+b)x + 9(a+b)$
$$= (a+b)(x^2 + 6x + 9)$$
$$= (a+b)\left[(x)^2 + 2(x)(3) + (3)^2\right]$$
$$= (a+b)(x+3)^2$$

71. $(x^2 + 20xy + 100y^2)a^2 - 16(x^2 + 20xy + 100y^2)$
$$= (x^2 + 20xy + 100y^2)(a^2 - 16)$$
$$= \left[(x)^2 + 2(x)(10) + (10y)^2\right]\left[(a)^2 - (4)^2\right]$$
$$= (x + 10y)^2 (a+4)(a-4)$$

73. $x_1^2 - x_2^2 = (x_1 + x_2)(x_1 - x_2)$

75. $\pi r_1^2 h - \pi r_2^2 h = \pi h(r_1^2 - r_2^2)$
$$= \pi h(r_1 + r_2)(r_1 - r_2)$$

77. **a.** $V(x) = 63x - 32x^2 + 4x^3 = x(63 - 32x + 4x^2) = x(9 - 2x)(7 - 2x)$

b. The height of the box is x in. The length of the box is $9 - 2x$ in. The width of the box is $7 - 2x$ in.

c. The factored form is the more meaningful form. (It gives us the dimensions of the box.)

79. **a.** The x-intercepts are $(-1, 0)$, $(0, 0)$, and $(1, 0)$.

   b. The zeros are $x = -1$, $x = 0$, and $x = 1$.

   c. $x^3 - x = x(x+1)(x-1)$

Cumulative Review

1. $5x + 6 - 2(3x + 7) = 5x + 6 - 6x - 14 = 5x - 6x + 6 - 14 = -x - 8$

2. Use the addition method. To eliminate y, multiply both sides of the second equation by 2, then add the two equations. Solve this equation for x.

$$3x + 4y = 32$$
$$5x - 2y = -3$$

$$\begin{array}{r} 3x + 4y = 32 \\ \underline{10x - 4y = -6} \\ 13x = 26 \\ x = 2 \end{array}$$

Back substitute 2 for x in the first equation to find y.

$$3x + 4y = 32$$
$$3(2) + 4y = 32$$
$$6 + 4y = 32$$
$$4y = 26$$
$$y = \frac{26}{4} = \frac{\cancel{2} \cdot 13}{\cancel{2} \cdot 2} = \frac{13}{2}$$

Solution: $\left(2, \dfrac{13}{2}\right)$

3. $\begin{array}{ll} 3x - 5 < 10 & \text{or} \quad 7 - x < -1 \\ 3x < 15 & \quad\;\; -x < -8 \\ x < 5 & \quad\;\;\;\; x > 8 \end{array}$

Solution: $(-\infty, 5) \cup (8, \infty)$

4. $\left(\dfrac{1}{3}\right)^{-2} + \left(\dfrac{2}{5}\right)^{-1} = \left(\dfrac{3}{1}\right)^{2} + \left(\dfrac{5}{2}\right)^{1} = \dfrac{9}{1} + \dfrac{5}{2}$

$= \dfrac{9}{1} \cdot \dfrac{2}{2} + \dfrac{5}{2} = \dfrac{18}{2} + \dfrac{5}{2}$

$= \dfrac{18 + 5}{2} = \dfrac{23}{2}$

5. $\dfrac{18x^{10}y^8}{3x^{-2}y^4} = \dfrac{\overset{6}{\cancel{18}} x^{10-(-2)} y^{8-4}}{\underset{1}{\cancel{3}}} = \dfrac{6x^{12}y^4}{1} = 6x^{12}y^4$

Section 6.5: Factoring by Grouping and a General Strategy for Factoring Polynomials

Quick Review 6.5

1. $a(x - y) - 3a = a\big[(x - y) - 3\big]$
$= a(x - y - 3)$

2. $2bx - 6b(y - 1) = 2b\big[x - 3(y - 1)\big]$
$= 2b(x - 3y + 3)$

3. $(3a - b)x^2 - 3(3a - b)x + 9(3a - b)$
$= (3a - b)(x^2 - 3x + 9)$

4. $(a + 2b)^2 - 9y^2 = (a + 2b)^2 - (3y)^2 = (a + 2b)^2 - (3y)^2$
$= \big[(a + 2b) + (3y)\big]\big[(a + 2b) - (3y)\big]$
$= (a + 2b + 3y)(a + 2b - 3y)$

5. $25x^2 - (a - 3b)^2 = (5x)^2 - (a - 3b)^2$
$= \big[(5x) + (a - 3b)\big]\big[(5x) - (a - 3b)\big]$
$= (5x + a - 3b)(5x - a + 3b)$

Exercises 6.5

1. $\quad x^2 - xy + 5x - 5y = x(x-y) + 5(x-y)$
$\qquad\qquad\qquad = (x+5)(x-y)$

3. $\quad x^2 - y^2 + 2y - 1 = x^2 - (y^2 - 2y + 1)$
$\qquad\qquad\qquad = x^2 - (y-1)^2$
$\qquad\qquad\qquad = [x + (y-1)][x - (y-1)]$
$\qquad\qquad\qquad = (x + y - 1)(x - y + 1)$

5. $\quad ac + bc + ad + bd = c(a+b) + d(a+b)$
$\qquad\qquad\qquad = (c+d)(a+b)$

7. $\quad 3a - 6b + 5ac - 10bc = 3(a-2b) + 5c(a-2b)$
$\qquad\qquad\qquad = (3+5c)(a-2b)$

9. $\quad ab + bc - ad - cd = b(a+c) - d(a+c)$
$\qquad\qquad\qquad = (b-d)(a+c)$

11. $\quad v^2 - vw - 7v + 7w = v(v-w) - 7(v-w)$
$\qquad\qquad\qquad = (v-7)(v-w)$

13. $\quad 4a^2 + 12a + 9 - 16b^2$
$\qquad = (4a^2 + 12a + 9) - 16b^2$
$\qquad = (2a+3)^2 - (4b)^2$
$\qquad = [(2a+3) + 4b][(2a+3) - 4b]$
$\qquad = (2a + 4b + 3)(2a - 4b + 3)$

15. $\quad 3mn + 15m - kn - 5k = 3m(n+5) - k(n+5)$
$\qquad\qquad\qquad = (3m - k)(n+5)$

17. $\quad az^3 + bz^3 + aw^2 + bw^2$
$\qquad = z^3(a+b) + w^2(a+b)$
$\qquad = (a+b)(z^3 + w^2)$

19. $\quad 9b^2 - 24b + 16 - a^2$
$\qquad = (9b^2 - 24b + 16) - a^2$
$\qquad = (3b-4)^2 - (a)^2$
$\qquad = [(3b-4) + a][(3b-4) - a]$
$\qquad = (3b + a - 4)(3b - a - 4)$

21. $\quad ay^2 + 2ay - y + a - 1$
$\qquad = ay^2 + 2ay + a - y - 1$
$\qquad = a(y^2 + 2y + 1) - (y+1)$
$\qquad = a(y+1)^2 - (1)(y+1)$
$\qquad = (y+1)[a(y+1) - 1]$
$\qquad = (y+1)(ay + a - 1)$

23. $\quad 64y^2 - 9z^2 = (8y)^2 - (3z)^2$
$\qquad\qquad\qquad = (8y + 3z)(8y - 3z)$

25. $\quad 16x^2 + 49y^2$ is prime

27. $\quad 12x^2 - 27x + 15 = 3(4x^2 - 9x + 5)$
$\qquad\qquad\qquad = 3(4x - 5)(x - 1)$

29. $\quad 49a^2 - 28a + 4 = (7a - 2)^2$

31. $\quad x(a-b) + y(a-b) = (a-b)(x+y)$

33. $\quad 10w^2 - 6w - 21$ is prime

35. $\quad 25v^2 - vw + 36w^2$ is prime

37. $4x^{10} + 12x^5 y^3 + 9y^6$

$\quad = \left(2x^5\right)^2 + 2\left(2x^5\right)\left(3y^3\right) + \left(3y^3\right)^2$

$\quad = \left(2x^5 + 3y^3\right)^2$

39. $12x^3 y - 12xy^3 = 12xy\left(x^2 - y^2\right)$

$\qquad\qquad\qquad = 12xy\left(x+y\right)\left(x-y\right)$

41. $cx + cy + dx + dy = c\left(x+y\right) + d\left(x+y\right)$

$\qquad\qquad\qquad\quad = \left(c+d\right)\left(x+y\right)$

43. $ax^2 + ax + bxy + by = ax\left(x+1\right) + by\left(x+1\right)$

$\qquad\qquad\qquad\qquad = \left(ax+by\right)\left(x+1\right)$

45. $x^6 + 4x^3 y + 4y^2 = \left(x^3\right)^2 + 2\left(x^3\right)\left(2y\right) + \left(2y\right)^2$

$\qquad\qquad\qquad = \left(x^3 + 2y\right)^2$

47. $64ax^2 - 104ax + 40a = 8a\left(8x^2 - 13x + 5\right)$

$\qquad\qquad\qquad\quad = 8a\left(8x^2 - 8x - 5x + 5\right)$

$\qquad\qquad\qquad\quad = 8a\left[8x\left(x-1\right) - 5\left(x-1\right)\right]$

$\qquad\qquad\qquad\quad = 8a\left[\left(x-1\right)\left(8x-5\right)\right]$

$\qquad\qquad\qquad\quad = 8a\left(x-1\right)\left(8x-5\right)$

49. $5x^2 - 55 = 5\left(x^2 - 11\right)$

51. $63a^3 b - 175ab = 7ab\left(9a^2 - 25\right)$

$\qquad\qquad\qquad = 7ab\left(3a+5\right)\left(3a-5\right)$

53. $-12x^2 + 12xy - 3y^2 = -3\left(4x^2 - 4xy + y^2\right)$

$\qquad\qquad\qquad\qquad = -3\left(2x - y\right)^2$

55. $144x^2 + 81 = 9\left(16x^2 + 9\right)$

57. $9x^2 - 6x + 1 - 25y^2$

$\quad = \left(9x^2 - 6x + 1\right) - \left(5y\right)^2$

$\quad = \left(3x - 1\right)^2 - \left(5y\right)^2$

$\quad = \left[\left(3x-1\right) + \left(5y\right)\right]\left[\left(3x-1\right) - \left(5y\right)\right]$

$\quad = \left(3x - 1 + 5y\right)\left(3x - 1 - 5y\right)$

$\quad = \left(3x + 5y - 1\right)\left(3x - 5y - 1\right)$

59. $12ax^2 - 10axy - 12ay^2 = 2a\left(6x^2 - 5xy - 6y^2\right)$

$\qquad\qquad\qquad\qquad\quad = 2a\left(3x + 2y\right)\left(2x - 3y\right)$

61. $7s^5 t - 7st^5 = 7st\left(s^4 - t^4\right)$

$\qquad\qquad = 7st\left[\left(s^2\right)^2 - \left(t^2\right)^2\right]$

$\qquad\qquad = 7st\left(s^2 + t^2\right)\left(s^2 - t^2\right)$

$\qquad\qquad = 7st\left(s^2 + t^2\right)\left(s+t\right)\left(s-t\right)$

63. $3ax^2 - 3ay^2 + 6ay - 3a$

$\quad = 3a\left(x^2 - y^2 + 2y - 1\right)$

$\quad = 3a\left[x^2 - \left(y^2 - 2y + 1\right)\right]$

$\quad = 3a\left[x^2 - \left(y - 1\right)^2\right]$

$\quad = 3a\left[x - \left(y-1\right)\right]\left[x + \left(y-1\right)\right]$

$\quad = 3a\left(x - y + 1\right)\left(x + y - 1\right)$

65. $2ax^3 + 10ax^2 - 28ax = 2ax\left(x^2 + 5x - 14\right)$

$\qquad\qquad\qquad\quad = 2ax\left(x^2 + 7x - 2x - 14\right)$

$\qquad\qquad\qquad\quad = 2ax\left[x\left(x+7\right) - 2\left(x+7\right)\right]$

$\qquad\qquad\qquad\quad = 2ax\left[\left(x+7\right)\left(x-2\right)\right]$

$\qquad\qquad\qquad\quad = 2ax\left(x+7\right)\left(x-2\right)$

67. $a^2 + 2a + 1 + ab + b = \left(a^2 + 2a + 1\right) + b\left(a+1\right)$

$\qquad\qquad\qquad\qquad = \left(a+1\right)\left(a+1\right) + b\left(a+1\right)$

$\qquad\qquad\qquad\qquad = \left(a+1\right)\left[\left(a+1\right) + b\right]$

$\qquad\qquad\qquad\qquad = \left(a+1\right)\left(a+b+1\right)$

69. $(a-2b)x^2 - 2(a-2b)x - 24(a-2b)$
$= (a-2b)(x^2 - 2x - 24)$
$= (a-2b)(x-6)(x+4)$

71. $(4x^2 - 12xy + 9y^2) + (72ay - 48ax) - 25a^2$
$= (2x-3y)^2 + 24a(3y-2x) - 25a^2$
$= (2x-3y)^2 - 24a(2x-3y) - 25a^2$
$= (2x-3y)^2 + a(2x-3y) - 25a(2x-3y) - 25a^2$
$= (2x-3y)\left[(2x-3y)+a\right] - 25a\left[(2x-3y)+a\right]$
$= \left[(2x-3y)-25a\right]\left[(2x-3y)+a\right]$
$= (2x-3y-25a)(2x-3y+a)$

Polynomial $P(x)$	x-intercepts of the graph of $y = P(x)$	Zeros of $P(x)$	Factored Form
73. $x^3 - 3x^2 - 10x + 24$	$(-3, 0), (2, 0), (4, 0)$	$x = -3,\ x = 2,\ x = 4$	$(x+3)(x-2)(x-4)$

75. $5ab^3 - 5a = 5a(b^3 - 1)$
$= 5a(b-1)(b^2 + b + 1)$

77. $x^3 + y^3 + x^2 - y^2$
$= (x^3 + y^3) + (x^2 - y^2)$
$= (x+y)(x^2 - xy + y^2) + (x+y)(x-y)$
$= (x+y)\left[(x^2 - xy + y^2) + (x-y)\right]$
$= (x+y)(x^2 - xy + y^2 + x - y)$

Cumulative Review

---

1. The x-intercepts are: $(-5, 0)$ and $(8, 0)$.

2. The zeros are: $x = 3$ and $x = -9$.

3. $2(x+3) = x+6$
$2x + 6 = x + 6$
$2x - x + 6 - 6 = x - x + 6 - 6$
$x = 0$
The equation is a condtional equation. The solution is $x = 0$

4. $2(x+3) = 2x+6$
$2x + 6 = 2x + 6$
$2x - 2x + 6 - 6 = 2x - 2x + 6 - 6$
$0 = 0$
The equation is an identity. The solution set is all real numbers: $\mathbb{R}$

5. $2(x+3) = 2x+5$
$2x + 6 = 2x + 5$
$2x - 2x + 6 = 2x - 2x + 5$
$6 = 5$
The equation is a contradiction. It does not have a solution.

Section 6.6: Solving Equations by Factoring

Quick Review 6.6

1.
$$3x - 45 = 0$$
$$3x - 45 + 45 = 0 + 45$$
$$3x = 45$$
$$\frac{3x}{3} = \frac{45}{3}$$
$$x = 15$$

2.
$$2x + 14 = 0$$
$$2x + 14 - 14 = 0 - 14$$
$$2x = -14$$
$$\frac{2x}{2} = \frac{-14}{2}$$
$$x = -7$$

3.
$$5x - 7 = 0$$
$$5x - 7 + 7 = 0 + 7$$
$$5x = 7$$
$$\frac{5x}{5} = \frac{7}{5}$$
$$x = \frac{7}{5}$$

4. Substitute $x = \dfrac{2}{3}$ for x in the equaiton and determine if the equation is satisfied.
$$(3x - 2)(x + 5) = 0$$
$$\left(3\left(\frac{2}{3}\right) - 2\right)\left(\left(\frac{2}{3}\right) + 5\right) = 0$$
$$(2 - 2)\left(\left(\frac{2}{3}\right) + 5\right) = 0$$
$$(0)\left(\left(\frac{2}{3}\right) + 5\right) = 0$$
$$0 = 0$$

$x = \dfrac{2}{3}$ is a solution.

5. Substitute $x = 3$ for x in the equaiton and determine if the equation is satisfied.
$$(x - 3)(x + 5) = 2$$
$$(3 - 3)(3 + 5) = 2$$
$$(0)(8) = 2$$
$$0 \neq 2$$

$x = 3$ is not a solution.

Exercises 6.6

1.
  a. $2x - 3 = 0$ is a linear equation with one real solution. Answer: **D**.
  b. $(2x - 3)^2 = 0$ is a quadratic equation with a double real solution. Answer: **C**.
  c. $(2x - 3)(x + 4) = 0$ is a quadratic equation with two distinct real solutions. Answer: **A**.
  d. $(2x - 3)(x + 4)$ is a quadratic polynomial, but not an equation. Answer: **B**.

3.
  a. $2x^2 - 7x + 3 = 0$ is written in standard form. $a = 2$, $b = -7$, $c = 3$
  b. $8x^2 = 3x$ is equivalent to $8x^2 - 3x = 0$. $a = 8$, $b = -3$, $c = 0$
  c. $7x^2 = -5$ is equivalent to $7x^2 + 5 = 0$. $a = 7$, $b = 0$, $c = 5$
  d. $(x - 1)(2x + 1) = 3$ is equivalent to $2x^2 - x - 1 = 3$ or $2x^2 - x - 4 = 0$. $a = 2$, $b = -1$, $c = -4$

5. $(m-8)(m+17)=0$

$m-8=0 \quad$ or $\quad m+17=0$

$m=8 \qquad\qquad m=-17$

7. $(2n-5)(3n+1)=0$

$2n-5=0 \quad$ or $\quad 3n+1=0$

$2n=5 \qquad\qquad 3n=-1$

$n=\dfrac{5}{2} \qquad\qquad n=-\dfrac{1}{3}$

9. $z(2z+7)=0$

$z=0, \ $ or $\ 2z+7=0$

$z=0 \ $ or $\ z=-\dfrac{7}{2}$

11. $v^2-121=0$

$(v-11)(v+11)=0$

$v-11=0 \quad$ or $\quad v+11=0$

$v=11 \qquad\qquad v=-11$

13. $x^2+3x+2=0$

$(x+2)(x+1)=0$

$x+2=0 \quad$ or $\quad x+1=0$

$x=-2 \qquad\qquad x=-1$

15. $y^2-3y=18$

$y^2-3y-18=0$

$(y-6)(y+3)=0$

$y-6=0 \quad$ or $\quad y+3=0$

$y=6 \qquad\qquad y=-3$

17. $3v^2=-v$

$3v^2+v=0$

$v(3v+1)=0$

$v=0 \quad$ or $\quad 3v+1=0$

$\qquad\qquad\qquad 3v=-1$

$\qquad\qquad\qquad v=-\dfrac{1}{3}$

19. $2w^2=7w+15$

$2w^2-7w-15=0$

$(2w+3)(w-5)=0$

$2w+3=0 \quad$ or $\quad w-5=0$

$2w=-3 \qquad\qquad w=5$

$w=-\dfrac{3}{2}$

21. $6x^2+19x+10=0$

$(2x+5)(3x+2)=0$

$2x+5=0 \quad$ or $\quad 3x+2=0$

$2x=-5 \qquad\qquad 3x=-2$

$x=-\dfrac{5}{2} \qquad\qquad x=-\dfrac{2}{3}$

23. $x^2=11x-24$

$x^2-11x+24=0$

$(x-3)(x-8)=0$

$x-3=0 \quad$ or $\quad x-8=0$

$x=3 \qquad\qquad x=8$

25. $70z^2=5z+15$

$70z^2-5z-15=0$

$5(14z^2-z-3)=0$

$5(7z+3)(2z-1)=0$

$7z+3=0 \quad$ or $\quad 2z-1=0$

$7z=-3 \qquad\qquad 2z=1$

$z=-\dfrac{3}{7} \qquad\qquad z=\dfrac{1}{2}$

27. $9x^2=25$

$9x^2-25=0$

$(3x-5)(3x+5)=0$

$3x-5=0 \quad$ or $\quad 3x+5=0$

$3x=5 \qquad\qquad 3x=-5$

$x=\dfrac{5}{3} \qquad\qquad x=-\dfrac{5}{3}$

29.
$$r(r+3)=10$$
$$r^2+3r-10=0$$
$$(r+5)(r-2)=0$$
$$r+5=0 \quad \text{or} \quad r-2=0$$
$$r=-5 \qquad r=2$$

31.
$$\frac{x^2}{2}-\frac{x}{2}-1=0$$
$$2\left(\frac{x^2}{2}-\frac{x}{2}-1\right)=2(0)$$
$$x^2-x-2=0$$
$$(x-2)(x+1)=0$$
$$x-2=0 \quad \text{or} \quad x+1=0$$
$$x=2 \qquad x=-1$$

33.
$$\frac{x^2}{10}-\frac{x}{5}=\frac{3}{10}$$
$$10\left(\frac{x^2}{10}-\frac{x}{5}\right)=10\left(\frac{3}{10}\right)$$
$$x^2-2x=3$$
$$x^2-2x-3=0$$
$$(x-3)(x+1)=0$$
$$x-3=0 \quad \text{or} \quad x+1=0$$
$$x=3 \qquad x=-1$$

35.
$$\frac{m^2}{18}-\frac{m}{6}-1=0$$
$$18\left(\frac{m^2}{18}-\frac{m}{6}-1\right)=18(0)$$
$$m^2-3m-18=0$$
$$(m-6)(m+3)=0$$
$$m-6=0 \quad \text{or} \quad m+3=0$$
$$m=6 \qquad m=-3$$

37.
$$\frac{x^2}{12}-\frac{x}{3}-1=0$$
$$12\left(\frac{x^2}{12}-\frac{x}{3}-1\right)=12(0)$$
$$x^2-4x-12=0$$
$$(x-6)(x+2)=0$$
$$x-6=0 \quad \text{or} \quad x+2=0$$
$$x=6 \qquad x=-2$$

39.
$$(v-12)(v+1)=-40$$
$$v^2-11v-12=-40$$
$$v^2-11v+28=0$$
$$(v-7)(v-4)=0$$
$$v-7=0 \quad \text{or} \quad v-4=0$$
$$v=7 \qquad v=4$$

41.
$$(v+2)(v+1)=8v+2$$
$$v^2+3v+1=8v+2$$
$$v^2+3v-8v+2-2=8v-8v+2-2$$
$$v^2-5v=0$$
$$v(v-5)=0$$
$$v=0 \quad \text{or} \quad v-5=0$$
$$v=5$$

43.
$$(2w-3)^2=25$$
$$4w^2-12w+9=25$$
$$4w^2-12w-16=0$$
$$4(w^2-3w-4)=0$$
$$4(w-4)(w+1)=0$$
$$w-4=0 \quad \text{or} \quad w+1=0$$
$$w=4 \qquad w=-1$$

45. $(3x-8)(x+1)=(x+1)(x-3)$

$3x^2-5x-8=x^2-2x-3$

$2x^2-3x-5=0$

$(2x-5)(x+1)=0$

$2x-5=0 \quad$ or $\quad x+1=0$

$2x=5 \qquad\qquad x=-1$

$x=\dfrac{5}{2}$

47. $(4x+5)(x+5)=45x$

$4x^2+25x+25=45x$

$4x^2-20x+25=0$

$(2x-5)^2=0$

$2x-5=0$

$2x=5$

$x=\dfrac{5}{2}$

49. $9m^2=42m-49$

$9m^2-42m+49=0$

$(3m-7)^2=0$

$3m-7=0$

$3m-7=0$

$m=\dfrac{7}{3}$

51. If the solutions are $x=1$ and $x=5$, then

$x-1=0 \quad$ and $\quad x-5=0$.

Thus, $(x-1)$ and $(x-5)$ must be factors and

equation is: $(x-1)(x-5)=0$

$x^2-5x-x+5=0$

$x^2-6x+5=0$

53. If the solutions are $x=-3$ and $x=6$, then

$x+3=0 \quad$ and $\quad x-6=0$.

Thus, $(x+3)$ and $(x-6)$ must be factors and

equation is: $(x+3)(x-6)=0$

$x^2-6x+3x-18=0$

$x^2-3x-18=0$

56. If the solutions are $x=-\dfrac{1}{2}$ and $x=\dfrac{3}{4}$, then

$x+\dfrac{1}{2}=0 \quad$ and $\quad x-\dfrac{3}{4}=0$.

These are equivalent to $2x+1=0 \quad$ and $\quad 4x-3=0$.

Thus, $(2x+1)$ and $(4x-3)$ must be factors and

equation is: $(2x+1)(4x-3)=0$

$8x^2-6x+4x-3=0$

$8x^2-2x-3=0$

57. If the solutions are $x=-\dfrac{7}{5}$ and $x=-\dfrac{2}{3}$, then

$x+\dfrac{7}{5}=0 \quad$ and $\quad x+\dfrac{2}{3}=0$.

These are equivalent to $5x+7=0 \quad$ and $\quad 3x+2=0$.

Thus, $(5x+7)$ and $(3x+2)$ must be factors and

equation is: $(5x+7)(3x+2)=0$

$15x^2+10x+21x+14=0$

$15x^2+31x+14=0$

59. **a.** The solution to the equation corresponds to the x-intercepts on the graph.

Solution: $x=-3,\ x=5$

b. The solution set corresponds to all values of x such that the graph is below the x-axis.

Solution: $(-3,\ 5)$

c. The solution set corresponds to all values of x such that the graph is above the x-axis.

Solution: $(-\infty,\ -3)\cup(5,\ \infty)$

61. a. The solution to the equation corresponds to the x-intercepts on the graph.
Solution: $x = -5$, $x = 2$

b. The solution set corresponds to all values of x such that the graph is below the x-axis.
Solution: $(-\infty, -5) \cup (2, \infty)$

c. The solution set corresponds to all values of x such that the graph is above the x-axis.
Solution: $(-5, 2)$

63. a. From the table, we can see that the zeros are $x = -10$ and $x = 4$.

b. The x-intercepts are $(-10, 0)$ and $(4, 0)$.

c. $x^2 + 6x - 40 = (x + 10)(x - 4)$

d. The solutions of $x^2 + 6x - 40 = 0$ are $x = -10$, $x = 4$.

65. a. The x-intercepts are $(0, 0)$, $(-1, 0)$, and $(2, 0)$.

b. The zeros are $x = 0$, $x = -1$, and $x = 2$.

c. $x^3 - x^2 - 2x = x(x + 1)(x - 2)$

d. The solutions to $x^3 - x^2 - 2x = 0$ are $x = 0$, $x = -1$, $x = 2$.

67. a. $(5m - 3)(m - 2) = 0$
$5m - 3 = 0 \quad$ or $\quad m - 2 = 0$
$5m = 3 \qquad\qquad m = 2$
$m = \dfrac{3}{5}$

b. $(5m - 3)(m - 2) = 5m^2 - 13m + 6$

69. a. $4(x - 3)(5x + 2) = 0$
$x - 3 = 0 \quad$ or $\quad 5x + 2 = 0$
$x = 3 \qquad\qquad 5x = -2$
$x = -\dfrac{2}{5}$

b. $4(x - 3)(5x + 2) = 4(5x^2 - 13x - 6)$
$= 20x^2 - 52x - 24$

Polynomial $P(x)$	Solutions of $P(x) = 0$	Solutions of $P(x) < 0$	Solutions of $P(x) > 0$
71. $(x - 2)(x + 7)$	$[-10, 10, 1]$ by $[-30, 30, 5]$ $x = -7$, $x = 2$	$(-7, 2)$	$(-\infty, -7) \cup (2, +\infty)$
73. $-3x^2 - 9x + 12$	$[-10, 10, 1]$ by $[-50, 50, 5]$ $x = -4$, $x = 1$	$(-\infty, -4) \cup (1, +\infty)$	$(-4, 1)$

75. Let w be the width of the rectangle. If the length is 2 cm more than three times the width, then the length is $l = 3w + 2$. If the area is 33 square centimeters and $A = l \cdot w$, then to determine the width we solve the equation.

$$l \cdot w = 33$$
$$(3w + 2)w = 33$$
$$3w^2 + 2w - 33 = 0$$
$$(3w + 11)(w - 3) = 0$$

Thus $w = 3$ cm and $l = 3(3) + 2$
$$l = 11 \text{ cm}$$

(Note: The width cannot be equal to a negative number.)

The dimensions must be 3 cm $\times$ 11 cm.

77. If the base of the triangle is 2 meters longer than the height, then $b = h + 2$ or $h = b - 2$. If the area is 24 square meters and $A = \frac{1}{2}bh$, then to find the base of the triangle we solve the following equation.

$$\frac{1}{2}bh = 24$$
$$\frac{1}{2}b(b - 2) = 24$$
$$b(b - 2) = 48$$
$$b^2 - 2b - 48 = 0$$
$$(b - 8)(b + 6) = 0$$

Thus $b = 8$ meters.

(Note: The base cannot be equal to a negative number.)

79. If the trough is made from a sheet of metal that is 60 cm wide, then $w + 2h = 60$ or $w = 60 - 2h$. If the cross-sectional area is 450 square centimeters and $A = w \cdot h$, then to determine the height we solve the following equation.

$$w \cdot h = 450$$
$$(60 - 2h)h = 450$$
$$60h - 2h^2 = 450$$
$$2h^2 - 60h + 450 = 0$$
$$2(h^2 - 30h + 225) = 0$$
$$2(h - 15)^2 = 0$$

Thus $h = 15$ cm.

Cumulative Review

1. $(xy)z = x(yz)$ is an example of the Associative Property of Multiplication since the factors have been regrouped. Answer: **B**.

2. $(x + y) + z = x + (y + z)$ is an example of the Associative Property of Addition since the terms have been regrouped. Answer: **A**.

3. $w(xy + z) = w(yx + z)$ is an example of the Commutative Property of Multiplication since the factors have been rearranged. Answer: **D**.

4. $w(xy + z) = wxy + wz$ is an example of the Distributive Property of Multiplication Over Addition. Answer: **E**.

5. $w(xy + z) = w(z + xy)$ is an example of the Commutative Property of Addition since the terms have been rearranged. Answer: **C**.

Review Exercises for Chapter 6

1. $4x - 36 = 4(x - 9)$

2. $2x^2 - 10x = 2x(x - 5)$

3. $12ax^2 - 24ax = 12ax(x - 2)$

4. $5x^3 - 15x = 5x(x^2 - 3)$

5. $ax + bx + ay + by = x(a + b) + y(a + b)$
$$= (x + y)(a + b)$$

6. $ax + 2ay - 3x - 6y = a(x + 2y) - 3(x + 2y)$
$$= (a - 3)(x + 2y)$$

7. $6x^2 + 21x - 10x - 35 = 3x(2x + 7) - 5(2x + 7)$
$$= (2x + 7)(3x - 5)$$

8. $24x^2 - 20x + 18x - 15 = 4x(6x - 5) + 3(6x - 5)$
$$= (6x - 5)(4x + 3)$$

9. $x^2 - 4 = (x)^2 - (2)^2$
$$= (x + 2)(x - 2)$$

10. $4x^2 - 1 = (2x)^2 - (1)^2$
$$= (2x + 1)(2x - 1)$$

11. $7x^2 - 28 = 7(x^2 - 4) = 7(x + 2)(x - 2)$

12. $2m^2 - 128 = 2(m^2 - 64) = 2(m^2 - 8^2)$
$$= 2(m - 8)(m + 8)$$

13. $x^2 - 11x + 18 = x^2 - 2x - 9x + 18$
$$= x(x - 2) - 9(x - 2)$$
$$= (x - 9)(x - 2)$$

14. $m^2 + 10m + 21 = m^2 + 3m + 7m + 21$
$$= m(m + 3) + 7(m + 3)$$
$$= (m + 7)(m + 3)$$

15. $10x^2 + 90x + 140 = 10(x^2 + 9x + 14)$
$$= 10(x^2 + 7x + 2x + 14)$$
$$10\left[(x^2 + 7x) + (2x + 14)\right]$$
$$= 10\left[x(x + 7) + 2(x + 7)\right]$$
$$= 10(x + 7)(x + 2)$$

16. $5x^2 - 45x + 40 = 5(x^2 - 9x + 8)$
$$= 5(x^2 - 8x - x + 8)$$
$$= 5\left[(x^2 - 8x) - (x - 8)\right]$$
$$= 5\left[x(x - 8) - 1(x - 8)\right]$$
$$= 5(x - 8)(x - 1)$$

17. $x^2 + 4x + 4 = (x)^2 + 2(x)(2) + (2)^2$
$$= (x + 2)^2$$

18. $m^2 + 10m + 25 = (m)^2 + 2(m)(5) + (5)^2$
$$= (m + 5)^2$$

19. $3x^2 - 18x + 27 = 3(x^2 - 6x + 9)$
$$= 3(x^2 - 3x - 3x + 9)$$
$$= 3\left[(x^2 - 3x) - (3x - 9)\right]$$
$$= 3\left[x(x - 3) - 3(x - 3)\right]$$
$$= 3(x - 3)(x - 3)$$
$$= 3(x - 3)^2$$

20. $2m^2 - 16m + 32 = 2(m^2 - 8m + 16)$
$$= 2(m^2 - 4m - 4m + 16)$$
$$= 2\left[(m^2 - 4m) - (4m - 16)\right]$$
$$= 2\left[m(m - 4) - 4(m - 4)\right]$$
$$= 2(m - 4)(m - 4)$$
$$= 2(m - 4)^2$$

21. $-4x^2 + 12xy - 9y^2 = -\left(4x^2 - 12xy + 9y^2\right)$

$\qquad = -\left(\left(2x\right)^2 - 2\left(2x\right)\left(3y\right) + \left(3y\right)^2\right)$

$\qquad = -\left(2x - 3y\right)^2$

22. $-9x^2 + 30xy - 25y^2 = -\left(9x^2 - 30xy + 25y^2\right)$

$\qquad = -\left(\left(3x\right)^2 - 2\left(3x\right)\left(5y\right) + \left(5y\right)^2\right)$

$\qquad = -\left(3x - 5y\right)^2$

23. $ax + 2ay - 7x - 14y = a\left(x + 2y\right) - 7\left(x + 2y\right)$

$\qquad = \left(a - 7\right)\left(x + 2y\right)$

24. $x^3y - 5x^2y + 4xy = xy\left(x^2 - 5x + 4\right)$

$\qquad = xy\left(x^2 - x - 4x + 4\right)$

$\qquad = xy\left[x\left(x - 1\right) - 4\left(x - 1\right)\right]$

$\qquad = xy\left(x - 1\right)\left(x - 4\right)$

25. $x^2\left(a + b\right) - 25\left(a + b\right) = \left(a + b\right)\left(x^2 - 25\right)$

$\qquad = \left(a + b\right)\left[\left(x\right)^2 - \left(5\right)^2\right]$

$\qquad = \left(a + b\right)\left[\left(x - 5\right)\left(x + 5\right)\right]$

$\qquad = \left(a + b\right)\left(x - 5\right)\left(x + 5\right)$

26. $11x^2 - 11y^2 + 33x + 33y$

$\qquad = 11\left[\left(x^2 - y^2\right) + 3\left(x + y\right)\right]$

$\qquad = 11\left[\left(x - y\right)\left(x + y\right) + 3\left(x + y\right)\right]$

$\qquad = 11\left[\left(x - y\right) + 3\right]\left(x + y\right)$

$\qquad = 11\left(x - y + 3\right)\left(x + y\right) = 11\left(x + y\right)\left(x - y + 3\right)$

27. $v^2 + 2v + 1 - w^2 = \left(v^2 + 2v + 1\right) - w^2$

$\qquad = \left(v + 1\right)^2 - w^2$

$\qquad = \left[\left(v + 1\right) + w\right]\left[\left(v + 1\right) - w\right]$

$\qquad = \left(v + w + 1\right)\left(v - w + 1\right)$

28. $5a\left(2x - 3y\right) + 3b\left(3y - 2x\right)$

$\qquad = 5a\left(2x - 3y\right) - 3b\left(2x - 3y\right)$

$\qquad = \left(5a - 3b\right)\left(2x - 3y\right)$

29. $v^2 + 9w^2$ is prime.

30. $v^2 - 9w^2 = \left(v\right)^2 - \left(3w\right)^2$

$\qquad = \left(v - 3w\right)\left(v + 3w\right)$

31. $100x^2 - 49y^2 = \left(10x\right)^2 - \left(7y\right)^2$

$\qquad = \left(10x - 7y\right)\left(10x + 7y\right)$

32. $100x^2 + 49y^2$ is prime.

33. $4x^2 + 2xy - 30y^2 = 2\left(2x^2 + xy - 15y^2\right)$

$\qquad = 2\left(2x^2 - 5xy + 6xy - 15y^2\right)$

$\qquad = 2\left[x\left(2x - 5y\right) + 3y\left(2x - 5y\right)\right]$

$\qquad = 2\left(x + 3y\right)\left(2x - 5y\right)$

34. $6x^2 - 7xy - 20y^2 = 6x^2 + 8xy - 15xy - 20y^2$

$\qquad = 2x\left(3x + 4y\right) - 5y\left(3x + 4y\right)$

$\qquad = \left(2x - 5y\right)\left(3x + 4y\right)$

35. $20x^2 + 50x - 30 = 10\left(2x^2 + 5x - 3\right)$

$\qquad = 10\left(2x^2 + 6x - x - 3\right)$

$\qquad = 10\left[2x\left(x + 3\right) - \left(x + 3\right)\right]$

$\qquad = 10\left[\left(x + 3\right)\left(2x - 1\right)\right]$

$\qquad = 10\left(x + 3\right)\left(2x - 1\right)$

36. $6x^2 + 61xy + 10y^2 = 6x^2 + xy + 60xy + 10y^2$

$\qquad = x\left(6x + x\right) + 10y\left(6x + y\right)$

$\qquad = \left(x + 10y\right)\left(6x + y\right)$

37. $v^4 - 1 = (v^2 + 1)(v^2 - 1)$

$= (v^2 + 1)(v + 1)(v - 1)$

38. $81w^4 - 16 = (9w^2)^2 - (4)^2$

$= (9w^2 - 4)(9w^2 + 4)$

$= \left[(3w)^2 - 2^2 \right](9w^2 + 4)$

$= (3w - 2)(3w + 2)(9w^2 + 4)$

39. $a^2(x + 5y) + 2ab(x + 5y) + b^2(x + 5y)$

$= (x + 5y)(a^2 + 2ab + b^2)$

$= (x + 5y)(a + b)^2$

40. $9x^2 - y^2 + 3x - y = \left[(3x)^2 - (y)^2 \right] + (3x - y)$

$= (3x - y)(3x + y) + (1)(3x - y)$

$= (3x - y)\left[(3x + y) + (1) \right]$

$= (3x - y)(3x + y + 1)$

41. a. $x^2 - 48x - 100 = x^2 - 50x + 2x - 100$

$= x(x - 50) + 2(x - 50)$

$= (x + 2)(x - 50)$

b. $x^2 - 15x - 100 = x^2 - 20x + 5x - 100$

$= x(x - 20) + 5(x - 20)$

$= (x + 5)(x - 20)$

c. $x^2 - 100 = x^2 - 10x + 10x - 100$

$= x(x - 10) + 10(x - 10)$

$= (x + 10)(x - 10)$

d. $x^2 - 20x - 100$ is prime.

42. a. $x^2 + 22x - 48 = x^2 + 24x - 2x - 48$

$= x(x + 24) - 2(x + 24)$

$= (x - 2)(x + 24)$

b. $x^2 + 13x - 48 = x^2 - 3x + 16x - 48$

$= x(x - 3) + 16(x - 3)$

$= (x + 16)(x - 3)$

c. $x^2 + 2x - 48 = x^2 + 8x - 6x - 48$

$= x(x + 8) - 6(x + 8)$

$= (x - 6)(x + 8)$

d. $x^2 + x - 48$ is prime.

43. a. $100x^2 + 52x + 1 = 100x^2 + 50x + 2x + 1$

$= 50x(2x + 1) + (2x + 1)$

$= (50x + 1)(2x + 1)$

b. $4x^2 + 52x + 25 = 4x^2 + 50x + 2x + 25$

$= 2x(2x + 25) + (1)(2x + 25)$

$= (2x + 1)(2x + 25)$

c. $5x^2 + 29xy + 20y^2 = 5x^2 + 25xy + 4xy + 20y^2$

$= 5x(x + 5y) + 4y(x + 5y)$

$= (5x + 4y)(x + 5y)$

d. $10x^2 + 29xy + 10y^2 = 10x^2 + 4xy + 25xy + 10y^2$

$= 2x(5x + 2y) + 5y(5x + 2y)$

$= (2x + 5y)(5x + 2y)$

44. a. $48x^2 - 19x + 1 = 48x^2 - 16x - 3x + 1$

$= 16x(3x - 1) - (1)(3x - 1)$

$= (16x - 1)(3x - 1)$

b. $3x^2 - 26x + 16 = 3x^2 - 24x - 2x + 16$

$= 3x(x - 8) - 2(x - 8)$

$= (3x - 2)(x - 8)$

c. $2x^2 - 49xy + 24y^2 = 2x^2 - 48xy - xy + 24y^2$

$\qquad = 2x(x - 24y) - y(x - 24y)$

$\qquad = (2x - y)(x - 24y)$

d. $16x^2 - 16xy + 3y^2 = 16x^2 - 4xy - 12xy + 3y^2$

$\qquad = 4x(4x - y) - 3y(4x - y)$

$\qquad = (4x - 3y)(4x - y)$

45. $8x^3 - y^3 = (2x)^3 - (y)^3$

$\qquad = (2x - y)\left[(2x)^2 + (2x)(y) + (y)^2\right]$

$\qquad = (2x - y)(4x^2 + 2xy + y^2)$

46. $x^3 + 64 = (x)^3 + (4)^3$

$\qquad = (x + 4)\left[(x)^2 - (x)(4) + (4)^2\right]$

$\qquad = (x + 4)(x^2 - 4x + 16)$

47. $2x^4 - 16x = 2x(x^3 - 8)$

$\qquad = 2x(x^3 - 8) = 2x\left[(x)^3 - (2)^3\right]$

$\qquad = 2x\left[(x - 2)((x)^2 + (x)(2) + (2)^2)\right]$

$\qquad = 2x(x - 2)(x^2 + 2x + 4)$

48. $v^4 - v^3 - v + 1 = v^3(v - 1) - (1)(v - 1)$

$\qquad = (v^3 - 1)(v - 1)$

$\qquad = (v - 1)(v^2 + v + 1)(v - 1)$

$\qquad = (v - 1)^2(v^2 + v + 1)$

49. $(x - 5)(x + 1) = 0$

$\qquad x - 5 = 0 \quad$ or $\quad x + 1 = 0$

$\qquad\quad x = 5 \qquad\qquad x = -1$

50. $(2x - 3)(3x + 2) = 0$

$\qquad 2x - 3 = 0 \quad$ or $\quad 3x + 2 = 0$

$\qquad\quad 2x = 3 \qquad\qquad 3x = -2$

$\qquad\quad x = \dfrac{3}{2} \qquad\qquad x = -\dfrac{2}{3}$

51. $x(x - 7)(7x - 2) = 0$

$\qquad x = 0,\ x - 7 = 0,\ $ or $\ 7x - 2 = 0$

$\qquad x = 0,\ x = 7,\ $ or $\ x = \dfrac{2}{7}$

52. $v^2 - 4v - 21 = 0$

$\qquad (v - 7)(v + 3) = 0$

$\qquad v - 7 = 0 \quad$ or $\quad v + 3 = 0$

$\qquad\quad v = 7 \qquad\qquad v = -3$

53. $10y^2 + 13y - 3 = 0$

$\qquad (5y - 1)(2y + 3) = 0$

$\qquad 5y - 1 = 0 \quad$ or $\quad 2y + 3 = 0$

$\qquad\quad 5y = 1 \qquad\qquad 2y = -3$

$\qquad\quad y = \dfrac{1}{5} \qquad\qquad y = -\dfrac{3}{2}$

54. $\qquad\qquad 6w^2 = 11w + 21$

$\qquad 6w^2 - 11w - 21 = 0$

$\qquad (w - 3)(6w + 7) = 0$

$\qquad w - 3 = 0 \quad$ or $\quad 6w + 7 = 0$

$\qquad\quad w = 3 \qquad\qquad 6w = -7$

$\qquad\qquad\qquad\qquad\qquad w = -\dfrac{7}{6}$

55.
$$\frac{v^2}{30} = \frac{v}{15} + \frac{1}{2}$$
$$30\left(\frac{v^2}{30}\right) = 30\left(\frac{v}{15} + \frac{1}{2}\right)$$
$$v^2 = 2v + 15$$
$$v^2 - 2v - 15 = 0$$
$$(v-5)(v+3) = 0$$
$$v - 5 = 0 \quad \text{or} \quad v + 3 = 0$$
$$v = 5 \qquad\qquad v = -3$$

56.
$$(x+6)(x-2) = 9$$
$$x^2 + 4x - 12 = 9$$
$$x^2 + 4x - 21 = 0$$
$$(x+7)(x-3) = 0$$
$$x + 7 = 0 \quad \text{or} \quad x - 3 = 0$$
$$x = -7 \qquad\qquad x = 3$$

57.
$$x\left(x^2 - 36\right) = 0$$
$$x(x-6)(x+6) = 0$$
$$x = 0, \ x - 6 = 0, \ \text{or} \ x + 6 = 0$$
$$x = 0, \ x = 6, \ \text{or} \ x = -6$$

58.
$$2x\left(x^2 - 10x + 25\right) = 0$$
$$2x(x-5)^2 = 0$$
$$2x = 0 \quad \text{or} \quad x - 5 = 0$$
$$x = 0 \qquad\qquad x = 5$$

59.
$$\frac{z^2}{12} = \frac{z+3}{3}$$
$$12\left(\frac{z^2}{12}\right) = 12\left(\frac{z+3}{3}\right)$$
$$z^2 = 4(z+3)$$
$$z^2 = 4z + 12$$
$$z^2 - 4z - 12 = 0$$
$$(z-6)(z+2) = 0$$
$$z - 6 = 0 \quad \text{or} \quad z + 2 = 0$$
$$z = 6 \qquad\qquad z = -2$$

60.
$$\frac{x^2}{9} + \frac{9}{4} = -x$$
$$36\left(\frac{x^2}{9} + \frac{9}{4}\right) = 36(-x)$$
$$4x^2 + 81 = -36x$$
$$4x^2 + 36x + 81 = 0$$
$$4x^2 + 36x + 81 = 0$$
$$(2x+9)^2 = 0$$
$$2x + 9 = 0$$
$$2x = -9$$
$$x = -\frac{9}{2}$$

61.
$$(3w+2)(w+1) = (2w+3)(w-2)$$
$$3w^2 + 5w + 2 = 2w^2 - w - 6$$
$$w^2 + 6w + 8 = 0$$
$$(w+2)(w+4) = 0$$
$$w + 2 = 0 \quad \text{or} \quad w + 4 = 0$$
$$w = -2 \qquad\qquad w = -4$$

62.
$$(x-3)(x+2) = (x+9)(2x-9)$$
$$x^2 - x - 6 = 2x^2 + 9x - 81$$
$$0 = x^2 + 10x - 75$$
$$(x-5)(x+15) = 0$$
$$x - 5 = 0 \quad \text{or} \quad x + 15 = 0$$
$$x = 5 \qquad\qquad x = -15$$

63. a.
$$(x-3)(x+12) = 0$$
$$x - 3 = 0 \quad \text{or} \quad x + 12 = 0$$
$$x = 3 \qquad\qquad x = -12$$

b.
$$(x-3)(x+12) = x^2 + 9x - 36$$

64.   **a.** $(3x-1)(2x+5)=0$ **b.** $(3x-1)(2x+5)=6x^2+13x-5$

$$3x-1=0 \quad \text{or} \quad 2x+5=0$$

$$3x=1 \qquad\qquad 2x=-5$$

$$x=\frac{1}{3} \qquad\qquad x=-\frac{5}{2}$$

65.   **a.** The zeros of $x^2+2x-24$ are $x=-6$ and $x=4$.

     b. The x-intercepts are $(-6,\,0)$ and $(4,\,0)$.

     c. $x^2+2x-24=(x+6)(x-4)$

     d. The solutions to $x^2+2x-24=0$ are $x=-6$ and $x=4$.

66.   **a.** The zeros of x^3+3x^2-x-3 are $x=-3$, $x=-1$ and $x=1$.

     b. The x-intercepts are $(-3,\,0)$, $(-1,\,0)$, and $(1,\,0)$.

     c. $x^3+3x^2-x-3=(x+3)(x+1)(x-1)$

     d. The solutions to $x^3+3x^2-x-3=0$ are $x=-3$, $x=-1$ and $x=1$.

67.   **a.** The solution to the equation corresponds to the x-intercepts on the graph.
     Solution: $x=-5$, $x=7$

     b. The solution set corresponds to all values of x such that the graph is below or on the x-axis.
     Solution: $[-5,\,7]$

     c. The solution set corresponds to all values of x such that the graph is above the x-axis.
     Solution: $(-\infty,\,-5)\cup(7,\,\infty)$

68.   **a.** The solution to the equation corresponds to the x-intercepts on the graph.
     Solution: $x=-5$, $x=4$

     b. The solution set corresponds to all values of x such that the graph is below the x-axis.
     Solution: $(-\infty,\,-5)\cup(4,\,\infty)$

     c. The solution set corresponds to all values of x such that the graph is above or on the x-axis.
     Solution: $[-5,\,4]$

69.   If the solutions are $x=3$ and $x=-\dfrac{4}{7}$, then

$$x-3=0 \quad \text{and} \quad x+\frac{4}{7}=0.$$

These are equivalent to $x-3=0$ and $7x+4=0$.

Thus, $(x-3)$ and $(7x+4)$ must be factors and

equation is: $(x-3)(7x+4)=0$

$$7x^2+4x-21x-12=0$$

$$7x^2-17x-12=0$$

70.   If the solutions are $x=-2$ and $x=\dfrac{5}{2}$, then

$$x+2=0 \quad \text{and} \quad x-\frac{5}{2}=0.$$

These are equivalent to $x+2=0$ and $2x-5=0$.

Thus, $(x+2)$ and $(2x-5)$ must be factors and

equation is: $(x+2)(2x-5)=0$

$$2x^2+4x-5x-10=0$$

$$2x^2-x-10=0$$

Polynomial $P(x)$	x-intercepts of the graph of $y = P(x)$	Factored Form	Zeros of $P(x)$	Solutions of $P(x)=0$
71. $x^2 + 4x - 77$	$(-11, 0), (7, 0)$	$(x+11)(x-7)$	$x=-11, x=7$	$x=-11, x=7$
72. $x^2 - 20x - 525$	$(35, 0), (-15, 0)$	$(x-35)(x+15)$	$x=35, x=-15$	$x=35, x=-15$

73. $2\pi r_1 - 2\pi r_2 = 2\pi(r_1 - r_2)$

74. $\pi L_1^2 - \pi L_2^2 = \pi\left(L_1^2 - L_2^2\right)$
$$= \pi(L_1 + L_2)(L_1 - L_2)$$

75. $\dfrac{4}{3}\pi r_1^3 - \dfrac{4}{3}\pi r_2^3 = \dfrac{4}{3}\pi\left(r_1^3 - r_2^3\right)$
$$= \dfrac{4}{3}\pi(r_1 - r_2)\left(r_1^2 + r_1 r_2 + r_2^2\right)$$

76. If the base of the triangle is 3 cm longer than the height, then $b = h + 3$ or $h = b - 3$. If the area is 14 square centimeters and $A = \dfrac{1}{2}bh$, then to find the height of the triangle we solve the following equation.
$$\dfrac{1}{2}bh = 14$$
$$\dfrac{1}{2}(h+3)h = 14$$
$$(h+3)h = 28$$
$$h^2 + 3h - 28 = 0$$
$$(h+7)(h-4) = 0$$
Thus $h = 4$ cm.
(Note: The height cannot be equal to a negative number.)

77. If the trough is made from a sheet of metal that is 60 cm wide, then $w + 2h = 60$ or $w = 60 - 2h$. If the cross-sectional area is 400 square centimeters and $A = w \cdot h$, then to determine the height we solve the following equation.
$$w \cdot h = 400$$
$$(60 - 2h)h = 400$$
$$60h - 2h^2 = 400$$
$$2h^2 - 60h + 400 = 0$$
$$2\left(h^2 - 30h + 200\right) = 0$$
$$2(h-10)(h-20) = 0$$
Thus there are two possible values for the height, $h = 20$ cm or $h = 10$ cm.

Mastery Test for Chapter 6

1.
  a. $18x^3 - 99x^2 = 9x^2(2x - 11)$
  b. $4x^3y^2 - 6x^2y^3 + 10xy^4 = 2xy^2\left(2x^2 - 3xy + 5y^2\right)$
  c. $(7x-2)(3x) + (7x-2)(4) = (7x-2)(3x+4)$
  d. $x(2x+3y) - 5y(2x+3y) = (2x+3y)(x-5y)$

2.
  a. $(7ax+a) + (21x+3) = a(7x+1) + 3(7x+1) = (7x+1)(a+3)$
  b. $(12ax-8a) - (15bx-10b) = 4a(3x-2) - 5b(3x-2) = (3x-2)(4a-5b)$
  c. $2x^2 - 6x + 4x - 12 = 2\left(x^2 - 3x + 2x - 6\right) = 2\left[x(x-3) + 2(x-3)\right] = 2\left[(x-3)(x+2)\right]$
      $= 2(x-3)(x+2)$
  d. $10x^2 - 15x - 12x + 18 = \left(10x^2 - 15x\right) - (12x-18) = 5x(2x-3) - 6(2x-3) = (2x-3)(5x-6)$

3.   **a.** The zeros of $x^2 + 10x - 24$ are $x = -12$ and $x = 2$.

     b. The x-intercepts are $(-12,\, 0)$ and $(2,\, 0)$.

     c. $x^2 + 10x - 24 = (x+12)(x-2)$

4.   **a.** $w^2 - 4w - 45 = w^2 - 9w + 5w - 45$

             $= w(w-9) + 5(w-9)$

             $= (w+5)(w-9)$

     b. $w^2 + 14w + 45 = w^2 + 5w + 9w + 45$

             $= w(w+5) + 9(w+5)$

             $= (w+9)(w+5)$

     c. $v^2 - 10v + 24 = v^2 - 4v - 6v + 24$

             $= v(v-4) - 6(v-4)$

             $= (v-6)(v-4)$

     d. $v^2 + 5v - 36 = v^2 - 4v + 9v - 36$

             $= v(v-4) + 9(v-4)$

             $= (v+9)(v-4)$

5.   **a.** $x^2 - 5x - 36 = x^2 - 9x + 4x - 36$

             $= (x^2 - 9x) + (4x - 36)$

             $= x(x-9) + 4(x-9)$

             $= (x-9)(x+4)$

     b. $x^2 - 5x + 36$ is prime.

     c. $x^2 + 17x + 30 = x^2 + 15x + 2x + 30$

             $= (x^2 + 15x) + (2x + 30)$

             $= x(x+15) + 2(x+15)$

             $= (x+15)(x+2)$

     d. $x^2 + 17x - 30$ is prime.

6.   **a.** $x^2 - xy - 12y^2 = x^2 + 3xy - 4xy - 12y^2$

             $= x(x+3y) - 4y(x+3y)$

             $= (x-4y)(x+3y)$

     b. $x^2 - 13xy + 12y^2 = x^2 - xy - 12xy + 12y^2$

             $= x(x-y) - 12y(x-y)$

             $= (x-12y)(x-y)$

     c. $a^2 + 30ab + 144b^2 = a^2 + 24ab + 6ab + 144b^2$

             $= a(a+24b) + 6b(a+24b)$

             $= (a+6b)(a+24b)$

     d. $a^2 + 2ab - 48b^2 = a^2 - 6ab + 8ab - 48b^2$

             $= a(a-6b) + 8b(a-6b)$

             $= (a+8b)(a-6b)$

7.   **a.** $5x^2 - 33x - 14 = 5x^2 - 35x + 2x - 14$

             $= (5x^2 - 35x) + (2x - 14)$

             $= 5x(x-7) + 2(x-7)$

             $= (x-7)(5x+2)$

     b. $6x^2 - 73x + 12 = 6x^2 - 72x - x + 12$

             $= (6x^2 - 72x) - (x - 12)$

             $= 6x(x-12) - (x-12)$

             $= (x-12)(6x-1)$

     c. $9x^2 + 21x + 10 = 9x^2 + 6x + 15x + 10$

             $= (9x^2 + 6x) + (15x + 10)$

             $= 3x(3x+2) + 5(3x+2)$

             $= (3x+2)(3x+5)$

     d. $12x^2 - 7xy - 12y^2 = 12x^2 - 16xy + 9xy - 12y^2$

             $= 4x(3x-4y) + 3y(3x-4y)$

             $= (4x+3y)(3x-4y)$

8.   **a.** $9x^2 + 21x - 8 = 9x^2 - 3x + 24x - 8$

$$= \left(9x^2 - 3x\right) + \left(24x - 8\right)$$
$$= 3x\left(3x - 1\right) + 8\left(3x - 1\right)$$
$$= \left(3x - 1\right)\left(3x + 8\right)$$

b. $12x^2 + x - 6 = 12x^2 - 8x + 9x - 6$

$$= \left(12x^2 - 8x\right) + \left(9x - 6\right)$$
$$= 4x\left(3x - 2\right) + 3\left(3x - 2\right)$$
$$= \left(3x - 2\right)\left(4x + 3\right)$$

c. $3x^2 + x - 24 = 3x^2 - 8x + 9x - 24$

$$= \left(3x^2 - 8x\right) + \left(9x - 24\right)$$
$$= x\left(3x - 8\right) + 3\left(3x - 8\right)$$
$$= \left(3x - 8\right)\left(x + 3\right)$$

d. $18x^2 + 71xy - 4y^2 = 18x^2 - xy + 72xy - 4y^2$

$$= \left(18x^2 - xy\right) + \left(72xy - 4y^2\right)$$
$$= x\left(18x - y\right) + 4y\left(18x - y\right)$$
$$= \left(18x - y\right)\left(x + 4y\right)$$

9.   **a.** $8x^2 - 14x - 3$ is prime.

b. $8x^2 - 14x + 3 = 8x^2 - 12x - 2x + 3$

$$= \left(8x^2 - 12x\right) - \left(2x - 3\right)$$
$$= 4x\left(2x - 3\right) - \left(2x - 3\right)$$
$$= \left(2x - 3\right)\left(4x - 1\right)$$

c. $9x^2 + 9x - 4 = 9x^2 + 12x - 3x - 4$

$$= \left(9x^2 + 12x\right) - \left(3x + 4\right)$$
$$= 3x\left(3x + 4\right) - \left(3x + 4\right)$$
$$= \left(3x + 4\right)\left(3x - 1\right)$$

d. $9x^2 + 9x + 4$ is prime.

10.   **a.** $x^2 + 14xy + 49y^2 = \left(x\right)^2 + 2\left(x\right)\left(7y\right) + \left(7y\right)^2$

$$= \left(x + 7y\right)^2$$

b. $x^2 - 16xy + 64y^2 = \left(x\right)^2 - 2\left(x\right)\left(8y\right) + \left(8y\right)^2$

$$= \left(x - 8y\right)^2$$

c. $9x^2 + 60xy + 100y^2$

$$= \left(3x\right)^2 + 2\left(3x\right)\left(10y\right) + \left(10y\right)^2$$
$$= \left(3x + 10y\right)^2$$

d. $25x^2 - 110xy + 121y^2$

$$= \left(5x\right)^2 - 2\left(5x\right)\left(11y\right) + \left(11y\right)^2$$
$$= \left(5x - 11y\right)^2$$

11.   **a.** $x^2 - 4y^2 = \left(x\right)^2 - \left(2y\right)^2$

$$= \left(x + 2y\right)\left(x - 2y\right)$$

b. $400a^2 - b^2 = \left(20a\right)^2 - \left(b\right)^2$

$$= \left(20a - b\right)\left(20a + b\right)$$

c. $16v^2 - 49w^2 = \left(4v\right)^2 - \left(7w\right)^2$

$$= \left(4v + 7w\right)\left(4v - 7w\right)$$

d. $36x^2 - 25y^2 = \left(6x\right)^2 - \left(5y\right)^2$

$$= \left(6x + 5y\right)\left(6x - 5y\right)$$

12.   **a.** $64v^3 - 1 = \left(4v\right)^3 - \left(1\right)^3$

$$= \left(4v - 1\right)\left[\left(4v\right)^2 + \left(4v\right)\left(1\right) + \left(1\right)^2\right]$$
$$= \left(4v - 1\right)\left(16v^2 + 4v + 1\right)$$

b. $v^3 + 125 = \left(v\right)^3 + \left(5\right)^3$

$$= \left(v + 5\right)\left[\left(v\right)^2 - \left(v\right)\left(5\right) + \left(5\right)^2\right]$$
$$= \left(v + 5\right)\left(v^2 - 5v + 25\right)$$

c. $8x^3 + 125y^3$

$= (2x)^3 + (5y)^3$

$= (2x+5y)\left[(2x)^2 - (2x)(5y) + (5y)^2\right]$

$= (2x+5y)\left(4x^2 - 10xy + 25y^2\right)$

d. $27a^3 - 1000b^3$

$= (3a)^3 - (10b)^3$

$= (3a-10b)\left[(3a)^2 + (3a)(10b) + (10b)^2\right]$

$= (3a-10b)\left(9a^2 + 30ab + 100b^2\right)$

13. a. $2ax + 3a + 2bx + 3b$

$= a(2x+3) + b(2x+3)$

$= (a+b)(2x+3)$

b. $14ax - 6bx - 35ay + 15by$

$= 2x(7a-3b) - 5y(7a-3b)$

$= (2x-5y)(7a-3b)$

c. $a^2 - 4b^2 + a - 2b$

$= (a^2 - 4b^2) + (a - 2b)$

$= (a-2b)(a+2b) + (1)(a-2b)$

$= \left[(a+2b)+1\right](a-2b)$

$= (a+2b+1)(a-2b)$

d. $x^2 + 10xy + 25y^2 - 4$

$= (x^2 + 10xy + 25y^2) - 4$

$= (x+5y)^2 - 4$

$= \left[(x+5y)-2\right]\left[(x+5y)+2\right]$

$= (x+5y-2)(x+5y+2)$

14. a. $5x^2 - 245 = 5(x^2 - 49) = 5(x+7)(x-7)$

b. $2ax^2 + 20ax + 50a = 2a(x^2 + 10x + 25)$

$= 2a(x+5)^2$

c. $5av^2 - 5ax^2 + 20axy - 20ay^2$

$= 5a(v^2 - x^2 + 4xy - 4y^2)$

$= 5a\left[v^2 - (x^2 - 4xy + 4y^2)\right]$

$= 5a\left[v^2 - (x-2y)^2\right]$

$= 5a\left[(v+(x-2y))(v-(x-2y))\right]$

$= 5a(v+x-2y)(v-x+2y)$

d. $19x^3 - 19 = 19(x^3 - 1)$

$= 19(x-1)(x^2 + x + 1)$

15. a. $2x - 5 = x^2$ is a quadratic equation equivalent to $-x^2 + 2x - 5 = 0$. $a = -1, b = 2, c = -5$.

b. $2x - 5 = x^3$ is not a quadratic equation. (It is a cubic equation.)

c. $2x - 5$ is not a quadratic equation. (It is a linear expression.)

d. $2x^2 - 5 = 0$ is a quadratic equation. $a = 2, b = 0, c = -5$.

16. a. $(2x+1)(x-3) = 0$

$2x+1 = 0$ or $x-3 = 0$

$2x = -1$ $x = 3$

$x = -\dfrac{1}{2}$

b. $x^2 - 2x - 99 = 0$

$(x-11)(x+9) = 0$

$x-11 = 0$ or $x+9 = 0$

$x = 11$ $x = -9$

c. $(2x-1)(x+5)=6$

$2x^2+10x-x-5=6$

$2x^2+9x-11=0$

$(2x+11)(x-1)=0$

$2x+11=0 \qquad \text{or} \quad x-1=0$

$2x=-11 \qquad\qquad x=1$

$x=-\dfrac{11}{2}$

d. $(3x+1)(2x+7)=4(x+1)$

$6x^2+21x+2x+7=4x+4$

$6x^2+23x+7=4x+4$

$6x^2+19x+3=0$

$(6x+1)(x+3)=0$

$6x+1=0 \qquad \text{or} \quad x+3=0$

$6x=-1 \qquad\qquad x=-3$

$x=-\dfrac{1}{6}$

17. **a.** If the solutions are $x=-7$ and $x=9$, then

$x+7=0 \quad$ and $\quad x-9=0$.

Thus, $(x+7)$ and $(x-9)$ must be factors and

equation is: $\quad (x+7)(x-9)=0$

$x^2-9x+7x-63=0$

$x^2-2x-63=0$

b. If the solutions are $x=-13$ and $x=13$, then

$x+13=0 \quad$ and $\quad x-13=0$.

Thus, $(x+13)$ and $(x-13)$ must be factors and

equation is: $\quad (x+13)(x-13)=0$

$x^2-169=0$

c. If the solutions are $x=\dfrac{1}{7}$ and $x=-4$, then

$x-\dfrac{1}{7}=0 \quad$ and $\quad x+4=0$.

These are equivalent to $7x-1=0 \quad$ and $\quad x+4=0$.

Thus, $(7x-1)$ and $(x+4)$ must be factors and

equation is: $\quad (7x-1)(x+4)=0$

$7x^2+28x-x-4=0$

$7x^2+27x-4=0$

c. If the solutions are $x=\dfrac{3}{7}$ and $x=\dfrac{4}{3}$, then

$x-\dfrac{3}{7}=0 \quad$ and $\quad x-\dfrac{4}{3}=0$.

These are equivalent to $7x-3=0 \quad$ and $\quad 3x-4=0$.

Thus, $(7x-3)$ and $(3x-4)$ must be factors and

equation is: $\quad (7x-3)(3x-4)=0$

$21x^2-28x-9x+12=0$

$21x^2-37x+12=0$

18. **a.** The solutions to $x^2+2x-15=0$ are $x=-5$ and $x=3$.

b. The solutions of $x^2+2x-15<0$ are the x values for which the graph is below the x-axis. Thus the solution set is $(-5,\,3)$.

c. The solutions of $x^2+2x-15>0$ are the x values for which the graph is above the x-axis. Thus the solution set is $(-\infty,\,-5)\cup(3,\,+\infty)$.

Chapter 7: Solving Quadratic Equations

Quick Review 7.1

1. $\sqrt{36} = 6$

2. $\sqrt{39} \approx 6.245$

3. $\dfrac{\sqrt{3}}{5} \approx 0.346$

4. $\dfrac{35}{77} = \dfrac{5 \cdot \cancel{7}}{\cancel{7} \cdot 11} = \dfrac{5}{11}$

5. $1 + \dfrac{x}{2} = 9$

$2\left(1 + \dfrac{x}{2}\right) = 2(9)$

$2 + x = 18$

$x = 16$

Exercises 7.1

1. $m^2 = 4$

$\sqrt{m^2} = \pm\sqrt{4}$

$m = \pm 2$

3. $x^2 = 2$

$\sqrt{x^2} = \pm\sqrt{2} \approx \pm 1.41$

5. $5y^2 = 45$

$\dfrac{5y^2}{5} = \dfrac{45}{5}$

$y^2 = 9$

$\sqrt{y^2} = \pm\sqrt{9}$

$y = \pm 3$

7. $2v^2 = 38$

$\dfrac{2v^2}{2} = \dfrac{38}{2}$

$v^2 = 19$

$\sqrt{v^2} = \pm\sqrt{19} \approx \pm 4.36$

9. $2w^2 - 72 = 0$

$2w^2 = 72$

$\dfrac{2w^2}{2} = \dfrac{72}{2}$

$w^2 = 36$

$\sqrt{w^2} = \pm\sqrt{36}$

$w = \pm 6$

11. $10z^2 - 50 = 0$

$10z^2 = 50$

$\dfrac{10z^2}{10} = \dfrac{50}{10}$

$z^2 = 5$

$\sqrt{z^2} = \pm\sqrt{5}$

$z = \pm\sqrt{5} \approx \pm 2.24$

13. $\sqrt{16 \cdot 5} = \sqrt{16} \cdot \sqrt{5} = 4\sqrt{5}$

15. $\sqrt{20} = \sqrt{4 \cdot 5} = \sqrt{4} \cdot \sqrt{5}$

$= 2\sqrt{5}$

17. $\sqrt{200} = \sqrt{100 \cdot 2}$

$= \sqrt{100} \cdot \sqrt{2}$

$= 10\sqrt{2}$

19. $x^2 = 18$

$\sqrt{x^2} = \pm\sqrt{18}$

$x = \pm\sqrt{9} \cdot \sqrt{2}$

$x = \pm 3\sqrt{2} \approx \pm 4.24$

21. $3y^2 = 81$

$y^2 = 27$

$\sqrt{y^2} = \pm\sqrt{27}$

$y = \pm\sqrt{9}\sqrt{3}$

$y = \pm 3\sqrt{3} \approx \pm 5.20$

23. $7a^2 - 56 = 0$

$7a^2 = 56$

$a^2 = 8$

$\sqrt{a^2} = \pm\sqrt{8}$

$a = \pm\sqrt{4}\sqrt{2}$

$a = \pm 2\sqrt{2} \approx \pm 2.83$

25. $\sqrt{\dfrac{4}{9}} = \dfrac{\sqrt{4}}{\sqrt{9}} = \dfrac{2}{3}$

27. $\sqrt{\dfrac{6}{49}} = \dfrac{\sqrt{6}}{\sqrt{49}} = \dfrac{\sqrt{6}}{7}$

29. $\dfrac{\sqrt{20}}{\sqrt{5}} = \sqrt{\dfrac{20}{5}} = \sqrt{4} = 2$

31. $\dfrac{\sqrt{18}}{\sqrt{50}} = \sqrt{\dfrac{18}{50}} = \sqrt{\dfrac{\cancel{2} \cdot 9}{\cancel{2} \cdot 25}}$

$= \sqrt{\dfrac{9}{25}} = \dfrac{\sqrt{9}}{\sqrt{25}} = \dfrac{3}{5}$

33. $4v^2 = 81$

$v^2 = \dfrac{81}{4}$

$\sqrt{v^2} = \pm\sqrt{\dfrac{81}{4}}$

$v = \pm\dfrac{\sqrt{81}}{\sqrt{4}} = \pm\dfrac{9}{2}$

35. $36x^2 - 7 = 0$

$36x^2 = 7$

$x^2 = \dfrac{7}{36}$

$\sqrt{x^2} = \pm\sqrt{\dfrac{7}{36}}$

$x = \pm\dfrac{\sqrt{7}}{\sqrt{36}} = \pm\dfrac{\sqrt{7}}{6}$

37. $\dfrac{3}{\sqrt{5}} = \dfrac{3}{\sqrt{5}} \cdot \dfrac{\sqrt{5}}{\sqrt{5}} = \dfrac{3\sqrt{5}}{5}$

39. $\dfrac{6}{\sqrt{10}} = \dfrac{6}{\sqrt{10}} \cdot \dfrac{\sqrt{10}}{\sqrt{10}} = \dfrac{\overset{3}{\cancel{6}}\sqrt{10}}{\underset{5}{\cancel{10}}} = \dfrac{3\sqrt{10}}{5}$

41. $\dfrac{\sqrt{2}}{\sqrt{3}} = \dfrac{\sqrt{2}}{\sqrt{3}} \cdot \dfrac{\sqrt{3}}{\sqrt{3}} = \dfrac{\sqrt{6}}{3}$

43. $\sqrt{\dfrac{5}{17}} = \dfrac{\sqrt{5}}{\sqrt{17}} = \dfrac{\sqrt{5}}{\sqrt{17}} \cdot \dfrac{\sqrt{17}}{\sqrt{17}} = \dfrac{\sqrt{85}}{17}$

45. $8x^2 = 20$

$x^2 = \dfrac{\overset{5}{\cancel{20}}}{\underset{2}{\cancel{8}}}$

$x^2 = \dfrac{5}{2}$

$\sqrt{x^2} = \pm\sqrt{\dfrac{5}{2}}$

$x = \pm\dfrac{\sqrt{5}}{\sqrt{2}} \cdot \dfrac{\sqrt{2}}{\sqrt{2}} = \pm\dfrac{\sqrt{10}}{2} \approx \pm1.58$

47. $10w^2 - 14 = 0$

$10w^2 = 14$

$w^2 = \dfrac{14}{10}$

$w^2 = \dfrac{7}{5}$

$\sqrt{w^2} = \pm\sqrt{\dfrac{7}{5}}$

$w = \pm\dfrac{\sqrt{7}}{\sqrt{5}} \cdot \dfrac{\sqrt{5}}{\sqrt{5}} = \pm\dfrac{\sqrt{35}}{5} \approx \pm1.18$

49. $(n-1)^2 = 36$

$\sqrt{(n-1)^2} = \pm\sqrt{36}$

$n - 1 = \pm6$

$n - 1 = -6 \quad$ or $\quad n - 1 = 6$

$n = -6 + 1 \qquad\qquad n = 6 + 1$

$n = -5 \qquad\qquad\quad n = 7$

51. $(2b+3)^2 = 49$

$\sqrt{(2b+3)^2} = \pm\sqrt{49}$

$2b + 3 = \pm7$

$2b + 3 = -7 \quad$ or $\quad 2b + 3 = 7$

$2b = -10 \qquad\qquad 2b = 4$

$b = -5 \qquad\qquad\quad b = 2$

53. $(3x-1)^2 + 7 = 32$

$(3x-1)^2 = 25$

$\sqrt{(3x-1)^2} = \pm\sqrt{25}$

$3x - 1 = \pm5$

$3x - 1 = -5 \quad$ or $\quad 3x - 1 = 5$

$3x = -4 \qquad\qquad\quad 3x = 6$

$x = -\dfrac{4}{3} \qquad\qquad\quad x = 2$

55.   **a.** $2x = 36$

$$\frac{2x}{2} = \frac{36}{2}$$

$$x = 18$$

b. $x^2 = 36$

$$\sqrt{x^2} = \pm\sqrt{36}$$

$$x = \pm 6$$

57.   **a.** $2m - 1 = 9$

$$2m = 10$$

$$m = 5$$

b. $(2m-1)^2 = 9$

$$\sqrt{(2m-1)^2} = \pm\sqrt{9}$$

$$2m - 1 = \pm 3$$

$2m - 1 = -3$	or	$2m - 1 = 3$
$2m = -2$		$2m = 4$
$m = -1$		$m = 2$

59.   **a.** The solutions to $(2x-1)^2 - 1 = 0$ are $x = 0$ and $x = 1$.

    b. The solutions of $(2x-1)^2 - 1 < 0$ are the x values for which the graph is below the x-axis. Thus the solution set is $(0, 1)$.

    c. The solutions of $(2x-1)^2 - 1 > 0$ are the x values for which the graph is above the x-axis. Thus the solution set is $(-\infty, 0) \cup (1, \infty)$.

61.   **a.** $x^2 - 6 = 0$

$$x^2 = 6$$

$$\sqrt{x^2} = \pm\sqrt{6}$$

$$x = \pm\sqrt{6}$$

    b. $x = \pm\sqrt{6}$

    c. $\left(\pm\sqrt{6}, 0\right)$

63.   **a.**   If the solutions are $x = -7$ and $x = 7$, then

$$x + 7 = 0 \quad \text{and} \quad x - 7 = 0.$$

Thus, $(x+7)$ and $(x-7)$ must be factors and equation is: $(x+7)(x-7) = 0$

$$x^2 - 49 = 0$$

    b.   If the solutions are $x = -\sqrt{7}$ and $x = \sqrt{7}$, then

$$x + \sqrt{7} = 0 \quad \text{and} \quad x - \sqrt{7} = 0.$$

Thus, $\left(x + \sqrt{7}\right)$ and $\left(x - \sqrt{7}\right)$ must be factors and equation is: $\left(x + \sqrt{7}\right)\left(x - \sqrt{7}\right) = 0$

$$x^2 - 7 = 0$$

65.

$$a^2 + b^2 = c^2$$

$$(29.5)^2 + (35.7)^2 = c^2$$

$$870.25 + 1274.49 = c^2$$

$$c^2 = 2144.74$$

$$\sqrt{c^2} = \sqrt{2144.74}$$

$$c = 46.3 \text{ cm}$$

(Only the principle square root is used here since c is the length of the hypotenuse.)

67.

$$A = P\left(1 + \frac{r}{2}\right)^2 \Rightarrow 923.79 = 850\left(1 + \frac{r}{2}\right)^2$$

$$\frac{923.79}{850} = \left(1 + \frac{r}{2}\right)^2$$

$$1.086812 \approx \left(1 + \frac{r}{2}\right)^2$$

$$\sqrt{1.086812} \approx \sqrt{\left(1 + \frac{r}{2}\right)^2}$$

$$\sqrt{1.086812} \approx 1 + \frac{r}{2}$$

$$\frac{r}{2} \approx \sqrt{1.086812} - 1$$

$$r \approx 2\left(\sqrt{1.086812} - 1\right) \approx 0.085$$

Thus $r \approx 8.5\%$

69. Let $d = 50$ and solve for t.

$$16t^2 = 50$$

$$t^2 = \frac{\overset{25}{\cancel{50}}}{\underset{8}{\cancel{16}}} = \frac{25}{8}$$

$$t = \sqrt{\frac{25}{8}} = \frac{5}{\sqrt{8}} = \frac{5}{\sqrt{8}} \cdot \frac{\sqrt{8}}{\sqrt{8}} = \frac{5\sqrt{8}}{8} \approx 1.8$$

It takes the hammer 1.8 seconds to fall 50 ft.

Cumulative Review

1. $4718.5 = 4.7185 \times 10^3$

2. $2.3 \times 10^{-4} = 0.00023$

3. $\left(5x^2 y^3\right)\left(4x^3 y^4\right) = 20x^{2+3} y^{3+4} = 20x^5 y^7$

4. $\left(5x^2 y^3\right)^2 = 5^2 \left(x^2\right)^2 \left(y^3\right)^2 = 25x^{2 \cdot 2} y^{3 \cdot 2} = 25x^4 y^6$

5.   1, 2, 3, 4

Section 7.2: Solving Quadratic Equations by Completing the Square

Quick Review 7.2

1. $\left(\dfrac{7}{2}\right)^2 = \dfrac{7^2}{2^2} = \dfrac{49}{4}$

2. $(x-7)^2 = x^2 - 2(x)(7) + (-7)^2$
$$= x^2 - 14x + 49$$

3. $\left(1-\sqrt{7}\right)^2 = 1^2 - 2(1)\sqrt{7} + \left(-\sqrt{7}\right)^2$
$$= 1 - 2\sqrt{7} + 7$$
$$= 8 - 2\sqrt{7}$$

4. $x^2 + 14x + 49 = x^2 + 2(7)x + (7)^2$
$$= (x+7)^2$$

5. $\dfrac{6-4\sqrt{5}}{2} = \dfrac{6}{2} - \dfrac{4\sqrt{5}}{2} = 3 - 2\sqrt{5}$

Exercises 7.2

1. $m^2 - 2m + 1 = 4$
$$(m-1)^2 = 4$$

3. $y^2 + 14y + 49 = 5$
$$(y+7)^2 = 5$$

5.   To complete the square we add the square of one-half the coefficient of x.

$x^2 + 12x + 36$ $\left(\dfrac{12}{2}\right)^2 = (6)^2 = 36$

7.   To complete the square we add the square of one-half the coefficient of v.

$v^2 - 18v + 81$ $\left(\dfrac{-18}{2}\right)^2 = (-9)^2 = 81$

9. To complete the square we add the square of one-half the coefficient of m.

$$m^2 + 4bm + 4b^2 \qquad \left(\frac{4b}{2}\right)^2 = (2b)^2 = 4b^2$$

11. To complete the square we add the square of one-half the coefficient of w to both sides of the equation and then solve the equation using the extraction of roots method.

$$w^2 - 4w = 0$$
$$w^2 - 4w + 4 = 0 + 4 \qquad \left(\frac{-4}{2}\right)^2 = (-2)^2 = 4$$
$$(w-2)^2 = 4$$
$$w - 2 = \pm\sqrt{4}$$
$$w - 2 = \pm 2$$
$$w - 2 = 2 \quad \text{or} \quad w - 2 = -2$$
$$w = 4 \qquad\qquad w = 0$$

13. To complete the square we add the square of one-half the coefficient of w to both sides of the equation and then solve the equation using the extraction of roots method.

$$w^2 - 4w = 12$$
$$w^2 - 4w + 4 = 12 + 4 \qquad \left(\frac{-4}{2}\right)^2 = (-2)^2 = 4$$
$$(w-2)^2 = 16$$
$$w - 2 = \pm\sqrt{16}$$
$$w - 2 = \pm 4$$
$$w - 2 = -4 \quad \text{or} \quad w - 2 = 4$$
$$w = -2 \qquad\qquad w = 6$$

15. To complete the square we add the square of one-half the coefficient of x to both sides of the equation and then solve the equation using the extraction of roots method.

$$y^2 + 6x = 0$$
$$y^2 + 6x + 9 = 0 + 9 \qquad \left(\frac{6}{2}\right)^2 = (3)^2 = 9$$
$$(y+3)^2 = 9$$
$$y + 3 = \pm\sqrt{9}$$
$$y + 3 = \pm 3$$
$$y + 3 = -3 \quad \text{or} \quad y + 3 = 3$$
$$y = -6 \qquad\qquad y = 0$$

17. To complete the square we add the square of one-half the coefficient of x to both sides of the equation and then solve the equation using the extraction of roots method.

$$y^2 + 6x = -5$$
$$y^2 + 6x + 9 = -5 + 9 \qquad \left(\frac{6}{2}\right)^2 = (3)^2 = 9$$
$$(y+3)^2 = 4$$
$$y + 3 = \pm\sqrt{4}$$
$$y + 3 = \pm 2$$
$$y + 3 = -2 \quad \text{or} \quad y + 3 = 2$$
$$y = -5 \qquad\qquad y = -1$$

19. To complete the square we add the square of one-half the coefficient of t to both sides of the equation and then solve the equation using the extraction of roots method.

$$t^2 + 2t + 2 = 6$$
$$t^2 + 2t = 4$$
$$t^2 + 2t + 1 = 4 + 1 \qquad \left(\frac{-2}{2}\right)^2 = (-1)^2 = 1$$
$$(t+1)^2 = 5$$
$$t + 1 = \pm\sqrt{5}$$
$$t = -1 \pm \sqrt{5}$$
$$t = -1 - \sqrt{5} \approx -3.24 \quad \text{or} \quad t = -1 + \sqrt{5} \approx 1.24$$

21. The left hand side is already a perfect square trinomial.

$$w^2 + 12w + 25 = \frac{1}{4}$$

$$(w+5)^2 = \frac{1}{4}$$

$$w+5 = \pm\sqrt{\frac{1}{4}}$$

$$w+5 = \pm\frac{1}{2}$$

$$w+5 = -\frac{1}{2} \quad \text{or} \quad w+5 = \frac{1}{2}$$

$$w = -\frac{1}{2} - 5 \qquad\qquad w = \frac{1}{2} - 5$$

$$w = -\frac{1}{2} - \frac{10}{2} \qquad\qquad w = \frac{1}{2} - \frac{10}{2}$$

$$w = -\frac{11}{2} \qquad\qquad w = -\frac{9}{2}$$

23. First, simplify the equation by dividing both sides by 2. To complete the square we add the square of one-half the coefficient of y to both sides of the equation and then solve the equation using the extraction of roots method.

$$2y^2 - 8y + 4 = 2$$

$$\frac{2y^2}{2} - \frac{8y}{2} + \frac{4}{2} = \frac{2}{2}$$

$$y^2 - 4y + 2 = 1$$

$$y^2 - 4y = -1$$

$$y^2 - 4y + 4 = -1 + 4$$

$$\boxed{\left(\frac{4}{2}\right)^2 = (2)^2 = 4}$$

$$(y-2)^2 = 3$$

$$y-2 = \pm\sqrt{3}$$

$$y = 2 \pm \sqrt{3}$$

$$y = 2 + \sqrt{3} \approx 3.73 \quad \text{or} \quad y = 2 - \sqrt{3} \approx 0.27$$

25. First, simplify the equation by dividing both sides by 3. To complete the square we add the square of one-half the coefficient of x to both sides of the equation and then solve the equation using the extraction of roots method.

$$3x^2 + 6x + 2 = 0$$

$$\frac{3x^2}{3} + \frac{6x}{3} + \frac{2}{3} = \frac{0}{3}$$

$$x^2 + 2x + \frac{2}{3} = 0$$

$$x^2 + 2x = -\frac{2}{3}$$

$$\boxed{\left(\frac{2}{2}\right)^2 = (1)^2 = 1}$$

$$x^2 + 2x + 1 = -\frac{2}{3} + 1$$

$$(x+1)^2 = \frac{1}{3}$$

$$x+1 = \pm\sqrt{\frac{1}{3}} = \pm\frac{1}{\sqrt{3}} = \pm\frac{\sqrt{3}}{3}$$

$$x = -1 \pm \frac{\sqrt{3}}{3} = -\frac{3}{3} \pm \frac{\sqrt{3}}{3} = \frac{-3 \pm \sqrt{3}}{3}$$

$$x = \frac{-3-\sqrt{3}}{3} \approx -1.58 \quad \text{or} \quad x = \frac{-3+\sqrt{3}}{3} \approx -4.22$$

27. To complete the square we add the square of one-half the coefficient of m to both sides of the equation and then solve the equation using the extraction of roots method.

$$m^2 - \frac{3}{2}m = 1$$

$$m^2 - \frac{3}{2}m + \frac{9}{16} = 1 + \frac{9}{16}$$

$$\left(m - \frac{3}{4}\right)^2 = \frac{16}{16}$$

$$\boxed{\left(\frac{1}{2}\cdot\frac{5}{2}\right)^2 = \left(\frac{5}{4}\right)^2 = \frac{25}{16}}$$

$$\left(m - \frac{3}{4}\right)^2 = \frac{25}{16}$$

$$\sqrt{\left(m - \frac{3}{4}\right)^2} = \pm\sqrt{\frac{25}{16}}$$

$$m - \frac{3}{4} = \pm\frac{5}{4}$$

$$m = \frac{3}{4} \pm \frac{5}{4}$$

$$m = \frac{3}{4} - \frac{5}{4} \quad \text{or} \quad m = \frac{3}{4} + \frac{5}{4}$$

$$m = -\frac{2}{4} = -\frac{1}{2} \qquad\qquad m = \frac{8}{4} = 2$$

29. First, divide both sides of the equation by 4. To complete the square we add the square of one-half the coefficient of v to both sides of the equation and then solve the equation using the extraction of roots method.

$$4v^2 - 4v - 1 = 0$$

$$\frac{4v^2}{4} - \frac{4v}{4} - \frac{1}{4} = \frac{0}{4}$$

$$v^2 - v - \frac{1}{4} = 0$$

$$v^2 - v = \frac{1}{4}$$

$$v^2 - v + \frac{1}{4} = \frac{1}{4} + \frac{1}{4} \quad \left(\frac{-1}{2}\right)^2 = \frac{1}{4}$$

$$\left(v - \frac{1}{2}\right)^2 = \frac{1}{2}$$

$$\sqrt{\left(v - \frac{1}{2}\right)^2} = \pm\sqrt{\frac{1}{2}}$$

$$v - \frac{1}{2} = \pm\frac{1}{\sqrt{2}} = \pm\frac{\sqrt{2}}{2}$$

$$v = \frac{1}{2} \pm \frac{\sqrt{2}}{2} = \frac{1 \pm \sqrt{2}}{2}$$

$$v = \frac{1 - \sqrt{2}}{2} \approx -0.21 \quad \text{or} \quad v = \frac{1 + \sqrt{2}}{2} \approx 1.21$$

31. First, combine like terms and divide both sides of the equation by 5. To complete the square we add the square of one-half the coefficient of v to both sides of the equation and then solve the equation using the extraction of roots method.

$$5v^2 + v + 1 = 3v + 2$$

$$5v^2 - 2v = 1$$

$$\frac{5v^2}{5} - \frac{2v}{5} = \frac{1}{5} \quad \left(\frac{1}{2} \cdot \frac{2}{5}\right)^2 = \left(\frac{1}{5}\right)^2 = \frac{1}{25}$$

$$v^2 - \frac{2}{5}v + \frac{1}{25} = \frac{1}{5} + \frac{1}{25}$$

$$\left(v - \frac{1}{5}\right)^2 = \frac{6}{25}$$

$$v - \frac{1}{5} = \pm\sqrt{\frac{6}{25}} = \pm\frac{\sqrt{6}}{5}$$

$$v = \frac{1}{5} \pm \frac{\sqrt{6}}{5} = \frac{1 \pm \sqrt{6}}{5}$$

$$v = \frac{1 - \sqrt{6}}{5} \approx -0.29 \quad \text{or} \quad v = \frac{1 + \sqrt{6}}{5} \approx 0.69$$

33. First, expand and combine like terms. To complete the square we add the square of one-half the coefficient of x to both sides of the equation and then solve the equation using the extraction of roots method.

$$(x - 3)(x + 2) = 1$$

$$x^2 - x - 6 = 1$$

$$x^2 - x = 7$$

$$x^2 - x + \frac{1}{4} = 7 + \frac{1}{4} \quad \left(\frac{-1}{2}\right)^2 = \frac{1}{4}$$

$$\left(x - \frac{1}{2}\right)^2 = \frac{7}{1} \cdot \frac{4}{4} + \frac{1}{4}$$

$$\left(x - \frac{1}{2}\right)^2 = \frac{28}{4} + \frac{1}{4} = \frac{29}{4}$$

$$x - \frac{1}{2} = \pm\sqrt{\frac{29}{4}} = \pm\frac{\sqrt{29}}{2}$$

$$x = \frac{1}{2} \pm \frac{\sqrt{29}}{2} = \frac{1 \pm \sqrt{29}}{2}$$

$$x = \frac{1 - \sqrt{29}}{2} \approx -2.19 \quad \text{or} \quad x = \frac{1 + \sqrt{29}}{2} \approx 3.19$$

35. a.
$$2x + x = 3$$
$$3x = 3$$
$$x = 1$$

b. To complete the square we add the square of one-half the coefficient of x to both sides of the equation and then solve the equation using the extraction of roots method.

$$x^2 + 2x = 3$$

$$x^2 + 2x + 1 = 3 + 1 \quad \left(\frac{2}{2}\right)^2 = (1)^2 = 1$$

$$(x + 1)^2 = 4$$

$$x + 1 = \pm\sqrt{4} = \pm 2$$

$$x = -1 \pm 2$$

$$x = -1 - 2 \quad \text{or} \quad x = -1 + 2$$

$$x = -3 \quad\quad\quad\quad x = 1$$

37.   **a.** The solutions to $x^2 - 3 = 0$ are $x = -\sqrt{3}$ and $x = \sqrt{3}$.

b. The solutions of $x^2 - 3 \leq 0$ are the x values for which the graph is below or on the x-axis. Thus the solution set is $\left[-\sqrt{3}, \sqrt{3}\right]$.

c. The solutions of $x^2 - 3 \geq 0$ are the x values for which the graph is above or on the x-axis. Thus the solution set is $\left(-\infty, -\sqrt{3}\right] \cup \left[\sqrt{3}, \infty\right)$.

39.   **a.** First, divide both sides of the equation by 2. To complete the square we add the square of one-half the coefficient of x to both sides of the equation and then solve the equation using the extraction of roots method.

$$2x^2 - 2x - 1 = 0$$

$$\frac{2x^2}{2} - \frac{2x}{2} - \frac{1}{2} = \frac{0}{2}$$

$$x^2 - x - \frac{1}{2} = 0$$

$$x^2 - x = \frac{1}{2}$$

$$x^2 - x + \frac{1}{4} = \frac{1}{2} + \frac{1}{4} \qquad \left(\frac{-1}{2}\right)^2 = \frac{1}{4}$$

$$\left(x - \frac{1}{2}\right)^2 = \frac{3}{4}$$

$$x - \frac{1}{2} = \pm\sqrt{\frac{3}{4}} = \pm\frac{\sqrt{3}}{2}$$

$$x = \frac{1}{2} \pm \frac{\sqrt{3}}{2} = \frac{1 \pm \sqrt{3}}{2}$$

b. The zeros of $x^2 - 2x - 5$ are $x = \dfrac{1 \pm \sqrt{3}}{2}$.

c. The x-intercepts of $y = x^2 - 2x - 5$ are $\left(\dfrac{1 - \sqrt{3}}{2}, 0\right)$ and $\left(\dfrac{1 + \sqrt{3}}{2}, 0\right)$.

41.   **a.** If the solutions are $x = -\dfrac{2}{3}$ and $x = \dfrac{2}{3}$, then

$$x + \frac{2}{3} = 0 \text{ and } x - \frac{2}{3} = 0.$$

These are equivalent to $3x - 2 = 0$ and $3x + 2 = 0$. Thus $(3x - 2)$ and $(3x + 2)$ are factors and the equation is $(3x - 2)(3x + 2) = 0$

$$9x^2 - 4 = 0$$

b. If the solutions are $x = -\dfrac{\sqrt{2}}{3}$ and $x = \dfrac{\sqrt{2}}{3}$, then

$$x + \frac{\sqrt{2}}{3} = 0 \text{ and } x - \frac{\sqrt{2}}{3} = 0.$$

These are equivalent to $3x - \sqrt{2} = 0$ and $3x + \sqrt{2} = 0$. Thus $(3x + \sqrt{2})$ and $(3x - \sqrt{2})$ are factors and the equation is $(3x + \sqrt{2})(3x - \sqrt{2}) = 0$

$$9x^2 - 2 = 0$$

43. The area of the photo is $A = (1.5x)(x)$. Let $A = 24$
and solve for x:

$$(1.5x)(x) = 24$$

$$1.5x^2 = 24$$

$$x^2 = \frac{24}{1.5} = 16$$

$$x = \sqrt{16} = 4$$

The width of the photo is $x = 4$ cm.

The length of the photo is $1.5(4) = 6$ cm.

45. The area of the metal ring is $A = \pi(2r)^2 - \pi r^2$.
Let $A = 15$ and solve for r.

$$\pi(2r)^2 - \pi r^2 = 15$$

$$\pi(4r^2 - r^2) = 15$$

$$\pi(3r^2) = 15$$

$$3\pi r^2 = 15$$

$$r^2 = \frac{15}{3\pi} = \frac{5}{\pi}$$

$$r = \sqrt{\frac{5}{\pi}} \approx 1.3 \text{ cm}$$

47.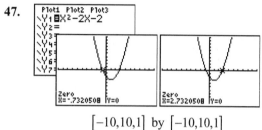

$[-10,10,1]$ by $[-10,10,1]$

Solutions: $x \approx -0.73$, $x \approx 2.73$

49.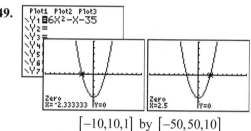

$[-10,10,1]$ by $[-50,50,10]$

Solutions: $w \approx -2.33$ or $w \approx 2.5$

Cumulative Review

1.
$$12 - 5(11 - 8 \div 2) = 12 - 5(11 - 4)$$
$$= 12 - 5(7)$$
$$= 12 - 35$$
$$= -23$$

2.
$$(12 - 5)(11 - 8 \div 2) = (7)(11 - 4)$$
$$= (7)(7)$$
$$= 49$$

3. If a line has a slope of $\dfrac{3}{5}$, then a parallel line has a slope of $\dfrac{3}{5}$.

4. If a line has a slope of $\dfrac{3}{5}$, then a perpendicular line has a slope of $-\dfrac{5}{3}$.

5. $\dfrac{36x^5 y^{10}}{2x^2 y^2} = \dfrac{\overset{18}{\cancel{36}}\, x^{5-2} y^{10-2}}{\underset{1}{\cancel{2}}} = 18x^3 y^8$

Section 7.3: Using the Quadratic Formula to Find Real Solutions

Quick Review 7.3

1. $\sqrt{20} = \sqrt{4}\sqrt{5} = 2\sqrt{5}$

2. $\dfrac{6 + 4\sqrt{5}}{2} = \dfrac{\overset{3}{\cancel{6}}}{\cancel{2}} + \dfrac{\overset{2}{\cancel{4}}\sqrt{5}}{\cancel{2}} = 3 + 2\sqrt{5}$

3. $y = 3x^2 + 2x - 1 = 3(0)^2 + 2(0) - 1 = -1$

4. $y = 3x^2 + 2x - 1 = 3\left(\dfrac{1}{3}\right)^2 + 2\left(\dfrac{1}{3}\right) - 1 = -1$

$= 3\left(\dfrac{1}{9}\right) + \dfrac{2}{3} - 1 = \dfrac{1}{3} + \dfrac{2}{3} - 1 = \dfrac{3}{3} - 1 = 1 - 1 = 0$

5.   The solutions are $x = -12$ and $x = 2.5$

Exercises 7.3

1.   Substitute a, b, and c in the quadratic formula.

$$a = 1, \quad b = -2, \quad c = -3$$

$$m = \frac{2 \pm \sqrt{(-2)^2 - 4(1)(-3)}}{2(1)}$$

$$= \frac{2 \pm \sqrt{4 + 12}}{2} = \frac{2 \pm \sqrt{16}}{2} = \frac{2 \pm 4}{2}$$

$$m = \frac{2 + 4}{2} \quad \text{or} \quad m = \frac{2 - 4}{2}$$

$$m = \frac{6}{2} \quad \text{or} \quad m = \frac{-2}{2}$$

$$m = 3 \quad \text{or} \quad m = -1$$

3.   First write the equation in standard form.

$$8y^2 = 2y + 1$$

$$8y^2 - 2y - 1 = 0$$

Substitute a, b, and c in the quadratic formula.

$$a = 8, \quad b = -2, \quad c = -1$$

$$y = \frac{-(-2) \pm \sqrt{(-2)^2 - 4(8)(-1)}}{2(8)}$$

$$= \frac{2 \pm \sqrt{4 + 32}}{16} = \frac{2 \pm \sqrt{36}}{16} = \frac{2 \pm 6}{16}$$

$$y = \frac{2 - 6}{16} \quad \text{or} \quad y = \frac{2 + 6}{16}$$

$$y = \frac{-4}{16} \quad \text{or} \quad y = \frac{8}{16}$$

$$y = -\frac{1}{4} \quad \text{or} \quad y = \frac{1}{2}$$

5.   First write the equation in standard form and simplify.

$$4x^2 = 4x + 35$$

$$4x^2 - 4x - 35 = 0$$

Substitute a, b, and c in the quadratic formula.

$$a = 4, \quad b = -4, \quad c = -35$$

$$x = \frac{-(-4) \pm \sqrt{(-4)^2 - 4(4)(-35)}}{2(4)}$$

$$= \frac{4 \pm \sqrt{16 + 560}}{8} = \frac{4 \pm \sqrt{576}}{8} = \frac{4 \pm 24}{8}$$

$$x = \frac{4 - 24}{8} \quad \text{or} \quad x = \frac{4 + 24}{8}$$

$$x = \frac{-20}{8} \quad \text{or} \quad x = \frac{28}{8}$$

$$x = -\frac{5}{2} \quad \text{or} \quad x = \frac{7}{2}$$

7.   Substitute a, b, and c in the quadratic formula.

$$a = 5, \quad b = -2, \quad c = -1$$

$$x = \frac{-(-2) \pm \sqrt{(-2)^2 - 4(5)(-1)}}{2(5)}$$

$$= \frac{2 \pm \sqrt{4 + 20}}{10} = \frac{2 \pm \sqrt{24}}{10} = \frac{2 \pm 2\sqrt{6}}{10} = \frac{\cancel{2}\left(1 \pm \sqrt{6}\right)}{\cancel{10}_{5}}$$

$$x = \frac{1 + \sqrt{6}}{5} \approx 0.69 \quad \text{or} \quad x = \frac{1 - \sqrt{6}}{5} \approx -0.29$$

9. First write the equation in standard form.

$$9v^2 + 1 = 12v$$

$$9v^2 - 12v + 1 = 0$$

Substitute a, b, and c in the quadratic formula.

$$a = 9, \quad b = -12, \quad c = 1$$

$$v = \frac{-(-12) \pm \sqrt{(-12)^2 - 4(9)(1)}}{2(9)}$$

$$= \frac{12 \pm \sqrt{144 - 36}}{18} = \frac{12 \pm \sqrt{108}}{18} = \frac{12 \pm 6\sqrt{3}}{18}$$

$$= \frac{\cancel{6}(2 \pm \sqrt{3})}{\cancel{18}_{3}} = \frac{2 \pm \sqrt{3}}{3}$$

$$v = \frac{2 + \sqrt{3}}{3} \approx 1.24 \quad \text{or} \quad v = \frac{2 - \sqrt{3}}{3} \approx 0.09$$

11. Substitute a, b, and c in the quadratic formula.

$$a = 6, \quad b = 5, \quad c = 0$$

$$t = \frac{-(5) \pm \sqrt{(5)^2 - 4(6)(0)}}{2(6)}$$

$$= \frac{-5 \pm \sqrt{25 - 0}}{12} = \frac{-5 \pm \sqrt{25}}{12} = \frac{-5 \pm 5}{12}$$

$$t = \frac{-5 + 5}{12} \quad \text{or} \quad t = \frac{-5 - 5}{12}$$

$$t = \frac{0}{12} \quad \text{or} \quad t = \frac{-10}{12}$$

$$t = 0 \quad \text{or} \quad t = -\frac{5}{6}$$

13. First write the equation in standard form.

$$z^2 = 8$$

$$z^2 - 8 = 0$$

Substitute a, b, and c in the quadratic formula.

$$a = 1, \quad b = 0, \quad c = -8$$

$$z = \frac{-(0) \pm \sqrt{(0)^2 - 4(1)(-8)}}{2(1)}$$

$$= \frac{\pm\sqrt{32}}{2} = \frac{\pm 4\sqrt{2}}{2} = \frac{\pm \cancel{4}^{2} \sqrt{2}}{\cancel{2}}$$

$$z = 2\sqrt{2} \approx 2.83 \quad \text{or} \quad z = -2\sqrt{2} \approx -2.83$$

15. Substitute a, b, and c in the quadratic formula.

$$a = 4, \quad b = -12, \quad c = 9$$

$$x = \frac{-(-12) \pm \sqrt{(-12)^2 - 4(4)(9)}}{2(4)}$$

$$= \frac{12 \pm \sqrt{144 - 144}}{8} = \frac{12 \pm \sqrt{0}}{8} = \frac{12}{8} = \frac{3}{2}$$

17. First write the equation in standard form and simplify.

$$(w + 4)(w + 5) = 12$$

$$w^2 + 9w + 20 = 12$$

$$w^2 + 9w + 8 = 0$$

Substitute a, b, and c in the quadratic formula.

$$a = 1, \quad b = 9, \quad c = 8$$

$$w = \frac{-(9) \pm \sqrt{(9)^2 - 4(1)(8)}}{2(1)}$$

$$= \frac{-9 \pm \sqrt{81 - 32}}{2} = \frac{-9 \pm \sqrt{49}}{2} = \frac{-9 \pm 7}{2}$$

$$w = \frac{-9 + 7}{2} = \frac{-2}{2} \quad \text{or} \quad w = \frac{-9 - 7}{2} = \frac{-16}{2}$$

$$w = -1 \quad \text{or} \quad w = -8$$

19. First write the equation in standard form and simplify.

$$x(x + 2) = 2x + 3$$

$$x^2 + 2x = 2x + 3$$

$$x^2 - 3 = 0$$

Substitute a, b, and c in the quadratic formula.

$$a = 1, \quad b = 0, \quad c = -3$$

$$x = \frac{-(0) \pm \sqrt{(0)^2 - 4(1)(-3)}}{2(1)}$$

$$= \frac{0 \pm \sqrt{12}}{2} = \frac{\pm \cancel{2}\sqrt{3}}{\cancel{2}} = \pm\sqrt{3} \approx \pm 1.73$$

21. **a.** A quadratic equation whose discriminant is negative will have no real solutions.
Thus the graph is **B**.

b. A quadratic equation whose discriminant is zero will have exactly one real solution.
Thus the graph is **C**.

c. A quadratic equation whose discriminant is positive will have exactly two real solutions.
Thus the graph is **A**.

23. $a = 1$, $b = -20$, $c = 100$

$b^2 - 4ac = (-20)^2 - 4(1)(100) = 400 - 400 = 0$

Thus the equation has a double real solution.

25. $a = 1$, $b = -5$, $c = 5$

$b^2 - 4ac = (-5)^2 - 4(1)(5) = 25 - 20 = 5 > 0$

Thus the equation has two distinct real solutions.

27. $a = 1$, $b = 0$, $c = 6$

$b^2 - 4ac = (0)^2 - 4(1)(6) = -24 < 0$

Thus the equation has complex solutions with imaginary parts.

29. To determine the y-intercept we let $x = 0$.

$y = (0)^2 - 6 = -6$. y-intercept: $(0, -6)$.

To determine the x-intercepts we let $y = 0$ and solve for x. $\quad x^2 - 6 = 0$

$$x^2 = 6$$

$$x = \pm\sqrt{6}$$

x-intercepts: $\left(\pm\sqrt{6}, 0\right) \approx (\pm 2.45, 0)$

31. To determine the y-intercept we let $x = 0$. $y = (0)^2 - 4(0) - 1 = -1$. y-intercept: $(0, -2)$.

To determine the x-intercepts we let $y = 0$ and solve for x.

$$x^2 - 4x - 1 = 0$$

$$a = 1, \quad b = -4, \quad c = -1$$

$$y = \frac{-(-4) \pm \sqrt{(-4)^2 - 4(1)(-1)}}{2(1)} = \frac{4 \pm \sqrt{16 + 4}}{2}$$

$$= \frac{4 \pm \sqrt{20}}{2} = \frac{4 \pm 2\sqrt{5}}{2} = \frac{\cancel{2}(2 \pm \sqrt{5})}{\cancel{2}} = 2 \pm \sqrt{5} \quad x\text{-intercepts: } \left(2 \pm \sqrt{5}, 0\right) \approx (4.24, 0) \text{ and } (-0.24, 0)$$

33. Let x be one the smaller number. If the other number is 6 more than x, and their product is 8 then to find the numbers we solve the following equation.

$$x(x + 6) = 8$$

$$x^2 + 6x - 8 = 0$$

$$a = 1, \quad b = 6, \quad c = -8$$

$$x = \frac{-(6) \pm \sqrt{(6)^2 - 4(1)(-8)}}{2(1)}$$

$$= \frac{-6 \pm \sqrt{36 + 32}}{2} = \frac{-6 \pm \sqrt{68}}{2}$$

$$= \frac{-6 \pm 2\sqrt{17}}{2} = \frac{2(-3 \pm \sqrt{17})}{2}$$

$$x = -3 + \sqrt{17} \quad \text{or} \quad x = -3 - \sqrt{17}$$

Thus there are two possible pairs of numbers:
The numbers are $-3 + \sqrt{17}$ and $3 + \sqrt{17}$

or $-3 - \sqrt{17}$ and $3 - \sqrt{17}$

35. Let w be the width of the rectangle. If the length of the rectangle is 4 cm longer than w and the area is 8 square cm, then to find the dimensions we solve the following equation.

$$w(w + 4) = 8$$

$$w^2 + 4w - 8 = 0$$

$$a = 1, \quad b = 4, \quad c = -8$$

$$x = \frac{-(4) \pm \sqrt{(4)^2 - 4(1)(-8)}}{2(1)}$$

$$= \frac{-4 \pm \sqrt{16 + 32}}{2} = \frac{-4 \pm \sqrt{48}}{2} = \frac{-4 \pm 4\sqrt{3}}{2}$$

$$= \frac{2(-2 \pm 2\sqrt{3})}{2} = \frac{2(-2 \pm 2\sqrt{3})}{2} = -2 \pm 2\sqrt{3}$$

Since the width must be a positive number, $-2 + 2\sqrt{3}$ cm is the only possible answer for w. In this way, we determine that the length must be $2 + 2\sqrt{3}$ cm (4 cm longer than the width)

37. a. $P(0) = -80(0)^2 + 5280(0) - 61200 = -61200$. The overhead costs are $61,200.

b. Solve the equation: $\qquad\qquad P(x) = 0$

$$-80x^2 + 5280x - 61200 = 0$$
$$-80\left(x^2 - 66x + 765\right) = 0$$
$$-80(x - 15)(x - 51) = 0$$

The company will break even if either 15 or 51 units are produced and sold

39. Solve the equation: $\quad 0.01v^2 + 0.03v = 100$

$$0.01v^2 + 0.03v - 100 = 0$$
$$a = 0.01, \quad b = 0.03, \quad c = -100$$

$$v = \frac{-(0.03) \pm \sqrt{(0.03)^2 - 4(0.01)(-100)}}{2(0.01)}$$

$$= \frac{-0.03 \pm \sqrt{4.0009}}{0.02} =$$

$$v \approx -102 \quad \text{or} \quad v \approx 99$$

A car with a speed of approximately 99 km/hr requires 100 m to stop.

41. $v(v - 4)(v + 7) = 0$

$$v = 0, \ v = 4, \text{ or } v = -7$$

43. $w\left(w^2 - 10\right) = 0$

$$w = 0 \quad \text{or} \quad w^2 - 10 = 0$$
$$w^2 = 10$$
$$w = \pm\sqrt{10}$$

Solution: $w = 0, \ w = -\sqrt{10}, \text{ or } w = \sqrt{10}$

45. a. The solutions of $-x^2 + 2x + 6 < 0$ are the x values for which the graph is below the x-axis. Thus the solution set is $\left(-\infty, 1 - \sqrt{7}\right) \cup \left(1 + \sqrt{7}, +\infty\right)$.

c. The solutions of $-x^2 + 2x + 6 > 0$ are the x values for which the graph is above the x-axis. Thus the solution set is $\left(1 - \sqrt{7}, 1 + \sqrt{7}\right)$.

47. a. Solve the equation:

$$f(x) = 0$$
$$-16x^2 + 48x - 18 = 0$$
$$-2\left(8x^2 - 24x + 9\right) = 0$$
$$a = 8, \quad b = -24, \quad c = 9$$

$$x = \frac{-(-24) \pm \sqrt{(-24)^2 - 4(8)(9)}}{2(8)}$$

$$= \frac{24 \pm \sqrt{288}}{16} = \frac{24 \pm 12\sqrt{2}}{16} = \frac{4\left(6 \pm 3\sqrt{2}\right)}{16} = \frac{6 \pm 3\sqrt{2}}{4}$$

$$x = \frac{6 - 3\sqrt{2}}{4} \approx 0.44 \text{ seconds} \quad \text{or} \quad x = \frac{6 - 3\sqrt{2}}{4} \approx 2.56 \text{ seconds}$$

b. The rocket is above ground level in the time interval: $(0.44, 2.56)$.

49. If the solutions are $x = \dfrac{3 - \sqrt{5}}{2}$ and $x = \dfrac{3 + \sqrt{5}}{2}$, then

Thus $\left(x - \dfrac{3 - \sqrt{5}}{2} \right)$ and $\left(x - \dfrac{3 + \sqrt{5}}{2} \right)$ are factors and the equation is

$$\left(x - \frac{3 - \sqrt{5}}{2} \right)\left(x - \frac{3 + \sqrt{5}}{2} \right) = 0$$

$$\left(\left(x - \frac{3}{2} \right) + \frac{\sqrt{5}}{2} \right)\left(\left(x - \frac{3}{2} \right) - \frac{\sqrt{5}}{2} \right) = 0$$

$$\left(x - \frac{3}{2} \right)^2 - \left(\frac{\sqrt{5}}{2} \right)^2 = 0$$

$$x^2 - 3x + \frac{9}{4} - \frac{5}{4} = 0$$

$$x^2 - 3x + \frac{4}{4} = 0$$

$$x^2 - 3x + 1 = 0$$

Cumulative Review

1. $-3y^2 + 2xy + 2x^3 - 5x^2y = 2x^3 - 5x^2y + 2xy - 3y^2$

2. $|x| < 4$ is equivalent to $-4 < x < 4$ or $(-4, 4)$

3. $(-1)^{333} = -1$

4. $(-4)(-3)(-2)(-1)(0)(1)(2)(3)(4) = 0$

5. Division by zero is undefined.

Section 7.4: Applications of Quadratic Equations

Quick Review 7.4

1. If n represents an even integer, then the next two intergers are $n + 1$ and $n + 2$.

2. If n represents an even integer, then the next two even intergers are $n + 2$ and $n + 4$.

3. $x^2 = 64$

$\sqrt{x^2} = \pm\sqrt{64}$

$x = \pm 8$

4.

5. **a.** 0   **b.** 20   **c.** $\{0, 1, 2, 3, ..., 19, 20\}$

Exercises 7.4

1. Let n = smaller of the two integers
$n+1$ = larger of the two integers

If the product of the integers is 156, then to find n we solve the following equation.

$$n(n+1) = 156$$
$$n^2 + n - 156 = 0$$
$$(n+13)(n-12) = 0$$

$n = -13$	or	$n = 12$
$n+1 = -12$		$n+1 = 13$

The consecutive integers are either -13 and -12 or 12 and 13.

3. Let n = smaller of the two even integers
$n+2$ = larger of the two even integers

If the product of the integers is 288, then to find n we solve the following equation.

$$n(n+2) = 288$$
$$n^2 + 2n - 288 = 0$$
$$(n+18)(n-16) = 0$$

$n = -18$	or	$n = 16$
$n+2 = -16$		$n+2 = 18$

The consecutive even integers are either -18 and -16 or 16 and 18.

5. Let n = smaller of the two integers
$n+1$ = larger of the two integers

If the sum of the squares of these integers is 113, then to find n we solve the following equation.

$$n^2 + (n+1)^2 = 113$$
$$n^2 + n^2 + 2n + 1 = 113$$
$$2n^2 + 2n - 112 = 0$$
$$2(n^2 + n - 56) = 0$$
$$2(n+8)(n-7) = 0$$

$n = -8$	or	$n = 7$
$n+1 = -7$		$n+1 = 8$

The consecutive integers are either -8 and -7 or 7 and 8.

7. Let n = first number
$3n+4$ = second number

If the product of the integers is 175, then to find n we solve the following equation.

$$n(3n+4) = 175$$
$$3n^2 + 4n - 175 = 0$$
$$(3n+25)(n-7) = 0$$

$$n = -\frac{25}{3} \qquad \text{or} \qquad n = 7$$

$$3n+4 = 3\left(-\frac{25}{3}\right)+4 \qquad 3n+4 = 3(7)+4$$
$$= -21 \qquad\qquad\qquad = 25$$

The numbers are either $-\frac{25}{3}$ and -21 or 7 and 25.

9. Let w = width of the rectangle
$l = 3w + 2$ = length of the rectangle

If the area of the rectangle is 21 square centimeters, then to find w we solve the following equation.

$$l \cdot w = Area$$

$$(3w + 2)w = 21$$

$$3w^2 + 2w - 21 = 0$$

$$(3w - 7)(w + 3) = 0$$

Note: This answer is not reasonable.

$$w = -3 \quad or \quad w = \frac{7}{3}$$

$$l = 3w + 2 = 3\left(\frac{7}{3}\right) + 2 = 9$$

The dimensions of the rectangle are $\frac{7}{3}$ cm by 9 cm.

11. Let h = height of the triangle
$b = h + 3$ = base of the triangle

If the area of the triangle is 77 square meters, then to find h we solve the following equation.

$$\frac{1}{2}b \cdot h = Area$$

$$\frac{1}{2}(h + 3)h = 77$$

$$(h + 3)h = 154$$

$$h^2 + 3h - 154 = 0$$

$$(h + 14)(h - 11) = 0$$

Note: This answer is not reasonable.

$$h = -14 \quad or \quad h = 11$$

$$b = h + 3 = 14$$

The base of the triangle is 14 m.

13. If the sum of the areas of the two square is 200 square centimeters, then to find x we solve the following equation.

$$x^2 + (x + 5)^2 = 200$$

$$x^2 + x^2 + 10x + 25 = 200$$

$$2x^2 + 10x - 175 = 0$$

$$a = 2, \ b = 10, \ c = -175$$

$$x = \frac{-(10) \pm \sqrt{(10)^2 - 4(2)(-175)}}{2(2)}$$

$$= \frac{-10 \pm \sqrt{1500}}{4} = \frac{-10 \pm 10\sqrt{15}}{4}$$

Note: This answer is not reasonable.

$$= \frac{2\left(-5 \pm 5\sqrt{15}\right)}{4} = \frac{-5 \pm 5\sqrt{15}}{2}$$

$$x = \frac{-5 + 5\sqrt{15}}{2} \approx 7.2 \quad or \quad x = \frac{-5 - 5\sqrt{15}}{2} \approx -12.2$$

The length of each side of the original square is approximately 7.2 cm.

15. To determine the time interval that the ball is above 50 meters we solve the following inequality.

$$-4.9t^2 + 29.4t + 34.3 > 50$$

We can solve the inequality using a graphing calculator and the intersect feature.

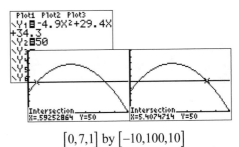

$[0, 7, 1]$ by $[-10, 100, 10]$

Thus the time interval in which the ball is above 50 meters is between 0.6 seconds and 5.4 seconds.

17. To determine the number of windmills that should be produced we solve the following inequality.

$$P(x) > 0$$

$$-x^2 + 70x - 600 > 0$$

We can solve the equation using a graphing calculator and the zero feature.

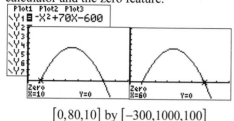

$$[0, 80, 10] \text{ by } [-300, 1000, 100]$$

Thus the company has a profit if between 10 and 60 windmills are produced.

19. If the area of the shaded region (the difference of the areas of the circles) is 54π square centimeters, then to determine r we solve the following equation.

$$\pi(\text{large radius})^2 - \pi(\text{small radius})^2 = 56\pi$$

$$\pi(2r-1)^2 - \pi r^2 = 56\pi$$

$$(2r-1)^2 - r^2 = 56$$

$$4r^2 - 4r + 1 - r^2 = 56$$

$$3r^2 - 4r - 55 = 0$$

$$(3r+11)(r-5) = 0$$

Note: This answer is not reasonable.

$$r = -\frac{11}{3} \quad \text{or} \quad r = 5$$

The radius of the smaller circle is 5 cm.

21. The radius of a 10 inch pizza is 5 inches. Thus the area of a 10 inch pizza is $\pi(5)^2 = 25\pi \text{ in}^2$. To determine the radius of a pizza that has twice the area we solve the following equation.

$$\pi r^2 = 50\pi$$

$$\frac{\pi r^2}{\pi} = \frac{50\pi}{\pi}$$

$$r^2 = 50$$

$$r = \sqrt{50} \approx 7.07 \text{ in}$$

Thus they should order a 14 inch pizza to double the area of a 10 inch pizza

23. If the perimeter of the large square is $2s - 8$, then each side is of length $\frac{1}{4}(2s-8)$ and the area of the square is $\left(\frac{1}{4}(2s-8)\right)^2$. In a similar way we determine that the area of the small square is $\left(\frac{1}{4}s\right)^2$. If the difference of the areas is 279 square meters, then to find s we solve the following equation.

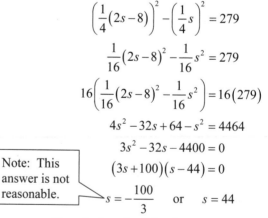

$$\left(\frac{1}{4}(2s-8)\right)^2 - \left(\frac{1}{4}s\right)^2 = 279$$

$$\frac{1}{16}(2s-8)^2 - \frac{1}{16}s^2 = 279$$

$$16\left(\frac{1}{16}(2s-8)^2 - \frac{1}{16}s^2\right) = 16(279)$$

$$4s^2 - 32s + 64 - s^2 = 4464$$

$$3s^2 - 32s - 4400 = 0$$

$$(3s+100)(s-44) = 0$$

Note: This answer is not reasonable.

$$s = -\frac{100}{3} \quad \text{or} \quad s = 44$$

Thus the length of the shorter rope is 44 meters.

25. Let $P = 1000$ and $A = 1095$ in $A = P\left(1 + \dfrac{r}{2}\right)^2$ and

solve for r.

$$1095 = 1000\left(1 + \frac{r}{2}\right)^2$$

$$1.095 = \left(1 + \frac{r}{2}\right)^2$$

$$\sqrt{1.095} = 1 + \frac{r}{2}$$

$$\frac{r}{2} = \sqrt{1.095} - 1$$

$$r = 2\left(\sqrt{1.095} - 1\right) \approx 0.0928 \quad \text{or} \quad 9.28\%$$

27. Let $d = 75$ in $16t^2 = d$ and solve for t.

$$16t^2 = 75$$

$$t^2 = \frac{75}{16}$$

$$\sqrt{t^2} = \sqrt{\frac{75}{16}}$$

$$t = \frac{\sqrt{75}}{4} = \frac{5\sqrt{3}}{4} \approx 2.2$$

It takes approximately 2.2 seconds for the hammer to fall 75 feet.

29. Let $d = 115$ in $d = 0.01v^2 + 0.02v$ and solve for v.

$$0.01v^2 + 0.02v = 100$$

$$0.01v^2 + 0.02v - 100 = 0$$

$$a = 0.01, \quad b = 0.02, \quad c = -100$$

$$x = \frac{-(0.02) \pm \sqrt{(0.02)^2 - 4(0.01)(-100)}}{2(0.01)}$$

$$= \frac{-0.02 \pm \sqrt{4.0004}}{0.02}$$

$$x \approx 99 \quad \text{or} \quad x \approx -101$$

Note: This answer is not reasonable.

A car with a speed of approximately 99 km/hr requires 100 m to stop.

31.

y 17 ft x

Using the Pythagorean Theorem we determine the following.

$$x^2 + y^2 = 17^2$$

$$y^2 = 289 - x^2$$

$$\sqrt{y^2} = \sqrt{289 - x^2}$$

$$y = \sqrt{289 - x^2}$$

With $x = 8$ we have $y = \sqrt{289 - (8)^2} = \sqrt{289 - 64} = \sqrt{225} = 15$

Thus the distance to the top of the ladder is 15 feet.

33.

Using the Pythagorean Theorem we determine the following.

$$x^2 + 30^2 = d^2$$

$$d^2 = x^2 + 900$$

$$\sqrt{d^2} = \sqrt{x^2 + 900}$$

$$d = \sqrt{x^2 + 900}$$

With $d = 35$ we have

$$\sqrt{x^2 + 900} = 35$$

$$\left(\sqrt{x^2 + 900}\right)^2 = (35)^2$$

$$x^2 + 900 = 1225$$

$$x^2 = 325$$

$$\sqrt{x^2} = \sqrt{325}$$

$$x \approx 18.0$$

Thus the ball can be positioned a distance of approximately 18.0 feet from center court.

35. If the 40-foot (240-inch) beam expands by a total of 0.5 inch then half of the beam will expand by a total of 0.25 inch.

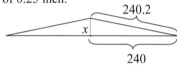

To determine x we use the Pythagorean Theorem.

$$x^2 + (240)^2 = (240.25)^2$$

$$x^2 = (240.25)^2 - (240)^2$$

$$x = \sqrt{(240.25)^2 - (240)^2} \approx 10.96$$

Thus the beam is displaced by approximately 10.96 inches in the middle.

37.

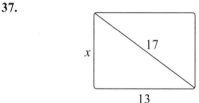

To determine the height of the monitor x we use the Pythagorean Theorem.

$$x^2 + 13^2 = 17^2$$

$$x^2 + 169 = 289$$

$$x^2 = 120$$

$$x = \sqrt{120} \approx 10.95$$

Thus the height of the monitor is approximately 10.95 inches.

39.

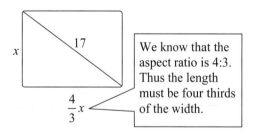

We know that the aspect ratio is 4:3. Thus the length must be four thirds of the width.

To determine the height of the monitor x we use the Pythagorean Theorem.

$$x^2 + \left(\frac{4}{3}x\right)^2 = 17^2$$

$$x^2 + \frac{16x^2}{9} = 289$$

$$9\left(x^2 + \frac{16x^2}{9}\right) = 9(289)$$

$$9x^2 + 16x^2 = 2601$$

$$25x^2 = 2601$$

$$x^2 = \frac{2601}{25}$$

$$x = \sqrt{\frac{2601}{25}} = 10.2$$

Thus the height of the monitor is approximately 10.2 inches and the length is $\frac{4}{3}(10.2) = 13.6$ inches.

41. Let $x =$ the distance flown south
$x + 17 =$ the distance flown east

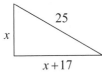

To determine how far south the plane had flown we use the Pythagorean Theorem.

$$x^2 + (x+17)^2 = 25^2$$
$$x^2 + x^2 + 34x + 289 = 625$$
$$2x^2 + 34x - 336 = 0$$
$$2(x^2 + 17x - 168) = 0$$
$$2(x+24)(x-7) = 0$$
$$x = 7 \quad \text{or} \quad x = -24$$

Note: This answer is not reasonable.

Thus the plane flew 7 miles south.

43. Let $x =$ speed of the plane flying south
$x + 30 =$ speed of the plane flying east

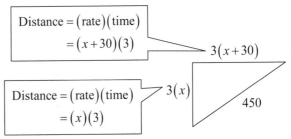

To determine x we use the Pythagorean Theorem.

$$(3(x+30))^2 + (3x)^2 = 450^2$$
$$9(x^2 + 60x + 900) + 9x^2 = 202500$$
$$9x^2 + 540x + 8100 + 9x^2 = 202500$$
$$18x^2 + 540x - 194400 = 0$$
$$18(x^2 + 30x - 10800) = 0$$
$$18(x+120)(x-90) = 0$$
$$x = -120 \quad \text{or} \quad x = 90$$

Thus speed of the plane flying south is 90 miles per hour and the speed of the plane flying east is $90 + 30 = 120$ miles per hour.

45. let $w =$ width of the room
$l = w + 17 =$ length of the room

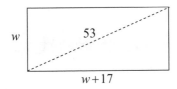

To determine the width of the room we use the Pythagorean Theorem.

$$w^2 + (w+17)^2 = 53^2$$
$$w^2 + w^2 + 34w + 289 = 2809$$
$$2w^2 + 34w - 2520 = 0$$
$$2(w^2 + 17w - 1260) = 0$$
$$2(w+45)(w-28) = 0$$
$$w = -45 \quad \text{or} \quad w = 28$$

Thus the width of the room is 28 feet.

47.

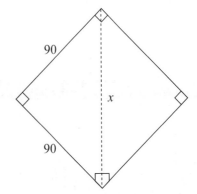

To determine the distance from home plate to second base x we use the Pythagorean Theorem.

$$x^2 = 90^2 + 90^2$$
$$x^2 = 16200$$
$$x = \sqrt{16200} \approx 127.3$$

Thus a throw from home plate must go about $127.3 - 90 = 37.3$ feet farther to reach second base than to reach third base.

49.

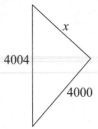

To determine x we use the Pythagorean Theorem.

$$x^2 + 4000^2 = 4004^2$$
$$x^2 = 4004^2 - 4000^2$$
$$x = \sqrt{4004^2 - 4000^2} \approx 179$$

Thus the distance to the horizon is about 180 miles.

51.

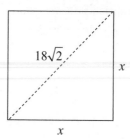

To determine x we use the Pythagorean Theorem.

$$x^2 + x^2 = \left(18\sqrt{2}\right)^2$$
$$2x^2 = 648$$
$$x^2 = 324$$
$$x = \sqrt{324} = 18 \text{ cm}$$

Cumulative Review

1. The slope of the line defined by $y = -3x + 5$ is $m = -3$.

2. The y-intercept of the line defined by $y = -3x + 5$ is $(0, 5)$.

3. Use the slope intercept form. $y = 2x - 3$

4. $2x + 3y = 3y + 2x$

5. $-2 < x \le 4$

Section 7.5: Complex Numbers and Solving Quadratic Equations with Complex Solutions

Quick Review 7.5

1. $37,469.21 = 3.746921 \times 10^4$

2. $4.06 \times 10^{-5} = 0.0000406$

3. $5x(2x - 3) + 4(2x - 3) = 10x^2 - 15x + 8x - 12$
$$= 10x^2 - 7x - 12$$

4. $5x(2x - 3) + 4(2x - 3) = (2x - 3)(5x + 4)$

5. $(5x + 3y)(5x - 3y) = (5x)^2 - (3y)^2$
$$= 25x^2 - 9y^2$$

Exercises 7.5

1. **a.** $-\sqrt{36} = -6$

b. $\sqrt{-36} = i\sqrt{36} = i(6) = 6i$

3. **a.** $\sqrt{-9} + \sqrt{16} = i\sqrt{9} + \sqrt{16} = i(3) + 4 = 4 + 3i$

b. $\sqrt{9} + \sqrt{-16} = \sqrt{9} + i\sqrt{16} = 3 + i(4) = 3 + 4i$

5. $(1+2i)+(8-3i)=1+2i+8-3i$
$$=(1+8)+(2-3)i$$
$$=9-i$$

7. $(5+3i)-(2+2i)=5+3i-2-2i$
$$=(5-2)+(3-2)i$$
$$=3+i$$

9. $6(10+4i)=(6)10+(6)4i=60+24i$

11. $(3+3i)+\frac{1}{2}(8-6i)=3+3i+\left(\frac{1}{2}\right)8-\left(\frac{1}{2}\right)6i$
$$=3+3i+4-3i$$
$$=(3+4)+(3-3)i=7$$

13. $\sqrt{-9-16}=\sqrt{-25}=i\sqrt{25}=i(5)=5i$

15. $\sqrt{-9}+\sqrt{-16}=i\sqrt{9}+i\sqrt{16}=i(3)+i(4)$
$$=3i+4i=7i$$

17. $(2i)(3i)=6i^2=6(-1)=-6$

19. $2i(3-5i)=(2i)3-(2i)5i=6i-10i^2$
$$=6i-10(-1)=6i+10=10+6i$$

21. $i(3+2i)+2(5-3i)=(i)3+(i)2i+(2)5-(2)3i$
$$=3i+2i^2+10-6i$$
$$=(3-6)i+2(-1)+10$$
$$=-3i+-2+10=-3i+8$$
$$=8-3i$$

23. $(2-7i)(2+7i)=(2)^2-(7i)^2=4-49i^2$
$$=4-49(-1)=4+49=53$$

25. $(5-2i)(4+7i)=5(4+7i)-2i(4+7i)$
$$=(5)4+(5)7i-(2i)4-(2i)7i$$
$$=20+35i-8i-14i^2$$
$$=20+(35-8)i-14(-1)$$
$$=20+14+27i=34+27i$$

27. $\sqrt{-4}\sqrt{-25}=i\sqrt{4}i\sqrt{25}=i^2\sqrt{4\cdot25}$
$$=(-1)\sqrt{100}=-10$$

29. $\sqrt{(-4)(-25)}=\sqrt{100}=10$

31. $(5+i)^2=(5)^2+2(5)(i)+(i)^2$
$$=25+10i+(-1)=24+10i$$

33. $(4-3i)^2=(4)^2-2(4)(3i)+(3i)^2$
$$=16-24i+9i^2=16-24i+9(-1)$$
$$=7-24i$$

35. $(4+7i)(7-4i)=28-16i+49i-28i^2$
$$=28+33i-28(-1)$$
$$=28+33i+28$$
$$=56+33i$$

37. $\sqrt{-3}\left(\sqrt{2}+\sqrt{-3}\right)=i\sqrt{3}\left(\sqrt{2}-i\sqrt{3}\right)$
$$=i\sqrt{6}-i^2\sqrt{9}$$
$$=i\sqrt{6}-(-1)3$$
$$=i\sqrt{6}+3$$
$$=3+i\sqrt{6}$$

39. $2\sqrt{-75}+\sqrt{-27}=2i\sqrt{25}\sqrt{3}+i\sqrt{9}\sqrt{3}$
$$=2i(5)\sqrt{3}+i(3)\sqrt{3}$$
$$=10i\sqrt{3}+3i\sqrt{3}$$
$$=13i\sqrt{3}$$

41. $\sqrt{4} + \sqrt{-9} - \sqrt{9} - \sqrt{-25} = 2 + 3i - 3 - 5i$

$$= 2 - 3 + 3i - 5i$$
$$= -1 - 2i$$

43. $i^9 = i^8 i = (1)i = i$

45. $i^{58} = i^{56}i^2 = (1)i^2 = -1$

47. The conjugate of $2 + 5i$ is $2 - 5i$

$$(2 + 5i)(2 - 5i) = (2)^2 - (5i)^2$$
$$= 4 - 25i^2 = 4 - 25(-1) = 29$$

49. The conjugate of $13i$ is $-13i$

$$(13i)(-13i) = -169i^2 = -169(-1) = 169$$

51. $\dfrac{4}{1+i} = \dfrac{4}{(1+i)} \cdot \dfrac{(1-i)}{(1-i)} = \dfrac{4(1-i)}{1-i^2}$

$$= \dfrac{4(1-i)}{1-(-1)} = \dfrac{4(1-i)}{2} = 2(1-i) = 2 - 2i$$

53. $\dfrac{5+i}{5-i} = \dfrac{(5+i)}{(5-i)} \cdot \dfrac{(5+i)}{(5+i)} = \dfrac{25 + 10i + i^2}{25 - i^2}$

$$= \dfrac{25 + 10i + (-1)}{25 - (-1)} = \dfrac{24 + 10i}{26} = \dfrac{24}{26} + \dfrac{10}{26}i$$

$$= \dfrac{12}{13} + \dfrac{5}{13}i$$

55. $\dfrac{3-2i}{i} = \dfrac{3-2i}{i} \cdot \dfrac{i}{i} = \dfrac{3i - 2i^2}{i^2}$

$$= \dfrac{3i - 2(-1)}{(-1)} = \dfrac{3i + 2}{-1} = -2 - 3i$$

57. $\dfrac{2+3i}{4-5i} = \dfrac{(2+3i)}{(4-5i)} \cdot \dfrac{(4+5i)}{(4+5i)} = \dfrac{8 + 10i + 12i + 15i^2}{16 - 25i^2}$

$$= \dfrac{8 + 22i + 15(-1)}{16 - 25(-1)} = \dfrac{8 + 22i - 15}{16 + 25}$$

$$= \dfrac{-7 + 22i}{41} = -\dfrac{7}{41} + \dfrac{22}{41}i$$

59. $85 \div (7 - 6i) = \dfrac{85}{(7-6i)} \cdot \dfrac{(7+6i)}{(7+6i)} = \dfrac{85(7+6i)}{49 - 36i^2}$

$$= \dfrac{85(7+6i)}{49 - 36(-1)} = \dfrac{85(7+6i)}{85} = 7 + 6i$$

61. $\sqrt{-\dfrac{25}{9}} = i\sqrt{\dfrac{25}{9}} = i\dfrac{\sqrt{25}}{\sqrt{9}} = i\left(\dfrac{5}{3}\right) = \dfrac{5}{3}i$

63. $\dfrac{\sqrt{25}}{\sqrt{-9}} = \dfrac{\sqrt{25}}{i\sqrt{9}} = \dfrac{5}{i(3)} = \dfrac{5}{3i} \cdot \dfrac{i}{i} = \dfrac{5i}{3i^2}$

$$= \dfrac{5i}{3(-1)} = -\dfrac{5i}{3}$$

65. $$x^2 - 4x + 29 = 0$$
Substitute a, b, and c in the quadratic formula.
$$a = 1, \quad b = -4, \quad c = 29$$

$$x = \dfrac{-(-4) \pm \sqrt{(-4)^2 - 4(1)(29)}}{2(1)}$$

$$= \dfrac{4 \pm \sqrt{-100}}{2} = \dfrac{4 \pm 10i}{2}$$

$$x = 2 + 5i \quad \text{or} \quad x = 2 - 5i$$

67. First write the equation in standard form.
$$x^2 = 6x - 13$$
$$x^2 - 6x + 13 = 0$$
Substitute a, b, and c in the quadratic formula.
$$a = 1, \quad b = -6, \quad c = 13$$

$$x = \dfrac{-(-6) \pm \sqrt{(-6)^2 - 4(1)(13)}}{2(1)}$$

$$= \dfrac{6 \pm \sqrt{-16}}{2} = \dfrac{6 \pm 4i}{2} = \dfrac{6}{2} \pm \dfrac{4i}{2} = 3 \pm 2i$$

$$x = 3 + 2i \quad \text{or} \quad x = 3 - 2i$$

69. First write the equation in standard form.

$$-2w(w-3) = 5$$
$$-2w^2 + 6w = 5$$
$$-2w^2 + 6w - 5 = 0$$

Substitute a, b, and c in the quadratic formula.

$$a = -2, \quad b = 6, \quad c = -5$$

$$w = \frac{-(6) \pm \sqrt{(6)^2 - 4(-2)(-5)}}{2(-2)}$$

$$= \frac{-6 \pm \sqrt{36 - 40}}{-4} = \frac{-6 \pm \sqrt{-4}}{-4} = \frac{-6 \pm 2i}{-4} = \frac{-6}{-4} \pm \frac{2i}{-4}$$

$$w = \frac{3}{2} + \frac{1}{2}i \quad \text{or} \quad w = \frac{3}{2} - \frac{1}{2}i$$

71. $x^2 = -16$

$$x = \pm\sqrt{-16}$$
$$x = \pm 4i$$

73. $(2x+3)^2 = -9$

$$2x + 3 = \pm\sqrt{-9}$$
$$2x + 3 = \pm 3i$$
$$2x = -3 \pm 3i$$
$$x = \frac{-3 \pm 3i}{2} = -\frac{3}{2} \pm \frac{3}{2}i$$

75. $a = 1, \quad b = -10, \quad c = 25$

$$b^2 = 4ac = (-10)^2 - 4(1)(25) = 100 - 100 = 0$$

Thus the equation has a double real solution.

77. $a = 1, \quad b = -10, \quad c = 26$

$$b^2 = 4ac = (-10)^2 - 4(1)(26) = 100 - 104 = -4 < 0$$

Thus the equation has complex solutions with imaginary parts.

79. $a = 1, \quad b = 0, \quad c = 2$

$$b^2 = 4ac = (0)^2 - 4(1)(2) = -8 < 0$$

Thus the equation has complex solutions with imaginary parts.

81. $x^2 - 6x + 13 = (3-2i)^2 - 6(3-2i) + 13$

$$= 9 - 12i + 4i^2 - 18 + 12i + 13$$
$$= 9 - 12i + 4(-1) - 18 + 12i + 13$$
$$= 9 - 18 - 4 + 13 - 12i + 12i$$
$$= 0$$

83. $x = -4i \quad \text{or} \quad x = 4i$

Write each equation so that the right side is zero.

$$x + 4i = 0 \quad \text{or} \quad x - 4i = 0$$

These factors equal zero, so their product is zero.

$$(x + 4i)(x - 4i) = 0$$
$$x^2 - (4i)^2 = 0$$
$$x^2 - 16i^2 = 0$$
$$x^2 - 16(-1) = 0$$
$$x^2 + 16 = 0$$

85. $x = 4 - i$ or $x = 4 + i$

Write each equation so that the right side is zero.
$$x - (4 - i) = 0 \quad \text{or} \quad x - (4 + i) = 0$$
These factors equal zero, so their product is zero.
$$\big(x - (4 - i)\big)\big(x - (4 + i)\big) = 0$$
$$(x - 4 + i)(x - 4 - i) = 0$$
$$\big((x - 4) + i\big)\big((x - 4) - i\big) = 0$$
$$(x - 4)^2 - i^2 = 0$$
$$x^2 - 8x + 16 - (-1) = 0$$
$$x^2 - 8x + 17 = 0$$

87. $(x - 2)(x^2 + x + 1) = 0$

$x - 2 = 0 \quad$ or $\quad x^2 + x + 1 = 0$
$\qquad x = 2 \qquad\qquad a = 1, \ b = 1, \ c = 1$

$$x = \frac{-(1) \pm \sqrt{(1)^2 - 4(1)(1)}}{2(1)}$$
$$= \frac{-1 \pm \sqrt{-3}}{2} = \frac{-1 \pm i\sqrt{3}}{2}$$
$$x = -\frac{1}{2} - \frac{\sqrt{3}}{2}i \quad \text{or} \quad x = -\frac{1}{2} + \frac{\sqrt{3}}{2}i$$

Solutions:
$$x = 2, \ x = -\frac{1}{2} - \frac{\sqrt{3}}{2}i, \ \text{or} \ x = -\frac{1}{2} + \frac{\sqrt{3}}{2}i$$

89. **a.** The conjugate of $3 - i$ is $3 + i$.

b. The additive inverse of $3 - i$ is $-(3 - i) = -3 + i$

c. The multiplicative inverse of $3 - i$ is
$$\frac{1}{3 - i} = \frac{1}{(3 - i)} \cdot \frac{(3 + i)}{(3 + i)} = \frac{3 + i}{9 - i^2}$$
$$= \frac{3 + i}{9 - (-1)} = \frac{3 + i}{10}$$
$$= \frac{3}{10} + \frac{1}{10}i$$

91. $i^{46} \approx -1 + 4 \times 10^{-13} i \approx -1 + 0i = -1$

Cumulative Review

1. $4x - 1 = 7$
$\quad 4x = 8$
$\quad\ \ x = 2$

2. $4(x - 1) = 7$
$$x - 1 = \frac{7}{4}$$
$$x = \frac{7}{4} + 1 = \frac{7}{4} + \frac{4}{4} = \frac{11}{4}$$

3. $|x - 1| = 7$ is equivalent to
$x - 1 = -7 \quad$ or $\quad x - 1 = 7$
$\quad\ x = -6 \qquad\qquad x = 8$

4. The perimeter is $P = 4s = 4 \cdot 5 = 20$ cm

5. The area is $A = s^2 = 5^2 = 25$ cm^2

Review Exercises for Chapter 7

1. $\sqrt{25 \cdot 7} = \sqrt{25}\sqrt{7} = 5\sqrt{7}$

2. $\sqrt{99} = \sqrt{9 \cdot 11} = \sqrt{9}\sqrt{11} = 3\sqrt{11}$

3. $\sqrt{\dfrac{25}{49}} = \dfrac{\sqrt{25}}{\sqrt{49}} = \dfrac{5}{7}$

4. $\sqrt{\dfrac{6}{25}} = \dfrac{\sqrt{6}}{\sqrt{25}} = \dfrac{\sqrt{6}}{5}$

5. $\dfrac{\sqrt{45}}{\sqrt{20}} = \sqrt{\dfrac{45}{20}} = \sqrt{\dfrac{\cancel{5} \cdot 9}{\cancel{5} \cdot 4}} = \sqrt{\dfrac{9}{4}} = \dfrac{3}{2}$

6. $\dfrac{4}{\sqrt{6}} = \dfrac{4}{\sqrt{6}} \cdot \dfrac{\sqrt{6}}{\sqrt{6}} = \dfrac{4\sqrt{6}}{6} = \dfrac{\overset{2}{\cancel{4}}\,\sqrt{6}}{\underset{3}{\cancel{6}}} = \dfrac{2\sqrt{6}}{3}$

7. $\dfrac{\sqrt{5}}{\sqrt{6}} = \dfrac{\sqrt{5}}{\sqrt{6}} \cdot \dfrac{\sqrt{6}}{\sqrt{6}} = \dfrac{\sqrt{30}}{6}$

8. $\sqrt{\dfrac{3}{11}} = \dfrac{\sqrt{3}}{\sqrt{11}} = \dfrac{\sqrt{3}}{\sqrt{11}} \cdot \dfrac{\sqrt{11}}{\sqrt{11}} = \dfrac{\sqrt{33}}{11}$

9. $x^2 - 12x + 36 = 0$

$\qquad (x-6)^2 = 0$

10. $x^2 + 30x + 225 = (x+15)^2$

$\qquad\qquad \left(\dfrac{30}{2}\right)^2 = (15)^2 = 225$

11. $x^2 - 20x + 100 = (x-10)^2$

$\qquad\qquad \left(\dfrac{-20}{2}\right)^2 = (-10)^2 = 100$

12. $v^2 - 8v = -7$

$\quad v^2 - 8v + 16 = -7 + 16 \qquad \left(\dfrac{-8}{2}\right)^2 = (-4)^2 = 16$

$\qquad (v-4)^2 = 9$

13. The solutions are $x = -2$ and $x = 4$.

14. The solutions are $x = -16$ and $x = 4$.

15. $x^2 - 7x + 12 = 0$

$\quad (x-3)(x-4) = 0$

$\quad x - 3 = 0 \quad \text{or} \quad x - 4 = 0$

$\qquad x = 3 \qquad\qquad x = 4$

16. $(2x-1)(4x-5) = 20$

$\quad 8x^2 - 10x - 4x + 5 = 20$

$\qquad 8x^2 - 14x - 15 = 0$

$\quad (2x-5)(4x+3) = 0$

$\quad 2x - 5 = 0 \quad \text{or} \quad 4x + 3 = 0$

$\qquad 2x = 5 \qquad\qquad 4x = -3$

$\qquad x = \dfrac{5}{2} \qquad\qquad x = -\dfrac{3}{4}$

17. $v^2 - 9v + 20 = 0$

$\quad a = 1, \quad b = -9, \quad c = 20$

$\quad v = \dfrac{-(-9) \pm \sqrt{(-9)^2 - 4(1)(20)}}{2(1)}$

$\quad = \dfrac{9 \pm \sqrt{81-80}}{2} = \dfrac{9 \pm \sqrt{1}}{2}$

$\quad v = \dfrac{9+1}{2} \quad \text{or} \quad v = \dfrac{9-1}{2}$

$\quad v = \dfrac{10}{2} \quad \text{or} \quad v = \dfrac{8}{2}$

$\quad v = 5 \quad \text{or} \quad v = 4$

18. $w^2 = 4w - 2$

$\quad w^2 - 4w + 2 = 0$

$\quad a = 1, \quad b = -4, \quad c = 2$

$\quad w = \dfrac{-(-4) \pm \sqrt{(-4)^2 - 4(1)(2)}}{2(1)}$

$\quad = \dfrac{4 \pm \sqrt{16-8}}{2} = \dfrac{4 \pm \sqrt{8}}{2} = \dfrac{4 \pm 2\sqrt{2}}{2} = \dfrac{4}{2} \pm \dfrac{2\sqrt{2}}{2}$

$\quad w = 2 - \sqrt{2} \quad \text{or} \quad w = 2 + \sqrt{2}$

19.

$$10(m^2 - 1) = 21m$$
$$10m^2 - 10 = 21m$$
$$10m^2 - 21m - 10 = 0$$
$$a = 10, \quad b = -21, \quad c = -10$$
$$m = \frac{-(-21) \pm \sqrt{(-21)^2 - 4(10)(-10)}}{2(10)}$$
$$= \frac{21 \pm \sqrt{441 + 400}}{20}$$
$$= \frac{21 \pm \sqrt{841}}{20} = \frac{21 \pm 29}{20}$$
$$m = \frac{21 - 29}{20} \quad \text{or} \quad m = \frac{21 + 29}{20}$$
$$m = \frac{-8}{20} \quad \text{or} \quad m = \frac{50}{20}$$
$$m = -\frac{2}{5} \quad \text{or} \quad m = \frac{5}{2}$$

20.

$$\frac{2}{3}x^2 = 2x + 3$$
$$3\left(\frac{2}{3}x^2\right) = 3(2x + 3)$$
$$2x^2 = 6x + 9$$
$$2x^2 - 6x - 9 = 0$$
$$a = 2, \quad b = -6, \quad c = -9$$
$$x = \frac{-(-6) \pm \sqrt{(-6)^2 - 4(2)(-9)}}{2(2)}$$
$$= \frac{6 \pm \sqrt{36 + 72}}{4} = \frac{6 \pm \sqrt{108}}{4}$$
$$= \frac{6 \pm 6\sqrt{3}}{4} = \frac{\cancel{2}\left(3 \pm 3\sqrt{3}\right)}{\cancel{2} \cdot 2}$$
$$x = \frac{3 - 3\sqrt{3}}{2} \quad \text{or} \quad x = \frac{3 + 3\sqrt{3}}{2}$$

21.

$$m^2 = 64$$
$$\sqrt{m^2} = \pm\sqrt{64}$$
$$m = \pm 8$$

22.

$$(2y - 3)^2 = 1$$
$$\sqrt{(2y - 3)^2} = \pm\sqrt{1}$$
$$2y - 3 = \pm 1$$
$$2y = 3 \pm 1$$
$$y = \frac{3 \pm 1}{2}$$
$$y = \frac{3 - 1}{2} \quad \text{or} \quad y = \frac{3 + 1}{2}$$
$$y = \frac{2}{2} \quad \text{or} \quad y = \frac{4}{2}$$
$$y = 1 \quad \text{or} \quad y = 2$$

23.

$$w^2 + 10w = 24$$
$$w^2 + 10w + 25 = 24 + 25$$
$$(w + 5)^2 = 49$$
$$w + 5 = \pm\sqrt{49}$$
$$w = -5 \pm 7$$
$$w = -5 - 7 \quad \text{or} \quad w = -5 + 7$$
$$w = -12 \quad \text{or} \quad w = 2$$

24.

$$v^2 - 18v = -65$$
$$v^2 - 18v + 81 = -65 + 81$$
$$(v - 9)^2 = 16$$
$$v - 9 = \pm\sqrt{16}$$
$$v = 9 \pm 4$$
$$v = 9 - 4 \quad \text{or} \quad v = 9 + 4$$
$$v = 5 \quad \text{or} \quad v = 13$$

25. **a.** The solutions to $x^2 + 6x - 7 = 0$ are $x = -7$ and $x = 1$.

b. The solutions of $x^2 + 6x - 7 \leq 0$ are the x values for which the graph is below or on the x-axis. Thus the solution set is $[-7, 1]$.

c. The solutions of $x^2 + 6x - 7 \geq 0$ are the x values for which the graph is above or on the x-axis. Thus the solution set is $(-\infty, -7] \cup [1, \infty)$.

26. If the solutions are $x = -3$ and $x = 5$, then
$$x + 3 = 0 \quad \text{and} \quad x - 5 = 0.$$
Thus, $(x+3)$ and $(x-5)$ must be factors and

equation is: $(x+3)(x-5) = 0$
$$x^2 - 5x + 3x - 15 = 0$$
$$x^2 - 2x - 15 = 0$$

27. If the solutions are $x = -\dfrac{2}{5}$ and $x = \dfrac{1}{4}$, then
$$x + \frac{2}{5} = 0 \text{ and } x - \frac{1}{4} = 0.$$
These are equivalent to $5x + 2 = 0$ and $4x - 1 = 0$.
Thus $(5x+2)$ and $(4x-1)$ are factors and the

equation is $(5x+2)(4x-1) = 0$
$$20x^2 - 5x + 8x - 2 = 0$$
$$20x^2 + 3x - 2 = 0$$

28. If the solutions are $x = -\sqrt{5}$ and $x = \sqrt{5}$, then
$$x + \sqrt{5} = 0 \quad \text{and} \quad x - \sqrt{5} = 0.$$
Thus, $\left(x + \sqrt{5}\right)$ and $\left(x - \sqrt{5}\right)$ must be factors and

equation is: $\left(x + \sqrt{5}\right)\left(x - \sqrt{5}\right) = 0$
$$x^2 - \left(\sqrt{5}\right)^2 = 0$$
$$x^2 - 5 = 0$$

29. If $x = \dfrac{5}{7}$ is a double solution, then $(7x - 5)$ must

be a repeated factor and the equation is:
$$(7x - 5)^2 = 0$$
$$49x^2 - 70x + 25 = 0$$

30. If the solutions are $x = 3 - \sqrt{5}$ and $x = 3 + \sqrt{5}$, then
$$x - \left(3 - \sqrt{5}\right) = 0 \quad \text{and} \quad x - \left(3 + \sqrt{5}\right) = 0.$$
Thus, $\left(x - \left(3 - \sqrt{5}\right)\right)$ and $\left(x - \left(3 + \sqrt{5}\right)\right)$ must be

factors and equation is:
$$\left(x - \left(3 - \sqrt{5}\right)\right)\left(x - \left(3 + \sqrt{5}\right)\right) = 0$$
$$\left((x-3) - \sqrt{5}\right)\left((x-3) - \sqrt{5}\right) = 0$$
$$(x-3)^2 - \left(\sqrt{5}\right)^2 = 0$$
$$x^2 - 6x + 9 - 5 = 0$$
$$x^2 - 6x + 4 = 0$$

Polynomial $P(x)$	x-intercepts of the graph of $y = P(x)$	Factored Form	Zeros of $P(x)$	Solutions of $P(x) = 0$
31. $-3x^2 + 8x + 3$	$[-5,5,1]$ by $[-10,10,1]$ x-intercepts: $\left(-\dfrac{1}{3}, 0\right)$ and $(3, 0)$	$-3x^2 + 8x + 3$ $= -\left(3x^2 - 8x - 3\right)$ $= -(3x+1)(x-3)$	$x = -\dfrac{1}{3}, \; x = 3$	$x = -\dfrac{1}{3}, \; x = 3$

Polynomial $P(x)$	x-intercepts of the graph of $y = P(x)$	Factored Form	Zeros of $P(x)$	Solutions of $P(x) = 0$
32. $x^3 + x^2 - 2x$	X= Plot1 Plot2 Plot3 \Y1◼X^3+X²-2X \Y2 \Y3 \Y4 \Y5 \Y6 \Y7 $[-5,5,1]$ by $[-10,10,1]$ x-intercepts: $(0, 0)$, $(-2, 0)$ and $(1, 0)$	$x^3 + x^2 - 2x$ $= x(x^2 + x - 2)$ $= x(x+2)(x-1)$	$x = -2$, $x = 0$, $x = 1$	$x = -2$, $x = 0$, $x = 1$

33. Let $P = 1000$ and $A = 1050$ in $A = P\left(1+\dfrac{r}{2}\right)^2$

and solve for r.

$$1050 = 1000\left(1+\frac{r}{2}\right)^2$$

$$1.05 = \left(1+\frac{r}{2}\right)^2$$

$$\sqrt{1.05} = 1+\frac{r}{2}$$

$$\frac{r}{2} = \sqrt{1.05} - 1$$

$$r = 2\left(\sqrt{1.05} - 1\right) \approx 0.049 \text{ or } 4.9\%$$

34. Set up a verbal equation.

$$\frac{\text{number of people}}{\text{area of opening}} = \frac{\text{number of people}}{\text{area of opening}}$$

Substitute the given values to translate the word equation into an algebraic one then solve the equation.

$$\frac{8}{\pi(3)^2} = \frac{4}{\pi r^2}$$

$$\pi\left(\frac{8}{9\pi}\right) = \pi\left(\frac{4}{\pi r^2}\right)$$

$$\frac{8}{9} = \frac{4}{r^2}$$

$$8r^2 = 36$$

$$r^2 = \frac{36}{8}$$

$$r^2 = \frac{9}{2}$$

$$r = \frac{3}{\sqrt{2}} \approx 2.12$$

Thus a diameter of 4.24 cm should be used.

35.

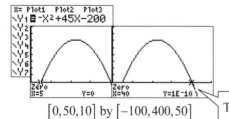

$[0,50,10]$ by $[-100,400,50]$

The profit interval is $(5, 40)$

36. a.

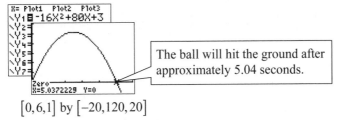

The ball will hit the ground after approximately 5.04 seconds.

$[0, 6, 1]$ by $[-20, 120, 20]$

b. From the graph in the text, we can see that the ball is higher than 67 ft between 1 second and 4 seconds.

37. Let $x =$ length of the short leg

$x + 7 =$ length of the longer leg

$(x + 7) + 2 = x + 9 =$ length of the hypotenuse.

To determine x we use the Pythagorean Theorem.

$$(x)^2 + (x+7)^2 = (x+9)^2$$

$$x^2 + x^2 + 14x + 49 = x^2 + 18x + 81$$

$$x^2 - 4x - 32 = 0$$

$$(x - 8)(x + 4) = 0$$

$$x = 8 \quad \text{or} \quad x = -4$$

Note: This answer is not reasonable.

Thus the short leg is 8 cm. The longer leg is $8 + 7 = 15$ cm. The hypotenuse is $15 + 2 = 17$ cm.

38. If the 40-foot (240 inch) beam expands by a total of 0.4 inch then half of the beam will expand by a total of 0.2 inch.

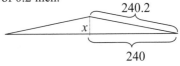

To determine x we use the Pythagorean Theorem.

$$x^2 + (240)^2 = (240.2)^2$$

$$x^2 = (240.2)^2 - (240)^2$$

$$x = \sqrt{(240.2)^2 - (240)^2} = 9.8$$

Thus the beam is displaced by 9.8 inches in the middle.

39.

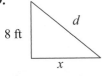

8 ft

d

x

a. Using the Pythagorean Theorem we determine the following.

$$x^2 + 8^2 = d^2$$

$$16^2 + 8^2 = d^2$$

$$320 = d^2$$

$$d \approx 17.9$$

Thus the distance between the speaker and the customer's ears is approximately 17.9 feet.

b. To determine this distance we solve the following equation for x.

$$x^2 + 8^2 = 20^2$$

$$x^2 = 400 - 64$$

$$x^2 = 336$$

$$\sqrt{x^2} = \sqrt{336}$$

$$x \approx 18.3$$

Thus, to the nearest foot, the customer can walk a distance of about 18 feet from the reference point.

40. Let $x =$ speed of the plane flying south

$x + 20 =$ speed of the plane flying east

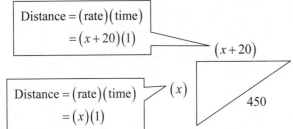

Distance $= (\text{rate})(\text{time})$

$= (x + 20)(1)$

Distance $= (\text{rate})(\text{time})$

$= (x)(1)$

$(x + 20)$

(x)

450

To determine x we use the Pythagorean Theorem.

$$(x + 20)^2 + (x)^2 = 450^2$$

$$x^2 + 40x + 400 + x^2 = 202500$$

$$2x^2 + 40x - 202100 = 0$$

$$2(x^2 + 20x - 101050) = 0$$

$$x \approx 308$$

Thus speed of the plane flying south is approximately 308 miles per hour and the speed of the plane flying east is approximately $308 + 20 = 328$ miles per hour.

41. $\sqrt{-100} = i\sqrt{100} = i(10) = 10i$

42. $\sqrt{64} - \sqrt{-64} = 8 - i\sqrt{64} = 8 - i(8) = 8 - 8i$

43. $(5 - 6i) - (3 - 2i) = 5 - 6i - 3 + 2i$
$$= (5 - 3) + (-6 + 2)i = 2 - 4i$$

44. $2(4 - 3i) - 5(2 + 6i) = 8 - 6i - 10 - 30i$
$$= (8 - 10) + (-6 - 30)i$$
$$= -2 - 36i$$

45. $2i(5 - 6i) = 10i - 12i^2 = 10i - 12(-1)$
$$= 10i + 12 = 12 + 10i$$

46. $(5 - 7i)(6 + 3i) = 30 + 15i - 42i - 21i^2$
$$= 30 - 27i - 21(-1)$$
$$= 30 + 21 - 27i = 51 - 27i$$

47. $(7 - 3i)^2 = (7)^2 - 2(7)(3i) + (3i)^2$
$$= 49 - 42i + 9i^2 = 49 - 28i + 9(-1)$$
$$= 49 - 9 - 42i = 40 - 42i$$

48. $(5 - 2i)(5 + 2i) = (5)^2 - (2i)^2 = 25 - 4i^2$
$$= 25 - 4(-1) = 25 + 4 = 29$$

49. $i^5 = i^4 \cdot i = (1)i = i$

50. $i^6 + i^7 = i^4 i^2 + i^4 i^3 = (1)(-1) + (1)(-i) = -1 - i$

51. $\dfrac{1+i}{1-i} = \dfrac{(1+i)}{(1-i)} \cdot \dfrac{(1+i)}{(1+i)} = \dfrac{1+2i+i^2}{1-i^2} = \dfrac{1+2i+(-1)}{1-(-1)}$
$$= \dfrac{2i}{2} = i$$

52. $\dfrac{58}{2+5i} = \dfrac{58}{(2+5i)} \cdot \dfrac{(2-5i)}{(2-5i)} = \dfrac{58(2-5i)}{4-25i^2}$
$$= \dfrac{58(2-5i)}{4-25(-1)} = \dfrac{58(2-5i)}{4+25}$$
$$= \dfrac{58(2-5i)}{29} = 2(2-5i) = 4 - 10i$$

53. $i^{-11} = \dfrac{1}{i^{11}} = \dfrac{1}{i^8 i^3} = \dfrac{1}{\left(i^4\right)^2 i^3} = \dfrac{1}{(1)^2 i^3} = \dfrac{1}{i^3} = \dfrac{1}{-i} = \dfrac{1}{-i} \cdot \dfrac{i}{i} = \dfrac{i}{-i^2} = \dfrac{i}{-(-1)} = \dfrac{i}{1} = i$

54. $i^{32} = \left(i^4\right)^8 = (1)^8 = 1$

55. **a.** There is only one x-intercept. Thus the discriminant is zero, and the quadratic equation has one double real solution.
   b. There are two x-intercepts. Thus the discriminant is positive, and the quadratic equation has two distinct real solutions.
   c. There aren't any x-intercepts. Thus the discriminant is negative, and the quadratic equation has complex solutions with imaginary parts.

56.
$$-3x^2 = 75 - 30x$$
$$-3x^2 + 30x - 75 = 0$$
$$a = -3, \quad b = 30, \quad c = -75$$
$$b^2 - 4ac = (30)^2 - 4(-3)(-75) = 0$$
Thus the equation has one double real solution.

57.
$$4v^2 + 2v + 1 = 0$$
$$a = 4, \quad b = 2, \quad c = 1$$
$$b^2 - 4ac = (2)^2 - 4(4)(1) = -12 < 0$$
Thus the equation has complex solutions with imaginary parts.

58.
$$x^2 + 3x = 2$$
$$x^2 + 3x - 2 = 0$$
$$a = 1, \quad b = 3, \quad c = -2$$
$$b^2 - 4ac = (3)^2 - 4(1)(-2) = 17 > 0$$
Thus the equation has two distinct real solutions.

59.
$$z^2 = -49$$
$$\sqrt{z^2} = \pm\sqrt{-49}$$
$$z = \pm 7i$$

60.
$$(2z+1)^2 = -9$$
$$\sqrt{(2z+1)^2} = \pm\sqrt{-9}$$
$$2z + 1 = \pm 3i$$
$$2z = -1 \pm 3i$$
$$z = \frac{-1 \pm 3i}{2} = -\frac{1}{2} \pm \frac{3}{2}i$$

61.
$$x^2 = 6x - 10$$
$$x^2 - 6x + 10 = 0$$
$$a = 1, \quad b = -6, \quad c = 10$$
$$x = \frac{-(-6) \pm \sqrt{(-6)^2 - 4(1)(10)}}{2(1)} = \frac{6 \pm \sqrt{-4}}{2}$$
$$= \frac{6 \pm 2i}{2} = \frac{6}{2} \pm \frac{2}{2}i = 3 \pm i$$

62.
$$(x-1)(x-5) = -6$$
$$x^2 - 6x + 5 = -6$$
$$x^2 - 6x + 11 = 0$$
$$a = 1, \quad b = -6, \quad c = 11$$
$$x = \frac{-(-6) \pm \sqrt{(-6)^2 - 4(1)(11)}}{2(1)} = \frac{6 \pm \sqrt{-8}}{2}$$
$$= \frac{6 \pm 2i\sqrt{2}}{2} = \frac{6}{2} \pm \frac{2i\sqrt{2}}{2} = 3 \pm i\sqrt{2}$$

63. $x = -11i$ or $x = 11i$
Write each equation so that the right side is zero.
$$x - 11i = 0 \quad \text{or} \quad x + 11i = 0$$
These factors equal zero, so their product is zero.
$$(x - 11i)(x + 11i) = 0$$
$$x^2 - 121i^2 = 0$$
$$x^2 + 121 = 0$$

64. $x = 5 - i$ or $x = 5 + i$
Write each equation so that the right side is zero.
$$x - 5 + i = 0 \quad \text{or} \quad x - 5 - i = 0$$
These factors equal zero, so their product is zero.
$$(x - 5 + i)(x - 5 - i) = 0$$
$$[(x-5) + i][(x-5) - i] = 0$$
$$(x-5)^2 - (i)^2 = 0$$
$$x^2 - 10x + 25 - i^2 = 0$$
$$x^2 - 10x + 25 + 1 = 0$$
$$x^2 - 10x + 26 = 0$$

65. **a.** The conjugate of $2 - 5i$ is $2 + 5i$.
b. The additive inverse of $2 - 5i$ is
$$-(2 - 5i) = -2 + 5i.$$
c. The multiplicative inverse of $2 - 5i$ is
$$\frac{1}{2 - 5i} = \frac{1}{(2-5i)} \cdot \frac{(2+5i)}{(2+5i)} = \frac{2+5i}{4 - 25i^2}$$
$$= \frac{2+5i}{4 - 25(-1)} = \frac{2+5i}{29} = \frac{2}{29} + \frac{5}{29}i$$

66. **a.** $3 - 4i$ is an example of a complex number that is not a real number.
b. It is not possible to write a real number that is not a complex number. All real numbers are also complex.
c. 5 is an example of a real number that is not imaginary.
d. It is not possible to write an imaginary number that is not complex. All imaginary numbers are also complex.

67. $i^{333} = 0 + i = i$

68. **a.** $2x+1=9$

$2x=8$

$x=4$

b. $(2x+1)^2=9$

$2x+1=\pm\sqrt{9}$

$2x+1=\pm3$

$2x=-1\pm3$

$x=\dfrac{-1\pm3}{2}$

$x=\dfrac{-1-3}{2}$ or $x=\dfrac{-1+3}{2}$

$x=\dfrac{-4}{2}$ or $x=\dfrac{2}{2}$

$x=-2$ or $x=1$

c. $|2x+1|=9$ is equivalent to

$2x+1=-9$ or $2x+1=9$

$2x=-10$ $2x=8$

$x=-5$ $x=4$

Mastery Test for Chapter 7

1. **a.** $x^2=400$

$\sqrt{x^2}=\pm\sqrt{400}$

$x=\pm20$

b. $(2v-5)^2-81=0$

$(2v-5)^2=81$

$\sqrt{(2v-5)^2}=\pm\sqrt{81}$

$2v-5=\pm9$

$2v-5=-9$ or $2v-5=9$

$2v=-4$ $2v=14$

$v=-2$ $v=7$

2. **a.** $\sqrt{36\cdot2}=\sqrt{36}\sqrt{2}=6\sqrt{2}$

b. $\sqrt{28}=\sqrt{4\cdot7}=\sqrt{4}\sqrt{7}=2\sqrt{7}$

3. **a.** $\sqrt{\dfrac{49}{64}}=\dfrac{\sqrt{49}}{\sqrt{64}}=\dfrac{7}{8}$

b. $\sqrt{\dfrac{11}{25}}=\dfrac{\sqrt{11}}{\sqrt{25}}=\dfrac{\sqrt{11}}{5}$

c. $\dfrac{\sqrt{48}}{\sqrt{3}}=\sqrt{\dfrac{48}{3}}=\sqrt{16}=4$

d. $\dfrac{\sqrt{18}}{\sqrt{98}}=\sqrt{\dfrac{18}{98}}=\sqrt{\dfrac{2\cdot9}{2\cdot49}}=\sqrt{\dfrac{9}{49}}=\dfrac{\sqrt{9}}{\sqrt{49}}=\dfrac{3}{7}$

4. **a.** $\dfrac{6}{\sqrt{2}}=\dfrac{6}{\sqrt{2}}\cdot\dfrac{\sqrt{2}}{\sqrt{2}}=\dfrac{6\sqrt{2}}{2}=\dfrac{\overset{3}{\cancel{6}}\sqrt{2}}{\underset{1}{\cancel{2}}}=3\sqrt{2}$

b. $\sqrt{\dfrac{3}{7}}=\dfrac{\sqrt{3}}{\sqrt{7}}=\dfrac{\sqrt{3}}{\sqrt{7}}\cdot\dfrac{\sqrt{7}}{\sqrt{7}}=\dfrac{\sqrt{21}}{7}$

5. **a.** $w^2-20w+100=(w-10)^2$

$\left(\dfrac{-20}{2}\right)^2=(-10)^2=100$

b. $w^2+8w+16=(w+4)^2$

$\left(\dfrac{8}{2}\right)^2=(4)^2=16$

6. **a.**
$$y^2 - 6y = 16$$
$$y^2 - 6y + 9 = 16 + 9$$
$$(y-3)^2 = 25$$
$$y - 3 = \pm\sqrt{25}$$
$$y - 3 = \pm 5$$
$$y = 3 \pm 5$$
$$y = 3 - 5 \quad \text{or} \quad y = 3 + 5$$
$$y = -2 \quad \text{or} \quad y = 8$$

b.
$$w^2 - 3w = \frac{7}{4}$$
$$w^2 - 3w + \frac{9}{4} = \frac{7}{4} + \frac{9}{4}$$
$$\left(w - \frac{3}{2}\right)^2 = \frac{16}{4}$$
$$w - \frac{3}{2} = \pm\sqrt{\frac{16}{4}} = \pm\sqrt{4}$$
$$w = \frac{3}{2} \pm 2$$
$$w = \frac{3}{2} - 2 \quad \text{or} \quad w = \frac{3}{2} + 2$$
$$w = -\frac{1}{2} \quad \text{or} \quad w = \frac{7}{2}$$

7. **a.**
$$x^2 + 6x - 5 = 0$$
$$a = 1, \quad b = 6, \quad c = -5$$
$$x = \frac{-(6) \pm \sqrt{(6)^2 - 4(1)(-5)}}{2(1)}$$
$$= \frac{-6 \pm \sqrt{36 + 20}}{2} = \frac{-6 \pm 2\sqrt{14}}{2} = \frac{-6 \pm 2\sqrt{14}}{2}$$
$$x = -3 - \sqrt{14} \quad \text{or} \quad x = -3 + \sqrt{14}$$
$$x \approx 0.74 \quad \text{or} \quad x \approx -6.74$$

b.
$$6m^2 - 11m - 4 = 6$$
$$6m^2 - 11m - 10 = 0$$
$$a =, \quad b =, \quad c =$$
$$m = \frac{-(-11) \pm \sqrt{(-11)^2 - 4(6)(-10)}}{2(6)}$$
$$= \frac{11 \pm \sqrt{121 + 240}}{12} = \frac{11 \pm \sqrt{361}}{12} = \frac{11 \pm 19}{12}$$
$$m = \frac{11 - 19}{12} \quad \text{or} \quad m = \frac{11 + 19}{12}$$
$$m = \frac{-8}{12} \quad \text{or} \quad m = \frac{30}{12}$$
$$m = \frac{-2}{3} \quad \text{or} \quad m = \frac{5}{2}$$

c.
$$4z^2 - 28z = -49$$
$$4z^2 - 28z + 49 = 0$$
$$a =, \quad b =, \quad c =$$
$$z = \frac{-(-28) \pm \sqrt{(-28)^2 - 4(4)(49)}}{2(4)}$$
$$= \frac{28 \pm \sqrt{784 - 784}}{8} = \frac{28 \pm \sqrt{0}}{8} = \frac{28}{8}$$
$$z = \frac{7}{2}$$

d.
$$(x-1)^2 = 2(x+1)$$
$$x^2 - 2x + 1 = 2x + 2$$
$$x^2 - 4x - 1 = 0$$
$$a = 1, \quad b = -4, \quad c = -1$$
$$x = \frac{-(-4) \pm \sqrt{(-4)^2 - 4(1)(-1)}}{2(1)}$$
$$= \frac{4 \pm \sqrt{16 + 4}}{2} = \frac{4 \pm \sqrt{20}}{2} = \frac{4 \pm 2\sqrt{5}}{2} = \frac{\cancel{2}\left(2 \pm \sqrt{5}\right)}{\cancel{2}}$$
$$x = 2 - \sqrt{5} \quad \text{or} \quad x = 2 + \sqrt{5}$$
$$x \approx -0.24 \quad \text{or} \quad x \approx 4.24$$

8. a. $5w^2 + 5w + 1 = 0$

$a = 5, \quad b = 5, \quad c = 1$

$b^2 - 4ac = (5)^2 - 4(5)(1) = 5 > 0$

Thus the equation has two distinct real solutions.

b. $7y^2 = 84y - 252$

$7y^2 - 84y + 252 = 0$

$a = 7, \quad b = -84, \quad c = 252$

$b^2 - 4ac = (-84)^2 - 4(7)(252) = 0$

Thus the equation has a double real solution.

c. $3x^2 + 2x - 1 = 0$

$a = 3, \quad b = 2, \quad c = -1$

$b^2 - 4ac = (2)^2 - 4(3)(-1) = 16 > 0$

Thus the equation has two distinct real solutions.

d. $(z+1)(z-2) = -3$

$z^2 - z - 2 = -3$

$z^2 - z + 1 = 0$

$a = 1, \quad b = -1, \quad c = 1$

$b^2 - 4ac = (-1)^2 - 4(1)(1) = -3 < 0$

Thus the equation has two complex conjugate solutions.

9.   Solve the equation: $-x^2 + 190x - 925 = 0$

$-(x^2 - 190x + 925) = 0$

$-(x - 185)(x - 5) = 0$

The company will break even if it sells either 5 or 185 units.

10. If the sum of the areas is 193 square centimeters, then to find x we solve the following equation.

$x^2 + (x+5)^2 = 193$

$x^2 + x^2 + 10x + 25 = 193$

$2(x^2 + 5x - 84) = 0$

$2(x - 7)(x + 12) = 0$ Note: This answer is not reasonable.

$x = 7 \quad \text{or} \quad x = -12$

Thus the lengths of the sides of the squares are 7 cm and 12 cm.

11. Let c be the length of the rafter and use the Pythagorean theorem:

$24^2 + 7^2 = c^2$

$c^2 = 625$

$c = \sqrt{625}$

$c = 25$

The length of the rafter is 25 ft.

12. Use the Pythagorean theorem:

$x^2 + 20^2 = 21^2$

$x^2 + 400 = 441$

$x^2 = 41$

$x = \sqrt{41} \approx 6.4$

The base of the ladder is approximately 6.4 ft from the wall.

13. a. $\sqrt{-81} = i\sqrt{81} = i(9) = 9i$

c. $\sqrt{-16} - \sqrt{25} = i\sqrt{16} - 5 = i(4) - 5 = -5 + 4i$

b. $\sqrt{16 - 25} = \sqrt{-9} = i\sqrt{9} = i(3) = 3i$

d. $i^2 + i^3 = (-1) + (-i) = -1 - i$

14. a. $2(4 - 5i) - 3(3 - 4i) = 8 - 10i - 9 + 12i$

$= (8 - 9) + (-10 + 12)i = -1 + 2i$

b. $(4 - 5i)(2 - 4i) = 8 - 16i - 10i + 20i^2$

$= 8 - 26i + 20(-1) = 8 - 26i + -20 = -12 - 26i$

c. $\dfrac{4 - 5i}{2 - 4i} = \dfrac{(4 - 5i)}{(2 - 4i)} \cdot \dfrac{(2 + 4i)}{(2 + 4i)} = \dfrac{8 + 16i - 10i - 20i^2}{4 - 16i^2}$

$= \dfrac{8 + 6i - 20(-1)}{4 - 16(-1)} = \dfrac{8 + 6i + 20}{4 + 16} = \dfrac{28 + 6i}{20}$

$= \dfrac{28}{20} + \dfrac{6i}{20} = \dfrac{7}{5} + \dfrac{3}{10}i$

d. $(3 - i)^2 = 9 - 6i + i^2 = 9 - 6i + (-1) = 8 - 6i$

15. **a.**
$$(y-1)^2 = -36$$
$$\sqrt{(y-1)^2} = \pm\sqrt{-36}$$
$$y-1 = \pm 6i$$
$$y = 1 \pm 6i$$

b.
$$x^2 + 29 = 10x$$
$$x^2 - 10x = -29$$
$$x^2 - 10x + 25 = -29 + 25$$
$$(x-5)^2 = -4$$
$$x-5 = \pm\sqrt{-4}$$
$$x = 5 \pm 2i$$

c.
$$(v-2)(v-4) = -26$$
$$v^2 - 6v + 8 = -26$$
$$v^2 - 6v = -34$$
$$v^2 - 6v + 9 = -34 + 9$$
$$(v-3)^2 = -25$$
$$v-3 = \pm\sqrt{-25}$$
$$v = 3 \pm 5i$$

Section 8.1: Functions and Representations of Functions

Quick Review 8.1

1. $3x^2 - 5x - 1 = 3(10)^2 - 5(10) - 1 = 3(100) - 50 - 1$
$= 300 - 50 - 1 = 249$

2.

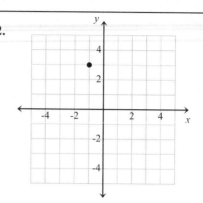

3.

-2 -1   0   1   2   3   4

4. $[-2, 2)$

5. $(-1, \infty)$

Exercises 8.1

1. **a.** The element 1 is not paired with exactly one element in the range. Thus the relation is not a function.
b. Each element in the domain is paired with exactly one output value in the range. Thus the relation is a function. Domain: $\{-3, -1, 1, 2\}$; Range: $\{1, 2, 3\}$
c. Each element in the domain is paired with exactly one output value in the range. Thus the relation is a function. Domain: $\{0, 1, 2, 3\}$; Range: $\{-1, 0, 1, 3\}$

3. **a.** Each element in the domain is paired with exactly one output value in the range. Thus the relation is a function. Domain: $\{-1, 1, 2\}$; Range: $\{0, 1\}$
b. The element 1 is not paired with exactly one element in the range. Thus the relation is not a function.
c. Each element in the domain is paired with exactly one output value in the range. Thus the relation is a function. Domain: $\{-3, -2, -1, 0, 1\}$; Range: $\{-1, 0, 1, 2, 3\}$

5. **a.** No vertical line will cross the function more than once. Thus the graph represents a function.
b. The vertical line $x = 2$ crosses the graph more than once. Thus the graph does not represent a function.
c. No vertical line will cross the function more than once. Thus the graph represents a function.

7. **a.** No vertical line will cross the function more than once. Thus the graph represents a function.
b. The vertical line $x = -3$ crosses the graph more than once. Thus the graph does not represent a function.
c. The vertical line $x = 1$ crosses the graph more than once. Thus the graph does not represent a function.

9. **a.** No vertical line will cross the function more than once. Thus the graph represents a function.
b. No vertical line will cross the function more than once. Thus the graph represents a function.
c. The vertical line $x = 2$ crosses the graph more than once. Thus the graph does not represent a function.

11. **a.** The domain of the function is the projection of its graph onto the x-axis. Domain $= \{-4, -3, -2, -1, 0\}$
The range of the function is the projection of its graph onto the y-axis. Range $= \{8, 6, 4, 2, 0\}$

    b. The domain of the function is the projection of its graph onto the x-axis. Domain $= \{1, 2, 3, 4, 5\}$

    The range of the function is the projection of its graph onto the y-axis. Range $= \{5\}$

13. **a.** The domain of the function is the projection of its graph onto the x-axis. Domain $= \{2, 5, 8, 11, 14\}$

    The range of the function is the projection of its graph onto the y-axis. Range $= \{-3, 1, 5, 9, 13\}$

    b. The domain of the function is the projection of its graph onto the x-axis. Domain $= \{5, 6, 8, 12\ 16\}$

    The range of the function is the projection of its graph onto the y-axis. Range $= \{9, 5, 2, 4\}$

15. **a.** The domain of the function is the projection of its graph onto the x-axis. Domain $= \{-3, -2, -1, 0, 1, 2, 3\}$

    The range of the function is the projection of its graph onto the y-axis. Range $= \{2\}$

    b. The domain of the function is the projection of its graph onto the x-axis. Domain $= (-\pi, \pi]$

    The range of the function is the projection of its graph onto the y-axis. Range $= [-1, 1]$

    c. The domain of the function is the projection of its graph onto the x-axis. Domain $= [-2, +\infty)$

    The range of the function is the projection of its graph onto the y-axis. Range $= (-\infty, 2]$

17. **a.** The domain of the function is the projection of its graph onto the x-axis. Domain $= [-2, 2]$

    The range of the function is the projection of its graph onto the y-axis. Range $= [0, 2]$

    b. The domain of the function is the projection of its graph onto the x-axis. Domain $= [-2, 4)$

    The range of the function is the projection of its graph onto the y-axis. Range $= [-1, 4]$

    c. The domain of the function is the projection of its graph onto the x-axis. Domain $= (-\infty, +\infty)$ or $\mathbb{R}$

    The range of the function is the projection of its graph onto the y-axis. Range $= [-2, 2]$

19. **a.** $f(-10) = 2(-10) - 7 = -27$

    b. $f(0) = 2(0) - 7 = -7$

    c. $f(5) = 2(5) - 7 = 3$

21. **a.** $f(0) = \sqrt{0} = 0$

    b. $f(9) = \sqrt{9} = 3$

    c. $f\left(\dfrac{1}{4}\right) = \sqrt{\dfrac{1}{4}} = \dfrac{1}{2}$

23. **a.** $f(0) = -|0 - 5| + 7 = -|-5| + 7 = -(5) + 7 = 2$

    b. $f(5) = -|5 - 5| + 7 = -|0| + 7 = -(0) + 7 = 7$

    c. $f(8) = -|8 - 5| + 7 = -|3| + 7 = -(3) + 7 = 4$

25. **a.** $f(-1) = (-1)^2 - 4(-1) - 5 = 1 + 4 - 5 = 0$

    b. $f(2) = (2)^2 - 4(2) - 5 = 4 - 8 - 5 = -9$

    c. $f(7) = (7)^2 - 4(7) - 5 = 49 - 28 - 5 = 16$

27. Using the given table, we determine the following.
    a. 3 is an output value.
    b. −1 is an input value.
    c. If 2 is the input value, 3 is the output.
    d. 7 is the output when 8 is the input.

29. Using the given graph, we determine the following.
    a. 3 is an input value.
    b. −1 is an output value.
    c. If 2 is the input value, 0 is the output.
    d. 1 is the output when 3 is the input.

31. Using the given table, we determine the following.
    a. $f(-3) = 8$
    b. $f(1) = -2$
    c. $f(2) = -5$

33. Using the given table, we determine the following.
    a. $f(0) = -1$
    b. $f(-1) = 0$
    c. $f(-3) = 8$

35. Using the given graph, we determine the following.

   a. $f(-2) = 4$

   b. $f(0) = 0$

   c. $f(3) = -3$

37. Using the given graph, we determine the following.

   a. $f(-2) = 4$

   b. $f(0) = 0$

   c. $f(2) = -2$

39. **a.**

D		R
-5	→	4
-3	→	2
-2	→	0
0	→	-2
1	→	-3
4	→	-4

b. $\{(-5, 4), (-3, 2), (-2, 0), (0, -2), (1, -3), (4, -4)\}$

c.

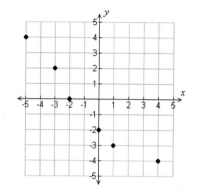

41. **a.**

D		R
-3	→	1
-2	→	-1
-1	→	3
1	→	-2
3	→	2

b. $\{(-3, 1), (-2, -1), (-1, 3), (1, -2), (3, 2)\}$

c.

x	-3	-2	-1	1	3
y	1	-1	3	-2	2

43. **a.**

x	-1	1	2	4
y	1	3	-1	-2

b. $\{(-1, 1), (1, 3), (2, -1), (4, -2)\}$

c.

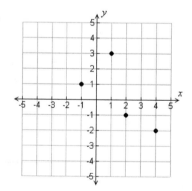

45. **a.**

x	−5	−3	1	2	3
y	4	4	4	4	4

c.

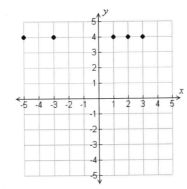

b.

D		R
−5	→	4
−3	→	4
1	→	4
2	→	4
3	→	4

47. **a.** The function that represents the doubling of an investment is $f(x) = 2x$.

b.

D		R
25000	→	50000
40000	→	80000
50000	→	100000
65000	→	130000

c.

x	25000	40000	50000	65000
y	50000	80000	100000	130000

d. $\{(25000,50000),(40000,80000),(50000,100000),(65000,130000)\}$

49. **a.** y represents the pressure in pounds per square inch.
b. From the histogram we can determine that if the pressure is 7.5 pounds per square inch, then the volume is 16 cubic inches.
c. From the histogram we can determine that if the pressure is 15 pounds per square inch, then the volume is 8 cubic inches.

51. **a.**

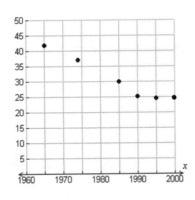

b. From the table, we can determine that 29.9% of U.S. adults smoked in 1985.

c. In 1974, the percent of U.S. adults who smoke was 37%.

53. **a.**

x, (number of years since 1970)	$C(x) = 200x + 1000$
0	$C(0) = 200(0) + 1000 = 1000$
10	$C(10) = 200(10) + 1000 = 3000$
20	$C(20) = 200(20) + 1000 = 5000$
30	$C(30) = 200(30) + 1000 = 7000$

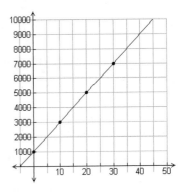

b. The cost of tuition and fees in 2010 is estimated to be $C(40) = 200(40) + 1000 = \$9000$.

c. The cost of tuition and fees in 1994 is estimated to be $5,800

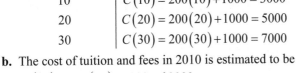

55. **a.** If x represents the purchase price, then the tax is 8.25% of x. Thus $T(x) = 0.0825x$

b.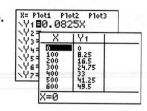

57. The domain of the function is the projection of its graph onto the x-axis. Domain $= (-\infty, +\infty)$ or $\mathbb{R}$
The range of the function is the projection of its graph onto the y-axis. Range $= [-1, \infty)$
The proper choice is **D**.

59. The domain of the function is the projection of its graph onto the x-axis. Domain $= [-2, 3)$
The range of the function is the projection of its graph onto the y-axis. Range $= (-1, 2]$
The proper choice is **B**.

61. a.

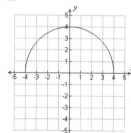

b.

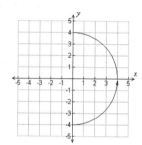

Cumulative Review

1.
$$\frac{x}{3} + \frac{1}{2} = \frac{2x-5}{4}$$
$$12\left(\frac{x}{3} + \frac{1}{2}\right) = 12\left(\frac{2x-5}{4}\right)$$
$$4x + 6 = 3(2x - 5)$$
$$4x + 6 = 6x - 15$$
$$-2x = -21$$
$$x = \frac{21}{2}$$

2.
$$\frac{-5x^3}{2y^7} \cdot \frac{12x^2 y^{-2}}{25x^{-1} y^{-4}} = \frac{-\cancel{5}x^3}{\cancel{2}y^7} \cdot \frac{\overset{6}{\cancel{12}} x^{2-(-1)} y^{-2-(-4)}}{\underset{5}{\cancel{25}}}$$
$$= \frac{-x^3}{y^7} \cdot \frac{6x^3 y^2}{5} = \frac{-6x^{3+3}}{5y^{7-2}} = -\frac{6x^6}{5y^5}$$

3. $25x^2 - 60xy + 36y^2 = (5x)^2 - 2(5x)(6y) + (6y)^2$
$$= (5x - 6y)^2$$

4. $25x^2 - 36y^2 = (5x)^2 - (6y)^2$
$$= (5x + 6y)(5x - 6y)$$

5. $-5x^2 + 20 = -5(x^2 - 4) = -5(x + 2)(x - 2)$

Quick Review 8.2

1. $(-\infty, 6)$

2. $[5, \infty)$

3. $-\dfrac{1}{3}x + 1 < 9$

$-\dfrac{1}{3}x < 8$

$-3\left(-\dfrac{1}{3}x\right) > -3(8)$

$x > -24$

Solution: $(-24, \infty)$

4.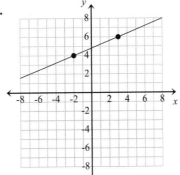

5.

x	y
-14	5
-7	8
0	11
7	14
14	17

The change in x in the table is 7. Thus the corresponding change in y must be 3, since the slope is

$$\dfrac{\Delta y}{\Delta x} = \dfrac{3}{7}$$

Exercises 8.2

1. $f(x) = 5x + 3$ is a line written in slope intercept form. The slope is $m = 5$.

3. $f(x) = 2$ is a horizontal line. The slope is $m = 0$.

5. In the table the change in the values of x is $\Delta x = 1$ while the corresponding change in y is $\Delta y = 2$. Thus the

slope is $m = \dfrac{\Delta y}{\Delta x} = \dfrac{2}{1} = 2$.

7. In the table the change in the values of x is $\Delta x = 3$ while the corresponding change in y is $\Delta y = -4$. Thus the

slope is $m = \dfrac{\Delta y}{\Delta x} = \dfrac{-4}{3} = -\dfrac{4}{3}$.

9. $m = \dfrac{y_2 - y_1}{x_2 - x_1} = \dfrac{-1-1}{2-0} = \dfrac{-2}{2} = -1$

11. The line is horizontal. The slope is $m = 0$.

13. a.

x	$f(x) = -x + 2$
-2	$-(-2) + 2 = 4$
-1	$-(-1) + 2 = 3$
0	$-(0) + 2 = 2$
1	$-(1) + 2 = 1$
2	$-(2) + 2 = 0$

b.   The values of y decrease by 1-unit for each 1-unit increase in x.

c.

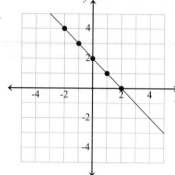

d.   The line decreases by 1-unit for every 1-unit move to the right.

15.

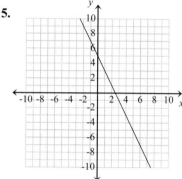

17.

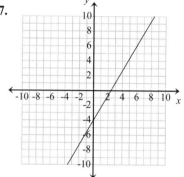

19.   Determine the slope of the line passing through the given points

$$m = \frac{y_2 - y_1}{x_2 - x_1} = \frac{7 - (-2)}{4 - 0} = \frac{9}{4}$$

The y-intercept is $(0, -2)$. Thus the equation of the line is $f(x) = \frac{9}{4}x - 2$.

21.   Determine the slope of the line passing through the given points

$$m = \frac{y_2 - y_1}{x_2 - x_1} = \frac{-6 - (-1)}{2 - 5} = \frac{-5}{-3} = \frac{5}{3}$$

Use the point-slope form with either point. Substitute $(5, -1)$ for (x_1, y_1) and 0 for m. Then write the equation in slope intercept form by solving for y.

$$y - y_1 = m(x - x_1)$$

$$y - (-1) = \frac{5}{3}(x - 5)$$

$$y + 1 = \frac{5}{3}x - \frac{25}{3}$$

$$y = \frac{5}{3}x - \frac{25}{3} - 1$$

$$y = \frac{5}{3}x - \frac{28}{3}$$

or $f(x) = \frac{5}{3}x - \frac{28}{3}$

23. **a.** In the table the change in the values of x is $\Delta x = 1$ while the corresponding change in y is $\Delta y = -2$. Thus the slope is $m = \dfrac{\Delta y}{\Delta x} = \dfrac{-2}{1} = -2$.

b. The y-intercept is $(0, 3)$.

c. The equation of the line is $f(x) = -2x + 3$

25. **a.** In the table the change in the values of x is $\Delta x = 4$ while the corresponding change in y is $\Delta y = 7$. Thus the slope is $m = \dfrac{\Delta y}{\Delta x} = \dfrac{7}{4}$.

b. Use the slope-intercept form of the line to find the y-intercept. Substitute $(11, 1)$ for (x, y) and $\dfrac{7}{4}$ for m and solve for b.

$$y = mx + b$$
$$1 = \frac{7}{4}(11) + b$$
$$1 = \frac{77}{4} + b$$
$$b = 1 - \frac{77}{4} = -\frac{73}{4}$$

The y-intercept is $\left(0, -\dfrac{73}{4}\right)$.

c. The equation of the line is $f(x) = \dfrac{7}{4}x - \dfrac{73}{4}$

27. **a.** The slope is $m = \dfrac{y_2 - y_1}{x_2 - x_1} = \dfrac{3 - (0)}{0 - (-2)} = \dfrac{3}{2}$.

b. The y-intercept is $(0, 3)$.

c. The equation of the line is $f(x) = \dfrac{3}{2}x + 3$.

29. **a.** The slope is

$$m = \frac{y_2 - y_1}{x_2 - x_1} = \frac{-4 - (-1)}{3 - (-2)} = \frac{-3}{5} = -\frac{3}{5}.$$

b. Use the slope-intercept form of the line to find the y-intercept. Substitute $(-2, -1)$ for (x, y) and $-\dfrac{3}{5}$ for m and solve for b.

$$y = mx + b$$
$$-1 = -\frac{3}{5}(-2) + b$$
$$-1 = \frac{6}{5} + b$$
$$b = -1 - \frac{6}{5} = -\frac{11}{5}$$

The y-intercept is $\left(0, -\dfrac{11}{5}\right)$.

c. The equation of the line is $f(x) = -\dfrac{3}{5}x - \dfrac{11}{5}$.

31. The x-intercept is $(3, 0)$.

The y-intercept is $(0, 3)$.

33. The x-intercept is $(1, 0)$.

The y-intercept is $(0, 4)$.

35. To find the y-intercept set $x = 0$.

$$f(0) = 2(0) - 4 = -4$$

The y-intercept is $(0, -4)$.

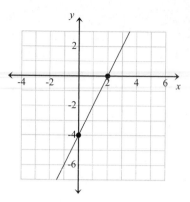

To find the x-intercept set $y = 0$ $(f(x) = 0)$ and solve for x.

$$0 = 2x - 4$$
$$2x = 4$$
$$x = 2$$

The x-intercept is $(2, 0)$.

37. To find the y-intercept set $x = 0$.

$$f(0) = -\frac{2}{3}(0) + 12 = 12$$

The y-intercept is $(0, 12)$.

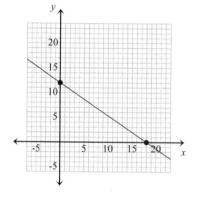

To find the x-intercept set $y = 0$ $(f(x) = 0)$ and solve for x.

$$0 = -\frac{2}{3}x + 12$$
$$\frac{3}{2}\left(\frac{2}{3}x\right) = \frac{3}{2}(12)$$
$$x = 18$$

The x-intercept is $(18, 0)$.

39. The linear function is negative (below the x-axis) on the interval $(-\infty, -4)$ and positve (above the x-axis) on the interval $(-4, \infty)$.

41. The linear function is negative on the interval $(-\infty, 6)$ and positve on the interval $(6, \infty)$.

43. First, find the x-intercept by letting $y = 0$ $(f(x) = 0)$ and solving for x.

$$0 = -10x + 500$$
$$10x = 500$$
$$x = 50$$

The x-intercept is $(50, 0)$.
The function is decreasing since the slope is negative $(m = -10)$. Thus the function is negative on the interval $(50, \infty)$ and positive on the interval $(-\infty, 50)$.

45. Use the point slope form. Substitute $(2, -3)$ for (x_1, y_1) and $\frac{3}{5}$ for m. Then write the equation in slope intercept form by solving for y.

$$y - y_1 = m(x - x_1)$$
$$y - (-3) = \frac{3}{5}(x - 2)$$
$$y + 3 = \frac{3}{5}x - \frac{6}{5}$$
$$y = \frac{3}{5}x - \frac{6}{5} - 3$$
$$y = \frac{3}{5}x - \frac{21}{5}$$

47. Use the point slope form. Substitute $(2, -3)$ for (x_1, y_1) and $\dfrac{3}{2}$ for m. Then write the equation in slope intercept form by solving for y.

$$y - y_1 = m(x - x_1)$$
$$y - (-3) = \frac{3}{2}(x - 2)$$
$$y + 3 = \frac{3}{2}x - 3$$
$$y = \frac{3}{2}x - 6$$

49.

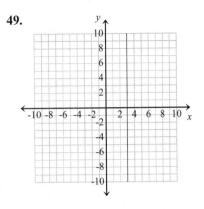

51.

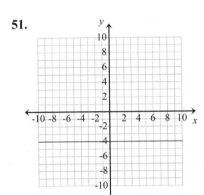

53.

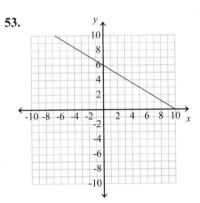

55.

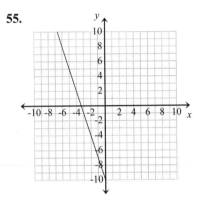

57. **a.**

n	$a_n = -n + 5$
1	$-1 + 5 = 4$
2	$-2 + 5 = 3$
3	$-3 + 5 = 2$
4	$-4 + 5 = 1$
5	$-5 + 5 = 0$

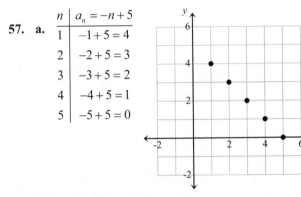

b.

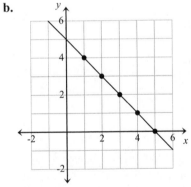

59. **a.** $f(12) = 5(12) - 8 = 52$

b. $f(x) = 12$
$$5x - 8 = 12$$
$$5x = 20$$
$$x = 4$$

61. **a.** $f(6) = 2$

b. If $f(x) = 6$ then $x = 8$.

63. **a.** $f(2) = 1$

b. If $f(x) = 2$ then $x = 0$.

65. a.

x	$C(x) = 0.20x$
0	$0.20(0) = 0$
500	$0.20(500) = 100$
1,000	$0.20(1000) = 200$
1,500	$0.20(1500) = 300$
2,000	$0.20(2000) = 400$
2,500	$0.20(2500) = 500$
3,000	$0.20(3000) = 600$

b. If the bill is $1000, then the patient's responsibility is $200.

c. If the cost to the patient is $425, then to find the original bill we solve the following equation:
$$0.20x = 425$$
$$\frac{0.20x}{0.20} = \frac{425}{0.20}$$
$$x = 2125$$
Thus, the original bill was $2,125.

67. The loss interval is the set of x-values for which the profit is negative. Therefore the loss interval is $[0, 50)$. The profit interval is the set of x-values for which the profit is posotove. Therefore the profit interval is $(50, 150]$.

69. a. To find the y-intercept set $x = 0$.
$$f(0) = 50(0) - 500 = -500$$
The y-intercept is $(0, -500)$.

The business has a loss of $500 when no units are produced and sold.

To find the x-intercept set $y = 0$ $(f(x) = 0)$ and solve for x.
$$0 = 50x - 500$$
$$50x = 500$$
$$x = 10$$
The x-intercept is $(10, 0)$.

The business breaks even when 10 units are produced and sold.

b. The profit interval is $(10, 30]$.
The loss interval is $[0, 10)$.

71. a. Determine the slope of the line passing through two of the given the given points
$$m = \frac{y_2 - y_1}{x_2 - x_1} = \frac{30 - 20}{750 - 500} = \frac{10}{250} = 0.04$$
Use the point-slope form with any of the points. Substitute $(500, 20)$ for (x_1, y_1) and 0.04 for m. Then write the equation in slope intercept form by solving for y.
$$y - y_1 = m(x - x_1)$$
$$y - 20 = 0.04(x - 500)$$
$$y - 20 = 0.04x - 20$$
$$y = 0.04x$$
or $V(x) = 0.04x$

b. $m = 0.04$ is the annual interest rate.

c. $b = 0$ is amount of interest earned when the balance in the account is $0.

d. $V(1100) = 0.04(1100) = 44$; If the balance in the savings account is $1,100, then the yearly interest is $44.

73. **a.** $V(x) = -50x + 500$

b. $V(7) = -50(7) + 150$; The value of the tools after 7 years is $150.

c. Let $V(x) = 50$ and solve for x.

$$50 = -50x + 500$$
$$50x = 450$$
$$x = 9$$

The value of the tools will be $50 after 9 years.

d.

x	$V(x) = -50x + 500$
0	$-50(0) + 500 = 500$
1	$-50(1) + 500 = 450$
2	$-50(2) + 500 = 400$
3	$-50(3) + 500 = 350$
4	$-50(4) + 500 = 300$
5	$-50(5) + 500 = 250$
6	$-50(6) + 500 = 200$

Cumulative Review

1.
$$\frac{5}{12} + \frac{1}{3} = \frac{5}{12} + \frac{1}{3} \cdot \frac{4}{4} = \frac{5}{12} + \frac{4}{12}$$
$$= \frac{5+4}{12} = \frac{9}{12} = \frac{\cancel{3} \cdot 3}{\cancel{3} \cdot 4} = \frac{3}{4}$$

2.
$$\frac{4x^8}{8x^4} = \frac{\overset{1}{\cancel{4}} x^{8-4}}{\underset{2}{\cancel{8}}} = \frac{x^4}{2}$$

3.
$$-3(x+4)(x-1) = -3(x^2 - x + 4x - 4)$$
$$= -3(x^2 + 3x - 4)$$
$$= -3x^2 - 9x + 12$$

4.
$$-2x^2 + 8x + 24 = -2(x^2 - 4x - 12)$$
$$= -2(x-6)(x+2)$$

5.
$$(x-2)(x+3) = 6$$
$$x^2 + 3x - 2x - 6 = 6$$
$$x^2 + x - 6 = 6$$
$$x^2 + x - 12 = 0$$
$$(x+4)(x-3) = 0$$
$$x = -4 \quad \text{or} \quad x = 3$$

Section 8.3: Absolute Value Functions

Quick Review 8.3

1. $-|3-8| = -|-5| = -(5) = -5$

2. $-|8-3| = -|5| = -(5) = -5$

3. $-3 < x < 3$ is equivalent to $(-3, 3)$

4.
$$-9 < 2x + 1 < 9$$
$$-9 - 1 < 2x + 1 - 1 < 9 - 1$$
$$-10 < 2x < 8$$
$$\frac{-10}{2} < \frac{2x}{2} < \frac{8}{2}$$
$$-5 < x < 4$$
Solution: $(-5, 4)$

5. $5x - 2 \le -10$ or $5x - 2 \ge 10$

$\qquad\qquad 5x \le -8 \qquad\qquad 5x \ge 12$

$\qquad\qquad x \le -\dfrac{8}{5} \qquad\qquad x \ge \dfrac{12}{5}$

Solution: $\left(-\infty, -\dfrac{8}{5}\right] \cup \left[\dfrac{12}{5}, \infty\right)$

Exercises 8.3

1. $f(0) = |2(0) - 1| - 3 = |0 - 1| - 3$

$\qquad = |-1| - 3 = 1 - 3 = -2$

3. $f(-4) = |2(-4) - 1| - 3 = |-8 - 1| - 3$

$\qquad = |-9| - 3 = 9 - 3 = 6$

5. Since the absolute value expression is positive, the graph will open up.

7. Since the absolute value expression is negative, the graph will open down.

9. The graph of $f(x) = |x + 1| - 2$ opens up and the vertex is $(-1, 2)$. Thus the answer is **C**.

11. The graph of $f(x) = |x - 1| + 2$ opens up and the vertex is $(1, 2)$. Thus the answer is **D**.

13.

x	$y = |x + 2|$
-3	$|(-3) + 2| = 1$
-2	$|(-2) + 2| = 0$
-1	$|(-1) + 2| = 1$
0	$|(0) + 2| = 2$
1	$|(1) + 2| = 3$
2	$|(2) + 2| = 4$
3	$|(3) + 2| = 5$

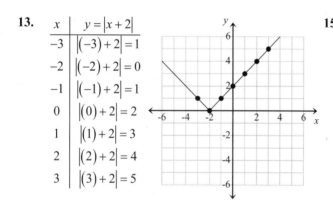

15.

x	$y = |x| - 1$
-3	$|-3| - 1 = 2$
-2	$|-2| - 1 = 1$
-1	$|-1| - 1 = 0$
0	$|0| - 1 = -1$
1	$|1| - 1 = 0$
2	$|2| - 1 = 1$
3	$|3| - 1 = 2$

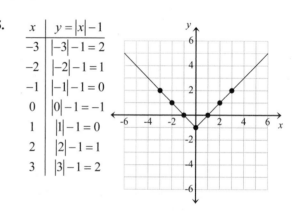

17.
  a. The vertex is $(3, 2)$.
  b. The minimum y-value is $y = 2$.
  c. The x-value at which the minimum y-value occurs is $x = 3$.

19.
  a. The vertex is $(-3, 4)$.
  b. The maximum y-value is $y = 4$.
  c. The x-value at which the maximum y-value occurs is $x = -3$.

21. a.

x	−3	−2	−1	0	1	2	3
y	−1	0	1	2	3	2	1

b.

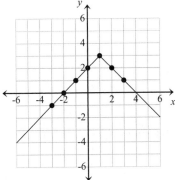

c. The graph opens downward.

d. The vertex is $(1, 3)$.

e. The maximum value of y is $y = 3$.

f. The domain is the projection of the graph onto the x-axis. In this case the domain is $\mathbb{R}$.

g. The range is the projection of the graph onto the y-axis. In this case the range is $(-\infty, 3]$.

23. a.

x	−3	−2	−1	0	1	2	3
y	−3	−4	−3	−2	−1	0	1

b.

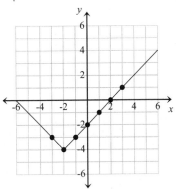

c. The graph opens upward.

d. The vertex is $(-2, -4)$.

e. The minimum value of y is $y = -4$.

f. The domain is the projection of the graph onto the x-axis. In this case the domain is $\mathbb{R}$.

g. The range is the projection of the graph onto the y-axis. In this case the range is $[-4, \infty)$.

25.

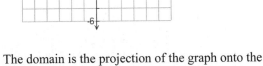

The domain is the projection of the graph onto the x-axis. In this case the domain is $\mathbb{R}$.

The range is the projection of the graph onto the y-axis. In this case the range is $[-1, \infty)$.

27.

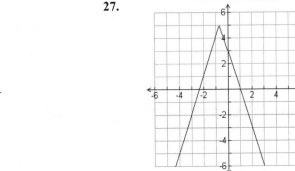

The domain is the projection of the graph onto the x-axis. In this case the domain is $\mathbb{R}$.

The range is the projection of the graph onto the y-axis. In this case the range is $(-\infty, 5]$.

29. The x-intercepts are $(-3, 0)$ and $(1, 0)$.

The y-intercept is $(0, 1)$.

31. The x-intercepts are $(-3, 0)$ and $(1, 0)$.

The y-intercept is $(0, -1)$.

33. To find the y-intercept set $x = 0$.
$$f(0) = |0 - 3| - 7 = |-3| - 7 = 3 - 7 = -4$$
The x-intercept is $(0, -4)$.

To find the x-intercept set $y = 0$ $(f(x) = 0)$ and solve for x.
$$|x - 3| - 7 = 0$$
$$|x - 3| = 7$$
is equivalent to
$$x - 3 = -7 \quad \text{or} \quad x - 3 = 7$$
$$x = -4 \qquad\qquad x = 10$$
The x-intercepts are $(-4, 0)$ and $(10, 0)$.

35. To find the y-intercept set $x = 0$.
$$f(0) = -|0 + 1| + 7 = -|1| + 7 = -1 + 7 = 6$$
The x-intercept is $(0, 6)$.

To find the x-intercept set $y = 0$ $(f(x) = 0)$ and solve for x.
$$-|x + 1| + 7 = 0$$
$$-|x + 1| = -7$$
$$|x + 1| = 7$$
is equivalent to
$$x + 1 = -7 \quad \text{or} \quad x + 1 = 7$$
$$x = -8 \qquad\qquad x = 6$$
The x-intercepts are $(-8, 0)$ and $(6, 0)$.

37. The function is positive (above the x-axis) for the x-values in the interval $(-\infty, -4) \cup (2, \infty)$ and negative (below the x-axis) in the interval $(-4, 2)$.

39. The function is positive (above the x-axis) for the x-values in the interval $(-4, 2)$ and negative (below the x-axis) in the interval $(-\infty, -4) \cup (2, \infty)$.

41. The function is positive for the x-values in the interval $(-4, -2)$ and negative in the interval $(-\infty, -4) \cup (-2, \infty)$.

43. The function is positive for the x-values in the interval $(-3, 1)$ and negative in the interval $(-\infty, -3) \cup (1, \infty)$

45. To determine the interval of x-values for which the fnction is positive we solve the inequality $f(x) > 0$.
$$|x + 5| - 7 > 0$$
$$|x + 5| > 7$$
is eqivalent to
$$x + 5 < -7 \quad \text{or} \quad x + 5 > 7$$
$$x < -12 \qquad\qquad x > 2$$
The function is positive for the x-values in the interval $(-\infty, -12) \cup (2, \infty)$.

To determine the interval of x-values for which the fnction is positive we solve the inequality $f(x) < 0$.
$$|x + 5| - 7 < 0$$
$$|x + 5| < 7$$
is eqivalent to
$$-7 < x + 5 < 7$$
$$-12 < x < 2$$
The function is negative for the x-values in the interval $(-12, 2)$.

47. To determine the interval of x-values for which the fnction is positive we solve the inequality $f(x) > 0$.
$$-|x + 2| + 3 > 0$$
$$-|x + 2| > -3$$
$$|x + 2| < 3 \quad \boxed{\text{Dividing by a } \textit{negative} \text{ number reverses the order of the inequality.}}$$
is eqivalent to
$$-3 < x + 2 < 3$$
$$-5 < x < 1$$
The function is positive for the x-values in the interval $(-5, 1)$.

To determine the interval of x-values for which the fnction is positive we solve the inequality $f(x) < 0$.
$$-|x + 2| + 3 < 0$$
$$-|x + 2| < -3 \quad \boxed{\text{Dividing by a } \textit{negative} \text{ number reverses the order of the inequality.}}$$
$$|x + 2| > 3$$
is eqivalent to
$$x + 2 < -3 \quad \text{or} \quad x + 2 > 3$$
$$x < -5 \qquad\qquad x > 1$$
The function is negative for the x-values in the interval $(-\infty, -5) \cup (1, \infty)$.

49. a.

$$|x-2|=8$$

is equivalent to

$$x-2=-8 \text{ or } x-2=8$$

$$x=-6 \qquad x=10$$

Answer: $x=-6$ or $x=10$

b.

$$|x-2|<8$$

is equivalent to

$$-8<x-2<8$$

$$-6<x<10$$

Answer: $(-6, 10)$

c.

$$|x-2|\geq 8$$

is equivalent to

$$x-2\leq -8 \text{ or } x-2\geq 8$$

$$x\leq -6 \qquad x\geq 10$$

Answer: $(-\infty, -6]\cup[10, \infty)$

51. a.

$$|3x-1|=5$$

is equivalent to

$$3x-1=5 \quad \text{ or } \quad 3x-1=-5$$

$$3x-1+1=5+1 \qquad 3x-1+1=-5+1$$

$$3x=6 \qquad\qquad 3x=-4$$

$$x=2 \qquad\qquad x=-\frac{4}{3}$$

Answer: $x=2$ or $x=-\dfrac{4}{3}$

b.

$$|3x-1|\leq 5$$

is equivalent to

$$-5\leq 3x-1\leq 5$$

$$-5+1\leq 3x-1+1\leq 5+1$$

$$-4\leq 3x\leq 6$$

$$-\frac{4}{3}\leq x\leq 2$$

Answer: $\left[-\dfrac{4}{3}, 2\right]$

c.

$$|3x-1|>5$$

is equivalent to

$$3x-1<-5 \quad \text{ or } \quad 3x-1>5$$

$$3x-1+1<-5+1 \qquad 3x-1+1>5+1$$

$$3x<-4 \qquad\qquad 3x>6$$

$$x<-\frac{4}{3} \qquad\qquad x>2$$

Answer: $\left(-\infty, -\dfrac{4}{3}\right)\cup(2, \infty)$

53. a.

$$f(x)=10$$

$$|x+5|-1=10$$

$$|x+5|=11$$

is equivalent to

$$x+5=-11 \text{ or } x+5=11$$

$$x=-16 \qquad x=6$$

Answer: $x=-16$ or $x=6$

b.

$$f(x)<10$$

$$|x+5|-1<10$$

$$|x+5|<11$$

is equivalent to

$$-11<x+5<11$$

$$-16<x<6$$

Answer: $(-16, 6)$

c.
$$f(x) \geq 10$$
$$|x+5| - 1 \geq 10$$
$$|x+5| \geq 11$$
is equivalent to
$$x + 5 \leq -11 \text{ or } x + 5 \geq 11$$
$$x \leq -16 \qquad x \geq 6$$
Answer: $(-\infty, -16] \cup [6, \infty)$

55. a. $f(-3) = -1$

 b. $f(-2) = 0$

 c. If $f(x) = -2$, then $x = -4$ or $x = 2$.

 d. If $f(x) = 0$, then $x = -2$ or $x = 0$.

57. a. $f(-2) = 1$

 b. $f(2) = -3$

 c. If $f(x) = -2$, then $x = 1$ or $x = 3$.

 d. If $f(x) = 2$, then $x = -3$ or $x = 7$.

59. a. $f(0) = |0 - 8| - 4 = |-8| - 4 = 8 - 4 = 4$

 b. $f(3) = |3 - 8| - 4 = |-5| - 4 = 5 - 4 = 1$

 c. If $f(x) = 3$, then
$$|x - 8| - 4 = 3$$
$$|x - 8| = 7$$
is equivalent to
$$x - 8 = -7 \quad \text{or} \quad x - 8 = 7$$
$$x = 1 \qquad x = 15$$

 d. If $f(x) = 12$, then
$$|x - 8| - 4 = 12$$
$$|x - 8| = 16$$
is equivalent to
$$x - 8 = -16 \quad \text{or} \quad x - 8 = 16$$
$$x = -8 \qquad x = 24$$

61. a. $P(2) = \dfrac{6 - |7 - 2|}{36} = \dfrac{1}{36}$. The probability that a sum of 2 is rolled on a pair of dice is $\dfrac{1}{36}$.

 b. $P(7) = \dfrac{6 - |7 - 7|}{36} = \dfrac{6}{36} = \dfrac{1}{6}$. The probability that a sum of 7 is rolled on a pair of dice is $\dfrac{1}{6}$.

 c. $P(12) = \dfrac{6 - |7 - 12|}{36} = \dfrac{1}{36}$. The probability that a sum of 12 is rolled on a pair of dice is $\dfrac{1}{36}$.

 d. The domain of the function is the set of possible outcomes when rolling a pair of dice. Therefore the domain is $\{2, 3, 4, 5, 6, 7, 8, 9, 10, 11, 12\}$

 e. From parts **a.** and **c.** we can see that the probability of rolling a 7 is greater than that of rolling a 2.

Cumulative Review

1. $\sqrt{24} = \sqrt{4}\sqrt{6} = 2\sqrt{6} \approx 4.90$

2.
$$x^2 = 8$$
$$\sqrt{x^2} = \pm\sqrt{8}$$
$$x = \pm\sqrt{4}\sqrt{2}$$
$$x = \pm 2\sqrt{2}$$

3.
$$3x^2 - 5x - 7 = 0$$

Substitute a, b, and c in the quadratic formula.

$$a = 3, \quad b = -5, \quad c = -7$$

$$x = \frac{-(-5) \pm \sqrt{(-5)^2 - 4(3)(-7)}}{2(3)}$$

$$= \frac{5 \pm \sqrt{25 + 84}}{6} = \frac{5 \pm \sqrt{109}}{6}$$

4. If the solutions are $x = -2$ and $x = 7$, then Thus $(x+2)$ and $(x-7)$ are factors and the equation is

$$(x+2)(x-7) = 0$$
$$x^2 - 7x + 2x - 14 = 0$$
$$x^2 - 5x - 14 = 0$$

5.
$$\frac{4+5i}{2-i} = \frac{(4+5i)}{(2-i)} \cdot \frac{(2+i)}{(2+i)} = \frac{8 + 4i + 10i + 5i^2}{4 - i^2}$$

$$= \frac{8 + 14i + 5(-1)}{4 - (-1)} = \frac{3 + 14i}{5} = \frac{3}{5} + \frac{14}{5}i$$

Section 8.4: Quadratic Functions

Quick Review 8.4

1. The equation $y = mx + b$ is known as the slope-intercept form of the line.
2. The fixed costs or the overhead costs for a company can include insurance, rent, electricity, and other fixed expenses when 0 units are produced.
3. If (x, y) lies in Quadrant II, then x is negative and y is positve.
4. If x and y have the same sign, then the point (x, y) lies in Quadrant I or Quadrant III.
5.
$$6x^2 - 13x + 6 = 0$$
$$(2x - 3)(3x - 2) = 0$$
$$2x - 3 = 0 \quad \text{or} \quad 3x - 2 = 0$$
$$2x = 3 \qquad\qquad 3x = 2$$
$$x = \frac{3}{2} \qquad\qquad x = \frac{2}{3}$$

Exercises 8.4

1. The graph is that of a parabola that opens downward. Thus, the function must be a quadratic with a negative quadratic term. Answer: **D**.
3. The graph is that of a line with positive slope. Thus the function must be linear with a positive leading term. Answer: **A**.
5. $y = -3x + 4$ is a line with a negative slope $(m = -3)$.

7. $y = 4x - 3$ is a line with a positive slope $(m = 4)$.

9. $y = 8x^2$ is a parabola that opens upward. (The leading term is positive.)

11. $y = -3x^2 + 8x + 9$ is a parabola that opens downward. (The leading term is negative.)

13. The vertex is $(-3, -20)$.

15. The vertex will have an x-coordinate that is midway between the x-intercepts. Thus the x-coordinate of the vertex is the average of 6 and -2 or $\dfrac{6+(-2)}{2} = \dfrac{4}{2} = 2$.

17. To find the x-value of the vertex we use the formula $x = -\dfrac{b}{2a} = -\dfrac{(-6)}{2(1)} = \dfrac{6}{2} = 3$.

    To find the corresponding value of y for the vertex we evaluate $f(3) = (3)^2 - 6(3) + 11 = 9 - 18 + 11 = 2$.
    Vertex: $(3, 2)$.

19. To find the x-value of the vertex we use the formula $x = -\dfrac{b}{2a} = -\dfrac{(10)}{2(-5)} = \dfrac{10}{10} = 1$.

    To find the corresponding value of y for the vertex we evaluate $f(1) = -5(1)^2 + 10(1) + 6 = -5 + 10 + 6 = 11$.
    Vertex: $(1, 11)$.

21. **a.** The y-intercept is found by letting $x = 0$.
    $$y = 2(0)^2 - 3(0) - 2 = -2$$, thus the y-intercept is $(0, -2)$

    b. The x-intercepts are found by letting $y = 0$ and solving for x.
    $$2x^2 - 3x - 2 = 0$$
    $$(2x+1)(x-2) = 0$$
    $$x = -\frac{1}{2}, \text{ or } x = 2$$
    The x-intercepts are $\left(-\dfrac{1}{2}, 0\right)$ and $(2, 0)$

    c. To find the x-value of the vertex we use the formula $x = \dfrac{-b}{2a} = \dfrac{-(-3)}{2(2)} = \dfrac{3}{4}$.

    To find the corresponding value of y for the vertex we evaluate
    $$y = 2\left(\frac{3}{4}\right)^2 - 3\left(\frac{3}{4}\right) - 2 = -\frac{25}{8}.$$
    Vertex: $\left(\dfrac{3}{4}, -\dfrac{25}{8}\right)$.

23. **a.** The y-intercept is found by letting $x = 0$.
    $$y = (2(0)-3)((0)+4) = (-3)(4) = -12$$, thus the y-intercept is $(0, -12)$

    b. The x-intercepts are found by letting $y = 0$ and solving for x.
    $$(2x-3)(x+4) = 0$$
    $$x = \frac{3}{2}, \text{ or } x = -4$$
    The x-intercepts are $\left(\dfrac{3}{2}, 0\right)$ and $(-4, 0)$

    c. In this case we will establish the x value of the vertex by finding the point midway between the x-intercepts: $\dfrac{\frac{3}{2}+(-4)}{2} = -\dfrac{5}{4}$

    To find the corresponding value of y for the vertex we evaluate
    $$y = \left(2\left(-\frac{5}{4}\right)-3\right)\left(\left(-\frac{5}{4}\right)+4\right) = -\frac{121}{8}.$$
    Vertex: $\left(-\dfrac{5}{4}, -\dfrac{121}{8}\right)$

25.

x	y
-3	-6
-2	-1
-1	2
0	3
1	2
2	-1
3	-6

27.

x	y
-3	0
-2	-4
-1	-6
0	-6
1	-4
2	0
3	6

29. **a.** The parabola is opening upward.

b. The vertex is $(1, -4)$.

c. The y-intercept is $(0, -3)$.

d. The x-intercepts are $(-1, 0)$ and $(3, 0)$.

e. The domain is $(-\infty, \infty)$ or $\mathbb{R}$..

f. The range is $[-4, \infty)$.

31. **a.** The parabola is opening downward.

b. The vertex is $(0, 4)$.

c. The y-intercept is $(0, 4)$.

d. The x-intercepts are $(-2, 0)$ and $(2, 0)$.

e. The domain is $(-\infty, \infty)$ or $\mathbb{R}$..

f. The range is $(-\infty, 4]$.

33. **a.** The parabola is opening upward.

b. The vertex is $(1, 0)$.

c. The y-intercept is $(0, 1)$.

d. The x-intercept is $(1, 0)$.

e. The domain is $(-\infty, \infty)$ or $\mathbb{R}$..

f. The range is $[0, \infty)$.

35. **a.** The parabola will open upward because the leading coefficient is positive.

b. To find the x-value of the vertex we use the formula

$$x = -\frac{b}{2a} = -\frac{5}{2(1)} = -\frac{5}{2} = -2.5 .$$

To find the corresponding value of y for the vertex we evaluate

$$y = (2.5)^2 + 5(2.5) - 6 = -12.25 .$$

Vertex: $(-2.50, -12.25)$.

c. The x-intercepts are found by letting $y = 0$ and solving for x.

$$x^2 + 5x - 6 = 0$$
$$(x + 6)(x - 1) = 0$$
$$x = -6, \quad \text{or} \quad x = 1$$

The x-intercepts are $(-6, 0)$ and $(1, 0)$

The y-intercept is found by letting $x = 0$. $y = (0)^2 + 5(0) - 6 = -6$, thus the y-intercept is $(0, -6)$.

d.

x	y
-5	-6
-4	-10
-3	-12
-2.5	-12.25
-2	-12
-1	-10
0	-6

e.

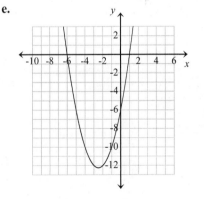

37. a. The parabola will open downward because the leading coefficient is negative.

d.

x	y
−2	5
−1	12
0	15
0.25	15.125
1	14
2	9
3	0

b. To find the x-value of the vertex we use the formula

$$x = -\frac{b}{2a} = -\frac{1}{2(-2)} = -\frac{1}{-4} = 0.25 \,.$$

To find the corresponding value of y for the vertex we evaluate

$$y = -2(0.25)^2 + (0.25) + 15 = 15.125 \,.$$

Vertex: $(0.25,\ 15.125)$.

c. The x-intercepts are found by letting $y = 0$ and solving for x.

$$-2x^2 + x + 15 = 0$$
$$-\left(2x^2 - x - 15\right) = 0$$
$$-(2x + 5)(x - 3) = 0$$
$$x = -\frac{5}{2}, \quad \text{or} \quad x = 3$$

The x-intercepts are $\left(-\frac{5}{2},\ 0\right)$ and $(3,\ 0)$.

e.

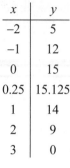

The y-intercept is found by letting $x = 0$.

$y = -2(0)^2 + (0) + 15 = 15$, thus the y-intercept is $(0,\ 15)$.

39. a. The overhead cost is equal to the profit when zero units are produced and sold. From the graph we can see that $P(0) = -15000$ thus the overhead cost is $15,000.

b. The break even values occur when the profit is zero. From the graph we can see that the break even values occur when $x = 20$ and $x = 80$.

c. From the graph we can see that the maximum profit is $9,000 and occurs when 50 units are produced and sold.

41. a. The overhead cost is equal to the profit when zero units are produced and sold. From the graph we can see that $P(0) = -1000$ thus the overhead cost is $1,000.

b. The break even values occur when the profit is zero. From the graph we can see that the break even values occur when $x = 1$ and $x = 9$.

c. From the graph we can see that the maximum profit is $1,500 and occurs when 5 units are produced and sold.

43. a.

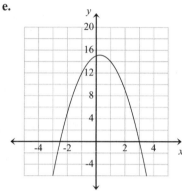

The overhead cost is $240,000.

$[0, 150, 10]$ by $[-300000, 300000, 100000]$

b.

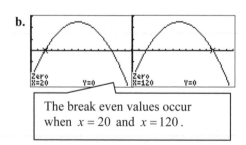

The break even values occur when $x = 20$ and $x = 120$.

c.

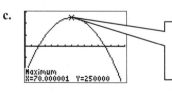

The maximum profit is $250,000 and occurs when 70 tons are produced and sold.

45. **a.**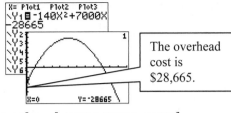

The overhead cost is $28,665.

$[0, 60, 10]$ by $[-70000, 70000, 10000]$

b.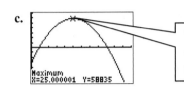

The break even values occur when $x = 4.5$ and $x = 45.5$.

c.

The maximum profit is $58,835 and occurs when 25 tons are produced and sold.

47. The ball will reach its highest point at the vertex. To find the x-value of the vertex we use the following formula $x = -\dfrac{b}{2a} = -\dfrac{96}{2(-16)} = \dfrac{96}{32} = 3$.

To find the y-value of the vertex we evaluate $f(3) = -16(3)^2 + 96(3) + 3 = 147$. The ball reaches a maximum height of 147 feet 3 seconds into its flight.

49. To maximize the number of grapefruit we find the vertex of $N(t) = (200 - 2t)(50 + t) = -2t^2 + 100t + 1000$.

Use the formula $t = -\dfrac{b}{2a} = -\dfrac{100}{2(-2)} = \dfrac{100}{4} = 25$. To maximize the number of grapefruit the plot will yield they should plant 75 (25 more than 50) trees on a lot this size

51. **a.** The area is
$$A(x) = lw = (20 - w)w = -w^2 + 20w$$

b. The maximum area occurs at the vertex. To find the w-value of the vertex we use the formula $w = -\dfrac{b}{2a} = -\dfrac{20}{2(-1)} = \dfrac{20}{2} = 10$.

Thus, the maximum area is
$$A(10) = -(10)^2 + 20(10) = 100 \text{ m}^2.$$

53. **a.** Let $w =$ the width of the storage area.
Let $l =$ the length of the storage area.
We know that the amount of fencing is 80 ft, thus $2w + l = 60$. If we solve for l we have $l = 60 - 2w$.
The area of the rectangle is $A = lw$
$$A = (60 - 2w)w$$
$$A = -2w^2 + 60w$$

b. The maximum area occurs at the vertex. To find the w-value of the vertex we use the formula $w = -\dfrac{b}{2a} = -\dfrac{60}{2(-2)} = \dfrac{60}{4} = 15$.

Thus, the maximum area is
$$A(15) = -2(15)^2 + 60(15) = 450 \text{ ft}^2.$$

55. **a.** Once the sides are turned up the cross section is a recatangle with dimensions: x by $(100 - 2x)$. Thus the cross-sectional area is $A(x) = x(100 - 2x) = -2x^2 + 100x$.

b. The maximum area occurs at the vertex. To find the x-value of the vertex we use the formula
$$x = -\frac{b}{2a} = -\frac{100}{2(-2)} = \frac{100}{4} = 25.$$

c. Thus, the maximum area is $A(20) = -2(25)^2 + 100(25) = 1250 \text{ cm}^2.$

57. To determine the interval of x-values for which the fnction is positive we solve the inequality

$f(x) > 0$.

$$-2x + 8 > 0$$
$$-2x > -8$$
$$x < 4$$

> Dividing by a *negative* number reverses the order of the inequality.

The function is positive for the x-values in the interval $(-\infty, 4)$.

In this way, the function must be negative on the interval $(4, \infty)$.

59. To determine the interval of x-values for which the fnction is positive we solve the inequality

$f(x) > 0$.

$$3x - 10 > 0$$
$$3x > 10$$
$$x > \frac{10}{3}$$

The function is positive for the x-values in the interval $\left(\frac{10}{3}, \infty\right)$.

In this way, the function must be negative on the interval $\left(-\infty, \frac{10}{3}\right)$.

61. First, find the x-intercepts by solving the equation

$$f(x) = 0$$
$$x^2 - 36 = 0$$
$$x^2 = 36$$
$$x = \pm\sqrt{36}$$
$$x = \pm 6$$

Since $f(x)$ is a parabola that opens up, the function is negative between the x-intercepts or on the interval: $(-6, 6)$. In this way, the function is negative on the interval: $(-\infty, -6) \cup (6, \infty)$.

63. First, find the x-intercepts by solving the equation

$$f(x) = 0$$
$$-x^2 + 4x + 5 = 0$$
$$-(x^2 - 4x - 5) = 0$$
$$-(x + 1)(x - 5) = 0$$
$$x = -1 \text{ or } x = 5$$

Since $f(x)$ is a parabola that opens down, the function is positive between the x-intercepts or on the interval: $(-1, 5)$. In this way, the function is negative on the interval: $(-\infty, -1) \cup (5, \infty)$.

65. a.
$$f(x) = 7$$
$$x^2 - 2x - 8 = 7$$
$$x^2 - 2x - 15 = 0$$
$$(x + 3)(x - 5) = 0$$
$$x = -3 \text{ or } x = 5$$

b. Since $f(x)$ is a parablola that opens up, the solution to $f(x) < 7$ is $(-3, 5)$.

c. Since $f(x)$ is a parablola that opens up, the solution to $f(x) \geq 7$ is $(-\infty, -3] \cup [5, \infty)$.

67. a. $f(-2) = 1$

b. If $f(x) = -2$, then $x = -3$ or $x = 1$.

69. a. $f(3) = 6$

b. If $f(x) = 3$, then $x = 0$ or $x = 4$.

71. a. $f(12) = (12)^2 - 9(12) - 10 = 144 - 108 - 10 = 26$

b. If $f(x) = 12$, then $x^2 - 9x - 10 = 12$
$$x^2 - 9x - 22 = 0$$
$$(x + 2)(x - 11)$$
$$x = -2 \text{ or } x = 11$$

Cumulative Review

1.

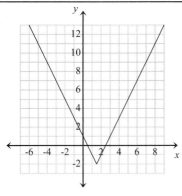

2. $|2x-3|-2<11$

$$|2x-3|<13$$

is equivalent to

$$-13<2x-3<13$$

$$-10<2x<16$$

$$-5<x<8$$

Answer: $(-5, 8)$

3. Determine the slope of the line passing through the given points

$$m=\frac{y_2-y_1}{x_2-x_1}=\frac{-4-(-5)}{3-(-2)}=\frac{1}{5}$$

Use the point-slope form with either point.

Substitute $(-2, -5)$ for (x_1, y_1) and $\frac{1}{5}$ for m.

Then write the equation in slope intercept form by solving for y.

$$y-y_1=m(x-x_1)$$

$$y-(-5)=\frac{1}{5}(x-(-2))$$

$$y+5=\frac{1}{5}x+\frac{2}{5}$$

$$y=\frac{1}{5}x-\frac{23}{5}$$

4. $2x^2-11x-21=2x^2-14x+3x-21$

$$=(2x^2-14x)+(3x-21)$$

$$=2x(x-7)+3(x-7)$$

$$=(x-7)(2x+3)$$

5. If the solutions are $x=3$ and $x=-\frac{5}{2}$, then

$$x-3=0 \text{ and } x+\frac{5}{2}=0 .$$

Thus, $(x-3)$ and $(2x+5)$ must be factors and the equation is $\quad (x-3)(2x+5)=0$

$$2x^2+5x-6x-15=0$$

$$2x^2-x-15=0$$

Section 8.5: Analyzing Graphs

Quick Review 8.5

1.

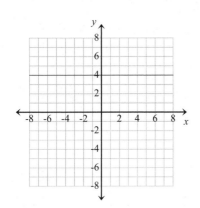

2.

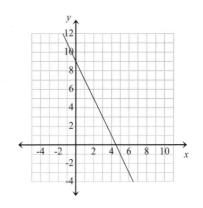

3.

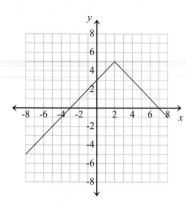

4.

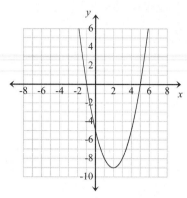

5.   **a.** The domain is the projection of the graph onto the x-axis. The range is the projection of the graph onto the y-axis. Using the graph in problem **1** we can conclude that the domain is $\mathbb{R}$ and the range is $\{4\}$.

   b. The domain is the projection of the graph onto the x-axis. The range is the projection of the graph onto the y-axis. Using the graph in problem **2** we can conclude that the domain is $\mathbb{R}$ and the range is $\mathbb{R}$.

   c. The domain is the projection of the graph onto the x-axis. The range is the projection of the graph onto the y-axis. Using the graph in problem **3** we can conclude that the domain is $\mathbb{R}$ and the range is $\left(-\infty, 5\right]$.

   d. The domain is the projection of the graph onto the x-axis. The range is the projection of the graph onto the y-axis. Using the graph in problem **4** we can conclude that the domain is $\mathbb{R}$ and the range is $\left[-9, \infty\right)$.

Exercises 8.5

1.   The function drops as x moves from left to right. Therefore the function is decreasing.

3.   The function rises as x moves from left to right. Therefore the function is increasing.

5.   The function $f(x) = -2x + 5$ is a line with a negative slope. Therefore the function is decreasing.

7.   The function $f(x) = 2x - 5$ is a line with a positive slope. Therefore the function is increasing.

9.   The function $f(x) = -3$ is a line with a slope of zero. Therefore the function is neither increasing nor decreasing. The function is constant.

11.   **a.** The price was increasing during the fifth and sixth months.

   b. The price was decreasing during the first three months.

   c. The price was constant during the fourth month.

13. a. Using the points $(0, -1)$ and $(2, 0)$, we can determine the slope of the line is $m = \dfrac{y_2 - y_1}{x_2 - x_1} = \dfrac{0 - (-1)}{2 - 0} = \dfrac{1}{2}$.

    b. The x-intercept is $(2, 0)$.

    c. The y-intercept is $(0, -1)$.

    d. The domain of the function is the projection of the graph onto the x-axis. Domain: $\mathbb{R}$.

    e. The range of the function is the projection of the graph onto the y-axis. Range: $\mathbb{R}$.

    f. The function is positive (above the x-axis) on the interval: $(2, \infty)$.

    g. The function is negative (below the x-axis) on the interval: $(-\infty, 2)$.

    h. The function is never decreasing.

    i. The function is increasing over its entire domain, $\mathbb{R}$.

15. a. Using the points $(0, 4)$ and $(3, 0)$, we can determine the slope of the line is $m = \dfrac{y_2 - y_1}{x_2 - x_1} = \dfrac{0 - 4}{3 - 0} = -\dfrac{4}{3}$.

    b. The x-intercept is $(3, 0)$.

    c. The y-intercept is $(0, 4)$.

    d. The domain of the function is the projection of the graph onto the x-axis. Domain: $\mathbb{R}$.

    e. The range of the function is the projection of the graph onto the y-axis. Range: $\mathbb{R}$.

    f. The function is positive (above the x-axis) on the interval: $(-\infty, 3)$.

    g. The function is negative (below the x-axis) on the interval: $(3, \infty)$.

    h. The function is decreasing over its entire domain, $\mathbb{R}$. (The slope is negative.)

    i. The function is never increasing. (The slope is negative.)

17. a. The slope of the line is $m = 5$.

    b. To find the x-intercept we let $y = 0$ and solve for x: $0 = 5x - 20 \Rightarrow x = 4$. x-intercept: $(4, 0)$

    c. To find the y-intercept we evaluate $f(0) = 5(0) - 20 = -20$. y-intercept: $(0, -20)$

    d. The domain of the function is the projection of the graph onto the x-axis. Domain: $\mathbb{R}$.

    e. The range of the function is the projection of the graph onto the y-axis. Range: $\mathbb{R}$.

    f. The function is positive (above the x-axis) on the interval: $(4, \infty)$.

    g. The function is negative (below the x-axis) on the interval: $(-\infty, 4)$.

    h. The function is never decreasing. (The slope is positive.)

    i. The function is increasing over its entire domain, $\mathbb{R}$. (The slope is positive.)

19. a. The slope of the line is $m = -150$.

    b. To find the x-intercept we let $y = 0$ and solve for x: $0 = -150x + 300 \Rightarrow x = 2$. x-intercept: $(2, 0)$

    c. To find the y-intercept we evaluate $f(0) = -150(0) + 300 = 300$. y-intercept: $(0, 300)$

    d. The domain of the function is the projection of the graph onto the x-axis. Domain: $\mathbb{R}$.

    e. The range of the function is the projection of the graph onto the y-axis. Range: $\mathbb{R}$.

    f. The function is positive (above the x-axis) on the interval: $(-\infty, 2)$.

    g. The function is negative (below the x-axis) on the interval: $(2, \infty)$.

    h. The function is decreasing over its entire domain, $\mathbb{R}$. (The slope is negative.)

    i. The function is never increasing. (The slope is negative.)

21. **a.** The vertex of the graph is $(-3, 1)$.

    b. The graph opens downward.

    c. The x-intercepts are $(-4, 0)$ and $(-2, 0)$.

    d. The y-intercept is $(0, -2)$.

    e. The domain of the function is the projection of the graph onto the x-axis. Domain: $\mathbb{R}$.

    f. The range of the function is the projection of the graph onto the y-axis. Range: $(-\infty, 1]$.

    g. The function is positive (above the x-axis) on the interval: $(-4, -2)$.

    h. The function is negative (below the x-axis) on the interval: $(-\infty, -4) \cup (-2, \infty)$.

    i. The function is decreasing over the interval: $(-3, \infty)$.

    j. The function is increasing over the interval: $(-\infty, -3)$.

23. **a.** The vertex of the graph is $(-1, -2)$.

    b. The graph opens upward.

    c. The x-intercepts are $(-3, 0)$ and $(1, 0)$.

    d. The y-intercept is $(0, -1)$.

    e. The domain of the function is the projection of the graph onto the x-axis. Domain: $\mathbb{R}$.

    f. The range of the function is the projection of the graph onto the y-axis. Range: $[-2, \infty)$.

    g. The function is positive (above the x-axis) on the interval: $(-\infty, -3) \cup (1, \infty)$.

    h. The function is negative (below the x-axis) on the interval: $(-3, 1)$.

    i. The function is decreasing over the interval: $(-\infty, -1)$.

    j. The function is increasing over the interval: $(-1, \infty)$.

25. The graph of $f(x) = |x + 7| - 12$ is shown here.

    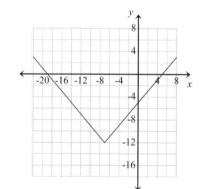

    a. The vertex of the graph is $(-7, -12)$.

    b. The graph opens upward.

    c. The x-intercepts are $(-19, 0)$ and $(5, 0)$.

    d. The y-intercept is $(0, -5)$.

    e. The domain of the function is the projection of the graph onto the x-axis. Domain: $\mathbb{R}$.

    f. The range of the function is the projection of the graph onto the y-axis. Range: $[-12, \infty)$.

    g. The function is positive (above the x-axis) on the interval: $(-\infty, -19) \cup (5, \infty)$.

    h. The function is negative (below the x-axis) on the interval: $(-19, 5)$.

    i. The function is decreasing over the interval: $(-\infty, -7)$.

    j. The function is increasing over the interval: $(-7, \infty)$.

27. The graph of $f(x) = -|x - 15| + 20$ is shown here.

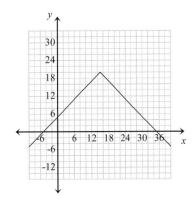

    a. The vertex of the graph is $(15\ 20)$.

    b. The graph opens downward.

    c. The x-intercepts are $(-5, 0)$ and $(35, 0)$.

    d. The y-intercept is $(0, 5)$.

    e. The domain of the function is the projection of the graph onto the x-axis. Domain: $\mathbb{R}$.

    f. The range of the function is the projection of the graph onto the y-axis. Range: $(-\infty, 20]$.

    g. The function is positive (above the x-axis) on the interval: $(-5, 35)$.

    h. The function is negative (below the x-axis) on the interval: $(-\infty, -5) \cup (35, \infty)$.

    i. The function is decreasing over the interval: $(15, \infty)$.

    j. The function is increasing over the interval: $(-\infty, 15)$.

29. **a.** The vertex of the graph is $(-2, 0)$.

    b. The graph opens downward.

    c. The x-intercept is $(-2, 0)$.

    d. The y-intercept is $(0, -4)$.

    e. The domain of the function is the projection of the graph onto the x-axis. Domain: $\mathbb{R}$.

    f. The range of the function is the projection of the graph onto the y-axis. Range: $(-\infty, 0]$.

    g. The function never positive.

    h. The function is negative (below the x-axis) on the interval: $(-\infty, -2) \cup (-2, \infty)$.

    i. The function is decreasing over the interval: $(-2, \infty)$.

    j. The function is increasing over the interval: $(-\infty, -2)$.

31. **a.** The vertex of the graph is $(2, -1)$.

    b. The graph opens upward.

    c. The x-intercepts are $(1, 0)$ and $(3, 0)$.

    d. The y-intercept is $(0, 3)$.

    e. The domain of the function is the projection of the graph onto the x-axis. Domain: $\mathbb{R}$.

    f. The range of the function is the projection of the graph onto the y-axis. Range: $[-1, \infty)$.

    g. The function is positive (above the x-axis) on the interval: $(-\infty, 1) \cup (3, \infty)$.

    h. The function is negative (below the x-axis) on the interval: $(1, 3)$.

    i. The function is decreasing over the interval: $(-\infty, 2)$.

    j. The function is increasing over the interval: $(2, \infty)$.

33. The graph of $f(x) = x^2 - 9x + 20$ is shown here.

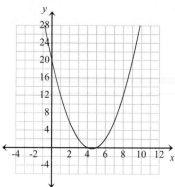

a. To find the x-value of the vertex we use the formula $x = -\dfrac{b}{2a} = -\dfrac{-9}{2(1)} = \dfrac{9}{2}$.

To find the corresponding value of y for the vertex we evaluate $f\left(\dfrac{9}{2}\right) = \left(\dfrac{9}{2}\right)^2 - 9\left(\dfrac{9}{2}\right) + 20 = -\dfrac{1}{4}$.

Vertex: $\left(\dfrac{9}{2}, -\dfrac{1}{4}\right)$.

b. The graph opens upward.

c. The x-intercepts are found by letting $y = 0$ and solving for x.
$$x^2 - 9x + 20 = 0$$
$$(x - 4)(x - 5) = 0$$
$$x = 4, \quad \text{or} \quad x = 5$$
The x-intercepts are $(4, 0)$ and $(5, 0)$.

d. The y-intercept is found by letting $x = 0$. $f(0) = (0)^2 - 9(0) + 20 = 20$, thus the y-intercept is $(0, 20)$.

e. The domain of the function is the projection of the graph onto the x-axis. Domain: $\mathbb{R}$.

f. The range of the function is the projection of the graph onto the y-axis. Range: $\left[-\dfrac{1}{4}, \infty\right)$.

g. The function is positive (above the x-axis) on the interval: $(-\infty, 4) \cup (5, \infty)$.

h. The function is negative (below the x-axis) on the interval: $(4, 5)$.

i. The function is decreasing over the interval: $\left(-\infty, \dfrac{9}{2}\right)$.

j. The function is increasing over the interval: $\left(\dfrac{9}{2}, \infty\right)$

35. The graph of $f(x) = -2x^2 + 9x + 26$ is shown here.

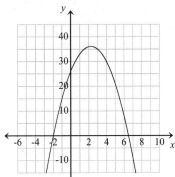

a. To find the x-value of the vertex we use the formula $x = -\dfrac{b}{2a} = -\dfrac{9}{2(-2)} = \dfrac{9}{4}$.

To find the corresponding value of y for the vertex we evaluate $f\left(\dfrac{9}{4}\right) = -2\left(\dfrac{9}{4}\right)^2 + 9\left(\dfrac{9}{4}\right) + 26 = \dfrac{289}{8}$.

Vertex: $\left(\dfrac{9}{4}, \dfrac{289}{4}\right)$.

b. The graph opens downward.

c. The x-intercepts are found by letting $y = 0$ and solving for x.
$$-2x^2 + 9x + 26 = 0$$
$$-\left(2x^2 - 9x - 26\right) = 0$$
$$-\left(2x - 13\right)\left(x + 2\right) = 0$$
$$x = \frac{13}{2}, \quad \text{or} \quad x = -2$$

The x-intercepts are $\left(\dfrac{13}{2}, 0\right)$ and $(-2, 0)$.

d. The y-intercept is found by letting $x = 0$. $f(0) = -2(0)^2 + 9(0) + 26 = 26$, thus the y-intercept is $(0, 26)$.

e. The domain of the function is the projection of the graph onto the x-axis. Domain: $\mathbb{R}$.

f. The range of the function is the projection of the graph onto the y-axis. Range: $\left(-\infty, \dfrac{289}{8}\right]$.

g. The function is positive (above the x-axis) on the interval: $\left(-2, \dfrac{13}{2}\right)$.

h. The function is negative (below the x-axis) on the interval: $(-\infty, -2) \cup \left(\dfrac{13}{2}, \infty\right)$.

i. The function is decreasing over the interval: $\left(\dfrac{9}{4}, \infty\right)$.

j. The function is increasing over the interval: $\left(-\infty, \dfrac{9}{4}\right)$.

37. **a.** The function is increasing. (The slope is positive.)
  b. The rate of increase is the profit in dollars per snow cone.
  c. The x-intercepts are found by letting $P = 0$ and solving for t.
$$0.25x - 400 = 0$$
$$x = \frac{400}{0.25} = 1600$$
  The x-intercept is $(1600, 0)$.

  The P-intercept is found by letting $x = 0$.
$$P(0) = 0.25(0) - 400 = -400$$, thus the P-intercept is $(0, -400)$.

  d. The company will break even when 1600 snow cones are sold. The company has an overhead of $400.
  e. The x-values for which the function is positive are in the interval $(1600, \infty)$
  f. The company will have a profit when more than 1600 snow cones are sold

39. **a.** To find the x-value of the vertex we use the formula $x = -\dfrac{b}{2a} = -\dfrac{24.5}{2(-4.9)} = 2.5$.

  To find the corresponding value of y for the vertex we evaluate
$$H(2.5) = -4.9(2.5)^2 + 48(2.5) \approx 30.6$$.
  Vertex: $(2.5, 30.6)$.

  b. The ball reaches a maximum height of 30.6 meters 2.5 seconds after the ball is hit.
  c. The t-intercepts are found by letting $H = 0$ and solving for x.
$$-4.9t^2 + 24.5t = 0$$
$$-t(4.9t - 24.5)$$
$$t = 0, \quad \text{or} \quad t = \frac{24.5}{4.9} = 5$$
  The t-intercepts are $(0, 0)$ and $(5, 0)$.

  The H-intercept is found by letting $t = 0$.
$$H(0) = -4.9(0)^2 + 24.5(0)$$, thus the H-intercept is $(0, 0)$.

  d. The ball is on the ground initially $(t = 0)$ and after 5 seconds.
  e. The function is increasing on the interval $(0, 2.5)$.
  f. The ball is rising for the first 2.5 seconds of its flight.

Cumulative Review

1. $5123 = 5.123 \times 10^3$

2. $-0.0078 = -7.8 \times 10^{-3}$

3. $4.5 \times 10^4 = 45000$

4. $-6.73 \times 10^{-3} = -0.00673$

5. The coefficient of $7x^3$ is 7.

Section 8.6: Curve Fitting

Quick Review 8.6

1. The slope is $m = 15$

2. To find the x-intercept let $y = 0$ and solve for x.
$$15x + 20 = 0$$
$$15x = -20$$
$$x = -\frac{20}{15} = -\frac{4}{3}$$
  The x-intercept is $\left(-\frac{4}{3}, 0\right)$.

  To find the y-intercept evaluate:
$$f(0) = 15(0) + 20 = 20$$
  The y-intercept is $(0, 20)$.

3. To find the x-value of the vertex we use the formula

$$x = -\frac{b}{2a} = -\frac{5}{2(-1)} = \frac{5}{2} = 2.5.$$

To find the corresponding value of y for the vertex we evaluate $f(2.5) = -(2.5)^2 + 5(2.5) + 6 = 12.25$.

Vertex: $(2.5, 12.25)$.

4. The graph opens downward, since the leading coefficient is negative.

5. To find the x-intercepts let $y = 0$ and solve for x.

$$-x^2 + 5x + 6 = 0$$
$$-(x^2 - 5x - 6) = 0$$
$$-(x+1)(x-6) = 0$$
$$x = -1 \text{ or } x = 6$$

The x-intercepts are $(-1, 0)$ and $(6, 0)$.

To find the y-intercept evaluate:

$$f(0) = -(0)^2 + 5(0) + 6 = 6$$

The y-intercept is $(0, 6)$.

Exercises 8.6

1. The scatter diagram that best matches a line with a positive slope is **B**.

3. The scatter diagram that best matches a parabola opening upward is **C**.

5.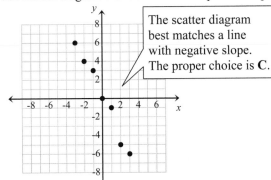

The scatter diagram best matches a line with negative slope. The proper choice is **C**.

7.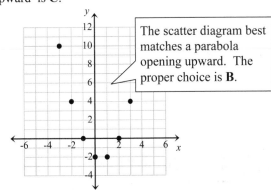

The scatter diagram best matches a parabola opening upward. The proper choice is **B**.

9.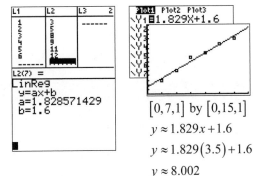

$[0,7,1]$ by $[0,15,1]$

$y \approx 1.829x + 1.6$

$y \approx 1.829(3.5) + 1.6$

$y \approx 8.002$

11.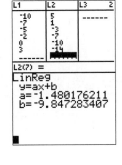

$[-15,5,1]$ by $[-15,5,1]$

$y \approx -1.480x - 9.84$

$y \approx -1.480(1) - 9.84$

$y \approx -11.327$

13. **a.**

b. The slope is the change in the birth weight per cigarette

c. $y \approx -.005x + 3.201$

$y \approx -.005(18) + 3.201$

$y \approx 3.11$ kg

d. $y \approx -.005x + 3.201$

$y \approx -.005(45) + 3.201$

$y \approx 2.98$ kg

15. a.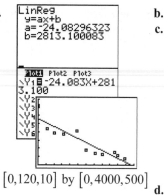

$[0,120,10]$ by $[0,4000,500]$

b. The slope represents the decrease in the Olympic marathon times per year.

c. The year 1984 corresponds to $x = 84$

$$y \approx -24.083x + 2813.100$$

$$y \approx -24.083(84) + 2813.100$$

$$y \approx 790$$

The Olympic marathon time for 1984 is estimated to be 790 seconds past 2 hours

$$\left(2\,\text{hours}, \frac{790}{60} = 13.17\,\text{minutes or 2 hour, 13 minutes, and 10 seconds}\right)$$

The actual record is 3 min and 49 sec faster.

d. To estimate when the Olympic marathon time will reach 2 hours we solve the following equation.

$$-24.083x + 2813.100 = 0$$

$$24.083x = 2813.100$$

$$x = \frac{2813.100}{24.083} \approx 116.8$$

Therefore it is estimated that the Olympic marathon time will reach 2 hours approximately 116.8 years past 1900 or in the Olympics of 2020.

17.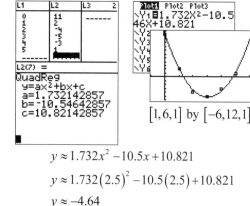

$[1,6,1]$ by $[-6,12,1]$

$$y \approx 1.732x^2 - 10.5x + 10.821$$

$$y \approx 1.732(2.5)^2 - 10.5(2.5) + 10.821$$

$$y \approx -4.64$$

19.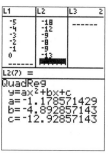

$[-6,1,1]$ by $[-20,0,1]$

$$y \approx -1.179x^2 - 4.893x - 12.929$$

$$y \approx -1.179(1)^2 - 4.893(1) - 12.929$$

$$y \approx -19.0$$

21.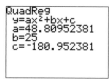

$[10,24,1]$ by $[0,30000,5000]$

b. $y \approx 48.810x^2 + 25x - 180.952$

$$y \approx 48.810(15)^2 + 25(15) - 180.952$$

$$y \approx 11176$$

It is estimated that a beam that is 15 cm deep can support a load of about 11,000 kilograms.

23. **a.**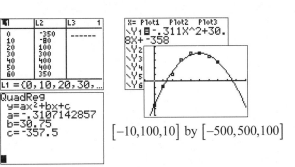

$f(x) \approx -0.000189x^2 + 0.791x - 4.96$

b. To find the point of maximum power for this engine, we locate the vertex of the parabola. To find the x-value of the vertex, use the formula $x = -\dfrac{b}{2a} = -\dfrac{0.791}{2(-0.000189)} \approx 2090$. To find the y-value of the vertex evaluate:

$f(2090) \approx -0.000189(2090)^2 + 0.791(2090) - 4.96 \approx 820$

c. The engine has a maximum power of 820 hp when running at 2090 rpm.

25. **a.**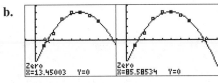

$[-10,100,10]$ by $[-500,500,100]$

c.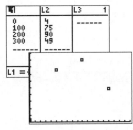

A maximum profit of approximately $405 is achieved when about 50 units are produced and sold.

b.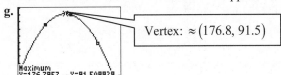

The business will break even when approximately 13 units or 86 units are produced and sold.

27. **a.**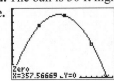

b. QuadReg
y=ax²+bx+c
a=-.0028
b=.99
c=4

$[0,380,20]$ by $[0,100,10]$

c. $f(325) = -0.0028(325)^2 + 0.99(325) + 4 = 30$

d. The ball is 30 ft high when it has traveled a horizontal distance of 325 ft.

e.

f. The ball travels a horizontal distance of approximately 357.6 ft.

g.

Vertex: $\approx (176.8, 91.5)$

h. The ball has a maximun height of 91.5 ft when it is 176.8 ft from homeplate.

Cumulative Review

1. $2x + 5 = 19$

$2x = 14$

$x = 7$

2. $1 - \dfrac{2x - 5}{3} = \dfrac{x}{2}$

$6\left(1 - \dfrac{2x - 5}{3}\right) = 6\left(\dfrac{x}{2}\right)$

$6 - 2(2x - 5) = 3x$

$6 - 4x + 10 = 3x$

$-4x + 16 = 3x$

$16 = 7x$

$x = \dfrac{16}{7}$

3. $|4x + 3| = 8$ is equivalent to

$4x + 3 = -8$ or $4x + 3 = 8$

$4x = -11$ $\qquad$ $4x = 5$

$x = -\dfrac{11}{4}$ $\qquad$ $x = \dfrac{5}{4}$

4. $(3x + 1)^2 = 12$

$3x + 1 = \pm\sqrt{12}$

$3x = -1 \pm 2\sqrt{3}$

$x = \dfrac{-1 \pm 2\sqrt{3}}{3}$

5. $(x + 5)(x - 4) = 22$

$x^2 - 4x + 5x - 20 = 22$

$x^2 + x - 20 = 22$

$x^2 + x - 42 = 0$

$(x + 7)(x - 6) = 0$

$x = -7$ or $x = 6$

Review Exercises for Chapter 8

1.
  a. Each element in the domain is paired with exactly one output value in the range. Thus the relation is a function.
  b. Each element in the domain is paired with exactly one output value in the range. Thus the relation is a function.
  c. The element 1 is not paired with exactly one element in the range. Thus the relation is not a function.
  d. Each element in the domain is paired with exactly one output value in the range. Thus the relation is a function.

2.
  a. The vertical line $x = -2$ crosses the graph more than once. Thus the graph does not represent a function.
  b. No vertical line will cross the function more than once. Thus the graph represents a function.
  c. No vertical line will cross the function more than once. Thus the graph represents a function.
  d. The vertical line $x = 1$ crosses the graph more than once. Thus the graph does not represent a function.

3.
  a. The domain of a function is the set of input values for the function. Domain $= \{5, 6, 7\}$.

  The range of a function is the set of output values for the function. Range $= \{8\}$.

  b. The domain of the function is the projection of its graph onto the x-axis. Domain $= (-1, 3]$.

  The range of the function is the projection of its graph onto the y-axis. Range $= [0, 2]$.

  c. The domain of a function is the set of input values for the function. Domain $= (-\infty, \infty)$ or $\mathbb{R}$.

  The range of a function is the set of output values for the function. The vertex of the absolute value function is $(-3, 4)$ and it opens down. Thus the range is $(-\infty, 4]$.

  d. The domain of a function is the set of input values for the function. Domain $= (-\infty, \infty)$ or $\mathbb{R}$.

  The range of a function is the set of output values for the function. The vertex of the parabola is $(3, -1)$ and it opens up. Thus the range is $[-1, \infty)$.

4. **a.** $f(-2) = ((-2) + 2)^2 + 3 = (0)^2 + 3 = 3$

  b. $f(0) = ((0) + 2)^2 + 3 = (2)^2 + 3 = 7$

  c. $f(1) = ((1) + 2)^2 + 3 = (3)^2 + 3 = 12$

  d. $f(8) = ((8) + 2)^2 + 3 = (10)^2 + 3 = 103$

5. Using the given table, we determine the following.

  a. $f(-2) = 4$

  b. $f(0) = 2$

  c. $f(2) = 8$

  d. $f(-1) = 3$

6. Using the given graph ,we determine the following.

  a. $f(-4) = -2$

  b. $f(3) = 2$

  c. $f(-1) = 0$

  d. $f(-2) = -1$

7. **a.**

D		R
-10	$\rightarrow$	4
-5	$\rightarrow$	3
0	$\rightarrow$	2
5	$\rightarrow$	1
10	$\rightarrow$	0
15	$\rightarrow$	-1
20	$\rightarrow$	-2

b. $\{(-10, 4), (-5, 3), (0, 2), (5, 1), (10, 0), (15, -1), (20, -2)\}$

c.

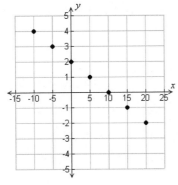

d. Using any two points from the table we can determine the slope of the line. For example, we can use the points $(10, 0)$ and $(5, 1)$.

$$m = \frac{y_2 - y_1}{x_2 - x_2} = \frac{1 - 0}{5 - 10} = \frac{1}{-5} = -\frac{1}{5}$$

The table includes the point $(0, 2)$. Thus we can use the slope intercept form to find the equation of the line.

$$y = mx + b$$

$$y = -\frac{1}{5}x + 2$$

8.   **a.** $\{(-4,-1),(-2,0),(0,1),(2,2),(4,3)\}$

b.

x	y
-4	-1
-2	0
0	1
2	2
4	3

c.

D		R
-4	→	-1
-2	→	0
0	→	1
2	→	2
4	→	3

d. Using any two points from the table we can determine the slope of the line. For example, we can use the points $(2,2)$ and $(4,3)$.

$$m = \frac{y_2 - y_1}{x_2 - x_2} = \frac{3-2}{4-2} = \frac{1}{2}$$

The table includes the point $(0,1)$. Thus we can use the slope intercept form to find the equation of the line.
$$y = mx + b$$
$$y = \frac{1}{2}x + 1$$

9. The slope of the line is
$$m = \frac{y_2 - y_1}{x_2 - x_1} = \frac{-1-1}{3-0} = \frac{-2}{3} = -\frac{2}{3}$$

10. The slope of the line is
$$m = \frac{y_2 - y_1}{x_2 - x_1} = \frac{-3-(-3)}{2-0} = \frac{0}{2} = 0$$

11.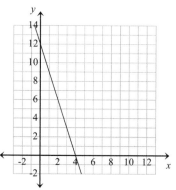

12.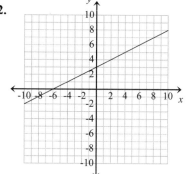

13. Determine the slope of the line passing through the given points
$$m = \frac{y_2 - y_1}{x_2 - x_1} = \frac{-3-2}{4-0} = \frac{-5}{4} = -\frac{5}{4}$$
Use the point-slope form with either point.

Substitute $(0,2)$ for (x_1, y_1) and $-\frac{5}{4}$ for m. Then write the equation in slope intercept form by solving for y.
$$y - y_1 = m(x - x_1)$$
$$y - 2 = -\frac{5}{4}(x - 0)$$
$$y - 2 = -\frac{5}{4}x$$
$$y = -\frac{5}{4}x + 2$$

14. Determine the slope of the line passing through the given points
$$m = \frac{y_2 - y_1}{x_2 - x_1} = \frac{5-3}{2-(-1)} = \frac{2}{3}$$
Use the point-slope form with either point.

Substitute $(2,5)$ for (x_1, y_1) and $\frac{2}{3}$ for m. Then write the equation in slope intercept form by solving for y.
$$y - y_1 = m(x - x_1)$$
$$y - 5 = \frac{2}{3}(x - 2)$$
$$y - 5 = \frac{2}{3}x - \frac{4}{3}$$
$$y = \frac{2}{3}x + \frac{11}{3}$$

15. The slope of the line is positive. The function is increasing.

16. The slope of the line is negative. The function is decreasing.

17. The slope of the line is negative. The function is decreasing.

18. The slope of the line is positive. The function is increasing.

19. **a.** Using the points $(0, 3)$ and $(-2, 0)$, we can determine the slope of the line is $m = \dfrac{y_2 - y_1}{x_2 - x_1} = \dfrac{3 - 0}{0 - (-2)} = \dfrac{3}{2}$.

 b. The x-intercept is $(-2, 0)$.

 c. The y-intercept is $(0, 3)$.

 d. The domain of the function is the projection of the graph onto the x-axis. Domain: $\mathbb{R}$.
 e. The range of the function is the projection of the graph onto the y-axis. Range: $\mathbb{R}$.
 f. The function is positive (above the x-axis) on the interval: $(-2, \infty)$.

 g. The function is negative (below the x-axis) on the interval: $(-\infty, -2)$.

 h. The function is never decreasing.
 i. The function is increasing over its entire domain, $\mathbb{R}$.

20. **a.** Using the points $(0, 2)$ and $(3, 0)$, we can determine the slope of the line is $m = \dfrac{y_2 - y_1}{x_2 - x_1} = \dfrac{0 - 2}{3 - 0} = -\dfrac{2}{3}$.

 b. The x-intercept is $(3, 0)$.

 c. The y-intercept is $(0, 2)$.

 d. The domain of the function is the projection of the graph onto the x-axis. Domain: $\mathbb{R}$.
 e. The range of the function is the projection of the graph onto the y-axis. Range: $\mathbb{R}$.
 f. The function is positive (above the x-axis) on the interval: $(-\infty, 3)$.

 g. The function is negative (below the x-axis) on the interval: $(3, \infty)$.

 h. The function is decreasing over its entire domain, $\mathbb{R}$.
 i. The function is never increasing.

21. **a.** The slope of the line is $m = -12.5$.
 b. To find the x-intercept we let $y = 0$ and solve for x: $0 = -12.5x + 125 \Rightarrow x = 10$. x-intercept: $(10, 0)$

 c. To find the y-intercept we evaluate $f(0) = -12.5(0) + 125 = 125$. y-intercept: $(0, 125)$

 d. The domain of the function is the projection of the graph onto the x-axis. Domain: $\mathbb{R}$.
 e. The range of the function is the projection of the graph onto the y-axis. Range: $\mathbb{R}$.
 f. The function is positive (above the x-axis) on the interval: $(-\infty, 10)$.

 g. The function is negative (below the x-axis) on the interval: $(10, \infty)$.

 h. The function is decreasing over its entire domain, $\mathbb{R}$. (The slope is negative.)
 i. The function is never increasing. (The slope is negative.)

22. **a.** The slope of the line is $m = 35$.
 b. To find the x-intercept we let $y = 0$ and solve for x: $0 = 35x - 210 \Rightarrow x = 6$. x-intercept: $(6, 0)$

 c. To find the y-intercept we evaluate $f(0) = 35(0) - 210 = -210$. y-intercept: $(0, -210)$

 d. The domain of the function is the projection of the graph onto the x-axis. Domain: $\mathbb{R}$.
 e. The range of the function is the projection of the graph onto the y-axis. Range: $\mathbb{R}$.
 f. The function is positive (above the x-axis) on the interval: $(6, \infty)$.

 g. The function is negative (below the x-axis) on the interval: $(-\infty, 6)$.

 h. The function is never decreasing. (The slope is positive.)
 i. The function is increasing over its entire domain, $\mathbb{R}$. (The slope is positive.)

23. **a.**

x	−3	−2	−1	0	1	2	3
y	0	1	2	1	0	−1	−2

b.

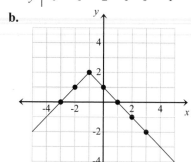

c. The graph opens downward.

d. The vertex is $(-1, 2)$.

e. The maximum value of y is $y = 2$.

f. The domain is the projection of the graph onto the x-axis. In this case the domain is $\mathbb{R}$.

g. The range is the projection of the graph onto the y-axis. In this case the range is $(-\infty, 2]$.

24. **a.**

x	−3	−2	−1	0	1	2	3
y	1	0	−1	−2	−3	−2	−1

b.

c. The graph opens upward.

d. The vertex is $(1, -3)$.

e. The minimum value of y is $y = -3$.

f. The domain is the projection of the graph onto the x-axis. In this case the domain is $\mathbb{R}$.

g. The range is the projection of the graph onto the y-axis. In this case the range is $[-3, \infty)$.

25.

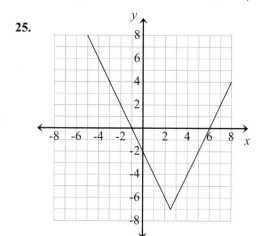

26.

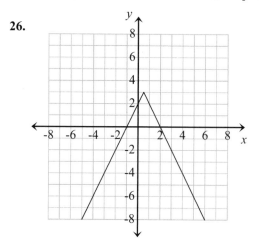

27. **a.**

$$|x + 1| = 8$$

is equivalent to

$$x + 1 = -8 \quad \text{or} \quad x + 1 = 8$$

$$x = -9 \qquad x = 7$$

Answer: $x = -9$ or $x = 7$

b.

$$|x + 1| < 8$$

is equivalent to

$$-8 < x + 1 < 8$$

$$-9 < x < 7$$

Answer: $(-9, 7)$

c.

$$|x + 1| \geq 8$$

is equivalent to

$$x + 1 \leq -8 \text{ or } x + 1 \geq 8$$

$$x \leq -9 \qquad x \geq 7$$

Answer: $(-\infty, -9] \cup [7, +\infty)$

28. a.
$$|2x+3| = 7$$
is equivalent to
$$2x + 3 = 7 \text{ or } 2x + 3 = -7$$
$$2x = 4 \qquad 2x = -10$$
$$x = 2 \qquad x = -5$$
Answer: $x = 2$ or $x = -5$

b.
$$|2x+3| \leq 7$$
is equivalent to
$$-7 \leq 2x + 3 \leq 7$$
$$-10 \leq 2x \leq 4$$
$$-5 \leq x \leq 2$$
Answer: $[-5, 2]$

c.
$$|2x+3| > 7$$
is equivalent to
$$2x + 3 < -7 \qquad 2x + 3 > 7$$
$$2x < -10 \text{ or } \quad 2x > 4$$
$$x < -5 \qquad x > 2$$
Answer: $(-\infty, -5) \cup (2, +\infty)$

29. a. The vertex of the graph is $(-1, 2)$.

b. The graph opens downward.

c. The x-intercepts are $(-3, 0)$ and $(1, 0)$.

d. The y-intercept is $(0, 1)$.

e. The domain of the function is the projection of the graph onto the x-axis. Domain: $\mathbb{R}$.

f. The range of the function is the projection of the graph onto the y-axis. Range: $(-\infty, 2]$.

g. The function is positive (above the x-axis) on the interval: $(-3, 1)$.

h. The function is negative (below the x-axis) on the interval: $(-\infty, -3) \cup (1, \infty)$.

i. The function is decreasing over the interval: $(-1, \infty)$.

j. The function is increasing over the interval: $(-\infty, -1)$.

30. a. The vertex of the graph is $(2, -1)$.

b. The graph opens upward.

c. The x-intercepts are $(1, 0)$ and $(3, 0)$.

d. The y-intercept is $(0, 1)$.

e. The domain of the function is the projection of the graph onto the x-axis. Domain: $\mathbb{R}$.

f. The range of the function is the projection of the graph onto the y-axis. Range: $[-1, \infty)$.

g. The function is positive (above the x-axis) on the interval: $(-\infty, 1) \cup (3, \infty)$.

h. The function is negative (below the x-axis) on the interval: $(1, 3)$.

i. The function is decreasing over the interval: $(-\infty, 2)$.

j. The function is increasing over the interval: $(2, \infty)$.

31. The graph of $f(x) = |x-8| - 9$ is shown here.

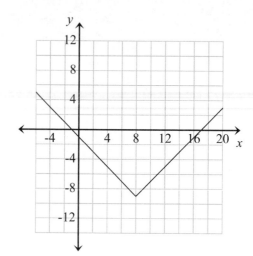

   a. The vertex of the graph is $(8, -9)$.

   b. The graph opens upward.

   c. The x-intercepts are $(-1, 0)$ and $(17, 0)$.

   d. The y-intercept is $(0, -1)$.

   e. The domain of the function is the projection of the graph onto the x-axis. Domain: $\mathbb{R}$.

   f. The range of the function is the projection of the graph onto the y-axis. Range: $[-9, \infty)$.

   g. The function is positive (above the x-axis) on the interval: $(-\infty, -1) \cup (17, \infty)$.

   h. The function is negative (below the x-axis) on the interval: $(-1, 17)$.

   i. The function is decreasing over the interval: $(-\infty, 8)$.

   j. The function is increasing over the interval: $(8, \infty)$.

32. The graph of $f(x) = -|x+7| + 12$ is shown here.

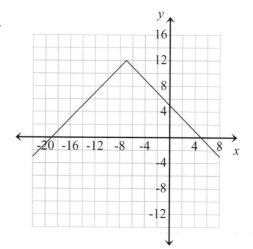

   a. The vertex of the graph is $(-7, 12)$.

   b. The graph opens downward.

   c. The x-intercepts are $(-19, 0)$ and $(5, 0)$.

   d. The y-intercept is $(0, 5)$.

   e. The domain of the function is the projection of the graph onto the x-axis. Domain: $\mathbb{R}$.

   f. The range of the function is the projection of the graph onto the y-axis. Range: $(-\infty, 12]$.

   g. The function is positive (above the x-axis) on the interval: $(-19, 5)$.

   h. The function is negative (below the x-axis) on the interval: $(-\infty, -19) \cup (5, \infty)$.

   i. The function is decreasing over the interval: $(-7, \infty)$.

   j. The function is increasing over the interval: $(-\infty, -7)$.

33. The graph is a line with negative slope. The proper choice is **B**.

34. The graph is a parabola that opens upward. The proper choice is **C**.

35. The graph is a line with positive slope. The proper choice is **A**.

36. The graph is a parabola that opens downward. The proper choice is **D**.

37. The parabola opens downward and has a vertex of $(2, 7)$.

38. The parabola opens upward and has a vertex of $(3, -2)$.

39. The graph opens upward, since the leading coefficient is positive.

To find the x-value of the vertex we use the formula

$$x = -\frac{b}{2a} = -\frac{10}{2(1)} = -5 .$$

To find the corresponding value of y for the vertex we evaluate

$$f(-5) = (-5)^2 + 10(-5) + 5 = -20 .$$

Vertex: $(-5, -20)$.

40. The graph opens downward, since the leading coefficient is negative.

To find the x-value of the vertex we use the formula

$$x = -\frac{b}{2a} = -\frac{4}{2(-1)} = 2 .$$

To find the corresponding value of y for the vertex we evaluate

$$f(2) = -(2)^2 + 4(2) + 7 = 11 .$$

Vertex: $(2, 11)$.

41. To find the x-value of the vertex we use the formula

$$x = -\frac{b}{2a} = -\frac{4}{2(-4)} = \frac{1}{2} .$$

To find the corresponding value of y for the vertex we evaluate $f\left(\frac{1}{2}\right) = -4\left(\frac{1}{2}\right)^2 + 4\left(\frac{1}{2}\right) + 3 = 4$;

Vertex: $\left(\frac{1}{2}, 4\right)$.

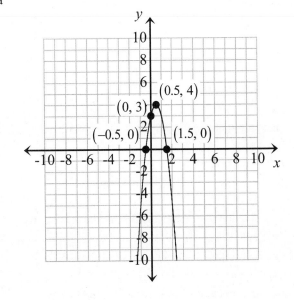

To find the x-intercepts let $y = 0$ and solve for x.

$$-4x^2 + 4x + 3 = 0$$

$$-(4x^2 - 4x - 3) = 0$$

$$-(2x + 1)(2x - 3) = 0$$

$$x = -\frac{1}{2} \text{ or } x = \frac{3}{2}$$

The x-intercepts are $\left(-\frac{1}{2}, 0\right)$ and $\left(\frac{3}{2}, 0\right)$.

To find the y-intercept evaluate

$$f(0) = -4(0)^2 + 4(0) + 3 = 3 .$$

The y-intercept is $(0, 3)$.

42. To find the x-value of the vertex we use the formula

$$x = -\frac{b}{2a} = -\frac{3}{2(2)} = -\frac{3}{4}.$$

To find the corresponding value of y for the vertex we evaluate

$$f\left(\frac{3}{4}\right) = 2\left(\frac{3}{4}\right)^2 + 3\left(\frac{3}{4}\right) - 9 = -\frac{81}{8} = -10.125;$$

Vertex: $\left(-\frac{3}{4}, -\frac{81}{8}\right)$.

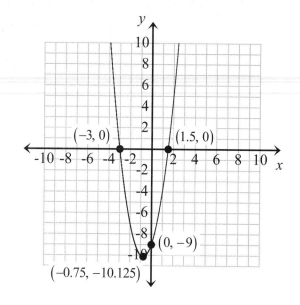

To find the x-intercepts let $y = 0$ and solve for x.

$$2x^2 + 3x - 9 = 0$$
$$(x - 3)(2x + 3) = 0$$
$$x = 3 \quad \text{or} \quad x = -\frac{3}{2}$$

The x-intercepts are $(3, 0)$ and $\left(-\frac{3}{2}, 0\right)$.

To find the y-intercept evaluate

$$f(0) = 2(0)^2 + 3(0) - 9 = -9.$$

The y-intercept is $(0, -9)$.

43.
   a. The vertex of the graph is $(3, -4)$.
   b. The graph opens upward.
   c. The x-intercepts are $(1, 0)$ and $(5, 0)$.
   d. The y-intercept is $(0, 5)$.
   e. The domain of the function is the projection of the graph onto the x-axis. Domain: $\mathbb{R}$.
   f. The range of the function is the projection of the graph onto the y-axis. Range: $[-4, \infty)$.
   g. The function is positive (above the x-axis) on the interval: $(-\infty, 1) \cup (5, \infty)$.
   h. The function is negative (below the x-axis) on the interval: $(1, 5)$.
   i. The function is decreasing over the interval: $(-\infty, 3)$.
   j. The function is increasing over the interval: $(3, \infty)$.

44.
   a. The vertex of the graph is $(-1, 9)$.
   b. The graph opens downward.
   c. The x-intercepts are $(-4, 0)$ and $(2, 0)$.
   d. The y-intercept is $(0, 8)$.
   e. The domain of the function is the projection of the graph onto the x-axis. Domain: $\mathbb{R}$.
   f. The range of the function is the projection of the graph onto the y-axis. Range: $(-\infty, 9]$.
   g. The function is positive (above the x-axis) on the interval: $(-4, 2)$.
   h. The function is negative (below the x-axis) on the interval: $(-\infty, -4) \cup (2, \infty)$.
   i. The function is decreasing over the interval: $(-1, \infty)$.
   j. The function is increasing over the interval: $(-\infty, -1)$.

45. The graph of $f(x) = x^2 + 12x - 28$ is shown here.

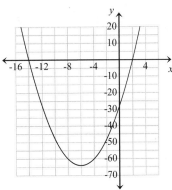

a. To find the x-value of the vertex we use the formula $x = -\dfrac{b}{2a} = -\dfrac{12}{2(1)} = -6$.

To find the corresponding value of y for the vertex we evaluate $y = (-6)^2 + 12(-6) - 28 = -64$.

Vertex: $(-6, -64)$.

b. The graph opens upward.

c. The x-intercepts are found by letting $y = 0$ and solving for x.
$$x^2 + 12x - 28 = 0$$
$$(x + 14)(x - 2) = 0$$
$$x = -14 \quad \text{or} \quad x = 2$$
The x-intercepts are $(-14, 0)$ and $(2, 0)$.

d. The y-intercept is found by letting $x = 0$; $f(0) = (0)^2 + 12(0) - 28 = -28$, thus the y-intercept is $(0, -28)$.

e. The domain of the function is the projection of the graph onto the x-axis. Domain: $\mathbb{R}$.

f. The range of the function is the projection of the graph onto the y-axis. Range: $[-64, \infty)$.

g. The function is positive (above the x-axis) on the interval: $(-\infty, -14) \cup (2, \infty)$.

h. The function is negative (below the x-axis) on the interval: $(-14, 2)$.

i. The function is decreasing over the interval: $(-\infty, -6)$.

j. The function is increasing over the interval: $(-6, \infty)$.

46. The graph of $f(x) = -x^2 + 6x + 27$ is shown here.

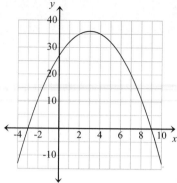

a. To find the x-value of the vertex we use the formula $\quad x = -\dfrac{b}{2a} = -\dfrac{6}{2(-1)} = 3$.

To find the corresponding value of y for the vertex we evaluate $\quad y = -(3)^2 + 6(3) + 27 = 36$.
Vertex: $(3, 36)$.

b. The graph opens downward.

c. The x-intercepts are found by letting $y = 0$ and solving for x.
$$-x^2 + 6x + 27 = 0$$
$$-\left(x^2 - 6x - 27\right) = 0$$
$$-(x + 3)(x - 9) = 0$$
$$x = -3 \quad \text{or} \quad x = 9$$
The x-intercepts are $(-3, 0)$ and $(9, 0)$.

d. The y-intercept is found by letting $x = 0$. $\; f(0) = -(0)^2 + 6(0) + 27 = 27$, thus the y-intercept is $(0, 27)$.

e. The domain of the function is the projection of the graph onto the x-axis. Domain: $\mathbb{R}$.

f. The range of the function is the projection of the graph onto the y-axis. Range: $(-\infty, 36]$.

g. The function is positive (above the x-axis) on the interval: . $(-3, 9)$

h. The function is negative (below the x-axis) on the interval: $(-\infty, -3) \cup (9, \infty)$.

i. The function is decreasing over the interval: $(3, \infty)$.

j. The function is increasing over the interval: $(-\infty, 3)$.

47. **a.** Determine the slope of the line passing through the given points

$$m = \frac{y_2 - y_1}{x_2 - x_1} = \frac{6.20 - 3.80}{7 - 3} = \frac{2.4}{4} = 0.60$$

Use the point-slope form with either point. Substitute $(3, 3.80)$ for (x_1, y_1) and 0.60 for m. Then write the equation in slope intercept form by solving for y.

$$y - y_1 = m(x - x_1)$$
$$y - 3.80 = 0.60(x - 3)$$
$$y - 3.80 = 0.60x - 1.8$$
$$y = 0.60x + 2.00$$

b. The telephone call costs $0.60 per minute.

c. The telephone call has a flat fee of $2 per call.

d. $C(15) = 0.60(15) + 2.00 = 11$; The total cost of a 15 minute phone call is $11.

48. **a.** To find the x-intercept let $y = 0$ and solve for x.

$$4x - 640 = 0$$
$$4x = 640$$
$$x = 160$$

The x-intercept is $(160, 0)$. The business will break even when 160 units are produced and sold.

To find the y-intercept evaluate
$$P(0) = 4(0) - 640 = -640$$

The y-intercept is $(0, -640)$. The business has a loss of $640 when zero units are produced and sold.

b. Profit Interval: $(160, 300]$;

Loss interval: $[0, 160)$

49. **a.** $P(0) = -100(0)^2 + 8500(0) - 150000$

$$= -150000$$

The overhead costs are $150,000$.

b. $$P(x) = 0$$
$$-100x^2 + 8500x - 150000 = 0$$
$$-100(x^2 - 85x + 1500) = 0$$
$$-100(x - 60)(x - 25) = 0$$
$$x = 25 \text{ or } x = 60$$

The company will break even when either 25 or 60 tons are produced.

c. The maximum profit occurs at the vertex. To find the x-value of the vertex we use the formula $x = -\dfrac{b}{2a} = -\dfrac{8500}{2(-100)} = 42.5$.

To find the corresponding value of y for the vertex we evaluate
$$P(42.5) = -100(42.5)^2 + 8500(42.5) - 150000$$
$$= 30625$$

Thus the vertex is $(42.5, 30625)$. The company has a maximum profit of $30,625 when 42.5 tons are produced and sold.

d. $(25, 60)$

e. The company has a profit when between 25 and 60 tons are produced.

50. **a.**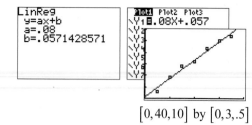

$[0,40,10]$ by $[0,3,.5]$

b. The slope of the line of best fit gives us the rate of centimeters stretched per kilogram of weight.

c.
$$y \approx 0.08x + 0.057$$
$$y \approx 0.08(12) + 0.057$$
$$y \approx 1.017$$

A mass of 12 kilograms would stretch the spring approximately 1.017 cm.

d. Solve the following equation.
$$0.08x + 0.057 = 2.4$$
$$0.08x + 0.057 - 0.057 = 2.4 - 0.057$$
$$0.08x = 2.343$$
$$\frac{0.08x}{0.08} = \frac{2.343}{0.08}$$
$$x \approx 29.29$$

A weight of approximately 29.29 kg is required to stretch the spring 2.4 cm.

51. **a.**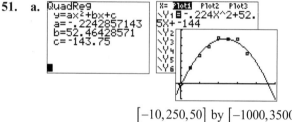

$[-10,250,50]$ by $[-1000,3500,500]$

b. $f(80) = -0.224(80)^2 + 52.5(80) - 144 \approx 2600$ (hundred dollars).

Thus the profit will be approximately \$260,000 when 80 units are sold in a quarter.

c.

The break-even values are $x = 3$ units and $x = 232$

d.

The maximum profit from parabola of best fit is approximately \$290,000 when 117 units are sold, but the table of data suggests that the maximum profit is \$300,000 and occurs when 100 units are sold.

52. The maximum height occurs at the vertex. To find the x-value of the vertex we use the formula

$$x = -\frac{b}{2a} = -\frac{56}{2(-16)} = 1.75 \, .$$

To find the corresponding value of y for the vertex we evaluate $H(4) = -16(1.75)^2 + 56(1.75) = 49$

Thus the vertex is $(1.75, \, 49)$. The ball reaches a maximum height of 49 feet 1.75 seconds after it is hit.

53. **a.** Let $w =$ the width of the storage area.

Let $l =$ the length of the storage area.

We know that the amount of fencing is 120 ft, thus $2w + l = 120$. If we solve for l we have $l = 120 - 2w$.

The area of the rectangle is $A = lw$

$$A = (120 - 2w)w$$

$$A = -2w^2 + 120w$$

b. The maximum area occurs at the vertex. To find the w-value of the vertex we use the formula

$$w = -\frac{b}{2a} = -\frac{120}{2(-2)} = \frac{120}{4} = 30.$$

Thus, the maximum area is $A(300) = -2(30)^2 + 120(30) = 1800 \text{ ft}^2$.

1. **a.** Each element in the domain is paired with exactly one output value in the range. Thus the relation is a function. Domain: $\{-3, 3, -4, 4\}$; Range: $\{9, 16\}$

b. The elements 9 and 16 are not paired with exactly one element in the range. Thus the relation is not a function.

c. No vertical line will cross the function more than once. Thus the graph represents a function. Domain: $\mathbb{R}$; Range: $[-1, \infty)$

d. No vertical line will cross the function more than once. Thus the graph represents a function. Domain: $\{-3, -2, 0, 1, 2\}$; Range: $\{-2, -1, 0, 1, 2\}$

e. The vertical line $x = 1$ crosses the graph more than once. Thus the graph does not represent a function.

f. Each element in the domain is paired with exactly one output value in the range. Thus the relation is a function.

2. **a.** $f(2) = 3(2)^2 + (2) - 12 = 2$

b. $f(-2) = 3(-2)^2 + (-2) - 12 = -2$

c. $f(0) = -3$

d. $f(2) = 0$

e. $f(-10) = -18$

f. $f(10) = 12$

3. **a.** In the table the change in the values of x is $\Delta x = 2$ while the corresponding change in y is $\Delta y = 3$.

Thus the slope is $m = \dfrac{\Delta y}{\Delta x} = \dfrac{3}{2}$.

b. $m = 1$

4. **a.**

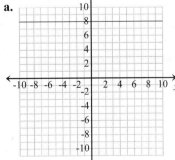

b.

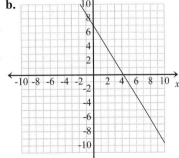

c.

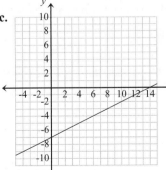

5. **a.** In the table the change in the values of x is $\Delta x = 2$ while the corresponding change in y is $\Delta y = -3$. The slope is $m = \dfrac{\Delta y}{\Delta x} = \dfrac{-3}{2} = -\dfrac{3}{2}$.

Also, in the table we can see that the y-intercept is $(0, -3)$. Thus the equation is $y = -\dfrac{3}{2}x - 3$.

b. In the table the change in the values of x is $\Delta x = 5$ while the corresponding change in y is $\Delta y = 4$.

Thus the slope is $m = \dfrac{\Delta y}{\Delta x} = \dfrac{4}{5}$.

Now, use the point slope form. Substitute $(4, -1)$ for (x_1, y_1) and $\dfrac{4}{5}$ for m. Then write the equation in slope intercept form by solving for y.

$$y - y_1 = m(x - x_1)$$
$$y - (-1) = \dfrac{4}{5}(x - 4)$$
$$y + 1 = \dfrac{4}{5}x - \dfrac{16}{5}$$
$$y = \dfrac{4}{5}x - \dfrac{21}{5}$$

6. **a.** The x-intercept is $(8, 0)$.

The y-intercept is $(0, -6)$.

b. To find the y-intercept set $x = 0$.
$$f(0) = -0.25(0) + 12 = 12$$
The y-intercept is $(0, 12)$.

To find the x-intercept set $y = 0$ $(f(x) = 0)$ and solve for x.
$$0 = -0.25x + 12$$
$$0.25x = 12$$
$$x = 48$$
The x-intercept is $(48, 0)$.

7. **a.** The linear function is negative (below the x-axis) on the interval $(-\infty, -2)$ and positve (above the x-axis) on the interval $(-2, \infty)$.

b. The linear function is negative if
$$-8x + 24 > 0$$
$$-8x > -24$$
$$x < 3$$

> Dividing by a *negative* number reverses the order of the inequality.

which is equivalent to the interval $(-\infty, 3)$.

The linear function is negative if
$$-8x + 24 < 0$$
$$-8x < -24$$
$$x > 3$$

> Dividing by a *negative* number reverses the order of the inequality.

which is equivalent to the interval $(3, \infty)$.

8. **a.** The graph opens upward.

b. The vertex is $(-2, -5)$

c.

d. The minimum value of y is -5.

e. The domain of the function is the projection of the graph onto the x-axis. Domain: $\mathbb{R}$.

f. The range of the function is the projection of the graph onto the y-axis. Range: $[-5, \infty)$

9. **a.** The y-intercept is found by letting $x = 0$. $f(0) = |0 + 2| - 5 = 2 - 5 = -3$, thus the y-intercept is $(0, -3)$

b. The x-intercepts are found by letting $y = 0$ and solving for x.

$$|x + 2| - 5 = 0$$
$$|x + 2| = 5$$

Is equivalent to

$$x + 2 = -5 \quad \text{or} \quad x + 2 = 5$$
$$x = -7 \qquad\qquad x = 3$$

The x-intercepts are $(-7, 0)$ and $(3, 0)$

10. **a.** Solve the inequality:

$$|x + 2| - 5 > 0$$
$$|x + 2| > 5$$

is equivalent to

$$x + 2 < -5 \quad \text{or} \quad x + 2 > 5$$
$$x < -7 \qquad\qquad x > 3$$

The function is positive on the interval

$$(-\infty, -7) \cup (3, \infty)$$

b. Solve the inequality:

$$|x + 2| - 5 < 0$$
$$|x + 2| < 5$$

is equivalent to

$$-5 < x + 2 < 5$$
$$-7 < x < 3$$

The function is negative on the interval

$$(-7, 3)$$

11. **a.** $y = -2x + 5$ is a line with a negative slope.

b. $y = 2x^2 - 5$ is a parabola that opens upward.

c. $y = 3x^2 - 4x + 5$ is a parabola that opens upward.

d. $y = 3x - 4$ is a line with a positive slope.

12. **a.** The vertex is $(1, -3)$.

b. To find the x-value of the vertex we use the formula $x = -\dfrac{b}{2a} = -\dfrac{8}{2(-1)} = 4$.

To find the corresponding value of y for the vertex we evaluate

$$f(4) = -(4)^2 + 8(4) - 15 = 1.$$

Vertex: $(4, 1)$.

13. **a.** The parabola will open upward because the leading coefficient is positive.

b. To find the x-value of the vertex we use the formula

$$x = -\frac{b}{2a} = -\frac{11}{2(2)} = -\frac{11}{4} = -2.75.$$

To find the corresponding value of y for the vertex we evaluate

$$y = 2(-2.75)^2 + 11(-2.75) - 41 = -55.125.$$

Vertex: $(-2.75, -55.125)$.

c. The x-intercepts are found by letting $y = 0$ and solving for x.

$$2x^2 + 11x - 40 = 0$$
$$(x + 8)(2x - 5) = 0$$
$$x = -8, \quad \text{or} \quad x = \frac{5}{2}$$

The x-intercepts are $(-8, 0)$ and $\left(\dfrac{5}{2}, 0\right)$

The y-intercept is found by letting $x = 0$.

$y = 2(0)^2 + 11(0) - 40 = -40$, thus the y-intercept is $(0, -40)$.

d.

x	y
-4	-52
-3	-55
-2	-54
-1	-49

e.

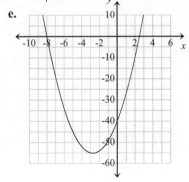

14. The maximum height occurs at the vertex. To find the *x*-value of the vertex we use the formula

$$x = -\frac{b}{2a} = -\frac{48}{2(-16)} = 1.5.$$

To find the corresponding value of *y* for the vertex we evaluate $y = -16(1.5)^2 + 48(1.5) + 4 = 40$

Thus the vertex is $(1.5, 40)$.

a. The ball reaches a maximum height of 40 feet.
b. It takes 1.5 seconds to reach its maximum height.

15. a. The function is decreasing.
b. The function is increasing.

16. a. To find the *x*-value of the vertex we use the formula $x = -\dfrac{b}{2a} = -\dfrac{3}{2(-1)} = \dfrac{3}{2}$.

To find the corresponding value of *y* for the vertex we evaluate

$$y = -\left(\frac{3}{2}\right)^2 + 3\left(\frac{3}{2}\right) + 10 = \frac{49}{4}.$$

Vertex: $\left(\dfrac{3}{2}, \dfrac{49}{4}\right)$.

b. The graph opens downward.
c. The *x*-intercepts are found by letting $y = 0$ and solving for *x*.

$$-x^2 + 3x + 10 = 0$$
$$-(x^2 - 3x - 10) = 0$$
$$-(x + 2)(x - 5)$$
$$x = -2 \quad \text{or} \quad x = 5$$

The *x*-intercepts are $(-2, 0)$ and $(5, 0)$

d. The *y*-intercept is found by letting $x = 0$;

$f(0) = -(0)^2 + 3(0) + 10 = 10$, thus the *y*-intercept is $(0, 10)$.

e. The domain of the function is the projection of the graph onto the *x*-axis. Domain: $\mathbb{R}$.

f. The range of the function is the projection of the graph onto the *y*-axis. Range: $\left(-\infty, \dfrac{49}{4}\right]$.

g. The function is positive (above the *x*-axis) on the interval: $(-2, 5)$.

h. The function is negative (below the *x*-axis) on the interval: $(-\infty, -2) \cup (5, \infty)$.

i. The function is decreasing over the interval: $\left(\dfrac{3}{2}, \infty\right)$.

j. The function is increasing over the interval: $\left(-\infty, \dfrac{3}{2}\right)$.

17. a.

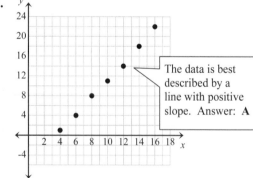

b.

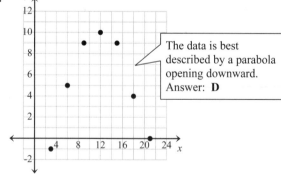

c.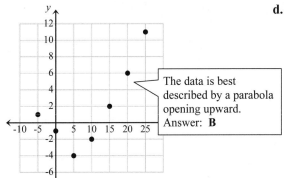

The data is best described by a parabola opening upward. Answer: **B**

d.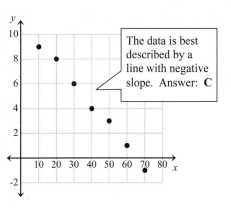

The data is best described by a line with negative slope. Answer: **C**

18. **a.**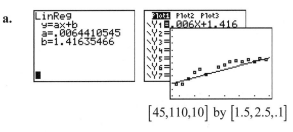

$[45, 110, 10]$ by $[1.5, 2.5, .1]$

b. The slope of the line of best fit gives us the rate at which the winning high jump heights are increasing per year. (0.6 cm per year)

c. $y \approx 0.006x + 1.416$

$y \approx 0.006(72) + 1.416$

$y \approx 1.848$

The winning high jump height is estimated to be approximately 1.848 m in 1972.

d. $y \approx 0.006x + 1.416$

$y \approx 0.006(112) + 1.416$

$y \approx 2.088$

The winning high jump height is estimated to be approximately 2.088 m in 2012.

19.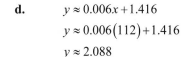

$[-10, 10, 1]$ by $[-40, 40, 4]$

The quadratic function of best fit is

$f(x) \approx 0.210x^2 - 0.497x - 3.49$

$f(7) \approx 0.210(7)^2 - 0.497(7) - 3.49 = 3.32$

Section 9.1: Graphs of Rational Functions and Reducing Rational Expressions

Quick Review 9.1

1. $56 = 2 \cdot 2 \cdot 2 \cdot 7 = 2^3 \cdot 7$

2. $\dfrac{36}{90} = \dfrac{\cancel{18} \cdot 2}{\cancel{18} \cdot 5} = \dfrac{2}{5}$

3. $-3x^3 + 4x^2 = -x^2(3x - 4)$

4. $x^3 - 6x^2 - 40x = x(x^2 - 6x - 40)$
   $$= x(x - 10)(x + 4)$$

5. $6x^2 + xy - 35y^2 = 6x^2 + 15xy - 14xy - 35y^2$
   $$= 3x(2x + 5y) - 7y(2x + 5y)$$
   $$= (2x + 5y)(3x - 7y)$$

Exercises 9.1

1. **a.** $f(x) = \dfrac{x}{x - 6}$ is a rational function whose graph will have a break. The proper choice is **C**.

    b. $f(x) = |5x - 2|$ is not a rational function. It is an absolute value function whose graph has a V-shape. The proper choice is **D**.

    c. $f(x) = 2x^2 - 3x - 4$ is a rational function whose graph is a parabola. The proper choice is **A**.

    d. $f(x) = 3x - 7$ is a rational function whose graph is a line. The proper choice is **B**.

3. **a.** $f(0) = \dfrac{2(0) + 1}{2(0) - 1} = \dfrac{1}{-1} = -1$

    b. $f(1) = \dfrac{2(1) + 1}{2(1) - 1} = \dfrac{3}{1} = 3$

    c. $f\left(\dfrac{1}{2}\right) = \dfrac{2\left(\dfrac{1}{2}\right) + 1}{2\left(\dfrac{1}{2}\right) - 1} = \dfrac{1 + 1}{1 - 1} = \dfrac{2}{0}$ is undefined.

5. **a.** Find the values that make the denominator zero.
    $$x - 4 = 0$$
    $$x = 4$$
    The excluded value is 4.

    b. The domain contains all real numbers except 4.
    Domain: $(-\infty, 4) \cup (4, +\infty)$ or $\mathbb{R} \sim \{4\}$

    c. Vertical asymptote: $x = 4$

7. If the excluded value is -3, then the domain is **C**. $(-\infty, -3) \cup (-3, +\infty)$.

9. If the excluded values are -3 and 0, then the domain is **D**. $(-\infty, -3) \cup (-3, 0) \cup (0, +\infty)$.

11. The excluded value of $f(x) = \dfrac{2x - 1}{x + 1}$ is $x = -1$ (The value that makes the denominator zero.) Answer: **D**.

13. The excluded values of $f(x) = \dfrac{2x - 1}{(x + 1)(2x + 1)}$ are $x = -1$ and $x = -\dfrac{1}{2}$ (The values that makes the denominator zero.) Answer: **C**.

15. a. Find the values that make the denominator zero.

$$2x - 1 = 0$$

$$x = \frac{1}{2}$$

The excluded value is $\frac{1}{2}$.

Domain: $\left(-\infty, \frac{1}{2}\right) \cup \left(\frac{1}{2}, \infty\right)$ or $\mathbb{R} \sim \left\{\frac{1}{2}\right\}$

b. Find the values that make the denominator zero.

$$x^2 - 81 = 0$$

$$(x + 9)(x - 9) = 0$$

The excluded values are -9 and 9.

Domain:

$$(-\infty, -9) \cup (-9, 9) \cup (9, \infty) \text{ or } \mathbb{R} \sim \{-9, 9\}$$

17. The value of x that gives us an error for y_1 is 1.5. Thus the excluded value is 1.5.

Domain: $(-\infty, 1.5) \cup (1.5, +\infty)$ or $\mathbb{R} \sim \{1.5\}$

19. The vertical asymptote of $f(x) = \dfrac{1}{x + 2}$ is $x = -2$. Thus the corresponding graph is **D**.

21. The vertical asymptote of $f(x) = \dfrac{1}{x - 4}$ is $x = 4$. Thus the corresponding graph is **B**.

23. C

25. D

27. $\dfrac{22a^2b^3}{33a^3b} = \dfrac{11a^2b\left(2b^2\right)}{11a^2b\left(3a\right)} = \dfrac{2b^2}{3a}$

29. $\dfrac{30x^2 - 45x}{5x} = \dfrac{5x\left(6x - 9\right)}{5x} = 6x - 9$

31. $\dfrac{7x}{14x^2 - 21x} = \dfrac{7x}{7x\left(2x - 3\right)} = \dfrac{1}{2x - 3}$

33. $\dfrac{a^2b\left(2x - 3y\right)}{-ab^2\left(2x - 3y\right)} = \dfrac{a\left[ab\left(2x - 3y\right)\right]}{-b\left[ab\left(2x - 3y\right)\right]} = -\dfrac{a}{b}$

35. $\dfrac{7x - 8y}{8y - 7x} = \dfrac{(-1)\left(8y - 7x\right)}{\left(8y - 7x\right)} = -1$

37. $\dfrac{ax - ay}{by - bx} = \dfrac{a\left(x - y\right)}{-b\left(x - y\right)} = -\dfrac{a}{b}$

39. $\dfrac{(x - 2y)(x + 5y)}{(x + 2y)(x + 5y)} = \dfrac{(x - 2y)\left(x + 5y\right)}{(x + 2y)\left(x + 5y\right)} = \dfrac{x - 2y}{x + 2y}$

41. $\dfrac{x^2 - y^2}{3x + 3y} = \dfrac{(x - y)\left(x + y\right)}{3\left(x + y\right)} = \dfrac{x - y}{3}$

43. $\dfrac{25x^2 - 4}{14 - 35x} = \dfrac{\left(5x - 2\right)(5x + 2)}{-7\left(5x - 2\right)} = -\dfrac{5x + 2}{7}$

45. $\dfrac{3x^2 - 2xy}{3x^2 - 5xy + 2y^2} = \dfrac{x\left(3x - 2y\right)}{\left(3x - 2y\right)(x - y)} = \dfrac{x}{x - y}$

47. $\dfrac{4x^2 + 12xy + 9y^2}{14x + 21y} = \dfrac{\left(2x + 3y\right)(2x + 3y)}{7\left(2x + 3y\right)} = \dfrac{2x + 3y}{7}$

49. $\dfrac{14ax + 21a}{35ay + 42a} = \dfrac{7a\left(2x + 3\right)}{7a\left(5y + 6\right)} = \dfrac{2x + 3}{5y + 6}$

51. $\dfrac{ax - y - z}{y + z - ax} = \dfrac{(-1)\left(y + z - ax\right)}{y + z - ax} = -1$

53. $\dfrac{2a^2 - ab - b^2}{a^2 - b^2} = \dfrac{(2a + b)\left(a - b\right)}{(a + b)\left(a - b\right)} = \dfrac{2a + b}{a + b}$

55. $\dfrac{vx + vy - wx - wy}{v^2 - w^2} = \dfrac{v(x + y) - w(x + y)}{(v - w)(v + w)}$

$$= \dfrac{\left(v - w\right)(x + y)}{\left(v - w\right)(v + w)} = \dfrac{x + y}{v + w}$$

57. $\dfrac{x^2 - 25}{3x^2 + 14x - 5} = \dfrac{(x - 5)\left(x + 5\right)}{(3x - 1)\left(x + 5\right)} = \dfrac{x - 5}{3x - 1}$

59. $\dfrac{5a^2+4ab-b^2}{5a^2-6ab+b^2}=\dfrac{(5a-b)(a+b)}{(5a-b)(a-b)}=\dfrac{a+b}{a-b}$

61. $\dfrac{(b^2-2b+1)-a^2}{5ab-5a+5a^2}=\dfrac{(b-1)^2-a^2}{5a(b-1+a)}$

$=\dfrac{[(b-1)+a][(b-1)-a]}{5a(b-1+a)}$

$=\dfrac{(b-1+a)(b-1-a)}{5a(b-1+a)}=\dfrac{b-a-1}{5a}$

$=\dfrac{-(a-b+1)}{5a}=-\dfrac{a-b+1}{5a}$

63. $\dfrac{4z^2-5w}{5w-4z^2}=\dfrac{(-1)(5w-4z^2)}{(5w-4z^2)}=-1$

65. $\dfrac{12x^2+24xy+12y^2}{16x^2-16y^2}=\dfrac{12(x^2+2xy+y^2)}{16(x^2-y^2)}$

$=\dfrac{3(x+y)(x+y)}{4(x-y)(x+y)}=\dfrac{3(x+y)}{4(x-y)}$

67. $\dfrac{14x^2-9xy+y^2}{y^2-7xy}=\dfrac{(7x-y)(2x-y)}{-y(7x-y)}$

$=-\dfrac{2x-y}{y}$

69. $\dfrac{b^4-1}{5b+5}=\dfrac{(b^2+1)(b^2-1)}{5(b+1)}=\dfrac{(b^2+1)(b-1)(b+1)}{5(b+1)}$

$=\dfrac{(b^2+1)(b-1)}{5}$

71. **a.** $T(6)=\dfrac{12}{6-2}=\dfrac{12}{4}=3$; A camper paddling at a rate of 6 miles per hour will travel the 12 miles upstream in 3 hours.

b. $T(8)=\dfrac{12}{8-2}=\dfrac{12}{6}=2$; A camper paddling at a rate of 8 miles per hour will travel the 12 miles upstream in 2 hours.

c. $T(2)=\dfrac{12}{2-2}=\dfrac{12}{0}$ is undefined ; A camper paddling at a rate of 2 miles per hour will never make it upstream (since the rate of the current is the same as that of the camper).

73. **a.** The average cost increases dramatically without bound.
   b. The average cost decreases and approaches \$4.00 per meter.

75. $\dfrac{7}{12}=\dfrac{7}{12}\cdot\dfrac{2}{2}=\dfrac{14}{24}$

77. $\dfrac{2x}{x-5}=\dfrac{2x}{(x-5)}\cdot\dfrac{7}{7}=\dfrac{14x}{7(x-5)}$

79. $\dfrac{7x-8y}{3a-5b}=\dfrac{(7x-8y)}{(3a-5b)}\cdot\dfrac{(-2)}{(-2)}=\dfrac{16y-14x}{10b-6a}$

81. $\dfrac{10}{a+b}=\dfrac{10}{(a+b)}\cdot\dfrac{(a-b)}{(a-b)}=\dfrac{10a-10b}{a^2-b^2}$

83. $\dfrac{5}{x-6}=\dfrac{5}{(x-6)}\cdot\dfrac{(x-1)}{(x-1)}=\dfrac{5x-5}{x^2-7x+6}$

85. $\dfrac{2x-y}{x+3y}=\dfrac{(2x-y)}{(x+3y)}\cdot\dfrac{(x+y)}{(x+y)}=\dfrac{2x^2+xy-y^2}{x^2+4xy+3y^2}$

Cumulative Review

1.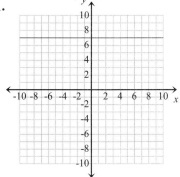

2.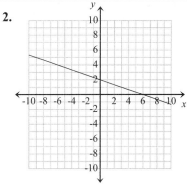

3.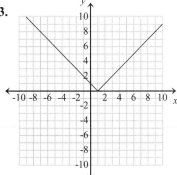

4.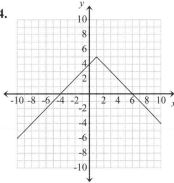

5.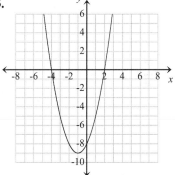

Section 9.2: Multiplying and Dividing Rational Expressions

Quick Review 9.2

1. $\dfrac{5}{3} \cdot \dfrac{2}{5} \cdot \dfrac{8}{5} = \dfrac{\cancel{5}}{3} \cdot \dfrac{2}{\cancel{5}} \cdot \dfrac{8}{5} = \dfrac{2 \cdot 8}{3 \cdot 5} = \dfrac{16}{15}$

2. $\dfrac{5}{3} \div \dfrac{2}{5} \cdot \dfrac{8}{5} = \dfrac{5}{3} \cdot \dfrac{5}{2} \cdot \dfrac{8}{5} = \dfrac{5}{3} \cdot \dfrac{\cancel{5}}{\cancel{2}} \cdot \dfrac{\overset{4}{\cancel{8}}}{\cancel{5}} = \dfrac{5 \cdot 4}{3} = \dfrac{20}{3}$

3. $\dfrac{5}{3} \div \left(\dfrac{2}{5} \cdot \dfrac{8}{5} \right) = \dfrac{5}{3} \div \left(\dfrac{2 \cdot 8}{5 \cdot 5} \right) = \dfrac{5}{3} \div \left(\dfrac{16}{25} \right)$

$\qquad = \dfrac{5}{3} \cdot \dfrac{25}{16} = \dfrac{5 \cdot 25}{3 \cdot 16} = \dfrac{125}{48}$

4. $\dfrac{3}{10} = \dfrac{3}{10} \cdot \dfrac{2}{2} = \dfrac{6}{20}; \quad \left(? = \dfrac{2}{2} \right)$

5. $\dfrac{5}{8} = \dfrac{5}{8} \cdot \dfrac{7}{7} = \dfrac{35}{56}; \quad \left(? = \dfrac{7}{7} \right)$

Exercises 9.2

1. $\dfrac{14}{15} \cdot \dfrac{55}{42} = \dfrac{(2)(7)(5)(11)}{(3)(5)(2)(3)(7)} = \dfrac{11}{9}$

3. $\dfrac{9}{35} \div \dfrac{27}{55} = \dfrac{9}{35} \cdot \dfrac{55}{27} = \dfrac{(9)(5)(11)}{(5)(7)(9)(3)} = \dfrac{11}{21}$

5. $\dfrac{7m}{9} \cdot \dfrac{6}{14m^2} = \dfrac{(7m)(2)(3)}{(3)(3)(2)(7m)(m)} = \dfrac{1}{3m}$

7. $\dfrac{66x^2}{30y} \div \dfrac{77x^8}{45y^3} = \dfrac{66x^2}{30y} \cdot \dfrac{45y^3}{77x^8}$

$= \dfrac{(2)(3)(11x^2)(15y)(3y^2)}{(2)(15y)(7)(11x^2)(x^6)} = \dfrac{9y^2}{7x^6}$

9. $\dfrac{x-2y}{6} \cdot \dfrac{3}{2y-x} = \dfrac{(x-2y)(3)}{(2)(3)(-1)(x-2y)} = -\dfrac{1}{2}$

11. $\dfrac{2x(x-1)}{6(x-3)} \cdot \dfrac{3(x+3)}{x^2(x+1)}$

$= \dfrac{(2)(x)(x-1)(3)(x+3)}{(2)(3)(x+3)(x)(x)(x+1)} = \dfrac{x-1}{x(x+1)}$

13. $\dfrac{(x-2)(x-3)}{10(x-2)} \cdot \dfrac{5(x-3)}{(x+3)(x-3)}$

$= \dfrac{(x-2)(x-3)(5)(x-3)}{(5)(2)(x-2)(x+3)(x-3)} = \dfrac{x-3}{2(x+3)}$

15. $\dfrac{x^2-y^2}{x^2-2xy+y^2} \div \dfrac{3x+3y}{7x-21} = \dfrac{x^2-y^2}{x^2-2xy+y^2} \cdot \dfrac{7x-21}{3x+3y}$

$= \dfrac{(x-y)(x+y)(7)(x-3)}{(x-y)(x-y)(3)(x+y)} = \dfrac{7(x-3)}{3(x-y)}$

17. $\dfrac{x^2-3x+2}{x^2-4x+4} \div \dfrac{x^2-2x+1}{3x^2-12} = \dfrac{x^2-3x+2}{x^2-4x+4} \cdot \dfrac{3x^2-12}{x^2-2x+1}$

$= \dfrac{(x-1)(x-2)(3)(x^2-4)}{(x-2)(x-2)(x-1)(x-1)} = \dfrac{3(x-2)(x+2)}{(x-2)(x-1)}$

$= \dfrac{3(x+2)}{x-1}$

19. $\dfrac{7(c-y)-a(c-y)}{2c^2-7cy+5y^2} \cdot \dfrac{2c-5y}{c-y}$

$= \dfrac{(7-a)(c-y)(2c-5y)}{(2c-5y)(c-y)(c-y)} = \dfrac{7-a}{c-y} = \dfrac{a-7}{y-c}$

21. $\dfrac{10y-14x}{x-1} \cdot \dfrac{x^2-2x+1}{21x-15y} = \dfrac{(2)(5y-7x)(x-1)(x-1)}{(x-1)(-3)(5y-7x)} = -\dfrac{2(x-1)}{3}$

23. $\dfrac{9x^2-9xy+9y^2}{5x^2y+5xy^2} \cdot \dfrac{2x^3y-2xy^3}{3x^2-3xy+3y^2} = \dfrac{\overset{3}{(9)}(x^2-xy+y^2)(2)(xy)(x^2-y^2)}{(5)(xy)(x+y)(3)(x^2-xy+y^2)} = \dfrac{6(x-y)(x+y)}{5(x+y)} = \dfrac{6(x-y)}{5}$

25. $\dfrac{4x^2-4}{18xy} \cdot \dfrac{30x^2y}{5-5x^2} = \dfrac{4(x^2-1)\left(30\,x^2\,y\right)}{18xy(-5)(x^2-1)} = -\dfrac{\overset{4}{120}\,x}{\underset{3}{90}} = -\dfrac{4x}{3}$

27. $(3x^2-14x-5) \cdot \dfrac{x^2-2x-35}{3x^2-20x-7} = \dfrac{(3x+1)(x-5)(x-7)(x+5)}{(3x+1)(x-7)} = (x-5)(x+5)$

29. $\dfrac{20x^2+3x-9}{21x-35x^2} \div \left(12x^2-11x-15\right) = \dfrac{\cancel{(5x-3)}\,\cancel{(4x+3)}}{(-7x)\,\cancel{(5x-3)}\,(3x-5)\,\cancel{(4x+3)}} = -\dfrac{1}{7x(3x-5)}$

31. $\dfrac{-4}{7} \cdot \left(\dfrac{15}{6} \div \dfrac{-10}{14}\right) = \dfrac{-4}{7} \cdot \left(\dfrac{15}{6} \cdot \dfrac{14}{-10}\right) = \dfrac{-4}{7} \cdot \left(\dfrac{\cancel{(5)}\,\cancel{(3)}\,\cancel{(2)}\,(7)}{-(2)\,\cancel{(3)}\,\cancel{(2)}\,\cancel{(5)}}\right) = \dfrac{-4}{\cancel{7}} \cdot \dfrac{\cancel{7}}{-2} = 2$

33. $\dfrac{18x^2}{5a} \cdot \dfrac{15ax}{81a^2} \cdot \dfrac{44ax}{24x^3} = \dfrac{(18)(15)(44)a^2x^4}{(5)(81)(24)a^3x^3}$

$= \dfrac{\cancel{(9)}\,\cancel{(2)}\,\cancel{(5)}\,\cancel{(3)}\,\cancel{(4)}\,(11)x^{4-3}}{\cancel{(5)}(3)(3)\,\cancel{(9)}\,\cancel{(4)}\,\cancel{(2)}\,\cancel{(3)}a^{3-2}} = \dfrac{11x}{9a}$

35. $\dfrac{x^2+x-y^2-y}{3x^2-3y^2} \div \dfrac{5x+5y+5}{7x^2y+7xy^2}$

$= \dfrac{\left(x^2-y^2\right)+(x-y)}{3\left(x^2-y^2\right)} \cdot \dfrac{7x^2y+7xy^2}{5x+5y+5}$

$= \dfrac{(x+y)(x-y)+(x-y)}{3(x+y)(x-y)} \cdot \dfrac{7xy(x+y)}{5(x+y+1)}$

$= \dfrac{\cancel{(x-y)}\left[\cancel{(x+y)+1}\right]}{3\cancel{(x+y)}\,\cancel{(x-y)}} \cdot \dfrac{7xy\,\cancel{(x+y)}}{5\cancel{(x+y+1)}} = \dfrac{7xy}{15}$

37. $\dfrac{2x-5}{2x^2-x-15} \cdot \dfrac{-2x^2-x+10}{3x+4} \cdot \dfrac{-15x-20}{2x^2-9x+10} = \dfrac{\cancel{(2x-5)}\,(-1)\left(2x^2+x-10\right)(-5)\,\cancel{(3x+4)}}{(2x+5)(x-3)\,\cancel{(3x+4)}\,\cancel{(2x-5)}\,(x-2)}$

$= \dfrac{(5)\,\cancel{(2x+5)}\,\cancel{(x-2)}}{\cancel{(2x+5)}\,(x-3)\,\cancel{(x-2)}} = \dfrac{5}{x-3}$

39. $\dfrac{5a-b}{a^2-5ab+4b^2} \div \left(\dfrac{6ab}{3a-12b} \cdot \dfrac{b^2-5ab}{4a-4b}\right)$

$= \dfrac{5a-b}{(a-4b)(a-b)} \div \left(\dfrac{(6ab)(b)(b-5a)}{3(a-4b)(4)(a-b)}\right)$

$= \dfrac{(-1)(b-5a)}{(a-4b)(a-b)} \cdot \dfrac{3(a-4b)(4)(a-b)}{(6ab)(b)(b-5a)}$

$= \dfrac{(-1)\,\cancel{(b-5a)}\,(3)\,\cancel{(a-4b)}\,(4)\,\cancel{(a-b)}}{\cancel{(a-4b)}\,\cancel{(a-b)}\,(6ab)(b)\,\cancel{(b-5a)}}$

$= \dfrac{-\overset{2}{\cancel{12}}}{\cancel{6}ab^2} = -\dfrac{2}{ab^2}$

41. $\dfrac{x^2-xy}{5x^2y^2} \div \dfrac{4x-4y}{3xy} \cdot \dfrac{20y}{11}$

$= \left(\dfrac{x(x-y)}{5x^2y^2} \cdot \dfrac{3xy}{4(x-y)}\right) \cdot \dfrac{20y}{11}$

$= \left(\dfrac{\cancel{(x-y)}\,(3)\,\cancel{(x^2)}\,\cancel{(y)}}{(5)\,\cancel{(x^2)}\,\cancel{(y^2)}\,(4)\,\cancel{(x-y)}}\right) \cdot \dfrac{20y}{11}$

$= \dfrac{3}{20y} \cdot \dfrac{\cancel{20y}}{11} = \dfrac{3}{11}$

43. $\dfrac{x(a-b+2c)-2y(a-b+2c)}{x^2-4xy+4y^2} \div \dfrac{2a^2-2ab+4ac}{7xy^2-14y^3} = \dfrac{\cancel{(x-2y)}\,\cancel{(a-b+2c)}}{\cancel{(x-2y)}\,\cancel{(x-2y)}} \cdot \dfrac{7y^2\,\cancel{(x-2y)}}{2a\,\cancel{(a-b+2c)}} = \dfrac{7y^2}{2a}$

45. $\dfrac{5x^2-5xy}{6x^2-6y^2} \div \dfrac{10xy}{x^2+2xy+y^2} = \dfrac{5x^2-5xy}{6x^2-6y^2} \cdot \dfrac{x^2+2xy+y^2}{10xy} = \dfrac{5x(x-y)}{6(x^2-y^2)} \cdot \dfrac{(x+y)(x+y)}{10xy}$

$$= \dfrac{\cancel{5}\,\cancel{x}\,\cancel{(x-y)}\,\cancel{(x+y)}\,(x+y)}{6\cancel{(x-y)}\,\cancel{(x+y)}\,\underset{2}{\cancel{10}}\,\cancel{x}y} = \dfrac{x+y}{12y}$$

	Problem	Mental Estimate	Calculator Approximation
47.	$\dfrac{(x+6)\,\cancel{(x-7)}}{\cancel{(x-7)}\,(x-6)}$	$\dfrac{(10+6)}{(10-6)} = \dfrac{16}{4} = 4$	3.99
49.	$\dfrac{x^2+50}{x^2-50}$	$\dfrac{(10)^2+50}{(10)^2-50} = \dfrac{150}{50} = 3$	2.99

51. Except for the excluded value, the table is equivalent to the one shown in **D**. Thus $y_1 = \dfrac{3x^2+6x+3}{(x+1)^2} = 3$.

53. Except for the excluded value, the table is equivalent to the one shown in **B**. Thus $y_1 = \dfrac{x^3+4x^2+4x}{(x+2)^2} = x$.

55. $12 \cdot (?) = 60$

$12 \cdot (?) = 12 \cdot 5$

$(?) = 5$

57. $\left(x^2 y^3\right) \div (?) = xy$

$(xy)\left(xy^2\right) \div (?) = xy$

$(?) = xy^2$

59. $\left(x^2-7x-8\right) \div (?) = x+1$

$(x-8)(x+1) \div (?) = x+1$

$(?) = (x-8)$

61. $\left(\dfrac{x+2}{x-3}\right) \cdot (?) = \dfrac{x^2-x-6}{x^2-6x+9}$

$\left(\dfrac{x+2}{x-3}\right) \cdot (?) = \dfrac{(x-3)(x+2)}{(x-3)(x-3)}$

$(?) = \left(\dfrac{x-3}{x-3}\right)$

63. $\left(\dfrac{2x^2-5x+2}{3x^2-4x+1}\right) \div (?) = \dfrac{2x-1}{3x-1}$

$\left(\dfrac{(2x-1)(x-2)}{(3x-1)(x-1)}\right) \div (?) = \dfrac{2x-1}{3x-1}$

$(?) = \dfrac{x-2}{x-1}$

65. **a.** $A(t) = \dfrac{C(t)}{N(t)} = \dfrac{200t + 200}{2t^2 - 2t} = \dfrac{\overset{100}{\cancel{200}}(t+1)}{\cancel{2}t(t-1)} = \dfrac{100(t+1)}{t(t-1)}$

b.

t	2	6	10	14	18	22
$A(t)$	150.00	23.33	12.22	8.24	6.21	4.98

c. The average cost increases without bound as the number of hours the factory operates is reduced to almost one hour.

d. The average cost decreases to about \$4.53 as the number of hours the factory operates is increased to almost 24 hours.

Cumulative Review

1. $2 - 5(3+1)^2 = 2 - 5(4)^2 = 2 - 5 \cdot 16$
$= 2 - 80 = -78$

2. $(2-5)(3+1)^2 = (-3)(4)^2 = -3 \cdot 16 = -48$

3. $2x - 5(3x+1)^2 = 2x - 5(9x^2 + 6x + 1)$
$= 2x - 45x^2 - 30x - 5$
$= -45x^2 - 30x + 2x - 5$
$= -45x^2 - 28x - 5$

4. $(2x-5)(3x+1)^2 = (2x-5)(9x^2 + 6x + 1)$
$= 18x^3 + 12x^2 + 2x - 45x^2 - 30x - 5$
$= 18x^3 + 12x^2 - 45x^2 + 2x - 30x - 5$
$= 18x^3 - 33x^2 - 28x - 5$

5. $\big((2x-5)(3x+1)\big)^2 = \big(6x^2 + 2x - 15x - 5\big)^2 = \big(6x^2 - 13x - 5\big)^2 = \big(6x^2 - 13x - 5\big)\big(6x^2 - 13x - 5\big)$
$= 36x^4 - 78x^3 - 30x^2 - 78x^3 + 169x^2 + 65x - 30x^2 + 65x + 25$
$= 36x^4 - 78x^3 - 78x^3 - 30x^2 + 169x^2 - 30x^2 + 65x + 65x + 25$
$= 36x^4 - 156x^3 + 109x^2 + 130x + 25$

Section 9.3: Adding and Subtracting Rational Expressions

Quick Review 9.3

1. $\dfrac{7}{12} + \dfrac{3}{12} = \dfrac{7+3}{12} = \dfrac{10}{12} = \dfrac{\cancel{2} \cdot 5}{\cancel{2} \cdot 6} = \dfrac{5}{6}$

2. $\dfrac{17}{24} - \dfrac{5}{24} = \dfrac{17-5}{24} = \dfrac{12}{24} = \dfrac{\cancel{12}}{2 \cdot \cancel{12}} = \dfrac{1}{2}$

3. $\dfrac{2}{3} - \dfrac{1}{12} = \dfrac{2}{3} \cdot \dfrac{4}{4} - \dfrac{1}{12} = \dfrac{8}{12} - \dfrac{1}{12} = \dfrac{8-1}{12} = \dfrac{7}{12}$

4. $\dfrac{3}{24} + \dfrac{5}{16} = \dfrac{\cancel{3}}{\cancel{3} \cdot 8} + \dfrac{5}{16} = \dfrac{1}{8} + \dfrac{5}{16}$
$= \dfrac{1}{8} \cdot \dfrac{2}{2} + \dfrac{5}{16} = \dfrac{2}{16} + \dfrac{5}{16} = \dfrac{2+5}{16} = \dfrac{7}{16}$

5. $\dfrac{1}{6} + \dfrac{2}{3} - \dfrac{1}{4} = \dfrac{1}{6} \cdot \dfrac{2}{2} + \dfrac{2}{3} \cdot \dfrac{4}{4} - \dfrac{1}{4} \cdot \dfrac{3}{3} = \dfrac{2}{12} + \dfrac{8}{12} - \dfrac{3}{12} = \dfrac{2+8-3}{12} = \dfrac{7}{12}$

Exercises 9.3

1. $\dfrac{5b+13}{3b^2} + \dfrac{b-4}{3b^2} = \dfrac{(5b+13) + (b-4)}{3b^2}$
$= \dfrac{5b+13+b-4}{3b^2} = \dfrac{6b+9}{3b^2} = \dfrac{\cancel{3}(2b+3)}{\cancel{3}b^2} = \dfrac{2b+3}{b^2}$

3. $\dfrac{7}{x-7} - \dfrac{x}{x-7} = \dfrac{7-x}{x-7} = \dfrac{(-1)\cancel{(x-7)}}{\cancel{(x-7)}} = -1$

5. $\dfrac{3s+7}{s^2-9}+\dfrac{s+5}{s^2-9}=\dfrac{(3s+7)+(s+5)}{s^2-9}$

$=\dfrac{3s+7+s+5}{s^2-9}=\dfrac{4s+12}{s^2-9}=\dfrac{4(s+3)}{(s-3)(s+3)}=\dfrac{4}{s-3}$

7. $\dfrac{x+a}{x(a+b)+y(a+b)}-\dfrac{x-b}{x(a+b)+y(a+b)}$

$=\dfrac{(x+a)-(x-b)}{x(a+b)+y(a+b)}=\dfrac{x+a-x+b}{(x+y)(a+b)}$

$=\dfrac{a+b}{(x+y)(a+b)}=\dfrac{1}{x+y}$

9. $\dfrac{1}{15xy^2}+\dfrac{2}{27x^2y}=\dfrac{1}{15xy^2}\left(\dfrac{9x}{9x}\right)+\dfrac{2}{27x^2y}\left(\dfrac{5y}{5y}\right)$

$=\dfrac{9x}{135x^2y^2}+\dfrac{10y}{135x^2y^2}$

$=\dfrac{9x+10y}{135x^2y^2}$

11. $\dfrac{a+b}{21(3a-b)}-\dfrac{a-b}{14(3a-b)}$

$=\dfrac{a+b}{21(3a-b)}\left(\dfrac{2}{2}\right)-\dfrac{a-b}{14(3a-b)}\left(\dfrac{3}{3}\right)$

$=\dfrac{2a+2b}{42(3a-b)}-\dfrac{3a-3b}{42(3a-b)}$

$=\dfrac{-a+5b}{42(3a-b)}$

13. $\dfrac{2}{(x-3)(x-15)}+\dfrac{1}{(x-3)(x+3)}=\dfrac{2}{(x-3)(x-15)}\left(\dfrac{x+3}{x+3}\right)+\dfrac{1}{(x-3)(x+3)}\left(\dfrac{x-15}{x-15}\right)$

$=\dfrac{2(x+3)}{(x-3)(x-15)(x+3)}+\dfrac{x-15}{(x-3)(x-15)(x+3)}$

$=\dfrac{3(x-3)}{(x-3)(x-15)(x+3)}$

$=\dfrac{3}{(x-15)(x+3)}$

15. $\dfrac{4}{9w}-\dfrac{7}{6w}=\dfrac{4}{9w}\cdot\dfrac{2}{2}-\dfrac{7}{6w}\cdot\dfrac{3}{3}=\dfrac{8}{18w}-\dfrac{21}{18w}$

$=\dfrac{8-21}{18w}=-\dfrac{13}{18w}$

17. $\dfrac{3v-1}{7v}-\dfrac{v-2}{14v}=\dfrac{3v-1}{7v}\cdot\dfrac{4}{4}-\dfrac{v-2}{14v}\cdot\dfrac{2}{2}$

$=\dfrac{4(3v-1)}{28v}-\dfrac{2(v-2)}{28v}=\dfrac{4(3v-1)-2(v-2)}{28v}$

$=\dfrac{12v-4-2v+4}{28v}=\dfrac{10v}{28v}=\dfrac{5}{14}$

19. $\dfrac{4}{b}+\dfrac{b}{b+4}=\dfrac{4}{b}\cdot\dfrac{b+4}{b+4}+\dfrac{b}{b+4}\cdot\dfrac{b}{b}=\dfrac{4(b+4)}{b(b+4)}+\dfrac{b^2}{b(b+4)}=\dfrac{4(b+4)+b^2}{b(b+4)}=\dfrac{4b+16+b^2}{b(b+4)}=\dfrac{b^2+4b+16}{b(b+4)}$

21. $5-\dfrac{1}{x}=\dfrac{5}{1}\cdot\dfrac{x}{x}-\dfrac{1}{x}=\dfrac{5x}{x}-\dfrac{1}{x}=\dfrac{5x-1}{x}$

23. $\dfrac{1}{x}-\dfrac{2}{x^2}+\dfrac{3}{x^3}=\dfrac{1}{x}\cdot\dfrac{x^2}{x^2}-\dfrac{2}{x^2}\cdot\dfrac{x}{x}+\dfrac{3}{x^3}=\dfrac{x^2}{x^3}-\dfrac{2x}{x^3}+\dfrac{3}{x^3}=\dfrac{x^2-2x+3}{x^3}$

25. $\dfrac{3}{x-2} - \dfrac{2}{x+3} = \dfrac{3}{x-2} \cdot \dfrac{x+3}{x+3} - \dfrac{2}{x+3} \cdot \dfrac{x-2}{x-2}$

$= \dfrac{3(x+3)}{(x-2)(x+3)} - \dfrac{2(x-2)}{(x+3)(x-2)}$

$= \dfrac{3(x+3) - 2(x-2)}{(x-2)(x+3)} = \dfrac{3x+9-2x+4}{(x-2)(x+3)}$

$= \dfrac{x+13}{(x-2)(x+3)}$

27. $\dfrac{x}{x-1} - \dfrac{x}{x+1} = \dfrac{x}{x-1} \cdot \dfrac{x+1}{x+1} - \dfrac{x}{x+1} \cdot \dfrac{x-1}{x-1}$

$= \dfrac{x(x+1)}{(x-1)(x+1)} - \dfrac{x(x-1)}{(x+1)(x-1)}$

$= \dfrac{x(x+1) - x(x-1)}{(x-1)(x+1)} = \dfrac{x^2+x-x^2+x}{(x-1)(x+1)}$

$= \dfrac{2x}{(x-1)(x+1)}$

29. $\dfrac{x+5}{x-4} - \dfrac{x+3}{x+2} = \dfrac{x+5}{x-4} \cdot \dfrac{x+2}{x+2} - \dfrac{x+3}{x+2} \cdot \dfrac{x-4}{x-4}$

$= \dfrac{(x+5)(x+2)}{(x-4)(x+2)} - \dfrac{(x+3)(x-4)}{(x+2)(x-4)}$

$= \dfrac{(x^2+7x+10) - (x^2-x-12)}{(x-4)(x+2)}$

$= \dfrac{x^2+7x+10 - x^2+x+12}{(x-4)(x+2)}$

$= \dfrac{8x+22}{(x-4)(x+2)} \text{ or } \dfrac{2(4x+11)}{(x-4)(x+2)}$

31. $\dfrac{x-1}{x+2} + \dfrac{x+2}{x-1} = \dfrac{x-1}{x+2} \cdot \dfrac{x-1}{x-1} + \dfrac{x+2}{x-1} \cdot \dfrac{x+2}{x+2}$

$= \dfrac{(x-1)(x-1)}{(x+2)(x-1)} + \dfrac{(x+2)(x+2)}{(x-1)(x+2)}$

$= \dfrac{(x^2-2x+1) + (x^2+4x+4)}{(x+2)(x-1)}$

$= \dfrac{x^2-2x+1+x^2+4x+4}{(x+2)(x-1)} = \dfrac{2x^2+2x+5}{(x+2)(x-1)}$

33. $\dfrac{x}{77x-121y} - \dfrac{y}{49x-77y} = \dfrac{x}{11(7x-11y)} - \dfrac{y}{7(7x-11y)} = \dfrac{x}{11(7x-11y)} \cdot \dfrac{7}{7} - \dfrac{y}{7(7x-11y)} \cdot \dfrac{11}{11}$

$= \dfrac{7x}{77(7x-11y)} - \dfrac{11y}{77(7x-11y)} = \dfrac{7x-11y}{77(7x-11y)} = \dfrac{\cancel{(7x-11y)}}{77\cancel{(7x-11y)}} = \dfrac{1}{77}$

35. $\dfrac{2}{(m+1)(m-2)} + \dfrac{3}{(m-2)(m+3)} = \dfrac{2}{(m+1)(m-2)} \cdot \dfrac{m+3}{m+3} + \dfrac{3}{(m-2)(m+3)} \cdot \dfrac{m+1}{m+1}$

$= \dfrac{2(m+3)}{(m+1)(m-2)(m+3)} + \dfrac{3(m+1)}{(m-2)(m+3)(m+1)} = \dfrac{(2m+6) + (3m+3)}{(m+1)(m-2)(m+3)}$

$= \dfrac{5m+9}{(m+1)(m-2)(m+3)}$

37. $\dfrac{m+2}{m^2-6m+8} - \dfrac{8-3m}{m^2-5m+6} = \dfrac{m+2}{(m-4)(m-2)} - \dfrac{8-3m}{(m-2)(m-3)} = \dfrac{m+2}{(m-4)(m-2)} \cdot \dfrac{m-3}{m-3} - \dfrac{8-3m}{(m-2)(m-3)} \cdot \dfrac{m-4}{m-4}$

$= \dfrac{(m+2)(m-3)}{(m-4)(m-2)(m-3)} - \dfrac{(8-3m)(m-4)}{(m-2)(m-3)(m-4)} = \dfrac{(m^2-m-6) - (-3m^2+20m-32)}{(m-4)(m-2)(m-3)}$

$= \dfrac{m^2-m-6+3m^2-20m+32}{(m-4)(m-2)(m-3)} = \dfrac{4m^2-21m+26}{(m-4)(m-2)(m-3)} = \dfrac{(4m-13)\cancel{(m-2)}}{(m-4)\cancel{(m-2)}(m-3)}$

$= \dfrac{4m-13}{(m-4)(m-3)}$

39. $\dfrac{1}{a-3b}+\dfrac{b}{a^2-7ab+12b^2}+\dfrac{1}{a-4b}=\dfrac{1}{a-3b}+\dfrac{b}{(a-3b)(a-4b)}+\dfrac{1}{a-4b}$

$$=\dfrac{1}{a-3b}\cdot\dfrac{a-4b}{a-4b}+\dfrac{b}{(a-3b)(a-4b)}+\dfrac{1}{a-4b}\cdot\dfrac{a-3b}{a-3b}$$

$$=\dfrac{(a-4b)}{(a-3b)(a-4b)}+\dfrac{b}{(a-3b)(a-4b)}+\dfrac{(a-3b)}{(a-4b)(a-3b)}$$

$$=\dfrac{(a-4b)+b+(a-3b)}{(a-3b)(a-4b)}=\dfrac{2a-6b}{(a-3b)(a-4b)}=\dfrac{2(a-3b)}{(a-3b)(a-4b)}=\dfrac{2}{a-4b}$$

41. $\dfrac{1}{2}(x)\left(\dfrac{1}{x-1}\right)+\left(\dfrac{1}{x-1}\right)(x+1)=\dfrac{x}{2(x-1)}+\dfrac{2(x+1)}{2(x-1)}$

$$=\dfrac{x+2x+2}{2(x-1)}$$

$$=\dfrac{3x+2}{2(x-1)}\ \text{cm}^2$$

43. a. $\dfrac{8}{t}+\dfrac{8}{t+5}=\dfrac{8}{t}\cdot\dfrac{t+5}{t+5}+\dfrac{8}{t+5}\cdot\dfrac{t}{t}$

$$=\dfrac{8(t+5)+8t}{t(t+5)}=\dfrac{8t+40+8t}{t(t+5)}$$

$$=\dfrac{16t+40}{t(t+5)}=\dfrac{8(2t+5)}{t(t+5)}$$

b.

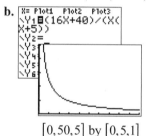

$[0,50,5]$ by $[0,5,1]$

If the time required to paint the house becomes very large, the fractional portion of the job completed in 8 hours approaches 0.

45. a. $\dfrac{90}{r}+\dfrac{165}{r+10}=\dfrac{90}{r}\cdot\dfrac{r+10}{r+10}+\dfrac{165}{r+10}\cdot\dfrac{r}{r}$

$$=\dfrac{90(r+10)+165r}{r(r+10)}$$

$$=\dfrac{90r+900+165r}{r(r+10)}=\dfrac{255r+900}{r(r+10)}$$

b. $\dfrac{255r+900}{r(r+10)}=\dfrac{255(45)+900}{(45)\big((45)+10\big)}=5\ \text{hours}$

47. The table is equivalent to the one shown in **A**. Thus $y_1=\dfrac{5}{x-1}+\dfrac{3}{x+2}=\dfrac{8x+7}{(x-1)(x+2)}$.

49. The table is equivalent to the one shown in **D**. Thus $y_1=\dfrac{2x}{x-1}-\dfrac{2x}{x+2}=\dfrac{6x}{(x-1)(x+2)}$.

51. $\dfrac{x^2+5}{x^2-3x+4}-2=\dfrac{x^2+5}{x^2-3x+4}-\dfrac{2}{1}\cdot\dfrac{x^2-3x+4}{x^2-3x+4}=\dfrac{(x^2+5)-2(x^2-3x+4)}{x^2-3x+4}=\dfrac{x^2+5-2x^2+6x-8}{x^2-3x+4}=\dfrac{-x^2+6x-3}{x^2-3x+4}$

53. $\dfrac{5}{2x+2}+\dfrac{x+5}{2x^2-2}-\dfrac{3}{x-1}=\dfrac{5}{2(x+1)}+\dfrac{x+5}{2(x-1)(x+1)}-\dfrac{3}{x-1}=\dfrac{5}{2(x+1)}\cdot\dfrac{x-1}{x-1}+\dfrac{x+5}{2(x-1)(x+1)}-\dfrac{3}{x-1}\cdot\dfrac{2(x+1)}{2(x+1)}$

$$=\dfrac{5(x-1)+(x+5)-6(x+1)}{2(x-1)(x+1)}=\dfrac{5x-5+x+5-6x-6}{2(x-1)(x+1)}=\dfrac{-6}{2(x-1)(x+1)}=\dfrac{-3}{(x-1)(x+1)}$$

55. $\dfrac{1}{x-5}+\dfrac{1}{x+5}-\dfrac{10}{x^2-25}=\dfrac{1}{x-5}\cdot\dfrac{x+5}{x+5}+\dfrac{1}{x+5}\cdot\dfrac{x-5}{x-5}-\dfrac{10}{(x-5)(x+5)}=\dfrac{(x+5)+(x-5)-10}{(x-5)(x+5)}$

$$=\dfrac{x+5+x-5-10}{(x-5)(x+5)}=\dfrac{2x-10}{(x-5)(x+5)}=\dfrac{2\cancel{(x-5)}}{\cancel{(x-5)}(x+5)}=\dfrac{2}{x+5}$$

57. $\dfrac{3}{s-5t}+\dfrac{7}{s-2t}-\dfrac{9t}{s^2-7st+10t^2}=\dfrac{3}{s-5t}\cdot\dfrac{s-2t}{s-2t}+\dfrac{7}{s-2t}\cdot\dfrac{s-5t}{s-5t}-\dfrac{9t}{(s-2t)(s-5t)}=\dfrac{3(s-2t)+7(s-5t)-9t}{(s-2t)(s-5t)}$

$$=\dfrac{3s-6t+7s-35t-9t}{(s-2t)(s-5t)}=\dfrac{10s-50t}{(s-2t)(s-5t)}=\dfrac{10\cancel{(s-5t)}}{(s-2t)\cancel{(s-5t)}}=\dfrac{10}{s-2t}$$

59. $\dfrac{2z+11}{z^2+z-6}+\dfrac{2}{z+3}-\dfrac{3}{z-2}=\dfrac{2z+11}{(z+3)(z-2)}+\dfrac{2}{z+3}\cdot\dfrac{z-2}{z-2}-\dfrac{3}{z-2}\cdot\dfrac{z+3}{z+3}=\dfrac{(2z+11)+2(z-2)-3(z+3)}{(z+3)(z-2)}$

$$=\dfrac{2z+11+2z-4-3z-9}{(z+3)(z-2)}=\dfrac{\cancel{(z-2)}}{(z+3)\cancel{(z-2)}}=\dfrac{1}{z+3}$$

61. $\dfrac{v+w}{vw}+\dfrac{w}{v^2-vw}-\dfrac{1}{w}=\dfrac{v+w}{vw}+\dfrac{w}{v(v-w)}-\dfrac{1}{w}=\dfrac{v+w}{vw}\cdot\dfrac{v-w}{v-w}+\dfrac{w}{v(v-w)}\cdot\dfrac{w}{w}-\dfrac{1}{w}\cdot\dfrac{v(v-w)}{v(v-w)}$

$$=\dfrac{(v+w)(v-w)+w^2-v(v-w)}{vw(v-w)}=\dfrac{v^2-w^2+w^2-v^2+vw}{vw(v-w)}=\dfrac{\cancel{vw}}{\cancel{vw}(v-w)}=\dfrac{1}{v-w}$$

63. $\dfrac{9w+2}{3w^2-2w-8}-\dfrac{7}{4-w-3w^2}=\dfrac{9w+2}{3w^2-2w-8}+\dfrac{7}{(-1)(4-w-3w^2)}=\dfrac{9w+2}{3w^2-2w-8}+\dfrac{7}{3w^2+w-4}$

$$=\dfrac{9w+2}{(3w+4)(w-2)}+\dfrac{7}{(3w+4)(w-1)}$$

$$=\dfrac{9w+2}{(3w+4)(w-2)}\cdot\dfrac{w-1}{w-1}+\dfrac{7}{(3w+4)(w-1)}\cdot\dfrac{w-2}{w-2}=\dfrac{(9w+2)(w-1)+7(w-2)}{(3w+4)(w-2)(w-1)}$$

$$=\dfrac{(9w^2-7w-2)+(7w-14)}{(3w+4)(w-2)(w-1)}=\dfrac{9w^2-7w-2+7w-14}{(3w+4)(w-2)(w-1)}=\dfrac{9w^2-16}{(3w+4)(w-2)(w-1)}$$

$$=\dfrac{\cancel{(3w+4)}(3w-4)}{\cancel{(3w+4)}(w-2)(w-1)}=\dfrac{3w-4}{(w-2)(w-1)}$$

65. $\dfrac{2w-7}{w^2-5w+6} - \dfrac{2-4w}{w^2-w-6} + \dfrac{5w+2}{4-w^2} = \dfrac{2w-7}{(w-2)(w-3)} - \dfrac{2-4w}{(w-3)(w+2)} - \dfrac{5w+2}{(w-2)(w+2)}$

$$= \dfrac{2w-7}{(w-2)(w-3)} \cdot \dfrac{w+2}{w+2} - \dfrac{2-4w}{(w-3)(w+2)} \cdot \dfrac{w-2}{w-2} - \dfrac{5w+2}{(w-2)(w+2)} \cdot \dfrac{w-3}{w-3}$$

$$= \dfrac{(2w-7)(w+2) - (2-4w)(w-2) - (5w+2)(w-3)}{(w-2)(w-3)(w+2)}$$

$$= \dfrac{(2w^2-3w-14) - (-4w^2+10w-4) - (5w^2-13w-6)}{(w-2)(w-3)(w+2)}$$

$$= \dfrac{2w^2-3w-14+4w^2-10w+4-5w^2+13w+6}{(w-2)(w-3)(w+2)} = \dfrac{w^2-4}{(w-2)(w-3)(w+2)}$$

$$= \dfrac{\cancel{(w-2)}\,\cancel{(w+2)}}{\cancel{(w-2)}\,(w-3)\,\cancel{(w+2)}} = \dfrac{1}{w-3}$$

67. $\dfrac{4m}{1-m^2} + \dfrac{2}{m+1} - 2 = \dfrac{-4m}{m^2-1} + \dfrac{2}{m+1} - 2 = \dfrac{-4m}{(m-1)(m+1)} + \dfrac{2}{m+1} \cdot \dfrac{m-1}{m-1} - \dfrac{2}{1} \cdot \dfrac{(m-1)(m+1)}{(m-1)(m+1)}$

$$= \dfrac{(-4m)+2(m-1)-2(m^2-1)}{(m-1)(m+1)} = \dfrac{-4m+2m-2-2m^2+2}{(m-1)(m+1)} = \dfrac{-2m^2-2m}{(m-1)(m+1)}$$

$$= \dfrac{-2m\,\cancel{(m+1)}}{(m-1)\,\cancel{(m+1)}} = \dfrac{-2m}{m-1}$$

69. Let $R(x)$ be the rational expression.

$$R(x) + \dfrac{1}{x+5} = \dfrac{4x}{2x^2+5x-25}$$

$$R(x) = \dfrac{4x}{2x^2+5x-25} - \dfrac{1}{x+5}$$

$$R(x) = \dfrac{4x}{(2x-5)(x+5)} - \dfrac{1}{x+5} \cdot \dfrac{2x-5}{2x-5}$$

$$R(x) = \dfrac{4x-(2x-5)}{(2x-5)(2x+5)}$$

$$R(x) = \dfrac{2x+5}{(2x-5)(x+5)}$$

Cumulative Review

1. A line that is parallel to $y = \dfrac{2}{5}x + 1$ will have a slope of $m = \dfrac{2}{5}$.

2. A line that is perpendicular to $y = \dfrac{2}{5}x + 1$ will have a slope of $m = -\dfrac{5}{2}$.

3. To eliminate x, multiply both sides of the first equation by -5, then multiply the second equation by 2 and add the two equations. Solve this equation for y.

$$2x + 3y = -10 \qquad 10x + 15y = -50$$
$$-5x + 7y = -62 \qquad \underline{-10x + 14y = -124}$$
$$29y = -174$$
$$y = -6$$

Back substitute -6 for y in the first equation to find x.
$$2x + 3y = -10$$
$$2x + 3(-6) = -10$$
$$2x - 18 = -10$$
$$2x = 8$$
$$x = 4$$

The system is a consistent system of independent equations. The solution is $(4, -6)$.

4. To eliminate x, multiply both sides of the first equation by 3, and add the two equations.

$$2x + 3y = 5 \qquad 6x + 9y = 15$$
$$-6x - 9y = 15 \qquad \underline{-6x - 9y = 15}$$
$$0 = 30$$

Since the resulting equation is a contradiction, the system is inconsistent. No solution.

5. To eliminate x, multiply both sides of the second equation by 3, and add the two equations.

$$2x + 3y = 12 \qquad 2x + 3y = 12$$
$$\frac{2}{3}x + y = 4 \qquad \underline{-2x - 3y = -12}$$
$$0 = 0$$

Since the resulting equation is an identity, the system is a consistent system of dependent equations. There are infinitely many solutions.

Section 9.4: Combining Operations and Simplifying Complex Rational Expressions

Quick Review 9.4

1. The LCD of $\dfrac{3}{20}$ and $\dfrac{17}{45}$ is 180.

2. The LCD of $\dfrac{x}{x-y}$ and $\dfrac{y}{x+y}$ is $(x-y)(x+y)$.

3. $-5^2 + 2(11-4) = -25 + 2(7) = -25 + 14 = -11$

4. $(-5)^2 + 2(11) - 4 = 25 + 22 - 4 = 47 - 4 = 43$

5. $x^{-1} + 3x^{-2} = \dfrac{1}{x} + \dfrac{3}{x^2}$

Exercises 9.4

1. a. $\dfrac{2x}{3} + \dfrac{x^2}{15} \cdot \dfrac{5}{x} = \dfrac{2x}{3} + \dfrac{5x^{\cancel{2}x}}{\cancel{15}x_3} = \dfrac{2x}{3} + \dfrac{x}{3}$

$$= \dfrac{2x + x}{3} = \dfrac{\cancel{3}x}{\cancel{3}} = x$$

b. $\left(\dfrac{2x}{3} + \dfrac{x^2}{15}\right) \cdot \dfrac{5}{x} = \left(\dfrac{2x}{3} \cdot \dfrac{5}{5} + \dfrac{x^2}{15}\right) \cdot \dfrac{5}{x} = \left(\dfrac{10x}{15} + \dfrac{x^2}{15}\right) \cdot \dfrac{5}{x}$

$$= \left(\dfrac{10x + x^2}{15}\right) \cdot \dfrac{5}{x} = \dfrac{5x(10 + x)}{15x}$$

$$= \dfrac{\cancel{5}x(10+x)}{\cancel{15}x_3} = \dfrac{x + 10}{3}$$

3. a. $-\dfrac{2y}{3} + \dfrac{y^2}{6} \div \dfrac{y}{9} = -\dfrac{2y}{3} + \dfrac{y^2}{6} \cdot \dfrac{9}{y} = -\dfrac{2y}{3} + \dfrac{9y^{\cancel{2}3y}}{\cancel{6}y_2}$

$$= -\dfrac{2y}{3} + \dfrac{3y}{2} = -\dfrac{2y}{3} \cdot \dfrac{2}{2} + \dfrac{3y}{2} \cdot \dfrac{3}{3}$$

$$= \dfrac{-4y}{6} + \dfrac{9y}{6} = \dfrac{-4y + 9y}{6} = \dfrac{5y}{6}$$

b. $\left(-\dfrac{2y}{3} + \dfrac{y^2}{6}\right) \div \dfrac{y}{9} = \left(-\dfrac{2y}{3} \cdot \dfrac{2}{2} + \dfrac{y^2}{6}\right) \div \dfrac{y}{9}$

$$= \left(-\dfrac{4y}{6} + \dfrac{y^2}{6}\right) \div \dfrac{y}{9} = \left(\dfrac{-4y + y^2}{6}\right) \div \dfrac{y}{9}$$

$$= \left(\dfrac{y(y-4)}{6}\right) \cdot \dfrac{9}{y} = \dfrac{\cancel{9}^3 \cancel{y}(y-4)}{\cancel{6}\cancel{y}_2}$$

$$= \dfrac{3(y-4)}{2} \text{ or } \dfrac{3y - 12}{2}$$

5. **a.** $\dfrac{v}{v-6} - \dfrac{3}{v+2} \cdot \dfrac{2v+4}{v^2-6v} = \dfrac{v}{v-6} - \dfrac{3}{v+2} \cdot \dfrac{2(v+2)}{v(v-6)} = \dfrac{v}{v-6} - \dfrac{3}{v+2} \cdot \dfrac{2(v+2)}{v(v-6)} = \dfrac{v}{v-6} - \dfrac{6(v+2)}{v(v+2)(v-6)}$

$= \dfrac{v}{v-6} \cdot \dfrac{v(v+2)}{v(v+2)} - \dfrac{6(v+2)}{v(v+2)(v-6)} = \dfrac{(v^3+2v^2)-6(v+2)}{v(v+2)(v-6)} = \dfrac{v^3+2v^2-6v-12}{v(v+2)(v-6)}$

$= \dfrac{v^2(v+2)-6(v+2)}{v(v+2)(v-6)} = \dfrac{(v^2-6)\cancel{(v+2)}}{v\cancel{(v+2)}(v-6)} = \dfrac{v^2-6}{v(v-6)}$

b. $\left(\dfrac{v}{v-6} - \dfrac{3}{v+2}\right) \cdot \dfrac{2v+4}{v^2-6v} = \left(\dfrac{v}{v-6} \cdot \dfrac{v+2}{v+2} - \dfrac{3}{v+2} \cdot \dfrac{v-6}{v-6}\right) \cdot \dfrac{2v+4}{v^2-6v} = \left(\dfrac{v(v+2)-3(v-6)}{(v-6)(v+2)}\right) \cdot \dfrac{2v+4}{v^2-6v}$

$= \left(\dfrac{v^2+2v-3v+18}{(v-6)(v+2)}\right) \cdot \dfrac{2v+4}{v^2-6v} = \dfrac{v^2-v+18}{(v-6)(v+2)} \cdot \dfrac{2v+4}{v^2-6v} = \dfrac{(v^2-v+18)(2)\cancel{(z+2)}}{(v-6)\cancel{(v+2)}(v)(v-6)}$

$= \dfrac{2(v^2-v+18)}{v(v-6)^2}$ or $\dfrac{2v^2-2v+36}{v(v-6)^2}$

7. $\dfrac{2-3x}{2x-3} + \dfrac{8-2x}{3x-6} \div \dfrac{4x-6}{3x-6} = \dfrac{2-3x}{2x-3} + \dfrac{8-2x}{3x-6} \cdot \dfrac{3x-6}{4x-6} = \dfrac{2-3x}{2x-3} + \dfrac{\cancel{2}(4-x)\cancel{(3x-6)}}{\cancel{2}\cancel{(3x-6)}(2x-3)} = \dfrac{2-3x}{2x-3} + \dfrac{4-x}{2x-3}$

$= \dfrac{(2-3x)+(4-x)}{2x-3} = \dfrac{-4x+6}{2x-3} = \dfrac{-2\cancel{(2x-3)}}{\cancel{(2x-3)}} = -2$

9. $\left(\dfrac{2}{v+3}+v\right)\left(v-\dfrac{3}{v+2}\right) = \left(\dfrac{2}{v+3}+\dfrac{v}{1} \cdot \dfrac{v+3}{v+3}\right)\left(\dfrac{v}{1} \cdot \dfrac{v+2}{v+2}-\dfrac{3}{v+2}\right) = \left(\dfrac{2+v(v+3)}{v+3}\right)\left(\dfrac{v(v+2)-3}{v+2}\right)$

$= \left(\dfrac{v^2+3v+2}{v+3}\right)\left(\dfrac{v^2+2v-3}{v+2}\right) = \left(\dfrac{(v+1)(v+2)}{v+3}\right)\left(\dfrac{(v+3)(v-1)}{v+2}\right)$

$= \dfrac{(v+1)\cancel{(v+2)}\cancel{(v+3)}(v-1)}{\cancel{(v+3)}\cancel{(v+2)}} = (v+1)(v-1) = v^2-1$

11. $\left(x-2-\dfrac{3}{x}\right) \div \left(1+\dfrac{1}{x}\right) = \left(\dfrac{x^2}{x}-\dfrac{2x}{x}-\dfrac{3}{x}\right) \div \left(\dfrac{x}{x}+\dfrac{1}{x}\right) = \left(\dfrac{x^2-2x-3}{x}\right) \div \left(\dfrac{x+1}{x}\right) = \dfrac{(x-3)(x+1)}{x} \cdot \dfrac{x}{x+1}$

$= \dfrac{\cancel{x}(x-3)\cancel{(x+1)}}{\cancel{x}\cancel{(x+1)}} = x-3$

13. $1-\dfrac{4}{x}-\left(1-\dfrac{2}{x}\right)^2 = 1-\dfrac{4}{x}-\left(1-\dfrac{4}{x}+\dfrac{4}{x^2}\right)$

$= 1-\dfrac{4}{x}-1+\dfrac{4}{x}-\dfrac{4}{x^2} = -\dfrac{4}{x^2}$

15. $\left(1+\dfrac{3}{5x}\right)^2-\left(1-\dfrac{3}{5x}\right)^2$

$= \left[\left(1+\dfrac{3}{5x}\right)-\left(1-\dfrac{3}{5x}\right)\right]\left[\left(1+\dfrac{3}{5x}\right)+\left(1-\dfrac{3}{5x}\right)\right]$

$= \left(1+\dfrac{3}{5x}-1+\dfrac{3}{5x}\right)\left(1+\dfrac{3}{5x}+1-\dfrac{3}{5x}\right)$

$= \left(\dfrac{6}{5x}\right)(2) = \dfrac{12}{5x}$

17. a. $\dfrac{\dfrac{4}{6}}{\dfrac{5}{8}} = \dfrac{4}{6} \div \dfrac{5}{8} = \dfrac{2}{3} \cdot \dfrac{8}{5} = \dfrac{16}{15}$

b. $\dfrac{\dfrac{4}{6}}{\dfrac{6}{5}} = \dfrac{4}{1} \div \dfrac{6}{5} = \dfrac{\overset{2}{\cancel{4}}}{1} \cdot \dfrac{5}{\underset{3}{\cancel{6}}} = \dfrac{10}{3}$

19. $\dfrac{1+\dfrac{1}{5}}{1-\dfrac{1}{5}} = \left(1+\dfrac{1}{5}\right) \div \left(1-\dfrac{1}{5}\right) = \left(\dfrac{5}{5}+\dfrac{1}{5}\right) \div \left(\dfrac{5}{5}-\dfrac{1}{5}\right)$

$= \dfrac{6}{5} \div \dfrac{4}{5} = \dfrac{\overset{3}{\cancel{6}}}{\cancel{5}} \cdot \dfrac{\cancel{5}}{\underset{2}{\cancel{4}}} = \dfrac{3}{2}$

21. $\dfrac{\dfrac{3}{5}-\dfrac{5}{3}}{\dfrac{1}{3}+\dfrac{1}{5}} = \left(\dfrac{3}{5}-\dfrac{5}{3}\right) \div \left(\dfrac{1}{3}+\dfrac{1}{5}\right)$

$= \left(\dfrac{3}{5} \cdot \dfrac{3}{3} - \dfrac{5}{3} \cdot \dfrac{5}{5}\right) \div \left(\dfrac{1}{3} \cdot \dfrac{5}{5} + \dfrac{1}{5} \cdot \dfrac{3}{3}\right)$

$= \left(\dfrac{9-25}{15}\right) \div \left(\dfrac{5+3}{15}\right) = \dfrac{-16}{15} \div \dfrac{8}{15}$

$= -\dfrac{\overset{2}{\cancel{16}}}{\cancel{15}} \cdot \dfrac{\cancel{15}}{\cancel{8}} = -2$

23. $\dfrac{\dfrac{12x^2}{5y}}{\dfrac{16x^2}{15y^2}} = \dfrac{12x^2}{5y} \div \dfrac{16x^2}{15y^2} = \dfrac{\overset{3}{\cancel{12}} \; \cancel{x^2}}{\cancel{5} \; \cancel{y}} \cdot \dfrac{\overset{3}{\cancel{15}} \; \overset{y}{\cancel{y^2}}}{\underset{4}{\cancel{16}} \; \cancel{x^2}} = \dfrac{9y}{4}$

25. $\dfrac{\dfrac{w-z}{x^2y^2}}{\dfrac{w^2-z^2}{2xy}} = \dfrac{w-z}{x^2y^2} \div \dfrac{w^2-z^2}{2xy} = \dfrac{w-z}{x^2y^2} \cdot \dfrac{2xy}{w^2-z^2}$

$= \dfrac{2\,\cancel{xy}\,\cancel{(w-z)}}{\underset{xy}{\cancel{x^2y^2}}\,\cancel{(w-z)}(w+z)} = \dfrac{2}{xy(w+z)}$

27. $\dfrac{\dfrac{x^2-9x+14}{34x^4}}{\dfrac{5x^2-20}{17x^5}} = \dfrac{x^2-9x+14}{34x^4} \div \dfrac{5x^2-20}{17x^5} = \dfrac{(x-2)(x-7)}{34x^4} \cdot \dfrac{17x^5}{5(x^2-4)} = \dfrac{\cancel{17}\;\overset{x}{\cancel{x^5}}\,\cancel{(x-2)}(x-7)}{\underset{2}{\cancel{34}}\,\cancel{x^4}\,(5)\,\cancel{(x-2)}(x+2)} = \dfrac{x(x-7)}{10(x+2)}$

29. $\dfrac{2-\dfrac{1}{x}}{4-\dfrac{1}{x^2}} = \dfrac{2-\dfrac{1}{x}}{4-\dfrac{1}{x^2}} \cdot \dfrac{x^2}{x^2} = \dfrac{\left(2-\dfrac{1}{x}\right)x^2}{\left(4-\dfrac{1}{x^2}\right)x^2}$

$= \dfrac{2x^2-x}{4x^2-1} = \dfrac{x\,\cancel{(2x-1)}}{\cancel{(2x-1)}(2x+1)} = \dfrac{x}{2x+1}$

31. $\dfrac{vw}{\dfrac{1}{v}+\dfrac{1}{w}} = \dfrac{vw}{\dfrac{1}{v}+\dfrac{1}{w}} \cdot \dfrac{vw}{vw} = \dfrac{(vw)vw}{\left(\dfrac{1}{v}+\dfrac{1}{w}\right)vw}$

$= \dfrac{v^2w^2}{\dfrac{1}{v}(vw)+\dfrac{1}{w}(vw)} = \dfrac{v^2w^2}{w+v}$

33. $\dfrac{\dfrac{3}{x^2}-\dfrac{6}{x}+3}{18-\dfrac{18}{x^2}} = \dfrac{\dfrac{3}{x^2}-\dfrac{6}{x}+3}{18-\dfrac{18}{x^2}} \cdot \dfrac{x^2}{x^2} = \dfrac{\left(\dfrac{3}{x^2}-\dfrac{6}{x}+3\right)x^2}{\left(18-\dfrac{18}{x^2}\right)x^2} = \dfrac{\dfrac{3}{x^2}(x^2)-\dfrac{6}{x}(x^2)+3(x^2)}{18(x^2)-\dfrac{18}{x^2}(x^2)} = \dfrac{3x-6x+3x^2}{18x^2-18} = \dfrac{\cancel{3}(x^2-2x+1)}{\underset{6}{\cancel{18}}(x^2-1)}$

$= \dfrac{\cancel{(x-1)}(x-1)}{6\cancel{(x-1)}(x+1)} = \dfrac{x-1}{6(x+1)}$

35.
$$\frac{3+\dfrac{9}{x}}{\dfrac{15}{x^3}+\dfrac{8}{x^2}+\dfrac{1}{x}} = \frac{3+\dfrac{9}{x}}{\dfrac{15}{x^3}+\dfrac{8}{x^2}+\dfrac{1}{x}}\cdot\frac{x^3}{x^3} = \frac{\left(3+\dfrac{9}{x}\right)x^3}{\left(\dfrac{15}{x^3}+\dfrac{8}{x^2}+\dfrac{1}{x}\right)x^3} = \frac{3\left(x^3\right)+\dfrac{9}{x}\left(x^3\right)}{\dfrac{15}{x^3}\left(x^3\right)+\dfrac{8}{x^2}\left(x^3\right)+\dfrac{1}{x}\left(x^3\right)} = \frac{3x^3+9x^2}{15+8x+x^2}$$

$$= \frac{3x^2\,\cancel{(x+3)}}{\cancel{(x+3)}\,(x+5)} = \frac{3x^2}{x+5}$$

37.
$$\frac{\dfrac{w-a}{w+a}-\dfrac{w+a}{w-a}}{\dfrac{w^2+a^2}{w^2-a^2}} = \frac{\dfrac{w-a}{w+a}-\dfrac{w+a}{w-a}}{\dfrac{w^2+a^2}{w^2-a^2}}\cdot\frac{(w+a)(w-a)}{(w+a)(w-a)} = \frac{\left(\dfrac{w-a}{w+a}-\dfrac{w+a}{w-a}\right)(w+a)(w-a)}{\left(\dfrac{w^2+a^2}{w^2-a^2}\right)(w+a)(w-a)}$$

$$= \frac{\dfrac{w-a}{w+a}(w+a)(w-a)-\dfrac{w+a}{w-a}(w+a)(w-a)}{\dfrac{w^2+a^2}{w^2-a^2}\left(w^2-a^2\right)} = \frac{(w-a)(w-a)-(w+a)(w+a)}{w^2+a^2}$$

$$= \frac{\left(w^2-2wa+a^2\right)-\left(w^2+2wa+a^2\right)}{w^2+a^2} = \frac{-4wa}{w^2+a^2}$$

39.
$$\frac{\dfrac{12}{v^2}+\dfrac{1}{v}-1}{\dfrac{24}{v^2}-\dfrac{2}{v}-1} = \frac{\dfrac{12}{v^2}+\dfrac{1}{v}-1}{\dfrac{24}{v^2}-\dfrac{2}{v}-1}\cdot\frac{v^2}{v^2} = \frac{\left(\dfrac{12}{v^2}+\dfrac{1}{v}-1\right)v^2}{\left(\dfrac{24}{v^2}-\dfrac{2}{v}-1\right)v^2} = \frac{\dfrac{12}{v^2}\left(v^2\right)+\dfrac{1}{v}\left(v^2\right)-\left(v^2\right)}{\dfrac{24}{v^2}\left(v^2\right)-\dfrac{2}{v}\left(v^2\right)-\left(v^2\right)} = \frac{12+v-v^2}{24-2v-v^2}$$

$$= \frac{\cancel{(-1)}\,\cancel{(v-4)}\,(v+3)}{\cancel{(-1)}\,(v+6)\,\cancel{(v-4)}} = \frac{v+3}{v+6}$$

	Problem	Mental Estimate	Calculator Approximation
41.	$\dfrac{\dfrac{211}{429}}{\dfrac{107}{325}}$	$\approx\dfrac{\dfrac{1}{2}}{\dfrac{1}{3}}=\dfrac{1}{2}\cdot\dfrac{3}{1}=\dfrac{3}{2}=1.5$	1.494
43.	$\dfrac{\dfrac{401}{99}}{\dfrac{499}{101}}$	$\approx\dfrac{4}{5}=0.8$	0.820

45.
$$\frac{a-b}{ab}+\frac{(a+b)^2}{a^3b^3}\cdot\frac{a^2b^2}{4a^2+8ab+4b^2} = \frac{a-b}{ab}+\frac{\cancel{a^2b^2}\,(a+b)(a+b)}{4\,\underset{ab}{\cancel{a^3b^3}}\left(a^2+2ab+b^2\right)} = \frac{a-b}{ab}+\frac{\cancel{(a+b)}\,\cancel{(a+b)}}{4ab\,\cancel{(a+b)}\,\cancel{(a+b)}}$$

$$= \frac{a-b}{ab}\cdot\frac{4}{4}+\frac{1}{4ab} = \frac{4(a-b)+1}{4ab} = \frac{4a-4b+1}{4ab}$$

47. $\dfrac{x^{-2}}{x^{-2}+y^{-2}} = \dfrac{\dfrac{1}{x^2}}{\dfrac{1}{x^2}+\dfrac{1}{y^2}} \cdot \dfrac{x^2 y^2}{x^2 y^2} = \dfrac{\left(\dfrac{1}{x^2}\right)x^2 y^2}{\left(\dfrac{1}{x^2}+\dfrac{1}{y^2}\right)x^2 y^2}$

$= \dfrac{y^2}{\dfrac{1}{x^2}\left(x^2 y^2\right)+\dfrac{1}{y^2}\left(x^2 y^2\right)} = \dfrac{y^2}{y^2+x^2}$

49. $\dfrac{v^{-1}+w^{-1}}{v^{-1}-w^{-1}} = \dfrac{\dfrac{1}{v}+\dfrac{1}{w}}{\dfrac{1}{v}-\dfrac{1}{w}} \cdot \dfrac{vw}{vw} = \dfrac{\left(\dfrac{1}{v}+\dfrac{1}{w}\right)vw}{\left(\dfrac{1}{v}-\dfrac{1}{w}\right)vw}$

$= \dfrac{\dfrac{1}{v}(vw)+\dfrac{1}{w}(vw)}{\dfrac{1}{v}(vw)-\dfrac{1}{w}(vw)} = \dfrac{w+v}{w-v}$

51. $\dfrac{m^2-n^2}{m^{-1}-n^{-1}} = \dfrac{m^2-n^2}{\dfrac{1}{m}-\dfrac{1}{n}} \cdot \dfrac{mn}{mn} = \dfrac{(m-n)(m+n)mn}{\left(\dfrac{1}{m}-\dfrac{1}{n}\right)mn} = \dfrac{(m-n)(m+n)mn}{\dfrac{1}{m}(mn)-\dfrac{1}{n}(mn)}$

$= \dfrac{\cancel{(m-n)}(m+n)mn}{\underset{(-1)}{\cancel{(n-m)}}} = -mn(m+n) = -m^2 n - mn^2$

53. $\dfrac{a^{-2}-b^{-2}}{a^{-1}-b^{-1}} = \dfrac{\dfrac{1}{a^2}-\dfrac{1}{b^2}}{\dfrac{1}{a}-\dfrac{1}{b}} \cdot \dfrac{a^2 b^2}{a^2 b^2} = \dfrac{\left(\dfrac{1}{a^2}-\dfrac{1}{b^2}\right)a^2 b^2}{\left(\dfrac{1}{a}-\dfrac{1}{b}\right)a^2 b^2}$

$= \dfrac{\dfrac{1}{a^2}\left(a^2 b^2\right)-\dfrac{1}{b^2}\left(a^2 b^2\right)}{\dfrac{1}{a}\left(a^2 b^2\right)-\dfrac{1}{b}\left(a^2 b^2\right)} = \dfrac{b^2-a^2}{ab^2-a^2 b}$

$= \dfrac{\cancel{(b-a)}(b+a)}{ab\cancel{(b-a)}} = \dfrac{b+a}{ab}$

55. $\dfrac{x^{-1}y^{-2}+x^{-2}y^{-1}}{y^{-2}-x^{-2}} = \dfrac{\dfrac{1}{xy^2}+\dfrac{1}{x^2 y}}{\dfrac{1}{y^2}-\dfrac{1}{x^2}} \cdot \dfrac{x^2 y^2}{x^2 y^2}$

$= \dfrac{\left(\dfrac{1}{xy^2}+\dfrac{1}{x^2 y}\right)x^2 y^2}{\left(\dfrac{1}{y^2}-\dfrac{1}{x^2}\right)x^2 y^2} = \dfrac{\dfrac{1}{xy^2}\left(x^2 y^2\right)+\dfrac{1}{x^2 y}\left(x^2 y^2\right)}{\dfrac{1}{y^2}\left(x^2 y^2\right)-\dfrac{1}{x^2}\left(x^2 y^2\right)}$

$= \dfrac{x+y}{x^2-y^2} = \dfrac{\cancel{(x+y)}}{\cancel{(x+y)}(x-y)} = \dfrac{1}{x-y}$

57. $\dfrac{\dfrac{\dfrac{1}{a}-\dfrac{1}{b}}{ab}}{\dfrac{1-\dfrac{a}{b}}{1+\dfrac{a}{b}}} = \dfrac{\dfrac{1}{a}-\dfrac{1}{b}}{ab} \div \dfrac{1-\dfrac{a}{b}}{1+\dfrac{a}{b}} = \dfrac{\dfrac{1}{a}-\dfrac{1}{b}}{ab} \cdot \dfrac{ab}{ab} \div \dfrac{1-\dfrac{a}{b}}{1+\dfrac{a}{b}} \cdot \dfrac{b}{b} = \dfrac{\left(\dfrac{1}{a}-\dfrac{1}{b}\right)ab}{a^2 b^2} \div \dfrac{\left(1-\dfrac{a}{b}\right)b}{\left(1+\dfrac{a}{b}\right)b} = \dfrac{\dfrac{1}{a}(ab)-\dfrac{1}{b}(ab)}{a^2 b^2} \div \dfrac{1(b)-\dfrac{a}{b}(b)}{1(b)+\dfrac{a}{b}(b)}$

$= \dfrac{b-a}{a^2 b^2} \div \dfrac{b-a}{b+a} = \dfrac{\cancel{b-a}}{a^2 b^2} \cdot \dfrac{b+a}{\cancel{b-a}} = \dfrac{b+a}{a^2 b^2}$

59. $\dfrac{\dfrac{1+\dfrac{x}{y}}{1-\dfrac{x}{y}}}{\dfrac{x+y}{x-\dfrac{y^2}{x}}} = \dfrac{1+\dfrac{x}{y}}{1-\dfrac{x}{y}} \div \dfrac{x+y}{x-\dfrac{y^2}{x}} = \dfrac{1+\dfrac{x}{y}}{1-\dfrac{x}{y}} \cdot \dfrac{y}{y} \div \dfrac{x+y}{x-\dfrac{y^2}{x}} \cdot \dfrac{x}{x} = \dfrac{\left(1+\dfrac{x}{y}\right)\cdot y}{\left(1-\dfrac{x}{y}\right)\cdot y} \div \dfrac{(x+y)\cdot x}{\left(x-\dfrac{y^2}{x}\right)\cdot x} = \dfrac{y+x}{y-x} \div \dfrac{(x+y)\cdot x}{x^2-y^2}$

$= \dfrac{y+x}{y-x} \cdot \dfrac{x^2-y^2}{(x+y)\cdot x} = \dfrac{(y+x)}{\cancel{(y-x)}} \cdot \dfrac{\cancel{(x+y)}\overset{-1}{\cancel{(x-y)}}}{\cancel{(x+y)}\cdot x} = -\dfrac{x+y}{x}$

61. The table is equivalent to the one shown in **B**. Thus $\dfrac{3}{x} + \dfrac{1}{4} \div \dfrac{3}{x} - \dfrac{1}{4} = \dfrac{x^2 - 3x + 36}{12x}$.

63. The table is equivalent to the one shown in **D**. Thus $\dfrac{3}{x} + \dfrac{1}{4} \div \left(\dfrac{3}{x} - \dfrac{1}{4} \right) = -\dfrac{x^2 - 3x + 36}{x(x-12)}$.

65. $A = \dfrac{h}{2}(a+b) = \dfrac{x}{2}\big((x+6)+(x+4)\big)$

$\quad = \dfrac{x}{2}(2x+10) = \dfrac{x}{\cancel{2}}\,\cancel{2}\,(x+5) = x(x+5) \text{ cm}^2$

67. a.

$A(t) = \dfrac{C(t)}{N(t)} = \dfrac{8400 - \dfrac{16800}{t}}{5t - 10}$

$= \dfrac{\left(8400 - \dfrac{16800}{t}\right)}{5(t-2)} \cdot \dfrac{t}{t} = \dfrac{\left(8400 - \dfrac{16800}{t}\right)t}{5(t-2)t}$

$= \dfrac{8400(t) - \dfrac{16800}{t}(t)}{5t(t-2)} = \dfrac{8400t - 16800}{5t(t-2)}$

$= \dfrac{\overset{1680}{\cancel{8400}}\,\cancel{(t-2)}}{\cancel{5}t\,\cancel{(t-2)}} = \dfrac{1680}{t} \text{ for } t \neq 2$

b. The function $N(t) = 5t - 10$ will produce a positive number of chairs only if t is greater than 2 hours. The maximum number of hours that a factory can run during the week is $24 \cdot 7 = 168$ hours. Thus the practical domain is $(0, 2) \cup (2, 168]$.

c.

$[0, 168, 10]$ by $[0, 500, 100]$

The average cost decreases to \$10 when the factory operates 168 h/wk.

69. a. $f = \dfrac{1}{\dfrac{1}{d_o} + \dfrac{1}{d_i}} = \dfrac{1}{\dfrac{1}{d_o} + \dfrac{1}{d_i}} \cdot \dfrac{d_o d_i}{d_o d_i}$

$= \dfrac{d_o d_i}{\left(\dfrac{1}{d_o} + \dfrac{1}{d_i}\right) d_o d_i} = \dfrac{d_o d_i}{\dfrac{1}{d_o}(d_o d_i) + \dfrac{1}{d_i}(d_o d_i)}$

$= \dfrac{d_o d_i}{d_i + d_o}$

b. $f = \dfrac{d_o d_i}{d_i + d_o} = \dfrac{(20)(0.5)}{(0.5)+(20)} \approx 0.488 \text{ ft}$

Cumulative Review

1. The y-intercept is $(0, 8)$.

2. The x-intercepts are $(-4, 0)$ and $(2, 0)$.

3. The maximum y-value of the function is 9.

4. x is equal to -1 when y is equal to 9.

5. The function is increasing on the interval $(-\infty, -1)$.

Section 9.5: Solving Equations Containing Rational Expressions

Quick Review 9.5

1.

$$\frac{x}{2} - \frac{x}{3} = 1$$

$$6\left(\frac{x}{2} - \frac{x}{3}\right) = 6(1)$$

$$3x - 2x = 6$$

$$x = 6$$

2.

$$x = \frac{36}{15} + \frac{x}{5}$$

$$15(x) = 15\left(\frac{36}{15} + \frac{x}{5}\right)$$

$$15x = 36 + 3x$$

$$12x = 36$$

$$x = 3$$

3.

$$\frac{x-1}{3} - \frac{x+3}{4} = 2$$

$$12\left(\frac{x-1}{3} - \frac{x+3}{4}\right) = 12(2)$$

$$4(x-1) - 3(x+3) = 24$$

$$4x - 4 - 3x - 9 = 24$$

$$4x - 3x - 4 - 9 = 24$$

$$x - 13 = 24$$

$$x = 37$$

4.

$$\frac{2x+3}{5} - 1 = \frac{x-2}{3}$$

$$15\left(\frac{2x+3}{5} - 1\right) = 15\left(\frac{x-2}{3}\right)$$

$$3(2x+3) - 15 = 5(x-2)$$

$$6x + 9 - 15 = 5x - 10$$

$$6x - 6 = 5x - 10$$

$$x = -4$$

5.

$$\frac{x}{2} + 5 = \frac{x}{2}$$

$$2\left(\frac{x}{2} + 5\right) = 2\left(\frac{x}{2}\right)$$

$$x + 10 = x$$

$$x - x + 10 = x - x$$

$$10 = 0$$

Since this is a contradiction, the equation has no solution.

Exercises 9.5

1. Find the values that make the denominators zero. The excluded values are $m = 3$ and $m = 2$.

3. Find the values that make the denominators zero. The excluded values are $y = -\frac{3}{2}$ and $y = \frac{2}{3}$.

5. Find the values that make the denominators zero.

$$2y^2 + 5y - 3 = 0 \qquad 6y^2 - y - 1 = 0$$

$$(2y - 1)(y + 3) = 0 \qquad (3y + 1)(2y - 1) = 0$$

$$y = \frac{1}{2} \text{ or } y = -3 \qquad y = -\frac{1}{3} \text{ or } y = \frac{1}{2}$$

The excluded values are $y = \frac{1}{2}$, $y = -3$ and $y = -\frac{1}{3}$.

7.
$$\frac{3}{z-1}+2=\frac{5}{z-1}$$
$$(z-1)\left(\frac{3}{z-1}+2\right)=(z-1)\left(\frac{5}{z-1}\right)$$
$$(z-1)\left(\frac{3}{z-1}\right)+(z-1)2=(z-1)\left(\frac{5}{z-1}\right)$$
$$3+2z-2=5$$
$$2z=4$$
$$z=2$$

9.
$$\frac{6w-1}{2w-1}-5=\frac{2w-3}{1-2w}$$
$$(2w-1)\left(\frac{6w-1}{2w-1}-5\right)=(2w-1)\left(\frac{2w-3}{1-2w}\right)$$
$$(2w-1)\left(\frac{6w-1}{2w-1}\right)-5(2w-1)=(2w-1)^{(-1)}\left(\frac{2w-3}{1-2w}\right)$$
$$6w-1-10w+5=-2w+3$$
$$-2w=-1$$
$$w=\frac{1}{2}$$

The value $w=\frac{1}{2}$ is an excluded value. Therefore there is no solution.

11.
$$\frac{-3}{p+2}=\frac{-8}{p-3}$$
$$(p+2)(p-3)\left[\frac{-3}{p+2}\right]=(p+2)(p-3)\left[\frac{-8}{p-3}\right]$$
$$-3p+9=-8p-16$$
$$5p=-25$$
$$p=-5$$

13.
$$\frac{7}{3n-1}=\frac{2}{n+2}$$
$$(3n-1)(n+2)\left[\frac{7}{3n-1}\right]=(3n-1)(n+2)\left[\frac{2}{n+2}\right]$$
$$7n+14=6n-2$$
$$n=-16$$

15.
$$\frac{4}{k+2}=\frac{1}{3k+6}+\frac{11}{9}$$
$$\frac{4}{k+2}=\frac{1}{3(k+2)}+\frac{11}{9}$$
$$9(k+2)\left[\frac{4}{k+2}\right]=9(k+2)\left[\frac{1}{3(k+2)}+\frac{11}{9}\right]$$
$$36=\overset{3}{9}(k+2)\frac{1}{3(k+2)}+9(k+2)\frac{11}{9}$$
$$36=3+11k+22$$
$$11=11k$$
$$k=1$$

17.
$$\frac{3y}{(y+4)(y-2)}=\frac{5}{y-2}+\frac{2}{y+4}$$
$$(y+4)(y-2)\left[\frac{3y}{(y+4)(y-2)}\right]=(y+4)(y-2)\left[\frac{5}{y-2}+\frac{2}{y+4}\right]$$
$$3y=(y+4)(y-2)\frac{5}{y-2}+(y+4)(y-2)\frac{2}{y+4}$$
$$3y=5y+20+2y-4$$
$$-16=4y$$
$$y=-4$$

The value $y=-4$ is an excluded value. Thus there is no solution.

19.

$$1 - \frac{14}{y^2 + 4y + 4} = \frac{7y}{y^2 + 4y + 4}$$

$$1 - \frac{14}{(y+2)^2} = \frac{7y}{(y+2)^2}$$

$$(y+2)^2\left(1 - \frac{14}{(y+2)^2}\right) = (y+2)^2\left(\frac{7y}{(y+2)^2}\right)$$

$$(y+2)^2 - (y+2)^2\frac{14}{(y+2)^2} = 7y$$

$$(y^2 + 4x + 4) - 14 = 7y$$

$$y^2 - 3x - 10 = 0$$

$$(y-5)(y+2) = 0$$

$$y = 5 \quad \text{or} \quad y = -2$$

The value $y = -2$ is an excluded value. Therefore the solution is $y = 5$.

21.

$$\frac{4}{x-5} + \frac{5}{x-2} = \frac{x+6}{3x-6}$$

$$\frac{4}{x-5} + \frac{5}{x-2} = \frac{x+6}{3(x-2)}$$

$$3(x-2)(x-5)\left[\frac{4}{x-5} + \frac{5}{x-2}\right] = \left[\frac{x+6}{3(x-2)}\right]3(x-2)(x-5)$$

$$3(x-2)(x-5)\frac{4}{x-5} + 3(x-2)(x-5)\frac{5}{x-2} = (x+6)(x-5)$$

$$12(x-2) + 15(x-5) = x^2 + x - 30$$

$$12x - 24 + 15x - 75 = x^2 + x - 30$$

$$x^2 - 26x + 69 = 0$$

$$(x-3)(x-23) = 0$$

$$x = 3 \quad \text{or} \quad x = 23$$

23.

$$\frac{1}{(t-1)^2} - 3 = \frac{2}{1-t}$$

$$(t-1)^2\left(\frac{1}{(t-1)^2} - 3\right) = \left(\frac{-2}{t-1}\right)(t-1)^2$$

$$(t-1)^2\frac{1}{(t-1)^2} - 3(t-1)^2 = -2(t-1)$$

$$1 - 3(t^2 - 2t + 1) = -2(t-1)$$

$$1 - 3t^2 + 6t - 3 = -2t + 2$$

$$3t^2 - 8t + 4 = 0$$

$$(3t-2)(t-2) = 0$$

$$t = 2 \quad \text{or} \quad t = \frac{2}{3}$$

25.

$$\frac{z}{(z-2)(z+1)} - \frac{z}{(z+1)(z+3)} = \frac{3z}{(z+3)(z-2)}$$

$$(z+1)(z+3)(z-2)\left[\frac{z}{(z-2)(z+1)} - \frac{z}{(z+1)(z+3)}\right] = \left[\frac{3z}{\cancel{(z+3)}\,\cancel{(z-2)}}\right](z+1)\cancel{(z+3)}\,\cancel{(z-2)}$$

$$\cancel{(z+1)}\,(z+3)\,\cancel{(z-2)}\frac{z}{\cancel{(z-2)}\,\cancel{(z+1)}} - \cancel{(z+1)}\,\cancel{(z+3)}\,(z-2)\frac{z}{\cancel{(z+1)}\,\cancel{(z+3)}} = 3z(z+1)$$

$$z(z+3) - z(z-2) = 3z(z+1)$$

$$z^2 + 3z - z^2 + 2z = 3z^2 + 3z$$

$$3z^2 - 2z = 0$$

$$z(3z-2) = 0$$

$$z = 0 \quad \text{or} \quad z = \frac{2}{3}$$

27.

$$\frac{2v-5}{3v^2 - v - 14} + \frac{7}{3v-7} = \frac{8}{v+2}$$

$$\frac{2v-5}{(3v-7)(v+2)} + \frac{7}{3v-7} = \frac{8}{v+2}$$

$$(3v-7)(v+2)\left[\frac{2v-5}{(3v-7)(v+2)} + \frac{7}{3v-7}\right] = (3v-7)\cancel{(v+2)}\left[\frac{8}{\cancel{v+2}}\right]$$

$$\cancel{(3v-7)}\,\cancel{(v+2)}\frac{2v-5}{\cancel{(3v-7)}\,\cancel{(v+2)}} + \cancel{(3v-7)}(v+2)\frac{7}{\cancel{3v-7}} = 8(3v-7)$$

$$2v-5 + 7(v+2) = 8(3v-7)$$

$$2v-5 + 7v + 14 = 24v - 56$$

$$15v = 65$$

$$v = \frac{13}{3}$$

29.

$$\frac{m+4}{6m^2 + 5m - 6} = \frac{m}{3m-2} - \frac{m}{2m+3}$$

$$\frac{m+4}{(3m-2)(2m+3)} = \frac{m}{3m-2} - \frac{m}{2m+3}$$

$$\cancel{(3m-2)}\,\cancel{(2m+3)}\left[\frac{m+4}{\cancel{(3m-2)}\,\cancel{(2m+3)}}\right] = (3m-2)(2m+3)\left[\frac{m}{3m-2} - \frac{m}{2m+3}\right]$$

$$m+4 = \cancel{(3m-2)}(2m+3)\frac{m}{\cancel{3m-2}} - (3m-2)\cancel{(2m+3)}\frac{m}{\cancel{2m+3}}$$

$$m+4 = m(2m+3) - m(3m-2)$$

$$m+4 = 2m^2 + 3m - 3m^2 + 2m$$

$$m^2 - 4m + 4 = 0$$

$$(m-2)^2 = 0$$

$$m = 2$$

31.

$$\frac{x+1}{3x^2-4x+1}-\frac{x+1}{2x^2+x-3}=\frac{2}{6x^2+7x-3}$$

$$\frac{x+1}{(3x-1)(x-1)}-\frac{x+1}{(2x+3)(x-1)}=\frac{2}{(3x-1)(2x+3)}$$

$$(2x+3)(x-1)(3x-1)\left[\frac{x+1}{(3x-1)(x-1)}-\frac{x+1}{(2x+3)(x-1)}\right]=\cancel{(2x+3)}(x-1)\cancel{(3x-1)}\left[\frac{2}{\cancel{(3x-1)}\cancel{(2x+3)}}\right]$$

$$(2x+3)\cancel{(x-1)}\cancel{(3x-1)}\frac{x+1}{\cancel{(3x-1)}\cancel{(x-1)}}-\cancel{(2x+3)}\cancel{(x-1)}(3x-1)\frac{x+1}{\cancel{(2x+3)}\cancel{(x-1)}}=2(x-1)$$

$$(2x+3)(x+1)-(3x-1)(x+1)=2(x-1)$$

$$2x^2+5x+3-\left(3x^2+2x-1\right)=2x-2$$

$$2x^2+5x+3-3x^2-2x+1=2x-2$$

$$x^2-x-6=0$$

$$(x-3)(x+2)=0$$

$$x=3 \quad \text{or} \quad x=-2$$

33.

$$\frac{2}{m+2}-\frac{1}{m+1}=\frac{1}{m}$$

$$m(m+2)(m+1)\left[\frac{2}{m+2}-\frac{1}{m+1}\right]=\cancel{m}(m+2)(m+1)\left[\frac{1}{\cancel{m}}\right]$$

$$m\cancel{(m+2)}(m+1)\frac{2}{\cancel{m+2}}-m(m+2)\cancel{(m+1)}\frac{1}{\cancel{m+1}}=(m+2)(m+1)$$

$$2m(m+1)-m(m+2)=(m+2)(m+1)$$

$$2m^2+2m-m^2-2m=m^2+3m+2$$

$$3m+2=0$$

$$m=-\frac{2}{3}$$

35.

$$\frac{z-2}{2z^2-5z+3}+\frac{3}{3z^2-2z-1}=\frac{3z}{6z^2-7z-3}$$

$$\frac{z-2}{(2z-3)(z-1)}+\frac{3}{(3z+1)(z-1)}=\frac{3z}{(3z+1)(2z-3)}$$

$$(2z-3)(3z+1)(z-1)\left[\frac{z-2}{(2z-3)(z-1)}+\frac{3}{(3z+1)(z-1)}\right]=\cancel{(2z-3)}\cancel{(3z+1)}(z-1)\left[\frac{3z}{\cancel{(3z+1)}\cancel{(2z-3)}}\right]$$

$$\cancel{(2z-3)}(3z+1)\cancel{(z-1)}\frac{z-2}{\cancel{(2z-3)}\cancel{(z-1)}}+(2z-3)\cancel{(3z+1)}\cancel{(z-1)}\frac{3}{\cancel{(3z+1)}\cancel{(z-1)}}=3z(z-1)$$

$$(3z+1)(z-2)+3(2z-3)=3z(z-1)$$

$$3z^2-5z-2+6z-9=3z^2-3z$$

$$4z=11$$

$$z=\frac{11}{4}$$

37.

$$\frac{1}{n^2-5n+6}-\frac{1}{n^2-n-2}+\frac{3}{n^2-2n-3}=0$$

$$\frac{1}{(n-3)(n-2)}-\frac{1}{(n-2)(n+1)}+\frac{3}{(n-3)(n+1)}=0$$

$$(n-3)(n-2)(n+1)\left[\frac{1}{(n-3)(n-2)}-\frac{1}{(n-2)(n+1)}+\frac{3}{(n-3)(n+1)}\right]=(n-3)(n-2)(n+1)[0]$$

$$(n+1)-(n-3)+3(n-2)=0$$

$$n+1-n+3+3n-6=0$$

$$3n=2$$

$$n=\frac{2}{3}$$

39.

$$\frac{x^2}{x^2-x-2}=\frac{2x}{x^2+x-6}$$

$$\frac{x^2}{(x-2)(x+1)}=\frac{2x}{(x+3)(x-2)}$$

$$(x+3)\cancel{(x-2)}\cancel{(x+1)}\left[\frac{x^2}{\cancel{(x-2)}\cancel{(x+1)}}\right]=\cancel{(x+3)}\cancel{(x-2)}(x+1)\left[\frac{2x}{\cancel{(x+3)}\cancel{(x-2)}}\right]$$

$$x^2(x+3)=2x(x+1)$$

$$x^3+3x^2=2x^2+2x$$

$$x^3+x^2-2x=0$$

$$x(x^2+x-2)=0$$

$$x(x+2)(x-1)=0$$

$$x=0,\quad x=-2\quad\text{or}\quad x=1$$

41.

$$\frac{a}{b}=\frac{c}{d}$$

$$\cancel{b}d\left(\frac{a}{\cancel{b}}\right)=b\cancel{d}\left(\frac{c}{\cancel{d}}\right)$$

$$da=bc$$

$$b=\frac{da}{c}$$

43.

$$\frac{a}{b-1}=\frac{c}{d+1}$$

$$\cancel{(b-1)}(d+1)\left[\frac{a}{\cancel{b-1}}\right]=(b-1)\cancel{(d+1)}\left[\frac{c}{\cancel{d+1}}\right]$$

$$a(d+1)=c(b-1)$$

$$ad+a=cb-c$$

$$ad+a+c=cb$$

$$b=\frac{ad+a+c}{c}$$

45.
$$I = \frac{k}{d}$$

$$d(I) = d\left(\frac{k}{d}\right)$$

$$dI = k$$

$$d = \frac{k}{I}$$

47.
$$\frac{1}{R} = \frac{1}{r_1} + \frac{1}{r_2}$$

$$Rr_1r_2\left[\frac{1}{R}\right] = Rr_1r_2\left[\frac{1}{r_1} + \frac{1}{r_2}\right]$$

$$r_1r_2 = Rr_1r_2\frac{1}{r_1} + Rr_1r_2\frac{1}{r_2}$$

$$r_1r_2 = Rr_2 + Rr_1$$

$$r_1r_2 = R(r_2 + r_1)$$

$$R = \frac{r_1r_2}{(r_2 + r_1)}$$

49.
$$h = \frac{2A}{B+b}$$

$$(B+b)[h] = (B+b)\left[\frac{2A}{B+b}\right]$$

$$Bh + bh = 2A$$

$$Bh = 2A - bh$$

$$B = \frac{2A - bh}{h}$$

51.
$$\frac{1}{x} = \frac{1}{y} - \frac{1}{z}$$

$$xyz\left[\frac{1}{x}\right] = xyz\left[\frac{1}{y} - \frac{1}{z}\right]$$

$$yz = xyz\frac{1}{y} - xyz\frac{1}{z}$$

$$yz = xz - xy$$

$$xz - yz = xy$$

$$z(x - y) = xy$$

$$z = \frac{xy}{x - y}$$

53. Let x be the radius of the window. Use the hint:

$$\frac{a}{b} = \frac{b}{c} \text{ With } a = x+1, \ c = x-1, \text{ and } b = 4.$$

$$\frac{x+1}{4} = \frac{4}{x-1}$$

$$(x+1)(x-1) = 4 \cdot 4$$

$$x^2 - 1 = 16$$

$$x^2 = 17$$

$$x = \sqrt{17} \approx 4.12 \text{ ft}$$

55.
$$\frac{1}{R} = \frac{1}{r_1} + \frac{1}{r_2}$$

$$\frac{1}{5} = \frac{1}{r_1} + \frac{1}{5r_1}$$

$$5r_1\left[\frac{1}{5}\right] = \left[\frac{1}{r_1} + \frac{1}{5r_1}\right]5r_1$$

$$r_1 = \frac{1}{r_1}(5r_1) + \frac{1}{5r_1}(5r_1)$$

$$r_1 = 5 + 1$$

$$r_1 = 6 \text{ ohms}$$

$$r_2 = 5(6) = 30 \text{ ohms}$$

57. a.

$$\frac{1}{p-1} - \frac{3}{p+1} = \frac{1}{p-1} \cdot \frac{p+1}{p+1} - \frac{3}{p+1} \cdot \frac{p-1}{p-1}$$

$$= \frac{(p+1) - 3(p-1)}{(p-1)(p+1)}$$

$$= \frac{p+1-3p+3}{(p-1)(p+1)}$$

$$= \frac{-2p+4}{(p-1)(p+1)}$$

$$= \frac{-2(p-2)}{(p-1)(p+1)}$$

b.

$$\frac{1}{p-1} = \frac{3}{p+1}$$

$$(p+1)\,\cancel{(p-1)}\left[\frac{1}{\cancel{p-1}}\right] = \cancel{(p+1)}\,(p-1)\left[\frac{3}{\cancel{p+1}}\right]$$

$$(p+1) = 3(p-1)$$

$$p+1 = 3p-3$$

$$-2p = -4$$

$$p = 2$$

59. a.

$$\frac{x-1}{x+1} - 1 - \frac{x-6}{x-2} = \frac{x-1}{x+1} \cdot \frac{x-2}{x-2} - 1 \cdot \frac{(x+1)(x-2)}{(x+1)(x-2)} - \frac{x-6}{x-2} \cdot \frac{x+1}{x+1} = \frac{(x-1)(x-2) - (x+1)(x-2) - (x-6)(x+1)}{(x+1)(x-2)}$$

$$= \frac{(x^2 - 3x + 2) - (x^2 - x - 2) - (x^2 - 5x - 6)}{(x+1)(x-2)} = \frac{x^2 - 3x + 2 - x^2 + x + 2 - x^2 + 5x + 6}{(x+1)(x-2)}$$

$$= \frac{-x^2 + 3x + 10}{(x+1)(x-2)} = \frac{-(x^2 - 3x - 10)}{(x+1)(x-2)} = \frac{-(x-5)(x+2)}{(x+1)(x-2)}$$

b.

$$\frac{x-1}{x+1} - 1 = \frac{x-6}{x-2}$$

$$(x-2)(x+1)\left[\frac{x-1}{x+1} - 1\right] = \cancel{(x-2)}\,(x+1)\left[\frac{x-6}{\cancel{x-2}}\right]$$

$$(x-2)\,\cancel{(x+1)}\,\frac{x-1}{\cancel{x+1}} - (x-2)(x+1)(1) = (x+1)(x-6)$$

$$(x-2)(x-1) - (x-2)(x+1) = (x+1)(x-6)$$

$$(x^2 - 3x + 2) - (x^2 - x - 2) = x^2 - 5x - 6$$

$$x^2 - 3x + 2 - x^2 + x + 2 = x^2 - 5x - 6$$

$$x^2 - 3x - 10 = 0$$

$$(x-5)(x+2) = 0$$

$$x = 5 \quad \text{or} \quad x = -2$$

61. a.

$$\frac{2x-8}{6x^2 + x - 2} - \frac{4}{3x+2} + \frac{2}{2x-1} = \frac{2x-8}{(3x+2)(2x-1)} - \frac{4}{3x+2} \cdot \frac{2x-1}{2x-1} + \frac{2}{2x-1} \cdot \frac{3x+2}{3x+2}$$

$$= \frac{(2x-8) - 4(2x-1) + 2(3x+2)}{(3x+2)(2x-1)} = \frac{2x - 8 - 8x + 4 + 6x + 4}{(3x+2)(2x-1)} = \frac{0}{(3x+2)(2x-1)} = 0$$

b.

$$\frac{2x-8}{6x^2+x-2}=\frac{4}{3x+2}-\frac{2}{2x-1}$$

$$\frac{2x-8}{(3x+2)(2x-1)}=\frac{4}{3x+2}-\frac{2}{2x-1}$$

$$(3x+2)(2x-1)\left[\frac{2x-8}{(3x+2)(2x-1)}\right]=(3x+2)(2x-1)\left[\frac{4}{3x+2}-\frac{2}{2x-1}\right]$$

$$2x-8=(3x+2)(2x-1)\frac{4}{3x+2}-(3x+2)(2x-1)\frac{2}{2x-1}$$

$$2x-8=4(2x-1)-2(3x+2)$$

$$2x-8=8x-4-6x-4$$

$$0=0$$

The solution set is all real numbers except for the excluded values or $\mathbb{R}\sim\left\{-\dfrac{2}{3},\dfrac{1}{2}\right\}$.

63. To find the x-intercept let $y=0$ and solve for x.

$$\frac{x+5}{x-2}=0$$

$$(x-2)\left[\frac{x+5}{(x-2)}\right]=(x-2)0$$

$$x+5=0$$

$$x=-5$$

The x-intercept is $(-5,0)$.

To find the y-intercept let $x=0$ and solve for y.

$$y=\frac{x+5}{x-2}$$

$$y=\frac{(0)+5}{(0)-2}$$

$$y=-\frac{5}{2}$$

The y-intercept is $\left(0,-\dfrac{5}{2}\right)$.

65. To find the x-intercept let $y=0$ and solve for x.

$$\frac{x^2-4}{x^2-1}=0$$

$$(x^2-1)\left[\frac{x^2-4}{(x^2-1)}\right]=(x^2-1)0$$

$$x^2-4=0$$

$$(x+2)(x-2)=0$$

$$x=-2\ \text{ or }\ x=2$$

The x-intercepts are $(-2,0)$ and $(2,0)$.

To find the y-intercept let $x=0$ and solve for y.

$$y=\frac{x^2-4}{x^2-1}$$

$$y=\frac{(0)^2-4}{(0)^2-1}=\frac{-4}{-1}=4$$

The y-intercept is $(0,4)$.

67. a.

$$\frac{5v+4}{2v^2+v-15}+\frac{3}{5-2v}-\frac{1}{v+3}=0$$

$$\frac{5v+4}{(2v-5)(v+3)}-\frac{3}{2v-5}-\frac{1}{v+3}=0$$

$$(2v-5)(v+3)\left[\frac{5v+4}{(2v-5)(v+3)}-\frac{3}{2v-5}-\frac{1}{v+3}\right]=(2v-5)(v+3)[0]$$

$$(2v-5)(v+3)\frac{5v+4}{(2v-5)(v+3)}-(2v-5)(v+3)\frac{3}{2v-5}-(2v-5)(v+3)\frac{1}{v+3}=0$$

$$5v+4-3(v+3)-(2v-5)=0$$

$$5v+4-3v-9-2v+5=0$$

$$0=0$$

The solution set is all real numbers except for the excluded values or $\mathbb{R} \sim \left\{-3, \frac{5}{2}\right\}$.

b.

$$\frac{5v+3}{2v^2+v-15}+\frac{3}{5-2v}-\frac{1}{v+3}=0$$

$$\frac{5v+3}{(2v-5)(v+3)}-\frac{3}{2v-5}-\frac{1}{v+3}=0$$

$$(2v-5)(v+3)\left[\frac{5v+3}{(2v-5)(v+3)}-\frac{3}{2v-5}-\frac{1}{v+3}\right]=(2v-5)(v+3)[0]$$

$$(2v-5)(v+3)\frac{5v+3}{(2v-5)(v+3)}-(2v-5)(v+3)\frac{3}{2v-5}-(2v-5)(v+3)\frac{1}{v+3}=0$$

$$5v+3-3(v+3)-(2v-5)=0$$

$$5v+3-3v-9-2v+5=0$$

$$-1=0 \text{ is false.}$$

Thus there is no solution.

69.

$$\frac{x^2}{2x^2+9x-5}+\frac{2x}{x^2+2x-15}=\frac{4x}{(2x-1)(x+5)(x-3)}$$

$$\frac{x^2}{(2x-1)(x+5)}+\frac{2x}{(x+5)(x-3)}=\frac{4x}{(2x-1)(x+5)(x-3)}$$

$$(2x-1)(x+5)(x-3)\left[\frac{x^2}{(2x-1)(x+5)}+\frac{2x}{(x+5)(x-3)}\right]=\cancel{(2x-1)}\cancel{(x+5)}\cancel{(x-3)}\left[\frac{4x}{\cancel{(2x-1)}\cancel{(x+5)}\cancel{(x-3)}}\right]$$

$$\cancel{(2x-1)}\cancel{(x+5)}(x-3)\frac{x^2}{\cancel{(2x-1)}\cancel{(x+5)}}+(2x-1)\cancel{(x+5)}\cancel{(x-3)}\frac{2x}{\cancel{(x+5)}\cancel{(x-3)}}=4x$$

$$x^2(x-3)+2x(2x-1)=4x$$

$$x^3-3x^2+4x^2-2x=4x$$

$$x^3+x^2-6x=0$$

$$x(x^2+x-6)=0$$

$$x(x+3)(x-2)=0$$

$$x=0,\ x=-3,\ \text{or}\ x=2$$

71.

$$\frac{z-2}{4z^2-29z+30}-\frac{z+2}{5z^2-27z-18}=\frac{z+1}{20z^2-13z-15}$$

$$\frac{z-2}{(4z-5)(z-6)}-\frac{z+2}{(5z+3)(z-6)}=\frac{z+1}{(4z-5)(5z+3)}$$

$$(5z+3)(z-6)(4z-5)\left[\frac{z-2}{(4z-5)(z-6)}-\frac{z+2}{(5z+3)(z-6)}\right]=\cancel{(5z+3)}(z-6)\cancel{(4z-5)}\left[\frac{z+1}{\cancel{(4z-5)}\cancel{(5z+3)}}\right]$$

$$(5z+3)\cancel{(z-6)}\cancel{(4z-5)}\frac{z-2}{\cancel{(4z-5)}\cancel{(z-6)}}-\cancel{(5z+3)}\cancel{(z-6)}(4z-5)\frac{z+2}{\cancel{(5z+3)}\cancel{(z-6)}}=(z-6)(z+1)$$

$$(5z+3)(z-2)-(4z-5)(z+2)=(z-6)(z+1)$$

$$5z^2-7z-6-(4z^2+3z-10)=z^2-5z-6$$

$$5z^2-7z-6-4z^2-3z+10=z^2-5z-6$$

$$-5z=-10$$

$$z=2$$

73.

$$\frac{z-1}{z^2-2z-3}+\frac{z+1}{z^2-4z+3}=\frac{z+8}{z^2-1}+\frac{20}{(z-1)(z+1)(z-3)}$$

$$\frac{z-1}{(z-3)(z+1)}+\frac{z+1}{(z-3)(z-1)}=\frac{z+8}{(z-1)(z+1)}+\frac{20}{(z-1)(z+1)(z-3)}$$

$$(z-1)(z+1)(z-3)\left[\frac{z-1}{(z-3)(z+1)}+\frac{z+1}{(z-3)(z-1)}\right]=(z-1)(z+1)(z-3)\left[\frac{z+8}{(z-1)(z+1)}+\frac{20}{(z-1)(z+1)(z-3)}\right]$$

$$(z-1)(z-1)+(z+1)(z+1)=(z-3)(z+8)+20$$

$$z^2-2z+1+z^2+2z+1=z^2+5z-24+20$$

$$z^2-5z+6=0$$

$$(z-2)(z-3)=0$$

$$z=2 \text{ or } z=3$$

The value $z=3$ is an excluded value. Therefore the solution is $z=2$.

Cumulative Review

1. If $x=3$ and $x=-\dfrac{1}{5}$ are solutions then $x-3=0$
and $5x+1=0$. Thus $(x-3)$ and $(5x+1)$ are
factors and the equation is $(x-3)(5x+1)=0$

$$5x^2+x-15x-3=0$$

$$5x^2-14x-3=0$$

2. If $x=-\sqrt{6}$ and $x=\sqrt{6}$ are solutions then
$x+\sqrt{6}=0$ and $x-\sqrt{6}=0$. Thus $\left(x-\sqrt{6}\right)$ and
$\left(x+\sqrt{6}\right)$ are factors and the equation is

$$\left(x-\sqrt{6}\right)\left(x+\sqrt{6}\right)=0$$

$$x^2-6=0$$

3. If $x=1-2i$ and $x=1+2i$ are solutions then
$x-(1-2i)=0$ and $x-(1+2i)=0$. Thus
$\left(x-(1-2i)\right)$ and $\left(x-(1+2i)\right)$ are factors and the
equation is $\left(x-(1-2i)\right)\left(x+(1-2i)\right)=0$

$$(x-1+2i)(x-1-2i)=0$$

$$((x-1)+2i)((x-1)-2i)=0$$

$$(x-1)^2-4i^2=0$$

$$x^2-2x+1-4(-1)=0$$

$$x^2-2x+1+4=0$$

$$x^2-2x+5=0$$

4. Find the values that make the denominator zero.

$$2x-6=0$$

$$x=3$$

The excluded value is 3.

Domain: $(-\infty, 3)\cup(3, +\infty)$ or $\mathbb{R}\sim\{3\}$

5. Find the values that make the denominator zero.

$$x^2+4=0$$

$$x^2=-4$$

$$x=\pm\sqrt{-4}$$

$$x=\pm 2i$$

Since there are no real solutions. There aren't any
excluded values and the domain is $\mathbb{R}$ or $(-\infty, \infty)$.

Section 9.6: Inverse and Joint Variation and Other Applications Yielding Equations with Fractions

Quick Review 9.6

1.
$$d = r \cdot t$$
$$240 = 60t$$
$$t = 4 \text{ hr}$$
It takes 4 hours to drive 240 miles while averaging 60 mi/hr.

2.
$$d = r \cdot t$$
$$240 = 50t$$
$$t = 4.8 \text{ hr}$$
It takes 4.8 hours (4 hours and 48 min) to drive 240 miles while averaging 50 mi/hr.

3.
$$d = r \cdot t$$
$$240 = r(0.5)$$
$$r = 480 \text{ mi/hr}$$
To travel 480 in 0.5 hours, one must average 480 mi/hr.

4.
$$I = PRT$$
$$I = (5000)(0.06)(1)$$
$$I = 300$$
The interest on an investment of $5000 for one year at 6% interest is $300.

5.
$$I = PRT$$
$$80 = (12000)(r)\left(\frac{1}{12}\right) \quad \text{(One month is 1/12 of one year.)}$$
$$80 = 1000r$$
$$r = \frac{80}{1000} = 0.8$$
The interest on an investment of $12000 for one month at 8% interest is $80.

Exercises 9.6

1. $C = \pi d$ is of the form $y = kx$. It is an example of direct variation.

3. $P = \dfrac{250}{R}$ is of the form $y = \dfrac{k}{x}$. It is an example of inverse variation.

5. The values of y are increasing as the values of x are increasing. This is an example of direct variation.

7. The values of T are decreasing as the values of N are increasing. This is an example of inverse variation.

9. The relationship is not linear. The values of T are decreasing as the values of R are increasing. This is an example of inverse variation.

11. $m = kn$

13. $m = \dfrac{k}{p}$

15. $v = k\sqrt{w}$

17. $v = \dfrac{k}{x^2}$

19. $m = \dfrac{kn}{p}$

21. $v = \dfrac{k\sqrt{w}}{x^2}$

23. $m = knp$

25. $v = k\sqrt{w}\,x^2$

27. If the electrical current I varies directly as the voltage V, then $I = kV$ for some constant k.

29. If the weight w of an astronaut varies inversely as the square of the distance d from the center of the earth, then $w = \dfrac{k}{d^2}$ for some constant k.

31. If the force of the wind resistance R on a moving automobile varies directly as the square of the velocity v of the automobile, then $R = kv^2$ for some constant k.

33. If the volume V of a cone varies jointly with the square of the radius r and the height h. Then $V = kr^2h$ for some constant k. The constant of variation in this problem is $k = \frac{1}{3}\pi$.

35. **a.** If y varies directly as x and $y = 24$ when $x = 8$, then

$$y = kx$$
$$24 = k(8)$$
$$k = 3$$

With $x = 10$ we have $y = 3x$

$$y = 3(10)$$
$$y = 30$$

b. If y varies inversely as x and $y = 24$ when $x = 8$, then

$$y = \frac{k}{x}$$
$$24 = \frac{k}{8}$$
$$k = 192$$

With $x = 10$ we have $y = \frac{192}{x}$

$$y = \frac{192}{10}$$
$$y = 19.2$$

37. a varies directly as b and inversely as c and $a = 3$ when $b = 9$ and $c = 12$.

$$a = \frac{kb}{c}$$
$$3 = \frac{k(9)}{12}$$
$$k = \frac{3 \cdot 12}{9} = 4$$

With $b = 15$ and $c = 6$ we have $a = \frac{4b}{c}$

$$a = \frac{4(15)}{6}$$
$$a = 10$$

39. a varies jointly as b and as c and $a = 27$ when $b = 9$ and $c = 12$.

$$a = kbc$$
$$27 = k(9)(12)$$
$$k = \frac{27}{(9)(12)} = \frac{1}{4}$$

With $b = 15$ and $c = 6$ we have

$$a = \frac{1}{4}bc$$
$$a = \frac{1}{4}(15)(6)$$
$$a = \frac{45}{2} = 22.5$$

41. **a.** Let n = the amount of newsprint
p = the number of people using the newsprint

$$n = kp$$
$$34800 = k(1000)$$
$$k = 34.8$$

b. $n = 34.8p$

c.

p	$n = 34.8p$
700,000	24,360,000
710,000	24,708,000
720,000	25,056,000
730,000	25,404,000
740,000	25,752,000
750,000	26,100,000

d. From the table we can see that a city with a population of 720,000 would require 25,056,000 kg of newsprint.

43. **a.** Let $T =$ the time required to distribute the fliers
$w =$ the number of workers

$$T = \frac{k}{w}$$

$$8 = \frac{k}{5}$$

$$k = 40$$

b. $T = \dfrac{40}{w}$

c.

w	$T = \dfrac{40}{w}$
5	8.00
10	4.00
15	2.67
20	2.00
25	1.60
30	1.33

d. From the table we can see that it would take 20 workers 2 hours to distribute the fliers.

45. Let $T =$ the time it takes to get a sun burn
$l =$ the ultraviolet light index

$$T = \frac{k}{l}$$

$$15 = \frac{k}{6}$$

$$k = 90$$

With $l = 10$ we have

$$T = \frac{90}{10}$$

$T = 9$ minutes to get a sun burn

47. Let $r =$ resistance of the wire
$d =$ diameter of the wire

$$r = \frac{k}{d^2}$$

$$4.5 = \frac{k}{4^2}$$

$$k = 72$$

With $d = 6$ we have $r = \dfrac{72}{d^2}$

$$r = \frac{72}{6^2} = 2 \text{ ohms}$$

49. Let $L =$ load that the beam can support
$w =$ width of the beam
$h =$ height of the beam
$l =$ length of the beam

$$L = \frac{kwh^2}{l}$$

$$800 = \frac{k(2)(6)^2}{120}$$

$$k = \frac{800(120)}{2(6)^2}$$

$$k = \frac{4000}{3}$$

With $w = 6$, $h = 2$, and $l = 120$ we have

$$L = \frac{kwh^2}{l}$$

$$L = \frac{4000}{3}\frac{(6)(2)^2}{120}$$

$$L = \frac{800}{3} = 266.6\overline{7} \approx 270 \text{ pounds}$$

51. Let $x =$ first integer
$x + 1 =$ second integer

$$\frac{1}{x} + \frac{1}{x+1} = \frac{11}{30}$$

$$30x(x+1)\left[\frac{1}{x} + \frac{1}{x+1}\right] = 30x(x+1)\left[\frac{11}{30}\right]$$

$$30x(x+1)\frac{1}{x} + 30x(x+1)\frac{1}{x+1} = 11x(x+1)$$

$$30(x+1) + 30x = 11x(x+1)$$

$$30x + 30 + 30x = 11x^2 + 11x$$

$$11x^2 - 49x - 30 = 0$$

$$(11x+6)(x-5) = 0$$

Note: This answer is not an integer.

$$x = -\frac{6}{11} \quad \text{or} \quad x = 5$$

The integers are 5 and $5 + 1 = 6$.

53. Let x = first integer

$x + 2$ = second integer

$$\frac{1}{x} + \frac{1}{x+2} = \frac{16}{x(x+2)}$$

$$x(x+2)\left[\frac{1}{x} + \frac{1}{x+2}\right] = \cancel{x}\cancel{(x+2)}\left[\frac{16}{\cancel{x}\cancel{(x+2)}}\right]$$

$$\cancel{x}(x+2)\frac{1}{\cancel{x}} + x\cancel{(x+2)}\frac{1}{\cancel{x+2}} = 16$$

$$(x+2) + x = 16$$

$$2x = 14$$

$$x = 7$$

The integers are 7 and $7 + 2 = 9$.

55. Let x = numerator

$$\frac{x}{x^2+4} = \frac{3}{20}$$

$$20\cancel{(x^2+4)}\left[\frac{x}{\cancel{x^2+4}}\right] = \cancel{20}(x^2+4)\left[\frac{3}{\cancel{20}}\right]$$

$$20x = 3(x^2+4)$$

$$3x^2 - 20x + 12 = 0$$

$$(3x-2)(x-6) = 0$$

$$x = \frac{2}{3} \quad \text{or} \quad x = 6$$

> Note: This answer is not an integer.

The numerator is 6.

57. Let x = number

$$x + \frac{1}{x} = \frac{13}{6}$$

$$6x\left[x + \frac{1}{x}\right] = \cancel{6}x\left[\frac{13}{\cancel{6}}\right]$$

$$(6x)x + (6\cancel{x})\frac{1}{\cancel{x}} = 13x$$

$$6x^2 + 6 = 13x$$

$$6x^2 - 13x + 6 = 0$$

$$(3x-2)(2x-3) = 0$$

$$x = \frac{2}{3} \quad \text{or} \quad x = \frac{3}{2}$$

The number is either $\frac{2}{3}$ or $\frac{3}{2}$.

59. Let x = normal reading

$$\frac{x+3}{x+5} = \frac{4}{5}$$

$$5\cancel{(x+5)}\left[\frac{x+3}{\cancel{x+5}}\right] = \cancel{5}(x+5)\left[\frac{4}{\cancel{5}}\right]$$

$$5(x+3) = 4(x+5)$$

$$5x + 15 = 4x + 20$$

$$x = 5$$

The normal reading is 5.

61. Let x = length of the first piece

$16 - x$ = length of the second piece.

$$\frac{16-x}{x} = \frac{3}{1}$$

$$\cancel{x}\left(\frac{16-x}{\cancel{x}}\right) = x\left(\frac{3}{1}\right)$$

$$16 - x = 3x$$

$$4x = 16$$

$$x = 4$$

The pieces of wire are 4 meters and $16 - 4 = 12$ meters long.

63.

$$\frac{1}{R} = \frac{1}{r_1} + \frac{1}{r_2}$$

$$\frac{1}{40} = \frac{1}{r_1} + \frac{1}{2r_1}$$

$$\cancel{40}r_1\left[\frac{1}{\cancel{40}}\right] = 40r_1\left[\frac{1}{r_1} + \frac{1}{2r_1}\right]$$

$$r_1 = (40r_1)\frac{1}{r_1} + (40r_1)\frac{1}{2r_1}$$

$$r_1 = (40\cancel{r_1})\frac{1}{\cancel{r_1}} + \left(\overset{20}{\cancel{40}}\cancel{r_1}\right)\frac{1}{\cancel{2}\cancel{r_1}}$$

$$r_1 = 40 + 20$$

$$r_1 = 60$$

$r_1 = 60$ ohms and $r_2 = 2(60) = 120$ ohms

65. Let x = first angle.
$90 - x$ = second angle.

$$\frac{90 - x}{x} = \frac{3}{2}$$

$$2x\left(\frac{90 - x}{x}\right) = 2x\left(\frac{3}{2}\right)$$

$$2(90 - x) = 3x$$

$$180 - 2x = 3x$$

$$5x = 180$$

$$x = 36$$

The angles are $36°$ and $90° - 36° = 54°$

67. Let x = amount in secure funds
$12000 - x$ = amount in high risk funds

$$\frac{x}{12000 - x} = \frac{7}{3}$$

$$3(12000 - x)\left[\frac{x}{12000 - x}\right] = 3(12000 - x)\left[\frac{7}{3}\right]$$

$$3x = 7(12000 - x)$$

$$3x = 84000 - 7x$$

$$10x = 84000$$

$$x = 8400$$

$8400 is invested in secure funds.

69.

$$\frac{500x + 10000}{100x + 14000} = \frac{5}{4}$$

$$(100x + 14000)\left(\frac{500x + 10000}{100x + 14000}\right) = (100x + 14000)\overset{25x + 3500}{\frac{5}{4}}$$

$$500x + 10000 = 5(25x + 3500)$$

$$500x + 10000 = 125x + 17500$$

$$375x = 7500$$

$$x = 20$$

Thus 20 vehicles were sold in January.

71. Let x = rate of each boat in still water
$x + 6$ = rate of boat going downstream
$x - 6$ = rate of boat going upstream

$$T = \frac{D}{R} = \frac{51}{x + 6} = \text{time of boat going}$$
downstream

$$T = \frac{D}{R} = \frac{15}{x - 6} = \text{time of boat going upstream}$$

Since the boats travel for the same amount of time we know:

$$\frac{51}{x + 6} = \frac{15}{x - 6}$$

$$(x - 6)(x + 6)\left[\frac{51}{x + 6}\right] = \left[\frac{15}{x - 6}\right](x - 6)(x + 6)$$

$$51(x - 6) = 15(x + 6)$$

$$51x - 306 = 15x + 90$$

$$36x = 396$$

$$x = 11$$

The rate of each boat in still water is 11 km per hour.

73. Let x = rate of slower plane

$x + 40$ = rate of faster plane

$T = \dfrac{D}{R} = \dfrac{1080}{x}$ = time of slower plane

$T = \dfrac{D}{R} = \dfrac{1170}{x+40}$ = time of faster plane

Since both planes travel for the same time we know:

$$\frac{1080}{x} = \frac{1170}{x+40}$$

$$\cancel{x}(x+40)\left[\frac{1080}{\cancel{x}}\right] = x\cancel{(x+40)}\left[\frac{1170}{\cancel{x+40}}\right]$$

$$1080(x+40) = 1170x$$

$$1080x + 43200 = 1170x$$

$$90x = 43200$$

$$x = 480$$

The rate of the slower plane is 480 miles per hour.
The rate of the faster plane is 520 miles per hour.

75. Let t = time for the two pipes to fill the tank

$\dfrac{1}{15}$ = rate of work for the small pipe

$\dfrac{1}{10}$ = rate of work for the hot faucet

$$\begin{pmatrix}\text{Rate}\\\text{of}\\\text{small}\\\text{pipe}\end{pmatrix}\begin{pmatrix}\text{Time}\\\text{of}\\\text{small}\\\text{pipe}\end{pmatrix} + \begin{pmatrix}\text{Rate}\\\text{of}\\\text{large}\\\text{pipe}\end{pmatrix}\begin{pmatrix}\text{Time}\\\text{of}\\\text{large}\\\text{pipe}\end{pmatrix} = \begin{pmatrix}\text{Total}\\\text{Work}\end{pmatrix}$$

$$\left(\frac{1}{15}\right)(t) \quad + \quad \left(\frac{1}{10}\right)(t) \quad = \quad 1$$

$$\frac{t}{15} + \frac{t}{10} = 1$$

$$30\left(\frac{t}{15} + \frac{t}{10}\right) = 30(1)$$

$$\overset{2}{\cancel{30}}\,\frac{t}{\cancel{15}} + \overset{3}{\cancel{30}}\,\frac{t}{\cancel{10}} = 30$$

$$2t + 3t = 30$$

$$5t = 30$$

$$t = 6$$

It would take 6 hour for both pipes to fill the tank.

77. Let t = time for the large pipe to fill the tank; $\dfrac{1}{t}$ = rate of work for the large pipe

$t + 6$ = time for the small pipe to fill the tank; $\dfrac{1}{t+6}$ = rate of work for the small pipe

$$\begin{pmatrix}\text{Rate of}\\\text{large pipe}\end{pmatrix}\begin{pmatrix}\text{Time of}\\\text{large pipe}\end{pmatrix} + \begin{pmatrix}\text{Rate of}\\\text{small pipe}\end{pmatrix}\begin{pmatrix}\text{Time of}\\\text{small pipe}\end{pmatrix} = \begin{pmatrix}\text{Total}\\\text{Work}\end{pmatrix}$$

$$\left(\frac{1}{t}\right)(4) \quad + \quad \left(\frac{1}{t+6}\right)(4) \quad = \quad 1$$

$$\frac{4}{t} + \frac{4}{t+6} = 1$$

$$t(t+6)\left[\frac{4}{t} + \frac{4}{t+6}\right] = t(t+6)[1]$$

$$\cancel{t}(t+6)\frac{4}{\cancel{t}} + t\cancel{(t+6)}\frac{4}{\cancel{t+6}} = t(t+6)$$

$$4(t+6) + 4t = t(t+6)$$

$$4t + 24 + 4t = t^2 + 6t$$

$$t^2 - 2t - 24 = 0$$

$$(t-6)(t+4) = 0$$

$$t = 6 \quad \text{or} \quad t = -4$$

Note: This answer is not appropriate.

It would take 6 hours for the large pipe to fill the tank alone.

79. Let $t =$ time for plane B to complete the search

$\dfrac{1}{t} =$ rate of work for plane B

$$\begin{pmatrix} \text{Rate} \\ \text{of} \\ \text{plane A} \end{pmatrix}\begin{pmatrix} \text{Time} \\ \text{of} \\ \text{plane A} \end{pmatrix} + \begin{pmatrix} \text{Rate} \\ \text{of} \\ \text{plane B} \end{pmatrix}\begin{pmatrix} \text{Time} \\ \text{of} \\ \text{plane B} \end{pmatrix} = \begin{pmatrix} \text{Total} \\ \text{Work} \end{pmatrix}$$

$$\left(\frac{1}{50}\right)(30) \quad + \quad \left(\frac{1}{t}\right)(30) \quad = \quad 1$$

$$\frac{30}{50} + \frac{30}{t} = 1$$

$$50t\left(\frac{30}{50} + \frac{30}{t}\right) = 50t(1)$$

$$50t\frac{30}{50} + 50t\frac{30}{t} = 50t$$

$$30t + 1500 = 50t$$

$$20t = 1500$$

$$t = 75$$

It would take 75 hours for new plane B to complete the search alone.

81. Let $r =$ rate of interest on the savings account.

$r + 0.02 =$ rate of interest on the money market account.

$I = PRT$; for $T = 1$ we can write $P = \dfrac{I}{R}$

$P = \dfrac{I}{R} = \dfrac{120}{r} =$ Principal in the savings account.

$P = \dfrac{I}{R} = \dfrac{200}{r+0.02} =$ Principal in the money market account.

$$\begin{pmatrix} \text{Principal in the} \\ \text{savings account} \end{pmatrix} = \begin{pmatrix} \text{Principal in the} \\ \text{money market account} \end{pmatrix}$$

$$\frac{120}{r} = \frac{200}{r+0.02}$$

$$r(r+0.02)\left(\frac{120}{r}\right) = r(r+0.02)\left(\frac{200}{r+0.02}\right)$$

$$120(r+0.02) = 200r$$

$$120r + 2.4 = 200r$$

$$80r = 2.4$$

$$r = 0.03$$

The interest rate for the savings account is 3% and the interest for the money market account is 5%.

83. Let $r =$ rate of interest on the 30-year mortgage.

$r - 0.015 =$ rate of interest on the 15-year mortgage.

$I = PRT$; we can write $P = \dfrac{I}{TR}$

$P = \dfrac{I}{TR} = \dfrac{10200}{r} =$ Principal on the 30-year mortgage. (I is the interest for 1 year: $I = 12 \cdot 850 = 10200$)

$P = \dfrac{I}{TR} = \dfrac{8400}{r - 0.015} =$ Principal on the 15-year mortgage. (I is the interest for 1 year: $I = 12 \cdot 700 = 8400$)

$$\begin{pmatrix} \text{Principal in the} \\ \text{30-year mortgage} \end{pmatrix} = \begin{pmatrix} \text{Principal in the} \\ \text{15-year mortgage} \end{pmatrix}$$

$$\frac{10200}{r} = \frac{8400}{r - 0.015}$$

$$\cancel{r}\,(r - 0.015)\left(\frac{10200}{\cancel{r}}\right) = r\,\cancel{(r - 0.015)}\left(\frac{8400}{\cancel{r - 0.015}}\right)$$

$$10200(r - 0.015) = 8400r$$

$$10200r - 153 = 8400r$$

$$1800r = 153$$

$$r = 0.085$$

The interest rate for the 30-year mortgage is 8.5% and the interest for the 15-year mortgage is 7%.

Cumulative Review

1.

$x + 2 = x + 3$

$x - x + 2 = x - x + 3$

$2 = 3$

This is a contradiction.

The proper choice is **C**.

2.

$x + 3 = x + 3$

$x - x + 3 = x - x + 3$

$3 = 3$

This is an identity.

The equation is an unconditional equation.

The proper choice is **B**.

3.

$x + 2 = 2x + 3$

$x - x + 2 = 2x - x + 3$

$2 = x - 3$

$x = 5$

There is only one solution.

The equation is a conditional equation.

The proper choice is **A**.

4. **Define the Variable:** Let x represent the number of liters of water added.

Verbal Equation:

Acid in Existing Mixture		Acid in Water Added		Total Acid in Desired Mixture
	$+$		$=$	

Algebraic Equation: $0.25(5) + (0.00)x = 0.20(5 + x)$

$$1.25 = 1.00 + 0.20x$$

$$0.20x = 0.25$$

$$x = 1.25$$

Answer: The chemist should add 1.25 liters of water.

5.   **Define the Variable:** Let x represent the speed of the faster train.

Verbal Equation: $\boxed{\begin{array}{c}\text{Distance Traveled} \\ \text{by the Faster Train}\end{array}} + \boxed{\begin{array}{c}\text{Distance Traveled} \\ \text{by the Slower Train}\end{array}} = \boxed{\begin{array}{c}\text{Total Distance} \\ \text{Traveled}\end{array}}$

Algebraic Equation: $0.5x + 0.5(x-8) = 99$

$$0.5x + .5x - 4 = 99$$

$$x = 103$$

Answer: The speed of the faster train is 103 km/hr.
The speed of the slower train is $103 - 8 = 95$ km/hr.

Review Exercises for Chapter 9

1. $f(0) = \dfrac{2(0)-9}{(0)^2-1} = \dfrac{-9}{-1} = 9$

2. $f(1) = \dfrac{2(1)-9}{(1)^2-1} = \dfrac{-7}{0}$ is undefined.

3. $f(4) = \dfrac{2(4)-9}{(4)^2-1} = \dfrac{-1}{15} = -\dfrac{1}{15}$

4. $f(10) = \dfrac{2(10)-9}{(10)^2-1} = \dfrac{11}{99} = \dfrac{1}{9}$

5.   The domain is the set of x values such that the function is defined. Thus the domain is all real numbers except -2 and 3. Domain: $(-\infty, -2) \cup (-2, 3) \cup (3, +\infty)$ or $\mathbb{R} \sim \{-2, 3\}$

6.   The domain is the set of x values such that the function is defined. Thus the domain is all real numbers except -5 and 3. Domain: $(-\infty, -5) \cup (-5, 3) \cup (3, +\infty)$ or $\mathbb{R} \sim \{-5, 3\}$

7.   The domain is the set of x values such that the function is defined. Thus the domain is all real numbers except -5 and $\dfrac{1}{3}$. Domain: $(-\infty, -5) \cup \left(-5, \dfrac{1}{3}\right) \cup \left(\dfrac{1}{3}, +\infty\right)$ or $\mathbb{R} \sim \left\{-5, \dfrac{1}{3}\right\}$

8.   The denominator is never zero. Thus the domain is all real numbers. Domain: $(-\infty, +\infty)$ or $\mathbb{R}$

9.   Find the values where the denominator is zero.
$$4x - 2 = 0$$
$$4x = 2$$
$$x = \frac{1}{2}$$
The vertical asymptote is $x = \dfrac{1}{2}$.

10.   Find the values where the denominator is zero.
$$x^2 - 36 = 0$$
$$(x-6)(x+6) = 0$$
$$x = 6 \ \text{ or } \ x = -6$$
The vertical asymptotes are $x = 6$ or $x = -6$.

11.   Find the values where the denominator is zero.
$$x^2 - 9x = 0$$
$$x(x-9) = 0$$
$$x = 0 \ \text{ or } \ x = 9$$
The vertical asymptotes are $x = 0$ or $x = 9$.

12. $\dfrac{36x^2y}{12xy^3} = \dfrac{\cancel{36}^{\,3}\,\cancel{x^2}^{\,x}\,\cancel{y}}{\cancel{12}\,\cancel{x}\,\cancel{y^3}_{\,y^2}} = \dfrac{3x}{y^2}$

13. $\dfrac{6a-18b}{12b-4a} = \dfrac{6\left(a-3b\right)}{-4\left(a-3b\right)} = -\dfrac{3}{2}$

14. $\dfrac{15x^2-15}{25x+25} = \dfrac{15\left(x^2-1\right)}{25\left(x+1\right)} = \dfrac{\overset{3}{\cancel{15}}\left(x-1\right)\left(x+1\right)}{\underset{5}{\cancel{25}}\left(x+1\right)}$

$\qquad\qquad = \dfrac{3\left(x-1\right)}{5}$

15. $\dfrac{x^2+x-30}{2x^2+11x-6} = \dfrac{\left(x+6\right)\left(x-5\right)}{\left(x+6\right)\left(2x-1\right)} = \dfrac{x-5}{2x-1}$

16. $\dfrac{cx-cy}{ax-ay+bx-by} = \dfrac{c\left(x-y\right)}{a\left(x-y\right)+b\left(x-y\right)}$

$\qquad\qquad = \dfrac{c\left(x-y\right)}{\left(a+b\right)\left(x-y\right)} = \dfrac{c}{a+b}$

17. $\dfrac{3-7m}{14m^2-6m} = \dfrac{\left(3-7m\right)}{-2m\left(3-7m\right)} = -\dfrac{1}{2m}$

18. $\dfrac{10x^2+29xy+10y^2}{6x^2+13xy-5y^2} = \dfrac{\left(5x+2y\right)\left(2x+5y\right)}{\left(2x+5y\right)\left(3x-y\right)}$

$\qquad\qquad = \dfrac{5x+2y}{3x-y}$

19. $\dfrac{9x^2-24xy+16y^2}{12x^2-25xy+12y^2} = \dfrac{\left(3x-4y\right)\left(3x-4y\right)}{\left(3x-4y\right)\left(4x-3y\right)}$

$\qquad\qquad = \dfrac{3x-4y}{4x-3y}$

20. $\dfrac{x^2-4y^2}{x^2-4xy+4y^2} = \dfrac{\left(x+2y\right)\left(x-2y\right)}{\left(x-2y\right)\left(x-2y\right)}$

$\qquad\qquad = \dfrac{x+2y}{x-2y}$

21. $\dfrac{2x+1}{x-3} = \dfrac{?}{x^2-6x+9}$

$\qquad \dfrac{2x+1}{x-3} = \dfrac{?}{\left(x-3\right)\left(x-3\right)}$

$\qquad \dfrac{2x+1}{x-3} = \dfrac{\left(x-3\right)\left(2x+1\right)}{\left(x-3\right)\left(x-3\right)}$

$\qquad\qquad ? = \left(x-3\right)\left(2x+1\right)$

22. $\dfrac{y-3}{y+4} = \dfrac{?}{2y^2+9y+4}$

$\qquad \dfrac{y-3}{y+4} = \dfrac{?}{\left(y+4\right)\left(2y+1\right)}$

$\qquad \dfrac{y-3}{y+4} = \dfrac{\left(2y+1\right)\left(y-3\right)}{\left(y+4\right)\left(2y+1\right)}$

$\qquad\qquad ? = \left(2y+1\right)\left(y-3\right)$

23. The table of values is the same as **D**. Thus $\dfrac{2x-1}{x-2}+\dfrac{x-2}{2x-1} = \dfrac{5x^2-8x+5}{\left(x-2\right)\left(2x-1\right)}$.

24. The table of values is the same as **C**. Thus $\dfrac{2x-1}{x-2}-\dfrac{x-2}{2x-1} = \dfrac{3x^2-3}{\left(x-2\right)\left(2x-1\right)}$.

25. Aside from the excluded values, the table is the same as **A**. Thus $\dfrac{2x-1}{x-2}\cdot\dfrac{x-2}{2x-1} = 1$.

26. The table of values is the same as **B**. Thus $\dfrac{2x-1}{x-2}\div\dfrac{x-2}{2x-1} = \dfrac{4x^2-4x+1}{\left(x-2\right)^2}$.

27. $\dfrac{36x^2 - 24x}{6x} = \dfrac{\cancel{6x}\,(6x-4)}{\cancel{6x}} = 6x - 4$

28. $\dfrac{6xy}{2x-y} \cdot \dfrac{4x^2 - y^2}{3x^2} = \dfrac{6xy}{2x-y} \cdot \dfrac{(2x-y)(2x+y)}{3x^2}$

$$= \dfrac{\overset{2}{\cancel{6}}\;\cancel{x}\,y\,\cancel{(2x-y)}\,(2x+y)}{\cancel{3}\;\underset{x}{\cancel{x^2}}\,\cancel{(2x-y)}}$$

$$= \dfrac{2y(2x+y)}{x}$$

29. $\dfrac{9t^2 - 4}{16st} \div \dfrac{3t+2}{16st^2 + 8st} = \dfrac{(3t-2)(3t+2)}{16st} \cdot \dfrac{8st(2t+1)}{3t+2}$

$$= \dfrac{\cancel{8st}\,(3t-2)\,\cancel{(3t+2)}\,(2t+1)}{\underset{2}{\cancel{16st}}\,\cancel{(3t+2)}}$$

$$= \dfrac{(3t-2)(2t+1)}{2}$$

30. $\dfrac{v^2 + 9vw + 8w^2}{v^2 - w^2} \div \dfrac{v^2 + 7vw - 8w^2}{v^2 + 5vw - 6w^2}$

$$= \dfrac{v^2 + 9vw + 8w^2}{v^2 - w^2} \cdot \dfrac{v^2 + 5vw - 6w^2}{v^2 + 7vw - 8w^2}$$

$$\dfrac{\cancel{(v+w)}\,\cancel{(v+8w)}}{\cancel{(v+w)}\,(v-w)} \cdot \dfrac{(v+6w)\,\cancel{(v-w)}}{\cancel{(v+8w)}\,\cancel{(v-w)}} = \dfrac{v+6w}{v-w}$$

31. $\dfrac{3x}{6x^2 + x - 1} - \dfrac{1}{6x^2 + x - 1} = \dfrac{3x-1}{6x^2 + x - 1} = \dfrac{\cancel{3x-1}}{\cancel{(3x-1)}(2x+1)} = \dfrac{1}{2x+1}$

32. $\dfrac{1}{w+1} - \dfrac{w}{w-2} + \dfrac{w^2 + 2}{w^2 - w - 2} = \dfrac{1}{w+1} \cdot \dfrac{w-2}{w-2} - \dfrac{w}{w-2} \cdot \dfrac{w+1}{w+1} + \dfrac{w^2 + 2}{(w-2)(w+1)} = \dfrac{(w-2) - w(w+1) + (w^2 + 2)}{(w-2)(w+1)}$

$$= \dfrac{w - 2 - w^2 - w + w^2 + 2}{(w-2)(w+1)} = \dfrac{0}{(w-2)(w+1)} = 0$$

33. $\dfrac{3v}{3v^2 - 5v + 2} - \dfrac{2v}{2v^2 - v - 1} = \dfrac{3v}{(3v-2)(v-1)} - \dfrac{2v}{(2v+1)(v-1)} = \dfrac{3v}{(3v-2)(v-1)} \cdot \dfrac{2v+1}{2v+1} - \dfrac{2v}{(2v+1)(v-1)} \cdot \dfrac{3v-2}{3v-2}$

$$= \dfrac{3v(2v+1) - 2v(3v-2)}{(3v-2)(v-1)(2v+1)} = \dfrac{6v^2 + 3v - 6v^2 + 4v}{(3v-2)(v-1)(2v+1)} = \dfrac{7v}{(3v-2)(v-1)(2v+1)}$$

34. $\dfrac{6x}{2x-3} - \dfrac{9x+18}{4x^2 - 9} \cdot \dfrac{2x^2 - x - 6}{x^2 - 4} = \dfrac{6x}{2x-3} - \dfrac{9\cancel{(x+2)}}{(2x-3)\cancel{(2x+3)}} \cdot \dfrac{\cancel{(2x+3)}\,\cancel{(x-2)}}{\cancel{(x-2)}\cancel{(x+2)}} = \dfrac{6x}{2x-3} - \dfrac{9}{2x-3} = \dfrac{6x-9}{2x-3}$

$$= \dfrac{3\cancel{(2x-3)}}{\cancel{2x-3}} = 3$$

35. $\dfrac{2w+4}{w^2+4w-12}+\dfrac{w^2-169}{2w^2-13w+21}\div\dfrac{w^2-15w+26}{2w-7}=\dfrac{2w+4}{w^2+4w-12}+\dfrac{w^2-169}{2w^2-13w+21}\cdot\dfrac{2w-7}{w^2-15w+26}$

$=\dfrac{2w+4}{(w+6)(w-2)}+\dfrac{(w+13)\,(w-13)}{(2w-7)\,(w-3)}\cdot\dfrac{2w-7}{(w-2)\,(w-13)}=\dfrac{2w+4}{(w+6)(w-2)}+\dfrac{w+13}{(w-3)(w-2)}$

$=\dfrac{2w+4}{(w+6)(w-2)}\cdot\dfrac{w-3}{w-3}+\dfrac{w+13}{(w-3)(w-2)}\cdot\dfrac{w+6}{w+6}=\dfrac{(2w+4)(w-3)+(w+13)(w+6)}{(w+6)(w-2)(w-3)}$

$=\dfrac{2w^2-2w-12+w^2+19w+78}{(w+6)(w-2)(w-3)}=\dfrac{3w^2+17w+66}{(w+6)(w-2)(w-3)}$

36. $\dfrac{6v^2-25v+4}{6v^2+5v-6}\div\dfrac{2v^2-3v-20}{4v^2+16v+15}=\dfrac{6v^2-25v+4}{6v^2+5v-6}\cdot\dfrac{4v^2+16v+15}{2v^2-3v-20}$

$=\dfrac{(6v-1)\,(v-4)}{(2v+3)\,(3v-2)}\cdot\dfrac{(2v+5)\,(2v+3)}{(2v+5)\,(v-4)}=\dfrac{6v-1}{3v-2}$

37. $\left(\dfrac{y}{4}-\dfrac{4}{y}\right)\left(y-\dfrac{y^2}{y+4}\right)=\left(\dfrac{y}{4}\cdot\dfrac{y}{y}-\dfrac{4}{y}\cdot\dfrac{4}{y}\right)\left(\dfrac{y}{1}\cdot\dfrac{y+4}{y+4}-\dfrac{y^2}{y+4}\right)=\left(\dfrac{y^2-16}{4y}\right)\left(\dfrac{y(y+4)-y^2}{y+4}\right)$

$=\left(\dfrac{(y-4)(y+4)}{4y}\right)\left(\dfrac{y^2+4y-y^2}{y+4}\right)=\dfrac{(y-4)\,(y+4)}{4y}\cdot\dfrac{4y}{y+4}=y-4$

38. $\dfrac{5z+5}{6z^2+13z+6}-\dfrac{1-4z}{3z^2-7z-6}-\dfrac{3z}{2x^2-3z-9}=\dfrac{5z+5}{(2z+3)(3z+2)}-\dfrac{1-4z}{(z-3)(3z+2)}-\dfrac{3z}{(2z+3)(z-3)}$

$=\dfrac{5z+5}{(2z+3)(3z+2)}\cdot\dfrac{z-3}{z-3}-\dfrac{1-4z}{(z-3)(3z+2)}\cdot\dfrac{2z+3}{2z+3}-\dfrac{3z}{(2z+3)(z-3)}\cdot\dfrac{3z+2}{3z+2}$

$=\dfrac{(5z+5)(z-3)-(1-4z)(2z+3)-3z(3z+2)}{(2z+3)(3z+2)(z-3)}=\dfrac{5z^2-10z-15-(-8z^2-10z+3)-9z^2-6z}{(2z+3)(3z+2)(z-3)}$

$=\dfrac{5z^2-10z-15+8z^2+10z-3-9z^2-6z}{(2z+3)(3z+2)(z-3)}=\dfrac{4z^2-6z-18}{(2z+3)(3z+2)(z-3)}=\dfrac{2(2z^2-3z-9)}{(2z+3)(3z+2)(z-3)}$

$=\dfrac{2(2z+3)\,(z-3)}{(2z+3)\,(3z+2)\,(z-3)}=\dfrac{2}{3z+2}$

39. $\dfrac{\dfrac{1}{a}+\dfrac{1}{a+1}}{\dfrac{1}{a}+\dfrac{1}{a^2}}=\left(\dfrac{1}{a}+\dfrac{1}{a+1}\right)\div\left(\dfrac{1}{a}+\dfrac{1}{a^2}\right)=\left(\dfrac{1}{a}\cdot\dfrac{a+1}{a+1}+\dfrac{1}{a+1}\cdot\dfrac{a}{a}\right)\div\left(\dfrac{1}{a}\cdot\dfrac{a}{a}+\dfrac{1}{a^2}\right)=\left(\dfrac{(a+1)+a}{a(a+1)}\right)\div\left(\dfrac{a+1}{a^2}\right)$

$=\dfrac{2a+1}{a(a+1)}\cdot\dfrac{a^2}{a+1}=\dfrac{a(2a+1)}{(a+1)^2}$

40.
$$\frac{x+\dfrac{44}{x+5}-10}{x+\dfrac{33}{x+5}-9}=\frac{x+\dfrac{44}{x+5}-10}{x+\dfrac{33}{x+5}-9}\cdot\frac{x+5}{x+5}=\frac{\left(x+\dfrac{44}{x+5}-10\right)(x+5)}{\left(x+\dfrac{33}{x+5}-9\right)(x+5)}=\frac{x(x+5)+\dfrac{44}{x+5}(x+5)-10(x+5)}{x(x+5)+\dfrac{33}{x+5}(x+5)-9(x+5)}$$

$$=\frac{x^2+5x+44-10x-50}{x^2+5x+33-9x-45}=\frac{x^2-5x-6}{x^2-4x-12}=\frac{\cancel{(x-6)}(x+1)}{\cancel{(x-6)}(x+2)}=\frac{x+1}{x+2}$$

41.
$$\left(\frac{3v^2+11v+6}{3v^2+5v+2}\right)^2\div\frac{v^2-9}{v^2+2v+1}=\left(\frac{\cancel{(3v+2)}(v+3)}{\cancel{(3v+2)}(v+1)}\right)^2\cdot\frac{v^2+2v+1}{v^2-9}$$

$$=\frac{\overset{v+3}{\cancel{(v+3)^2}}}{\cancel{(v+1)^2}}\cdot\frac{\cancel{(v+1)^2}}{(v-3)\cancel{(v+3)}}=\frac{v+3}{v-3}$$

42.
$$\frac{x^{-2}-x^{-1}}{x^{-2}+x^{-1}}=\frac{\dfrac{1}{x^2}-\dfrac{1}{x}}{\dfrac{1}{x^2}+\dfrac{1}{x}}=\frac{\dfrac{1}{x^2}-\dfrac{1}{x}}{\dfrac{1}{x^2}+\dfrac{1}{x}}\cdot\frac{x^2}{x^2}=\frac{\left(\dfrac{1}{x^2}-\dfrac{1}{x}\right)x^2}{\left(\dfrac{1}{x^2}+\dfrac{1}{x}\right)x^2}=\frac{\dfrac{1}{x^2}(x^2)-\dfrac{1}{x}(x^2)}{\dfrac{1}{x^2}(x^2)+\dfrac{1}{x}(x^2)}=\frac{1-x}{1+x}=\frac{-(x-1)}{x+1}=-\frac{x-1}{x+1}$$

43.
$$\frac{x+y^{-1}}{x-y^{-1}}=\frac{x+\dfrac{1}{y}}{x-\dfrac{1}{y}}=\frac{x+\dfrac{1}{y}}{x-\dfrac{1}{y}}\cdot\frac{y}{y}=\frac{\left(x+\dfrac{1}{y}\right)y}{\left(x-\dfrac{1}{y}\right)y}=\frac{xy+\dfrac{1}{y}y}{xy-\dfrac{1}{y}y}=\frac{xy+1}{xy-1}$$

44.
$$\frac{36w^{-2}+23w^{-1}-8}{24-5w^{-1}-36w^{-2}}=\frac{\dfrac{36}{w^2}+\dfrac{23}{w}-8}{24-\dfrac{5}{w}-\dfrac{36}{w^2}}=\frac{\dfrac{36}{w^2}+\dfrac{23}{w}-8}{24-\dfrac{5}{w}-\dfrac{36}{w^2}}\cdot\frac{w^2}{w^2}=\frac{\left(\dfrac{36}{w^2}+\dfrac{23}{w}-8\right)w^2}{\left(24-\dfrac{5}{w}-\dfrac{36}{w^2}\right)w^2}=\frac{\dfrac{36}{w^2}w^2+\dfrac{23}{w}w^2-8w^2}{24w^2-\dfrac{5}{w}w^2-\dfrac{36}{w^2}w^2}$$

$$=\frac{36+23w-8w^2}{24w^2-5w-36}=\frac{-(8w^2-23w-36)}{(8w+9)(3w-4)}=\frac{-\cancel{(8w+9)}(w-4)}{\cancel{(8w+9)}(3w-4)}=-\frac{w-4}{3w-4}$$

45.
$$\left(m-\frac{15}{m+2}\right)\div\left(m-1-\frac{10}{m+2}\right)=\left(\frac{m}{1}\cdot\frac{m+2}{m+2}-\frac{15}{m+2}\right)\div\left(\frac{m-1}{1}\cdot\frac{m+2}{m+2}-\frac{10}{m+2}\right)$$

$$=\left(\frac{m(m+2)-15}{m+2}\right)\div\left(\frac{(m-1)(m+2)-10}{m+2}\right)$$

$$=\left(\frac{m^2+2m-15}{m+2}\right)\div\left(\frac{m^2+m-2-10}{m+2}\right)=\left(\frac{m^2+2m-15}{m+2}\right)\cdot\left(\frac{m+2}{m^2+m-12}\right)$$

$$=\frac{(m+5)\cancel{(m-3)}}{\cancel{m+2}}\cdot\frac{\cancel{m+2}}{(m+4)\cancel{(m-3)}}=\frac{m+5}{m+4}$$

46. $\dfrac{6y}{3y+2}+\dfrac{20y+4}{15y^2+7y-2}\div\dfrac{5y^2-24y-5}{5y^2-26y+5}=\dfrac{6y}{3y+2}+\dfrac{20y+4}{15y^2+7y-2}\cdot\dfrac{5y^2-26y+5}{5y^2-24y-5}$

$$=\dfrac{6y}{3y+2}+\dfrac{4\cancel{(5y+1)}}{\cancel{(5y-1)}(3y+2)}\cdot\dfrac{\cancel{(5y-1)}\cancel{(y-5)}}{\cancel{(5y+1)}\cancel{(y-5)}}$$

$$=\dfrac{6y}{3y+2}+\dfrac{4}{3y+2}=\dfrac{6y+4}{3y+2}=\dfrac{2\cancel{(3y+2)}}{\cancel{3y+2}}=2$$

47. $\dfrac{3y}{25y^2-1}+\dfrac{2y-1}{25y^2-1}=\dfrac{3y+(2y-1)}{25y^2-1}=\dfrac{\cancel{(5y-1)}}{\cancel{(5y-1)}(5y+1)}=\dfrac{1}{5y+1}$

48. $\dfrac{z^2-2z+1}{z^5-z^4}\cdot\dfrac{2z^4}{z^2-1}+\dfrac{2z^2+2z}{z^2+2z+1}=\dfrac{\cancel{(z-1)}\cancel{(z-1)}}{z^4\cancel{(z-1)}}\cdot\dfrac{2z^{\cancel{4}}}{\cancel{(z-1)}(z+1)}+\dfrac{2z\cancel{(z+1)}}{\cancel{(z+1)}(z+1)}=\dfrac{2}{(z+1)}+\dfrac{2z}{(z+1)}$

$$=\dfrac{2+2z}{(z+1)}=\dfrac{2\cancel{(z+1)}}{\cancel{(z+1)}}=2$$

49. a. $\dfrac{1}{m+2}-\dfrac{3}{m+4}=\dfrac{1}{m+2}\cdot\dfrac{m+4}{m+4}-\dfrac{3}{m+4}\cdot\dfrac{m+2}{m+2}$

$$=\dfrac{(m+4)-3(m+2)}{(m+2)(m+4)}=\dfrac{m+4-3m-6}{(m+2)(m+4)}$$

$$=\dfrac{-2m-2}{(m+2)(m+4)}=\dfrac{-2(m+1)}{(m+2)(m+4)}$$

$$=-\dfrac{2(m+1)}{(m+2)(m+4)}$$

b. $\dfrac{1}{m+2}=\dfrac{3}{m+4}$

$$\cancel{(m+2)}(m+4)\left[\dfrac{1}{\cancel{m+2}}\right]=(m+2)\cancel{(m+4)}\left[\dfrac{3}{\cancel{m+4}}\right]$$

$$m+4=3(m+2)$$

$$m+4=3m+6$$

$$-2m=2$$

$$m=-1$$

50. a. $\dfrac{x-2}{x+1}-\dfrac{x-4}{x-6}=\dfrac{x-2}{x+1}\cdot\dfrac{x-6}{x-6}-\dfrac{x-4}{x-6}\cdot\dfrac{x+1}{x+1}$

$$=\dfrac{(x-2)(x-6)-(x-4)(x+1)}{(x+1)(x-6)}$$

$$=\dfrac{(x^2-8x+12)-(x^2-3x-4)}{(x+1)(x-6)}$$

$$=\dfrac{x^2-8x+12-x^2+3x+4}{(x+1)(x-6)}=\dfrac{-5x+16}{(x+1)(x-6)}$$

b. $\dfrac{x-2}{x+1}=\dfrac{x-4}{x-6}$

$$\cancel{(x+1)}(x-6)\left[\dfrac{x-2}{\cancel{x+1}}\right]=(x+1)\cancel{(x-6)}\left[\dfrac{x-4}{\cancel{x-6}}\right]$$

$$(x-6)(x-2)=(x+1)(x-4)$$

$$x^2-8x+12=x^2-3x-4$$

$$-5x=-16$$

$$x=\dfrac{16}{5}$$

51. a. $\dfrac{x}{x-3}+\dfrac{x+4}{x-2}=\dfrac{x}{x-3}\cdot\dfrac{x-2}{x-2}+\dfrac{x+4}{x-2}\cdot\dfrac{x-3}{x-3}$

$=\dfrac{x(x-2)+(x+4)(x-3)}{(x-3)(x-2)}$

$=\dfrac{x^2-2x+x^2+x-12}{(x-3)(x-2)}=\dfrac{2x^2-x-12}{(x-3)(x-2)}$

$=\dfrac{2x^2-x-12}{(x-3)(x-2)}$

b. $\dfrac{x}{x-3}=\dfrac{x+4}{x-2}$

$(x-3)(x-2)\left[\dfrac{x}{x-3}\right]=(x-3)(x-2)\left[\dfrac{x+4}{x-2}\right]$

$x(x-2)=(x-3)(x+4)$

$x^2-2x=x^2+x-12$

$-3x=-12$

$x=4$

52. a. $\dfrac{2x}{x^2-1}+\dfrac{2}{x^2-1}=\dfrac{2x+2}{x^2-1}$

$=\dfrac{2(x+1)}{(x-1)(x+1)}=\dfrac{2}{x-1}$

b. $\dfrac{2x}{x^2-1}=\dfrac{2}{x^2-1}$

$(x^2-1)\left[\dfrac{2x}{x^2-1}\right]=(x^2-1)\left[\dfrac{2}{x^2-1}\right]$

$2x=2$

$x=1$

Since $x=1$ is an excluded value, there is no solution.

53. $\dfrac{7}{2x}=\dfrac{2}{x}-\dfrac{3}{2}$

$2x\left(\dfrac{7}{2x}\right)=2x\left(\dfrac{2}{x}-\dfrac{3}{2}\right)$

$7=(2x)\dfrac{2}{x}-(2x)\dfrac{3}{2}$

$7=4-3x$

$-3x=3$

$x=-1$

54. $\dfrac{15}{w^2+5w}+\dfrac{w+4}{w+5}=\dfrac{w+3}{w}$

$\dfrac{15}{w(w+5)}+\dfrac{w+4}{w+5}=\dfrac{w+3}{w}$

$w(w+5)\left[\dfrac{15}{w(w+5)}+\dfrac{w+4}{w+5}\right]=w(w+5)\left[\dfrac{w+3}{w}\right]$

$w(w+5)\dfrac{15}{w(w+5)}+w(w+5)\dfrac{w+4}{w+5}=(w+5)(w+3)$

$15+w(w+4)=(w+5)(w+3)$

$15+w^2+4w=w^2+8w+15$

$4w=8w$

$4w=0$

$w=0$

The value $w=0$ is an excluded value. Thus there is no solution.

55.

$$\frac{1}{y^2+5y+6}-\frac{2}{y+3}=\frac{7}{y+2}$$

$$\frac{1}{(y+3)(y+2)}-\frac{2}{y+3}=\frac{7}{y+2}$$

$$(y+3)(y+2)\left[\frac{1}{(y+3)(y+2)}-\frac{2}{y+3}\right]=(y+3)(y+2)\left[\frac{7}{y+2}\right]$$

$$(y+3)(y+2)\frac{1}{(y+3)(y+2)}-(y+3)(y+2)\frac{2}{y+3}=7(y+3)$$

$$1-2(y+2)=7(y+3)$$

$$1-2y-4=7y+21$$

$$-9y=24$$

$$y=-\frac{24}{9}=-\frac{8}{3}$$

56.

$$1-\frac{14}{y^2+4y+4}=\frac{7y}{y^2+4y+4}$$

$$(y^2+4y+4)\left[1-\frac{14}{y^2+4y+4}\right]=(y^2+4y+4)\left[\frac{7y}{y^2+4y+4}\right]$$

$$(y^2+4y+4)-(y^2+4y+4)\frac{14}{y^2+4y+4}=7y$$

$$y^2+4y+4-14=7y$$

$$y^2-3y-10=0$$

$$(y-5)(y+2)=0$$

$$y=5 \quad\text{or}\quad y=-2$$

Since $y=-2$ is an excluded value, the solution is $y=5$.

57.

$$\frac{w}{w^2-9w+20}+\frac{14}{w^2-3w-4}=\frac{18}{w^2-4w-5}$$

$$\frac{w}{(w-5)(w-4)}+\frac{14}{(w-4)(w+1)}=\frac{18}{(w-5)(w+1)}$$

$$(w-5)(w-4)(w+1)\left[\frac{w}{(w-5)(w-4)}+\frac{14}{(w-4)(w+1)}\right]=(w-5)(w-4)(w+1)\left[\frac{18}{(w-5)(w+1)}\right]$$

$$(w-5)(w-4)(w+1)\frac{w}{(w-5)(w-4)}+(w-5)(w-4)(w+1)\frac{14}{(w-4)(w+1)}=18(w-4)$$

$$w(w+1)+14(w-5)=18w-72$$

$$w^2+w+14w-70=18w-72$$

$$w^2-3w+2=0$$

$$(w-2)(w-1)=0$$

$$w=2 \quad\text{or}\quad w=1$$

58.

$$\frac{4}{v^2 + 7v + 10} - \frac{3}{v+2} + \frac{8}{v+5} = 0$$

$$\frac{4}{(v+2)(v+5)} - \frac{3}{v+2} + \frac{8}{v+5} = 0$$

$$(v+2)(v+5)\left[\frac{4}{(v+2)(v+5)} - \frac{3}{v+2} + \frac{8}{v+5}\right] = (v+2)(v+5)[0]$$

$$\cancel{(v+2)}\,\cancel{(v+5)}\,\frac{4}{\cancel{(v+2)}\,\cancel{(v+5)}} - \cancel{(v+2)}\,(v+5)\frac{3}{\cancel{v+2}} + (v+2)\,\cancel{(v+5)}\,\frac{8}{\cancel{v+5}} = 0$$

$$4 - 3(v+5) + 8(v+2) = 0$$

$$4 - 3v - 15 + 8v + 16 = 0$$

$$5v = -5$$

$$v = -1$$

59.

$$\frac{5z+11}{2z^2 + 7z - 4} = \frac{1}{z+4} - \frac{3}{1-2z}$$

$$\frac{5z+11}{(2z-1)(z+4)} = \frac{1}{z+4} + \frac{3}{2z-1}$$

$$\cancel{(2z-1)}\,\cancel{(z+4)}\left[\frac{5z+11}{\cancel{(2z-1)}\,\cancel{(z+4)}}\right] = (2z-1)(z+4)\left[\frac{1}{z+4} + \frac{3}{2z-1}\right]$$

$$5z+11 = (2z-1)\,\cancel{(z+4)}\,\frac{1}{\cancel{z+4}} + \cancel{(2z-1)}\,(z+4)\frac{3}{\cancel{2z-1}}$$

$$5z+11 = (2z-1) + 3(z+4)$$

$$5z+11 = 2z-1 + 3z+12$$

$$12 = 12 \text{ is true.}$$

The solution set is $\mathbb{R} \sim \left\{-4, \dfrac{1}{2}\right\}$.

60..

$$\frac{1}{2z^2 - 9z - 5} - \frac{1}{2z^2 - 6z - 20} = \frac{3}{(2z+1)(2z+4)(z-5)}$$

$$\frac{1}{(2z+1)(z-5)} - \frac{1}{(2z+4)(z-5)} = \frac{3}{(2z+1)(2z+4)(z-5)}$$

$$(2z+1)(2z+4)(z-5)\left[\frac{1}{(2z+1)(z-5)} - \frac{1}{(2z+4)(z-5)}\right] = \cancel{(2z+1)}\,\cancel{(2z+4)}\,\cancel{(z-5)}\left[\frac{3}{\cancel{(2z+1)}\,\cancel{(2z+4)}\,\cancel{(z-5)}}\right]$$

$$\cancel{(2z+1)}\,(2z+4)\,\cancel{(z-5)}\,\frac{1}{\cancel{(2z+1)}\,\cancel{(z-5)}} - (2z+1)\,\cancel{(2z+4)}\,\cancel{(z-5)}\,\frac{1}{\cancel{(2z+4)}\,\cancel{(z-5)}} = 3$$

$$(2z+4) - (2z+1) = 3$$

$$2z+4 - 2z-1 = 3$$

$$3 = 3 \text{ is true.}$$

The solution set is $\mathbb{R} \sim \left\{-2, -\dfrac{1}{2}, 5\right\}$.

61.

$$\frac{a}{b+1} = \frac{a+1}{b}$$

$$b(b+1)\left(\frac{a}{b+1}\right) = b(b+1)\left(\frac{a+1}{b}\right)$$

$$ab = (b+1)(a+1)$$

$$ab = ab + a + b + 1$$

$$ab - ab = ab - ab + a + b + 1$$

$$0 = a + b + 1$$

$$b = -a - 1$$

62.

$$I = \frac{E}{r_1 + r_2}$$

$$(r_1 + r_2)(I) = (r_1 + r_2)\left(\frac{E}{r_1 + r_2}\right)$$

$$r_1 I + r_2 I = E$$

$$r_2 I = E - r_1 I$$

$$r_2 = \frac{E - r_1 I}{I}$$

Problem	Mental Estimate	Calculator Approximation
63. $f(1.01)$	$f(1.01) \approx \dfrac{(1+5)(1-8)}{(1)^2 - 4} = \dfrac{-42}{-3} = 14$	14.10
64. $f(-4.99)$	$f(-4.99) \approx \dfrac{(-5+5)(-5-8)}{(-5)^2 - 4} = \dfrac{0}{21} = 0$	-0.01

65. a.

$$P = \frac{4x+8}{x-2} + \frac{6x+12}{x-2} + \frac{x+3}{5x} + \frac{x+1}{5x} = \frac{4x+8+6x+12}{x-2} + \frac{x+3+x+1}{5x} = \frac{10x+20}{x-2} + \frac{2x+4}{5x}$$

$$= \frac{10x+20}{x-2} \cdot \frac{5x}{5x} + \frac{2x+4}{5x} \cdot \frac{x-2}{x-2} = \frac{10x+20}{x-2} \cdot \frac{5x}{5x} + \frac{2x+4}{5x} \cdot \frac{x-2}{x-2} = \frac{50x^2+100x}{5x(x-2)} + \frac{2x^2-8}{5x(x-2)}$$

$$= \frac{50x^2+100x+2x^2-8}{5x(x-2)} = \frac{52x^2+100x-8}{5x(x-2)} = \frac{4(13x-1)(x+2)}{5x(x-2)} \text{ cm}$$

b.

$$A = \frac{h}{2}(a+b) = \frac{\left(\frac{x-2}{5x}\right)}{2}\left(\frac{4x+8}{x-2} + \frac{6x+12}{x-2}\right) = \left(\frac{x-2}{10x}\right)\left(\frac{4x+8+6x+12}{x-2}\right)$$

$$= \left(\frac{x-2}{10x}\right)\left(\frac{10x+20}{x-2}\right) = \frac{10(x+2)}{10x} = \frac{x+2}{x} \text{ cm}^2$$

66. $A = \dfrac{1}{2}(2x+6)\left(\dfrac{5}{x+3}\right) + (2x+6)\left(\dfrac{20}{x+3}\right) = \dfrac{2(x+3)}{2}\left(\dfrac{5}{x+3}\right) + \dfrac{2(x+3)}{1}\left(\dfrac{20}{x+3}\right) = 5 + 40 = 45 \text{ cm}^2$

67. $V = l \cdot w \cdot h = \dfrac{4x+8}{7} \cdot \dfrac{35}{x^2-4} \cdot \dfrac{5x+10}{x} = \dfrac{4(x+2)}{7} \cdot \dfrac{\overset{5}{35}}{(x+2)(x-2)} \cdot \dfrac{5(x+2)}{x} = \dfrac{100(x+2)}{x(x-2)} \text{ cm}^3$

68. a. The plant can operate anywhere between zero and 24 hours a day. The practical domain is $[0, 24]$.

b. $A(t) = \dfrac{C(t)}{N(t)} = \dfrac{100t + 500}{0.5t^2 + 10t} = \dfrac{100(t+5)}{0.5t(t+20)} = \dfrac{200(t+5)}{t(t+20)}$

c. $N(10) = 0.5(10)^2 + 10(10) = 150$. The plant can produce 150 units when it operates for 10 hours a day.

d. $C(10) = 100(10) + 500 = 1500$. It costs \$1,500 to operate the plant for 10 hours a day.

e. $A(10) = \dfrac{1500}{150} = 10$. It costs an average of \$10 per unit to operate the plant for 10 hours a day.

f. As t approaches zero, $A(t)$ increases without bound.

g. When the plant approaches operating around the clock the average cost approaches

$$A(24) = \frac{200(24+5)}{24(24+20)} = 5.49 \text{ dollars per unit.}$$

69. Let $t = $ time

$s = $ speed

$$t = \frac{k}{s} \text{ for some constant } k.$$

$$5 = \frac{k}{60}$$

$$k = 300$$

With $s = 50$ we have $t = \dfrac{300}{50} = 6$ hours.

The constant of variation k represents the distance between Chicago and St. Louis.

70. Let $r = $ revolutions per minute.

$d = $ diameter of the pulley

$$r = \frac{k}{d} \text{ for some constant } k.$$

$$1500 = \frac{k}{6}$$

$$k = 9000$$

With $r = 2000$ we have $\quad 2000 = \dfrac{9000}{d}$

$$2000d = 9000$$

$$d = 4.5 \text{ in}$$

71. Let $F = $ force of the wind

$a = $ effective area of the front of the car

$s = $ speed of the wind

$$F = kas^2 \text{ for some constant } k.$$

$$80 = k(25)(40)^2$$

$$k = \frac{80}{(25)(40)^2} = 0.002$$

With $s = 60$ we have

$$F = (0.002)(25)(60)^2 = 180 \text{ lbs}$$

72. Let $x = $ numerator

$$\frac{x}{x+6} = -1$$

$$(x+6)\left(\frac{x}{x+6}\right) = (-1)(x+6)$$

$$x = -x - 6$$

$$2x = -6$$

$$x = -3$$

The numerator is -3.

73. Let $x = $ second number

$3x - 5 = $ first number

$$\frac{3x-5}{x} = \frac{5}{2}$$

$$2x\left(\frac{3x-5}{x}\right) = 2x\left(\frac{5}{2}\right)$$

$$2(3x-5) = 5x$$

$$6x - 10 = 5x$$

$$x = 10$$

The numbers are 10 and $3(10) - 5 = 25$.

74.

$$\frac{1}{x} + \frac{1}{x+2} = \frac{12}{x(x+2)}$$

$$x(x+2)\left[\frac{1}{x} + \frac{1}{x+2}\right] = x(x+2)\left[\frac{12}{x(x+2)}\right]$$

$$x(x+2)\frac{1}{x} + x(x+2)\frac{1}{x+2} = 12$$

$$(x+2) + x = 12$$

$$2x = 10$$

$$x = 5$$

The integers are 5 and $5 + 2 = 7$.

75.

$$\frac{1}{R} = \frac{1}{r_1} + \frac{1}{r_2}$$

$$\frac{1}{3} = \frac{1}{r_1} + \frac{1}{3r_1}$$

$$3r_1\left[\frac{1}{3}\right] = 3r_1\left[\frac{1}{r_1} + \frac{1}{3r_1}\right]$$

$$r_1 = \left(3r_1\right)\frac{1}{r_1} + \left(3r_1\right)\frac{1}{3r_1}$$

$$r_1 = 3 + 1$$

$$r_1 = 4$$

$$r_1 = 4 \text{ ohms} \quad \text{and} \quad r_2 = 3(4) = 12 \text{ ohms}$$

76. Let $t = $ time for the cold faucet to fill the tub

$t + 7 = $ time for the hot faucet to fill the tub

$\dfrac{1}{t} = $ rate of work for the cold faucet

$\dfrac{1}{t+7} = $ rate of work for the hot faucet

$$\left(\begin{matrix}\text{Rate} \\ \text{of cold}\end{matrix}\right)\left(\begin{matrix}\text{Time} \\ \text{of cold}\end{matrix}\right) + \left(\begin{matrix}\text{Rate} \\ \text{of hot}\end{matrix}\right)\left(\begin{matrix}\text{Time} \\ \text{of cold}\end{matrix}\right) = \text{Total Work}$$

$$\left(\frac{1}{t}\right)(12) \quad + \quad \left(\frac{1}{t+7}\right)(12) \quad = \quad 1$$

$$\frac{12}{t} + \frac{12}{t+7} = 1$$

$$t(t+7)\left[\frac{12}{t} + \frac{12}{t+7}\right] = t(t+7)[1]$$

$$t(t+7)\frac{12}{t} + t(t+7)\frac{12}{t+7} = t(t+7)$$

$$12(t+7) + 12t = t^2 + 7t$$

$$12t + 84 + 12t = t^2 + 7t$$

$$t^2 - 17t - 84 = 0$$

$$(t+4)(t-21) = 0$$

Note: This answer is not appropriate.

$$t = -4 \quad \text{or} \quad t = 21$$

It would take 21 minutes for the cold water faucet alone.

77. Let $x = $ number desks produced

Average Cost per Unit:

$$= \frac{\text{Total Cost}}{\text{Number of Desks}}$$

$$= \frac{54x + 20000}{x}$$

Solve the equation:

$$\frac{54x + 20000}{x} = 74$$

$$x\left(\frac{54x + 20000}{x}\right) = x(74)$$

$$54x + 20000 = 74x$$

$$20x = 20000$$

$$x = 1000$$

The company should produce 1000 desks.

78.

$$(w-1)(w+5) = \frac{13}{16}(w)(w+6)$$

$$16\left[(w-1)(w+5)\right] = 16\left[\frac{13}{16}(w)(w+6)\right]$$

$$16\left(w^2 + 4w - 5\right) = 13\left(w^2 + 6w\right)$$

$$16w^2 + 64w - 80 = 13w^2 + 78w$$

$$3w^2 - 14w - 80 = 0$$

$$(3w+10)(w-8) = 0$$

$$w = -\frac{10}{3} \quad \text{or} \quad w = 8$$

The original dimensions are 8 cm by 14 cm.

79. Let x = rate of each boat in still water

$x + 6$ = rate of boat going downstream

$x - 6$ = rate of boat going upstream

$T = \dfrac{D}{R} = \dfrac{54}{x+6}$ = time of boat going downstream

$T = \dfrac{D}{R} = \dfrac{30}{x-6}$ = time of boat going upstream

Since both boats travel for the same time we know:

$$\frac{54}{x+6} = \frac{30}{x-6}$$

$$\cancel{(x+6)}\,(x-6)\left[\frac{54}{\cancel{x+6}}\right] = (x+6)\,\cancel{(x-6)}\left[\frac{30}{\cancel{x-6}}\right]$$

$$54(x-6) = 30(x+6)$$

$$54x - 324 = 30x + 180$$

$$24x = 504$$

$$x = 21$$

The rate of each boat in still water is 21 miles per hour.

80. a. Directly. As the distance the car travels increases, the distance on the map increases.

b. Inversely. As the time between stations increases, the rate of the train decreases.

c. Inversely. As the number of feet the balloon is submerged increases, the volume of the balloon decreases.

d. Directly. As the number of feet the balloon is submerged increases, the pressure on the helium increases.

1. **a.** $f(x) = -x^2 + 4x = +5$ is a rational function whose graph is a parabola. The proper choice is **B**.

b. $f(x) = \dfrac{5}{x-1}$ is a rational function whose graph will have a break. The proper choice is **C**.

c. $f(x) = |3x+2| - 1$ is not a rational function. It is an absolute value function. The proper choice is **D**,

d. $f(x) = -\dfrac{3}{4}x - \dfrac{2}{3}$ is a rational function whose graph is a line. The proper choice is **A**.

2. a. Find the values that make the denominator zero.

$$2x - 12 = 0$$
$$2x = 12$$
$$x = 6$$

The domain is $\mathbb{R} \sim \{6\}$

b. Find the values that make the denominator zero.

$$(x-1)(x+6) = 0$$
$$x = 1 \ \text{ or } \ x = -6$$

The domain is $\mathbb{R} \sim \{1, -6\}$

c. Find the values that make the denominator zero.

$$x^2 - 64 = 0$$
$$(x-8)(x+8) = 0$$
$$x = 8 \ \text{ or } \ x = -8$$

The domain $\mathbb{R} \sim \{-8, 8\}$

d. The denominator is never zero. Thus the domain is $\mathbb{R}$.

3. a. $\dfrac{6x}{12x^2 - 18x} = \dfrac{\cancel{6x}}{\cancel{6x}(2x-3)} = \dfrac{1}{2x-3}$

b. $\dfrac{2x-6}{x^2-9} = \dfrac{2\cancel{(x-3)}}{\cancel{(x-3)}(x+3)} = \dfrac{2}{x+3}$

c. $\dfrac{2x^2-7x-15}{x^2-25} = \dfrac{(2x+3)\cancel{(x-5)}}{(x+5)\cancel{(x-5)}} = \dfrac{2x+3}{x+5}$

d. $\dfrac{4x^2-12xy+9y^2}{3ay-6by-2ax+4bx} = \dfrac{(2x-3y)(2x-3y)}{3y(a-2b)-2x(a-2b)}$

$$= \dfrac{(-1)\cancel{(2x-3y)}(2x-3y)}{\cancel{(3y-2x)}(a-2b)}$$

$$= -\dfrac{2x-3y}{a-2b}$$

4.   a. $\dfrac{ax-bx}{x^2} \cdot \dfrac{5x}{4a-4b} = \dfrac{x(a-b)}{x^2} \cdot \dfrac{5x}{4(a-b)}$

$$= \dfrac{5\cancel{x^2}\cancel{(a-b)}}{4\cancel{x^2}\cancel{(a-b)}} = \dfrac{5}{4}$$

b. $\dfrac{x^2-1}{x+1} \div \dfrac{x^2-3x+2}{x-2} = \dfrac{x^2-1}{x+1} \cdot \dfrac{x-2}{x^2-3x+2}$

$$= \dfrac{\cancel{(x-1)}\cancel{(x+1)}}{\cancel{x+1}} \cdot \dfrac{\cancel{x-2}}{\cancel{(x-1)}\cancel{(x-2)}} = 1$$

c. $\dfrac{v^2-v-20}{v^2-16} \div \dfrac{3v-15}{2v-8} = \dfrac{v^2-v-20}{v^2-16} \cdot \dfrac{2v-8}{3v-15}$

$$= \dfrac{\cancel{(v-5)}\cancel{(v+4)}}{\cancel{(v-4)}\cancel{(v+4)}} \cdot \dfrac{2\cancel{(v-4)}}{3\cancel{(v-5)}} = \dfrac{2}{3}$$

d. $\dfrac{x^2-4}{x^2-4x-21} \cdot \dfrac{x^2-2x-35}{x^2-7x+10}$

$$= \dfrac{(x+2)\cancel{(x-2)}}{\cancel{(x-7)}(x+3)} \cdot \dfrac{\cancel{(x-7)}(x+5)}{(x-5)\cancel{(x-2)}} = \dfrac{(x+2)(x+5)}{(x+3)(x-5)}$$

5.   a. $\dfrac{3x-4}{2x-3} + \dfrac{x-2}{2x-3} = \dfrac{(3x-4)+(x-2)}{2x-3}$

$$= \dfrac{3x-4+x-2}{2x-3} = \dfrac{4x-6}{2x-3}$$

$$= \dfrac{2\cancel{(2x-3)}}{\cancel{2x-3}} = 2$$

b. $\dfrac{3x+7}{x^2+x-12} - \dfrac{2x+3}{x^2+x-12} = \dfrac{(3x+7)-(2x+3)}{x^2+x-12}$

$$= \dfrac{3x+7-2x-3}{x^2+x-12} = \dfrac{x+4}{x^2+x-12}$$

$$= \dfrac{\cancel{x+4}}{\cancel{(x+4)}(x-3)} = \dfrac{1}{x-3}$$

c. $\dfrac{7}{w^2+w-12} + \dfrac{2}{w^2-8w+15} = \dfrac{7}{(w+4)(w-3)} + \dfrac{2}{(w-3)(w-5)}$

$$= \dfrac{7}{(w+4)(w-3)} \cdot \dfrac{w-5}{w-5} + \dfrac{2}{(w-3)(w-5)} \cdot \dfrac{w+4}{w+4} = \dfrac{7(w-5)+2(w+4)}{(w+4)(w-3)(w-5)} = \dfrac{7w-35+2w+8}{(w+4)(w-3)(w-5)}$$

$$= \dfrac{9w-27}{(w+4)(w-3)(w-5)} = \dfrac{9\cancel{(w-3)}}{(w+4)\cancel{(w-3)}(w-5)} = \dfrac{9}{(w+4)(w-5)}$$

5.   d. $\dfrac{1}{x+y} + \dfrac{3}{x-y} + \dfrac{2y}{x^2-y^2} = \dfrac{1}{x+y} + \dfrac{3}{x-y} + \dfrac{2y}{(x-y)(x+y)} = \dfrac{1}{x+y} \cdot \dfrac{x-y}{x-y} + \dfrac{3}{x-y} \cdot \dfrac{x+y}{x+y} + \dfrac{2y}{(x-y)(x+y)}$

$$= \dfrac{(x-y)+3(x+y)+2y}{(x-y)(x+y)} = \dfrac{x-y+3x+3y+2y}{(x-y)(x+y)} = \dfrac{4x+4y}{(x-y)(x+y)} = \dfrac{4\cancel{(x+y)}}{(x-y)\cancel{(x+y)}} = \dfrac{4}{x-y}$$

6. a. $\dfrac{4x}{5} + \dfrac{\overset{x}{\cancel{x^2}}}{\cancel{15}} \cdot \dfrac{\cancel{3}}{\cancel{x}} = \dfrac{4x}{5} + \dfrac{x}{5} = \dfrac{4x+x}{5} = \dfrac{\cancel{5}x}{\cancel{5}} = x$

b. $\left(\dfrac{4x}{5} + \dfrac{x^2}{15}\right) \cdot \dfrac{3}{x} = \left(\dfrac{4x}{5} \cdot \dfrac{3}{3} + \dfrac{x^2}{15}\right) \cdot \dfrac{3}{x} = \left(\dfrac{12x}{15} + \dfrac{x^2}{15}\right) \cdot \dfrac{3}{x}$

$= \left(\dfrac{12x}{15} + \dfrac{x^2}{15}\right) \cdot \dfrac{3}{x} = \dfrac{12x + x^2}{\underset{5}{\cancel{15}}} \cdot \dfrac{\cancel{3}}{x}$

$= \dfrac{\cancel{x}(12+x)}{5} \cdot \dfrac{1}{\cancel{x}} = \dfrac{x+12}{5}$

c. $\dfrac{x-y}{x+y} + \dfrac{3x-21y}{x^2-y^2} \div \dfrac{15x^2 - 105xy}{10x^2y - 10xy^2} = \dfrac{x-y}{x+y} + \dfrac{3x-21y}{x^2-y^2} \cdot \dfrac{10x^2y - 10xy^2}{15x^2 - 105xy}$

$= \dfrac{x-y}{x+y} + \dfrac{3(x-7y)}{(x-y)(x+y)} \cdot \dfrac{10xy(x-y)}{15x(x-7y)} = \dfrac{x-y}{x+y} + \dfrac{\overset{2}{\cancel{30}}\,\cancel{x}y\,(\cancel{x-7y})\,(\cancel{x-y})}{\cancel{15}\,\cancel{x}\,(\cancel{x-y})(x+y)(\cancel{x-7y})}$

$= \dfrac{x-y}{x+y} + \dfrac{2y}{x+y} = \dfrac{x-y+2y}{x+y} = \dfrac{\cancel{x+y}}{\cancel{x+y}} = 1$

d. $\left(\dfrac{w}{w-2} + \dfrac{1}{w-3}\right) \div \dfrac{w^2 - 2w - 2}{w^2 - w - 2} = \left(\dfrac{w}{w-2} \cdot \dfrac{w-3}{w-3} + \dfrac{1}{w-3} \cdot \dfrac{w-2}{w-2}\right) \div \dfrac{w^2 - 2w - 2}{w^2 - w - 2}$

$= \dfrac{w(w-3) + (w-2)}{(w-2)(w-3)} \cdot \dfrac{w^2 - w - 2}{w^2 - 2w - 2} = \dfrac{w^2 - 3w + w - 2}{(w-2)(w-3)} \cdot \dfrac{(w-2)(w+1)}{w^2 - 2w - 2}$

$= \dfrac{(\cancel{w^2 - 2w - 2})\,(\cancel{w-2})\,(w+1)}{(\cancel{w-2})\,(w-3)\,(\cancel{w^2 - 2w - 2})} = \dfrac{w+1}{w-3}$

7. a. $\dfrac{\frac{4}{5}}{\frac{5}{6}} = \dfrac{4}{1} \div \dfrac{5}{6} = \dfrac{4}{1} \div \dfrac{6}{5} = \dfrac{24}{5}$

b. $\dfrac{\frac{x}{3} - 2 + \frac{3}{x}}{1 - \frac{3}{x}} = \dfrac{\frac{x}{3} - 2 + \frac{3}{x}}{1 - \frac{3}{x}} \cdot \dfrac{3x}{3x} = \dfrac{\left(\frac{x}{3} - 2 + \frac{3}{x}\right)3x}{\left(1 - \frac{3}{x}\right)3x}$

$= \dfrac{\frac{x}{\cancel{3}}(\cancel{3}x) - 2(3x) + \frac{3}{\cancel{x}}(3\cancel{x})}{1(3x) - \frac{3}{\cancel{x}}(3\cancel{x})} = \dfrac{x^2 - 6x + 9}{3x - 9}$

$= \dfrac{(x-3)(\cancel{x-3})}{3(\cancel{x-3})} = \dfrac{x-3}{3}$

c. $\dfrac{36x^{-2} - 3x^{-1} - 18}{12x^{-2} - 25x^{-1} + 12} = \dfrac{\frac{36}{x^2} - \frac{3}{x} - 18}{\frac{12}{x^2} - \frac{25}{x} + 12} \cdot \dfrac{x^2}{x^2} = \dfrac{\left(\frac{36}{x^2} - \frac{3}{x} - 18\right)x^2}{\left(\frac{12}{x^2} - \frac{25}{x} + 12\right)x^2} = \dfrac{\frac{36}{\cancel{x^2}}\left(\cancel{x^2}\right) - \frac{3}{\cancel{x}}\left(\overset{x}{\cancel{x^2}}\right) - 18\left(x^2\right)}{\frac{12}{\cancel{x^2}}\left(\cancel{x^2}\right) - \frac{25}{\cancel{x}}\left(\overset{x}{\cancel{x^2}}\right) + 12\left(x^2\right)}$

$= \dfrac{36 - 3x - 18x^2}{12 - 25x + 12x^2} = \dfrac{-3(6x^2 + x - 12)}{12x^2 - 25x + 12} = \dfrac{-3(3x-4)(2x+3)}{(3x-4)(4x-3)} = -\dfrac{3(2x+3)}{4x-3}$

d. $\dfrac{\dfrac{v}{v-4}-\dfrac{2v}{v+3}}{\dfrac{v^2-4v}{2v+6}} = \left(\dfrac{v}{v-4}-\dfrac{2v}{v+3}\right)\div\left(\dfrac{v^2-4v}{2v+6}\right) = \left(\dfrac{v}{v-4}\cdot\dfrac{v+3}{v+3}-\dfrac{2v}{v+3}\cdot\dfrac{v-4}{v-4}\right)\cdot\dfrac{2v+6}{v^2-4v}$

$= \left(\dfrac{v(v+3)-2v(v-4)}{(v-4)(v+3)}\right)\cdot\dfrac{2(v+3)}{v(v-4)} = \dfrac{v^2+3v-2v^2+8v}{(v-4)(v+3)}\cdot\dfrac{2(v+3)}{v(v-4)} = \dfrac{-v^2+11v}{(v-4)\,\cancel{(v+3)}}\cdot\dfrac{2\,\cancel{(v+3)}}{v(v-4)}$

$= \dfrac{-2\cancel{v}(v-11)}{\cancel{v}(v-4)^2} = -\dfrac{2(v-11)}{(v-4)^2}$

8. a.
$$\dfrac{z-4}{z-2}=\dfrac{1}{z-2}$$
$$(z-2)\left(\dfrac{z-4}{z-2}\right)=(z-2)\left(\dfrac{1}{z-2}\right)$$
$$\cancel{(z-2)}\,\dfrac{z-4}{\cancel{z-2}}=\cancel{(z-2)}\,\dfrac{1}{\cancel{z-2}}$$
$$z-4=1$$
$$z=5$$

b.
$$\dfrac{z-2}{z-1}+\dfrac{z-3}{2z-5}=1$$
$$(z-1)(2z-5)\left[\dfrac{z-2}{z-1}+\dfrac{z-3}{2z-5}\right]=(z-1)(2z-5)[1]$$
$$\cancel{(z-1)}\,(2z-5)\dfrac{z-2}{\cancel{z-1}}+(z-1)\,\cancel{(2z-5)}\,\dfrac{z-3}{\cancel{2z-5}}=(z-1)(2z-5)$$
$$(2z-5)(z-2)+(z-1)(z-3)=(z-1)(2z-5)$$
$$2z^2-9z+10+z^2-4z+3=2z^2-7z+5$$
$$z^2-6z+8=0$$
$$(z-2)(z-4)=0$$
$$z=2\ \text{ or }\ z=4$$

c.
$$\dfrac{z+11}{z^2-5z+4}=\dfrac{5}{z-4}+\dfrac{3}{1-z}$$
$$\dfrac{z+11}{(z-4)(z-1)}=\dfrac{5}{z-4}-\dfrac{3}{z-1}$$
$$(z-4)(z-1)\left[\dfrac{z+11}{(z-4)(z-1)}\right]=(z-4)(z-1)\left[\dfrac{5}{z-4}-\dfrac{3}{z-1}\right]$$
$$\cancel{(z-4)}\,\cancel{(z-1)}\,\dfrac{z+11}{\cancel{(z-4)}\cancel{(z-1)}}=\cancel{(z-4)}\,(z-1)\dfrac{5}{\cancel{z-4}}-(z-4)\,\cancel{(z-1)}\,\dfrac{3}{\cancel{z-1}}$$
$$z+11=5(z-1)-3(z-4)$$
$$z+11=5z-5-3z+12$$
$$z=4$$
Since 4 is an excluded value, there is no solution.

d.

$$\frac{x}{x-2}+\frac{1}{x-4}=\frac{2}{x^2-6x+8}$$

$$\frac{x}{x-2}+\frac{1}{x-4}=\frac{2}{(x-2)(x-4)}$$

$$(x-2)(x-4)\left(\frac{x}{x-2}+\frac{1}{x-4}\right)=(x-2)(x-4)\left(\frac{2}{(x-2)(x-4)}\right)$$

$$(x-2)(x-4)\frac{x}{(x-2)}+(x-2)(x-4)\frac{1}{(x-4)}=(x-2)(x-4)\frac{2}{(x-2)(x-4)}$$

$$(x-4)x+(x-2)=2$$

$$x^2-4x+x-2=2$$

$$x^2-3x-4=0$$

$$(x+1)(x-4)=0$$

$$x=-1 \ \text{ or } \ x=4$$

Since 4 is an excluded value, the only solution is $x=-1$.

9. **a.**

$$\frac{2A}{h}=b$$

$$h\left(\frac{2A}{h}\right)=h(b)$$

$$2A=hb$$

$$\frac{2A}{b}=\frac{hb}{b}$$

$$h=\frac{2A}{b}$$

b.

$$\frac{1}{x}-\frac{1}{y}=\frac{1}{z}$$

$$xyz\left(\frac{1}{x}-\frac{1}{y}\right)=xyz\left(\frac{1}{z}\right)$$

$$xyz\frac{1}{x}-xyz\frac{1}{y}=xy$$

$$yz-xz=xy$$

$$z(y-x)=xy$$

$$\frac{z(y-x)}{(y-x)}=\frac{xy}{(y-x)}$$

$$z=\frac{xy}{y-x} \ \text{ or } \ -\frac{xy}{x-y}$$

c.

$$\frac{x+4}{x-5}=y$$

$$(x-5)\left(\frac{x+4}{x-5}\right)=(x-5)y$$

$$x+4=xy-5y$$

$$5y+4=xy-x$$

$$5y+4=x(y-1)$$

$$\frac{5y+4}{y-1}=\frac{x(y-1)}{y-1}$$

$$x=\frac{5y+4}{y-1}$$

d.

$$\frac{ac}{a-c}=b$$

$$(a-c)\left(\frac{ac}{a-c}\right)=(a-c)b$$

$$ac=ab-bc$$

$$ac-ab=-bc$$

$$a(c-b)=-bc$$

$$\frac{a(c-b)}{c-b}=\frac{-bc}{c-b}$$

$$a=-\frac{bc}{c-b} \ \text{ or } \ \frac{bc}{b-c}$$

10. **a.** The values of y are decreasing as the values of x are increasing. This is an example of inverse variation.

   b. The values of y are increasing as the values of x are increasing. This is an example of direct variation.

11. **a.** $a = kb$　　　**b.** $a = \dfrac{k}{b}$　　　**c.** $a = \dfrac{kb}{c^2}$　　　**d.** $a = kbc$

12. **a.** If y varies inversely as x and $y = 12$ when $x = 6$, then
$$y = \frac{k}{x}$$
$$12 = \frac{k}{6}$$
$$k = 72$$
With $x = 4$ we have $y = \dfrac{72}{x}$
$$y = \frac{72}{4}$$
$$y = 18$$

   b. If V varies inversely as p and $V = 4$ when $p = 6$, then
$$V = \frac{k}{p}$$
$$6 = \frac{k}{4}$$
$$k = 24$$
With $V = 3$ we have
$$V = \frac{24}{p}$$
$$3 = \frac{24}{p}$$
$$3p = 24$$
$$p = 8 \text{ Newtons per square centimeter}$$

13. **a.** Let $x =$ normal number of units for the indicator
$$\frac{x-2}{x+2} = \frac{2}{3}$$
$$3(x+2)\left(\frac{x-2}{x+2}\right) = 3(x+2)\left(\frac{2}{3}\right)$$
$$3(x-2) = 2(x+2)$$
$$3x - 6 = 2x + 4$$
$$x = 10$$
The normal number of units for the indicator is 10.

b. Let $t =$ time for the larger end loader

$t + 5 =$ time for the smaller end loader

$\dfrac{1}{t} =$ rate of work for the larger end loader

$\dfrac{1}{t+5} =$ rate of work for the smaller end loader

$$\left(\begin{array}{c}\text{Rate of larger}\\\text{end loader}\end{array}\right)\left(\begin{array}{c}\text{Time of larger}\\\text{end loader}\end{array}\right)+\left(\begin{array}{c}\text{Rate of smaller}\\\text{end loader}\end{array}\right)\left(\begin{array}{c}\text{Time of smaller}\\\text{end loader}\end{array}\right)=\left(\begin{array}{c}\text{Total}\\\text{Work}\end{array}\right)$$

$$\left(\frac{1}{t}\right)(6)\qquad+\qquad\left(\frac{1}{t+5}\right)(6)\qquad=\quad 1$$

$$\frac{6}{t}+\frac{6}{t+5}=1$$

$$t(t+5)\left[\frac{6}{t}+\frac{6}{t+5}\right]=t(t+5)[1]$$

$$\cancel{t}(t+5)\frac{6}{\cancel{t}}+t\cancel{(t+5)}\frac{6}{\cancel{t+5}}=t(t+5)$$

$$6(t+5)+6t=t(t+5)$$

$$6t+30+6t=t^2+5t$$

$$t^2-7t-30=0$$

$$(t-10)(t+3)=0$$

$$t=10 \quad\text{or}\quad t=-3$$

Note: This answer is not appropriate.

It would take 10 hours for the larger end loader and 15 hours for the smaller end loader to move the pile.

c. Let $r =$ rate of interest on shorter-term bond; $r + 0.025 =$ rate of interest on longer-term bond.

$I = PRT$; for $T = 1$ we can write $P = \dfrac{I}{R}$

$P = \dfrac{I}{R} = \dfrac{480}{r} =$ Principal in the shorter-term bond; $P = \dfrac{I}{R} = \dfrac{680}{r+0.025} =$ Principal in longer-term bond

$$\left(\begin{array}{c}\text{Principal in the}\\\text{shorter-term bond}\end{array}\right)=\left(\begin{array}{c}\text{Principal in the}\\\text{longer-term bond}\end{array}\right)$$

$$\frac{480}{r}=\frac{680}{r+0.025}$$

$$480(r+0.025)=680r$$

$$480r+12=680r$$

$$200r=12$$

$$r=6$$

The interest rate for the shorter-term bond is 6% and the interest for the longer-term bond is 8.5%.

d. Let x = rate of slower plane

$x + 50$ = rate of faster plane

$T = \dfrac{D}{R} = \dfrac{950}{x}$ = time of slower plane

$T = \dfrac{D}{R} = \dfrac{1050}{x+50}$ = time of faster plane

Since both planes travel for the same time we know:

$$\frac{950}{x} = \frac{1050}{x+50}$$

$$950(x+50) = 1050x$$

$$950x + 47500 = 1050x$$

$$950x + 47500 = 1050x$$

$$100x = 47500$$

$$x = 475$$

The rate of the slower plane is 475 miles per hour. The rate of the faster plane is 525 miles per hour.

Section 10.1: Evaluating Radical Expressions and Graphing Square Root and Cube Root Functions

Quick Review 10.1

1. $4^2 + (-4)^2 = 16 + 16 = 32$

2. $-3^2 + (3i)^2 = -9 + 9i^2 = -9 + 9(-1) = -9 - 9 = -18$

3. Find the values that make the denominator zero.
$$2x - 6 = 0$$
$$x = 3$$
The excluded value is 3.
Domain: $(-\infty, 3) \cup (3, +\infty)$ or $\mathbb{R} \sim \{3\}$

4. The domain is the projection of the graph onto the x-axis. Domain: $(-3, 4]$

5. The range is the projection of the graph onto the y-axis. Range: $[-1, 3]$

Exercises 10.1

1. The principal cube root of w is represented by $\sqrt[3]{w}$.

3. The principal seventh root of v is represented by $\sqrt[7]{v}$.

5. The principal square root of 4 is represented by $\sqrt{4} = 2$.

7. The principal fifth root of 32 is represented by $\sqrt[5]{32} = 2$.

9. **a.** $\sqrt{16} = 4$
b. $\sqrt[4]{16} = 2$

11. **a.** $\sqrt{36} = 6$
b. $-\sqrt{36} = -6$

13. **a.** $\sqrt[3]{8} = 2$
b. $\sqrt[3]{-8} = -2$

15. $\sqrt[3]{0} = 0$

17. $\sqrt[5]{1} = 1$

19. $\sqrt{10,000} = 100$

21. $\sqrt[4]{10,000} = 10$

23. $\sqrt[3]{0.125} = 0.5$

25. $\sqrt{\dfrac{81}{36}} = \dfrac{\sqrt{81}}{\sqrt{36}} = \dfrac{\cancel{3} \cdot 3}{\cancel{3} \cdot 2} = \dfrac{3}{2}$

27. $\sqrt[3]{-\dfrac{1}{8}} = \dfrac{\sqrt[3]{-1}}{\sqrt[3]{8}} = \dfrac{-1}{2} = -\dfrac{1}{2}$

29. $\sqrt{9} + \sqrt{16} + \sqrt{144} = 3 + 4 + 12 = 19$

31. $\sqrt{64 + 81 + 144} = \sqrt{289} = 17$

	Problem	Mental Estimate	Calculator Approximation
33.	$\sqrt[3]{9}$	$\sqrt[3]{9} \approx \sqrt[3]{8} = 2$	$\sqrt[3]{9} \approx 2.080$
35.	$\sqrt[4]{80}$	$\sqrt[4]{80} \approx \sqrt[4]{81} = 3$	$\sqrt[4]{80} \approx 2.991$

37. a.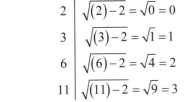

x	$\sqrt{x-2}$
2	$\sqrt{(2)-2} = \sqrt{0} = 0$
3	$\sqrt{(3)-2} = \sqrt{1} = 1$
6	$\sqrt{(6)-2} = \sqrt{4} = 2$
11	$\sqrt{(11)-2} = \sqrt{9} = 3$

b.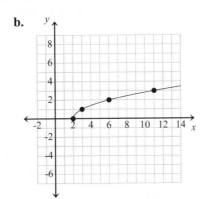

c. The domain is the projection of the graph onto the x-axis.
Domain: $[2, \infty)$

39. a.

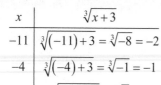

x	$\sqrt[3]{x+3}$
-11	$\sqrt[3]{(-11)+3} = \sqrt[3]{-8} = -2$
-4	$\sqrt[3]{(-4)+3} = \sqrt[3]{-1} = -1$
-3	$\sqrt[3]{(-3)+3} = \sqrt[3]{0} = 0$
-2	$\sqrt[3]{(-2)+3} = \sqrt[3]{1} = 1$
5	$\sqrt[3]{(5)+3} = \sqrt[3]{8} = 2$

b.

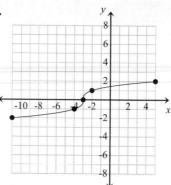

c. The domain is the projection of the graph onto the x-axis.

Domain: $\mathbb{R}$ or $(-\infty, \infty)$

41. The domain of $f(x) = 3x - 15$ is $\mathbb{R}$ or $(-\infty, \infty)$.

43. The domain of $f(x) = \sqrt{3x-15}$ is the set of all real numbers such that
$$3x - 15 \geq 0$$
$$3x \geq 15$$
$$x \geq 5$$
Domain: $[5, \infty)$

45. Find the values that make the denominator zero.
$$3x - 15 = 0$$
$$3x = 15$$
$$x = 5$$
The excluded value is 5.
Domain: $(-\infty, 5) \cup (5, +\infty)$ or $\mathbb{R} \sim \{5\}$

47. The domain of $f(x) = |3x - 15|$ is $\mathbb{R}$ or $(-\infty, \infty)$.

49. $c = \sqrt{a^2 + b^2} = \sqrt{5^2 + 12^2} = \sqrt{25 + 144} = \sqrt{169} = 13$ cm.

51. $s = \sqrt[3]{V} = \sqrt[3]{216} = 6$ cm.

53. $T(60) = 0.064\sqrt{60} \approx 0.5$ seconds.

55. $r = \sqrt[3]{\dfrac{3V}{4\pi}} = \sqrt[3]{\dfrac{3(216)}{4\pi}} \approx 3.7$ cm.

57. $C(0) = 1200\sqrt{(0)^2 + 1} = 1200$. The cost of running the cable from A to C if $x = 0$ is \$1,200.

59. $C(5) = 1200\sqrt{(5)^2 + 1} \approx 6120$. The cost of running the cable from A to C if $x = 5$ is approximately \$6,120.

61. A linear function whose a graph has a positive slope is represented in graph **E**.

63. An absolute value function whose graph opens upward is represented in graph **B**.

65. A quadratic function whose graph opens upward is represented in graph **G**.

67. A square root function is represented in graph **A**.

69. $f(x) = 2x + 1$ is a linear function with a positive slope. Its graph is **H**. The domain is $\mathbb{R}$.

71. $f(x) = \sqrt{2 - x}$ is a square root function with a domain equal to $(-\infty, 2]$. Its graph is **B**.

73. $f(x) = |x - 2| + 1$ is an absolute value function whose graph opens upward. Its graph is **C**. The domain is $\mathbb{R}$.

75. $f(x) = -|x+1| + 2$ is an absolute value function whose graph opens downward. Its graph is **F**. The domain is $\mathbb{R}$.

77. $f(x) = -\sqrt[3]{x} + 2$ is a cube root function that has been reflected vertically and shifted up two units. Its graph is **D**. The domain is $\mathbb{R}$.

79. $\sqrt[3]{-64} = -4$

81. $\sqrt{-1} = i$

83. $\sqrt[3]{-8000} + \sqrt{-81} = -20 + 9i$

Cumulative Review

1.
$$
\begin{aligned}
5(2x-4y) + 7(x-3y) &= 10x - 20y + 7x - 21y \\
&= 10x + 7x - 20y - 21y \\
&= 17x - 41y
\end{aligned}
$$

2.
$$
\begin{aligned}
-6(2x-4y) - (x-3y) &= -12x + 24y - x + 3y \\
&= -12x - x + 24y + 3y \\
&= -13x + 27y
\end{aligned}
$$

3.
$$
\begin{aligned}
(2a^3b^4)(5a^6b^7) &= 10a^{3+6}b^{4+7} \\
&= 10a^9b^{11}
\end{aligned}
$$

4. $\dfrac{12a^6b^4}{3a^3b^3} = \dfrac{\overset{4}{\cancel{12}}\, a^{6-3}b^{4-3}}{\cancel{3}} = 4a^3b$

5. $\left(5a^2b^4\right)^3 = 5^3\left(a^2\right)^3\left(b^4\right)^3 = 125a^{2\cdot3}b^{4\cdot3} = 125a^6b^{12}$

Section 10.2: Adding and Subtracting Radical Expressions

Quick Review 10.2

1.
$$
\begin{aligned}
(5x+3y) + (4x-9y) &= 5x + 3y + 4x - 9y \\
&= 5x + 4x + 3y - 9y \\
&= 9x - 6y
\end{aligned}
$$

2.
$$
\begin{aligned}
3(2x-y) - (4x-9y) &= 6x - 3y - 4x + 9y \\
&= 6x - 4x - 3y + 9y \\
&= 2x + 6y
\end{aligned}
$$

3. $|17| = 17$

4. $|-22| = 22$

5.

x	x^2	x^3
0	0	0
1	1	1
2	4	8
3	9	27
4	16	64
5	25	125

Exercises 10.2

1. Like radicals must have the same index and radicand. Thus $7\sqrt{5}$ is like **D.** $-2\sqrt{5}$.

3. $\sqrt{25} + \sqrt{49} = 5 + 7 = 12$

5. $2\sqrt{9} - 3\sqrt{16} = 2(3) - 3(4) = 6 - 12 = -6$

7. $19\sqrt{2} + 11\sqrt{2} = (19+11)\sqrt{2} = 30\sqrt{2}$

9. $9\sqrt{7} - 13\sqrt{7} = (9-13)\sqrt{7} = -4\sqrt{7}$

11. $4\sqrt[3]{6} + 2\sqrt[3]{6} - 11\sqrt[3]{6} = (4 + 2 - 11)\sqrt[3]{6} = -5\sqrt[3]{6}$

13. $5\sqrt[4]{13} + 6\sqrt[4]{13} - \sqrt[4]{13} = (5 + 6 - 1)\sqrt[4]{13} = 10\sqrt[4]{13}$

15. $7\sqrt{5} - 5\sqrt{7} - \sqrt{5} + \sqrt{7} = 7\sqrt{5} - \sqrt{5} - 5\sqrt{7} + \sqrt{7}$
$= (7 - 1)\sqrt{5} + (-5 + 1)\sqrt{7}$
$= 6\sqrt{5} - 4\sqrt{7}$

17. $6\sqrt{7x} - 9\sqrt{7x} = (6 - 9)\sqrt{7x} = -3\sqrt{7x}$

19. $7\sqrt[4]{17w} - 8\sqrt[4]{17w} + \sqrt[4]{17w} = (7 - 8 + 1)\sqrt[4]{17w}$
$= (0)\sqrt[4]{17w} = 0$

21. $\sqrt{75} = \sqrt{25 \cdot 3} = \sqrt{25}\sqrt{3} = 5\sqrt{3}$

23. $\sqrt{63} = \sqrt{9 \cdot 7} = \sqrt{9}\sqrt{7} = 3\sqrt{7}$

25. $\sqrt[3]{24} = \sqrt[3]{8 \cdot 3} = \sqrt[3]{8}\sqrt[3]{3} = 2\sqrt[3]{3}$

27. $\sqrt[4]{48} = \sqrt[4]{16 \cdot 3} = \sqrt[4]{16}\sqrt[4]{3} = 2\sqrt[4]{3}$

29. $\sqrt{28} + \sqrt{63} = \sqrt{4 \cdot 7} + \sqrt{9 \cdot 7} = \sqrt{4}\sqrt{7} + \sqrt{9}\sqrt{7}$
$= 2\sqrt{7} + 3\sqrt{7} = (2 + 3)\sqrt{7} = 5\sqrt{7}$

31. $\sqrt{75} - \sqrt{48} = \sqrt{25 \cdot 3} - \sqrt{16 \cdot 3} = \sqrt{25}\sqrt{3} - \sqrt{16}\sqrt{3}$
$= 5\sqrt{3} - 4\sqrt{3} = (5 - 4)\sqrt{3} = \sqrt{3}$

33. $3\sqrt{50v} - 7\sqrt{32v} = 3\sqrt{25 \cdot 2v} - 7\sqrt{16 \cdot 2v}$
$= 3\sqrt{25}\sqrt{2v} - 7\sqrt{16}\sqrt{2v} = 3(5)\sqrt{2v} - 7(4)\sqrt{2v}$
$= 15\sqrt{2v} - 28\sqrt{2v} = (15 - 28)\sqrt{2v} = -13\sqrt{2v}$

35. $5\sqrt{28w} - 4\sqrt{63w} = 5\sqrt{4 \cdot 7w} - 4\sqrt{9 \cdot 7w}$
$= 5\sqrt{4}\sqrt{7w} - 4\sqrt{9}\sqrt{7w} = 5(2)\sqrt{7w} - 4(3)\sqrt{7w}$
$= 10\sqrt{7w} - 12\sqrt{7w} = (10 - 12)\sqrt{7w} = -2\sqrt{7w}$

37. $\sqrt[3]{24} - \sqrt[3]{375} = \sqrt[3]{8 \cdot 3} - \sqrt[3]{125 \cdot 3} = \sqrt[3]{8}\sqrt[3]{3} - \sqrt[3]{125}\sqrt[3]{3}$
$= 2\sqrt[3]{3} - 5\sqrt[3]{3} = (2 - 5)\sqrt[3]{3} = -3\sqrt[3]{3}$

39. $20\sqrt[3]{-81t^3} - 7\sqrt[3]{24t^3} = 20\sqrt[3]{-27t^3 \cdot 3} - 7\sqrt[3]{8t^3 \cdot 3}$
$= 20\sqrt[3]{-27t^3}\sqrt[3]{3} - 7\sqrt[3]{8t^3}\sqrt[3]{3}$
$= 20(-3t)\sqrt[3]{3} - 7(2t)\sqrt[3]{3} = -60t\sqrt[3]{3} - 14t\sqrt[3]{3}$
$= (-60 - 14)t\sqrt[3]{3} = -74t\sqrt[3]{3}$

41. $9\sqrt[3]{40z^2} - 2\sqrt[3]{5000z^2}$
$= 9\sqrt[3]{8 \cdot 5z^2} - 2\sqrt[3]{1000 \cdot 5z^2}$
$= 9\sqrt[3]{8}\sqrt[3]{5z^2} - 2\sqrt[3]{1000}\sqrt[3]{5z^2}$
$= 9(2)\sqrt[3]{5z^2} - 2(10)\sqrt[3]{5z^2}$
$= 18\sqrt[3]{5z^2} - 20\sqrt[3]{5z^2}$
$= (18 - 20)\sqrt[3]{5z^2} = -2\sqrt[3]{5z^2}$

43. $\sqrt{\dfrac{5}{4}} + \sqrt{\dfrac{5}{9}} = \dfrac{\sqrt{5}}{\sqrt{4}} + \dfrac{\sqrt{5}}{\sqrt{9}} = \dfrac{\sqrt{5}}{2} + \dfrac{\sqrt{5}}{3} = \dfrac{3\sqrt{5}}{6} + \dfrac{2\sqrt{5}}{6} = \dfrac{3\sqrt{5} + 2\sqrt{5}}{6} = \dfrac{(3 + 2)\sqrt{5}}{6} = \dfrac{5\sqrt{5}}{6}$

45. $2\sqrt{\dfrac{11x}{25}} - \sqrt{\dfrac{11x}{49}} = \dfrac{2\sqrt{11x}}{\sqrt{25}} - \dfrac{\sqrt{11x}}{\sqrt{49}}$
$= \dfrac{2\sqrt{11x}}{5} - \dfrac{\sqrt{11x}}{7} = \dfrac{14\sqrt{11x}}{35} - \dfrac{5\sqrt{11x}}{35}$
$= \dfrac{14\sqrt{11x} - 5\sqrt{11x}}{35} = \dfrac{(14 - 5)\sqrt{11x}}{35} = \dfrac{9\sqrt{11x}}{35}$

47. $7\sqrt{0.98} + 2\sqrt{0.75} - \sqrt{0.12} + 5\sqrt{0.72}$
$= 7\sqrt{0.49 \cdot 2} + 2\sqrt{0.25 \cdot 3} - \sqrt{0.04 \cdot 3} + 5\sqrt{0.36 \cdot 2}$
$= 7\sqrt{0.49}\sqrt{2} + 2\sqrt{0.25}\sqrt{3} - \sqrt{0.04}\sqrt{3} + 5\sqrt{0.36}\sqrt{2}$
$= 7(0.7)\sqrt{2} + 2(0.5)\sqrt{3} - 0.2\sqrt{3} + 5(0.6)\sqrt{2}$
$= 4.9\sqrt{2} + \sqrt{3} - 0.2\sqrt{3} + 3\sqrt{2}$
$= (4.9 + 3)\sqrt{2} + (1 - 0.2)\sqrt{3} = 7.9\sqrt{2} + 0.8\sqrt{3}$

49. $\sqrt{x^2 + 2xy + y^2} - \sqrt{x^2} - \sqrt{y^2} = \sqrt{(x + y)^2} - x - y = (x + y) - x - y = x + y - x - y = 0$

		For $x \geq 0$	For any real number x
51.	$\sqrt{25x^2}$	**a.** $\sqrt{25x^2} = 5x$	**b.** $\sqrt{25x^2} = \vert 5x \vert = 5\vert x \vert$
53.	$\sqrt[3]{8x^3}$	**a.** $\sqrt[3]{8x^3} = 2x$	**b.** $\sqrt[3]{8x^3} = 2x$
55.	$\sqrt{1000000x^6}$	**a.** $\sqrt{1000000x^6} = 1000x^3$	**b.** $\sqrt{1000000x^6} = \vert 1000x^3 \vert = 1000\vert x^3 \vert$
57.	$\sqrt[5]{x^{30}}$	**a.** $\sqrt[5]{x^{30}} = x^6$	**b.** $\sqrt[5]{x^{30}} = x^6$

59. $\sqrt{50x^3} = \sqrt{25x^2}\sqrt{2x} = 5x\sqrt{2x}$

61. $\sqrt[3]{16x^4} = \sqrt[3]{8x^3}\sqrt[3]{2x} = 2x\sqrt[3]{2x}$

63. $\sqrt[3]{x^4 y^8} = \sqrt[3]{x^3 y^6}\sqrt[3]{xy^2} = xy^2\sqrt[3]{xy^2}$

65. Let $V = 750$, $h = 5$ ft $(h = 60$ in$)$ and solve for r.

$$V = \pi r^2 h$$
$$750 = \pi r^2 (60)$$
$$r^2 = \frac{750}{60\pi} = \frac{25}{2\pi}$$
$$r = \sqrt{\frac{25}{2\pi}} \approx 2.0 \text{ in}$$

67. $L = \sqrt{w^2 + l^2 + h^2} = \sqrt{(5.2)^2 + (9.4)^2 + (6.5)^2}$
≈ 12.6 m

69. $s = \sqrt{26} \approx \sqrt{25} = 5$ cm The proper choice is **C**.

	Integer Estimate	Inequality	Approximation
Example $\sqrt[4]{79}$	3	$3 > \sqrt[4]{79}$	2.981
71. $\sqrt[3]{63}$	4	$\sqrt[3]{63} < 4$	3.979
73. $\dfrac{1 + \sqrt{9.05}}{2}$	2	$\dfrac{1 + \sqrt{9.05}}{2} > 2$	2.004

75. The graph of $f(x) = x + 3$ is a line. The proper choice is **E**.

77. The graph of $f(x) = \sqrt{x} + 3$ is a radical function with a domain $[0, \infty)$ shifted up 3 units.
The proper choice is **C**.

79. The graph of $f(x) = \vert x \vert + 3$ is the absolute value function with vertex: $(0, 3)$.
The proper choice is **A**.

Cumulative Review

1. $f(x) = -3x + 35$ is a function that is decreasing over its whole domain. The proper choice is **B**.

2. $f(x) = \sqrt{x - 4}$ is a function that is increasing over its whole domain. The proper choice is **A**.

3. $f(x) = -x^2 + 9$ is a function whose graph has a single highest point. The proper choice is **D**.

4. $f(x) = \vert x + 6 \vert$ is a function whose graph has a single lowest point. The proper choice is **E**.

5. $f(x) = -3$ is a function that is neither increasing nor decreasing. The proper choice is **C**.

Section 10.3: Multiplying and Dividing Radical Expressions

Quick Review 10.3

1. $5xy(3x-2y)=15x^2y-10xy^2$

2. $(2x+5y)(7x-3y)=14x^2-6xy+35xy-15y^2$
$$=14x^2+29xy-15y^2$$

3. $(4x+5y)(4x-5y)=(4x)^2-(5y)^2$
$$=16x^2-25y^2$$

4. $(4x+5y)^2=(4x)^2+2(4x)(5y)+(5y)^2$
$$=16x^2+40xy+25y^2$$

5. The conjugate of $5-7i$ is $5+7i$.

Exercises 10.3

1. $\sqrt{2}\sqrt{6}=\sqrt{2\cdot6}=\sqrt{12}=\sqrt{4\cdot3}=\sqrt{4}\sqrt{3}=2\sqrt{3}$

3. $\sqrt{2}(5\sqrt{2}-1)=5\sqrt{2}\sqrt{2}-\sqrt{2}(1)=5\sqrt{4}-\sqrt{2}$
$$=5(2)-\sqrt{2}=10-\sqrt{2}$$

5. $(2\sqrt{3})(4\sqrt{5})=8\sqrt{15}$

7. $(7\sqrt{15})(4\sqrt{21})=28\sqrt{315}=28\sqrt{9\cdot35}=28\sqrt{9}\sqrt{35}$
$$=28(3)\sqrt{35}=28(3)\sqrt{35}=84\sqrt{35}$$

9. $\sqrt{3}(\sqrt{2}+\sqrt{5})=\sqrt{3}\sqrt{2}+\sqrt{3}\sqrt{5}=\sqrt{6}+\sqrt{15}$

11. $3\sqrt{5}(2\sqrt{15}-7\sqrt{35})$
$$=(3\sqrt{5})(2\sqrt{15})-(3\sqrt{5})(7\sqrt{35})$$
$$=6\sqrt{75}-21\sqrt{175}=6\sqrt{25\cdot3}-21\sqrt{25\cdot7}$$
$$=6\sqrt{25}\sqrt{3}-21\sqrt{25}\sqrt{7}=6(5)\sqrt{3}-21(5)\sqrt{7}$$
$$=30\sqrt{3}-105\sqrt{7}$$

13. $\sqrt{2}(5\sqrt{6})(8\sqrt{3})=5\cdot8\sqrt{6}\sqrt{2}\sqrt{3}=40\sqrt{6\cdot2\cdot3}$
$$=40\sqrt{36}=40(6)=240$$

15. $\sqrt{8w}\sqrt{2w}=\sqrt{16w^2}=4w$

17. $(2\sqrt{6z})(4\sqrt{3z})=8\sqrt{18z^2}=8\sqrt{9z^2\cdot2}=8\sqrt{9z^2}\sqrt{2}$
$$=8(3z)\sqrt{2}=24z\sqrt{2}$$

19. $3\sqrt{x}(2\sqrt{x}-5)=(3\sqrt{x})(2\sqrt{x})-(3\sqrt{x})(5)$
$$=6(\sqrt{x})^2-15\sqrt{x}=6x-15\sqrt{x}$$

21. $(\sqrt{3x}-\sqrt{y})(\sqrt{3x}+4\sqrt{y})$
$$=\sqrt{3x}(\sqrt{3x})+\sqrt{3x}(4\sqrt{y})-\sqrt{y}(\sqrt{3x})-\sqrt{y}(4\sqrt{y})$$
$$=(\sqrt{3x})^2+4\sqrt{3xy}-\sqrt{3xy}+4y$$
$$=3x+3\sqrt{3xy}-4y$$

23. $(2\sqrt{3}-\sqrt{2})^2=(2\sqrt{3})^2-2(2\sqrt{3})(\sqrt{2})+(\sqrt{2})^2$
$$=4(3)-4\sqrt{6}+2=12-4\sqrt{6}+2$$
$$=14-4\sqrt{6}$$

25. $\left(\sqrt{a}+5\sqrt{3b}\right)^2$

$=\left(\sqrt{a}\right)^2+2\left(\sqrt{a}\right)\left(5\sqrt{3b}\right)+\left(5\sqrt{3b}\right)^2$

$=a+10\sqrt{3ab}+25(3b)$

$=a+10\sqrt{3ab}+75b$

27. $\left(\sqrt{v-2}+3\right)\left(\sqrt{v-2}-3\right)=\left(\sqrt{v-2}\right)^2-(3)^2$

$=(v-2)-9$

$=v-11$

29. $\sqrt[3]{7}\sqrt[3]{49}=\sqrt[3]{343}=7$

31. $\sqrt[3]{9v}\sqrt[3]{-3v^2}=\sqrt[3]{-27v^3}=-3v$

33. $-\sqrt[3]{4}\left(2\sqrt[3]{2}+\sqrt[3]{5}\right)=\left(-\sqrt[3]{4}\right)\left(2\sqrt[3]{2}\right)+\left(-\sqrt[3]{4}\right)\left(\sqrt[3]{5}\right)$

$=-2\sqrt[3]{8}-\sqrt[3]{20}=-2(2)-\sqrt[3]{20}$

$=-4-\sqrt[3]{20}$

35. $\left(\sqrt[3]{xy^2}\right)^2=\sqrt[3]{\left(xy^2\right)^2}=\sqrt[3]{x^2y^4}$

$=\sqrt[3]{y^3}\sqrt[3]{x^2y}=y\sqrt[3]{x^2y}$

37. $-\sqrt{2}\left(3\sqrt{2}-5\sqrt{6}-7\right)=\left(-\sqrt{2}\right)\left(3\sqrt{2}\right)-\left(-\sqrt{2}\right)\left(5\sqrt{6}\right)-\left(-\sqrt{2}\right)(7)=-3\left(\sqrt{2}\right)^2+5\sqrt{12}+7\sqrt{2}$

$=-3(2)+5\sqrt{4}\sqrt{3}+7\sqrt{2}=-6+5(2)\sqrt{3}+7\sqrt{2}=-6+10\sqrt{3}+7\sqrt{2}$

39. $\left(2-\sqrt{2}\right)\left(2+\sqrt{2}\right)=2^2-\left(\sqrt{2}\right)^2=4-2=2$

41. $\left(x+\sqrt{3y}\right)\left(x-\sqrt{3y}\right)=(x)^2-\left(\sqrt{3y}\right)^2$

$=x^2-3y$

43. $\left(v+\sqrt{3v-1}\right)\left(v-\sqrt{3v-1}\right)$

$=v^2-\left(\sqrt{3v-1}\right)^2=v^2-(3v-1)=v^2-3v+1$

45. $\sqrt{\dfrac{3}{4}}=\dfrac{\sqrt{3}}{\sqrt{4}}=\dfrac{\sqrt{3}}{2}$

47. $\dfrac{2}{\sqrt{6}}=\dfrac{2}{\sqrt{6}}\cdot\dfrac{\sqrt{6}}{\sqrt{6}}=\dfrac{2\sqrt{6}}{6}=\dfrac{\sqrt{6}}{3}$

49. $\dfrac{\sqrt{5}}{\sqrt{8}}=\dfrac{\sqrt{5}}{\sqrt{4}\sqrt{2}}=\dfrac{\sqrt{5}}{2\sqrt{2}}\cdot\dfrac{\sqrt{2}}{\sqrt{2}}=\dfrac{\sqrt{10}}{2(2)}=\dfrac{\sqrt{10}}{4}$

51. $\dfrac{\sqrt{10}}{\sqrt{2}}=\sqrt{\dfrac{10}{2}}=\sqrt{5}$

53. $\dfrac{12}{\sqrt[3]{4}}=\dfrac{12}{\sqrt[3]{4}}\cdot\dfrac{\sqrt[3]{2}}{\sqrt[3]{2}}=\dfrac{12\sqrt[3]{2}}{\sqrt[3]{8}}=\dfrac{\overset{6}{\cancel{12}}\sqrt[3]{2}}{\cancel{2}}=6\sqrt[3]{2}$

55. $\dfrac{\sqrt[3]{5}}{\sqrt[3]{16}}=\dfrac{\sqrt[3]{5}}{\sqrt[3]{16}}\cdot\dfrac{\sqrt[3]{4}}{\sqrt[3]{4}}=\dfrac{\sqrt[3]{20}}{\sqrt[3]{64}}=\dfrac{\sqrt[3]{20}}{4}$

57. $\sqrt[3]{\dfrac{22}{99}}=\sqrt[3]{\dfrac{\cancel{11}\cdot2}{\cancel{11}\cdot9}}=\dfrac{\sqrt[3]{2}}{\sqrt[3]{9}}=\dfrac{\sqrt[3]{2}}{\sqrt[3]{9}}\cdot\dfrac{\sqrt[3]{3}}{\sqrt[3]{3}}=\dfrac{\sqrt[3]{6}}{\sqrt[3]{27}}=\dfrac{\sqrt[3]{6}}{3}$

59. $18\div\sqrt{6}=\dfrac{18}{\sqrt{6}}=\dfrac{18}{\sqrt{6}}\cdot\dfrac{\sqrt{6}}{\sqrt{6}}=\dfrac{18\sqrt{6}}{6}=3\sqrt{6}$

61. $\dfrac{26}{\sqrt{10}}=\dfrac{26}{\sqrt{10}}\cdot\dfrac{\sqrt{10}}{\sqrt{10}}=\dfrac{26\sqrt{10}}{10}=\dfrac{13\sqrt{10}}{5}$

63. $\dfrac{15}{\sqrt{3x}}=\dfrac{15}{\sqrt{3x}}\cdot\dfrac{\sqrt{3x}}{\sqrt{3x}}=\dfrac{15\sqrt{3x}}{3x}=\dfrac{5\sqrt{3x}}{x}$

65. $\dfrac{3}{1+\sqrt{7}}=\dfrac{3}{\left(1+\sqrt{7}\right)}\cdot\dfrac{\left(1-\sqrt{7}\right)}{\left(1-\sqrt{7}\right)}=\dfrac{3\left(1-\sqrt{7}\right)}{1-7}$

$=\dfrac{3\left(1-\sqrt{7}\right)}{-6}=-\dfrac{1-\sqrt{7}}{2}=\dfrac{\sqrt{7}-1}{2}$

67. $\dfrac{36}{\sqrt{13}-5}=\dfrac{36}{\left(\sqrt{13}-5\right)}\cdot\dfrac{\left(\sqrt{13}+5\right)}{\left(\sqrt{13}+5\right)}=\dfrac{36\left(\sqrt{13}+5\right)}{13-25}$

$=\dfrac{36\left(5+\sqrt{13}\right)}{-12}=-3\left(\sqrt{13}+5\right)$

$=-15-3\sqrt{13}$

69. $\dfrac{-15}{\sqrt{7}-\sqrt{2}} = \dfrac{-15}{\left(\sqrt{7}-\sqrt{2}\right)} \cdot \dfrac{\left(\sqrt{7}+\sqrt{2}\right)}{\left(\sqrt{7}+\sqrt{2}\right)}$

$= \dfrac{-15\left(\sqrt{7}+\sqrt{2}\right)}{7-2} = \dfrac{-15\left(\sqrt{7}+\sqrt{2}\right)}{5}$

$= -3\left(\sqrt{7}+\sqrt{2}\right) = -3\sqrt{7}-3\sqrt{2}$

71. $\dfrac{\sqrt{a}}{\sqrt{a}-\sqrt{b}} = \dfrac{\sqrt{a}}{\left(\sqrt{a}-\sqrt{b}\right)} \cdot \dfrac{\left(\sqrt{a}+\sqrt{b}\right)}{\left(\sqrt{a}+\sqrt{b}\right)}$

$= \dfrac{\sqrt{a}\left(\sqrt{a}+\sqrt{b}\right)}{a-b} = \dfrac{a+\sqrt{ab}}{a-b}$

73. $\dfrac{12}{\sqrt[3]{3}} = \dfrac{12}{\sqrt[3]{3}} \cdot \dfrac{\sqrt[3]{9}}{\sqrt[3]{9}} = \dfrac{12\sqrt[3]{9}}{\sqrt[3]{27}} = \dfrac{12\sqrt[3]{9}}{3} = 4\sqrt[3]{9}$

75. $\sqrt[3]{\dfrac{3}{4}} = \dfrac{\sqrt[3]{3}}{\sqrt[3]{4}} \cdot \dfrac{\sqrt[3]{2}}{\sqrt[3]{2}} = \dfrac{\sqrt[3]{6}}{\sqrt[3]{8}} = \dfrac{\sqrt[3]{6}}{2}$

77. $\sqrt[3]{\dfrac{v}{9w^2}} = \dfrac{\sqrt[3]{v}}{\sqrt[3]{9w^2}} \cdot \dfrac{\sqrt[3]{3w}}{\sqrt[3]{3w}} = \dfrac{\sqrt[3]{3vw}}{\sqrt[3]{27w^3}} = \dfrac{\sqrt[3]{3vw}}{3w}$

79. $\sqrt[3]{\dfrac{4v^2}{2vw^2}} = \sqrt[3]{\dfrac{2v \cdot 2v}{2v\,w^2}} = \dfrac{\sqrt[3]{2v}}{\sqrt[3]{w^2}} \cdot \dfrac{\sqrt[3]{w}}{\sqrt[3]{w}} = \dfrac{\sqrt[3]{2vw}}{\sqrt[3]{w^3}} = \dfrac{\sqrt[3]{2vw}}{w}$

81. $\dfrac{5}{\sqrt{3x}+\sqrt{2y}} = \dfrac{5}{\left(\sqrt{3x}+\sqrt{2y}\right)} \cdot \dfrac{\left(\sqrt{3x}-\sqrt{2y}\right)}{\left(\sqrt{3x}-\sqrt{2y}\right)}$

$= \dfrac{5\left(\sqrt{3x}-\sqrt{2y}\right)}{3x-2y}$

	Integer Estimate	Inequality	Approximation
Example $\dfrac{6}{\sqrt{4.1}}$	3	$3 > \dfrac{6}{\sqrt{4.1}}$	2.963
83. $\dfrac{100}{\sqrt{24}}$	20	$20 < \dfrac{100}{\sqrt{24}}$	20.412

85. $\sqrt[3]{x^7 y^5} = \sqrt[3]{x^6 y^3}\,\sqrt[3]{x^1 y^2} = x^2 y \sqrt[3]{xy^2}$

87. $\dfrac{\sqrt[3]{4z}}{\sqrt[3]{z^2}} = \dfrac{\sqrt[3]{4z}}{\sqrt[3]{z^2}} \cdot \dfrac{\sqrt[3]{z}}{\sqrt[3]{z}} = \dfrac{\sqrt[3]{4z^2}}{\sqrt[3]{z^3}} = \dfrac{\sqrt[3]{4z^2}}{z}$

89. $\dfrac{10}{\sqrt[5]{8z^3}} = \dfrac{10}{\sqrt[5]{8z^3}} \cdot \dfrac{\sqrt[5]{4z^2}}{\sqrt[5]{4z^2}} = \dfrac{10\sqrt[5]{4z^2}}{\sqrt[5]{32z^5}} = \dfrac{10\,\sqrt[5]{4z^2}}{2z} = \dfrac{5\sqrt[5]{4z^2}}{z}$

Cumulative Review

1. $5(2v-3)-3(2v-4)=5$

$10v-15-6v+12=5$

$10v-6v-15+12=5$

$4v-3=5$

$4v=8$

$v=2$

2. $|2w-3|=5$

is equivalent to

$2w-3=-5 \quad \text{or} \quad 2w-3=5$

$2w=-2 \qquad\qquad 2w=8$

$w=-1 \qquad\qquad w=4$

3. $(2x-3)^2 = 25$

$$2x-3 = \pm\sqrt{25}$$

$2x-3 = -5$ or $2x-3 = 5$

$\quad 2x = -2 \qquad\qquad 2x = 8$

$\qquad x = -1 \qquad\qquad\; x = 4$

4. $(2y-3)(y-4) = 7$

$$2y^2 - 8y - 3y + 12 = 7$$
$$2y^2 - 11y + 12 = 7$$
$$2y^2 - 11y + 5 = 0$$
$$(y-5)(2y-1) = 0$$

$y-5 = 0$ or $2y-1 = 0$

$\quad y = 5 \qquad\qquad y = \dfrac{1}{2}$

5. $\dfrac{3}{m-7} + 5 = \dfrac{8}{m-7}$

$$(m-7)\left(\dfrac{3}{m-7} + 5\right) = (m-7)\left(\dfrac{8}{m-7}\right)$$
$$3 + 5(m-7) = 8$$
$$3 + 5m - 35 = 8$$
$$5m - 32 = 8$$
$$5m = 40$$
$$m = 8$$

Section 10.4: Solving Equations Containing Radical Expressions

Quick Review 10.4

1. $5x - 1 = 64$

$$5x = 65$$
$$x = 13$$

2. $(5x-1)^2 = 64$

$$5x - 1 = \pm\sqrt{64}$$
$$5x - 1 = \pm 8$$

$5x-1 = -8$ or $5x-1 = 8$

$\quad 5x = -7 \qquad\qquad 5x = 9$

$\quad x = -\dfrac{7}{5} \qquad\qquad x = \dfrac{9}{5}$

3. $\sqrt{2x-1} + 2 = x$

$$\sqrt{2(1)-1} + 2 = (1)$$
$$\sqrt{1} + 2 = 1$$
$$1 + 2 = 1$$
$$3 \neq 1$$

No, $x = 1$ is not a solution to $\sqrt{2x-1} + 2 = x$.

4. $\sqrt{2x-1} + 2 = x$

$$\sqrt{2(5)-1} + 2 = (5)$$
$$\sqrt{9} + 2 = 5$$
$$3 + 2 = 5$$
$$5 = 5$$

Yes, $x = 5$ is a solution to $\sqrt{2x-1} + 2 = x$.

5. From the graph we can see that the point of intersection is $(4, 3)$. Thus the solution to the equation is $x = 4$.

Exercises 10.4

1. The solution to the equation is the x value of the point of intersection. Answer: $x = 5$.

3. The solution to the equation is determined by the x-intercept. Answer: $x = -1$.

5. $\sqrt{x} = 4$

    $\left(\sqrt{x}\right)^2 = (4)^2$

    $x = 16$

    Check:

    $\sqrt{16} = 4$

    $4 = 4$ is true.

    Answer: $x = 16$

7. $\sqrt{x} - 7 = -6$

    $\sqrt{x} = 1$

    $\left(\sqrt{x}\right)^2 = (1)^2$

    $x = 1$

    Check:

    $\sqrt{x} - 7 = -6$

    $\sqrt{1} - 7 = -6$

    $1 - 7 = -6$

    $-6 = -6$ is true.

    Answer: $x = 1$

9. $\sqrt{t-4} = 3$

    $\left(\sqrt{t-4}\right)^2 = (3)^2$

    $t - 4 = 9$

    $t = 13$

    Check:

    $\sqrt{(13)-4} = 3$

    $\sqrt{9} = 3$

    $3 = 3$ is true.

    Answer: $t = 13$

11. $\sqrt{c+7} + 23 = 43$

    $\sqrt{c+7} = 20$

    $\left(\sqrt{c+7}\right)^2 = (20)^2$

    $c + 7 = 400$

    $c = 393$

    Check:

    $\sqrt{(393)+7} + 23 = 43$

    $\sqrt{400} + 23 = 43$

    $20 + 23 = 43$

    $43 = 43$ is true.

    Answer: $c = 393$

13. $\sqrt{3x-21} + 7 = 2$

    $\sqrt{3x-21} = -5$

    $\left(\sqrt{3x-21}\right)^2 = (-5)^2$

    $3x - 21 = 25$

    $3x = 46$

    $x = \dfrac{46}{3}$

    Check:

    $\sqrt{3\left(\dfrac{46}{3}\right)-21} + 7 = 2$

    $\sqrt{46-21} + 7 = 2$

    $\sqrt{25} + 7 = 2$

    $5 + 7 = 2$

    $12 = 2$ is false.

    No Solution

15. $\sqrt[3]{2w+1} = -2$

    $\left(\sqrt[3]{2w+1}\right)^3 = (-2)^3$

    $2w + 1 = -8$

    $2w = -9$

    $w = -\dfrac{9}{2}$

    Check:

    $\sqrt[3]{2\left(-\dfrac{9}{2}\right)+1} = -2$

    $\sqrt[3]{-9+1} = -2$

    $\sqrt[3]{-8} = -2$

    $-2 = -2$ is true.

    Answer: $w = -\dfrac{9}{2}$

17. $\sqrt[4]{6v-2} = 2$

    $\left(\sqrt[4]{6v-2}\right)^4 = (2)^4$

    $6v - 2 = 16$

    $6v = 18$

    $v = 3$

    Check:

    $\sqrt[4]{6(3)-2} = 2$

    $\sqrt[4]{18-2} = 2$

    $\sqrt[4]{16} = 2$

    $2 = 2$ is true.

    Answer: $v = 3$

19. $\sqrt[5]{w^2-4w} = 2$

    $\left(\sqrt[5]{w^2-4w}\right)^5 = (2)^5$

    $w^2 - 4w = 32$

    $w^2 - 4w - 32 = 0$

    $(w-8)(w+4) = 0$

    $w = 8$ or $w = -4$

    Check:

    $\sqrt[5]{(8)^2-4(8)} = 2$

    $\sqrt[5]{64-32} = 2$

    $\sqrt[5]{32} = 2$

    $2 = 2$ is true.

    Check:

    $\sqrt[5]{(-4)^2-4(-4)} = 2$

    $\sqrt[5]{16+16} = 2$

    $\sqrt[5]{32} = 2$

    $2 = 2$ is true.

    Answer: $w = 8$ or $w = -4$

21. $\sqrt{y^2 - y + 13} - y = 1$

$\sqrt{y^2 - y + 13} = 1 + y$

$\left(\sqrt{y^2 - y + 13}\right)^2 = (1 + y)^2$

$y^2 - y + 13 = 1 + 2y + y^2$

$-3y = -12$

$y = 4$

Check:

$\sqrt{(4)^2 - (4) + 13} - (4) = 1$

$\sqrt{16 - 4 + 13} - 4 = 1$

$\sqrt{25} - 4 = 1$

$5 - 4 = 1$

$1 = 1$ is true.

Answer: $y = 4$

23. $\sqrt{7t + 2} = 2t$

$\left(\sqrt{7t + 2}\right)^2 = (2t)^2$

$7t + 2 = 4t^2$

$4t^2 - 7t - 2 = 0$

$(4t + 1)(t - 2) = 0$

$t = -\dfrac{1}{4}$ or $t = 2$

Check:

$\sqrt{7\left(-\dfrac{1}{4}\right) + 2} = 2\left(-\dfrac{1}{4}\right)$

$\sqrt{\dfrac{-7}{4} + \dfrac{8}{4}} = -\dfrac{1}{2}$

$\sqrt{\dfrac{1}{4}} = -\dfrac{1}{2}$

$\dfrac{1}{2} = -\dfrac{1}{2}$ is false.

Check:

$\sqrt{7(2) + 2} = 2(2)$

$\sqrt{14 + 2} = 4$

$\sqrt{16} = 4$

$4 = 4$ is true.

Answer: $t = 2$

25. $\sqrt{w^2 - 2w + 1} = 2w$

$\left(\sqrt{w^2 - 2w + 1}\right)^2 = (2w)^2$

$w^2 - 2w + 1 = 4w^2$

$3w^2 + 2w - 1 = 0$

$(3w - 1)(w + 1) = 0$

$w = \dfrac{1}{3}$ or $w = -1$

Check:

$\sqrt{\left(\dfrac{1}{3}\right)^2 - 2\left(\dfrac{1}{3}\right) + 1} = 2\left(\dfrac{1}{3}\right)$

$\sqrt{\dfrac{1}{9} - \dfrac{2}{3} + 1} = \dfrac{2}{3}$

$\sqrt{\dfrac{1}{9} - \dfrac{6}{9} + \dfrac{9}{9}} = \dfrac{2}{3}$

$\sqrt{\dfrac{4}{9}} = \dfrac{2}{3}$

$\dfrac{2}{3} = \dfrac{2}{3}$ is true.

Check:

$\sqrt{w^2 - 2w + 1} = 2w$

$\sqrt{(-1)^2 - 2(-1) + 1} = 2(-1)$

$\sqrt{1 + 2 + 1} = -2$

$\sqrt{4} = -2$

$2 = -2$ is false.

Answer: $w = \dfrac{1}{3}$

27. $\sqrt{2x + 1} + 5 = 2x$

$\sqrt{2x + 1} = 2x - 5$

$\left(\sqrt{2x + 1}\right)^2 = (2x - 5)^2$

$2x + 1 = 4x^2 - 20x + 25$

$4x^2 - 22x + 24 = 0$

$2(2x^2 - 11x + 12) = 0$

$2(2x - 3)(x - 4) = 0$

$x = \dfrac{3}{2}$ or $x = 4$

Check:

$\sqrt{2\left(\dfrac{3}{2}\right) + 1} + 5 = 2\left(\dfrac{3}{2}\right)$

$\sqrt{3 + 1} + 5 = 3$

$\sqrt{4} + 5 = 3$

$2 + 5 = 3$

$7 = 3$ is false.

Check:

$\sqrt{2(4) + 1} + 5 = 2(4)$

$\sqrt{8 + 1} + 5 = 8$

$\sqrt{9} + 5 = 8$

$3 + 5 = 8$

$8 = 8$ is true.

Answer: $x = 4$

29.

$$\sqrt{6u+7} = \sqrt{11u+7}$$
$$\left(\sqrt{6u+7}\right)^2 = \left(\sqrt{11u+7}\right)^2$$
$$6u+7 = 11u+7$$
$$-5u = 0$$
$$u = 0$$

Check:
$$\sqrt{6(0)+7} = \sqrt{11(0)+7}$$
$$\sqrt{7} = \sqrt{7} \text{ is true.}$$
Answer: $u = 0$

31.

$$d = \sqrt{(x_2-x_1)^2 + (y_2-y_1)^2}$$
$$= \sqrt{[3-(-2)]^2 + (6-6)^2}$$
$$= \sqrt{5^2 + 0^2} = \sqrt{25} = 5$$

33.

$$d = \sqrt{(x_2-x_1)^2 + (y_2-y_1)^2}$$
$$= \sqrt{[(-6)-2]^2 + [8-(-7)]^2}$$
$$= \sqrt{(-8)^2 + 15^2} = \sqrt{64+225} = \sqrt{289} = 17$$

35.

$$d = \sqrt{(x_2-x_1)^2 + (y_2-y_1)^2}$$
$$= \sqrt{\left[\left(\frac{1}{2}\right)-\left(-\frac{1}{2}\right)\right]^2 + \left[\left(-\frac{1}{3}\right)-\left(\frac{2}{3}\right)\right]^2}$$
$$= \sqrt{\left(\frac{2}{2}\right)^2 + \left(-\frac{3}{3}\right)^2} = \sqrt{1+1} = \sqrt{2}$$

37.

$$d = \sqrt{(x_2-x_1)^2 + (y_2-y_1)^2} = \sqrt{\left(-\sqrt{2}-0\right)^2 + \left(\sqrt{7}-0\right)^2} = \sqrt{\left(-\sqrt{2}\right)^2 + \left(\sqrt{7}\right)^2} = \sqrt{2+7} = \sqrt{9} = 3$$

39.

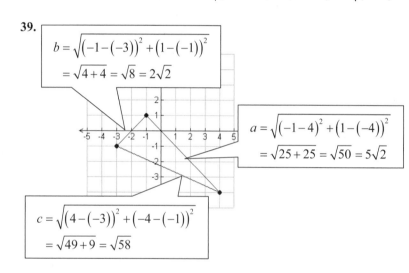

$$b = \sqrt{(-1-(-3))^2 + (1-(-1))^2}$$
$$= \sqrt{4+4} = \sqrt{8} = 2\sqrt{2}$$

$$a = \sqrt{(-1-4)^2 + (1-(-4))^2}$$
$$= \sqrt{25+25} = \sqrt{50} = 5\sqrt{2}$$

$$c = \sqrt{(4-(-3))^2 + (-4-(-1))^2}$$
$$= \sqrt{49+9} = \sqrt{58}$$

Perimeter:
$$a+b+c = 2\sqrt{2} + 5\sqrt{2} + \sqrt{58}$$
$$= 7\sqrt{2} + \sqrt{58}$$

To determine if the triangle is a right triangle we check the values of a, b, and c in the Pythagorean theorem.
$$a^2 + b^2 = c^2$$
$$\left(5\sqrt{2}\right)^2 + \left(2\sqrt{2}\right)^2 = \left(\sqrt{58}\right)^2$$
$$25(2) + 4(2) = 58$$
$$50 + 8 = 58$$
$$58 = 58 \text{ is true}$$
Thus the triangle is a right triangle.

41.

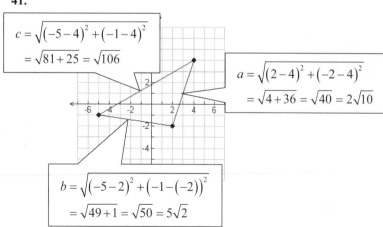

$$c = \sqrt{(-5-4)^2 + (-1-4)^2}$$
$$= \sqrt{81+25} = \sqrt{106}$$

$$a = \sqrt{(2-4)^2 + (-2-4)^2}$$
$$= \sqrt{4+36} = \sqrt{40} = 2\sqrt{10}$$

$$b = \sqrt{(-5-2)^2 + (-1-(-2))^2}$$
$$= \sqrt{49+1} = \sqrt{50} = 5\sqrt{2}$$

Perimeter:
$$a+b+c = 2\sqrt{10} + 5\sqrt{2} + \sqrt{106}$$

To determine if the triangle is a right triangle we check the values of a, b, and c in the Pythagorean theorem.
$$a^2 + b^2 = c^2$$
$$\left(2\sqrt{10}\right)^2 + \left(5\sqrt{2}\right)^2 = \left(\sqrt{106}\right)^2$$
$$4(10) + 25(2) = 106$$
$$40 + 50 = 106$$
$$90 = 106 \text{ is false}$$
Thus the triangle is not a right triangle.

43.
$$c^2 = 5^2 + 12^2$$
$$c^2 = 25 + 144$$
$$c^2 = 169$$
$$\sqrt{c^2} = \sqrt{169}$$
$$c = 13 \text{ cm}$$

45.
$$b^2 + 40^2 = 41^2$$
$$b^2 + 1600 = 1681$$
$$b^2 = 81$$
$$\sqrt{b^2} = \sqrt{81}$$
$$b = 9 \text{ cm}$$

47.
$$c^2 = 7^2 + 8^2$$
$$c^2 = 49 + 64$$
$$c^2 = 113$$
$$\sqrt{c^2} = \sqrt{113}$$
$$c = \sqrt{113} \approx 10.63 \text{ cm}$$

49. To find all points with an x-coordinate of 5 that are 10 units from the point $(13, 2)$ we solve the equation formed by letting the distance between $(13, 2)$ and $(5, y)$ equal 10.
$$\sqrt{(5-13)^2 + (y-2)^2} = 10$$
$$\sqrt{64 + y^2 - 4y + 4} = 10$$
$$\sqrt{y^2 - 4y + 68} = 10$$
$$\left(\sqrt{y^2 - 4y + 68}\right)^2 = (10)^2$$
$$y^2 - 4y + 68 = 100$$
$$y^2 - 4y - 32 = 0$$
$$(y-8)(y+4) = 0$$
$$y = 8 \quad \text{or} \quad y = -4$$

Thus the two points are $(5, 8)$ and $(5, -4)$.

51.
$$\sqrt{x+5} = 3$$
$$\left(\sqrt{x+5}\right)^2 = (3)^2$$
$$x + 5 = 9$$
$$x = 4$$

Check:
$$\sqrt{(4)+5} = 3$$
$$\sqrt{9} = 3$$
$3 = 3$ is true.
Answer: $x = 4$

53.
$$4\sqrt{x} = 3(x-5)$$
$$\left(4\sqrt{x}\right)^2 = \left[3(x-5)\right]^2$$
$$16x = 3^2(x-5)^2$$
$$16x = 9\left(x^2 - 10x + 25\right)$$
$$16x = 9x^2 - 90x + 225$$
$$9x^2 - 106x + 225 = 0$$
$$(9x-25)(x-9) = 0$$
$$x = \frac{25}{9} \quad \text{or} \quad x = 9$$

Check:
$$4\sqrt{\frac{25}{9}} = 3\left(\frac{25}{9} - 5\right)$$
$$4\left(\frac{5}{3}\right) = 3\left(\frac{25}{9} - \frac{45}{9}\right)$$
$$\frac{20}{3} = 3\left(-\frac{20}{9}\right)$$
$$\frac{20}{3} = -\frac{20}{3} \quad \text{is false.}$$

Check:
$$4\sqrt{9} = 3(9-5)$$
$$4(3) = 3(4)$$
$12 = 12$ is true.
Answer: $x = 9$

55. To find the x-intercepts we let $y = 0$ and solve for x.

$$y = \sqrt{x+9} - 2$$
$$0 = \sqrt{x+9} - 2$$
$$2 = \sqrt{x+9}$$
$$(2)^2 = \left(\sqrt{x+9}\right)^2$$
$$4 = x+9$$
$$x = -5$$

The x-intercept is $(-5, 0)$

To find the y-intercept we let $x = 0$ and solve for y

$$y = \sqrt{x+9} - 2$$
$$y = \sqrt{(0)+9} - 2$$
$$y = \sqrt{9} - 2$$
$$y = 3 - 2$$
$$y = 1$$

The y-intercept is $(0, 1)$

57. To find the x-intercepts we let $y = 0$ and solve for x.

$$y = \sqrt[3]{x+1} + 2$$
$$0 = \sqrt[3]{x+1} + 2$$
$$-2 = \sqrt[3]{x+1}$$
$$(-2)^3 = \left(\sqrt[3]{x+1}\right)^3$$
$$-8 = x+1$$
$$x = -9$$

The x-intercept is $(-9, 0)$

To find the y-intercept we let $x = 0$ and solve for y

$$y = \sqrt[3]{x+1} + 2$$
$$y = \sqrt[3]{(0)+1} + 2$$
$$y = 1 + 2$$
$$y = 3$$

The y-intercept is $(0, 3)$

59.
$$\sqrt{2x+6} = x$$
$$\left(\sqrt{2x+6}\right)^2 = (x)^2$$
$$2x+6 = x^2$$
$$x^2 - 2x - 6 = 0$$
$$a = 1, \quad b = -2, \quad c = -6$$
$$x = \frac{-(-2) \pm \sqrt{(-2)^2 - 4(1)(-6)}}{2(1)}$$
$$= \frac{2 \pm \sqrt{4+24}}{2} = \frac{2 \pm \sqrt{28}}{2} = \frac{2 \pm 2\sqrt{7}}{2}$$
$$= \frac{2\left(1 \pm \sqrt{7}\right)}{2} = 1 \pm \sqrt{7}$$

Check:
$$x = 1 + \sqrt{7}$$

```
1+√(7)→X
          3.645751311
√(2X+6)
          3.645751311
X
          3.645751311
■
```

The left hand side of the equation is equal to the right hand side of the equation. Thus $x = 1 + \sqrt{7}$ is a solution.

Check:
$$x = 1 - \sqrt{7}$$

```
1-√(7)→X
         -1.645751311
√(2X+6)
          1.645751311
X
         -1.645751311
■
```

The left hand side of the equation is not equal to the right hand side of the equation. Thus $x = 1 - \sqrt{7}$ is an extraneous solution.

61.
$$\sqrt{2x^2+3x} - 1 = x$$
$$\sqrt{2x^2+3x} = x+1$$
$$\left(\sqrt{2x^2+3x}\right)^2 = (x+1)^2$$
$$2x^2 + 3x = x^2 + 2x + 1$$
$$x^2 + x - 1 = 0$$
$$a = 1, \quad b = 1, \quad c = -1$$
$$x = \frac{-(1) \pm \sqrt{(1)^2 - 4(1)(-1)}}{2(1)} = \frac{-1 \pm \sqrt{5}}{2}$$

Check:
$$x = \frac{-1 + \sqrt{5}}{2}$$

```
(-1+√(5))/2→X
           .6180339887
√(2X²+3X)-1
           .6180339887
X
           .6180339887
```

The left hand side of the equation is equal to the right hand side of the equation. Thus $x = \frac{-1 + \sqrt{5}}{2}$ is a solution

Check:
$$x = \frac{-1 - \sqrt{5}}{2}$$

```
(-1-√(5))/2→X
         -1.618033989
√(2X²+3X)-1
          -.3819660113
X
         -1.618033989
■
```

The left hand side of the equation is not equal to the right hand side of the equation. Thus $x = \frac{-1 - \sqrt{5}}{2}$ is extraneous.

63.
$$\sqrt[3]{x^3 - 6x^2 + 12x} = x$$
$$\left(\sqrt[3]{x^3 - 6x^2 + 12x}\right)^3 = (x)^3$$
$$-6x^2 + 12x = 0$$
$$-6x(x - 2) = 0$$
$$x = 0 \quad \text{or} \quad x = 2$$

Check:
$$\sqrt[3]{(0)^3 - 6(0)^2 + 12(0)} = (0)$$
$$\sqrt[3]{0} = 0$$
$$0 = 0 \text{ is true.}$$

Check:
$$\sqrt[3]{x^3 - 6x^2 + 12x} = x$$
$$\sqrt[3]{(2)^3 - 6(2)^2 + 12(2)} = 2$$
$$\sqrt[3]{8 - 24 + 24} = 2$$
$$\sqrt[3]{8} = 2$$
$$2 = 2 \text{ is true.}$$
Answer: $x = 0$ or $x = 2$

65.
$$\sqrt{4w^2 + 12w + 6} = 2w$$
$$\left(\sqrt{4w^2 + 12w + 6}\right)^2 = (2w)^2$$
$$4w^2 + 12w + 6 = 4w^2$$
$$12w + 6 = 0$$
$$12w = -6$$
$$w = -\frac{1}{2}$$

Check:
$$\sqrt{4\left(-\frac{1}{2}\right)^2 + 12\left(-\frac{1}{2}\right) + 6} = 2\left(-\frac{1}{2}\right)$$
$$\sqrt{4\left(\frac{1}{4}\right) - 6 + 6} = -1$$
$$\sqrt{1 - 6 + 6} = -1$$
$$\sqrt{1} = -1$$
$$1 = -1 \text{ is false. No solution}$$

67. From the table we can see that the last column is equal to 3 when $x = 10$.
Thus the solution is $x = 10$.

69. From the table we can see that the last two columns are equal to each other when $x = 6$.
Thus the solution is $x = 6$.

71. $d = \sqrt{(37.8 - 3.0)^2 + (29.6 - 5.2)^2}$
$= \sqrt{34.8^2 + 24.4^2} \approx 42.5 \text{ m}$

73. $C(0) = 18\sqrt[3]{(0)^2} + 450 = 450$.
The overhead cost is $450.

75. To determine the number of solar cells produced when the cost is $738 we solve the following equation for n.
$$18\sqrt[3]{n^2} + 450 = 738$$
$$18\sqrt[3]{n^2} = 288$$
$$\sqrt[3]{n^2} = 16$$
$$\left(\sqrt[3]{n^2}\right)^3 = 16^3$$
$$n^2 = 4096$$
$$\sqrt{n^2} = \sqrt{4096}$$
$$n = 64$$
The cost of producing 64 solar cells is $738.

77. $S(1000) = 750\sqrt[3]{(1000)^2} = 75,000$. The strength of a beam with a volume of 1000 cubic centimeters is 75,000 newtons.

79.

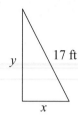

a. Using the Pythagorean Theorem we determine the following.

$$x^2 + y^2 = 17^2$$

$$y^2 = 289 - x^2$$

$$\sqrt{y^2} = \sqrt{289 - x^2}$$

$$y = \sqrt{289 - x^2}$$

Thus the function is

$$f(x) = \sqrt{289 - x^2}$$

b. 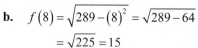 $f(8) = \sqrt{289 - (8)^2} = \sqrt{289 - 64}$

$$= \sqrt{225} = 15$$

Thus the distance to the top of the ladder is 15 feet.

81.

a. Using the Pythagorean Theorem we determine the following.

$$L(x) = \sqrt{x^2 + 11^2} = \sqrt{x^2 + 121}$$

b. $L(30) = \sqrt{30^2 + 121} = \sqrt{1021} \approx 32$

Thus the length of the rope is approximately 32 ft when the horse is 30 ft from the pole.

c. To determine the distance x that corresponds to a rope length of 35 ft we solve the following equation for x.

$$\sqrt{x^2 + 11^2} = 35$$

$$\left(\sqrt{x^2 + 121}\right)^2 = (35)^2$$

$$x^2 + 121 = 1225$$

$$x^2 = 325$$

$$\sqrt{x^2} = \sqrt{1104}$$

$$x = \sqrt{1104} \text{ ft}$$

This value of x gives the radius of the circle that the horse can occupy with a rope length of 35 ft. The area of this circle is $A = \pi\left(\sqrt{1104}\right)^2 \approx 3{,}470 \text{ ft}^2$.

83. To determine the distance x we solve the following equation.

$$\sqrt{16 + x^2} + (10 - x) = 12$$

$$\sqrt{16 + x^2} = x + 2$$

$$\left(\sqrt{16 + x^2}\right)^2 = (x + 2)^2$$

$$16 + x^2 = x^2 + 4x + 4$$

$$16 = 4x + 4$$

$$12 = 4x$$

$$x = 3$$

Thus x must be 3 miles long.

Cumulative Review

1. $a + b = b + a$

2. $a(b \cdot c) = (a \cdot b)c$

3. $a(b + c) = ab + ac$

4. $b^2 - 4ac = (-3)^2 - 4(2)(5) = 9 - 40 = -31 < 0$

Thus the equation has two non-real solutions.

5. $b^2 - 4ac = (-3)^2 - 4(2)(-5) = 9 + 40 = 49 > 0$

Thus the equation has two distinct real solutions.

Section 10.5: Rational Exponents and Radicals

Quick Review 10.5

1. $\left(\dfrac{4}{5}\right)^{-2} = \left(\dfrac{5}{4}\right)^{2} = \dfrac{5^2}{4^2} = \dfrac{25}{16}$

2. $x^7 x^{11} = x^{7+11} = x^{18}$

3. $\left(x^{11}\right)^7 = x^{11 \cdot 7} = x^{77}$

4. $\dfrac{x^{11}}{x^7} = x^{11-7} = x^4$

5. $\left(\dfrac{x^5}{x^{-3}}\right)^2 = \left(x^{5-(-3)}\right)^2 = \left(x^8\right)^2 = x^{8 \cdot 2} = x^{16}$

Exercises 10.5

1. The principal cube root of w is represented by $w^{1/3}$.

3. The principal sixth root of x is represented by $x^{1/6}$.

5. The principal cube root of 125 is represented by $\sqrt[3]{125} = 125^{1/3} = 5$.

7. The principal fourth root of 81 is represented by $81^{1/4} = 3$.

9. **a.** $\sqrt{16} = 16^{1/2} = 4$
  b. $\sqrt[4]{16} = 16^{1/4} = 2$

11. **a.** $\sqrt[5]{0} = 0^{1/5} = 0$
  b. $\sqrt[6]{0} = 0^{1/6} = 0$

13. **a.** $\sqrt[3]{-1} = (-1)^{1/3} = -1$
  b. $\sqrt[5]{-1} = (-1)^{1/5} = -1$

15. **a.** $36^{1/2} = \sqrt{36} = 6$
  b. $36^{-1/2} = \dfrac{1}{\sqrt{36}} = \dfrac{1}{6}$

17. **a.** $27^{1/3} = \sqrt[3]{27} = 3$
  b. $27^{-1/3} = \dfrac{1}{\sqrt[3]{27}} = \dfrac{1}{3}$

19. **a.** $0.09^{1/2} = \sqrt{0.09} = 0.3$
  b. $-0.09^{1/2} = -\sqrt{0.09} = -0.3$

21. **a.** $0.008^{1/3} = \sqrt[3]{0.008} = 0.2$
  b. $(-0.008)^{1/3} = \sqrt[3]{-0.008} = -0.2$

23. **a.** $64^{1/3} = \sqrt[3]{64} = 4$
  b. $64^{-1/3} = \dfrac{1}{\sqrt[3]{64}} = \dfrac{1}{4}$

25. **a.** $\left(\dfrac{8}{125}\right)^{2/3} = \left(\sqrt[3]{\dfrac{8}{125}}\right)^2 = \left(\dfrac{2}{5}\right)^2 = \dfrac{4}{25}$
  b. $\left(\dfrac{8}{125}\right)^{-2/3} = \left(\sqrt[3]{\dfrac{125}{8}}\right)^2 = \left(\dfrac{5}{2}\right)^2 = \dfrac{25}{4}$

27. **a.** $25^{1/2} + 144^{1/2} = \sqrt{25} + \sqrt{144} = 5 + 12 = 17$
  b. $(25 + 144)^{1/2} = \sqrt{25 + 144} = \sqrt{169} = 13$

29. **a.** $8^{1/3} + 1^{1/3} = \sqrt[3]{8} + \sqrt[3]{1} = 2 + 1 = 3$
  b. $(26 + 1)^{1/3} = \sqrt[3]{26 + 1} = \sqrt[3]{27} = 3$

31. **a.** $0.000001^{1/2} = \sqrt{0.000001} = 0.001$
  b. $0.000001^{1/3} = \sqrt[3]{0.000001} = 0.01$

33. $5^{1/2} \cdot 5^{3/2} = 5^{1/2 + 3/2} = 5^{4/2} = 5^2 = 25$

35. $\left(8^{5/3}\right)^{2/5} = 8^{(5/3)(2/5)} = 8^{2/3} = \left(8^{1/3}\right)^2 = 2^2 = 4$

37. $\dfrac{11^{4/3}}{11^{1/3}} = 11^{4/3 - 1/3} = 11^{3/3} = 11^1 = 11$

39. $\left(27^{1/12} \cdot 27^{-5/12}\right)^{-2} = \left(27^{1/12 - 5/12}\right)^{-2} = \left(27^{-4/12}\right)^{-2}$

$$= \left(27^{-1/3}\right)^{-2} = \left(\frac{1}{\sqrt[3]{27}}\right)^{-2}$$

$$= \left(\frac{1}{3}\right)^{-2} = 3^2 = 9$$

41. $x^{1/3} \cdot x^{1/2} = x^{1/3 + 1/2} = x^{2/6 + 3/6} = x^{5/6}$

43. $\dfrac{x^{1/2}}{x^{1/3}} = x^{1/2 - 1/3} = x^{3/6 - 2/6} = x^{1/6}$

45. $\left(z^{3/4}\right)^{2/7} = z^{(3/4)(2/7)} = z^{3/14}$

47. $\dfrac{w^{-2/3}}{w^{-5/3}} = w^{-2/3 - (-5/3)} = w^{-2/3 + 5/3} = w^{3/3} = w^1 = w$

49. $\left(v^{-10} w^{-15}\right)^{-1/5} = v^{(-10)(-1/5)} w^{(-15)(-1/5)} = v^2 w^3$

51. $\left(16v^{-2/5}\right)^{3/2} = 16^{3/2} v^{(-2/5)(3/2)}$

$$= \left(16^{1/2}\right)^3 v^{-3/5} = \frac{4^3}{v^{3/5}} = \frac{64}{v^{3/5}}$$

53. $\left(\dfrac{16n^{2/3}}{81n^{-2/3}}\right)^{-3/4} = \left(\dfrac{16n^{2/3 - (-2/3)}}{81}\right)^{-3/4}$

$$= \left(\frac{16n^{2/3 + 2/3}}{81}\right)^{-3/4} = \left(\frac{16n^{4/3}}{81}\right)^{-3/4}$$

$$= \left(\frac{81}{16n^{4/3}}\right)^{3/4} = \frac{81^{3/4}}{16^{3/4} n^{(4/3)(3/4)}}$$

$$= \frac{\left(81^{1/4}\right)^3}{\left(16^{1/4}\right)^3 n^1} = \frac{3^3}{2^3 n} = \frac{27}{8n}$$

55. $\dfrac{\left(27x^2 y\right)^{1/2} \left(3xy\right)^{1/2}}{5x^{1/2} y^2} = \dfrac{\left(\left(27x^2 y\right)\left(3xy\right)\right)^{1/2}}{5x^{1/2} y^2}$

$$= \frac{\left(81x^{2+1} y^{1+1}\right)^{1/2}}{5x^{1/2} y^2} = \frac{\left(81x^3 y^2\right)^{1/2}}{5x^{1/2} y^2}$$

$$= \frac{81^{1/2} x^{(3)(1/2)} y^{(2)(1/2)}}{5x^{1/2} y^2} = \frac{9x^{3/2} y^1}{5x^{1/2} y^2}$$

$$= \frac{9x^{3/2 - 1/2}}{5y^{2-1}} = \frac{9x^1}{5y^1} = \frac{9x}{5y}$$

57. $x^{3/5}\left(x^{2/5} - x^{-3/5}\right) = \left(x^{3/5}\right)\left(x^{2/5}\right) - \left(x^{3/5}\right)\left(x^{-3/5}\right)$

$$= x^{3/5 + 2/5} - x^{3/5 - 3/5} = x^{5/5} - x^{0/5}$$

$$= x^1 - x^0 = x - 1$$

59. $y^{-7/4}\left(2y^{11/4} - 3y^{7/4}\right) = \left(y^{-7/4}\right)\left(2y^{11/4}\right) - \left(y^{-7/4}\right)\left(3y^{7/4}\right)$

$$= 2y^{-7/4 + 11/4} - 3y^{-7/4 + 7/4}$$

$$= 2y^{4/4} - 3y^0 = 2y - 3$$

61.

$$3w^{5/11}\left(2w^{17/11} - 5w^{6/11} - 9w^{-5/11}\right)$$

$$= \left(3w^{5/11}\right)\left(2w^{17/11}\right) - \left(3w^{5/11}\right)\left(5w^{6/11}\right) - \left(3w^{5/11}\right)\left(9w^{-}\right)$$

$$= 6w^{5/11+17/11} - 15w^{5/11+6/11} - 27w^{5/11-5/11}$$

$$= 6w^{22/11} - 15w^{11/11} - 27w^{0} = 6w^{2} - 15w - 27$$

63. $\left(a^{1/2} + 3\right)\left(a^{1/2} - 3\right) = \left(a^{1/2}\right)^{2} - (3)^{2} = a - 9$

65. $\left(b^{3/5} - c^{5/3}\right)\left(b^{3/5} + c^{5/3}\right) = \left(b^{3/5}\right)^{2} - \left(c^{5/3}\right)^{2}$

$$= b^{6/5} - c^{10/3}$$

67. $\left(b^{3/5} - c^{5/3}\right)^{2} = \left(b^{3/5}\right)^{2} - 2\left(b^{3/5}\right)\left(c^{5/3}\right) + \left(c^{5/3}\right)^{2}$

$$= b^{6/5} - 2b^{3/5}c^{5/3} + c^{10/3}$$

69. $\left(x^{-1/2} + x^{1/2}\right)^{2} = \left(x^{-1/2}\right)^{2} + 2\left(x^{-1/2}\right)\left(x^{1/2}\right) + \left(x^{1/2}\right)^{2}$

$$= x^{-1} + 2x^{0} + x^{1} = \frac{1}{x} + 2 + x$$

71.
73.
75.

75^(1/4)	2.943
85^(1/6)	2.097
361^(1/6)	2.668
■	

77. Mental Estimate: $30^{1/3} = \sqrt[3]{30} \approx \sqrt[3]{27} = 3$
Calculator Approximation: $30^{1/3} \approx 3.107$

79. $S(1000) = 750(1000)^{2/3} = 75000$. A square box beam with a volume of $1000 \ cm^{3}$ has a load strength of 75,000 N.

81. $S(8000) = 750(8000)^{2/3} = 300000$. This load strength is four times that in Exercise **79**.

83. Let $T = 86400$ and solve for r.

$$\left(3.1469 \times 10^{-7}\right)r^{3/2} = 86400$$

$$r^{3/2} = \frac{86400}{\left(3.1469 \times 10^{-7}\right)}$$

$$\left(r^{3/2}\right)^{2/3} = \left(\frac{86400}{\left(3.1469 \times 10^{-7}\right)}\right)^{2/3}$$

$$r = \left(\frac{86400}{\left(3.1469 \times 10^{-7}\right)}\right)^{2/3} \approx 42,242,914$$

Thus, the radius of a geosynchronous orbit around the center of the Earth is $42,242,914$ meters.
The distance above the Earth's surface is
$42,242,914 - 6,378,100 = 35,864,814$ meters.

Cumulative Review

1. $x > 5$ is equivalent to $(5, \infty)$.

2. $(-\infty, 4)$ is equivalent to $x < 4$

3. $(-2, 4)$ is equivalent to $-2 < x < 4$.

4. The interval given is the set of points less than 4 units from the origin (0). Thus, in absolute-value notation, the set is the solution to $|x - 0| < 4$ or $|x| < 4$.

5. The interval given is the set of points greater than 3 units from the origin (0). Thus, in absolute-value notation, the set is the solution to $|x - 0| > 3$ or $|x| > 3$.

Review Exercises for Chapter 10

1. $\sqrt{81} = 9$

2. $\sqrt[3]{-27} = -3$

3. $\sqrt[4]{81} = 3$

4. $\sqrt[5]{-32} = -2$

5. $\sqrt{625 - 576} = \sqrt{49} = 7$

6. $\sqrt{625} - \sqrt{576} = 25 - 24 = 1$

7. $\sqrt{\dfrac{16}{81}} = \dfrac{\sqrt{16}}{\sqrt{81}} = \dfrac{4}{9}$

8. $\sqrt[3]{0.125} = 0.5$

9.

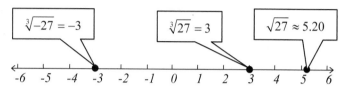

($\sqrt{-27}$ is not a real number and cannot be located on the number line.)

10. $\sqrt{70} \approx 8.37$

11. $\sqrt[3]{70} \approx 4.12$

12. $\sqrt[5]{-70} \approx -2.34$

13. $12\sqrt{3} + 8\sqrt{3} = (12 + 8)\sqrt{3} = 20\sqrt{3}$

14. $12\sqrt{3} - 8\sqrt{3} = (12 - 8)\sqrt{3} = 4\sqrt{3}$

15. $\left(5\sqrt{2} - 7\sqrt{3}\right) - \left(\sqrt{2} - 4\sqrt{3}\right)$
$= 5\sqrt{2} - 7\sqrt{3} - \sqrt{2} + 4\sqrt{3}$
$= (5 - 1)\sqrt{2} + (-7 + 4)\sqrt{3} = 4\sqrt{2} - 3\sqrt{3}$

16. $6\sqrt[3]{5} - 2\sqrt[3]{5} = (6 - 2)\sqrt[3]{5} = 4\sqrt[3]{5}$

17. $\dfrac{6\sqrt[3]{5}}{2\sqrt[3]{5}} = \dfrac{6\cancel{\sqrt[3]{5}}}{2\cancel{\sqrt[3]{5}}} = 3$

18. $\left(6\sqrt[3]{5}\right)\left(2\sqrt[3]{5}\right) = 12\sqrt[3]{5 \cdot 5} = 12\sqrt[3]{25}$

19. $\sqrt{20} = \sqrt{4 \cdot 5} = \sqrt{4}\sqrt{5} = 2\sqrt{5}$

20. $\sqrt[3]{24} = \sqrt[3]{8 \cdot 3} = \sqrt[3]{8}\sqrt[3]{3} = 2\sqrt[3]{3}$

21. $3\sqrt{72} - 2\sqrt{98} = 3\sqrt{36}\sqrt{2} - 2\sqrt{49}\sqrt{2}$
$= 3(6)\sqrt{2} - 2(7)\sqrt{2} = 18\sqrt{2} - 14\sqrt{2}$
$= (18 - 14)\sqrt{2} = 4\sqrt{2}$

22. $5\sqrt{3x} + 9\sqrt{3x} = (5 + 9)\sqrt{3x} = 14\sqrt{3x}$

23. $2\sqrt{50v} - 3\sqrt{8v} = 2\sqrt{25}\sqrt{2v} - 3\sqrt{4}\sqrt{2v}$
$= 2(5)\sqrt{2v} - 3(2)\sqrt{2v} = 10\sqrt{2v} - 6\sqrt{2v}$
$= (10 - 6)\sqrt{2v} = 4\sqrt{2v}$

24. $2\sqrt[3]{8v} - \sqrt[3]{125v} = 2\sqrt[3]{8}\sqrt[3]{v} - \sqrt[3]{125}\sqrt[3]{v}$
$= 2(2)\sqrt[3]{v} - 5\sqrt[3]{v} = 4\sqrt[3]{v} - 5\sqrt[3]{v}$
$= (4 - 5)\sqrt[3]{v} = -\sqrt[3]{v}$

25. $\dfrac{\sqrt{175}}{\sqrt{7}} = \sqrt{\dfrac{175}{7}} = \sqrt{25} = 5$

26. $\sqrt[3]{\dfrac{27x^3}{y^6}} = \dfrac{\sqrt[3]{27}\sqrt[3]{x^3}}{\sqrt[3]{y^6}} = \dfrac{3x}{y^2}$

27. $\sqrt[3]{\dfrac{25}{27}} = \dfrac{\sqrt[3]{25}}{\sqrt[3]{27}} = \dfrac{\sqrt[3]{25}}{3}$

28. $3\sqrt{8} - 7\sqrt{50} = 3\sqrt{4}\sqrt{2} - 7\sqrt{25}\sqrt{2} = 3(2)\sqrt{2} - 7(5)\sqrt{2} = 6\sqrt{2} - 35\sqrt{2} = (6 - 35)\sqrt{2} = -29\sqrt{2}$

29. $3\sqrt{3}\left(2\sqrt{12} - 9\sqrt{75}\right) = 3\sqrt{3}\left(2\sqrt{4}\sqrt{3} - 9\sqrt{25}\sqrt{3}\right) = 3\sqrt{3}\left(2(2)\sqrt{3} - 9(5)\sqrt{3}\right) = 3\sqrt{3}\left(4\sqrt{3} - 45\sqrt{3}\right)$

$$= 3\sqrt{3}\left((4 - 45)\sqrt{3}\right) = 3\sqrt{3}\left(-41\sqrt{3}\right) = -123(3) = -369$$

30. $\left(2\sqrt{2} - 5\sqrt{3}\right)\left(2\sqrt{2} + 5\sqrt{3}\right) = \left(2\sqrt{2}\right)^2 - \left(5\sqrt{3}\right)^2 = 4(2) - 25(3) = 8 - 75 = -67$

31. $\left(3\sqrt{14}\right)\left(15\sqrt{2}\right) = 45\sqrt{14 \cdot 2} = 45\sqrt{28} = 45\sqrt{4}\sqrt{7}$

$$= 45(2)\sqrt{7} = 90\sqrt{7}$$

32. $\dfrac{3\sqrt{14}}{15\sqrt{2}} = \dfrac{\sqrt{14}}{5\sqrt{2}} = \dfrac{1}{5}\sqrt{\dfrac{14}{2}} = \dfrac{1}{5}\sqrt{7} = \dfrac{\sqrt{7}}{5}$

33. $\dfrac{15\sqrt{2}}{3\sqrt{14}} = \dfrac{5\sqrt{2}}{\sqrt{14}} = 5\sqrt{\dfrac{2}{14}} = 5\sqrt{\dfrac{1}{7}} = \dfrac{5}{\sqrt{7}} \cdot \dfrac{\sqrt{7}}{\sqrt{7}} = \dfrac{5\sqrt{7}}{7}$

34. $\left(\sqrt{2} - \sqrt{3}\right)^2 = \left(\sqrt{2}\right)^2 - 2\left(\sqrt{2}\right)\left(\sqrt{3}\right) + \left(\sqrt{3}\right)^2$

$$= 2 - 2\sqrt{6} + 3 = 5 - 2\sqrt{6}$$

35. $\dfrac{\sqrt{2} - \sqrt{3}}{\sqrt{2} + \sqrt{3}} = \dfrac{\left(\sqrt{2} - \sqrt{3}\right)}{\left(\sqrt{2} + \sqrt{3}\right)} \cdot \dfrac{\left(\sqrt{2} - \sqrt{3}\right)}{\left(\sqrt{2} - \sqrt{3}\right)}$

$$= \dfrac{2 - 2\sqrt{6} + 3}{2 - 3} = \dfrac{5 - 2\sqrt{6}}{-1} = -5 + 2\sqrt{6}$$

36. $\dfrac{12}{\sqrt{7} - \sqrt{3}} = \dfrac{12}{\left(\sqrt{7} - \sqrt{3}\right)} \dfrac{\left(\sqrt{7} + \sqrt{3}\right)}{\left(\sqrt{7} + \sqrt{3}\right)}$

$$= \dfrac{12\left(\sqrt{7} + \sqrt{3}\right)}{7 - 3} = \dfrac{12\left(\sqrt{7} + \sqrt{3}\right)}{4}$$

$$= 3\left(\sqrt{7} + \sqrt{3}\right)$$

37. $\left(2\sqrt{3}\right)\left(3\sqrt{2}\right)\left(5\sqrt{6}\right) = 30\sqrt{3 \cdot 2 \cdot 6}$

$$= 30\sqrt{36} = 30(6) = 180$$

38. $\dfrac{\left(15\sqrt{2}\right)\left(2\sqrt{3}\right)}{10\sqrt{6}} = \dfrac{30\sqrt{6}}{10\sqrt{6}} = 3$

39. $\left(2\sqrt{3}\right)\left(3\sqrt{2}\right) - 5\sqrt{6} = 6\sqrt{6} - 5\sqrt{6}$

$$= (6 - 5)\sqrt{6} = \sqrt{6}$$

40. $\left(\sqrt[3]{5} - \sqrt[3]{2}\right)\left(\sqrt[3]{25} + \sqrt[3]{10} + \sqrt[3]{4}\right)$

$$= \sqrt[3]{125} + \sqrt[3]{50} + \sqrt[3]{20} - \sqrt[3]{50} - \sqrt[3]{20} - \sqrt[3]{8}$$

$$= 5 + \cancel{\sqrt[3]{50}} + \cancel{\sqrt[3]{20}} - \cancel{\sqrt[3]{50}} - \cancel{\sqrt[3]{20}} - 2$$

$$= 5 - 2 = 3$$

41. $\sqrt{32x^7} = \sqrt{16x^6}\sqrt{2x} = 4x^3\sqrt{2x}$

42. $\sqrt[3]{32x^7} = \sqrt[3]{8x^6}\sqrt[3]{4x} = 2x^2\sqrt[3]{4x}$

43. $\sqrt[4]{32x^7} = \sqrt[4]{16x^4}\sqrt[4]{2x^3} = 2x\sqrt[4]{2x^3}$

44. $\sqrt{12x^3y^{11}} = \sqrt{4x^2y^{10}}\sqrt{3xy} = 2xy^5\sqrt{3xy}$

45. $\sqrt{x} = x^{1/2}$

46. $\sqrt[3]{x^2} = \left(x^2\right)^{1/3} = x^{2/3}$

47. $\dfrac{1}{\sqrt[3]{x}} = \dfrac{1}{x^{1/3}} = x^{-1/3}$

48. $x^{1/4} = \sqrt[4]{x}$

49. $x^{-1/4} = \dfrac{1}{x^{1/4}} = \dfrac{1}{\sqrt[4]{x}}$

50. $x^{3/4} = \left(x^3\right)^{1/4} = \sqrt[4]{x^3}$

51. Twice the principal square root of w is $2\sqrt{w} = 2w^{1/2}$

52. The principal square root of two w is $\sqrt{2w} = (2w)^{\frac{1}{2}}$

53. The principal cube root of the quantity x plus 4 is $\sqrt[3]{x+4} = (x+4)^{\frac{1}{3}}$

54. $49^{\frac{1}{2}} = \sqrt{49} = 7$

55. $-49^{\frac{1}{2}} = -\sqrt{49} = -7$

56. $49^{-\frac{1}{2}} = \dfrac{1}{49^{\frac{1}{2}}} = \dfrac{1}{\sqrt{49}} = \dfrac{1}{7}$

57. $\left(\dfrac{27}{125}\right)^{\frac{2}{3}} = \left(\sqrt[3]{\dfrac{27}{125}}\right)^2 = \left(\dfrac{3}{5}\right)^2 = \dfrac{9}{25}$

58. $\left(-\dfrac{27}{125}\right)^{\frac{2}{3}} = \left(\sqrt[3]{-\dfrac{27}{125}}\right)^2 = \left(-\dfrac{3}{5}\right)^2 = \dfrac{9}{25}$

59. $\left(\dfrac{27}{125}\right)^{-\frac{2}{3}} = \left(\dfrac{125}{27}\right)^{\frac{2}{3}} = \left(\sqrt[3]{\dfrac{125}{27}}\right)^2 = \left(\dfrac{5}{3}\right)^2 = \dfrac{25}{9}$

60. $1,000,000^{\frac{1}{2}} = \sqrt{1,000,000} = 1,000$

61. $1,000,000^{\frac{1}{3}} = \sqrt[3]{1,000,000} = 100$

62. $1,000,000^{\frac{1}{6}} = \sqrt[6]{1,000,000} = 10$

63. $16^{\frac{5}{8}}16^{\frac{3}{8}} = 16^{\frac{5}{8}+\frac{3}{8}} = 16^{\frac{8}{8}} = 16^1 = 16$

64. $\dfrac{16^{\frac{5}{8}}}{16^{\frac{1}{8}}} = 16^{\frac{5}{8}-\frac{1}{8}} = 16^{\frac{4}{8}} = 16^{\frac{1}{2}} = 4$

65. $\left(16^{\frac{3}{8}}\right)^{\frac{2}{3}} = 16^{\left(\frac{3}{8}\right)\left(\frac{2}{3}\right)} = 16^{\frac{1}{4}} = 2$

66. $\left(8x^{-6}y^9\right)^{\frac{2}{3}} = \left(\dfrac{8y^9}{x^6}\right)^{\frac{2}{3}} = \dfrac{8^{\frac{2}{3}}y^{(9)\left(\frac{2}{3}\right)}}{x^{(6)\left(\frac{2}{3}\right)}} = \dfrac{\left(\sqrt[3]{8}\right)^2 y^6}{x^4}$

$= \dfrac{2^2 y^6}{x^4} = \dfrac{4y^6}{x^4}$

67. $\left(-32x^{\frac{5}{3}}y^{\frac{3}{2}}\right)^{\frac{2}{5}} = (-32)^{\frac{2}{5}} x^{\left(\frac{5}{3}\right)\left(\frac{2}{5}\right)} y^{\left(\frac{3}{2}\right)\left(\frac{2}{5}\right)}$

$= \left(\sqrt[5]{-32}\right)^2 x^{\frac{2}{3}} y^{\frac{3}{5}} = (-2)^2 x^{\frac{2}{3}} y^{\frac{3}{5}}$

$= 4x^{\frac{2}{3}} y^{\frac{3}{5}}$

68. $\dfrac{\left(x^2 y^2 z^2\right)^{\frac{1}{3}}}{(xyz)^{-\frac{4}{3}}} = \dfrac{x^{\frac{2}{3}} y^{\frac{2}{3}} z^{\frac{2}{3}}}{x^{-\frac{4}{3}} y^{-\frac{4}{3}} z^{-\frac{4}{3}}} = x^{\frac{2}{3}+\frac{4}{3}} y^{\frac{2}{3}+\frac{4}{3}} z^{\frac{2}{3}+\frac{4}{3}}$

$= x^{\frac{6}{3}} y^{\frac{6}{3}} z^{\frac{6}{3}} = x^2 y^2 z^2$

69. $2x^{\frac{1}{2}}\left(3x^{\frac{1}{2}} - 5x^{-\frac{1}{2}}\right)$

$= \left(2x^{\frac{1}{2}}\right)\left(3x^{\frac{1}{2}}\right) - \left(2x^{\frac{1}{2}}\right)\left(5x^{-\frac{1}{2}}\right)$

$= 6x^{\frac{1}{2}+\frac{1}{2}} - 10x^{\frac{1}{2}-\frac{1}{2}} = 6x - 10x^0 = 6x - 10$

70. $\left(3x^{\frac{1}{2}} + 5\right)\left(3x^{\frac{1}{2}} - 5\right) = \left(3x^{\frac{1}{2}}\right)^2 - (5)^2 = 9x - 25$

71. $\left(x^2 + 2xy + y^2\right)^{\frac{1}{2}} = \left((x+y)^2\right)^{\frac{1}{2}} = x + y$

72.
a. The function matches the graph in **C**.
b. The function matches the graph in **G**.
c. The function matches the graph in **D**.
d. The function matches the graph in **E**.
e. The function matches the graph in **B**.
f. The function matches the graph in **A**.
g. The function matches the graph in **F**.

73. The domain of a function is the projection of the graph onto the x-axis.
Using the given graphs we are able to conclude the following:

a. Domain: $\mathbb{R}$ or $(-\infty, \infty)$
b. Domain: $\mathbb{R}$ or $(-\infty, \infty)$
c. Domain: $[4, \infty)$
d. Domain: $(-\infty, 4]$
e. Domain: $\mathbb{R}$ or $(-\infty, \infty)$
f. Domain: $\mathbb{R}$ or $(-\infty, \infty)$
g. Domain: $\mathbb{R}$ or $(-\infty, \infty)$

74. **a.** The function matches the table in **E**. **d.** The function matches the table in **C**.
   b. The function matches the table in **D**. **e.** The function matches the table in **B**.
   c. The function matches the table in **A**.

75. Domain: $(-\infty, \infty)$ or $\mathbb{R}$ **76.** Domain: $(-\infty, \infty)$ or $\mathbb{R}$

77. Domain: $[5, \infty)$ **78.** Domain: $(-\infty, \infty)$ or $\mathbb{R}$

79. Domain: $(-\infty, 5)\cup(5, \infty)$ or $\mathbb{R} \sim \{5\}$ **80.** Domain: $(-\infty, -3)\cup(-3, 3)\cup(3, \infty)$

or $\mathbb{R} \sim \{-3, 3\}$

81. From the graph we can see that the two curves intersect where $x = 2$. Thus the solution is $x = 2$.

82. From the table we can see that the $f(x)$ column is equal to 3 where $x = 2$. Thus the solution is $x = 2$.

83. $\sqrt{x-5} = 4$

$\left(\sqrt{x-5}\right)^2 = (4)^2$

$x - 5 = 16$

$x = 21$

Check:

$\sqrt{x-5} = 4$

$\sqrt{(21)-5} = 4$

$\sqrt{16} = 4$

$4 = 4$ is true.

Answer: $x = 21$

84. $\sqrt{x+12} - x = 0$

$\sqrt{x+12} = x$

$\left(\sqrt{x+12}\right)^2 = (x)^2$

$x + 12 = x^2$

$x^2 - x - 12 = 0$

$(x-4)(x+3) = 0$

$x = 4$ or $x = -3$

Check:

$\sqrt{(4)+12} - (4) = 0$

$\sqrt{16} - 4 = 0$

$4 - 4 = 0$

$0 = 0$ is true.

Check:

$\sqrt{(-3)+12} - (-3) = 0$

$\sqrt{9} + 3 = 0$

$3 + 3 = 0$

$6 = 0$ is false.

Answer: $x = 4$

85. $\sqrt{2v-1} + 2 = v$

$\sqrt{2v-1} = v - 2$

$\left(\sqrt{2v-1}\right)^2 = (v-2)^2$

$2v - 1 = v^2 - 4v + 4$

$v^2 - 6v + 5 = 0$

$(v-5)(v-1) = 0$

$v = 5$ or $v = 1$

Check:

$\sqrt{2(5)-1} + 2 = (5)$

$\sqrt{9} + 2 = 5$

$3 + 2 = 5$

$5 = 5$ is true.

Check:

$\sqrt{2(1)-1} + 2 = (1)$

$\sqrt{1} + 2 = 1$

$1 + 2 = 1$

$3 = 1$ is false.

Answer: $v = 5$

86. $\sqrt[3]{4w+5} = -3$

$\left(\sqrt[3]{4w+5}\right)^3 = (-3)^3$

$4w + 5 = -27$

$4w = -32$

$w = -8$

Check:

$\sqrt[3]{4(-8)+5} = -3$

$\sqrt[3]{-32+5} = -3$

$\sqrt[3]{-27} = -3$

$-3 = -3$ is true.

Answer: $w = -8$

87. To find the x-intercepts we let $y = 0$ and

solve for x.
$$y = \sqrt{x+25} - 7$$
$$0 = \sqrt{x+25} - 7$$
$$7 = \sqrt{x+25}$$
$$(7)^2 = \left(\sqrt{x+25}\right)^2$$
$$49 = x + 25$$
$$x = 24$$

The x-intercept is $(24, 0)$

To find the y-intercept we let $x = 0$ and solve for y
$$y = \sqrt{x+25} - 7$$
$$y = \sqrt{(0)+25} - 7$$
$$y = \sqrt{25} - 7$$
$$y = 5 - 7$$
$$y = -2$$

The y-intercept is $(0, -2)$

88. $d = \sqrt{\left(1-(-4)\right)^2 + \left(-4-8\right)^2} = \sqrt{(5)^2 + (-12)^2} = \sqrt{25+144} = \sqrt{169} = 13$

89.

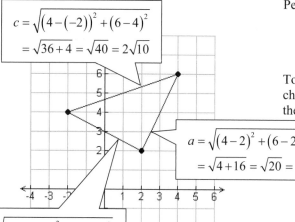

$$c = \sqrt{\left(4-(-2)\right)^2 + \left(6-4\right)^2}$$
$$= \sqrt{36+4} = \sqrt{40} = 2\sqrt{10}$$

$$a = \sqrt{\left(4-2\right)^2 + \left(6-2\right)^2}$$
$$= \sqrt{4+16} = \sqrt{20} = 2\sqrt{5}$$

$$b = \sqrt{\left(2-(-2)\right)^2 + \left(2-4\right)^2}$$
$$= \sqrt{16+4} = \sqrt{20} = 2\sqrt{5}$$

Perimeter:
$$a + b + c = 2\sqrt{5} + 2\sqrt{5} + 2\sqrt{10}$$
$$= 4\sqrt{5} + 2\sqrt{10}$$

To determine if the triangle is a right triangle we check the values of a, b, and c in the Pythagorean theorem.

$$a^2 + b^2 = c^2$$
$$\left(2\sqrt{5}\right)^2 + \left(2\sqrt{5}\right)^2 = \left(2\sqrt{10}\right)^2$$
$$4(5) + 4(5) = 4(10)$$
$$20 + 20 = 40$$
$$40 = 40 \text{ is true}$$

Thus the triangle is a right triangle.

90. Let x = length of the short leg
$x + 7$ = length of the longer leg
$(x+7) + 2 = x + 9$ = length of the hypotenuse.
To determine x we use the Pythagorean Theorem.
$$(x)^2 + (x+7)^2 = (x+9)^2$$
$$x^2 + x^2 + 14x + 49 = x^2 + 18x + 81$$
$$x^2 - 4x - 32 = 0$$
$$(x-8)(x+4) = 0$$
$$x = 8 \text{ or } x = -4$$

Note: This answer is not reasonable.

Thus the short leg is 8 cm. The longer leg is $8 + 7 = 15$ cm. The hypotenuse is $15 + 2 = 17$ cm.

91. To find all points with an x-coordinate of 8 that are 5 units from the point $(4, 4)$ we solve the equation formed by letting the distance between $(4, 4)$ and $(8, y)$ equal 5.
$$\sqrt{(8-4)^2 + (y-4)^2} = 5$$
$$\left(\sqrt{(8-4)^2 + (y-4)^2}\right)^2 = (5)^2$$
$$16 + \left(y^2 - 8y + 16\right) = 25$$
$$y^2 - 8y + 7 = 0$$
$$(y-1)(y-7) = 0$$
$$y = 1 \text{ or } y = 7$$

Thus the two points are $(8, 1)$ and $(8, 7)$.

92. The volume of a sphere is $V = \frac{4}{3}\pi r^3$. Let $V = 17000$ and solve for r.

$$\frac{4}{3}\pi r^3 = 17000$$

$$\left(\frac{3}{4\pi}\right)\left(\frac{4}{3}\pi r^3\right) = \left(\frac{3}{4\pi}\right)(17000)$$

$$r^3 = \frac{12750}{\pi}$$

$$r = \sqrt[3]{\frac{12750}{\pi}} \approx 16.0 \text{ ft}$$

93. The volume of a cubical box is $V = s^3$. Let $V = 3197$ and solve for s.

$$s^3 = 3197$$

$$s = \sqrt[3]{3197} \approx 14.7 \text{ cm}$$

94. Let $T(x) = 0.6$ and solve for x.

$$0.064\sqrt{x} = 0.6$$

$$\sqrt{x} = \frac{0.6}{0.064}$$

$$x = (9.375)^2 \approx 87.9 \text{ cm}$$

95. **a.** The overhead cost can be found by evaluating

$$C(0) = 20\sqrt[3]{0^2} + 200 = 0 + 200 = 200 .$$

The overhead cost is $200.

b. $C(512) = 20\sqrt[3]{512^2} + 200 = 1480$

The cost of producing 512 boxes is $1,480.

c. Let $C(n) = 1,480$ and solve for n. From part **b.** we can see that the solution will be $n = 512$ boxes.

Mastery Test for Chapter 10

1. **a.** The principle cube root of v is $\sqrt[3]{v}$.
  b. The principle fourth root of w is $\sqrt[4]{w}$.

2. **a.** $\sqrt[3]{27} = 3$
  b. $\sqrt[3]{-64} = -4$
  c. $\sqrt[4]{16} = 2$
  d. $\sqrt[5]{-100,000} = -10$

3. **a.** The function matches the graph in **D**.
  b. The function matches the graph in **B**.
  c. The function matches the graph in **C**.
  d. The function matches the graph in **A**.

4. **a.** To find the domain of $f(x) = \sqrt{x-3}$ we solve the inequality: $x - 3 \geq 0$
$$x \geq 3$$
The domain is $[3, \infty)$.

  b. The domain of $f(x) = \sqrt[3]{x-3}$ is all real numbers, $\mathbb{R}$ or $(-\infty, \infty)$.

  c. The domain of $f(x) = \frac{x+4}{x-3}$ is $\mathbb{R} \sim \{3\}$ or $(-\infty, 3) \cup (3, \infty)$. ($x = 3$ is the excluded value.)

  d. The domain of $f(x) = (x-3)^2$ is all real numbers, $\mathbb{R}$ or $(-\infty, \infty)$.

5.   **a.** $8\sqrt{7} - 3\sqrt{7} = (8-3)\sqrt{7} = 5\sqrt{7}$

   b. $\left(5\sqrt{2} - 3\sqrt{5}\right) - \left(2\sqrt{2} - 7\sqrt{5}\right)$

   $= 5\sqrt{2} - 3\sqrt{5} - 2\sqrt{2} + 7\sqrt{5}$

   $= (5-2)\sqrt{2} + (-3+7)\sqrt{5} = 3\sqrt{2} + 4\sqrt{5}$

   c. $4\sqrt[3]{7} - 11\sqrt[3]{7} + 6\sqrt[3]{7} = (4-11+6)\sqrt[3]{7} = -\sqrt[3]{7}$

   d. $13\sqrt{2x} - 5\sqrt{2x} = (13-5)\sqrt{2x} = 8\sqrt{2x}$

6.   **a.** $\sqrt{40} = \sqrt{4}\sqrt{10} = 2\sqrt{10}$

   b. $\sqrt[3]{24} = \sqrt[3]{8}\sqrt[3]{3} = 2\sqrt[3]{3}$

   c. $3\sqrt{28} - 5\sqrt{63} = 3\sqrt{4}\sqrt{7} - 5\sqrt{9}\sqrt{7}$

   $= 3(2)\sqrt{7} - 5(3)\sqrt{7} = 6\sqrt{7} - 15\sqrt{7}$

   $= (6-15)\sqrt{7} = -9\sqrt{7}$

   d. $\sqrt[3]{40x^5 y^4} = \sqrt[3]{8x^3 y^3}\sqrt[3]{5x^2 y} = 2xy\sqrt[3]{5x^2 y}$

7.   **a.** $\left(3\sqrt{2}\right)\left(5\sqrt{2}\right) = 15\sqrt{4} = 15(2) = 30$

   b. $2\sqrt{5}\left(3\sqrt{5} - 2\sqrt{10}\right)$

   $= \left(2\sqrt{5}\right)\left(3\sqrt{5}\right) - \left(2\sqrt{5}\right)\left(2\sqrt{10}\right)$

   $= 6\sqrt{25} - 4\sqrt{50} = 6(5) - 4\sqrt{25}\sqrt{2}$

   $= 30 - 4(5)\sqrt{2} = 30 - 20\sqrt{2}$

   c. $\sqrt[3]{16x^5}\sqrt[3]{-4x} = \sqrt[3]{-64x^6} = -4x^2$

   d. $\left(2\sqrt{3x} - \sqrt{5}\right)\left(2\sqrt{3x} + \sqrt{5}\right) = \left(2\sqrt{3x}\right)^2 - \left(\sqrt{5}\right)^2$

   $= 4(3x) - 5$

   $= 12x - 5$

8.   **a.** $\dfrac{\sqrt{18}}{\sqrt{2}} = \sqrt{\dfrac{18}{2}} = \sqrt{9} = 3$

   b. $\dfrac{18}{\sqrt{6}} = \dfrac{18}{\sqrt{6}} \cdot \dfrac{\sqrt{6}}{\sqrt{6}} = \dfrac{18\sqrt{6}}{6} = 3\sqrt{6}$

   c. $\dfrac{40}{\sqrt{7} - \sqrt{2}} = \dfrac{40}{\left(\sqrt{7} - \sqrt{2}\right)} \cdot \dfrac{\left(\sqrt{7} + \sqrt{2}\right)}{\left(\sqrt{7} + \sqrt{2}\right)}$

   $= \dfrac{40\left(\sqrt{7} + \sqrt{2}\right)}{7-2} = \dfrac{40\left(\sqrt{7} + \sqrt{2}\right)}{5} = 8\left(\sqrt{7} + \sqrt{2}\right)$

   d. $\dfrac{12}{2 - \sqrt{7}} = \dfrac{12}{\left(2 - \sqrt{7}\right)} \cdot \dfrac{\left(2 + \sqrt{7}\right)}{\left(2 + \sqrt{7}\right)} = \dfrac{12\left(2 + \sqrt{7}\right)}{4-7}$

   $= \dfrac{12\left(\sqrt{7} + 2\right)}{-3} = -4\left(\sqrt{7} + 2\right) = -8 - 4\sqrt{7}$

9.   **a.** $\sqrt{x-3} = 11$

   $\left(\sqrt{x-3}\right)^2 = (11)^2$

   $x - 3 = 121$

   $x = 124$

   Check:

   $\sqrt{x-3} = 11$

   $\sqrt{124 - 3} = 11$

   $\sqrt{121} = 11$

   $11 = 11$ is true.

   Answer: $x = 124$

   b. $\sqrt[3]{2x - 17} = -3$

   $\left(\sqrt[3]{2x - 17}\right)^3 = (-3)^3$

   $2x - 17 = -27$

   $2x = -10$

   $x = -5$

   Check:

   $\sqrt[3]{2x - 17} = -3$

   $\sqrt[3]{2(-5) - 17} = -3$

   $\sqrt[3]{-10 - 17} = -3$

   $\sqrt[3]{-27} = -3$

   $-3 = -3$ is true.

   Answer: $x = -5$

   c. $\sqrt{x+4} = x + 11$

   $\left(\sqrt{x+4}\right)^2 = (x+11)^2$

   $x + 4 = x^2 + 22x + 121$

   $x^2 + 21x + 117 = 0$

   The solutions to this quadratic are non-real since $b^2 - 4ac < 0$. No real solution.

d.
$$\sqrt{3x+1}+3=x$$
$$\sqrt{3x+1}=x-3$$
$$\left(\sqrt{3x+1}\right)^2=(x-3)^2$$
$$3x+1=x^2-6x+9$$
$$x^2-9x+8=0$$
$$(x-8)(x-1)=0$$
$$x=8 \text{ or } x=1$$

Check:
$$\sqrt{3x+1}+3=x$$
$$\sqrt{3(8)+1}+3=(8)$$
$$\sqrt{25}+3=8$$
$$5+3=8$$
$$8=8 \text{ is true.}$$

Check:
$$\sqrt{3x+1}+3=x$$
$$\sqrt{3(1)+1}+3=(1)$$
$$\sqrt{4}+3=1$$
$$2+3=1$$
$$5=1 \text{ is false.}$$
Answer: $x=8$

10. a. $d=\sqrt{(-5-3)^2+(9-9)^2}$
$$=\sqrt{(-8)^2+(0)^2}=\sqrt{64}=8$$

b. $d=\sqrt{(-4-(-4))^2+(-5-7)^2}$
$$=\sqrt{(0)^2+(-12)^2}=\sqrt{144}=12$$

c. $d=\sqrt{(7-1)^2+(6-(-2))^2}$
$$=\sqrt{(6)^2+(8)^2}=\sqrt{36+64}=\sqrt{100}=10$$

d. $d=\sqrt{(-4-1)^2+(3-1)^2}$
$$=\sqrt{(-5)^2+(2)^2}=\sqrt{25+4}=\sqrt{29}\approx5.39$$

11. a. $81^{\frac{1}{2}}=\sqrt{81}=9$

b. $(-1000)^{\frac{1}{3}}=\sqrt[3]{-1000}=-10$

c. $81^{\frac{3}{4}}=\left(\sqrt[4]{81}\right)^3=(3)^3=27$

d. $81^{-\frac{3}{4}}=\dfrac{1}{81^{\frac{3}{4}}}=\dfrac{1}{\left(\sqrt[4]{81}\right)^3}=\dfrac{1}{3^3}=\dfrac{1}{27}$

e. $100^{1/2}-64^{1/2}=\sqrt{100}-\sqrt{64}=10-8=2$

f. $(100-64)^{1/2}=\sqrt{100-64}=\sqrt{36}=6$

12. a. $\left(8v^6w^9\right)^{2/3}=8^{2/3}\left(v^6\right)^{2/3}\left(w^9\right)^{2/3}=\left(\sqrt[3]{8}\right)^2 v^{\frac{\cancel{6}^2}{1}\cdot\frac{2}{\cancel{3}}}w^{\frac{\cancel{9}^3}{1}\cdot\frac{2}{\cancel{3}}}=(2)^2 v^{2\cdot2}w^{3\cdot2}=4v^4w^6$

b. $\left(5x^{2/3}y^{2/5}\right)\left(2x^{1/3}y^{8/5}\right)=5\cdot2x^{2/3}x^{1/3}y^{2/5}y^{8/5}=10x^{2/3+1/3}y^{2/5+8/5}=10x^{3/3}y^{10/5}=10xy^2$

c. $\dfrac{12m^{5/8}n^{-4/7}}{8m^{-3/8}n^{3/7}}=\dfrac{\cancel{12}^3 m^{5/8-(-3/8)}n^{-4/7-3/7}}{\cancel{8}_2}=\dfrac{3mn^{-1}}{2}=\dfrac{3m}{2n}$

d. $\left(\dfrac{320x^{-4}y^5}{40x^2y^{-4}}\right)^{-2/3}=\left(\dfrac{\cancel{320}^8\, x^{-4-2}y^{5-(-4)}}{\cancel{40}_1}\right)^{-2/3}=\left(8x^{-6}y^9\right)^{-2/3}=\left(\dfrac{8y^9}{x^6}\right)^{-2/3}=\left(\dfrac{x^6}{8y^9}\right)^{2/3}=\dfrac{\left(x^6\right)^{2/3}}{8^{2/3}\left(y^9\right)^{2/3}}$

$$=\dfrac{x^{\frac{\cancel{6}^2}{1}\cdot\frac{2}{\cancel{3}}}}{\left(\sqrt[3]{8}\right)^2 y^{\frac{\cancel{9}^3}{1}\cdot\frac{2}{\cancel{3}}}}=\dfrac{x^{2\cdot2}}{(2)^2 y^{3\cdot2}}=\dfrac{x^4}{4y^6}$$

Section 11.1: Geometric Sequences and Graphs of Exponential Functions

Quick Review 11.1

1. The subscript notation a_n is read *a* sub *n*.

2. The function is increasing on the interval $(-1, 1)$. Note: This is an *interval* of x. It is not a point in the plane.

3. The function is decreasing on the interval $(1, 2)$. Note: This is an *interval* of x. It is not a point in the plane.

4. The domain of a function is the projection of the graph onto the x-axis. Domain: $(-1, 2)$ Note: This is an *interval* of x. It is not a point in the plane.

5. The range of a function is the projection of the graph onto the y-axis. Range: $(1, 3]$

Exercises 11.1

1. **a.** The sequence is geometric. The common ratio is $r = \dfrac{5}{1} = \dfrac{25}{5} = \dots = \dfrac{3125}{625} = 5$

    b. The sequence is geometric. The common ratio is $r = \dfrac{-5}{1} = \dfrac{25}{-5} = \dots = \dfrac{-3125}{625} = -5$

3. **a.** The sequence is geometric. The common ratio is $r = \dfrac{625}{3125} = \dfrac{125}{625} = \dots = \dfrac{1}{5}$

    b. The sequence is geometric. The common ratio is $r = \dfrac{-625}{3125} = \dfrac{125}{-625} = \dots = -\dfrac{1}{5}$

5. **a.** The sequence is geometric. The common ratio is $r = \dfrac{24}{36} = \dfrac{16}{24} = \dots = \dfrac{\left(\frac{64}{9}\right)}{\left(\frac{32}{3}\right)} = \dfrac{2}{3}$

    b. The sequence is not geometric. It is arithmetic with a common difference: $d = -12$.

7. **a.** The sequence is not geometric since the ratio between consecutive terms is not constant.

    b. The sequence is geometric. The common ratio is $r = \dfrac{2\sqrt{2}}{2} = \dfrac{4}{2\sqrt{2}} = \dots = \dfrac{8}{4\sqrt{2}} = \sqrt{2}$.

9. **a.** $a_1 = 10$
    $a_2 = 2(10) = 20$
    $a_3 = 2(20) = 40$
    $a_4 = 2(40) = 80$
    $a_5 = 2(80) = 160$

    b. $a_1 = 10$
    $a_2 = -2(10) = -20$
    $a_3 = -2(-20) = 40$
    $a_4 = -2(40) = -80$
    $a_5 = -2(-80) = 160$

11. **a.** $f(1) = 4^1 = 4$

    b. $f(2) = 4^2 = 16$

    c. $f(0) = 4^0 = 1$

    d. $f(-2) = 4^{-2} = \dfrac{1}{4^2} = \dfrac{1}{16}$

    e. $f\left(\dfrac{1}{2}\right) = 4^{1/2} = \sqrt{4} = 2$

13.

x	$f(x) = 4^x$
-2	$4^{-2} = \dfrac{1}{4^2} = \dfrac{1}{16}$
-1	$4^{-1} = \dfrac{1}{4^1} = \dfrac{1}{4}$
0	$4^0 = \dfrac{1}{4^0} = \dfrac{1}{1} = 1$
1	$4^1 = 4$
2	$4^2 = 16$

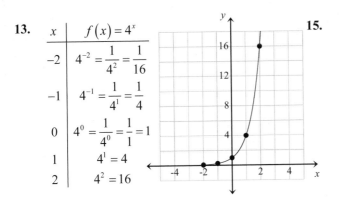

15.

x	$f(x) = \left(\dfrac{2}{3}\right)^x$
-2	$\left(\dfrac{2}{3}\right)^{-2} = \left(\dfrac{3}{2}\right)^2 = \dfrac{9}{4}$
-1	$\left(\dfrac{2}{3}\right)^{-1} = \left(\dfrac{3}{2}\right)^1 = \dfrac{3}{2}$
0	$\left(\dfrac{2}{3}\right)^0 = 1$
1	$\left(\dfrac{2}{3}\right)^1 = \dfrac{2}{3}$
2	$\left(\dfrac{2}{3}\right)^2 = \dfrac{4}{9}$

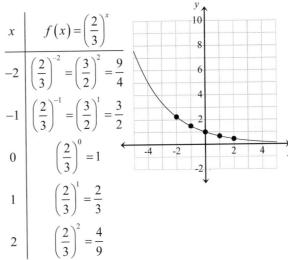

17.
$$4^m = 4$$
$$4^m = 4^1$$
$$m = 1$$
The exponents are equal since the bases are the same.

19.
$$4^x = 16$$
$$4^x = 4^2$$
$$x = 2$$
The exponents are equal since the bases are the same.

21.
$$5^{v+1} = 125$$
$$5^{v+1} = 5^3$$
$$v + 1 = 3$$
$$v = 2$$
The exponents are equal since the bases are the same.

23.
$$\left(\frac{2}{3}\right)^w = \frac{8}{27}$$
$$\left(\frac{2}{3}\right)^w = \left(\frac{2}{3}\right)^3$$
$$w = 3$$
The exponents are equal since the bases are the same.

25.
$$2^m = \frac{1}{2}$$
$$2^m = 2^{-1}$$
$$m = -1$$
The exponents are equal since the bases are the same.

27.
$$5^n = 1$$
$$5^n = 5^0$$
$$n = 0$$
The exponents are equal since the bases are the same.

29.
$$25^x = 5$$
$$25^x = 25^{1/2}$$
$$x = \frac{1}{2}$$
The exponents are equal since the bases are the same.

31.
$$49^x = 7$$
$$49^x = 49^{1/2}$$
$$x = \frac{1}{2}$$
The exponents are equal since the bases are the same.

33.
$$7^x = \frac{1}{49}$$
$$7^x = 7^{-2}$$
$$x = -2$$
The exponents are equal since the bases are the same.

35.
$$\left(\frac{2}{5}\right)^w = \frac{125}{8}$$
$$\left(\frac{2}{5}\right)^w = \left(\frac{2}{5}\right)^{-3}$$
$$w = -3$$
The exponents are equal since the bases are the same.

37. $32^{3n-5} = 2$

$\left(2^5\right)^{3n-5} = 2$

$2^{5(3n-5)} = 2^1$

$5(3n-5) = 1$ — The exponents are equal since the bases are the same.

$15n - 25 = 1$

$15n = 26$

$n = \dfrac{26}{15}$

39. $3^v = \sqrt{3}$

$3^v = 3^{\frac{1}{2}}$

$v = \dfrac{1}{2}$ — The exponents are equal since the bases are the same.

41. $10^x = 10,000$

$10^x = 10^4$

$x = 4$ — The exponents are equal since the bases are the same.

43. $10^y = 0.001$

$10^y = 10^{-3}$

$y = -3$ — The exponents are equal since the bases are the same.

45. $5^{x+7} = 25$

$5^{x+7} = 5^2$

$x + 7 = 2$ — The exponents are equal since the bases are the same.

$x = -5$

47. $7^{3x} = \sqrt{7}$

$7^{3x} = 7^{\frac{1}{2}}$

$3x = \dfrac{1}{2}$ — The exponents are equal since the bases are the same.

$x = \dfrac{1}{6}$

49. $\left(\dfrac{3}{7}\right)^x = \dfrac{49}{9}$

$\left(\dfrac{3}{7}\right)^x = \left(\dfrac{3}{7}\right)^{-2}$ — The exponents are equal since the bases are the same.

$x = -2$

51. **a.** $e^{\wedge}(\sqrt(8)) \qquad 16.919$

 b. $e^{\wedge}(-1.6) \qquad .202$

 c. $e^{\wedge}(\pi) \qquad 23.141$

Problem	Mental Estimate	Calculator Approximation
53. $f(2)$	$f(2) \approx (4)^2 = 16$	15.21
55. $f(-1)$	$f(-1) \approx (4)^{-1} = \dfrac{1}{4} = 0.25$	0.26

57. **a.** End of the first year: $100 + 10 = \$110$

End of the second year: $110 + 10 = \$120$

End of the third year: $120 + 10 = \$130$

End of the fourth year: $130 + 10 = \$140$

b. End of the first year: $100 - 10 = \$90$

End of the second year: $90 - 10 = \$80$

End of the third year: $80 - 10 = \$70$

End of the fourth year: $70 - 10 = \$60$

c. End of the first year: $(1.10)100 = \$110$

End of the second year: $(1.10)110 = \$121$

End of the third year: $(1.10)121 = \$133.10$

End of the fourth year: $(1.10)133.10 = \$146.41$

d. End of the first year: $(0.90)100 = \$90$

End of the second year: $(0.90)90 = \$81$

End of the third year: $(0.90)81 = \$72.90$

End of the fourth year: $(0.90)72.90 = \$65.61$

59. First bounce: $(0.5)36 = 18$ meters

Second bounce: $(0.5)18 = 9$ meters

Third bounce: $(0.5)9 = 4.5$ meters

Fourth bounce: $(0.5)4.5 = 2.25$ meters

61. $A = P(1+r)^t$

$A = 1000(1+0.06)^7 \approx \$1,503.63$

63. $A(10) = 100e^{-0.0248(10)} \approx 78.0$ mg

65. **a.** $a_1 = 6$

$a_2 = 6+5 = 11$

$a_3 = 11+5 = 16$

$a_4 = 16+5 = 21$

$a_5 = 21+5 = 26$

b. $a_1 = 6$

$a_2 = 6 \cdot 5 = 30$

$a_3 = 30 \cdot 5 = 150$

$a_4 = 150 \cdot 5 = 750$

$a_5 = 750 \cdot 5 = 3750$

67. The linear growth function is found in graph **B**.

69. The exponential growth function is found in graph **D**.

71. The geometric decay sequence is found in graph **E**.

73. $2x = 64$

$\dfrac{2x}{2} = \dfrac{64}{2}$

$x = 32$

75. $2^x = 64$

$2^x = 2^6$

$x = 6$ — The exponents are equal since the bases are the same.

77. $3z = \dfrac{1}{9}$

$\dfrac{1}{3}(3z) = \dfrac{1}{3}\left(\dfrac{1}{9}\right)$

$z = \dfrac{1}{27}$

Cumulative Review

1. $2x(3x-5) - 7(3x-5) = (3x-5)(2x-7)$

2. $2x(3x-5) - 7(3x-5) = 6x^2 - 10x - 21x + 35$

$= 6x^2 - 31x + 35$

3. The slope of the line that is parallel to $y = 3x - 4$ is $m = 3$.

4. The slope of the line that is perpendicular to $y = 3x - 4$ is $m = -\dfrac{1}{3}$.

5. $-5 \le 4x - 1 < 11$

$-5 + 1 \le 4x - 1 + 1 < 11 + 1$

$-4 \le 4x < 12$

$\dfrac{-4}{4} \le \dfrac{4x}{4} < \dfrac{12}{4}$

$-1 \le x < 3$

Solution: $[-1, 3)$

Section 11.2: Inverse Functions

Quick Review 11.2

1. The graph passes the vertical line test, therefore it represents a function.

2. The graph does not pass the vertical line test, therefore it does not represent a function.

3. The graph passes the vertical line test, therefore it represents a function.

4.

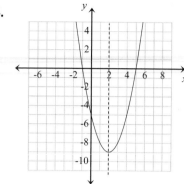

5.

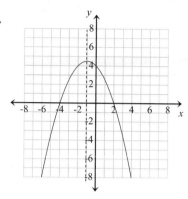

Exercises 11.2

1. $\{(4,1),(11,3),(2,8)\}$

3. $\{(2,-3),(2,-1),(2,0),(2,2)\}$

5. $\{(b,a),(d,c)\}$

7. $\{(7,4),(9,e),(-2,-3)\}$

9. $\{(0,9),(3,4),(-2,6),(5,-4)\}$

11. $f=\{(-3,2),(-1,1),(1,0),(3,-1)\}$

$f^{-1}=\{(2,-3),(1,-1),(0,1),(-1,3)\}$

13. Verbally: f^{-1} increases x by 2

Algebraically: $f^{-1}(x)=x+2$

15. Verbally: f^{-1} takes one-fourth of x

Algebraically: $f^{-1}(x)=\dfrac{x}{4}$

17. Verbally: f^{-1} adds 3 and divides the quantity by 2

Algebraically: $f^{-1}(x)=\dfrac{x+3}{2}$

19. First, replace $f(x)$ with y.

$$f(x)=5x+2$$
$$y=5x+2$$

Next, exchange x and y, then solve for y.

$$x=5y+2$$
$$x-2=5y$$
$$y=\dfrac{x-2}{5}$$

Rewrite the inverse using functional notation.

$$f^{-1}(x)=\dfrac{x-2}{5}$$

21. First, replace $f(x)$ with y.

$$f(x)=\dfrac{1}{3}x-7$$
$$y=\dfrac{1}{3}x-7$$

Next, exchange x and y, then solve for y.

$$x=\dfrac{1}{3}y-7$$
$$x+7=\dfrac{1}{3}y$$
$$y=3(x+7)$$

Rewrite the inverse using functional notation.

$$f^{-1}(x)=3(x+7)$$

23. First, replace $f(x)$ with y.
$$f(x) = \sqrt[3]{x} + 2$$
$$y = \sqrt[3]{x} + 2$$
Next, exchange x and y, then solve for y.
$$x = \sqrt[3]{y} + 2$$
$$x - 2 = \sqrt[3]{y}$$
$$y = (x-2)^3$$
Rewrite the inverse using functional notation.
$$f^{-1}(x) = (x-2)^3$$

25. First, replace $f(x)$ with y.
$$f(x) = -x$$
$$y = -x$$
Next, exchange x and y, then solve for y.
$$x = -y$$
$$y = -x$$
Rewrite the inverse using functional notation.
$$f^{-1}(x) = -x$$

27. The function is one-to-one since different input values produce different output values.

29. The function is not on-to-one since both 7.5 and 7.8 are paired with 7.

31. The function is one-to-one since any horizontal line will pass through exactly one point of the graph.

33. The function is not one-to-one since the horizontal line $y = 1$ passes through more than one point of the graph.

35. The function is not one-to-one since the horizontal line $y = 0$ passes through more than one point of the graph.

37. The function is not one-to-one since the horizontal line $y = 4$ passes through more than one point of the graph.

39. The function is not one-to-one since the horizontal line $y = 1$ passes through more than one point of the graph.

41.

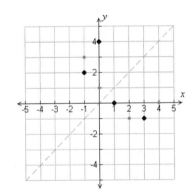

43.

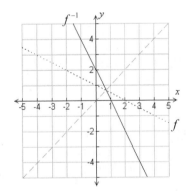

45.

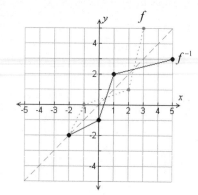

47.

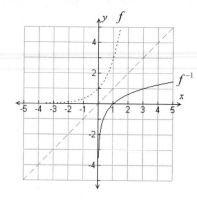

49.

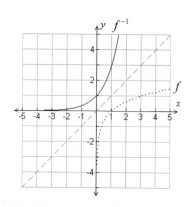

51. **a.** $f(5) = 4(5) - 3 = 17$

b. $f^{-1}(17) = \dfrac{17 + 3}{4} = 5$

53. **a.** $f(2) = 4(2) - 3 = 5$

b. $f^{-1}(5) = \dfrac{5 + 3}{4} = 2$

55. **a.** $f(1) = 4(1) - 3 = 1$

b. $f^{-1}(1) = \dfrac{1 + 3}{4} = 1$

57. Domain of f: $\{0, 1, 2, 3, 4\}$

Range of f: $\{-3, -2, -1, 0, 1\}$

$f^{-1} = \{(-3, 0), (-2, 1), (-1, 2), (0, 3), (1, 4)\}$

Domain of f^{-1}: $\{-3, -2, -1, 0, 1\}$

Range of f^{-1}: $\{0, 1, 2, 3, 4\}$

59. Domain of f: $\{-2, 0, 2\}$

Range of f: $\{0, 3, 1\}$

$f^{-1} = \{(0, -2), (3, 0), (1, 2)\}$

Domain of f^{-1}: $\{0, 3, 1\}$

Range of f^{-1}: $\{-2, 0, 2\}$

61.

European Size	US Size
39	7
40.5	8
42	9
43	10
44	11

63.

Monthly payment	Loan amount
$120.89	$5,000
$241.79	$10,000
$362.68	$15,000
$483.58	$20,000
$604.47	$25,000

65.

Celsius temperature	Fahrenheit temperature
−17.8°	0°
−6.7°	20°
4.4°	40°
15.6°	60°
26.7°	80°
37.8°	100°

67. **a.** x represents the number of units produced.

b. $C(x)$ represents the cost of producing x units.

c. First, replace $C(x)$ with y.

$$C(x) = 12x + 350$$
$$y = 12x + 350$$

Next, exchange x and y, then solve for y.

$$x = 12y + 350$$
$$x - 350 = 12y$$
$$y = \frac{x - 350}{12}$$

Rewrite the inverse using functional notation.

$$C^{-1}(x) = \frac{x - 350}{12}$$

d. x represents the cost in $C^{-1}(x)$.

e. $C^{-1}(x)$ represents the number of units that can be produced for x dollars.

f. $C(100) = 12(100) + 350 = \$1550$

g. $C^{-1}(1934) = \dfrac{1934 - 350}{12} = 132$ units

Cumulative Review

1. $2x^2 y^2 - 3xy^3 + 4x^3 y - 5x^4 = -5x^4 + 4x^3 y + 2x^2 y^2 - 3xy^3$

2. The polynomial $7x^3 - 2x^2 y^2 = -2x^2 y^2 + 7x^3$ is a 4th degree polynomial.

3. A horizontal line has a slope of $m = 0$.

4. The parabola defined by $y = ax^2 + bx + c$ opens upward if $a > 0$.

5. The parabola defined by $y = ax^2 + bx + c$ opens downward if $a < 0$.

Section 11.3: Logarithmic Functions

Quick Review 11.3

1. $x^0 = 1$ if $x \neq 0$.

2. x^0 is undefined if $x = 0$.

3. $\left(\dfrac{2}{3}\right)^{-1} = \left(\dfrac{3}{2}\right)^{1} = \dfrac{3}{2}$

4. $2x - 1 = 8$
$$2x = 9$$
$$x = \frac{9}{2}$$

5. $x^2 - 1 = 8$
$$x^2 = 9$$
$$x = \pm\sqrt{9}$$
$$x = \pm 3$$

Exercises 11.3

Logarithmic Form	Verbal Description	Exponential Form
Example: $\log_7 49 = 2$	The log base 7 of 49 is 2.	$7^2 = 49$
1. $\log_5 125 = 3$	The log base 5 of 125 is 3.	$5^3 = 125$
3. $\log_3 \sqrt{3} = \frac{1}{2}$	The log base 3 of $\sqrt{3}$ is $\frac{1}{2}$.	$3^{\frac{1}{2}} = \sqrt{3}$
5. $\log_5 \dfrac{1}{5} = -1$	The log base 5 of $\frac{1}{5}$ is -1.	$5^{-1} = \frac{1}{5}$
7. $\log_{16} 4 = \frac{1}{2}$	The log base 16 of 4 is $\frac{1}{2}$	$16^{\frac{1}{2}} = 4$
9. $\log_8 4 = \frac{2}{3}$	The log base 8 of 4 is $\frac{2}{3}$.	$8^{\frac{2}{3}} = 4$
11. $\log_3 \dfrac{1}{9} = -2$	The log base 3 of $\frac{1}{9}$ is -2.	$3^{-2} = \dfrac{1}{9}$

Logarithmic Form	**Verbal Description**	**Exponential Form**
13. $\log_m n = p$	The log base m of n is p.	$m^p = n$
15. $\log_n m = k$	The log base n of m is k.	$n^k = m$

17. $\log_{10} 100 = 2$ $\left(\text{since } 10^2 = 100\right)$

19. $\log_{10} 0.001 = -3$ $\left(\text{since } 10^{-3} = 0.001\right)$

21. $\log_{10} \sqrt[3]{10} = \dfrac{1}{3}$ $\left(\text{since } 10^{1/3} = \sqrt[3]{10}\right)$

23. $\log_2 32 = 5$ $\left(\text{since } 2^5 = 32\right)$

25. $\log_3 \dfrac{1}{3} = -1$ $\left(\text{since } 3^{-1} = \dfrac{1}{3}\right)$

27. $\log_{18} 1 = 0$ $\left(\text{since } 18^0 = 1\right)$

29. $\log_{\frac{3}{4}} \dfrac{4}{3} = -1$ $\left(\text{since } \left(\dfrac{3}{4}\right)^{-1} = \dfrac{4}{3}\right)$

31. $\log_3 81 = 4$ $\left(\text{since } 3^4 = 81\right)$

33. $\log_2 64 = 6$ $\left(\text{since } 2^6 = 64\right)$

35. $\log_3 27 = 3$ $\left(\text{since } 3^3 = 27\right)$

37. $\log_{16} 2 = \dfrac{1}{4}$ $\left(\text{since } 16^{1/4} = 2\right)$

39. $\log_{25} 125 = \dfrac{3}{2}$ $\left(\text{since } 25^{3/2} = \left(\sqrt{25}\right)^3 = 5^3 = 125\right)$

41. $\log_{19} 19 = 1$ $\left(\text{since } 19^1 = 19\right)$

43. $\log_5 5^{2.7} = 2.7$ $\left(\text{since } 5^{2.7} = 5^{2.7}\right)$

45. $\log_{3/4} \dfrac{16}{9} = -2$ $\left(\text{since } \left(\dfrac{3}{4}\right)^{-2} = \left(\dfrac{4}{3}\right)^2 = \dfrac{16}{9}\right)$

47. **a.** $\log_7 10$ is defined.

    b. $\log_7 0$ is undefined since no exponent of 7 will yield 0.

49. **a.** $\log_5 (-5)$ is undefined since no exponent of 5 will yield -5.

    b. $\log_5 1$ is defined

51. $\log_6 36 = x$ is equivalent to $6^x = 36$

$$6^x = 6^2$$
$$x = 2$$

53. $\log_6 x = 1$ is equivalent to $6^1 = x$

$$x = 6$$

55. $\log_6 x = -1$ is equivalent to $6^{-1} = x$

$$x = \dfrac{1}{6}$$

57. $\log_6 x = \dfrac{1}{2}$ is equivalent to $6^{1/2} = x$

$$x = \sqrt{6}$$

59. $\log_x 4 = 2$ is equivalent to $x^2 = 4$

Note: A base of -2 is not acceptable.
$$x = 2$$

61. $\log_x 125 = 3$ is equivalent to $x^3 = 125$

$$\sqrt[3]{x^3} = \sqrt[3]{125}$$
$$x = 5$$

63. $\log_b \sqrt[5]{b} = x$ is equivalent to $b^x = \sqrt[5]{b}$

$$b^x = b^{1/5}$$
$$x = \dfrac{1}{5}$$

65. $\log_3 1 = 2x + 1$ is equivalent to $3^{2x+1} = 1$

$$3^{2x+1} = 3^0$$
$$2x + 1 = 0$$
$$x = -\dfrac{1}{2}$$

67. $\log_2 (3x - 4) = 3$ is equivalent to $2^3 = 3x - 4$

$$8 = 3x - 4$$
$$x = 4$$

69.

x	$f(x)$
1/4	−1
1	0
4	1
16	2

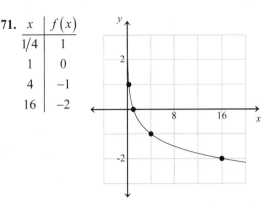

71.

x	$f(x)$
1/4	1
1	0
4	−1
16	−2

73. The exponential decay function $f(x) = e^x$ is found in graph **B**.

75. The logarithmic growth function $f(x) = \log_e x$ is found in graph **C**.

77. The domain of the function is the projection of the graph onto the x-axis. Domain: $(0, \infty)$.

The range of the function is the projection of the graph onto the y-axis. Domain: $\mathbb{R}$ or $(-\infty, \infty)$.

Cumulative Review

1. $\begin{aligned} 5m^2 - 45 &= 5(m^2 - 9) \\ &= 5(m+3)(m-3) \end{aligned}$

2. $21x^2 - 14x = 7x(3x - 2)$

3. $4v^2 - w^2 = (2v + w)(2v - w)$

4. $4v^2 + 4vw + w^2 = (2v + w)^2$

5. $\begin{aligned} a^2 - b^2 + 5a - 5b &= (a^2 - b^2) + (5a - 5b) \\ &= (a+b)(a-b) + 5(a-b) \\ &= (a-b)((a+b) + 5) \\ &= (a-b)(a+b+5) \end{aligned}$

Section 11.4: Evaluating Logarithms

Quick Review 11.4

1. $\dfrac{0}{10} = 0$

2. $\dfrac{10}{0}$ is undefined.

3. $10^{-4} = \dfrac{1}{10^4} = \dfrac{1}{10000}$

4. $75,345,247 = 7.5345247 \times 10^7$

5. $0.000087 = 8.7 \times 10^{-5}$

Exercises 11.4

1. $\log 10 = \log_{10} 10 = 1$ $\left(\text{since: } 10^1 = 10\right)$

3. $\log 0.0001 = \log_{10} 0.0001 = -4$ $\left(\text{since: } 10^{-4} = 0.0001\right)$

5. $\log 10^{-8} = \log_{10} 10^{-8} = -8$ $\left(\text{since: } 10^{-8} = 10^{-8}\right)$

7. $\log \sqrt[4]{10} = \log_{10} \sqrt[4]{10} = \dfrac{1}{4}$ $\left(\text{since: } \sqrt[4]{10} = 10^{1/4}\right)$

Chapter 11: Exponential and Logarithmic Functions

9. $\log 1 = \log_{10} 1 = 0$ $\left(\text{since: } 10^0 = 1\right)$

11. $\ln e^6 = \log_e e^6 = 6$ $\left(\text{since: } e^6 = e^6\right)$

13. $\ln e^{-3} = \log_e e^{-3} = -3$ $\left(\text{since: } e^{-3} = e^{-3}\right)$

15. $\ln \sqrt{e} = \log_e \sqrt{e} = \dfrac{1}{2}$ $\left(\text{since: } \sqrt{e} = e^{1/2}\right)$

17. $\ln 0 = \log_e 0$ is undefined since there is no exponent of e that will yield 0.

19. $\log(-10) = \log_{10}(-10)$ is undefined since there is no exponent of 10 that will yield -10.

21. $\ln \dfrac{1}{e} = \log_e \dfrac{1}{e} = -1$ $\left(\text{since: } e^{-1} = \dfrac{1}{e}\right)$

23.
25.
27.
```
log(47)
            1.672
ln(0.0034)
           -5.684
log(876)
            2.943
■
```

29.
31.
33.
```
log(4.5E6)
            6.653
ln(4.5E-5)
          -10.009
ln(√(134))
            2.449
■
```

35.
37.
39.
```
log(π)
            .497
log(ln(932))
            .835
ln(11/4)
            1.012
■
```

41.
43.
45.
```
ln(11)/ln(4)
            1.730
log(25*18)
            2.653
log(25)*log(18)
            1.755
■
```

47. The expression $\ln(-8)$ is not defined. The argument of a logarithmic function must be positive.

49. The expression $\ln(23 \cdot 0) = \ln(0)$ is not defined. The argument of a logarithmic function must be positive.

51. The expression $\ln(17 - 19) = \ln(-2)$ is not defined. The argument of a logarithmic function must be positive.

Problem	Mental Estimate
53. $\log_8 63$	$\log_8 63 \approx \log_8 64 = 2$ $\left(\text{since } 8^2 = 64\right)$
55. $2.99^{4.01}$	$2.99^{4.01} \approx 3^4 = 81$

57. **a.**
b.
```
log(2.472)
            .393
10^0.393
            2.472
■
```

59. **a.**
b.
```
ln(0.094)
           -2.364
e^(-2.364)
            .094
■
```

61. $\log x = 2.477$ is equivalent to $x = 10^{2.477} \approx 299.916$

63. $\log x = -0.301$ is equivalent to $x = 10^{-0.301} \approx 0.500$

65. $\ln x = 2.079$ is equivalent to $x = e^{2.079} \approx 7.996$

67. $\ln x = -2.996$ is equivalent to $x = e^{-2.996} \approx 0.050$

Cumulative Review

1. $\dfrac{12x^2 y^3}{24xy} = \dfrac{\cancel{12}x^{2-1}y^{3-1}}{\underset{2}{\cancel{24}}} = \dfrac{xy^2}{2}$

2. $\dfrac{5x}{10x^2 - 15x} = \dfrac{\cancel{5x}}{\cancel{5x}(2x-3)} = \dfrac{1}{2x-3}$

3. $\dfrac{2x+2}{7x+7} = \dfrac{2\cancel{(x+1)}}{7\cancel{(x+1)}} = \dfrac{2}{7}$

4. $\dfrac{(x+2)(5x-1)}{(x+2)(3x-4)} = \dfrac{\cancel{(x+2)}(5x-1)}{\cancel{(x+2)}(3x-4)} = \dfrac{5x-1}{3x-4}$

5. $\dfrac{x^2-16}{x^2-x-20} = \dfrac{\cancel{(x+4)}(x-4)}{\cancel{(x+4)}(x-5)} = \dfrac{x-4}{x-5}$

Section 11.5: Properties of Logarithms

Quick Review 11.5

1. $3x^4y^2\left(5x^3y^7\right) = 3\cdot5x^{4+3}y^{2+7} = 15x^7y^9$

2. $\dfrac{15x^4y^2}{5x^3y^7} = \dfrac{\cancel{15}^3\, x^{4-3}y^{2-7}}{\cancel{5}} = 3x^1y^{-5} = \dfrac{3x}{y^5}$

3. $\left(5x^3y^7\right)^2 = 5^2\left(x^3\right)^2\left(y^7\right)^2 = 25x^{3\cdot2}y^{7\cdot2} = 25x^6y^{14}$

4. $x\sqrt{y} = xy^{1/2}$

5. $\sqrt[3]{xy^2} = \left(xy^2\right)^{1/3} = x^{1/3}\left(y^2\right)^{1/3} = x^{1/3}y^{2\cdot\frac{1}{3}} = x^{1/3}y^{2/3}$

Exercises 11.5

1. $\log\, abc = \log a + \log b + \log c$

3. $\ln\dfrac{x}{11} = \ln x - \ln 11$

5. $\log\, y^5 = 5\log y$

7. $\ln x^2y^3 = \ln x^2 + \ln y^3 = 2\ln x + 3\ln y$

9. $\ln(x+2)(3x-1) = \ln(x+2) + \ln(3x-1)$

11. $\ln\dfrac{2x+3}{x+7} = \ln(2x+3) - \ln(x+7)$

13. $\log\sqrt{4x+7} = \log(4x+7)^{1/2} = \dfrac{1}{2}\log(4x+7)$

15. $\ln\dfrac{\sqrt{x+4}}{(y+5)^2} = \ln(x+4)^{1/2} - \ln(y+5)^2$

$$= \dfrac{1}{2}\ln(x+4) - 2\ln(y+5)$$

17. $\log\sqrt{\dfrac{xy}{z-8}} = \log\left(\dfrac{xy}{z-8}\right)^{1/2} = \dfrac{1}{2}\log\left(\dfrac{xy}{z-8}\right)$

$$= \dfrac{1}{2}\left[\log xy - \log(z-8)\right]$$

$$= \dfrac{1}{2}\left[\log x + \log y - \log(z-8)\right]$$

19. $\log\dfrac{x^2(2y+3)^3}{z^4} = \log\left[x^2(2y+3)^3\right] - \log z^4$

$$= \log x^2 + \log(2y+3)^3 - 4\log z$$

$$= 2\log x + 3\log(2y+3) - 4\log z$$

21. $\ln\left(\dfrac{xy^2}{z^3}\right) = \ln xy^2 - \ln z^3 = \ln x + \ln y^2 - \ln z^3$

$$= \ln x + 2\ln y - 3\ln z$$

23. $\ln x + \ln y = \ln xy$

25. $\ln w - \ln z = \ln\dfrac{w}{z}$

27. $3\ln w = \ln w^3$

29. $2 \log x + 5 \log y = \log x^2 + \log y^5 = \log x^2 y^5$

31. $3 \ln x + 7 \ln y - \ln z = \ln x^3 + \ln y^7 - \ln z$
$$= \ln x^3 y^7 - \ln z = \ln \left(\frac{x^3 y^7}{z} \right)$$

33. $\dfrac{1}{2} \ln x = \ln x^{1/2} = \ln \sqrt{x}$

35. $\dfrac{1}{2} \log(x+1) - \log(2x+3)$
$$= \log(x+1)^{1/2} - \log(2x+3)$$
$$= \log \sqrt{x+1} - \log(2x+3)$$
$$= \log \left(\frac{\sqrt{x+1}}{2x+3} \right)$$

37. $\dfrac{1}{3} \left[\ln(2x+7) + \ln(7x+1) \right]$
$$= \frac{1}{3} \ln(2x+7)(7x+1)$$
$$= \ln \left[(2x+7)(7x+1) \right]^{1/3}$$
$$= \ln \sqrt[3]{(2x+7)(7x+1)}$$

39. $2 \log_5 x + \dfrac{2}{3} \log_5 y = \log_5 x^2 + \log_5 y^{2/3}$
$$= \log_5 \left(x^2 y^{2/3} \right) = \log_5 \left(x^2 \sqrt[3]{y^2} \right)$$

41. $10^{\log 37} = 37$

43. $e^{\ln 0.045} = 0.045$

45. $e^{\ln x} = x$

47. $\log_3 37.1 = \dfrac{\ln 37.1}{\ln 3}$

49. $\log_{13} 7.9 = \dfrac{\ln 7.9}{\ln 13}$

51. 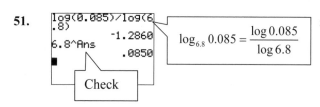 $\log_{6.8} 0.085 = \dfrac{\log 0.085}{\log 6.8}$

53. 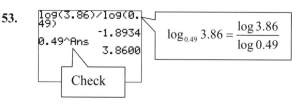 $\log_{0.49} 3.86 = \dfrac{\log 3.86}{\log 0.49}$

Problem	Mental Estimate	Calculator Approximation
55. $\log_4 63$	$\log_4 63 \approx \log_4 64 = 3$	$\log_4 63 = \dfrac{\log 63}{\log 4} \approx 2.989$
57. $1.99^{5.02}$	$1.99^{5.02} \approx 2^5 = 32$	$1.99^{5.02} \approx 31.640$

59. $\log_b 10 = \log_b(2 \cdot 5) = \log_b 2 + \log_b 5$
$$\approx 0.3562 + 0.8271 = 1.1833$$

61. $\log_b 25 = \log_b \left(5^2 \right) = 2 \log_b 5 \approx 2(0.8271) = 1.6542$

63. $\log_b \sqrt[3]{2} = \log_b 2^{1/3} = \dfrac{1}{3} \log_b 2 \approx \dfrac{1}{3}(0.3562) = 0.1187$

65. $\log_b 2b = \log_b 2 + \log_b b \approx 0.3562 + 1 = 1.3562$

67. $\log_b 0.4 = \log_b \left(\dfrac{2}{5} \right) = \log_b 2 - \log_b 5$
$$\approx 0.3562 - 0.8271 = -0.4709$$

69. $\log_b \dfrac{b}{2} = \log_b b - \log_b 2 \approx 1 - 0.3562 = 0.6438$

71. $\log \dfrac{x}{y} = \log x - \log y$; Answer: **C.**

73. $\log xy = \log x + \log y$ Answer: **B.**

75. $\log(x-y)$ cannot be simplified; Answer: **F.**

77. $\log x^y = y \log x$; Answer: **E.**

79. $10^{\log x} = x$; Answer: **A.**

81. $f(x) = 5^x = e^{x \ln 5}$

83. $f(x) = \left(\dfrac{1}{5}\right)^x = e^{x \ln\left(\frac{1}{5}\right)} = e^{x \ln\left(5^{-1}\right)} = e^{-x \ln 5}$

85. $\ln\left(\dfrac{1}{2}\right) = \ln 1 - \ln 2 = 0 - \ln 2 = -\ln 2$

Cumulative Review

1. $x^2 = 25$
$x = \pm\sqrt{25}$
$x = \pm 5$

2. $(x-4)^2 = 25$
$x - 4 = \pm\sqrt{25}$
$x = 4 \pm 5$
$x = 9 \;\; \text{or} \;\; x = -1$

3. $(x-4)(2x+7) = 0$
$x - 4 = 0 \;\; \text{or} \;\; 2x + 7 = 0$
$\qquad x = 4 \qquad\qquad 2x = -7$
$\qquad\qquad\qquad\qquad x = -\dfrac{7}{2}$

4. $(x-4)(2x+7) = -25$
$2x^2 + 7x - 8x - 28 = -25$
$2x^2 - x - 3 = 0$
$(2x-3)(x+1) = 0$
$2x - 3 = 0 \;\; \text{or} \;\; x + 1 = 0$
$\quad 2x = 3 \qquad\qquad x = -1$
$\quad\; x = \dfrac{3}{2}$

5. $2x^2 + 7x + 6 = 0$
$(2x+3)(x+2) = 0$
$2x + 3 = 0 \;\; \text{or} \;\; x + 2 = 0$
$\; 2x = -3 \qquad\qquad x = -2$
$\;\; x = -\dfrac{3}{2}$

Section 11.6: Solving Exponential and Logarithmic Equations

Quick Review 11.6

1.
2.
3.

```
log(48/5)
         .982
log(48)/5
         .336
48/ln(5)
       29.824
■
```

4. The last two columns (the y-columns) of the table are equal to each other when $x = 5$ and $y = -2$.

Thus the solution to the system is $(5, -2)$.

5. From the graph we can see that the intersection is $(1, 2.5)$. The solution to the system of equations is $(1, 2.5)$.

Exercises 11.6

1. $7^x = 49$
$7^x = 7^2$
$x = 2$

3. $\log_5 x = -3$ is equivalent to $x = 5^{-3}$
$$x = \frac{1}{5^3}$$
$$x = \frac{1}{125}$$

5. $3^{w-5} = 27$
$3^{w-5} = 3^3$
$w - 5 = 3$
$w = 8$

7. $\left(\dfrac{2}{3}\right)^{x^2} = \dfrac{16}{81}$
$\left(\dfrac{2}{3}\right)^{x^2} = \left(\dfrac{2}{3}\right)^4$
$x^2 = 4$
$x = \pm 2$

9. $\log(y - 5) = 1$ is equivalent to $y - 5 = 10^1$
$y = 15$

11. $\log(3n - 5) = 2$ is equivalent to $3n - 5 = 10^2$
$3n = 105$
$n = 35$

13. $\ln(3m - 7) = \ln(2m + 9)$
$3m - 7 = 2m + 9$
$m = 16$

15. $\log(4w + 3) = \log(8w + 5)$
$4w + 3 = 8w + 5$
$-4w = 2$
$w = -\dfrac{1}{2}$

17. $\ln(3 - x) = \ln(1 - 2x)$
$3 - x = 1 - 2x$
$x = -2$

19. $\log(t + 3) + \log(t - 1) = \log 5$
$\log(t + 3)(t - 1) = \log 5$
$(t + 3)(t - 1) = 5$
$t^2 + 2t - 3 = 5$
$t^2 + 2t - 8 = 0$
$(t + 4)(t - 2) = 0$
$t = -4$ or $t = 2$

$t = -4$ is an extraneous solution since it causes the argument of the logarithms to be negative. Thus $t = 2$ is the only solution.

21. $\ln(v^2 - 9) - \ln(v + 3) = \ln 7$

$$\ln\left(\frac{v^2 - 9}{v + 3}\right) = \ln 7$$

$$\frac{\cancel{(v+3)}(v - 3)}{\cancel{v+3}} = 7$$

$$v - 3 = 7$$

$$v = 10$$

23. $\ln(5x - 7) - \ln(2x + 3) = \ln 3$

$$\ln\left(\frac{5x - 7}{2x + 3}\right) = \ln 3$$

$$\frac{5x - 7}{2x + 3} = 3$$

$$5x - 7 = 3(2x + 3)$$

$$5x - 7 = 6x + 9$$

$$x = -16$$

$x = -16$ is an extraneous solution since it causes the argument of the logarithms to be negative. Thus there is no solution.

25. $\log(1 - y) + \log(4 - y) = \log(18 - 10y)$

$$\log(1 - y)(4 - y) = \log(18 - 10y)$$

$$(1 - y)(4 - y) = 18 - 10y$$

$$4 - 5y + y^2 = 18 - 10y$$

$$y^2 + 5y - 14 = 0$$

$$(y + 7)(y - 2) = 0$$

$$y = -7 \quad \text{or} \quad y = 2$$

$y = 2$ is an extraneous solution since it causes the argument of two of the logarithms to be negative or zero. Thus $y = -7$ is the only solution.

27. $\log(w - 3) - \log(w^2 + 9w - 32) = -1$

$$\log\left(\frac{w - 3}{w^2 + 9w - 32}\right) = -1$$

is equivalent to

$$\frac{w - 3}{w^2 + 9w - 32} = 10^{-1}$$

$$\frac{w - 3}{w^2 + 9w - 32} = \frac{1}{10}$$

$$10(w - 3) = w^2 + 9w - 32$$

$$10w - 30 = w^2 + 9w - 32$$

$$w^2 - w - 2 = 0$$

$$(w - 2)(w + 1) = 0$$

$$w = 2 \quad \text{or} \quad w = -1$$

Both values are extraneous since they each cause the arguments of the logarithms to be negative. Thus there are no solutions.

29. The solution to the equation $4^x = 32$ is the value of x in the table such that $y_1 = 32$. Thus the solution is $x = 2.5$.

31. The solution to the equation $\log(5x - 9.99) = -2$ is the value of x in the table such that $y_1 = -2$. Thus the solution is $x = 2$.

33. The solution to the equation $8^{\frac{x+2}{3}} = 16$ is the x value of the point of intersection. Thus the solution is $x = 2$.

35. The solution to the equation $\log(100x^2) = 2$ is the x values of the points of intersection. Thus the solutions are $x = -1$ and $x = 1$.

37. $4^v = 15$

$$\log 4^v = \log 15$$

$$v \log 4 = \log 15$$

$$v = \frac{\log 15}{\log 4} \approx 1.953$$

39. $3^{-w+7} = 22$

$$\log 3^{-w+7} = \log 22$$

$$(-w + 7)\log 3 = \log 22$$

$$-w \log 3 + 7 \log 3 = \log 22$$

$$-w \log 3 = \log 22 - 7 \log 3$$

$$w = \frac{\log 22 - 7 \log 3}{-\log 3} \approx 4.186$$

41.
$$9.2^{2t+1} = 11.3^t$$
$$\log 9.2^{2t+1} = \log 11.3^t$$
$$(2t+1)\log 9.2 = t\log 11.3$$
$$2t\log 9.2 + \log 9.2 = t\log 11.3$$
$$2t\log 9.2 - t\log 11.3 = -\log 9.2$$
$$t(2\log 9.2 - \log 11.3) = -\log 9.2$$
$$t = \frac{-\log 9.2}{2\log 9.2 - \log 11.3}$$
$$t \approx -1.102$$

43.
$$7.6^{-2z} = 5.3^{2z-1}$$
$$\log 7.6^{-2z} = \log 5.3^{2z-1}$$
$$-2z\log 7.6 = (2z-1)\log 5.3$$
$$-2z\log 7.6 = 2z\log 5.3 - \log 5.3$$
$$2z\log 5.3 + 2z\log 7.6 = \log 5.3$$
$$z(2\log 5.3 + 2\log 7.6) = \log 5.3$$
$$z = \frac{\log 5.3}{2\log 5.3 + 2\log 7.6}$$
$$z \approx 0.226$$

45. $e^{3x} = 78.9$
$$3x = \ln 78.9$$
$$x = \frac{\ln 78.9}{3} \approx 1.456$$

47. $10^{2y+1} = 51.3$
$$2y + 1 = \log 51.3$$
$$2y = \log 51.3 - 1$$
$$y = \frac{\log 51.3 - 1}{2} \approx 0.355$$

49.
$$0.83^{v^2} = 0.68$$
$$\log 0.83^{v^2} = \log 0.68$$
$$v^2 \log 0.83 = \log 0.68$$
$$v^2 = \frac{\log 0.68}{\log 0.83}$$
$$v = \pm\sqrt{\frac{\log 0.68}{\log 0.83}} \approx \pm 1.439$$

51. $3.7e^{x^2+1} = 689.7$
$$e^{x^2+1} = \frac{689.7}{3.7}$$
$$e^{x^2+1} = 186.405$$
$$x^2 + 1 = \ln 186.405$$
$$x^2 = \ln 186.405 - 1$$
$$x = \pm\sqrt{\ln 186.405 - 1} \approx \pm 2.056$$

53. $\log(5x - 17) = 0.83452$
$$5x - 17 = 10^{0.83452}$$
$$5x = 10^{0.83452} + 17$$
$$x = \frac{10^{0.83452} + 17}{5} \approx 4.766$$

55. $\ln(\ln y) = 1$
$$\ln y = e^1$$
$$y = e^e \approx 15.154$$

57.
$$\ln(v-4) + \ln(v-3) = \ln(5-v)$$
$$\ln(v-4)(v-3) = \ln(5-v)$$
$$(v-4)(v-3) = 5-v$$
$$v^2 - 7v + 12 = 5 - v$$
$$v^2 - 6v + 7 = 0$$
$$a = 1, \quad b = -6, \quad c = 7$$
$$v = \frac{-(-6) \pm \sqrt{(-6)^2 - 4(1)(7)}}{2(1)} = \frac{6 \pm 2\sqrt{2}}{2}$$
$$v \approx 4.414 \quad \text{or} \quad v \approx 1.586$$

$v \approx 1.586$ is an extraneous solution since it causes the argument of two of the logarithms to be negative. Thus $v \approx 4.414$ is the only solution.

59.
$$\ln(11 - 5x) - \ln(x-2) = \ln(x-6)$$
$$\ln\left(\frac{11-5x}{x-2}\right) = \ln(x-6)$$
$$\frac{11-5x}{x-2} = x - 6$$
$$11 - 5x = (x-6)(x-2)$$
$$11 - 5x = x^2 - 8x + 12$$
$$x^2 - 3x + 1 = 0$$
$$a = 1, \quad b = -3, \quad c = 1$$
$$x = \frac{-(-3) \pm \sqrt{(-3)^2 - 4(1)(1)}}{2(1)} = \frac{3 \pm \sqrt{5}}{2}$$
$$x \approx 2.618 \quad \text{or} \quad x \approx 0.382$$

Both values are extraneous since they each cause the arguments of the logarithms to be negative. Thus there are no solutions

61.
$$(\ln x)^2 = \ln x^2$$
$$(\ln x)^2 = 2\ln x$$
$$(\ln x)^2 - 2\ln x = 0$$
$$\ln x(\ln x - 2) = 0$$
$$\ln x = 0 \quad \text{or} \quad \ln x = 2$$
$$x = 1 \quad \text{or} \quad x = e^2 \approx 7.389$$

63.

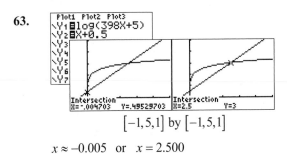

$$[-1, 5, 1] \text{ by } [-1, 5, 1]$$
$$x \approx -0.005 \quad \text{or} \quad x = 2.500$$

65.

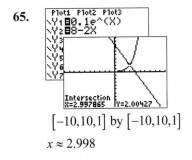

$$[-10, 10, 1] \text{ by } [-10, 10, 1]$$
$$x \approx 2.998$$

67.
$$10^{-\log x} = 10^{(-1)\log x} = 10^{\log x^{-1}} = 10^{\log\left(\frac{1}{x}\right)} = \frac{1}{x}$$

69.
$$e^{-x\ln 3} = e^{\ln 3^{-x}} = e^{\ln\left(3^{-1}\right)^x} = e^{\ln\left(\frac{1}{3}\right)^x} = \left(\frac{1}{3}\right)^x$$

71.
$$\log 60^x - \log 6^x = \log(10 \cdot 6)^x - \log 6^x$$
$$= \log(10^x \cdot 6^x) - \log 6^x$$
$$= \log 10^x + \log 6^x - \log 6^x$$
$$= \log 10^x = x$$

73.
$$\ln\left(\frac{4}{5}\right)^x + \ln\left(\frac{5}{3}\right)^x + \ln\left(\frac{3}{4}\right)^x$$
$$= x\ln\left(\frac{4}{5}\right) + x\ln\left(\frac{5}{3}\right) + x\ln\left(\frac{3}{4}\right)$$
$$= x\left[\ln\left(\frac{4}{5}\right) + \ln\left(\frac{5}{3}\right) + \ln\left(\frac{3}{4}\right)\right]$$
$$= x\ln\left(\frac{\cancel{4}}{\cancel{5}} \cdot \frac{\cancel{5}}{\cancel{3}} \cdot \frac{\cancel{3}}{\cancel{4}}\right) = x\ln(1) = x(0) = 0$$

75.
$$V = 10000$$
$$35000e^{-0.2t} + 1000 = 10000$$
$$35000e^{-0.2t} = 9000$$
$$e^{-0.2t} = \frac{9000}{35000}$$
$$-0.2t = \ln\left(\frac{9}{35}\right)$$
$$t = \frac{\ln\left(\frac{9}{35}\right)}{-0.2} \approx 6.8$$

It will take approximately 6.8 years for the value to depreciate to $10,000.

Cumulative Review

1. From the graph we can see that the y-intercept is $(0, 2)$.
2. From the graph we can see that the x-intercepts are $(-6, 0)$ and $(2, 0)$.
3. From the graph we can see that the maximum value of y is $y = 4$.
4. From the graph we can see that the value of x when y is at its maximum is $x = -2$.
5. From the graph we can see that the interval of x-values for which the function is increasing is $(-\infty, -2)$.

Section 11.7: Exponential Curve Fitting and Other Applications of Exponential and Logarithmic Equations

Quick Review 11.7

1. $10^4 = 10,000$ is equivalent to $\log 10,000 = 4$.

2. $\log 0.001 = -3$ is equivalent to $10^{-3} = 0.001$.

3. $\ln 78 \approx 4.357$ is equivalent to $e^{4.357} \approx 78$.

4.
5.
```
log(2.58E4)
              4.41
log(2.58E-4)
             -3.59
■
```

Section 11.7: Exponential Curve Fitting and Other Applications of Exponential and Logarithmic Equations

Exercises 11.7

1. Substitute $P = 150$, $r = 0.09$, $n = 4$, and $t = 5$

$$A = P\left(1 + \frac{r}{n}\right)^{nt}$$

$$A = 150\left(1 + \frac{0.09}{4}\right)^{(4)(5)} \approx \$234.08$$

3. Substitute $A = 2P$, $r = 0.08$, $n = 1$, and solve for t.

$$A = P\left(1 + \frac{r}{n}\right)^{nt}$$

$$2P = P\left(1 + \frac{0.08}{1}\right)^{(1)t}$$

$$\frac{2\cancel{P}}{\cancel{P}} = \frac{\cancel{P}(1.08)^t}{\cancel{P}}$$

$$2 = 1.08^t$$

$$\ln 2 = \ln 1.08^t$$

$$\ln 2 = t \ln 1.08$$

$$t = \frac{\ln 2}{\ln 1.08} \approx 9 \text{ years}$$

5. Substitute $A = 3P$, $r = 0.06$, $n = 12$, and solve for t.

$$A = P\left(1 + \frac{r}{n}\right)^{nt}$$

$$3P = P\left(1 + \frac{0.06}{12}\right)^{(12)t}$$

$$\frac{3\cancel{P}}{\cancel{P}} = \frac{\cancel{P}(1.005)^{12t}}{\cancel{P}}$$

$$3 = 1.005^{12t}$$

$$\ln 3 = \ln 1.005^{12t}$$

$$\ln 3 = 12t \ln 1.005$$

$$t = \frac{\ln 3}{12 \ln 1.005} \approx 18.4 \text{ years}$$

7. Substitute $A = 1.5P$, $r = 0.08$, $n = 2$, and solve for t.

$$A = P\left(1 + \frac{r}{n}\right)^{nt}$$

$$1.5P = P\left(1 + \frac{0.08}{2}\right)^{2t}$$

$$\frac{1.5\cancel{P}}{\cancel{P}} = \frac{\cancel{P}\left(1 + \frac{0.08}{2}\right)^{2t}}{\cancel{P}}$$

$$1.5 = \left(1 + \frac{0.08}{2}\right)^{2t}$$

$$\ln 1.5 = \ln\left(1 + \frac{0.08}{2}\right)^{2t}$$

$$\ln 1.5 = 2t \ln\left(1 + \frac{0.08}{2}\right)$$

$$t = \frac{\ln 1.5}{2 \ln\left(1 + \frac{0.08}{2}\right)} \approx 5.2$$

It will take approximately 5.2 years to increase in value by 50%.

9. Use $A = Pe^{rt}$. Substitute $A = 2P$, $t = 10$, and solve for r.

$$2P = Pe^{r(10)}$$

$$\frac{2\cancel{P}}{\cancel{P}} = \frac{\cancel{P}e^{10r}}{\cancel{P}}$$

$$2 = e^{10r}$$

$$10r = \ln 2$$

$$r = \frac{\ln 2}{10} \approx 0.069 \quad \text{or} \quad 6.9\%$$

11. Use $A = Pe^{rt}$. Substitute $A = 2P$, $r = 0.07$, and solve for t.

$$2P = Pe^{(0.07)t}$$

$$\frac{2\cancel{P}}{\cancel{P}} = \frac{\cancel{P}e^{0.07t}}{\cancel{P}}$$

$$2 = e^{0.07t}$$

$$0.07t = \ln 2$$

$$t = \frac{\ln 2}{0.07} \approx 9.9 \text{ years}$$

13. Use $A = Pe^{rt}$. Substitute
$A = 0.05P$, $r = -0.0001245$, and solve for t.

$$0.05P = Pe^{(-0.0001245)t}$$

$$\frac{0.05\cancel{P}}{\cancel{P}} = \frac{\cancel{P}e^{-0.0001245t}}{\cancel{P}}$$

$$0.05 = e^{-0.0001245t}$$

$$-0.0001245t = \ln 0.05$$

$$t = \frac{\ln 0.05}{-0.0001245} \approx 24,000 \text{ years}$$

15. **a.** $B(0) = 4.0e^{0.24(0)} = 4.0$; Initially, there are 4 units of bacteria present.

b. $B(5) = 4.0e^{0.24(5)} \approx 13.3$; After 5 days, there are 13.3 units of bacteria present.

c. $B(10) = 4.0e^{0.24(10)} \approx 44.1$; After 10 days, there are 44.1 units of bacteria present.

d. Solve the following equation for t.

$$B(t) = 100$$

$$4.0e^{0.24t} = 100$$

$$e^{0.24t} = 25$$

$$0.24t = \ln 25$$

$$t = \frac{\ln 25}{0.24} \approx 13.4 \text{ days}$$

There will be 100 units of bacteria present after 13.4 days.

17. Use $A = Pe^{rt}$. Substitute $A = \frac{1}{100}P$, $r = -0.0005$, and solve for t.

$$\frac{1}{100}P = Pe^{(-0.0005)t}$$

$$\frac{0.01\cancel{P}}{\cancel{P}} = \frac{\cancel{P}e^{-0.0005t}}{\cancel{P}}$$

$$0.01 = e^{-0.0005t}$$

$$-0.0005t = \ln 0.01$$

$$t = \frac{\ln 0.01}{-0.0005} \approx 9,200 \text{ days}$$

19. Use $A = Pe^{rt}$. Substitute $P = 15000$, $r = -0.04$. To find the population 10 years from now, we let $t = 10$.

$$15000e^{(-0.04)(10)} \approx 10,000 \text{ whales.}$$

To determine the number of years from now the population will have declined to 5000 we solve the following equation.

$$15000e^{-0.04t} = 5000$$

$$e^{-0.04t} = \frac{1}{3}$$

$$-0.04t = \ln\left(\frac{1}{3}\right)$$

$$t = \frac{\ln\left(\frac{1}{3}\right)}{-0.04} \approx 27.5 \text{ years}$$

21. Use $A = Pe^{rt}$. Substitute
$P = 1200$, $A = 1800$, $t = 3$, and solve for r.

$$1800 = 1200e^{r(3)}$$

$$1800 = 1200e^{3r}$$

$$1.5 = e^{3r}$$

$$3r = \ln(1.5)$$

$$r = \frac{\ln(1.5)}{3} \approx .135 \text{ or } 13.5\%$$

The population is increasing at approximately 13.5% per year.

23. Use $R = \log\dfrac{A}{a}$. Substitute $A = 63000000a$

$$R = \log\frac{63000000\cancel{a}}{\cancel{a}} \approx 7.8$$

25. To determine the intensity of the Izmit earthquake we use $R = \log \dfrac{A}{a}$ where $R = 7.4$.

$$7.4 = \log \dfrac{A}{a}$$

$$\dfrac{A}{a} = 10^{7.4}$$

Thus the Izmit earthquake had an amplitude that was $10^{7.4}$ times the reference amplitude.

To determine the intensity of the San Francisco earthquake we use $R = \log \dfrac{A}{a}$ where $R = 8.25$.

$$8.25 = \log \dfrac{A}{a}$$

$$\dfrac{A}{a} = 10^{8.25}$$

Thus the San Francisco earthquake had an amplitude that was $10^{8.25}$ times the reference amplitude.

Finally, we can determine that the San Francisco earthquake was about 7 times as intense since $\dfrac{10^{8.25}}{10^{7.4}} \approx 7$.

27. Use the formula $D = 10 \log \dfrac{I}{I_o}$ where $I_o = 10^{-16}$ and $I = 3 \times 10^{-14}$.

$$D = 10 \log \dfrac{3 \times 10^{-14}}{10^{-16}} \approx 24.8 \text{ decibels}$$

29. Use the formula $D = 10 \log \dfrac{I}{I_o}$ where $I_o = 10^{-16}$ and $D = 85$. Solve for I.

$$85 = 10 \log \dfrac{I}{10^{-16}}$$

$$8.5 = \log \dfrac{I}{10^{-16}}$$

$$\dfrac{I}{10^{-16}} = 10^{8.5}$$

$$I = 10^{8.5} \cdot 10^{-16} \approx 3.2 \times 10^{-8} \text{ watts/cm}^2$$

31. Use the formula $pH = -\log H^+$ where $H^+ = 0.000109$.

$$pH = -\log 0.000109 \approx 3.96$$

33. Use the formula $pH = -\log H^+$ where $pH = 9.13$. Solve for H^+.

$$9.13 = -\log H^+$$

$$-9.13 = \log H^+$$

$$H^+ = 10^{-9.13} \approx 7.41 \times 10^{-10} \text{ moles/liter}$$

35. Use the given formula. Substitute $A = 47400$, $n = 30$, $R = 0.09875$

$$P = \dfrac{A\left(\dfrac{R}{12}\right)}{1 - \left(1 + \dfrac{R}{12}\right)^{-12n}}$$

$$P = \dfrac{47400\left(\dfrac{0.09875}{12}\right)}{1 - \left(1 + \dfrac{0.09875}{12}\right)^{-12(30)}} \approx \$411.60$$

The monthly payments are \$411.60.

37. Use the given formula. Substitute $P = 253.59$, $A = 7668$, $R = 0.117$

$$n = -\frac{\log\left(1 - \dfrac{AR}{12P}\right)}{\log\left(1 + \dfrac{R}{12}\right)}$$

$$n = -\frac{\log\left(1 - \dfrac{(7668)(0.117)}{12(253.59)}\right)}{\log\left(1 + \dfrac{0.117}{12}\right)} \approx 36$$

There will be 36 monthly payments.

39. Use the given formula. Substitute $k = -3.8065$, $r = 22$, $b = 29$, and $b_0 = 37$.

$$t = k \ln \frac{b - r}{b_0 - r}$$

$$t = -3.8065 \ln \frac{29 - 22}{37 - 22} \approx 2.9 \text{ hours.}$$

41. a.

L1	L2	L3	1
1	2.5	------	
2	2		
3	1.5		
4	1.2		
5	1		
6	.8		

L1 ={1,2,3,4,5,6}

$[0,7,1]$ by $[0,3,0.5]$

b. ExpReg
y=a*b^x
a=3.092528853
b=.795674997

$$f(x) \approx 3.09(0.796)^x$$

c. The function $f(x)$ represents exponential decay.

d. $f(2.5) \approx 3.09(0.796)^{2.5} \approx 1.7$

43. a.

L1	L2	L3	1
0	40	------	
1	60		
2	90		
3	150		
4	200		
5	300		

L1 ={0,1,2,3,4,5}

$[0,6,1]$ by $[0,350,50]$

b. ExpReg
y=a*b^x
a=40.52307366
b=1.500256323

$$f(x) \approx 40.5(1.50)^x$$

c. $f(6) \approx 40.5(1.50)^6 \approx 460 \text{ GB.}$

Cumulative Review

1. $5(4 - 3i) = 20 - 15i$

2. $(5 + 2i) - (4 - 3i) = 5 + 2i - 4 + 3i$
$= 5 - 4 + 2i + 3i$
$= 1 + 5i$

3. $(5+2i)(4-3i) = 20-15i+8i-6i^2$
$$= 20-7i-6(-1)$$
$$= 20+6-7i$$
$$= 26-7i$$

4. $(5+2i)^2 = (5+2i)(5+2i)$
$$= 25+10i+10i+4i^2$$
$$= 25+20i+4(-1)$$
$$= 25-4+20i$$
$$= 21+20i$$

5. $\dfrac{5+2i}{4-3i} = \dfrac{(5+2i)}{(4-3i)} \cdot \dfrac{(4+3i)}{(4+3i)} = \dfrac{20+15i+8i+6i^2}{16-9i^2}$

$$= \dfrac{20+23i+6(-1)}{16-9(-1)} = \dfrac{20-6+23i}{16+9}$$

$$= \dfrac{14+23i}{25} = \dfrac{14}{25}+\dfrac{23}{25}i$$

Review Exercises for Chapter 11

1. **a.** The sequence is arithmetic. The common difference is $d = (4-2) = (6-4) = \ldots = (10-8) = 2$.

b. The sequence is geometric. The common ratio is $r = \dfrac{4}{2} = \dfrac{8}{4} = \ldots = \dfrac{32}{16} = 2$.

c. The sequence is neither arithmetic nor geometric.

2. **a.** The sequence is arithmetic with a common difference of $d = 0$.
It is also geometric with a common ratio of $r = 1$.

b. The sequence is arithmetic. The common difference is $d = (3-7) = (-1-3) = \ldots = (-9-(-5)) = -4$.

c. The sequence is geometric. The common ratio is $r = \dfrac{-5}{5} = \dfrac{5}{-5} = \dfrac{-5}{5} = \ldots = \dfrac{5}{-5} = -1$.

3. The sequence is defined by
$$a_n = 0.90(a_{n-1}); \quad a_1 = 100$$
$100, 90, 81, 72.9, 65.61, 59.049, \ldots$

4. **a.** $f(0) = 9^0 = 1$

b. $f(-1) = 9^{-1} = \dfrac{1}{9}$

c. $f(2) = 9^2 = 81$

d. $f\left(\dfrac{1}{2}\right) = 9^{1/2} = \sqrt{9} = 3$

5. **a.** **b.**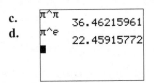
  c. **d.**

6. The graph in **B** is not a function since it does not satisfy the vertical line test.

7. The graph in **C** is a function of x but not a one-to-one function since it does not satisfy the horizontal line test.

8. The graph in **A** is a one-to-one function in x since it satisfies the horizontal and vertical line tests.

9. a.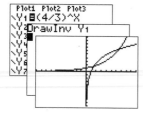

b.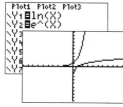

10. Verbally: f^{-1} increases x by 2 then takes a third of the quantity.

Algebraically: $f^{-1}(x) = \dfrac{x+2}{3}$

11. Verbally: f^{-1} decreases x by 6 then quadruples the quantity.

Algebraically: $f^{-1}(x) = 4(x-6)$

12. $f^{-1} = \{(-5,-4),(-3,-3),(3,0),(7,2),(9,3)\}$

13. $f^{-1} = \{(0,-2),(2,-1),(4,0),(6,1),(8,2),(10,3)\}$

14. First, replace $f(x)$ with y.

$$f(x) = \frac{1}{3}x - 4$$

$$y = \frac{1}{3}x - 4$$

Next, exchange x and y, then solve for y.

$$x = \frac{1}{3}y - 4$$

$$x + 4 = \frac{1}{3}y$$

$$y = 3(x+4)$$

Rewrite the inverse using functional notation.

$$f^{-1}(x) = 3(x+4)$$

15. First, replace $f(x)$ with y.

$$f(x) = 3^x$$

$$y = 3^x$$

Next, exchange x and y, then solve for y.

$$x = 3^y$$

$$y = \log_3 x$$

Rewrite the inverse using functional notation.

$$f^{-1}(x) = \log_3 x$$

16. a. x represents the number of pizzas produced.

b. First, replace $C(x)$ with y.

$$C(x) = 2x + 250$$

$$y = 2x + 250$$

Next, exchange x and y, then solve for y.

$$x = 2y + 250$$

$$x - 250 = 2y$$

$$y = \frac{x - 250}{2}$$

Rewrite the inverse using functional notation.

$$C^{-1}(x) = \frac{x - 250}{2}$$

c. x represents the cost in $C^{-1}(x)$.

d. $C^{-1}(x)$ represents the number of pizzas that can be produced for x dollars.

e. $C(100) = 2(100) + 250 = \$450$

f. $C^{-1}(398) = \dfrac{398 - 250}{2} = 74$ pizzas

17.

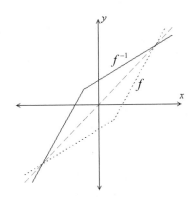

18.

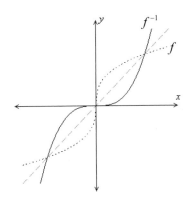

19. **a.** $\log_6 \sqrt{6} = \dfrac{1}{2}$ is equilalent to $6^{1/2} = \sqrt{6}$

b. $\log_{17} 1 = 0$ is equilalent to $17^0 = 1$

c. $\log_8 \dfrac{1}{64} = -2$ is equilalent to $8^{-2} = \dfrac{1}{64}$

20. **a.** $\log_b a = c$ is equilalent to $b^c = a$

b. $\ln a = c$ is equilalent to $e^c = a$

c. $\log c = d$ is equilalent to $10^d = c$

21. **a.** $7^3 = 343$ is equilalent to $\log_7 343 = 3$

b. $19^{1/3} = \sqrt[3]{19}$ is equilalent to $\log_{19} \sqrt[3]{19} = \dfrac{1}{3}$

c. $\left(\dfrac{4}{7}\right)^{-2} = \dfrac{49}{16}$ is equilalent to $\log_{4/7}\left(\dfrac{49}{16}\right) = -2$

22. **a.** $e^{-1} = \dfrac{1}{e}$ is equilalent to $\ln\left(\dfrac{1}{e}\right) = -1$

b. $10^{-4} = 0.0001$ is equilalent to $\log(0.0001) = -4$

c. $8^x = y$ is equilalent to $\log_8 y = x$

23. **a.** $\log_{12} 144 = 2 \quad \left(\text{since } 12^2 = 144\right)$

b. $\log_{12} \sqrt{12} = \dfrac{1}{2} \quad \left(\text{since } 12^{1/2} = \sqrt{12}\right)$

c. $\log_{12} \dfrac{1}{12} = -1 \quad \left(\text{since } 12^{-1} = \dfrac{1}{12}\right)$

24. **a.** $\log_{12} 1 = 0 \quad \left(\text{since } 12^0 = 1\right)$

b. $\log_{12} 12^{0.23} = 0.23 \quad \left(\text{since } 12^{0.23} = 12^{0.23}\right)$

c. $\log_{12} \dfrac{1}{\sqrt[3]{12}} = -\dfrac{1}{3} \quad \left(\text{since } 12^{-1/3} = \dfrac{1}{\sqrt[3]{12}}\right)$

25. **a.**
b.
```
e^(7.83)
           2514.929
10^7.83
         67608297.54
■
```

26. **a.**
b.
```
e^(-2.4)
              .091
10^-2.4
              .004
■
```

27. **a.**
b.
```
log(113.58)
            2.055
ln(113.58)
            4.733
■
```

28. **a.**
b.
```
log(8.1E-4)
           -3.092
ln(8.1E-4)
           -7.118
■
```

29. **a.**
b.
```
ln(23)/ln(19)
            1.065
ln(23/19)
            .191
■
```

30. **a.**
b.
```
ln(6+5)
            2.398
ln(6)+ln(5)
            3.401
■
```

31.
```
log(50)/log(7)
             2.010
log(63)/log(4)
             2.989
■
```
32.

33. $11^x = \dfrac{1}{121}$

$11^x = 11^{-2}$

$x = -2$

34. $125^x = 25$

$\left(5^3\right)^x = 5^2$

$5^{3x} = 5^2$

$3x = 2$

$x = \dfrac{2}{3}$

35. $2^y = \sqrt[3]{4}$

$2^y = 4^{1/3}$

$2^y = \left(2^2\right)^{1/3}$

$2^y = 2^{2/3}$

$y = \dfrac{2}{3}$

36. $\left(\dfrac{4}{9}\right)^y = \dfrac{3}{2}$

$\left(\left(\dfrac{3}{2}\right)^{-2}\right)^y = \dfrac{3}{2}$

$\left(\dfrac{3}{2}\right)^{-2y} = \left(\dfrac{3}{2}\right)^1$

$-2y = 1$

$y = -\dfrac{1}{2}$

37. $2^{4w-1} = 8$

$2^{4w-1} = 2^3$

$4w - 1 = 3$

$4w = 4$

$w = 1$

38. $9^{2v+1} = 27$

$\left(3^2\right)^{2v+1} = 3^3$

$3^{2(2v+1)} = 3^3$

$4v + 2 = 3$

$4v = 1$

$v = \dfrac{1}{4}$

39. $2^{x^2-1} = 8$

$2^{x^2-1} = 2^3$

$x^2 - 1 = 3$

$x^2 = 4$

$x = \pm 2$

40. $9^{x^2} = 3^{x+1}$

$\left(3^2\right)^{x^2} = 3^{x+1}$

$3^{2x^2} = 3^{x+1}$

$2x^2 = x + 1$

$2x^2 - x - 1 = 0$

$(2x + 1)(x - 1) = 0$

$x = -\dfrac{1}{2}$ or $x = 1$

41. $\log_8 64 = z$ is equivalent to $8^z = 64$

$$8^z = 8^2$$
$$z = 2$$

42. $\log_{16} 64 = x$ is equivalent to $16^x = 64$

$$\left(2^4\right)^x = 2^6$$
$$2^{4x} = 2^6$$
$$4x = 6$$
$$x = \frac{3}{2}$$

43. $\log_2 x = 2$ is equivalent to $2^2 = x$

$$x = 4$$

44. $\log_{13} x = \frac{1}{2}$ is equivalent to $13^{1/2} = x$

$$x = \sqrt{13}$$

45. $\log_3 w = -2$ is equivalent to $3^{-2} = w$

$$w = \frac{1}{9}$$

46. $\log_3 (-2) = w$ has no solution. $\log_3 (-2)$ is undefined.

47. $\log_{-2} 3 = y$ has no solution. $\log_{-2} 3$ is undefined.

48. $\log_t 169 = 2$ is equivalent to $t^2 = 169$

$$t = 13$$

(The base of a logarithm must be positive.)

49. $\log_t 8 = -3$ is equivalent to $t^{-3} = 8$

$$\left(t^{-3}\right)^{-1/3} = (8)^{-1/3}$$
$$t = \frac{1}{2}$$

50. $5^{\log_5 11} = x$

$$x = 11$$

51. $\log_5 5^{17} = x$

$$x = 17$$

52. $\log_7 x = 1$ is equivalent to $x = 7^1$

$$x = 7$$

53. $\ln 0 = x$ has no solution. $\ln 0$ is undefined.

54. $\log(3n - 4) = \log(2n - 1)$

$$3n - 4 = 2n - 1$$
$$n = 3$$

55. $\log_3 20 + \log_3 7 = \log_3 y$

$$\log_3 (20)(7) = \log_3 y$$
$$y = 140$$

56. $\log(3x + 1) = 2$

$$3x + 1 = 10^2$$
$$3x = 99$$
$$x = 33$$

57. $\log_3 \left(x^2 - 19\right) = 4$

$$x^2 - 19 = 3^4$$
$$x^2 - 19 = 81$$
$$x^2 = 100$$
$$x = \pm 10$$

58.
$$\ln(w+2)+\ln w = \ln 3$$
$$\ln(w+2)w = \ln 3$$
$$(w+2)w = 3$$
$$w^2 + 2w = 3$$
$$w^2 + 2w - 3 = 0$$
$$(w+3)(w-1) = 0$$
$$w = -3 \quad \text{or} \quad w = 1$$

$w = -3$ is an extraneous solution since it makes the argument in one of the logarithms negative. Thus the solution is $w = 1$.

59.
$$\ln(1-w)+\ln(1-2w) = \ln(7-4w)$$
$$\ln(1-w)(1-2w) = \ln(7-4w)$$
$$(1-w)(1-2w) = 7-4w$$
$$1-3w+2w^2 = 7-4w$$
$$2w^2 + w - 6 = 0$$
$$(2w-3)(w+2) = 0$$
$$w = \frac{3}{2} \quad \text{or} \quad w = -2$$

$w = \frac{3}{2}$ is an extraneous solution since it makes the argument in one of the logarithms negative. Thus the solution is $w = -2$.

60.
$$\log(5-2v) - \log(1-v) = \log(3-2v)$$
$$\log\left(\frac{5-2v}{1-v}\right) = \log(3-2v)$$
$$\frac{5-2v}{1-v} = 3-2v$$
$$5-2v = (3-2v)(1-v)$$
$$5-2v = 3-5v+2v^2$$
$$2v^2 - 3v - 2 = 0$$
$$(2v+1)(v-2) = 0$$
$$v = -\frac{1}{2} \quad \text{or} \quad v = 2$$

$v = 2$ is an extraneous solution since it makes the argument in one of the logarithms negative. Thus the solution is $v = -\frac{1}{2}$.

61.
$$\ln(5v+3) = \ln(3v+9)$$
$$5v+3 = 3v+9$$
$$2v = 6$$
$$v = 3$$

62.
$$\log_5 27 - \log_5 2 = \log_5 y$$
$$\log_5 \frac{27}{2} = \log_5 y$$
$$y = \frac{27}{2}$$

63. $\log(2-6v) - \log(2-v) = \log(1-v)$

$$\log\left(\frac{2-6v}{2-v}\right) = \log(1-v)$$

$$\frac{2-6v}{2-v} = 1-v$$

$$2-6v = (1-v)(2-v)$$

$$2-6v = 2-3v+v^2$$

$$v^2 + 3v = 0$$

$$v(v+3) = 0$$

$$v = 0 \quad \text{or} \quad v = -3$$

64. $\ln(5-x) + \ln(x+1) = \ln(3x-1)$

$$\ln(5-x)(x+1) = \ln(3x-1)$$

$$(5-x)(x+1) = 3x-1$$

$$-x^2 + 4x + 5 = 3x - 1$$

$$x^2 - x - 6 = 0$$

$$(x-3)(x+2) = 0$$

$$x = 3 \quad \text{or} \quad x = -2$$

$x = -2$ is an extraneous solution since it makes the argument in a logarithm negative. Thus the solution is $x = 3$.

65. $\log x + \log(x-9) = 1$

$$\log x(x-9) = 1$$

$$x(x-9) = 10^1$$

$$x^2 - 9x - 10 = 0$$

$$(x-10)(x+1) = 0$$

$$x = 10 \quad \text{or} \quad x = -1$$

$x = -1$ is an extraneous solution since it makes the argument in a logarithm negative. Thus the solution is $x = 10$.

66. $\log_2 x + \log_2(x-2) = 3$

$$\log_2 x(x-2) = 3$$

$$x(x-2) = 2^3$$

$$x^2 - 2x - 8 = 0$$

$$(x-4)(x+2) = 0$$

$$x = 4 \quad \text{or} \quad x = -2$$

$x = -2$ is an extraneous solution since it makes the argument in a logarithm negative. Thus the solution is $x = 4$.

67. $\log x^3 y^5 = \log x^3 + \log y^5$
$$= 3\log x + 5\log y$$

68. $\ln\dfrac{7x-9}{2x+3} = \ln(7x-9) - \ln(2x+3)$

69. $\ln\dfrac{\sqrt{2x+1}}{5x+9} = \ln\sqrt{2x+1} - \ln(5x+9)$

$$= \ln(2x+1)^{1/2} - \ln(5x+9)$$

$$= \frac{1}{2}\ln(2x+1) - \ln(5x+9)$$

70. $\log\sqrt{\dfrac{x^2 y^3}{z}} = \log\left(\dfrac{x^2 y^3}{z}\right)^{1/2} = \dfrac{1}{2}\log\left(\dfrac{x^2 y^3}{z}\right)$

$$= \frac{1}{2}\left[\log(x^2 y^3) - \log z\right]$$

$$= \frac{1}{2}\left(\log x^2 + \log y^3 - \log z\right)$$

$$= \frac{1}{2}\left(2\log x + 3\log y - \log z\right)$$

71. $2\ln x + 3\ln y = \ln x^2 + \ln y^3 = \ln\left(x^2 y^3\right)$

72. $5\ln x - 4\ln y = \ln x^5 - \ln y^4 = \ln\dfrac{x^5}{y^4}$

73. $\ln(x^2 - 3x - 4) - \ln(x-4)$

$$= \ln\left(\frac{x^2 - 3x - 4}{x-4}\right)$$

$$= \ln\left(\frac{(x-4)(x+1)}{x-4}\right) = \ln(x+1) \text{ for } x > 4$$

74. $\dfrac{1}{2}(\ln x - \ln y) = \dfrac{1}{2}\ln\dfrac{x}{y} = \ln\left(\dfrac{x}{y}\right)^{1/2} = \ln\sqrt{\dfrac{x}{y}}$

75.
$$\log(5x-2)+\log(x-1)=\log 10$$
$$\log(5x-2)(x-1)=\log 10$$
$$(5x-2)(x-1)=10$$
$$5x^2-7x+2=10$$
$$5x^2-7x-8=0$$
$$a=5,\quad b=-7,\quad c=-8$$
$$x=\frac{-(-7)\pm\sqrt{(-7)^2-4(5)(-8)}}{2(5)}=\frac{7\pm\sqrt{209}}{10}$$
$$x\approx 2.146\quad\text{or}\quad x\approx -0.746$$

$x\approx -0.746$ is an extraneous solution since it makes the argument in a logarithm negative. Thus the solution is $x\approx 2.146$.

76.
$$\ln(2w+3)+\ln(w+1)=\ln(w+2)$$
$$\ln(2w+3)(w+1)=\ln(w+2)$$
$$(2w+3)(w+1)=w+2$$
$$2w^2+5w+3=w+2$$
$$2w^2+4w+1=0$$
$$a=2,\quad b=4,\quad c=1$$
$$x=\frac{-(4)\pm\sqrt{(4)^2-4(2)(1)}}{2(2)}=\frac{-2\pm\sqrt{2}}{2}$$
$$x\approx -0.293\quad\text{or}\quad x\approx -1.707$$

$x\approx -1.707$ is an extraneous solution since it makes the argument in a logarithm negative. Thus the solution is $x\approx -0.293$.

77. $y=5^x=e^{x\ln 5}$

78.
$$\log 50^x+\log 6^x-\log 3^x$$
$$=x\log 50+x\log 6-x\log 3$$
$$=x(\log 50+\log 6-\log 3)$$
$$=x\log\left(\frac{50\cdot 6}{3}\right)=x\log 100$$
$$=x(2)=2x$$

79. $1000^{\log x}=\left(10^3\right)^{\log x}=10^{3\log x}=10^{\log\left(x^3\right)}=x^3$

	Problem	Mental Estimate	Calculator Approximation
80.	$\log 990$	$\log 990\approx\log 1000=3$	$\log 990\approx 2.996$
81.	$\ln 3$	$\ln 3\approx\ln 2.718\approx\ln e=1$	$\ln 3\approx 1.099$
82.	$\log_3 30$	$\log_3 30\approx\log_3 27=3$	$\log_3 30\approx 3.096$
83.	$\log_5 120$	$\log_5 120\approx\log_5 125=3$	$\log_5 120\approx 2.975$

84. **a.** $f(3)=5(3)-2=15-2=13$

b. $f^{-1}(13)=3\quad\left(\text{since } f(3)=13\right)$

c. $\dfrac{1}{f(3)}=\dfrac{1}{13}$

85. A linear growth function is shown in graph **D**.
86. A logarithmic growth function is shown in graph **E**.
87. An exponential growth function is shown in graph **C**.
88. An exponential decay function is shown in graph **B**.
89. A constant function is shown in graph **A**.

90. **a.** Use $A=P\left(1+\dfrac{r}{n}\right)^{nt}$.

Substitute $P=2000$, $r=0.08$, $n=1$, and $t=5$

$$A=2000\left(1+\frac{0.08}{1}\right)^{(1)(5)}\approx\$2938.66$$

b. Use $A=P\left(1+\dfrac{r}{n}\right)^{nt}$.

Substitute $P=2000$, $r=0.08$, $n=12$, and $t=5$

$$A=2000\left(1+\frac{0.08}{12}\right)^{(12)(5)}\approx\$2979.69$$

90. **c.** Use $A = Pe^{rt}$.

Substitute $P = 2000$, $r = 0.08$, and $t = 5$

$A = Pe^{rt} = 2000e^{(0.08)(5)} \approx \$2983.65$

91. Use $A = Pe^{rt}$. Substitute

$A = \dfrac{1}{100}P$, $r = -0.00045$, and solve for t.

$\dfrac{1}{100}P = Pe^{(-0.00045)t}$

$\dfrac{0.01\cancel{P}}{\cancel{P}} = \dfrac{\cancel{P}e^{-0.00045t}}{\cancel{P}}$

$0.01 = e^{-0.00045t}$

$-0.00045t = \ln 0.01$

$t = \dfrac{\ln 0.01}{-0.00045} \approx 10,200$ days

92. Use $A = P\left(1 + \dfrac{r}{n}\right)^{nt}$.

Substitute $A = 2P$, $r = 0.075$, $n = 1$, and solve for t.

$2P = P\left(1 + \dfrac{0.075}{1}\right)^{(1)t}$

$\dfrac{2\cancel{P}}{\cancel{P}} = \dfrac{\cancel{P}(1.075)^{t}}{\cancel{P}}$

$2 = 1.075^{t}$

$\ln 2 = \ln 1.075^{t}$

$\ln 2 = t \ln 1.075$

$t = \dfrac{\ln 2}{\ln 1.075} \approx 9.6$ years

93. Use $A = Pe^{rt}$. Substitute $A = 2P$, $t = 8$, and solve for r.

$2P = Pe^{r(8)}$

$\dfrac{2\cancel{P}}{\cancel{P}} = \dfrac{\cancel{P}e^{8r}}{\cancel{P}}$

$2 = e^{8r}$

$8r = \ln 2$

$r = \dfrac{\ln 2}{8} \approx 0.087$ or 8.7%

94. Use $R = \log \dfrac{A}{a}$. Substitute $A = 6310000a$

$R = \log \dfrac{6310000\cancel{a}}{\cancel{a}} \approx 6.8$

95. **a.** $B(0) = 3.0e^{0.29(0)} = 3.0$; Initially, there are 3 units of bacteria present.

b. $B(5) = 3.0e^{0.29(5)} \approx 12.8$; After 5 days, there are 12.8 units of bacteria present.

c. $B(10) = 3.0e^{0.29(10)} \approx 54.5$; After 10 days, there are 54.5 units of bacteria present.

d. Solve the following equation for t.

$$B(t) = 100$$

$$3.0e^{0.29t} = 100$$

$$e^{0.29t} = \left(\dfrac{100}{3}\right)$$

$$0.29t = \ln\left(\dfrac{100}{3}\right)$$

$$t = \dfrac{\ln\left(\dfrac{100}{3}\right)}{0.29} \approx 12.1 \text{ days}$$

There will be 100 units of bacteria present after 12.1 days.

Mastery Test for Chapter 11

1. **a.** The sequence is geometric. The common ratio is $r = \dfrac{5}{1} = \dfrac{25}{5} = \ldots = \dfrac{625}{125} = 5$.

   b. The sequence is not geometric. It is arithmetic. The common difference is
   $d = (5-1) = (9-5) = \ldots = (17-13) = 4$.

   c. The sequence is geometric. The common ratio is $r = \dfrac{24}{48} = \dfrac{12}{24} = \ldots = \dfrac{3}{6} = \dfrac{1}{2}$.

   d. The sequence is geometric. The common ratio is $r = \dfrac{0.09}{0.9} = \dfrac{0.009}{0.09} = \ldots = \dfrac{0.00009}{0.0009} = 0.10$.

2. **a.**

   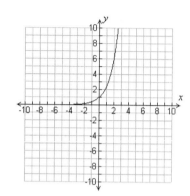

   b.

   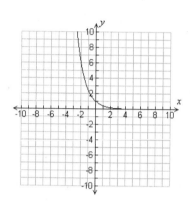

   c. $f(-1) = 16^{-1} = \dfrac{1}{16}$

   d. $f\left(\dfrac{1}{2}\right) = 16^{\frac{1}{2}} = \sqrt{16} = 4$

3. **a.** $6^x = 36$ **b.** $6^x = 1$ **c.** $6^x = \dfrac{1}{6}$ **d.** $6^x = \sqrt[5]{6}$

   $6^x = 6^2$ $6^x = 6^0$ $6^x = 6^{-1}$ $6^x = 6^{1/5}$

   $x = 2$ $x = 0$ $x = -1$ $x = \dfrac{1}{5}$

4. **a.** $f^{-1} = \{(4,-1),(9,8),(11,-7)\}$

   b. First, replace $f(x)$ with y.
   $$f(x) = 3x - 6$$
   $$y = 3x - 6$$
   Next, exchange x and y, then solve for y.
   $$x = 3y - 6$$
   $$x + 6 = 3y$$
   $$y = \dfrac{1}{3}(x+6)$$
   Rewrite the inverse using functional notation.
   $$f^{-1}(x) = \dfrac{x+6}{3}$$

   c. $f^{-1} = \{(-1,-2),(0,-1),(1,0),(2,1),(-2,3)\}$

   d. $f^{-1} = \left\{\left(2,\dfrac{1}{2}\right),\left(3,\dfrac{1}{3}\right),\left(\dfrac{1}{6},6\right),(1,1)\right\}$

5. **a.** The function is one-to-one since no two distinct ordered pairs have the same y-value.

      b. The function is not one-to-one since there are distinct ordered pairs that have the same y-value.

      c. The function is not one-to-one since it fails the horizontal line test.

      d. The function is one-to-one since it passes the horizontal line test.

6. **a.**

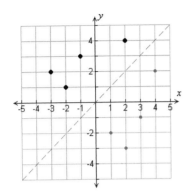

      b.

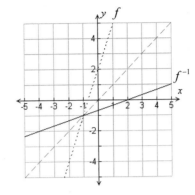

7. **a.** $\log_5 \sqrt[3]{25} = \dfrac{2}{3}$ is equilalent to $5^{2/3} = \sqrt[3]{25}$

      b. $\log_5 \dfrac{1}{125} = -3$ is equilalent to $5^{-3} = \dfrac{1}{125}$

      c. $\log_b (y+1) = x$ is equilalent to $b^x = y+1$

      d. $\log_b x = y+1$ is equilalent to $b^{y+1} = x$

8. **a.** $\log_8 1 = 0 \quad \left(\text{since } 8^0 = 1\right)$

      b. $\log_8 8 = 1 \quad \left(\text{since } 8^1 = 8\right)$

      c. $\log_8 \dfrac{1}{8} = -1 \quad \left(\text{since } 8^{-1} = \dfrac{1}{8}\right)$

      d. $\log_8 8^{17} = 17 \quad \left(\text{since } 8^{17} = 8^{17}\right)$

9.

x	$\log_5 x$
0.2	-1
1	0
5	1
25	2

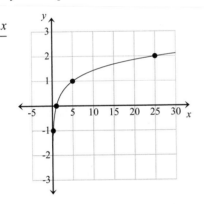

10. **a.**
        b.

```
log(19.1)
           1.2810
ln(19.1)
           2.9497
■
```

      c.
      d.

```
log(4.876E12)
           12.6881
ln(3.04E-5)
          -10.4011
```

11. **a.** $\log x^4 y^5 = \log x^4 + \log y^5$
$$= 4\log x + 5\log y$$

      b. $\ln \dfrac{x^3}{\sqrt{y}} = \ln x^3 - \ln \sqrt{y} = \ln x^3 - \ln y^{1/2}$
$$= 3\ln x - \dfrac{1}{2}\ln y$$

      c. $2\ln(7x+9) - \ln x = \ln(7x+9)^2 - \ln x$
$$= \ln \dfrac{(7x+9)^2}{x}$$

      d. $\dfrac{1}{2}\log(x+3) + \ln x = \log(x+3)^{1/2} + \ln x$
$$= \log \sqrt{x+3} + \ln x$$
$$= \log x\sqrt{x+3}$$

12. **a.**
b.

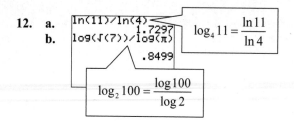

$$\log_4 11 = \frac{\ln 11}{\ln 4}$$

$$\log_2 100 = \frac{\log 100}{\log 2}$$

c.
d.

$$\log_\pi \sqrt{7} = \frac{\log \sqrt{7}}{\log \pi}$$

$$\log_\pi 5\pi = \frac{\log 5\pi}{\log \pi}$$

13. **a.** $3^x = \dfrac{1}{81}$

$3^x = 3^{-4}$

$x = -4$

b. $16^w = 64$

$\left(2^4\right)^w = 2^6$

$2^{4w} = 2^6$

$4w = 6$

$w = \dfrac{6}{4} = \dfrac{3}{2}$

c. $\log_2 x = 4$

$2^4 = x$

$x = 16$

d. $\log_8 2 = y$

$8^y = 2$

$\left(2^3\right)^y = 2^1$

$2^{3y} = 2^1$

$3y = 1$

$y = \dfrac{1}{3}$

e. $\log(1-4t) - \log(5+t) = \log 3$

$\log\left(\dfrac{1-4t}{5+t}\right) = \log 3$

$\dfrac{1-4t}{5+t} = 3$

$1-4t = 3(5+t)$

$1-4t = 15+3t$

$-7t = 14$

$t = -2$

f. $\ln(1-z) + \ln(2-z) = \ln(17-z)$

$\ln(1-z)(2-z) = \ln(17-z)$

$(1-z)(2-z) = 17-z$

$2-3z+z^2 = 17-z$

$z^2 - 2z - 15 = 0$

$(z-5)(z+3) = 0$

$z = 5 \quad \text{or} \quad z = -3$

$z = 5$ is an extraneous solution since it makes the argument in one of the logarithms negative. Thus the solution is $z = -3$.

g.
$$3^{4y+1} = 17.83$$
$$\ln 3^{4y+1} = \ln 17.83$$
$$(4y+1)\ln 3 = \ln 17.83$$
$$4y\ln 3 + \ln 3 = \ln 17.83$$
$$4y\ln 3 = \ln 17.83 - \ln 3$$
$$y = \frac{\ln 17.83 - \ln 3}{4\ln 3} = 0.406$$

h.
$$\ln(x+1) + \ln(3x-1) = \ln(6x)$$
$$\ln(x+1)(3x-1) = \ln(6x)$$
$$(x+1)(3x-1) = 6x$$
$$3x^2 + 2x - 1 = 6x$$
$$3x^2 - 4x - 1 = 0$$
$$a = 3, \quad b = -4, \quad c = -1$$
$$x = \frac{-(-4) \pm \sqrt{(-4)^2 - 4(3)(-1)}}{2(3)} = \frac{2 \pm \sqrt{7}}{3}$$
$$x \approx 1.549 \quad \text{or} \quad x \approx -0.215$$

$x \approx -0.215$ is an extraneous solution since it makes the argument in one of the logarithms negative. Thus the solution is $z \approx 1.549$

14. a. Use $A = Pe^{rt}$. Substitute
$P = 500, \ A = 3000, \ r = 0.05$, and solve for t.
$$3000 = 500e^{(0.05)t}$$
$$3000 = 500e^{0.05t}$$
$$6 = e^{0.05t}$$
$$0.05t = \ln 6$$
$$t = \frac{\ln 6}{0.05} \approx 35.8 \text{ years}$$

b. Use $A = P\left(1 + \dfrac{r}{n}\right)^{nt}$.

Substitute $A = 2P, \ r = 0.0825, \ n = 12$, and solve for t.
$$2P = P\left(1 + \frac{0.0825}{12}\right)^{(12)t}$$
$$\frac{2\cancel{P}}{\cancel{P}} = \frac{\cancel{P}(1.0069)^{12t}}{\cancel{P}}$$
$$2 = 1.0069^{12t}$$
$$\ln 2 = \ln 1.0069^{12t}$$
$$\ln 2 = 12t\ln 1.0069$$
$$t = \frac{\ln 2}{12\ln 1.0069} \approx 8.4 \text{ years}$$

Comprehensive Review of Intermediate Algebra

1. **a.** From the graph we can see that the zeros are $x=-1$, $x=3$, and $x=5$. Thus the factors are $(x+1)$, $(x-3)$, and $(x-5)$ and the factored form of $P(x)$ is $P(x)=(x+1)(x-3)(x-5)$.

   b. From the graph we can see that the zeros are $x=-5$ and $x=-3$. Thus the factors are $(x+5)$ and $(x+3)$ and the factored form of the polynomial is $x^2+8x+15=(x+3)(x+5)$.

2. **a.** $14x^3-35x^2=7x^2(2x-5)$

   b. $5x(2x-3)-6(2x-3)=(2x-3)(5x-6)$

3. **a.** $2ax+10bx+3ay+15by$
   $=2x(a+5b)+3y(a+5b)$
   $=(a+5b)(2x+3y)$

   b. $8x^2-24x-5x+15$
   $=8x(x-3)-5(x-3)$
   $=(x-3)(8x-5)$

4. **a.** $x^2+4x-45$
   $=x^2+9x-5x-45$
   $=x(x+9)-5(x+9)$
   $=(x+9)(x-5)$

   b. $x^2-10x-24$
   $=x^2-12x+2x-24$
   $=x(x-12)+2(x-12)$
   $=(x+2)(x-12)$

5. **a.** $6x^2-17x-10$
   $=6x^2+3x-20x-10$
   $=3x(2x+1)-10(2x+1)$
   $=(2x+1)(3x-10)$

   b. $6x^2-13x-10$ is prime.

6. **a.** $x^2+20x+100$
   $=(x)^2+2x(10)+(10)^2$
   $=(x+10)^2$

   b. $x^2-14xy+49y^2$
   $=(x)^2-2x(7y)+(7y)^2$
   $=(x-7y)^2$

7. **a.** x^2-64
   $=(x)^2-(8)^2$
   $=(x+8)(x-8)$

   b. x^3-64
   $=(x)^3-(4)^3$
   $=(x-4)((x)^2+4x+(4)^2)$
   $=(x-4)(x^2+4x+16)$

8. **a.** $a^2-b^2+5a-5b$
   $=(a^2-b^2)+5(a-b)$
   $=(a+b)(a-b)+5(a-b)$
   $=(a-b)[(a+b)+5]$
   $=(a-b)(a+b+5)$

   b. $a^2-x^2+10x-25$
   $=a^2-(x^2-10x+25)$
   $=a^2-(x-5)^2$
   $=[a+(x-5)][a-(x-5)]$
   $=(a+x-5)(a-x+5)$

9. **a.** $5x^2-80=5(x^2-16)=5(x+4)(x-4)$

   b. $-3ax^2+21ax-18a=-3a(x^2-7x+6)$
   $=-3a(x-6)(x+1)$

10. a. $2x^2 + 13x - 24 = 0$

$(x+8)(2x-3) = 0$

$x+8 = 0$ or $2x-3 = 0$

$x = -8$ $2x = 3$

$$x = \frac{3}{2}$$

b. $(x+3)(x-7) = 24$

$x^2 - 4x - 21 = 24$

$x^2 - 4x - 45 = 0$

$(x+5)(x-9) = 0$

$x+5 = 0$ or $x-9 = 0$

$x = -5$ $x = 9$

11. a. $\sqrt{72} = \sqrt{36}\sqrt{2} = 6\sqrt{2}$

b. $\sqrt{500} = \sqrt{100}\sqrt{5} = 10\sqrt{5}$

12. a. $\sqrt{\dfrac{4}{25}} = \dfrac{\sqrt{4}}{\sqrt{25}} = \dfrac{2}{5}$

b. $\dfrac{\sqrt{32}}{\sqrt{8}} = \sqrt{\dfrac{32}{8}} = \sqrt{4} = 2$

13. a. $\dfrac{12}{\sqrt{3}} = \dfrac{12}{\sqrt{3}} \cdot \dfrac{\sqrt{3}}{\sqrt{3}} = \dfrac{\overset{4}{\cancel{12}}\sqrt{3}}{\cancel{3}} = 4\sqrt{3}$

b. $\dfrac{\sqrt{3}}{\sqrt{5}} = \dfrac{\sqrt{3}}{\sqrt{5}} \cdot \dfrac{\sqrt{5}}{\sqrt{5}} = \dfrac{\sqrt{15}}{5}$

14. a. $(2x-3)^2 = 7$

$\sqrt{(2x-3)^2} = \pm\sqrt{7}$

$2x-3 = \pm\sqrt{7}$

$2x = 3 \pm \sqrt{7}$

$$x = \frac{3 \pm \sqrt{7}}{2} = \frac{3}{2} \pm \frac{\sqrt{7}}{2}$$

b. $(3x-4)^2 = -9$

$\sqrt{(3x-4)^2} = \pm\sqrt{-9}$

$3x-4 = \pm 3i$

$3x = 4 \pm 3i$

$$x = \frac{4 \pm 3i}{3}$$

$$x = \frac{4}{3} \pm \frac{3i}{3}$$

$$x = \frac{4}{3} \pm i$$

15. a. $x^2 - 10x - 3 = 0$

$x^2 - 10x = 3$

$x^2 - 10x + 25 = 3 + 25$

$(x-5)^2 = 28$

$x - 5 = \pm\sqrt{28} = \pm\sqrt{4}\sqrt{7}$

$x = 5 \pm 2\sqrt{7}$

$x \approx -0.29$ or $x \approx 10.29$

b. $2x^2 - 5x = 6$

$\dfrac{2x^2}{2} - \dfrac{5x}{2} = \dfrac{6}{2}$

$x^2 - \dfrac{5}{2}x = 3$

$x^2 - \dfrac{5}{2}x + \dfrac{25}{16} = 3 + \dfrac{25}{16}$

$\left(x - \dfrac{5}{4}\right)^2 = \dfrac{73}{16}$

$x - \dfrac{5}{4} = \pm\sqrt{\dfrac{73}{16}}$

$x = \dfrac{5}{4} \pm \dfrac{\sqrt{73}}{4}$

$x = \dfrac{5 \pm \sqrt{73}}{4}$

$x \approx -0.87$ or $x \approx 3.39$

16. **a.** $b^2 - 4ac = (3)^2 - 4(4)(-2) = 9 + 32 = 41 > 0$; The equation has two distinct real solutions.

b. First rewrite the equation: $2x^2 - 6x - 1 = -8$

$$2x^2 - 6x + 7 = 0$$

$b^2 - 4ac = (-6)^2 - 4(2)(7) = 36 - 56 = -20 < 0$; The equation has two imaginary solutions that are complex conjugates.

c. First rewrite the equation: $4x^2 - 12x = -9$

$$4x^2 - 12x + 9 = 0$$

$b^2 - 4ac = (-12)^2 - 4(4)(9) = 144 - 144 = 0$; The equation has a double real solution.

17. **a.**
$$4x^2 - 3x + 2 = 0$$
Substitute a, b, and c in the quadratic formula.
$$a = 4, \quad b = -3, \quad c = 2$$
$$x = \frac{-(-3) \pm \sqrt{(-3)^2 - 4(4)(2)}}{2(4)}$$
$$= \frac{3 \pm \sqrt{9 - 32}}{8} = \frac{3 \pm \sqrt{-23}}{8}$$
$$= \frac{3 \pm i\sqrt{23}}{8} = \frac{3}{8} \pm \frac{i\sqrt{23}}{8}$$

b.
$$4x^2 - 36x + 81 = 0$$
Substitute a, b, and c in the quadratic formula.
$$a = 4, \quad b = -36, \quad c = 81$$
$$x = \frac{-(-36) \pm \sqrt{(-36)^2 - 4(4)(81)}}{2(4)}$$
$$= \frac{36 \pm \sqrt{1296 - 1296}}{8} = \frac{36 \pm 0}{8} = \frac{36}{8} = \frac{9}{2}$$

c.
$$3x^2 + 5x - 7 = 0$$
Substitute a, b, and c in the quadratic formula.
$$a = 3, \quad b = 5, \quad c = -7$$
$$x = \frac{-(5) \pm \sqrt{(5)^2 - 4(3)(-7)}}{2(3)}$$
$$= \frac{-5 \pm \sqrt{25 + 84}}{6} = \frac{-5 \pm \sqrt{109}}{6} = \frac{-5}{6} \pm \frac{\sqrt{109}}{6}$$

18.

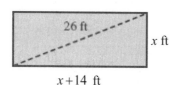

Using the Pythagorean Theorem we have:
$$x^2 + (x + 14)^2 = 26^2$$
$$x^2 + x^2 + 28x + 196 = 676$$
$$2x^2 + 28x - 480 = 0$$
$$2(x^2 + 14x - 240) = 0$$
$$2(x - 10)(x + 24) = 0$$
$$x = 10 \quad \text{or} \quad x = -24$$

Note: This answer is not reasonable.

The width of the room is 10 ft.

19. **a.** $\sqrt{-36} + \sqrt{-64} = 6i + 8i = 14i$

b. $\sqrt{-100} = 10i$

20. a. $(2-3i)(4+7i)$

$= 8 + 14i - 12i - 21i^2$

$= 8 + 2i - 21(-1)$

$= 8 + 2i + 21$

$= 29 + 2i$

b. $\dfrac{29+2i}{2-3i} = \dfrac{(29+2i)}{(2-3i)} \cdot \dfrac{(2+3i)}{(2+3i)} = \dfrac{58 + 87i + 4i + 6i^2}{4 - 9i^2}$

$= \dfrac{58 + 91i + 6(-1)}{4 - 9(-1)} = \dfrac{58 + 91i - 6}{4 + 9}$

$= \dfrac{52 + 91i}{13} = \dfrac{52}{13} + \dfrac{91i}{13} = 4 + 7i$

21. a. No vertical line will cross the function more than once. Thus the graph represents a function.

   b. The vertical line $x = 1$ crosses the graph more than once. Thus the graph does not represent a function.

22. a. This is the horizontal line $y = -3$. The domain of the function is the projection of its graph onto the x-axis.

     Domain $= (-\infty, +\infty)$ or $\mathbb{R}$

     The range of the function is the projection of its graph onto the y-axis. Range $= \{-3\}$

   b. The domain of the function is the projection of its graph onto the x-axis. Domain $= [-2, +\infty)$

     The range of the function is the projection of its graph onto the y-axis. Range $= [-3, +\infty)$

23. a. $f(-2) = 3(-2)^2 + 2(-2) - 4 = 4$ **b.** $f(5) = 3(5)^2 + 2(5) - 4 = 81$

24. a. $f(0) = 2$ **b.** $f(x) = 0;\ x = 3$

25. a. $f(2) = -10$ **b.** $f(x) = 2;\ x = -1$

26. a.

x	$y = 2x - 5$
1	$2(1) - 5 = -3$
2	$2(2) - 5 = -1$
3	$2(3) - 5 = 1$
4	$2(4) - 5 = 3$
5	$2(5) - 5 = 5$

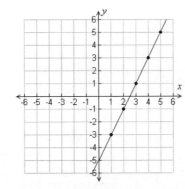

   b.

x	$y = -3x + 4$
1	$-3(1) + 4 = 1$
2	$-3(2) + 4 = -2$
3	$-3(3) + 4 = -5$
4	$-3(4) + 4 = -8$
5	$-3(5) + 4 = -11$

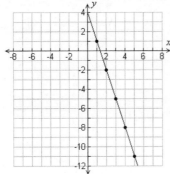

27. a. The x-intercept is the point on the graph that has a y coordinate of 0. Thus, the x-intercept is $(-1, 0)$.

The y-intercept is the point on the graph that has a x coordinate of 0. Thus, the y-intercept is $(0, -3)$.

b. The x-intercept is the point on the graph that has a y coordinate of 0. Thus, the x-intercept is $(10, 0)$.

The y-intercept is the point on the graph that has a x coordinate of 0. Thus, the y-intercept is $(0, 6)$.

c. To find the x-intercept, we let y equal zero and solve for x.

$$2x - 3y = 36$$
$$2x - 3(0) = 36$$
$$2x = 36$$
$$x = 18$$

x-intercept: $(18, 0)$

To find the y-intercept, we let x equal zero and solve for y.

$$2x - 3y = 36$$
$$2(0) - 3y = 36$$
$$-3y = 36$$
$$y = -12$$

y-intercept: $(0, -12)$

28. a. The total cost of running the ice cream shop is the sum of the fixed cost of \$200 and the variable cost of $0.25x$. The total cost is $f(x) = 0.25x + 200$.

b.

x	0	50	100	150	200	250
$f(x)$	200	212.50	225	237.50	250	262.50

c. $f(75) = 0.25(75) + 200 = 218.75$. If the ice cream shop sells 75 ice cream cones in a month, the total operating costs for the month will be \$218.75.

d.
$$f(x) = 260$$
$$0.25x + 200 = 260$$
$$.25x = 60$$
$$x = 240$$

If the ice cream shop sells 240 ice cream cones in a month, the total operating costs for the month will be \$260.

29. a. Use $x_1 = -3$, $y_1 = 5$, $x_2 = 0$, $y_2 = 1$

$$m = \frac{y_2 - y_1}{x_2 - x_1} = \frac{1 - 5}{0 - (-3)} = \frac{-4}{3} = -\frac{4}{3}$$

b. The equation is written in point-slope $y - y_1 = m(x - x_1)$ form. The slope is $m = \frac{2}{3}$.

30. a. Use the slope-intercept form. Substitute $-\frac{5}{3}$ for m and -2 for b.

$$y = mx + b$$
$$y = -\frac{5}{3}x - 2$$

b. Use the point slope form. Substitute $(-2, 4)$ for (x_1, y_1) and $-\frac{3}{2}$ for m (This is the slope of a line perpendicular to one with a slope of $\frac{2}{3}$). Then write the equation in slope intercept form by solving for y. $y - y_1 = m(x - x_1)$

$$y - 4 = -\frac{3}{2}(x - (-2))$$
$$y - 4 = -\frac{3}{2}(x + 2)$$
$$y - 4 = -\frac{3}{2}x - 3$$
$$y = -\frac{3}{2}x + 1$$

31. **a.**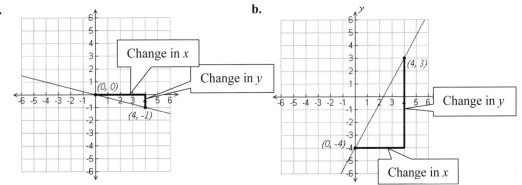

b.

32. **a.** The line has a negative slope. It represents a decreasing function.

    b. The line has a positive slope $(m=4)$. It represents an increasing function.

33. **a.**

x	$f(x)=\|x-2\|-3$
-2	$\|-2-2\|-3=1$
-1	$\|-1-2\|-3=0$
0	$\|0-2\|-3=-1$
1	$\|1-2\|-3=-2$
2	$\|2-2\|-3=-3$
3	$\|3-2\|-3=-2$
4	$\|4-2\|-3=-1$

b.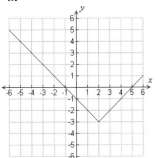

c. x-intercepts: $(-1,0)$ and $(5,0)$

d. y-intercept: $(0,-1)$

e. vertex: $(2,-3)$

f. The minimum value of y is -3.

g. Domain: $(-\infty,+\infty)$ or $\mathbb{R}$

h. Range: $[-3,+\infty)$

i. Interval of decrease: $(-\infty,2)$

j. Interval of increase: $(2,\infty)$

k. $f(x)$ is positive on $(-\infty,-1)\cup(5,+\infty)$

l. $f(x)$ is negative on $(-1,5)$

34. The minimum value of y is $y=-4$ and occurs at $x=-2$.

35. **a.** The leading coefficient is negative. Therfore the parabola will open downward.

    b. To find the x-value of the vertex we use the formula: $x=-\dfrac{b}{2a}=-\dfrac{2}{2(-1)}=1$. To find the y-value of the vertex we evaluate: $f(1)=-(1)^2+2(1)+8=9$.

The vertex is $(1,9)$.

To find the x-intercepts we solve the following equation:
$$-x^2+2x+8=0$$
$$-(x^2-2x-8)=0$$
$$-(x+2)(x-4)=0$$
$$x=-2 \text{ or } x=4$$
The x-intercepts are $(-2,0)$ and $(4,0)$.

c.

x	y
-1	5
0	8
1	9
2	8
3	5

d. To find the y-intercept we evaluate:
$$f(0)=-(0)^2+2(0)+8=8$$
The y-intercept is $(0,8)$.

e.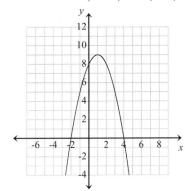

36.

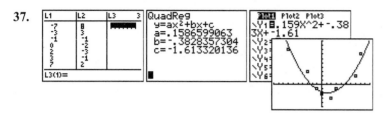

The maximum height of the ball is 59.3 ft and occurs 1.9 seconds after impact.

$[0, 4, 1]$ by $[-10, 70, 10]$

37.

$f(x) = 0.159x^2 - 0.383x - 1.61$

$f(7) = 0.159(7)^2 - 0.383(7) - 1.61 = 3.5$

38. **a.** The excluded values of $f(x) = \dfrac{x-2}{(x-1)(x+3)}$ are $x = 1$ and $x = -3$ (The values of x that make the

denominator zero.) The domain is $(-\infty, -3) \cup (-3, 1) \cup (1, +\infty)$ or $\mathbb{R} \sim \{-3, 1\}$.

b. There are no excluded values of $f(x) = \dfrac{3x+1}{x^2+4}$ (The denominator is never zero.)

The domain is $(-\infty, +\infty)$ or $\mathbb{R}$.

39. **a.** The vertical asymptotes of $f(x) = \dfrac{x+5}{(x-3)(x+4)}$ are $x = 3$ and $x = -4$.

b. The vertical asymptote of the graph is $x = -1$.

40. **a.** $\dfrac{4x}{12x^2 - 20x} = \dfrac{4x}{4x(3x-5)} = \dfrac{1}{3x-5}$

b. $\dfrac{2x^2 - x - 15}{x^2 - 9} = \dfrac{(2x+5)(x-3)}{(x+3)(x-3)} = \dfrac{2x+5}{x+3}$

41. **a.** $\dfrac{2x^2 - 6x}{10x^2} \cdot \dfrac{5x^2}{x-3} = \dfrac{2x(x-3)(5x^2)}{10x^2(x-3)} = \dfrac{10x^2 x}{10x^2} = x$

b. $\dfrac{x^2 - 16}{x^2 - 2x - 24} \div \dfrac{x^2 - 7x + 12}{x^2 - 3x - 18} = \dfrac{x^2 - 16}{x^2 - 2x - 24} \cdot \dfrac{x^2 - 3x - 18}{x^2 - 7x + 12} = \dfrac{(x+4)(x-4)}{(x+4)(x-6)} \cdot \dfrac{(x-6)(x+3)}{(x-4)(x-3)}$

$= \dfrac{(x+4)(x-4)(x-6)(x+3)}{(x+4)(x-6)(x-4)(x-3)} = \dfrac{x+3}{x-3}$

42. **a.** $\dfrac{5x+4}{3x-5} + \dfrac{x-14}{3x-5} = \dfrac{(5x+4)+(x-14)}{3x-5} = \dfrac{6x-10}{3x-5} = \dfrac{2(3x-5)}{(3x-5)} = 2$

b. $\dfrac{3x}{3x-y}-\dfrac{3x}{3x+y}-\dfrac{2y^2}{9x^2-y^2}=\dfrac{3x}{(3x-y)}\cdot\dfrac{(3x+y)}{(3x+y)}-\dfrac{3x}{(3x+y)}\cdot\dfrac{(3x-y)}{(3x-y)}-\dfrac{2y^2}{(3x+y)(3x-y)}$

$$=\dfrac{3x(3x+y)-3x(3x-y)-2y^2}{(3x-y)(3x+y)}=\dfrac{9x^2+3xy-9x^2+3xy-2y^2}{(3x-y)(3x+y)}$$

$$=\dfrac{6xy-2y^2}{(3x-y)(3x+y)}=\dfrac{2y\cancel{(3x-y)}}{\cancel{(3x-y)}(3x+y)}=\dfrac{2y}{3x+y}$$

43. a. $\dfrac{5x}{4}+\dfrac{x^3}{6}\cdot\dfrac{3}{2x^2}=\dfrac{5x}{4}+\dfrac{\overset{x}{\cancel{3x^3}}}{\underset{4}{\cancel{12x^2}}}=\dfrac{5x}{4}+\dfrac{x}{4}=\dfrac{5x+x}{4}=\dfrac{6x}{4}=\dfrac{3x}{2}$

b. $\left(\dfrac{4}{5x+25}+\dfrac{1}{5x-25}\right)\div\dfrac{x^2-x-6}{x+5}=\left(\dfrac{4}{5(x+5)}+\dfrac{1}{5(x-5)}\right)\cdot\dfrac{x+5}{x^2-x-6}$

$$=\left(\dfrac{4}{5(x+5)}\cdot\dfrac{(x-5)}{(x-5)}+\dfrac{1}{5(x-5)}\cdot\dfrac{(x+5)}{(x+5)}\right)\cdot\dfrac{x+5}{x^2-x-6}$$

$$=\dfrac{4(x-5)+(x+5)}{5(x+5)(x-5)}\cdot\dfrac{x+5}{(x-3)(x+2)}=\dfrac{4x-20+x+5}{5(x+5)(x-5)}\cdot\dfrac{x+5}{(x-3)(x+2)}$$

$$=\dfrac{5x-15}{5(x+5)(x-5)}\cdot\dfrac{x+5}{(x-3)(x+2)}=\dfrac{\cancel{5}\cancel{(x-3)}\cancel{(x+5)}}{\cancel{5}\cancel{(x+5)}(x-5)\cancel{(x-3)}(x+2)}$$

$$=\dfrac{1}{(x-5)(x+2)}$$

44.

a. $\dfrac{\dfrac{x}{4}-2+\dfrac{3}{x}}{1-\dfrac{6}{x}}=\dfrac{\left(\dfrac{x}{4}-2+\dfrac{3}{x}\right)}{\left(1-\dfrac{6}{x}\right)}\cdot\dfrac{4x}{4x}=\dfrac{x^2-8x+12}{4x-24}=\dfrac{(x-2)\cancel{(x-6)}}{4\cancel{(x-6)}}=\dfrac{x-2}{4}$

b. $\dfrac{\dfrac{3x}{x+1}-\dfrac{2x}{x-2}}{\dfrac{x^2-8x}{2x-4}}=\dfrac{\left(\dfrac{3x}{x+1}-\dfrac{2x}{x-2}\right)}{\left(\dfrac{x(x-8)}{2(x-2)}\right)}\cdot\dfrac{2(x+1)(x-2)}{2(x+1)(x-2)}=\dfrac{3x(2)(x-2)-2x(2)(x+1)}{x(x-8)(x+1)}=\dfrac{6x^2-12x-4x^2-4x}{x(x-8)(x+1)}$

$$=\dfrac{2x^2-16x}{x(x-8)(x+1)}=\dfrac{2x^2-16x}{x(x-8)(x+1)}=\dfrac{2\cancel{x}\cancel{(x-8)}}{\cancel{x}\cancel{(x-8)}(x+1)}=\dfrac{2}{x+1}$

45.   a.

$$\frac{x^2-13x-10}{x^2+2x-15} = \frac{2}{x+5} + \frac{5}{3-x}$$

$$\frac{x^2-13x-10}{(x+5)(x-3)} = \frac{2}{x+5} + \frac{5}{3-x}$$

$$(x+5)(x-3)\left(\frac{x^2-13x-10}{(x+5)(x-3)}\right) = \left(\frac{2}{x+5} + \frac{5}{3-x}\right)(x+5)(x-3)$$

$$x^2-13x-10 = 2(x-3)-5(x+5)$$

$$x^2-13x-10 = 2x-6-5x-25$$

$$x^2-13x-10 = -3x-31$$

$$x^2-10x+21 = 0$$

$$(x-7)(x-3) = 0$$

$$x = 7 \quad \text{or} \quad x = 3$$

Note: $x = 3$ is a restricted value.

Answer: $x = 7$

b.

$$\frac{x-3}{x+2} = y$$

$$(x+2)\left(\frac{x-3}{x+2}\right) = y(x+2)$$

$$x-3 = xy+2y$$

$$x-xy = 2y+3$$

$$x(1-y) = 2y+3$$

$$\frac{x\cancel{(1-y)}}{\cancel{(1-y)}} = \frac{2y+3}{(1-y)}$$

$$x = \frac{2y+3}{1-y}$$

46.   a. If y varies inversely as x and $y = 2$ when $x = 12$, then

$$y = \frac{k}{x}$$

$$2 = \frac{k}{12}$$

$$k = 24$$

$$y = \frac{24}{x}$$

With $x = 4$ we have $y = \frac{24}{4}$

$$y = 6$$

b.   Let V = Volume of the gas
p = pressure

$$V = \frac{k}{p}$$

$$10 = \frac{k}{6}$$

$$k = 60$$

With $p = 4$ we have $V = \frac{60}{p}$

$$4 = \frac{60}{p}$$

$$4p = 60$$

$$p = 15 \text{ N/cm}^2$$

47. **a.** Let t = time for the experienced worker

$t+3$ = time for the inexperienced worker

$\dfrac{1}{t}$ = rate of work for the experienced worker

$\dfrac{1}{t+3}$ = rate of work for the inexperienced worker

$$\left(\begin{array}{l}\text{Rate}\\\text{of}\\\text{experienced}\\\text{worker}\end{array}\right)\left(\begin{array}{l}\text{Time}\\\text{of}\\\text{experienced}\\\text{worker}\end{array}\right)+\left(\begin{array}{l}\text{Rate}\\\text{of}\\\text{inexperienced}\\\text{worker}\end{array}\right)\left(\begin{array}{l}\text{Time}\\\text{of}\\\text{inexperienced}\\\text{worker}\end{array}\right)=\left(\begin{array}{l}\text{Total}\\\text{Work}\end{array}\right)$$

$$\left(\frac{1}{t}\right)(2)\qquad+\qquad\left(\frac{1}{t+3}\right)(2)\qquad=\quad 1$$

$$\frac{2}{t}+\frac{2}{t+3}=1$$

$$t(t+3)\left(\frac{2}{t}+\frac{2}{t+3}\right)=t(t+3)(1)$$

$$2(t+3)+2t=t^2+3t$$

$$2t+6+2t=t^2+3t$$

$$4t+6=t^2+3t$$

$$t^2-t-6$$

$$(t-3)(t+2)=0$$

$$t=3 \ \text{ or } \ t=-2$$

Note: This answer is not appropriate.

It would take 3 hours for the experienced worker to complete the roof.

b. Let x = rate of slower plane

$x+40$ = rate of faster plane

$$T=\frac{D}{R}=\frac{660}{x}=\text{time of slower plane}$$

$$T=\frac{D}{R}=\frac{780}{x+40}=\text{time of faster plane}$$

Since both planes travel for the same time we know:

$$\frac{660}{x}=\frac{780}{x+40}$$

$$660(x+40)=780x$$

$$660x+26400=780x$$

$$120x=26400$$

$$x=220$$

The rate of the slower plane is 220 miles per hour. The rate of the faster plane is 260 miles per hour.

48. **a.** The function $f(x)=(x-2)^2+1$ matches graph **B**.

b. The function $f(x)=x/2+1$ matches graph **E**.

c. The function $f(x)=\sqrt{x-2}$ matches graph **A**.

d. The function $f(x)=\sqrt[3]{2-x}$ matches graph **C**.

e. The function $f(x)=|x-2|-1$ matches graph **D**.

49. **a.** The domain of $f(x) = 3x - 15$ is $(-\infty, +\infty)$ or $\mathbb{R}$.

  b. The domain of $f(x) = \dfrac{2}{3x - 15}$ is $(-\infty, 5) \cup (5, +\infty)$ or $\mathbb{R} \sim \{5\}$.

  c. The domain of $f(x) = \sqrt[3]{3x - 15}$ is $(-\infty, +\infty)$ or $\mathbb{R}$.

  d. The domain of $f(x) = \sqrt{3x - 15}$ is $[5, +\infty)$.

50. **a.** $\sqrt{64} = 8$

  b. $\sqrt[3]{64} = 4$

  c. $\sqrt[3]{-0.125} = -0.5$

  d. $\sqrt[4]{16} = 2$

51. **a.** $15\sqrt{3x} - 7\sqrt{3x} = 8\sqrt{3x}$

  b. $5\sqrt{72} - 3\sqrt{8} = 5\sqrt{36}\sqrt{2} - 3\sqrt{4}\sqrt{2}$

$$= 5(6)\sqrt{2} - 3(2)\sqrt{2}$$

$$= 30\sqrt{2} - 6\sqrt{2}$$

$$= 24\sqrt{2}$$

52. **a.** $\sqrt{48} = \sqrt{16}\sqrt{3} = 4\sqrt{3}$ **b.** $\sqrt[3]{48} = \sqrt[3]{8}\sqrt[3]{6} = 2\sqrt[3]{6}$

53. **a.** $\sqrt{x + 8} = x - 4$

$$\left(\sqrt{x + 8}\right)^2 = (x - 4)^2$$

$$x + 8 = x^2 - 8x + 16$$

$$x^2 - 9x + 8 = 0$$

$$(x - 8)(x - 1) = 0$$

$$x = 8 \quad \text{or} \quad x = 1$$

Answer: $x = 8$

Note: This answer is extraneous. It does not satisfy the original equation.

  b. $\sqrt[3]{2x - 3} = 5$

$$\left(\sqrt[3]{2x - 3}\right)^3 = (5)^3$$

$$2x - 3 = 125$$

$$2x = 128$$

$$x = 64$$

54. **a.** $d = \sqrt{(x_2 - x_1)^2 + (y_2 - y_1)^2}$

$$= \sqrt{[3 - (-2)]^2 + [(-7) - 5]^2}$$

$$= \sqrt{5^2 + (-12)^2} = \sqrt{25 + 144} = \sqrt{169} = 13$$

  b. $d = \sqrt{(x_2 - x_1)^2 + (y_2 - y_1)^2}$

$$= \sqrt{(3 - 1)^2 + [(-7) - (-3)]^2}$$

$$= \sqrt{2^2 + (-4)^2} = \sqrt{4 + 16} = \sqrt{20} = \sqrt{4}\sqrt{5} = 2\sqrt{5}$$

55. **a.** $-25^{1/2} = -\sqrt{25} = -5$

  b. $\left(x^{3/8}x^{1/8}\right)^{2/3} = \left(x^{3/8 + 1/8}\right)^{2/3} = \left(x^{4/8}\right)^{2/3} = \left(x^{1/2}\right)^{2/3} = x^{(1/2)(2/3)} = x^{1/3}$

  c. $25^{3/2} - 9^{3/2} = \left(\sqrt{25}\right)^3 - \left(\sqrt{9}\right)^3 = 5^3 - 3^3 = 125 - 27 = 98$

  d. $(25 - 9)^{3/2} = (16)^{3/2} = \left(\sqrt{16}\right)^3 = 4^3 = 64$

56. **a.** Mental Estimate: $\sqrt{26} \approx \sqrt{25} = 5$; Calculator Approximation: $\sqrt{26} \approx 5.099$

  b. Mental Estimate: $\sqrt[3]{26} \approx \sqrt[3]{27} = 3$; Calculator Approximation: $\sqrt[3]{26} \approx 2.962$

57. **a.** The sequence is geometric. The common ratio is $r = \dfrac{10}{2} = \dfrac{50}{10} = \ldots = \dfrac{1250}{250} = 5$

  b. The sequence is not geometric. It is arithmetic with a common difference: $d = 3$.

58.   **a.**

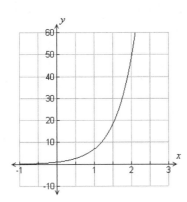

b.

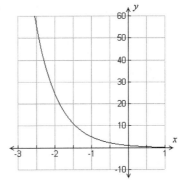

59.   **a.** $f(-1) = 9^{-1} = \dfrac{1}{9}$

b. $f\left(\dfrac{1}{2}\right) = 9^{1/2} = \sqrt{9} = 3$

60.   **a.**

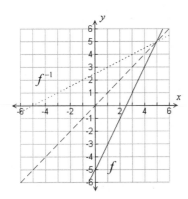

b.

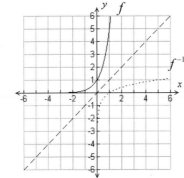

61.   **a.** $\log_4 x = \dfrac{3}{2}$ is equivalent to $4^{3/2} = x$.

b. $\log_3(y-2) = x$ is equivalent to $3^x = y-2$

62.   **a.** $\log_4 1 = 0$ (since $4^0 = 1$)

b. $\log_4 4 = 1$ (since $4^1 = 4$)

c. $\log_4 \dfrac{1}{4} = -1$ (since $4^{-1} = \dfrac{1}{4}$)

d. $\log_4\left(4^7\right) = 7$ (since $4^7 = \left(4^7\right)$)

63.   **a.** $\log x^5 y^3 = \log x^5 + \log y^3 = 5\log x + 3\log y$

b. $\ln \dfrac{x^2}{\sqrt[3]{y}} = \ln \dfrac{x^2}{y^{1/3}} = \ln x^2 - \ln y^{1/3} = 2\ln x - \dfrac{1}{3}\ln y$

64.   **a.** $2\ln x - \ln(x-5) = \ln x^2 - \ln(x-5) = \ln\left(\dfrac{x^2}{x-5}\right)$

b. $\dfrac{1}{2}\log x + \log(x+2) = \log x^{1/2} + \log(x+2)$

$$= \log\left(x^{1/2}(x+2)\right)$$

$$= \log\left(\sqrt{x}(x+2)\right)$$

65.   **a.** $2^x = \dfrac{1}{32}$

$2^x = 2^{-5}$

$x = -5$

b. $9^x = 27$

$\left(3^2\right)^x = 3^3$

$3^{2x} = 3^3$

$2x = 3$

$x = \dfrac{3}{2}$

66. **a.** $\log_3 x = 4$ is equivalent to $x = 3^4$

$$x = 81$$

b. $\log_{64} 4 = y$ is equivalent to $64^y = 4$

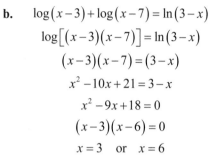

$$\left(4^3\right)^y = 4^1$$
$$4^{3y} = 4^1$$
$$3y = 1$$
$$y = 1/3$$

67. **a.** $\log(x-4) + \log(x+3) = \log 8$

$$\log\left[(x-4)(x+3)\right] = \log 8$$
$$(x-4)(x+3) = 8$$
$$x^2 - x - 12 = 8$$
$$x^2 - x - 20 = 0$$
$$(x-5)(x+4) = 0$$
$$x = 5 \text{ or } x = -4$$

$x = -4$ is an extraneous solution since it causes the argument of the logarithms to be negative. Thus $x = 5$ is the only solution.

b. $\log(x-3) + \log(x-7) = \ln(3-x)$

$$\log\left[(x-3)(x-7)\right] = \ln(3-x)$$
$$(x-3)(x-7) = (3-x)$$
$$x^2 - 10x + 21 = 3 - x$$
$$x^2 - 9x + 18 = 0$$
$$(x-3)(x-6) = 0$$
$$x = 3 \text{ or } x = 6$$

Both of these solutions are extraneous since they cause the argument of the logarithms to be zero or negative. Thus there is no solution.

68. Use the formula $A = Pe^{rt}$.

$$2500 = 1000e^{0.0825t}$$

$$\frac{2500}{1000} = \frac{1000e^{0.0825t}}{1000}$$

$$2.5 = e^{0.0825t}$$

$$\ln 2.5 = 0.0825t$$

$$t = \frac{\ln 2.5}{0.0825} \approx 11.1 \text{ years}$$

69. **a.** $\log 25 \approx 1.398$

b. $\ln\left(2.89 \times 10^{-4}\right) \approx -8.149$

70. **a.** $\log_3 7 = \dfrac{\ln 7}{\ln 3} \approx 1.771$

b. $\log_5 26 = \dfrac{\ln 26}{\ln 5} \approx 2.024$

71. **a.**

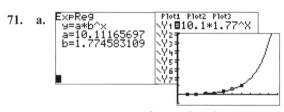

$$[0, 11, 1] \text{ by } [-500, 3500, 500]$$

b. $f(10) \approx 10.1\left(1.77^{10}\right) \approx 3050$ thousand bateria.

(There will be approximately 3,050,000 bacteria present after 10 days.)

Section 12.1: Solving Systems of Linear Equations by Using Augmented Matrices

Quick Review 12.1

1. Check the point $(-2, 5)$ in both equations.

First Equation	**Second Equation**
$4x + 3y = 7$	$5x + 2y = 1$
$4(-2) + 3(5) = 7$	$5(-2) + 2(5) = 1$
$-8 + 15 = 7$	$-10 + 10 = 1$
$7 = 7$	$0 \neq 1$

The point $(-2, 5)$ is not a solution to the system of linear equations.

2. Let $x = 5$ in either equation and solve for y.

$$2x + 3y = 4$$
$$2(5) + 3y = 4$$
$$10 + 3y = 4$$
$$3y = -6$$
$$y = -2$$

3.
$$\frac{x}{2} - \frac{y}{3} = 1$$
$$6\left(\frac{x}{2} - \frac{y}{3}\right) = 6(1)$$
$$\frac{\overset{3}{\cancel{6}}}{1} \cdot \frac{x}{\cancel{2}} - \frac{\overset{2}{\cancel{6}}}{1} \cdot \frac{y}{\cancel{3}} = 6$$
$$3x - 3y = 6$$

4.

Step 1	**Step 2**	**Step 3**
Solve the second equation for x.	Substitute $2y + 2$ for x in the first equation and then solve for y.	Back-substitute 1 for y in the equation obtained in step 1.
$3x - 4y = 8$	$3x - 4y = 8$	$x = 2(1) + 2$
$x - 2y = 2$	$3(2y + 2) - 4y = 8$	$x = 4$
Second equation: $x = 2y + 2$	$6y + 6 - 4y = 8$	Solution: $(4, 1)$
	$2y = 2$	
	$y = 1$	

5. To eliminate y, multiply both sides of the first equation by 4, then multiply the second equation by 5 and add the two equations. Solve this equation for x.

$$2x + 5y = 1$$
$$3x - 4y = 13$$

$$\begin{aligned} 8x + 20y &= 4 \\ \underline{15x - 20y} &= \underline{65} \\ 23x &= 69 \\ x &= 3 \end{aligned}$$

Back substitute 3 for x in the first equation to find y.
$$2x + 5y = 1$$
$$2(3) + 5y = 1$$
$$6 + 5y = 1$$
$$5y = -5$$
$$y = -1$$

Solution: $(3, -1)$

Exercises 12.1

1. $\begin{bmatrix} 3 & 1 & | & 0 \\ 2 & -1 & | & -5 \end{bmatrix}$

3. $\begin{bmatrix} 4 & 0 & | & 12 \\ 3 & 2 & | & 1 \end{bmatrix}$

5. $\begin{bmatrix} 1 & 0 & | & 5 \\ 0 & 1 & | & -6 \end{bmatrix}$

7. $\begin{cases} 2x + 3y = 2 \\ 4x - 3y = 1 \end{cases}$

9. $\begin{cases} 2x + y = 1 \\ x + 3y = 0 \end{cases}$

11. $\begin{cases} x = 7 \\ y = -8 \end{cases}$

13. $\begin{bmatrix} 2 & 1 & | & 1 \\ 1 & 3 & | & 0 \end{bmatrix} \xrightarrow{r_1 \leftrightarrow r_2} \begin{bmatrix} 1 & 3 & | & 0 \\ 2 & 1 & | & 1 \end{bmatrix}$

15. $\begin{bmatrix} 1 & -3 & | & -2 \\ 2 & -5 & | & 4 \end{bmatrix} \xrightarrow{r_2' = r_2 - 2r_1} \begin{bmatrix} 1 & -3 & | & -2 \\ 0 & 1 & | & 8 \end{bmatrix}$

17. $\begin{bmatrix} 3 & -1 & | & 3 \\ 6 & 4 & | & -6 \end{bmatrix} \xrightarrow{r_1' = \frac{1}{3}r_1} \begin{bmatrix} 1 & -\frac{1}{3} & | & 1 \\ 6 & 4 & | & -6 \end{bmatrix}$

19. $\begin{bmatrix} 1 & 5 & | & 16 \\ 0 & 1 & | & 3 \end{bmatrix} \xrightarrow{r_1' = r_1 - 5r_2} \begin{bmatrix} 1 & 0 & | & 1 \\ 0 & 1 & | & 3 \end{bmatrix}$

21. Answer: $(-5, 9)$

23. The last row of the matrix implies $0 = 7$ which is a contradiction. Thus there is no solution.

25. Since the last row of the matrix gives us an identity, we have a dependent system of equations with an infinite number of solutions. Solving for x in the first equation we obtain: $x = 5 - 3y$. Thus the general solution of the system is $(5 - 3y, y)$. For $y = 0$, $y = 1$, and $y = -1$, we obtain the following particular solutions: $(5, 0), (2, 1),$ and $(8, -1)$.

27. $\begin{bmatrix} 2 & 6 & | & 8 \\ 3 & 7 & | & 10 \end{bmatrix} \xrightarrow{r_1' = \frac{1}{2}r_1} \begin{bmatrix} 1 & 3 & | & 4 \\ 3 & 7 & | & 10 \end{bmatrix}$

29. $\begin{bmatrix} 1 & 5 & | & 8 \\ 3 & 2 & | & -2 \end{bmatrix} \xrightarrow{r_2' = r_2 - 3r_1} \begin{bmatrix} 1 & 5 & | & 8 \\ 0 & -13 & | & -26 \end{bmatrix}$

31. $\begin{bmatrix} 1 & -2 & | & 8 \\ 0 & 3 & | & -9 \end{bmatrix} \xrightarrow{r_2' = \frac{1}{3}r_2} \begin{bmatrix} 1 & -2 & | & 8 \\ 0 & 1 & | & -3 \end{bmatrix}$

33. $\begin{bmatrix} 1 & 2 & | & 6 \\ 0 & 1 & | & 1 \end{bmatrix} \xrightarrow{r_1' = r_1 - 2r_2} \begin{bmatrix} 1 & 0 & | & 4 \\ 0 & 1 & | & 1 \end{bmatrix}$

35. $\begin{bmatrix} 1 & 3 & | & 5 \\ 2 & 1 & | & -5 \end{bmatrix} \xrightarrow{r_2' = r_2 - 2r_1} \begin{bmatrix} 1 & 3 & | & 5 \\ 0 & -5 & | & -15 \end{bmatrix} \xrightarrow{r_2' = -\frac{1}{5}r_2} \begin{bmatrix} 1 & 3 & | & 5 \\ 0 & 1 & | & 3 \end{bmatrix} \xrightarrow{r_1' = r_1 - 3r_2} \begin{bmatrix} 1 & 0 & | & -4 \\ 0 & 1 & | & 3 \end{bmatrix}$; Answer: $(-4, 3)$

37. $\begin{bmatrix} 1 & 3 & | & 1 \\ 3 & 7 & | & 7 \end{bmatrix} \xrightarrow{r_2' = r_2 - 3r_1} \begin{bmatrix} 1 & 3 & | & 1 \\ 0 & -2 & | & 4 \end{bmatrix} \xrightarrow{r_2' = -\frac{1}{2}r_2} \begin{bmatrix} 1 & 3 & | & 1 \\ 0 & 1 & | & -2 \end{bmatrix} \xrightarrow{r_1' = r_1 - 3r_2} \begin{bmatrix} 1 & 0 & | & 7 \\ 0 & 1 & | & -2 \end{bmatrix}$; Answer: $(7, -2)$

39. $\begin{bmatrix} 2 & 5 & | & -4 \\ 4 & 3 & | & 6 \end{bmatrix} \xrightarrow{r_1' = \frac{1}{2}r_1} \begin{bmatrix} 1 & \frac{5}{2} & | & -2 \\ 4 & 3 & | & 6 \end{bmatrix} \xrightarrow{r_2' = r_2 - 4r_1} \begin{bmatrix} 1 & \frac{5}{2} & | & -2 \\ 0 & -7 & | & 14 \end{bmatrix} \xrightarrow{r_2' = -\frac{1}{7}r_2} \begin{bmatrix} 1 & \frac{5}{2} & | & -2 \\ 0 & 1 & | & -2 \end{bmatrix}$

$\xrightarrow{r_1' = r_1 - \frac{5}{2}r_2} \begin{bmatrix} 1 & 0 & | & 3 \\ 0 & 1 & | & -2 \end{bmatrix}$; Answer: $(3, -2)$

41. $\begin{bmatrix} 4 & -9 & | & 5 \\ 3 & 12 & | & 10 \end{bmatrix} \xrightarrow{r_1'=\frac{1}{4}r_1} \begin{bmatrix} 1 & -\frac{9}{4} & | & \frac{5}{4} \\ 3 & 12 & | & 10 \end{bmatrix} \xrightarrow{r_2'=r_2-3r_1} \begin{bmatrix} 1 & -\frac{9}{4} & | & \frac{5}{4} \\ 0 & \frac{75}{4} & | & \frac{25}{4} \end{bmatrix} \xrightarrow{r_2'=\frac{4}{75}r_2} \begin{bmatrix} 1 & -\frac{9}{4} & | & \frac{5}{4} \\ 0 & 1 & | & \frac{1}{3} \end{bmatrix}$

$\xrightarrow{r_1'=r_1+\frac{9}{4}r_2} \begin{bmatrix} 1 & 0 & | & 2 \\ 0 & 1 & | & \frac{1}{3} \end{bmatrix}$; Answer: $\left(2, \frac{1}{3}\right)$

43. $\begin{bmatrix} 3 & -1 & | & 2 \\ 2 & 1 & | & 6 \end{bmatrix} \xrightarrow{r_1'=\frac{1}{3}r_1} \begin{bmatrix} 1 & -\frac{1}{3} & | & \frac{2}{3} \\ 2 & 1 & | & 6 \end{bmatrix} \xrightarrow{r_2'=r_2-2r_1} \begin{bmatrix} 1 & -\frac{1}{3} & | & \frac{2}{3} \\ 0 & \frac{5}{3} & | & \frac{14}{3} \end{bmatrix} \xrightarrow{r_2'=\frac{3}{5}r_2} \begin{bmatrix} 1 & -\frac{1}{3} & | & \frac{2}{3} \\ 0 & 1 & | & \frac{14}{5} \end{bmatrix}$

$\xrightarrow{r_1'=r_1+\frac{1}{3}r_2} \begin{bmatrix} 1 & 0 & | & \frac{8}{5} \\ 0 & 1 & | & \frac{14}{5} \end{bmatrix}$; Answer: $\left(\frac{8}{5}, \frac{14}{5}\right)$

45. $\begin{bmatrix} 6 & 4 & | & 11 \\ 10 & 6 & | & 17 \end{bmatrix} \xrightarrow{r_1'=\frac{1}{6}r_1} \begin{bmatrix} 1 & \frac{2}{3} & | & \frac{11}{6} \\ 10 & 6 & | & 17 \end{bmatrix} \xrightarrow{r_2'=r_2-10r_1} \begin{bmatrix} 1 & \frac{2}{3} & | & \frac{11}{6} \\ 0 & -\frac{2}{3} & | & -\frac{4}{3} \end{bmatrix} \xrightarrow{r_2'=-\frac{3}{2}r_2} \begin{bmatrix} 1 & \frac{2}{3} & | & \frac{11}{6} \\ 0 & 1 & | & 2 \end{bmatrix}$

$\xrightarrow{r_1'=r_1-\frac{2}{3}r_2} \begin{bmatrix} 1 & 0 & | & \frac{1}{2} \\ 0 & 1 & | & 2 \end{bmatrix}$; Answer: $\left(\frac{1}{2}, 2\right)$

47. $\begin{bmatrix} 3 & 4 & | & 7 \\ 6 & 8 & | & 10 \end{bmatrix} \xrightarrow{r_1'=\frac{1}{3}r_1} \begin{bmatrix} 1 & \frac{4}{3} & | & \frac{7}{3} \\ 6 & 8 & | & 10 \end{bmatrix} \xrightarrow{r_2'=r_2-6r_1} \begin{bmatrix} 1 & \frac{4}{3} & | & \frac{7}{3} \\ 0 & 0 & | & -4 \end{bmatrix}$

The last row is a contradiction. Thus there is no solution.

49. $\begin{bmatrix} 2 & -1 & | & 5 \\ 4 & -2 & | & 10 \end{bmatrix} \xrightarrow{r_1'=\frac{1}{2}r_1} \begin{bmatrix} 1 & -\frac{1}{2} & | & \frac{5}{2} \\ 4 & -2 & | & 10 \end{bmatrix} \xrightarrow{r_2'=r_2-4r_1} \begin{bmatrix} 1 & -\frac{1}{2} & | & \frac{5}{2} \\ 0 & 0 & | & 0 \end{bmatrix}$

Since the last row of the matrix gives us an identity, we have a dependent system of equations with an infinite number of solutions. Solving for x in the first equation we obtain: $x = \frac{5}{2} + \frac{1}{2}y$. Thus the general solution of the system is $\left(\frac{5}{2} + \frac{1}{2}y, y\right)$.

51. Let x and y be the two numbers. If their sum is 160 and their difference is 4, then to find the numbers we solve the following system.

$\begin{cases} x + y = 160 \\ x - y = 4 \end{cases} \rightarrow \begin{bmatrix} 1 & 1 & | & 160 \\ 1 & -1 & | & 4 \end{bmatrix} \xrightarrow{r_2'=r_2-r_1} \begin{bmatrix} 1 & 1 & | & 160 \\ 0 & -2 & | & -156 \end{bmatrix} \xrightarrow{r_2'=-\frac{1}{2}r_2} \begin{bmatrix} 1 & 1 & | & 160 \\ 0 & 1 & | & 78 \end{bmatrix} \xrightarrow{r_1'=r_1-r_2} \begin{bmatrix} 1 & 0 & | & 82 \\ 0 & 1 & | & 78 \end{bmatrix}$

Thus the two numbers are 82 and 78.

53. Let x and y be the two angles. If they are complementary and one angle is $32°$ larger than the other, then to find the angles we solve the following system.

$$\begin{cases} x + y = 90 \\ x - y = 32 \end{cases} \rightarrow \begin{bmatrix} 1 & 1 & | & 90 \\ 1 & -1 & | & 32 \end{bmatrix} \xrightarrow{r_2' = r_2 - r_1} \begin{bmatrix} 1 & 1 & | & 90 \\ 0 & -2 & | & -58 \end{bmatrix} \xrightarrow{r_2' = -\frac{1}{2}r_2} \begin{bmatrix} 1 & 1 & | & 90 \\ 0 & 1 & | & 29 \end{bmatrix} \xrightarrow{r_1' = r_1 - r_2} \begin{bmatrix} 1 & 0 & | & 61 \\ 0 & 1 & | & 29 \end{bmatrix}$$

Thus the two angles are $61°$ and $29°$.

55. Let x be the fixed cost and y be the variable cost per costume. To find these values, we solve the following system.

$$\begin{cases} x + 20y = 3200 \\ x + 30y = 4300 \end{cases} \rightarrow \begin{bmatrix} 1 & 20 & | & 3200 \\ 1 & 30 & | & 4300 \end{bmatrix} \xrightarrow{r_2' = r_2 - r_1} \begin{bmatrix} 1 & 20 & | & 3200 \\ 0 & 10 & | & 1100 \end{bmatrix} \xrightarrow{r_2' = \frac{1}{10}r_2} \begin{bmatrix} 1 & 20 & | & 3200 \\ 0 & 1 & | & 110 \end{bmatrix} \xrightarrow{r_1' = r_1 - 20r_2} \begin{bmatrix} 1 & 20 & | & 1000 \\ 0 & 1 & | & 110 \end{bmatrix}$$

Thus the fixed cost is $1,000 and the variable cost is $110 per costume.

57. Let x be the rate of the boat and y be the rate of the current. To find these values, solve the following system.

$$\begin{cases} x + y = 30 \\ x - y = 14 \end{cases} \rightarrow \begin{bmatrix} 1 & 1 & | & 30 \\ 1 & -1 & | & 14 \end{bmatrix} \xrightarrow{r_2' = r_2 - r_1} \begin{bmatrix} 1 & 1 & | & 30 \\ 0 & -2 & | & -16 \end{bmatrix} \xrightarrow{r_2' = -\frac{1}{2}r_2} \begin{bmatrix} 1 & 1 & | & 30 \\ 0 & 1 & | & 8 \end{bmatrix} \xrightarrow{r_1' = r_1 - r_2} \begin{bmatrix} 1 & 0 & | & 22 \\ 0 & 1 & | & 8 \end{bmatrix}$$

Thus the speed of the boat is 22 km/hr and the speed of the current is 8 km/hr.

59. Let x be amount of the fruit concentrate and y be the amount of pure water used. To find these values, solve the following system.

$$\begin{cases} x + y = 100 \\ .15x + (1)y = 100(.83) \end{cases} \rightarrow \begin{bmatrix} 1 & 1 & | & 100 \\ .15 & 1 & | & 83 \end{bmatrix} \xrightarrow{r_2' = r_2 - .15r_1} \begin{bmatrix} 1 & 1 & | & 100 \\ 0 & .85 & | & 68 \end{bmatrix} \xrightarrow{r_2' = \frac{1}{.85}r_2} \begin{bmatrix} 1 & 1 & | & 100 \\ 0 & 1 & | & 80 \end{bmatrix}$$

$$\xrightarrow{r_1' = r_1 - r_2} \begin{bmatrix} 1 & 0 & | & 20 \\ 0 & 1 & | & 80 \end{bmatrix}$$

Thus they should use 20 liters of the fruit concentrate and 80 liters of pure water.

61. If the inside wheel covers 111.5 inches per revolution, then the circumference of the inside wheel is 111.5 inches and $2\pi r_1 = 111.5$. Thus $r_1 = \dfrac{111.5}{2\pi} \approx 17.75$ inches. The radius of the outside wheel is $r_2 = 17.75 + .25 = 18$ inches.

Cumulative Review

1.

n	$a_n = 2n + 1$
1	$2(1) + 1 = 3$
2	$2(2) + 1 = 5$
3	$2(3) + 1 = 7$
4	$2(4) + 1 = 9$
5	$2(5) + 1 = 11$

2. $a_{50} = 2(50) + 1 = 101$

3.

n	$a_n = 2^{n+1}$
1	$2^{1+1} = 2^2 = 4$
2	$2^{2+1} = 2^3 = 8$
3	$2^{3+1} = 2^4 = 16$
4	$2^{4+1} = 2^5 = 32$
5	$2^{5+1} = 2^6 = 64$

4. $(12a + 3b)^0 + (12a)^0 + (3b)^0 + 12a^0 + 3b^0$
$= 1 + 1 + 1 + 12(1) + 3(1) = 18$

5. $(-1)^4 + 4^{-1} + (1)^{1/4} = 1 + \dfrac{1}{4} + \sqrt[4]{1} = 1 + \dfrac{1}{4} + 1$

$= 2 + \dfrac{1}{4} = \dfrac{2}{1} \cdot \dfrac{4}{4} + \dfrac{1}{4} = \dfrac{8}{4} + \dfrac{1}{4} = \dfrac{9}{4}$

Quick Review 12.2

1. Check the point $(4, -3)$ in both equations.

First Equation	**Second Equation**
$2x + 3y = -1$	$6x + 5y = 9$
$2(4) + 3(-3) = -1$	$6(4) + 5(-3) = 9$
$8 + (-9) = -1$	$24 - 15 = 9$
$-1 = -1$	$9 = 9$

The point $(4, -3)$ is a solution to the system of linear equations.

2.

Step 1

Solve the first equation for y.

$$2x - y = 5$$

$$\frac{x}{2} - \frac{y}{3} = 1$$

First equation: $y = 2x - 5$

Step 2

Substitute $2x - 5$ for y in the second equation and then solve for x.

$$\frac{x}{2} - \frac{y}{3} = 1$$

$$\frac{x}{2} - \frac{2x - 5}{3} = 1$$

$$6\left(\frac{x}{2} - \frac{2x - 5}{3}\right) = 6(1)$$

$$3x - 2(2x - 5) = 6$$

$$3x - 4x + 10 = 6$$

$$-x = -4$$

$$x = 4$$

Step 3

Back-substitute 4 for x in the equation obtained in step 1.

$$y = 2x - 5$$

$$y = 2(4) - 5$$

$$y = 3$$

Solution: $(4, 3)$

3. The system represents two parallel lines with different y-intercepts. It is an inconsistent system. The proper choice is **C**.

4. The system represents two lines that are identical. It is a consistent system of dependent equations. The proper choice is **B**.

5. The system represents two lines with different slopes. It is a consistent system of independent equations. The proper choice is **A**.

Exercises 12.2

1. First, produce a 2×2 system of equations by eliminating x from equations **(1)** and **(2)** and then again from equations **(1)** and **(3)**.

(1) $x + 2y + z = 11$
(2) $-x - y + 2z = 1$
(3) $2x - y + z = 4$

(1) $x + 2y + z = 11$
(2) $-x - y + 2z = 1$
$y + 3z = 12$

$-2x - 4y - 2z = -22$
(3) $2x - y + z = 4$
$-5y - z = -18$

Multiply both sides of the first equation by -2.

The 2×2 system is $\begin{cases} y + 3z = 12 \\ -5y - z = -18 \end{cases}$

Use the addition method to solve this 2×2 system of equations. Multiply both sides of the second equation by 3 then add the equations to eliminate y.

$y + 3z = 12$
$-15y - 3z = -54$
$-14y \quad = -42$
$y = 3$

Back substitute:
$y + 3z = 12$
$(3) + 3z = 12$
$3z = 9$
$z = 3$

(1) $x + 2y + z = 11$
$x + 2(3) + (3) = 11$
$x + 9 = 11$
$x = 2$

The answer as an ordered triple is $(2, 3, 3)$

3. First, produce a 2×2 system of equations by eliminating z from equations **(1)** and **(2)** and then again from equations **(1)** and **(3)**.

(1) $x + y - z = 1$
(2) $2x + y + z = 4$
(3) $x - y - 2z = -2$

(1) $x + y - z = 1$
(2) $2x + y + z = 4$
$3x + 2y = 5$

$-2x - 2y + 2z = -2$
(3) $x - y - 2z = -2$
$-x - 3y = -4$

Multiply both sides of the first equation by -2.

The 2×2 system is $\begin{cases} 3x + 2y = 5 \\ -x - 3y = -4 \end{cases}$

Use the addition method to solve this 2×2 system of equations. Multiply both sides of the second equation by 3 then add the equations to eliminate x.

$3x + 2y = 5$
$-3x - 9y = -12$
$-7y = -7$
$y = 1$

Back substitute:
$3x + 2y = 5$
$3x + 2(1) = 5$
$3x = 3$
$x = 1$

(1) $x + y - z = 1$
$(1) + (1) - z = 1$
$-z = -1$
$z = 1$

The answer as an ordered triple is $(1, 1, 1)$

5. First, produce a 2×2 system of equations by eliminating y from equations **(1)** and **(2)** and then again from equations **(1)** and **(3)**.

(1) $\begin{cases} 5x + y + 3z = -1 \\ 2x - y + 4z = -6 \\ 3x + y - 2z = 7 \end{cases}$
(2)
(3)

$\begin{array}{l} \textbf{(1)} \quad 5x + y + 3z = -1 \\ \textbf{(2)} \quad \underline{2x - y + 4z = -6} \\ \quad 7x + 7z = -7 \end{array}$

$\begin{array}{l} \; -5x - y - 3z = 1 \\ \textbf{(3)} \quad \underline{3x + y - 2z = 7} \\ \; -2x - 5z = 8 \end{array}$ $\longleftarrow$ Multiply both sides of the first equation by -1.

or

$x + z = -1$

The 2×2 system is $\begin{cases} x + z = -1 \\ -2x - 5z = 8 \end{cases}$

Use the addition method to solve this 2×2 system of equations. Multiply both sides of the first equation by 2 then add the equations to eliminate x.

$\begin{array}{l} 2x + 2z = -2 \\ \underline{-2x - 5z = 8} \\ -3z = 6 \\ z = -2 \end{array}$

Back substitute:

$\begin{array}{ll} x + z = -1 & \textbf{(1)} \quad 5x + y + 3z = -1 \\ x + (-2) = -1 & \quad 5(1) + y + 3(-2) = -1 \\ x = 1 & y = 0 \end{array}$

The answer as an ordered triple is $(1, 0, -2)$

7. First, produce a 2×2 system of equations by eliminating x from equations **(1)** and **(2)** and then again from equations **(1)** and **(3)**.

(1) $\begin{cases} x - 10y + 3z = -5 \\ 2x - 15y + z = 7 \\ 3x + 5y - 2z = 8 \end{cases}$
(2)
(3)

$\begin{array}{l} \; -2x + 20y - 6z = 10 \\ \textbf{(2)} \quad \underline{2x - 15y + z = 7} \\ \quad 5y - 5z = 17 \end{array}$

$\begin{array}{l} \; -3x + 30y - 9z = 15 \\ \textbf{(3)} \quad \underline{3x + 5y - 2z = 8} \\ \quad 35y - 11z = 23 \end{array}$ $\longleftarrow$ Multiply both sides of the first equation by -3.

Multiply both sides of the first equation by -2.

The 2×2 system is $\begin{cases} 5y - 5z = 17 \\ 35y - 11z = 23 \end{cases}$

Use the addition method to solve this 2×2 system of equations. Multiply both sides of the first equation by -7 then add the equations to eliminate y.

$\begin{array}{l} -35y + 35z = -119 \\ \underline{35y - 11z = 23} \\ 24z = -96 \\ z = -4 \end{array}$

Back substitute:

$\begin{array}{ll} 5y - 5z = 17 & \textbf{(1)} \quad x - 10y + 3z = -5 \\ 5y - 5(-4) = 17 & \\ 5y = -3 & \quad x - 10\left(-\dfrac{3}{5}\right) + 3(-4) = -5 \\ y = \dfrac{-3}{5} & x = 1 \end{array}$

The answer as an ordered triple is $\left(1, -\dfrac{3}{5}, -4\right)$

9. First, produce a 2×2 system of equations by eliminating y from equations **(1)** and **(2)** ..

$$\begin{array}{ll}\textbf{(1)} & x+y \quad\; =-2 \\ \textbf{(2)} & \quad\; -y+z=2 \\ \textbf{(3)} & x \quad\; -z=-1\end{array}$$

$$\begin{array}{ll}\textbf{(1)} & x+y \quad\; =-2 \\ \textbf{(2)} & \quad\; -y+z=2 \\ \hline & x \qquad +z=0\end{array}$$

The 2×2 system is $\begin{cases} x+z=0 \\ x-z=-1 \end{cases}$ — We simply use equation **(3)** here.

Use the addition method to solve this 2×2 system of equations. Add the equations to eliminate z.

$$\begin{array}{l} x+z=0 \\ \underline{x-z=-1} \\ 2x=-1 \\ \quad x=-\dfrac{1}{2} \end{array}$$

Back substitute:

$$\begin{array}{l} x+z=0 \\ -\dfrac{1}{2}+z=0 \\ \quad z=\dfrac{1}{2} \end{array}$$

$$\begin{array}{ll}\textbf{(1)} & x+y=-2 \\ & -\dfrac{1}{2}+y=-2 \\ & \quad y=-\dfrac{3}{2} \end{array}$$

The answer as an ordered triple is

$$\left(-\dfrac{1}{2}, -\dfrac{3}{2}, \dfrac{1}{2}\right)$$

11. First, produce a 2×2 system of equations by eliminating x from equations **(1)** and **(3)**.

$$\begin{array}{ll}\textbf{(1)} & 2x \quad\; +z=7 \\ \textbf{(2)} & \quad\; y-2z=-5 \\ \textbf{(3)} & x+2y \quad\; =4\end{array}$$

$$\begin{array}{ll}\textbf{(1)} & 2x \qquad +z=7 \\ & -2x-4y \qquad =-8 \\ \hline & \quad -4y \;+z=-1\end{array}$$

Multiply both sides of the third equation by -2.

The 2×2 system is $\begin{cases} y-2z=-5 \\ -4y+z=-1 \end{cases}$ — We simply use equation **(2)** here.

Use the addition method to solve this 2×2 system of equations. Multiply both sides of the second equation by 2 then add the equations to eliminate z.

$$\begin{array}{l} y-2z=-5 \\ \underline{-8y+2z=-2} \\ \quad -7y=-7 \\ \qquad y=1 \end{array}$$

Back substitute:

$$\begin{array}{l} y-2z=-5 \\ (1)-2z=-5 \\ \quad -2z=-6 \\ \qquad z=3 \end{array}$$

$$\begin{array}{ll}\textbf{(1)} & 2x+z=7 \\ & 2x+(3)=7 \\ & \quad 2x=4 \\ & \quad\; x=2 \end{array}$$

The answer as an ordered triple is $(2, 1, 3)$

13. If we multiply the first equation by -2 and add it to the third equation we obtain the following:

$$-4x + 8y - 4z = -12$$

$$\underline{4x - 8y + 4z = 11}$$

$$0 = -1$$

This is a contradiction. Therefore there is no solution. The system is inconsistent.

15. $\begin{bmatrix} 1 & 1 & 1 & | & 2 \\ -1 & 1 & -2 & | & 1 \\ 1 & 1 & -1 & | & 0 \end{bmatrix}$

17. $\begin{bmatrix} 1 & 2 & -1 & | & 19 \\ 2 & -1 & 0 & | & -1 \\ 3 & -2 & 4 & | & -32 \end{bmatrix}$

19. $\begin{cases} x - 2y + 5z = 0 \\ 2x + 4y - 3z = 8 \\ 3x + 5y + 7z = 11 \end{cases}$

21. $\begin{cases} x + 2z = 5 \\ x + y = 0 \\ y + z = 4 \end{cases}$

23. $\begin{cases} x = 7 \\ y = -5 \\ z = 8 \end{cases}$

25. $\begin{bmatrix} 2 & 1 & -2 & | & -11 \\ 1 & 2 & 3 & | & 16 \\ 3 & 2 & 1 & | & 3 \end{bmatrix} \xrightarrow{r_1 \leftrightarrow r_2} \begin{bmatrix} 1 & 2 & 3 & | & 16 \\ 2 & 1 & -2 & | & -11 \\ 3 & 2 & 1 & | & 3 \end{bmatrix}$

27. $\begin{bmatrix} 2 & 4 & 8 & | & 6 \\ 3 & 5 & 7 & | & 1 \\ 4 & 9 & 2 & | & 8 \end{bmatrix} \xrightarrow{r_1' = \frac{1}{2}r_1} \begin{bmatrix} 1 & 2 & 4 & | & 3 \\ 3 & 5 & 7 & | & 1 \\ 4 & 9 & 2 & | & 8 \end{bmatrix}$

29. $\begin{bmatrix} 1 & 3 & 5 & | & 11 \\ 2 & 7 & 9 & | & 13 \\ 4 & 8 & 3 & | & 7 \end{bmatrix} \xrightarrow{r_2' = r_2 - 2r_1} \begin{bmatrix} 1 & 3 & 5 & | & 11 \\ 0 & 1 & -1 & | & -9 \\ 4 & 8 & 3 & | & 7 \end{bmatrix}$

31. $\begin{bmatrix} 1 & 2 & 2 & | & 3 \\ 2 & 1 & 3 & | & -1 \\ 3 & -1 & 4 & | & -8 \end{bmatrix} \xrightarrow[r_3' = r_3 - 3r_1]{r_2' = r_2 - 2r_1} \begin{bmatrix} 1 & 2 & 2 & | & 3 \\ 0 & -3 & -1 & | & -7 \\ 0 & -7 & -2 & | & -17 \end{bmatrix}$

33. $\begin{bmatrix} 1 & 3 & -2 & | & 19 \\ 0 & 2 & 4 & | & -10 \\ 0 & 4 & 1 & | & 8 \end{bmatrix} \xrightarrow{r_2' = \frac{1}{2}r_2} \begin{bmatrix} 1 & 3 & -2 & | & 19 \\ 0 & 1 & 2 & | & -5 \\ 0 & 4 & 1 & | & 8 \end{bmatrix}$

35. $\begin{bmatrix} 1 & 2 & 4 & | & 9 \\ 0 & 1 & 2 & | & 3 \\ 0 & -3 & 5 & | & 13 \end{bmatrix} \xrightarrow[r_3' = r_3 + 3r_2]{r_1' = r_1 - 2r_2} \begin{bmatrix} 1 & 0 & 0 & | & 3 \\ 0 & 1 & 2 & | & 3 \\ 0 & 0 & 11 & | & 22 \end{bmatrix}$

37. Answer: $(-2, 7, 3)$

39. The last row of the matrix is a contradiction. Thus there is no solution.

41. Since the last row of the matrix gives us an identity, we have a dependent system of equations with an infinite number of solutions. Solving for x in the first equation we obtain: $x = 2 - 3z$. Solving for y in the second equation we obtain: $y = -5 - 2z$. Thus the general solution of the system is $(2 - 3z, -5 - 2z, z)$. For $z = 0$, $z = 1$, and $z = 2$, we obtain the following particular solutions:

$(2, -5, 0), (-1, -7, 1)$, and $(-4, -9, 2)$.

43. $\begin{bmatrix} 2 & 4 & 6 & | & -6 \\ 3 & 1 & -1 & | & 6 \\ 1 & 2 & -4 & | & 11 \end{bmatrix} \xrightarrow{r_1' = \frac{1}{2}r_1} \begin{bmatrix} 1 & 2 & 3 & | & -3 \\ 3 & 1 & -1 & | & 6 \\ 1 & 2 & -4 & | & 11 \end{bmatrix}$

45. $\begin{bmatrix} 1 & 3 & -2 & | & -3 \\ -3 & 1 & 1 & | & -16 \\ 4 & 2 & -1 & | & 15 \end{bmatrix} \xrightarrow{r_2' = r_2 + 3r_1} \begin{bmatrix} 1 & 3 & -2 & | & -3 \\ 0 & 10 & -5 & | & -25 \\ 4 & 2 & -1 & | & 15 \end{bmatrix}$

47. $\begin{bmatrix} 1 & -3 & 2 & | & 10 \\ 0 & 1 & 5 & | & -12 \\ 0 & -2 & -1 & | & 1 \end{bmatrix} \xrightarrow{r_1' = r_1 + 3r_2} \begin{bmatrix} 1 & 0 & 17 & | & -26 \\ 0 & 1 & 5 & | & -12 \\ 0 & -2 & -1 & | & 1 \end{bmatrix}$

49. $\begin{bmatrix} 2 & 1 & 0 & | & 7 \\ 0 & 1 & -1 & | & 2 \\ 1 & 0 & 1 & | & 2 \end{bmatrix} \xrightarrow{r_1 \leftrightarrow r_3} \begin{bmatrix} 1 & 0 & 1 & | & 2 \\ 0 & 1 & -1 & | & 2 \\ 2 & 1 & 0 & | & 7 \end{bmatrix} \xrightarrow{r_2'=r_2-2r_1} \begin{bmatrix} 1 & 0 & 1 & | & 2 \\ 0 & 1 & -1 & | & 2 \\ 0 & 1 & -2 & | & 3 \end{bmatrix} \xrightarrow{r_3'=r_3-r_2} \begin{bmatrix} 1 & 0 & 1 & | & 2 \\ 0 & 1 & -1 & | & 2 \\ 0 & 0 & -1 & | & 1 \end{bmatrix}$

$\xrightarrow{r_3'=(-1)r_3} \begin{bmatrix} 1 & 0 & 1 & | & 2 \\ 0 & 1 & -1 & | & 2 \\ 0 & 0 & 1 & | & -1 \end{bmatrix} \xrightarrow[r_2'=r_2+r_3]{r_1'=r_1-r_3} \begin{bmatrix} 1 & 0 & 0 & | & 3 \\ 0 & 1 & 0 & | & 1 \\ 0 & 0 & 1 & | & -1 \end{bmatrix}$; Answer: $(3, 1, -1)$

51. $\begin{bmatrix} 1 & 2 & 1 & | & 11 \\ -1 & -1 & 2 & | & 1 \\ 2 & -1 & 1 & | & 4 \end{bmatrix} \xrightarrow[r_3'=r_3-2r_1]{r_2'=r_2+r_1} \begin{bmatrix} 1 & 2 & 1 & | & 11 \\ 0 & 1 & 3 & | & 12 \\ 0 & -5 & -1 & | & -18 \end{bmatrix} \xrightarrow[r_3'=r_3+5r_2]{r_1'=r_1-2r_2} \begin{bmatrix} 1 & 0 & -5 & | & -13 \\ 0 & 1 & 3 & | & 12 \\ 0 & 0 & 14 & | & 42 \end{bmatrix} \xrightarrow{r_3'=\frac{1}{14}r_3} \begin{bmatrix} 1 & 0 & -5 & | & -13 \\ 0 & 1 & 3 & | & 12 \\ 0 & 0 & 1 & | & 3 \end{bmatrix}$

$\xrightarrow[r_2'=r_2-3r_3]{r_1'=r_1+5r_3} \begin{bmatrix} 1 & 0 & 0 & | & 2 \\ 0 & 1 & 0 & | & 3 \\ 0 & 0 & 1 & | & 3 \end{bmatrix}$; Answer: $(2, 3, 3)$

53. $\begin{bmatrix} 1 & 2 & -2 & | & -7 \\ -2 & 3 & -17 & | & -14 \\ 4 & 2 & 10 & | & -4 \end{bmatrix} \xrightarrow[r_3'=r_3-4r_1]{r_2'=r_2+2r_1} \begin{bmatrix} 1 & 2 & -2 & | & -7 \\ 0 & 7 & -21 & | & -28 \\ 0 & -6 & 18 & | & 24 \end{bmatrix} \xrightarrow{r_2'=\frac{1}{7}r_2} \begin{bmatrix} 1 & 2 & -2 & | & -7 \\ 0 & 1 & -3 & | & -4 \\ 0 & -6 & 18 & | & 24 \end{bmatrix}$

$\xrightarrow[r_3'=r_3+6r_2]{r_1'=r_1-2r_2} \begin{bmatrix} 1 & 0 & 4 & | & 1 \\ 0 & 1 & -3 & | & -4 \\ 0 & 0 & 0 & | & 0 \end{bmatrix}$

Since the last row of the matrix gives us an identity, we have a dependent system of equations with an infinite number of solutions. Solving for x_1 in the first equation we obtain: $x_1 = 1 - 4x_3$. Solving for x_2 in the second equation we obtain: $x_2 = -4 + 3x_3$. Thus the general solution of the system is $(1 - 4x_3, \, -4 + 3x_3, \, x_3)$.

55. $\begin{bmatrix} 5 & 1 & -2 & | & -3 \\ 2 & 4 & 1 & | & -3 \\ -3 & 5 & -6 & | & -21 \end{bmatrix} \xrightarrow{r_1'=\frac{1}{5}r_1} \begin{bmatrix} 1 & \frac{1}{5} & -\frac{2}{5} & | & -\frac{3}{5} \\ 2 & 4 & 1 & | & -3 \\ -3 & 5 & -6 & | & -21 \end{bmatrix} \xrightarrow[r_3'=r_3+3r_1]{r_2'=r_2-2r_1} \begin{bmatrix} 1 & \frac{1}{5} & -\frac{2}{5} & | & -\frac{3}{5} \\ 0 & \frac{18}{5} & \frac{9}{5} & | & -\frac{9}{5} \\ 0 & \frac{28}{5} & -\frac{36}{5} & | & -\frac{114}{5} \end{bmatrix}$

$\xrightarrow{r_2'=\frac{5}{18}r_2} \begin{bmatrix} 1 & \frac{1}{5} & -\frac{2}{5} & | & -\frac{3}{5} \\ 0 & 1 & \frac{1}{2} & | & -\frac{1}{2} \\ 0 & \frac{28}{5} & -\frac{36}{5} & | & -\frac{114}{5} \end{bmatrix} \xrightarrow[r_3'=r_3-\frac{28}{5}r_2]{r_1'=r_1-\frac{1}{5}r_2} \begin{bmatrix} 1 & 0 & -\frac{1}{2} & | & -\frac{1}{2} \\ 0 & 1 & \frac{1}{2} & | & -\frac{1}{2} \\ 0 & 0 & -10 & | & -20 \end{bmatrix}$

$\xrightarrow{r_3'=-\frac{1}{10}r_3} \begin{bmatrix} 1 & 0 & -\frac{1}{2} & | & -\frac{1}{2} \\ 0 & 1 & \frac{1}{2} & | & -\frac{1}{2} \\ 0 & 0 & 1 & | & 2 \end{bmatrix} \xrightarrow[r_2'=r_2-\frac{1}{2}r_3]{r_1'=r_1+\frac{1}{2}r_3} \begin{bmatrix} 1 & 0 & 0 & | & \frac{1}{2} \\ 0 & 1 & 0 & | & -\frac{3}{2} \\ 0 & 0 & 1 & | & 2 \end{bmatrix}$; Answer: $\left(\frac{1}{2}, -\frac{3}{2}, 2 \right)$

57. $\begin{bmatrix} 1 & 2 & -5 & | & 4 \\ 3 & -1 & 2 & | & 3 \\ 1 & 9 & -22 & | & 10 \end{bmatrix} \xrightarrow[r_3'=r_3-r_1]{r_2'=r_2-3r_1} \begin{bmatrix} 1 & 2 & -5 & | & 4 \\ 0 & -7 & 17 & | & -9 \\ 0 & 7 & -17 & | & 6 \end{bmatrix} \xrightarrow{r_2'=-\frac{1}{7}r_2} \begin{bmatrix} 1 & 2 & -5 & | & 4 \\ 0 & 1 & -\frac{17}{7} & | & \frac{9}{7} \\ 0 & 7 & -17 & | & 6 \end{bmatrix} \xrightarrow[r_3'=r_3-7r_2]{r_1'=r_1-2r_2} \begin{bmatrix} 1 & 0 & -\frac{1}{7} & | & \frac{10}{7} \\ 0 & 1 & -\frac{17}{7} & | & \frac{9}{7} \\ 0 & 0 & 0 & | & -3 \end{bmatrix}$

The last row of the matrix is a contradiction. Thus there is no solution.

59. $\begin{bmatrix} 2 & -1 & -3 & | & -5 \\ 3 & 1 & -2 & | & -10 \end{bmatrix} \xrightarrow{r_1'=\frac{1}{2}r_1} \begin{bmatrix} 1 & -\frac{1}{2} & -\frac{3}{2} & | & -\frac{5}{2} \\ 3 & 1 & -2 & | & -10 \end{bmatrix} \xrightarrow{r_2'=r_2-3r_1} \begin{bmatrix} 1 & -\frac{1}{2} & -\frac{3}{2} & | & -\frac{5}{2} \\ 0 & \frac{5}{2} & \frac{5}{2} & | & -\frac{5}{2} \end{bmatrix}$

$\xrightarrow{r_2'=\frac{2}{5}r_2} \begin{bmatrix} 1 & -\frac{1}{2} & -\frac{3}{2} & | & -\frac{5}{2} \\ 0 & 1 & 1 & | & -1 \end{bmatrix} \xrightarrow{r_1'=r_1+\frac{1}{2}r_2} \begin{bmatrix} 1 & 0 & -1 & | & -3 \\ 0 & 1 & 1 & | & -1 \end{bmatrix}$

Solving for a in the first equation we obtain: $a = -3 + c$. Solving for b in the second equation we obtain: $b = -1 - c$. Thus the general solution of the system is $(-3 + c, -1 - c, c)$. For $c = 0$ and $c = 2$, we obtain the following particular solutions: $(-3, -1, 0)$, and $(-1, -3, 2)$.

61. Let x be the smallest number, z be the largest number, and y be the third number.

$\begin{cases} x + y + z = 108 \\ -x - y + z = -16 \\ x - 2y + z = 0 \end{cases} \rightarrow \begin{bmatrix} 1 & 1 & 1 & | & 108 \\ -1 & -1 & 1 & | & -16 \\ 1 & -2 & 1 & | & 0 \end{bmatrix} \xrightarrow[r_3'=r_3-r_1]{r_2'=r_2+r_1} \begin{bmatrix} 1 & 1 & 1 & | & 108 \\ 0 & 0 & 2 & | & 92 \\ 0 & -3 & 0 & | & -108 \end{bmatrix} \xrightarrow{r_2 \leftrightarrow r_3} \begin{bmatrix} 1 & 1 & 1 & | & 108 \\ 0 & -3 & 0 & | & -108 \\ 0 & 0 & 2 & | & 92 \end{bmatrix}$

$\xrightarrow{r_2'=-\frac{1}{3}r_2} \begin{bmatrix} 1 & 1 & 1 & | & 108 \\ 0 & 1 & 0 & | & 36 \\ 0 & 0 & 2 & | & 92 \end{bmatrix} \xrightarrow{r_1'=r_1-r_2} \begin{bmatrix} 1 & 0 & 1 & | & 72 \\ 0 & 1 & 0 & | & 36 \\ 0 & 0 & 2 & | & 92 \end{bmatrix} \xrightarrow{r_3'=\frac{1}{3}r_3} \begin{bmatrix} 1 & 0 & 1 & | & 72 \\ 0 & 1 & 0 & | & 36 \\ 0 & 0 & 1 & | & 46 \end{bmatrix} \xrightarrow{r_1'=r_1-r_3} \begin{bmatrix} 1 & 0 & 0 & | & 26 \\ 0 & 1 & 0 & | & 36 \\ 0 & 0 & 1 & | & 46 \end{bmatrix}$

The numbers are 26, 36, and 46.

63. Let x be the smallest side, z be the largest side, and y be the third side.

$\begin{cases} x + y + z = 168 \\ -2x + z = 0 \\ x - y + z = 48 \end{cases} \rightarrow \begin{bmatrix} 1 & 1 & 1 & | & 168 \\ -2 & 0 & 1 & | & 0 \\ 1 & -1 & 1 & | & 48 \end{bmatrix} \xrightarrow[r_3'=r_3-r_1]{r_2'=r_2+2r_1} \begin{bmatrix} 1 & 1 & 1 & | & 168 \\ 0 & 2 & 3 & | & 336 \\ 0 & -2 & 0 & | & -120 \end{bmatrix} \xrightarrow{r_2'=\frac{1}{2}r_2} \begin{bmatrix} 1 & 1 & 1 & | & 168 \\ 0 & 1 & \frac{3}{2} & | & 168 \\ 0 & -2 & 0 & | & -120 \end{bmatrix}$

$\xrightarrow[r_3'=r_3+2r_2]{r_1'=r_1-r_2} \begin{bmatrix} 1 & 0 & -\frac{1}{2} & | & 0 \\ 0 & 1 & \frac{3}{2} & | & 168 \\ 0 & 0 & 3 & | & 216 \end{bmatrix} \xrightarrow{r_3'=\frac{1}{3}r_3} \begin{bmatrix} 1 & 0 & -\frac{1}{2} & | & 0 \\ 0 & 1 & \frac{3}{2} & | & 168 \\ 0 & 0 & 1 & | & 72 \end{bmatrix} \xrightarrow[r_1'=r_1-\frac{3}{2}r_2]{r_1'=r_1+\frac{1}{2}r_3} \begin{bmatrix} 1 & 0 & 0 & | & 36 \\ 0 & 1 & 0 & | & 60 \\ 0 & 0 & 1 & | & 72 \end{bmatrix}$

The lengths of the sides are 36 cm, 60 cm, and 72 cm.

65.

$$\begin{cases} A+B+C=180 \\ A-B-C=9 \\ -2B+C=0 \end{cases} \rightarrow \begin{bmatrix} 1 & 1 & 1 & | & 180 \\ 1 & -1 & -1 & | & 9 \\ 0 & -2 & 1 & | & 0 \end{bmatrix} \xrightarrow{r_2'=r_2-r_1} \begin{bmatrix} 1 & 1 & 1 & | & 180 \\ 0 & -2 & -2 & | & -171 \\ 0 & -2 & 1 & | & 0 \end{bmatrix} \xrightarrow{r_2'=-\frac{1}{2}r_2} \begin{bmatrix} 1 & 1 & 1 & | & 180 \\ 0 & 1 & 1 & | & 85.5 \\ 0 & -2 & 1 & | & 0 \end{bmatrix}$$

$$\xrightarrow[r_3'=r_3+2r_2]{r_1'=r_1-r_2} \begin{bmatrix} 1 & 0 & 0 & | & 94.5 \\ 0 & 1 & 1 & | & 85.5 \\ 0 & 0 & 3 & | & 171 \end{bmatrix} \xrightarrow{r_3'=\frac{1}{3}r_3} \begin{bmatrix} 1 & 0 & 0 & | & 94.5 \\ 0 & 1 & 1 & | & 85.5 \\ 0 & 0 & 1 & | & 57 \end{bmatrix} \xrightarrow{r_2'=r_2-r_3} \begin{bmatrix} 1 & 0 & 0 & | & 94.5 \\ 0 & 1 & 0 & | & 28.5 \\ 0 & 0 & 1 & | & 57 \end{bmatrix}$$

The angles are $94.5°$, $28.5°$, and $57°$.

67. $\begin{cases} .06A+.04B+.05C=133 \\ .15A+.18B+.20C=494 \\ .45A+.65B+.70C=1700 \end{cases} \rightarrow \begin{bmatrix} .06 & .04 & .05 & | & 133 \\ .15 & .18 & .20 & | & 494 \\ .45 & .65 & .70 & | & 1700 \end{bmatrix} \rightarrow ... \rightarrow \begin{bmatrix} 1 & 0 & 0 & | & 600 \\ 0 & 1 & 0 & | & 800 \\ 0 & 0 & 1 & | & 1300 \end{bmatrix}$

The zookeeper should use 600 grams of A, 800 grams of B and 1300 grams of C.

69. The intercepts of $2x+y+3z=6$ are $(0, 0, 2)$, $(0, 6, 0)$, and $(3, 0, 0)$. Thus the graph is **B**.

71. The intercepts of $4x+2y+3z=12$ are
$(0, 0, 4)$, $(0, 6, 0)$, and $(3, 0, 0)$.

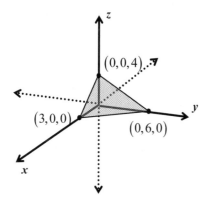

Cumulative Review

1. $d=\sqrt{(x_2-x_1)^2+(y_2-y_1)^2}$
$=\sqrt{(10-2)^2+(12-(-3))^2}$
$=\sqrt{8^2+15^2}=\sqrt{64+225}$
$=\sqrt{289}=17$

2. $c^2=a^2+b^2$
$c^2=(7)^2+(24)^2$
$c^2=49+576$
$c^2=625$
$c=25$

3. $(x-5)(x^2+5x+25)=x^3+5x^2+25x-5x^2-25x-125$
$=x^3+\cancel{5x^2}-\cancel{5x^2}+\cancel{25x}-\cancel{25x}-125$
$=x^3-125$

4. The integer factors of 36 between 1 and 36 are: 1, 2, 3, 4, 6, 9, 12, 18, and 36 .

5. 37 is prime. Its only factors are 1 and 37.

Section 12.3: Horizontal and Vertical Translations of the Graphs of Functions

Quick Review 12.3

1.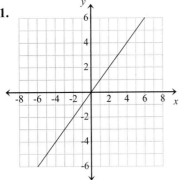

2.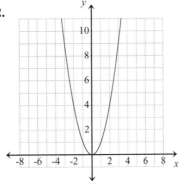

3.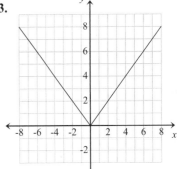

4.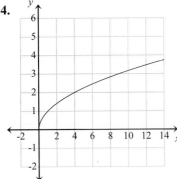

5.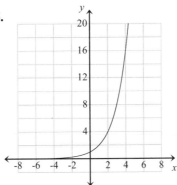

Exercises 12.3

1. The graph of $f(x) = |x| + 3$ is the graph of $y = |x|$ shifted up 3 units. Thus the answer is **C**.

3. The graph of $f(x) = |x| - 3$ is the graph of $y = |x|$ shifted down 3 units. Thus the answer is **D**.

5. The graph of $f(x) = x^2 - 5$ is the graph of $y = x^2$ shifted down 5 units. Thus the answer is **D**.

7. The graph of $f(x) = (x + 5)^2$ is the graph of $y = x^2$ shifted left 5 units. Thus the answer is **B**.

9. The graph of $f(x) = \sqrt{x - 4}$ is the graph of $y = \sqrt{x}$ shifted right 4 units. Thus the answer is **C**.

11. The graph of $f(x) = \sqrt{x} + 4$ is the graph of $y = \sqrt{x}$ shifted up 4 units. Thus the answer is **D**.

13. The graph of $f(x) = |x - 1| + 2$ is the graph of $y = |x|$ shifted right 1 unit and up 2 units. Thus the answer is **B**.

15. The graph of $f(x) = |x + 1| + 2$ is the graph of $y = |x|$ shifted left 1 unit and up 2 units. Thus the answer is **D**.

17. The graph of $y = f(x) - 3$ is the graph of $y = f(x)$ shifted down three units.

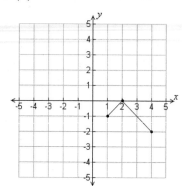

19. The graph of $y = f(x+4)$ is the graph of $y = f(x)$ shifted left four units.

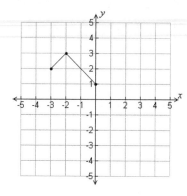

21. The graph of $y = f(x-1) + 2$ is the graph of $y = f(x)$ shifted right one unit down three units.

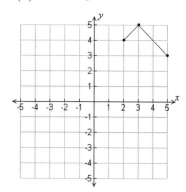

23. The graph shown is the graph of $y = \dfrac{x}{2}$ shifted up 3 units. Thus the equation is $y = \dfrac{x}{2} + 3$. y-intercept: $(0, 3)$

25.

x	$y = f(x) + 10$
-3	$0 + 10 = 10$
-2	$8 + 10 = 18$
-1	$6 + 10 = 16$
0	$0 + 10 = 10$
1	$-4 + 10 = 6$
2	$0 + 10 = 10$

27. The elements in the y_2 column are 7 units less than the elements in the $y_1 = f(x)$ column. Thus the equation for y_2 is $y_2 = f(x) - 7$.

29.

x	$y_1 = f(x)$
0	-3
1	-1
2	1
3	3
4	5
5	7

x	$y_2 = f(x-4)$
4	-3
5	-1
6	1
7	3
8	5
9	7

For the same y value in y_1 and y_2, the x-value is 4 units more for y_2 than for y_1.

31. For the same y value in y_1 and y_2, the x-value is 3 units more for y_2 than for y_1.

Thus the equation for y_2 is $y_2 = f(x-3)$.

33. The graph of $y = (x-6)^2$ is the graph of $y = x^2$ shifted right 6 units. Thus the vertex is $(6, 0)$.

35. The graph of $f(x) = x^2 + 11$ is the graph of $y = x^2$ shifted up 11 units. Thus the vertex is $(0, 11)$.

37. The graph of $f(x) = (x+5)^2 - 8$ is the graph of $y = x^2$ shifted left 5 units and down 8 units. Thus the vertex is $(-5, -8)$.

39. The graph of $f(x) = |x| - 13$ is the graph of $y = |x|$ shifted down 13 units. Thus the vertex is $(0, -13)$.

41. The graph of $f(x) = |x+15|$ is the graph of $y = |x|$ shifted left 15 units. Thus the vertex is $(-15, 0)$.

43. The graph of $f(x) = |x-7| - 6$ is the graph of $y = |x|$ shifted right 7 units and down 6 units. Thus the vertex is $(7, -6)$.

45. A translation of the graph of $y = f(x)$ eleven units left is obtained in the graph of $y = f(x+11)$. Answer: **E.**

47. A translation of the graph of $y = f(x)$ eleven units down is obtained in the graph of $y = f(x) - 11$. Answer: **D.**

49. A translation of the graph of $y = f(x)$ eleven units up and eleven units right is obtained in the graph of $y = f(x-11) + 11$. Answer: **A.**

51. Domain: $[0+3, 5+3) = [3, 8)$; Range: $[2, 4)$

53. Domain: $[0, 5)$; Range: $[2-7, 4-7) = [-5, -3)$

55. Domain: $[0-4, 5-4) = [-4, 1)$; Range: $[2+5, 4+5) = [7, 9)$

57. The graph of $f(x) = x - 6$ is the graph of the linear equation $y = x$ shifted down 6 units. Answer: **D.**

59. The graph of $f(x) = |x+5|$ is the graph of the absolute value equation $y = |x|$ shifted left 5 units. Answer: **A.**

61. The graph of $f(x) = \sqrt{x} + 3$ is the graph of the square root equation $y = \sqrt{x}$ shifted up 3 units. Answer: **E.**

63. The graph of $f(x) = \sqrt[3]{x} - 5$ is the graph of the cube root equation $y = \sqrt[3]{x}$ shifted down 5 units. Answer: **H.**

65. a.

n	$a_n = 2n$
1	$a_1 = 2(1) = 2$
2	$a_2 = 2(2) = 4$
3	$a_3 = 2(3) = 6$
4	$a_4 = 2(4) = 8$
5	$a_5 = 2(5) = 10$

b.

n	$a_n = 2n+3$
1	$a_1 = 2(1)+3 = 5$
2	$a_2 = 2(2)+3 = 7$
3	$a_3 = 2(3)+3 = 9$
4	$a_4 = 2(4)+3 = 11$
5	$a_5 = 2(5)+3 = 13$

c.

n	$a_n = 2(n+3)$
1	$a_1 = 2(1+3) = 2(4) = 8$
2	$a_2 = 2(2+3) = 2(5) = 10$
3	$a_3 = 2(3+3) = 2(6) = 12$
4	$a_4 = 2(4+3) = 2(7) = 14$
5	$a_5 = 2(5+3) = 2(8) = 16$

d.

n	$a_n = -2n$
1	$a_1 = -2(1) = -2$
2	$a_2 = -2(2) = -4$
3	$a_3 = -2(3) = -6$
4	$a_4 = -2(4) = -8$
5	$a_5 = -2(5) = -10$

67.

t Celsius	V $V(t) = 4t$
200	800
150	600
100	400
50	200
0	0

t Kelvin	V $V = 4(t-273)$
473	800
423	600
373	400
323	200
273	0

For the same V value in the tables, the x-value is 273 units more for the second table than the first table.

69.

x item #	$P(x)+1$ price
1	$24.95 + 1 = 25.95$
2	$33.79 + 1 = 34.79$
3	$12.98 + 1 = 13.98$
4	$26.78 + 1 = 27.78$
5	$19.95 + 1 = 20.95$

Cumulative Review

1.
$$\frac{x}{x-2} + \frac{1}{x} = \frac{x}{x-2} \cdot \frac{x}{x} + \frac{1}{x} \cdot \frac{x-2}{x-2}$$
$$= \frac{x^2}{x(x-2)} + \frac{x-2}{x(x-2)}$$
$$= \frac{x^2+x-2}{x(x-2)} = \frac{x^2+x-2}{x(x-2)}$$
$$= \frac{(x+2)(x-1)}{x(x-2)}$$

2.
$$\frac{x}{x-2} \cdot \frac{1}{x} = \frac{\not{x}}{x-2} \cdot \frac{1}{\not{x}} = \frac{1}{x-2}$$

3.
$$\frac{x}{x-2} \div \frac{1}{x} = \frac{x}{x-2} \cdot \frac{x}{1} = \frac{x^2}{x-2}$$

4.
$$(x-y)^2 - x^2 - y^2 = x^2 - 2xy + y^2 - x^2 - y^2$$
$$= x^2 - x^2 - 2xy + y^2 - y^2$$
$$= -2xy$$

5.
$$5(2x-3y) - 4(x-2y) + 3x - y = 10x - 15y - 4x + 8y + 3x - y$$
$$= 10x + 3x - 4x - 15y + 8y - y$$
$$= 9x - 8y$$

Section 12.4: Stretching, Shrinking, and Reflecting Graphs of Functions

Quick Review 12.4

1. $f(2) = 3(2)^2 - 4 = 3 \cdot 4 - 4 = 12 - 4 = 8$

2. $-f(2) = -\left(3(2)^2 - 4\right) = -(3 \cdot 4 - 4) = -(12 - 4) = -8$

3. $f(-2) = 3(-2)^2 - 4 = 3 \cdot 4 - 4 = 12 - 4 = 8$

4. $f(0) = 3(0)^2 - 4 = 3 \cdot 0 - 4 = -4$

5. $-f(0) = -\left(3(0)^2 - 4\right) = -(3 \cdot 0 - 4) = -(-4) = 4$

Exercises 12.4

1. The graph of the absolute value function $f(x) = |x|$ is given in choice **G**.

3. The graph of the linear function $f(x) = x$ is given in choice **B**.

5. The graph of the square root function $f(x) = \sqrt{x}$ is given in choice **E**.

7. The graph of the cubic function $f(x) = x^3$ is given in choice **D**.

9.

x	$f(x)$	$-f(x)$
0	4	−4
1	2	−2
2	2	−2
3	4	−4
4	6	−6

11.

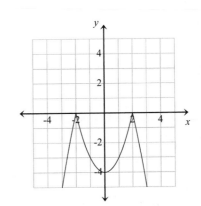

13. The graph of the scaled function $f(x) = 2x^2$ can be found by vertically stretching the graph of $y = x^2$ by a factor of 2. Thus the answer is **B**.

15. The graph of the scaled function $f(x) = \dfrac{1}{2}x^2$ can be found by vertically shrinking the graph of $y = x^2$ by a factor of $1/2$. Thus the answer is **A**.

17. The graph of the linear function $f(x) = 5x$ is the graph that has the greatest positive slope. Thus the answer is **D**.

19. The graph of the linear function $f(x) = -2x$ is the graph that has the greatest negative slope. Thus the answer is **A**.

21. The graph of the scaled function $f(x) = \frac{3}{4}|x|$ can be found by vertically shrinking the graph of $y = |x|$ by a factor of $3/4$. Thus the answer is **D**.

23. The graph of the scaled function $f(x) = \frac{3}{2}|x|$ can be found by vertically stretching the graph of $y = |x|$ by a factor of $3/2$. Thus the answer is **A**. (Note that the graph in **B** is stretched more than the graph in **A**.)

25. The graph of the scaled function $f(x) = 4\sqrt{x}$ can be found by vertically stretching the graph of $y = \sqrt{x}$ by a factor of 4. Thus the answer is **B**.

27. The graph of the scaled function $f(x) = \frac{3}{4}\sqrt{x}$ can be found by vertically shrinking the graph of $y = \sqrt{x}$ by a factor of $3/4$. Thus the answer is **A**. (Note that the graph in **C** is compressed more than the graph in **A**.)

29. The graph of $y = -f(x)$ is the graph of $y = f(x)$ reflected across the x-axis.

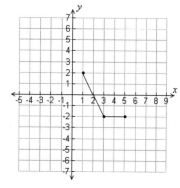

31. The graph of $y = 2f(x)$ is obtained by vertically stretching the graph of $y = f(x)$ by a factor of 2.

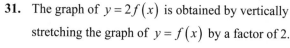
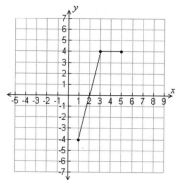

33. The graph of $y = f(x) + 2$ is the graph of $y = f(x)$ shifted up two units.

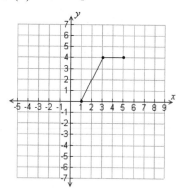

35.

x	$-f(x)$
-2	-18
-1	-9
0	-3
1	-1
2	-3

37.

x	$2f(x)$
-2	$2(18) = 36$
-1	$2(9) = 18$
0	$2(3) = 6$
1	$2(1) = 2$
2	$2(3) = 6$

39. For each value of x, $y_2 = \frac{1}{2}y_1$. Thus $y_2 = \frac{1}{2}f(x)$.

41. For each value of x, $y_2 = -\frac{1}{4}y_1$. Thus $y_2 = -\frac{1}{4}f(x)$.

43. For each value of x, $y_2 = y_1 - 8$. Thus $y_2 = f(x) - 8$.

45. For the same y value in y_1 and y_2, the x-value is 3 units less for y_2 than for y_1. Thus the equation for y_2 is $y_2 = f(x+3)$.

47. The graph of $f(x) = 8x^2$ is obtained by vertically stretching the graph of $f(x) = x^2$ by a factor of 8. The location of the vertex $(0, 0)$ will not change.

49. The graph of $f(x) = 8x^2 - 7$ is obtained by vertically stretching the graph of $f(x) = x^2$ by a factor of 8 and then shifting the graph down 7 units. Thus the vertex is $(0, -7)$.

51. The graph of $f(x) = (x-8)^2 - 7$ is obtained by shifting the graph of $f(x) = x^2$ right 8 units and down 7 units. Thus the vertex is $(8, -7)$.

53. The graph of $f(x) = -(x-8)^2 + 7$ is obtained by shifting the reflection of the graph of $f(x) = x^2$ right 8 units and up 7 units. Thus the vertex is $(8, 7)$.

55.

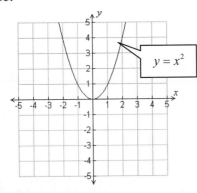

$y = x^2$

a.

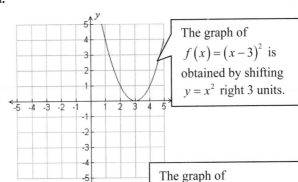

The graph of $f(x) = (x-3)^2$ is obtained by shifting $y = x^2$ right 3 units.

b.

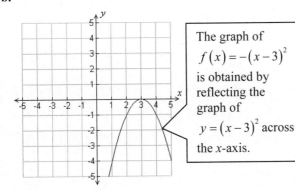

The graph of $f(x) = -(x-3)^2$ is obtained by reflecting the graph of $y = (x-3)^2$ across the x-axis.

c.

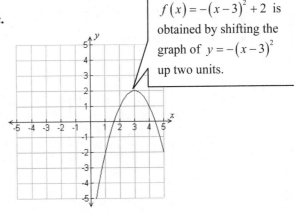

The graph of $f(x) = -(x-3)^2 + 2$ is obtained by shifting the graph of $y = -(x-3)^2$ up two units.

57. A vertical stretching of $y = f(x)$ by a factor of 7 is obtained by multiplying the function by 7. Answer: **B**.

59. A reflection of $y = f(x)$ is obtained by multiplying the function by -1. Answer: **D**.

61. A horizontal shift of $y = f(x)$ right 7 units is obtained by subtracting 7 to x within the function. Answer: **F**.

63. Range: $[2+2, 6+2) = [4, 8)$ **65.** Range: $[2(2), 2(6)) = [4, 12)$

67. Range: $(-6, -2]$

69. a.

n	$a_n = n^3$
1	$a_1 = (1)^3 = 1$
2	$a_2 = (2)^3 = 8$
3	$a_3 = (3)^3 = 27$
4	$a_4 = (4)^3 = 64$
5	$a_5 = (5)^3 = 125$

b.

n	$a_n = -n^3$
1	$a_1 = -(1)^3 = -1$
2	$a_2 = -(2)^3 = -8$
3	$a_3 = -(3)^3 = -27$
4	$a_4 = -(4)^3 = -64$
5	$a_5 = -(5)^3 = -125$

c.

n	$a_n = 2n^3$
1	$a_1 = 2(1)^3 = 2$
2	$a_2 = 2(2)^3 = 16$
3	$a_3 = 2(3)^3 = 54$
4	$a_4 = 2(4)^3 = 128$
5	$a_5 = 2(5)^3 = 250$

d.

n	$a_n = n^3 - 2$
1	$a_1 = (1)^3 - 2 = -1$
2	$a_2 = (2)^3 - 2 = 6$
3	$a_3 = (3)^3 - 2 = 25$
4	$a_4 = (4)^3 - 2 = 62$
5	$a_5 = (5)^3 - 2 = 123$

71. **a.** $A_n = n$

   b. $V_n = 50n$

73.

Investment I

T years	I interest
5	4000
10	8000
15	12000
20	16000

Investment II

T years	I interest
5	$\frac{3}{4}(4000) = 3,000$
10	$\frac{3}{4}(8000) = 6,000$
15	$\frac{3}{4}(12000) = 9,000$
20	$\frac{3}{4}(16000) = 12,000$

Cumulative Review

1. The horizontal line through $(2, -3)$ is $y = -3$

2. The vertical line through $(2, -3)$ is $x = 2$

3. Use the point-slope form of the line:
$$y - y_1 = m(x - x_1)$$
$$y - (-3) = \frac{3}{5}(x - 2)$$
$$y + 3 = \frac{3}{5}x - \frac{6}{5}$$
$$y = \frac{3}{5}x - \frac{6}{5} - 3$$
$$y = \frac{3}{5}x - \frac{21}{5}$$

4. First, find the slope: $m = \dfrac{2 - (-3)}{7 - 2} = \dfrac{5}{5} = 1$.

Use the slope intercept form:
$$y - y_1 = m(x - x_1)$$
$$y - (-3) = 1(x - 2)$$
$$y + 3 = x - 2$$
$$y = x - 5$$

5. Using the point-slope form we know that the
    equation of the line is:

$$y - y_1 = m(x - x_1)$$

$$y - (-3) = -\frac{3}{4}(x - 2)$$

$$y + 3 = -\frac{3}{4}x + \frac{6}{4}$$

$$y + 3 = -\frac{3}{4}x + \frac{6}{4}$$

$$y = -\frac{3}{4}x + \frac{6}{4} - 3$$

$$y = -\frac{3}{4}x - \frac{3}{2}$$

With $x = 6$ we have

$$y = -\frac{3}{4}(6) - \frac{3}{2} = -\frac{9}{2} - \frac{3}{2} = -\frac{12}{2} = -6$$

Section 12.5: Algebra of Functions

Quick Review 12.5

1. $(2x^2 - 7x - 15) + (2x + 3) = 2x^2 - 7x - 15 + 2x + 3$

    $= 2x^2 - 7x + 2x - 15 + 3$

    $= 2x^2 - 5x - 12$

2. $(2x^2 - 7x - 15) - (2x + 3) = 2x^2 - 7x - 15 - 2x - 3$

    $= 2x^2 - 7x - 2x - 15 - 3$

    $= 2x^2 - 9x - 18$

3. $(2x^2 - 7x - 15)(2x + 3)$

    $= 4x^3 + 6x^2 - 14x^2 - 21x - 30x - 45$

    $= 4x^3 - 8x^2 - 51x - 45$

4. $\dfrac{2x^2 - 7x - 15}{2x + 3} = \dfrac{(2x+3)(x-5)}{(2x+3)} = x - 5$

5. First, write $y = 2x + 3$.

    Next, swap all values of x and y.

    $$x = 2y + 3$$

    Now, solve for y.

    $$x = 2y + 3$$

    $$x - 3 = 2y$$

    $$y = \frac{x - 3}{2}$$

    The inverse of $f(x)$ is $f^{-1}(x) = \dfrac{x - 3}{2}$.

Exercises 12.5

1.　**a.**　$(f+g)(2)=f(2)+g(2)$
$$=\left(\left(2\right)^2-1\right)+\left(2(2)+5\right)$$
$$=(3)+(9)=12$$

　b.　$(f-g)(2)=f(2)-g(2)$
$$=\left(\left(2\right)^2-1\right)-\left(2(2)+5\right)$$
$$=(3)-(9)=-6$$

　c.　$(f\cdot g)(2)=f(2)\cdot g(2)$
$$=\left(\left(2\right)^2-1\right)\cdot\left(2(2)+5\right)$$
$$=(3)\cdot(9)=27$$

　d.　$\left(\dfrac{f}{g}\right)(2)=\dfrac{f(2)}{g(2)}$
$$=\dfrac{\left(\left(2\right)^2-1\right)}{\left(2(2)+5\right)}$$
$$=\dfrac{3}{9}=\dfrac{1}{3}$$

3.

x	$f+g$
0	$(-2)+(-1)=-3$
3	$(0)+(5)=5$
8	$(7)+(9)=16$

5.

x	$g-f$
0	$(-1)-(-2)=1$
3	$(5)-(0)=5$
8	$(9)-(7)=2$

7.

x	$g\cdot f$
0	$(-1)\cdot(-2)=2$
3	$(5)\cdot(0)=0$
8	$(9)\cdot(7)=63$

9.

x	$f-g$
-2	$3-4=-1$
1	$5-(-1)=6$
4	$7-6=1$

$f-g=\{(-2,-1),(1,6),(4,1)\}$

11.

x	$f+g$
-2	$\dfrac{3}{4}$
1	$\dfrac{5}{-1}=-5$
4	$\dfrac{7}{6}$

$f-g=\left\{\left(-2,\dfrac{3}{4}\right),(1,-5),\left(4,\dfrac{7}{6}\right)\right\}$

13.

x	$f+g$
-3	$1+2=3$
-1	$2+(-1)=1$
1	$3+1=4$
3	$(-2)+1=-1$
5	$1+1=2$

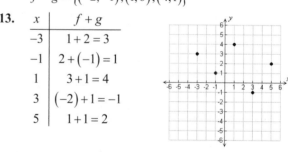

15.

x	$f\cdot g$
-3	$1\cdot2=2$
-1	$2\cdot(-1)=-2$
1	$3\cdot1=3$
3	$(-2)\cdot1=-2$
5	$1\cdot1=1$

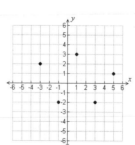

17.　f and g are not equal.　$f(2)$ is defined and $g(2)$ is not defined.　(The functions do not have the same domains.)

19. f and g are not equal. They do not have the same domains.

21. f and g are equal.

23. a. $(f \circ g)(2) = f(g(2))$
$= f(2(2)+5)$
$= f(9) = (9)^2 - 1 = 80$

b. $(g \circ f)(2) = g(f(2))$
$= g((2)^2 - 1)$
$= g(3) = 2(3) + 5 = 11$

c. $(f \circ f)(2) = f(f(2))$
$= f((2)^2 - 1)$
$= f(3) = 3^2 - 1 = 8$

d. $(g \circ g)(2) = g(g(2))$
$= g(2(2)+5)$
$= g(9) = 2(9) + 5 = 23$

25.

$x \xrightarrow{g} g(x) \xrightarrow{f} f(g(x))$	$x \longrightarrow f(g(x))$
$3 \longrightarrow 5 \longrightarrow 9$	$3 \longrightarrow 9$
$4 \longrightarrow 2 \longrightarrow 8$	$4 \longrightarrow 8$
$7 \longrightarrow 1 \longrightarrow 0$	$7 \longrightarrow 0$
$8 \longrightarrow 4 \longrightarrow 6$	$8 \longrightarrow 6$

27. a.

$x \xrightarrow{g} g(x) \xrightarrow{f} f(g(x))$	$x \longrightarrow f(g(x))$
$-3 \longrightarrow 2 \longrightarrow -1$	$-3 \longrightarrow -1$
$-1 \longrightarrow 3 \longrightarrow 4$	$-1 \longrightarrow 4$
$2 \longrightarrow -2 \longrightarrow 0$	$2 \longrightarrow 0$
$4 \longrightarrow 0 \longrightarrow -2$	$4 \longrightarrow -2$

$(f \circ g)(x) = \{(-3,-1),(-1,4),(2,0),(4,-2)\}$

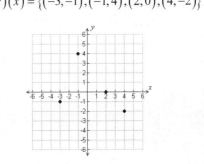

29. $(f \circ g)(x) = f(g(x)) = f(4x-2) = (4x-2)^2 - 5(4x-2) + 3 = 16x^2 - 16x + 4 - 20x + 10 + 3$
$= 16x^2 - 36x + 17$
$(g \circ f)(x) = g(f(x)) = g(x^2 - 5x + 3) = 4(x^2 - 5x + 3) - 2 = 4x^2 - 20x + 12 - 2 = 4x^2 - 20x + 10$

31. $(f \circ g)(x) = f(g(x)) = f(x+5) = \sqrt{x+5}$
$(g \circ f)(x) = g(f(x)) = g(\sqrt{x}) = \sqrt{x} + 5$

33. $(f \circ g)(x) = f(g(x)) = f(x^2 - 4) = \dfrac{1}{(x^2-4)+2} = \dfrac{1}{x^2 - 2}$

$(g \circ f)(x) = g(f(x)) = g\left(\dfrac{1}{x+2}\right) = \left(\dfrac{1}{x+2}\right)^2 - 4 = \dfrac{1}{(x+2)^2} - 4 = \dfrac{1-4(x+2)^2}{(x+2)^2}$

$= \dfrac{1-4x^2-16x-16}{(x+2)^2} = -\dfrac{4x^2+16x+15}{(x+2)^2} = -\dfrac{(2x+3)(2x+5)}{(x+2)^2}$

35. $(f+g)(x) = (6x^2 - x - 15) + (3x - 5) = 6x^2 - x - 15 + 3x - 5 = 6x^2 + 2x - 20;$ Domain: $(-\infty, \infty)$ or $\mathbb{R}$

$(f-g)(x) = (6x^2 - x - 15) - (3x - 5) = 6x^2 - x - 15 - 3x + 5 = 6x^2 - 4x - 10;$ Domain: $(-\infty, \infty)$ or $\mathbb{R}$

$(f \cdot g)(x) = (6x^2 - x - 15) \cdot (3x - 5) = 6x^2(3x-5) - x(3x-5) - 15(3x-5)$
$\qquad = 18x^3 - 30x^2 - 3x^2 + 5x - 45x + 75 = 18x^3 - 33x^2 - 40x + 75;$ Domain: $(-\infty, \infty)$ or $\mathbb{R}$

$(f+g)(x) = \dfrac{6x^2 - x - 15}{3x - 5} = \dfrac{\cancel{(3x-5)}(2x+3)}{\cancel{3x-5}} = 2x + 3;$ Domain: $\left(-\infty, \dfrac{5}{3}\right) \cup \left(\dfrac{5}{3}, \infty\right)$ or $\mathbb{R} \sim \left\{\dfrac{5}{3}\right\}$

$(f \circ g)(x) = f(g(x)) = f(3x - 5) = 6(3x - 5)^2 - (3x - 5) - 15 = 6(9x^2 - 30x + 25) - 3x + 5 - 15$
$\qquad = 54x^2 - 180x + 150 - 3x - 10 = 54x^2 - 183x + 140;$ Domain: $(-\infty, \infty)$ or $\mathbb{R}$

37. $(f+g)(x) = (5x - 7) + (3) = 5x - 4;$ Domain: $(-\infty, \infty)$ or $\mathbb{R}$

$(f-g)(x) = (5x - 7) - (3) = 5x - 10;$ Domain: $(-\infty, \infty)$ or $\mathbb{R}$

$(f \cdot g)(x) = (5x - 7) \cdot (3) = 15x - 21;$ Domain: $(-\infty, \infty)$ or $\mathbb{R}$

$\left(\dfrac{f}{g}\right)(x) = \dfrac{5x - 7}{3};$ Domain: $(-\infty, \infty)$ or $\mathbb{R}$

$(f \circ g)(x) = f(g(x)) = f(3) = 5(3) - 7 = 8;$ Domain: $(-\infty, \infty)$ or $\mathbb{R}$

39.

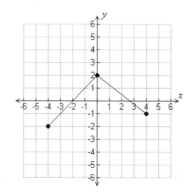

41. $(f \circ f^{-1})(x) = f(f^{-1}(x))$

$\qquad = f\left(\dfrac{3x+1}{2}\right) = \dfrac{\cancel{2}\left(\dfrac{3x+1}{\cancel{2}}\right) - 1}{3}$

$\qquad = \dfrac{(3x+1) - 1}{3} = \dfrac{\cancel{3}x}{\cancel{3}} = x$

$(f^{-1} \circ f)(x) = f^{-1}(f(x))$

$\qquad = f^{-1}\left(\dfrac{2x-1}{3}\right) = \dfrac{\cancel{3}\left(\dfrac{2x-1}{\cancel{3}}\right) + 1}{2}$

$\qquad = \dfrac{(2x-1) + 1}{2} = \dfrac{\cancel{2}x}{\cancel{2}} = x$

43. $h(x) = (f+g)(x) = f(x) + g(x)$
$\qquad = (x^2 + 1) + (\sqrt{x}) = x^2 + \sqrt{x} + 1$

45. $h(x) = (g \circ f)(x) = g(f(x))$
$\qquad = g(x^2 + 1) = \sqrt{x^2 + 1}$

47. Let $g(x) = x^2 + 4$ (the "inside" function)

and $f(x) = \sqrt[3]{x}$ (the "outside" function)

49. Let $g(x) = x + 2$ (the "inside" function)

and $f(x) = x^2 + 3x + 5$ (the "outside" function)

51. $P(x) = R(x) - C(x)$

$= (4u^2 - 3u) - (10u + 25)$

$= 4u^2 - 3u - 10u - 25$

$= 4u^2 - 13u - 25$

$P(10) = 4(10)^2 - 13(10) - 25 = \$245$

53.
  a. $V(b) = 10b$

  b. $f(b) = 3000$

  c. $C(b) = 10b + 3000$

  d. $A(b) = \dfrac{C(b)}{b} = \dfrac{10b + 3000}{b}$

  e. $R(b) = 12b$

  f. $P(b) = R(b) - C(b)$

     $= (12b) - (10b - 3000)$

     $= 2b - 3000$

  g. $P(1000) = 2(1000) - 3000 = -\$1000$

  h. $P(1500) = 2(1500) - 3000 = \$0$

  i. $P(2000) = 2(2000) - 3000 = \$1000$

  j. From part **h** we can determine that the company breaks even when 1,500 units are produced and sold.

55.
  a. $S(10) = 5(10) = 50$; The factory produces 50 sofas in 10 hours.

  b. $C(50) = (50)^2 - 6(50) + 500 = 2700$; The cost of producing 50 sofas is \$2700.

  c. $(C \circ S)(10) = C(S(10)) = C(50) = 2700$; The cost of operating the factory for 10 hours is \$2700.

  d. $(C \circ S)(t) = C(S(t)) = C(5t) = (5t)^2 - 6(5t) + 500 = 25t^2 - 30t + 500$

  e. $(C \circ S)(40) = 25(40)^2 - 30(40) + 500 = 39,300$; The cost of operating the factory for 40 hours is \$39,300.

  f. $(C \circ S)(100) = 25(100)^2 - 30(100) + 500 = 247,500$; The cost of operating the factory for 100 hours is \$247,500.

57.
  a. $r(s) = \dfrac{1}{2}s$

  b. $A(r) = \pi r^2$

  c. $(A \circ r)(s) = A(r(s))$

    $= A\left(\dfrac{1}{2}s\right) = \pi\left(\dfrac{1}{2}s\right)^2 = \dfrac{1}{4}\pi s^2$

59.
  a. $A = w^2$

  b. $w = 44 - 2x$

  c. $(A \circ w)(x) = A(w(x))$

    $= A(44 - 2x) = (44 - 2x)^2$

  d. $V = (\text{height})(\text{Area of Base})$

    $= x(44 - 2x)^2$

Cumulative Review

1. The additive identity is 0.

2. The multiplicative identity is 1.

3. The additive inverse of 6 is -6.

4. The multiplicative inverse of 6 is $\dfrac{1}{6}$.

5. The property that justifies rewriting $7x(3x - 2) + 5(3x - 2)$ as $(7x + 5)(3x - 2)$ is the distributive property of multiplication over addition.

Chapter 12: A preview of College Algebra

![Section bar] **Section 12.6:** Sequences, Series, and Summation Notation

Quick Review 12.6

1. $a_5 = 23$ **2.** $a_n = 4n + 8$

3.

n	$a_n = 3n + 5$
1	$3(1) + 5 = 8$
2	$3(2) + 5 = 11$
3	$3(3) + 5 = 14$
4	$3(4) + 5 = 17$
5	$3(5) + 5 = 20$

4.

n	$a_n = n^2 - 5n + 8$
1	$(1)^2 - 5(1) + 8 = 4$
2	$(2)^2 - 5(2) + 8 = 2$
3	$(3)^2 - 5(3) + 8 = 2$
4	$(4)^2 - 5(4) + 8 = 4$
5	$(5)^2 - 5(5) + 8 = 8$

5.

n	$a_n = 5 \cdot 2^{n-1}$
1	$5 \cdot 2^{1-1} = 5 \cdot 2^0 = 5$
2	$5 \cdot 2^{2-1} = 5 \cdot 2^1 = 10$
3	$5 \cdot 2^{3-1} = 5 \cdot 2^2 = 20$
4	$5 \cdot 2^{4-1} = 5 \cdot 2^3 = 40$
5	$5 \cdot 2^{5-1} = 5 \cdot 2^4 = 80$

Exercises 12.6

1.   **a.**   The sequence is geometric. The common ratio is $r = \dfrac{6}{1} = \dfrac{36}{6} = \dots = \dfrac{7776}{1296} = 6$.

   b.   The sequence is arithmetic. The common difference is $d = (6-1) = (11-5) = \dots = (26-21) = 5$.

   c.   The sequence is neither arithmetic nor geometric. (The sequence does not have a common ratio or common difference.)

   d.   The sequence is arithmetic with a common difference of $d = (6-6) = (6-6) = \dots = (6-6) = 0$.

   It is also geometric with a common ratio of $r = \dfrac{6}{6} = \dfrac{6}{6} = \dots = \dfrac{6}{6} = 1$.

3.   **a.**   The sequence: $-2, 1, 4, 7, 10, 13, \dots$ is arithmetic.

   The common difference is $d = (1-(-2)) = (4-1) = \dots = (13-10) = \dots = 3$.

   b.   The sequence: $1, 4, 9, 16, 25, 36, \dots$ is neither arithmetic nor geometric. (The sequence does not have a common ratio or common difference.)

   c.   The sequence: $4, 16, 64, 256, 1024, \dots$ is geometric.

   The common ratio is $r = \dfrac{4}{1} = \dfrac{16}{4} = \dots = \dfrac{1024}{256} = \dots = 4$.

   d.   The sequence: $7, 7, 7, 7, 7, \dots$ is arithmetic with a common difference of

   $d = (7-7) = (7-7) = \dots = (7-7) = \dots = 0$.

   It is also geometric with a common ratio of $r = \dfrac{7}{7} = \dfrac{7}{7} = \dots = \dfrac{7}{7} = \dots = 1$.

5.   **a.** $a_1 = 5(1) + 3 = 8$
   $a_2 = 5(2) + 3 = 13$
   $a_3 = 5(3) + 3 = 18$
   $a_4 = 5(4) + 3 = 23$
   $a_5 = 5(5) + 3 = 28$
   $a_6 = 5(6) + 3 = 33$
   Answer: 8, 13, 18, 23, 28, 33,...

   b. $a_1 = (1)^2 - (1) + 1 = 1$
   $a_2 = (2)^2 - (2) + 1 = 3$
   $a_3 = (3)^2 - (3) + 1 = 7$
   $a_4 = (4)^2 - (4) + 1 = 13$
   $a_5 = (5)^2 - (5) + 1 = 21$
   $a_6 = (6)^2 - (6) + 1 = 31$
   Answer: 1, 3, 7, 13, 21, 31,...

c.
$$a_1 = 16\left(\frac{1}{2}\right)^1 = 8$$

$$a_2 = 16\left(\frac{1}{2}\right)^2 = 4$$

$$a_3 = 16\left(\frac{1}{2}\right)^3 = 2$$

$$a_4 = 16\left(\frac{1}{2}\right)^4 = 1$$

$$a_5 = 16\left(\frac{1}{2}\right)^5 = \frac{1}{2}$$

$$a_6 = 16\left(\frac{1}{2}\right)^6 = \frac{1}{4}$$

Answer: $8, 4, 2, 1, \dfrac{1}{2}, \dfrac{1}{4}, \dots$

d.
$$a_1 = 5(-2)^1 = -10$$

$$a_2 = 5(-2)^2 = 20$$

$$a_3 = 5(-2)^3 = -40$$

$$a_4 = 5(-2)^4 = 80$$

$$a_5 = 5(-2)^5 = -160$$

$$a_6 = 5(-2)^6 = 320$$

Answer: $-10, 20, -40, 80, -160, 320\dots$

7. a.
$$a_1 = 18$$

$$a_2 = 18 - 4 = 14$$

$$a_3 = 14 - 4 = 10$$

$$a_4 = 10 - 4 = 6$$

$$a_5 = 6 - 4 = 2$$

$$a_6 = 2 - 4 = -2$$

Answer: $18, 14, 10, 6, 2, -2, \dots$

b.
$$a_1 = 18$$

$$a_2 = 18 - 2 = 16$$

$$a_3 = 16 - 2 = 14$$

$$a_4 = 14 - 2 = 12$$

$$a_5 = 12 - 2 = 10$$

$$a_6 = 10 - 2 = 8$$

Answer: $18, 16, 14, 12, 10, 8, \dots$

c.
$$a_1 = 7$$

$$a_2 = 7 - 2 = 5$$

$$a_3 = 5 - 2 = 3$$

$$a_4 = 3 - 2 = 1$$

$$a_5 = 1 - 2 = -1$$

$$a_6 = -1 - 2 = -3$$

Answer: $7, 5, 3, 1, -1, -3, \dots$

d.
$$a_1 = -9$$

$$a_2 = -9 + 3 = -6$$

$$a_3 = -6 + 3 = -3$$

$$a_4 = -3 + 3 = 0$$

$$a_5 = 0 + 3 = 3$$

$$a_6 = 3 + 3 = 6$$

Answer: $-9, -6, -3, 0, 3, 6, \dots$

9. a.
$$a_1 = 1$$

$$a_2 = 4 \cdot 1 = 4$$

$$a_3 = 4 \cdot 4 = 16$$

$$a_4 = 4 \cdot 16 = 64$$

$$a_5 = 4 \cdot 64 = 256$$

Answer: $1, 4, 16, 64, 256, \dots$

b.
$$a_1 = 1$$

$$a_2 = 2 \cdot 1 = 2$$

$$a_3 = 2 \cdot 2 = 4$$

$$a_4 = 2 \cdot 4 = 8$$

$$a_5 = 2 \cdot 8 = 16$$

Answer:
$1, 2, 4, 8, 16, \dots$

or $a_1 = 1$

$$a_2 = (-2) \cdot 1 = -2$$

$$a_3 = (-2) \cdot (-2) = 4$$

$$a_4 = (-2) \cdot 4 = -8$$

$$a_5 = (-2) \cdot (-8) = 16$$

Answer:
$1, -2, 4, -8, 16, \dots$

c. $a_1 = 16$

$$a_2 = \frac{1}{2}(16) = 8$$

$$a_3 = \frac{1}{2}(8) = 4$$

$$a_4 = \frac{1}{2}(4) = 2$$

$$a_5 = \frac{1}{2}(2) = 1$$

Answer: 16, 8, 4, 2, 1,...

d. $a_1 = 5$

$$a_2 = -3 \cdot (5) = -15$$

$$a_3 = -3 \cdot (-15) = 45$$

$$a_4 = -3 \cdot (45) = -135$$

$$a_5 = -3 \cdot (-135) = 405$$

Answer: 5, −15, 45, −135, 405,...

11. The nth term for an arithmetic sequence is determined by $a_n = a_1 + (n-1)d$.

a. $a_n = a_1 + (n-1)d$

$$a_{83} = 6 + (83-1)5 = 416$$

b. $d = 15 - 17 = -2$

$$a_n = a_1 + (n-1)d$$

$$a_{51} = 17 + (51-1)(-2) = -83$$

c. $d = 33 - 25 = 8$

$$a_{82} = a_{81} + d$$

$$a_{82} = 33 + 8 = 41$$

d. First, find d.

$$a_3 = a_1 + (3-1)d$$

$$12 = 2 + 2d$$

$$2d = 10$$

$$d = 5$$

$$a_n = a_1 + (n-1)d$$

$$a_{101} = 2 + (101-1)(5) = 502$$

13. $a_n = a_1 + (n-1)d$

$$-62 = 18 + (n-1)(-4)$$

$$-80 = (n-1)(-4)$$

$$n - 1 = 20$$

$$n = 21$$

15. $a_n = a_1 + (n-1)d$

$$216 = a_1 + (44-1)(12)$$

$$216 = a_1 + 516$$

$$a_1 = -300$$

17. $a_{31} = a_{11} + (20)d$

$$14 = 4 + 20d$$

$$20d = 10$$

$$d = \frac{1}{2}$$

19. $a_n = a_1 + (n-1)d$

$$14 = 5 + (n-1)\left(\frac{1}{5}\right)$$

$$9 = (n-1)\left(\frac{1}{5}\right)$$

$$n - 1 = 45$$

$$n = 46$$

21. $a_n = a_1 r^{n-1}$

$$\frac{1}{3} = 243\left(\frac{1}{3}\right)^{n-1}$$

$$\frac{1}{729} = \left(\frac{1}{3}\right)^{n-1}$$

$$\left(\frac{1}{3}\right)^6 = \left(\frac{1}{3}\right)^{n-1}$$

$$n - 1 = 6$$

$$n = 7$$

23. $a_n = a_1 r^{n-1}$

$$24 = a_1 (2)^{5-1}$$

$$24 = a_1 (16)$$

$$a_1 = \frac{3}{2}$$

25. $a_{11} = a_9 r^2$

$288 = 32(r)^2$

$r^2 = 9$

$r = 3 \ \text{or} \ -3$

27. $a_n = a_1 r^{n-1}$

$a_9 = \left(\dfrac{1}{3125}\right)(5)^{9-1} = 125$

29. a. $\displaystyle\sum_{i=1}^{6}(2i+3) = (2(1)+3)+(2(2)+3)+(2(3)+3)+(2(4)+3)+(2(5)+3)+(2(6)+3)$

$\qquad\qquad = 5+7+9+11+13+15 = 60$

b. $\displaystyle\sum_{i=1}^{5}(i^2-1) = (1^2-1)+(2^2-1)+(3^2-1)+(4^2-1)+(5^2-1) = 0+3+8+15+24 = 50$

c. $\displaystyle\sum_{j=1}^{6}2^j = 2^1+2^2+2^3+2^4+2^5+2^6 = 2+4+8+16+32+64 = 126$

d. $\displaystyle\sum_{k=1}^{10}5 = 5+5+5+5+5+5+5+5+5+5 = 50$

31. $S_n = \dfrac{n}{2}(a_1 + a_n)$

$S_{40} = \dfrac{40}{2}(2+80) = 1,640$

33. $S_n = \dfrac{n}{2}(a_1 + a_n)$

$S_{12} = \dfrac{12}{2}\left(\dfrac{1}{2}+\dfrac{1}{3}\right) = 5$

35. $S_n = \dfrac{n}{2}(2a_1 + (n-1)d)$

$S_{66} = \dfrac{66}{2}(2(10)+(66-1)4) = 9,240$

37. $\displaystyle\sum_{i=1}^{61}(2i+3) = 5+7+9+11+...+125$

$S_n = \dfrac{n}{2}(a_1 + a_n)$

$S_n = \dfrac{61}{2}(5+125) = 3,965$

39. $\displaystyle\sum_{k=1}^{24}\dfrac{k+3}{5} = \dfrac{4}{5}+\dfrac{5}{5}+\dfrac{6}{5}+\dfrac{7}{5}+...+\dfrac{27}{5}$

$S_n = \dfrac{n}{2}(a_1 + a_n)$

$S_n = \dfrac{24}{2}\left(\dfrac{4}{5}+\dfrac{27}{5}\right) = \dfrac{372}{5}$

41. $S_n = \dfrac{a_1(1-r^n)}{1-r}$

$S_7 = \dfrac{3(1-2^7)}{1-2} = 381$

43. $S_n = \dfrac{a_1(1-r^n)}{1-r}$

$S_5 = \dfrac{0.2(1-0.1^5)}{1-0.1} = 0.22222$

45. $S_n = \dfrac{a_1(1-r^n)}{1-r}$

$S_8 = \dfrac{48\left(1-\left(-\dfrac{1}{2}\right)^8\right)}{1-\left(-\dfrac{1}{2}\right)} = \dfrac{255}{8}$

47. $S_n = \dfrac{a_1 - r a_n}{1-r}$

$S_n = \dfrac{1-(1.3)(3.71293)}{1-1.3} = 12.75603$

49. $S_n = \dfrac{a_1(1-r^n)}{1-r}$

$S_7 = \dfrac{0.8(1-0.1^7)}{1-0.1} = 0.8888888$

51. $S_n = \dfrac{a_1\left(1-r^n\right)}{1-r}$

$$S_6 = \dfrac{40\left(1-\left(\dfrac{1}{5}\right)^6\right)}{1-\left(\dfrac{1}{5}\right)} = \dfrac{31{,}248}{625}$$

53. Since $|r| < 1$ we may use the following formula to evaluate the infinite geometric series.

$$S = \dfrac{a_1}{1-r}$$

$$S = \dfrac{5}{1-\dfrac{2}{3}} = 15$$

55. Since $|r| < 1$ we may use the following formula to evaluate the infinite geometric series.

$$S = \dfrac{a_1}{1-r}$$

$$S = \dfrac{14}{1-\left(-\dfrac{3}{4}\right)} = 8$$

57. Since $|r| < 1$ we may use the following formula to evaluate the infinite geometric series.

$$S = \dfrac{a_1}{1-r}$$

$$S = \dfrac{0.12}{1-\dfrac{1}{100}} = \dfrac{4}{33}$$

59. Since $|r| < 1$ we may use the following formula to evaluate the infinite geometric series.

$$S = \dfrac{a_1}{1-r}$$

$$S = \dfrac{\left(\dfrac{4}{9}\right)}{1-\left(\dfrac{4}{9}\right)} = \dfrac{4}{5}$$

61. Since $|r| < 1$ we may use the following formula to evaluate the infinite geometric series.

$$S = \dfrac{a_1}{1-r}$$

$$S = \dfrac{6}{1-\left(-\dfrac{2}{3}\right)} = \dfrac{18}{5}$$

63. Since $|r| < 1$ we may use the following formula to evaluate the infinite geometric series.

$$S = \dfrac{a_1}{1-r}$$

$$S = \dfrac{24}{1-\dfrac{3}{8}} = \dfrac{192}{5}$$

65. a. $0.444\ldots = 0.4 + 0.04 + 0.004 + \ldots$

$$= 4(0.1) + 4(0.1)^2 + 4(0.1)^3 + \ldots$$

$$S = \dfrac{a_1}{1-r} = \dfrac{0.4}{1-0.1} = \dfrac{4}{9}$$

b. $0.212121\ldots = 0.21 + 0.0021 + 0.000021 + \ldots$

$$= 21(0.01) + 21(0.01)^2 + 21(0.01)^3 + \ldots$$

$$S = \dfrac{a_1}{1-r} = \dfrac{0.21}{1-0.01} = \dfrac{7}{33}$$

c. $0.409409\ldots = 0.409 + 0.000409 + 0.000000409 + \ldots$

$$= 409(0.001) + 409(0.001)^2 + 409(0.001)^3 + \ldots$$

$$S = \dfrac{a_1}{1-r} = \dfrac{0.409}{1-0.001} = \dfrac{409}{999}$$

d. $2.5555\ldots = 2 + 0.5 + 0.05 + 0.005 + \ldots$

$$= 2 + 5(0.1) + 5(0.1)^2 + 5(0.1)^3 + \ldots$$

$$S = 2 + \dfrac{a_1}{1-r} = 2 + \dfrac{.5}{1-0.1} = \dfrac{23}{9}$$

67. First determine a_1 by using the formula for the nth term of an arithmetic sequence.

$$a_n = a_1 + (n-1)d$$
$$19 = a_1 + (77-1)(-11)$$
$$19 = a_1 + (-836)$$
$$a_1 = 855$$

Now use the formula for the sum of the first n terms of an arithmetic sequence.

$$S_n = \frac{n}{2}(a_1 + a_n)$$
$$S_{77} = \frac{77}{2}(855 + 19) = 33,649$$

69.
$$S_n = \frac{n}{2}(a_1 + a_n)$$
$$1560 = \frac{30}{2}(a_1 + 93)$$
$$104 = a_1 + 93$$
$$a_1 = 11$$

71.
$$S_n = \frac{n}{2}(2a_1 + (n-1)d)$$
$$680 = \frac{40}{2}(2(11) + (40-1)d)$$
$$34 = 22 + 39d$$
$$39d = 12$$
$$d = \frac{4}{13}$$

73.
$$S_n = \frac{a_1(1-r^n)}{1-r}$$
$$6138 = \frac{a_1(1-2^{10})}{1-2}$$
$$a_1 = 6138\left(\frac{-1}{1-2^{10}}\right)$$
$$a_1 = 6$$

75.
$$S_n = \frac{a_1 - ra_n}{1-r}$$
$$32766 = \frac{6 - r(24576)}{1-r}$$
$$32766(1-r) = 6 - 24576r$$
$$32766 - 32766r = 6 - 24576r$$
$$-8190r = -32760$$
$$r = 4$$

77.
$$S = \frac{a_1}{1-r}$$
$$21 = \frac{a_1}{1 - \frac{2}{9}}$$
$$a_1 = 21\left(1 - \frac{2}{9}\right)$$
$$a_1 = \frac{49}{3}$$

79. Find the following sum.
$$8 + 9 + 10 + 11 + \ldots + 24$$
There are 17 terms in the arithmetic series. Thus the sum is
$$S_n = \frac{n}{2}(a_1 + a_n)$$
$$S_{17} = \frac{17}{2}(8 + 24) = 272$$
There are 272 logs in the stack.

81. Given the following arithmetic series, find S_{12}.
$$4000 + 4500 + 5000 + \ldots$$
$$S_n = \frac{n}{2}(2a_1 + (n-1)d)$$
$$S_{12} = \frac{12}{2}(2(4000) + (12-1)500) = \$81,000$$

Chapter 12: A preview of College Algebra

83. Given the following geometric series, find S_8.
$$1+4+16+64+...$$
$$S_n = \frac{a_1\left(1-r^n\right)}{1-r}$$
$$S_8 = \frac{1\left(1-4^8\right)}{1-4} = 21,845 \text{ participants}$$

85. The terms in the following sequence give us the percent of air that is left in the vessel after each cycle.
$$100\left(\frac{2}{3}\right), 100\left(\frac{2}{3}\right)^2, 100\left(\frac{2}{3}\right)^3,...$$

After the 8th cycle, there will be $100\left(\frac{2}{3}\right)^8$ % left.

Thus $\left[100-100\left(\frac{2}{3}\right)^8\right]\% \approx 96.1\%$ of the air has been removed.

87. Determine the following infinite sum.
$$600000\left(\frac{3}{4}\right)+600000\left(\frac{3}{4}\right)^2+600000\left(\frac{3}{4}\right)^2+...$$
$$S = \frac{a_1}{1-r}$$
$$S = \frac{600000\left(\frac{3}{4}\right)}{1-\frac{3}{4}} = \$1,800,000$$

Cumulative Review

1. $12,000 = 1.2\times10^4$

2. $0.0045 = 4.5\times10^{-3}$

3. $-3 \le x < 5$

4. $x \le 2$

5. $[2, 7]$

Section 12.7: Conic Sections

Quick Review 12.7

1. The vertex of the parabola defined by $y = ax^2 + bx + c$ has an x-coordinate of $x = -\frac{b}{2a}$ and a y-coordinate of $f\left(-\frac{b}{2a}\right)$.

2. The x-coordinate of the vertex of $f(x) = 2x^2 + 4x + 3$ is
$$x = -\frac{b}{2a} = -\frac{4}{2(2)} = -1.$$
The y-coordinate is
$$f(-1) = 2(-1)^2 + 4(-1) + 3 = 2-4+3 = 1$$
Vertex: $(-1, 1)$

3. $9(x-2)^2 + 4(y+1)^2 - 36$

$= 9(x^2 - 4x + 4) + 4(y^2 + 2y + 1) - 36$

$= 9x^2 - 36x + 36 + 4y^2 + 8y + 4 - 36$

$= 9x^2 + 4y^2 - 36x + 8y + 36 + 4 - 36$

$= 9x^2 + 4y^2 - 36x + 8y + 4$

4. $2x^2 + 5x + 7 = 0$

$\dfrac{2x^2}{2} + \dfrac{5x}{2} = \dfrac{-7}{2}$

$x^2 + \dfrac{5}{2}x + \dfrac{25}{16} = \dfrac{-7}{2} + \dfrac{25}{16}$

$\left(x + \dfrac{5}{4}\right)^2 = -\dfrac{31}{16}$

$x + \dfrac{5}{4} = \pm\sqrt{-\dfrac{31}{16}}$

$x = -\dfrac{5}{4} \pm \dfrac{i\sqrt{31}}{4}$

$x = \dfrac{-5 \pm i\sqrt{31}}{4} = \dfrac{-5}{4} \pm \dfrac{i\sqrt{31}}{4}$

5. $f(x) = x^2 + 12x - 30$

$= x^2 + 12x + 36 - 30 - 36$

$= \left(x^2 + 12x + 36\right) - 30 - 36$

$= (x+6)^2 - 66$

Exercises 12.7

---

1. Distance: $d = \sqrt{(x_2 - x_1)^2 + (y_2 - y_1)^2}$

$= \sqrt{(1-(-3))^2 + ((-1)-2)^2}$

$= \sqrt{(4)^2 + (-3)^2}$

$= \sqrt{16+9} = \sqrt{25} = 5$

Midpoint: $\left(\dfrac{x_1+x_2}{2}, \dfrac{y_1+y_2}{2}\right) = \left(\dfrac{(-3)+1}{2}, \dfrac{2+(-1)}{2}\right)$

$= \left(\dfrac{-2}{2}, \dfrac{1}{2}\right) = \left(-1, \dfrac{1}{2}\right)$

3. Distance: $d = \sqrt{(x_2 - x_1)^2 + (y_2 - y_1)^2}$

$= \sqrt{(0-1)^2 + (1-2)^2}$

$= \sqrt{(-1)^2 + (-1)^2}$

$= \sqrt{1+1} = \sqrt{2}$

Midpoint: $\left(\dfrac{x_1+x_2}{2}, \dfrac{y_1+y_2}{2}\right) = \left(\dfrac{0+1}{2}, \dfrac{1+2}{2}\right)$

$= \left(\dfrac{1}{2}, \dfrac{3}{2}\right)$

5. Use the distance formula:

$r = \sqrt{(x_2 - x_1)^2 + (y_2 - y_1)^2}$

$= \sqrt{(7-0)^2 + (24-0)^2}$

$= \sqrt{(7)^2 + (24)^2} = \sqrt{49 + 576} = 25$

7. Use the midpoint formula:

$\left(\dfrac{x_1+x_2}{2}, \dfrac{y_1+y_2}{2}\right) = \left(\dfrac{(-1)+5}{2}, \dfrac{5+(-3)}{2}\right)$

$= \left(\dfrac{4}{2}, \dfrac{2}{2}\right) = (2, 1)$

9. The equation $x^2 + y^2 = 4$ is in the standard form of a circle. Thus the graph is **B**.

11. The equation $\dfrac{x^2}{1} - \dfrac{y^2}{4} = 1$ is in the standard form of a hyperbola. Thus the graph is **D**.

13. Substitute: $(h, k) = (0, 0)$ and $r = 10$ in the standard form of the equation of a circle.

$$(x - h)^2 + (y - k)^2 = r^2$$
$$(x - 0)^2 + (y - 0)^2 = 10^2$$
$$x^2 + y^2 = 100$$

15. Substitute: $(h, k) = (2, 6)$ and $r = \sqrt{2}$ in the standard form of the equation of a circle.

$$(x - h)^2 + (y - k)^2 = r^2$$
$$(x - 2)^2 + (y - 6)^2 = \left(\sqrt{2}\right)^2$$
$$(x - 2)^2 + (y - 6)^2 = 2$$

17. Substitute: $(h, k) = \left(0, \dfrac{1}{2}\right)$ and $r = \dfrac{1}{2}$ in the standard form of the equation of a circle.

$$(x - h)^2 + (y - k)^2 = r^2$$
$$(x - 0)^2 + \left(y - \dfrac{1}{2}\right)^2 = \left(\dfrac{1}{2}\right)^2$$
$$x^2 + \left(y - \dfrac{1}{2}\right)^2 = \dfrac{1}{4}$$

19. Write the equation in the standard form of the equation of a circle.

$$(x + 5)^2 + (y - 4)^2 = 64$$
$$(x - (-5))^2 + (y - 4)^2 = 8^2$$

The circle has a center $(-5, 4)$ and radius 8.

21. Write the equation in the standard form of the equation of a circle by completing the square.

$$x^2 + y^2 - 6x = 0$$
$$x^2 - 6x + 9 + y^2 = 0 + 9$$
$$(x - 3)^2 + y^2 = 9$$
$$(x - 3)^2 + (y - 0)^2 = 3^2$$

The circle has a center $(3, 0)$ and radius 3.

23. Write the equation in the standard form of the equation of a circle by completing the square.

$$x^2 + y^2 - 2x + 10y + 22 = 0$$
$$x^2 - 2x + 1 + y^2 + 10y + 25 = -22 + 1 + 25$$
$$(x - 1)^2 + (y + 5)^2 = 4$$
$$(x - 1)^2 + (y - (-5))^2 = 2^2$$

The circle has a center $(1, -5)$ and radius 2.

25. Write the equation in the standard form of the equation of an ellipse.

$$\dfrac{x^2}{36} + \dfrac{y^2}{16} = 1$$
$$\dfrac{(x - 0)^2}{36} + \dfrac{(y - 0)^2}{16} = 1$$

Center: $(0, 0)$

$$a^2 = 36 \qquad b^2 = 16$$
$$a = 6 \qquad b = 4$$

Length of major axis: $2a = 2(6) = 12$

Length of major axis: $2b = 2(4) = 8$

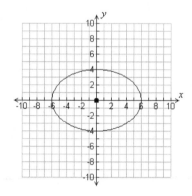

27. Write the equation in the standard form of the equation of an ellipse.

$$\frac{(y-3)^2}{25}+\frac{(x+4)^2}{16}=1$$

$$\frac{(y-3)^2}{25}+\frac{(x-(-4))^2}{16}=1$$

Center: $(-4, 3)$

$$a^2 = 25 \qquad b^2 = 16$$
$$a = 5 \qquad b = 4$$

Length of major axis: $2a = 2(5) = 10$

Length of major axis: $2b = 2(4) = 8$

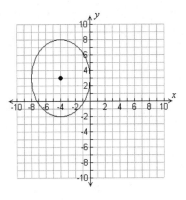

29. $(h, k) = (0, 0)$

$a = 9; \quad b = 5$

$$\frac{(x-h)^2}{a^2}+\frac{(y-k)^2}{b^2}=1$$

$$\frac{(x-0)^2}{9^2}+\frac{(y-0)^2}{5^2}=1$$

$$\frac{x^2}{81}+\frac{y^2}{25}=1$$

31. $(h, k) = (3, 4)$

$$a = \left(\frac{1}{2}\right)4 = 2; \qquad b = \left(\frac{1}{2}\right)2 = 1$$

$$\frac{(x-h)^2}{a^2}+\frac{(y-k)^2}{b^2}=1$$

$$\frac{(x-3)^2}{2^2}+\frac{(y-4)^2}{1^2}=1$$

$$\frac{(x-3)^2}{4}+\frac{(y-4)^2}{1}=1$$

33. $(h, k) = (6, -2)$

$$a = \left(\frac{1}{2}\right)10 = 5; \qquad b = \left(\frac{1}{2}\right)6 = 3$$

$$\frac{(x-h)^2}{b^2}+\frac{(y-k)^2}{a^2}=1$$

$$\frac{(x-6)^2}{3^2}+\frac{(y-(-2))^2}{5^2}=1$$

$$\frac{(x-6)^2}{9}+\frac{(y+2)^2}{25}=1$$

35. $(h, k) = (-3, -4)$

$a = 6; \quad b = 2$

$$\frac{(x-h)^2}{b^2}+\frac{(y-k)^2}{a^2}=1$$

$$\frac{(x-(-3))^2}{2^2}+\frac{(y-(-4))^2}{6^2}=1$$

$$\frac{(x+3)^2}{4}+\frac{(y+4)^2}{36}=1$$

37. Write the equation in the standard form of the equation of a hyperbola.

$$\frac{(x-0)^2}{25}-\frac{(y-0)^2}{81}=1$$

Center: $(0, 0)$

$$a^2 = 25 \qquad b^2 = 81$$
$$a = 5 \qquad b = 9$$

The hyperbola opens horizontally.

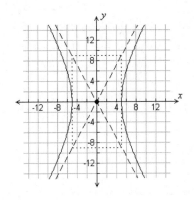

39. Write the equation in the standard form of the equation of a hyperbola.

$$25x^2 = 100y^2 + 100$$

$$25x^2 - 100y^2 = 100$$

$$\frac{(x-0)^2}{4} - \frac{(y-0)^2}{1} = 1$$

Center: $(0, 0)$

$a^2 = 4$	$b^2 = 1$
$a = 2$	$b = 1$

The hyperbola opens horizontally.

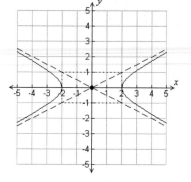

41. Write the equation in the standard form of the equation of a hyperbola.

$$\frac{(y-6)^2}{9} - \frac{(x-4)^2}{49} = 1$$

Center: $(4, 6)$

$a^2 = 9$	$b^2 = 49$
$a = 3$	$b = 7$

The hyperbola opens vertically.

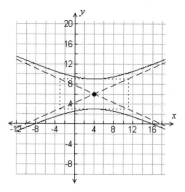

43. $(h, k) = (0, 0)$

$a = \left(\frac{1}{2}\right)10 = 5; \quad b = \left(\frac{1}{2}\right)8 = 4$

$$\frac{(y-k)^2}{a^2} - \frac{(x-h)^2}{b^2} = 1$$

$$\frac{(y-0)^2}{5^2} - \frac{(x-0)^2}{4^2} = 1$$

$$\frac{y^2}{25} - \frac{x^2}{16} = 1$$

45. $(h, k) = (0, 0)$

$a = 3; \quad b = \left(\frac{1}{2}\right)14 = 7$

$$\frac{(x-h)^2}{a^2} - \frac{(y-k)^2}{b^2} = 1$$

$$\frac{(x-0)^2}{3^2} - \frac{(y-0)^2}{7^2} = 1$$

$$\frac{x^2}{9} - \frac{y^2}{49} = 1$$

47. a.

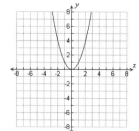

b.

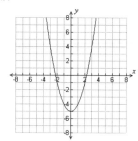

c.

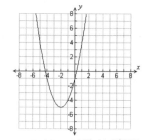

49. **a.**

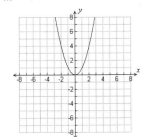

b.

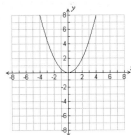

c.

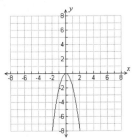

51. **a.** The solutions to the system of equations are the points of intersection: $(-2, 7)$ and $(2, -1)$.

53. **a.** The solutions to the system of equations are the points of intersection: $(-2, -2)$ and $(2, 2)$.

b.

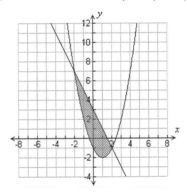

b.

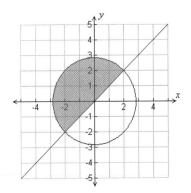

Cumulative Review

1.
$$3(2x-1)+5 = 7(4x-5)-34$$
$$6x-3+5 = 28x-35-34$$
$$6x+2 = 28x-69$$
$$-22x = -71$$
$$x = \frac{71}{22}$$

2. $|2x-1| = 25$
is equivalent to
$$2x-1 = -25 \quad \text{or} \quad 2x-1 = 25$$
$$2x = -24 \qquad\qquad 2x = 26$$
$$x = -12 \qquad\qquad x = 13$$

3.
$$(2x-1)^2 = 25$$
$$2x-1 = \pm\sqrt{25}$$
$$2x-1 = \pm 5$$
$$2x = 1 \pm 5$$
$$x = \frac{1 \pm 5}{2}$$
$$x = -2 \quad \text{or} \quad x = 3$$

4.
$$\frac{3x+2}{2x-7} = 4$$
$$(2x-7)\left(\frac{3x+2}{2x-7}\right) = (2x-7)4$$
$$3x+2 = 8x-28$$
$$-5x = -30$$
$$x = 6$$

5.
$$\log(3x+1) = 2$$
$$\log_{10}(3x+1) = 2$$
is equivalent to $3x+1 = 10^2$
$$3x+1 = 100$$
$$3x = 99$$
$$x = 33$$

Review Exercises for Chapter 12

1. **a.** $\begin{bmatrix} 2 & -5 & | & 17 \\ 3 & 4 & | & 14 \end{bmatrix}$

    b. $\begin{bmatrix} 3 & -4 & 2 & | & -11 \\ 2 & 2 & 3 & | & -3 \\ 4 & -1 & 5 & | & -13 \end{bmatrix}$

2. **a.** Answer: $(-2,\,6)$

    b. Answer: $(4,\,5,\,8)$

3. Solving for x in the first equation we obtain: $x = 5 - 3z$. Solving for y in the second equation we obtain: $y = 4 + 2z$. Thus the general solution of the system is $(5 - 3z,\, 4 + 2z,\, z)$. For $z = 0$, $z = 1$, and $z = 5$, we obtain the following particular solutions: $(5,\,4,\,0)$, $(2,\,6,\,1)$, and $(-10,\,14,\,5)$.

4. $\begin{bmatrix} 3 & 5 & | & 13 \\ 1 & 4 & | & 2 \end{bmatrix} \xrightarrow{r_1 \leftrightarrow r_2} \begin{bmatrix} 1 & 4 & | & 2 \\ 3 & 5 & | & 13 \end{bmatrix}$

5. $\begin{bmatrix} 2 & 4 & | & -10 \\ 3 & 2 & | & -3 \end{bmatrix} \xrightarrow{r_1'=\frac{1}{2}r_1} \begin{bmatrix} 1 & 2 & | & -5 \\ 3 & 2 & | & -3 \end{bmatrix}$

6. $\begin{bmatrix} 1 & 2 & | & 14 \\ 3 & -1 & | & 13 \end{bmatrix} \xrightarrow{r_2'=r_2-3r_1} \begin{bmatrix} 1 & 2 & | & 14 \\ 0 & -7 & | & -29 \end{bmatrix}$

7. $\begin{bmatrix} 1 & 3 & -2 & | & -6 \\ 0 & 1 & 2 & | & 3 \\ 0 & 2 & 3 & | & 4 \end{bmatrix} \xrightarrow[r_3'=r_3-2r_2]{r_1'=r_1-3r_2} \begin{bmatrix} 1 & 0 & -8 & | & -15 \\ 0 & 1 & 2 & | & 3 \\ 0 & 0 & -1 & | & -2 \end{bmatrix}$

8. $\begin{bmatrix} 1 & 2 & | & 17 \\ 2 & 5 & | & 41 \end{bmatrix} \xrightarrow{r_2'=r_2-2r_1} \begin{bmatrix} 1 & 2 & | & 17 \\ 0 & 1 & | & 7 \end{bmatrix} \xrightarrow{r_1'=r_1-2r_2} \begin{bmatrix} 1 & 0 & | & 3 \\ 0 & 1 & | & 7 \end{bmatrix}$; Answer: $(3,\,7)$

9. $\begin{bmatrix} 3 & -2 & | & -16 \\ 1 & 3 & | & 13 \end{bmatrix} \xrightarrow{r_1 \leftrightarrow r_2} \begin{bmatrix} 1 & 3 & | & 13 \\ 3 & -2 & | & -16 \end{bmatrix} \xrightarrow{r_2'=r_2-3r_1} \begin{bmatrix} 1 & 3 & | & 13 \\ 0 & -11 & | & -55 \end{bmatrix} \xrightarrow{r_2'=-\frac{1}{11}r_2} \begin{bmatrix} 1 & 3 & | & 13 \\ 0 & 1 & | & 5 \end{bmatrix}$

    $\xrightarrow{r_1'=r_1-3r_2} \begin{bmatrix} 1 & 0 & | & -2 \\ 0 & 1 & | & 5 \end{bmatrix}$; Answer: $(-2,\,5)$

10. $\begin{bmatrix} 3 & 4 & | & -1 \\ 2 & -3 & | & 5 \end{bmatrix} \xrightarrow{r_1'=\frac{1}{3}r_1} \begin{bmatrix} 1 & \frac{4}{3} & | & -\frac{1}{3} \\ 2 & -3 & | & 5 \end{bmatrix} \xrightarrow{r_2'=r_2-2r_1} \begin{bmatrix} 1 & \frac{4}{3} & | & -\frac{1}{3} \\ 0 & -\frac{17}{3} & | & \frac{17}{3} \end{bmatrix} \xrightarrow{r_2'=-\frac{3}{17}r_2} \begin{bmatrix} 1 & \frac{4}{3} & | & -\frac{1}{3} \\ 0 & 1 & | & -1 \end{bmatrix}$

    $\xrightarrow{r_1'=r_1-\frac{4}{3}r_2} \begin{bmatrix} 1 & 0 & | & 1 \\ 0 & 1 & | & -1 \end{bmatrix}$; Answer: $(1,\,-1)$

11. $\begin{bmatrix} 1 & -5 & | & 8 \\ -3 & 15 & | & 10 \end{bmatrix} \xrightarrow{r_2'=r_2+3r_1} \begin{bmatrix} 1 & -5 & | & 8 \\ 0 & 0 & | & 34 \end{bmatrix}$; The last row is a contradiction. Thus there is no solution.

12. $\begin{bmatrix} 1 & 2 & -1 & | & -2 \\ 2 & -1 & 1 & | & 4 \\ 3 & 2 & 2 & | & 3 \end{bmatrix} \xrightarrow[r_3'=r_3-3r_1]{r_2'=r_2-2r_1} \begin{bmatrix} 1 & 2 & -1 & | & -2 \\ 0 & -5 & 3 & | & 8 \\ 0 & -4 & 5 & | & 9 \end{bmatrix} \xrightarrow{r_2'=-\frac{1}{5}r_2} \begin{bmatrix} 1 & 2 & -1 & | & -2 \\ 0 & 1 & -\frac{3}{5} & | & -\frac{8}{5} \\ 0 & -4 & 5 & | & 9 \end{bmatrix} \xrightarrow[r_3'=r_3+4r_2]{r_1'=r_1-2r_2} \begin{bmatrix} 1 & 0 & \frac{1}{5} & | & \frac{6}{5} \\ 0 & 1 & -\frac{3}{5} & | & -\frac{8}{5} \\ 0 & 0 & \frac{13}{5} & | & \frac{13}{5} \end{bmatrix}$

$\xrightarrow{r_3'=\frac{5}{13}r_3} \begin{bmatrix} 1 & 0 & \frac{1}{5} & | & \frac{6}{5} \\ 0 & 1 & -\frac{3}{5} & | & -\frac{8}{5} \\ 0 & 0 & 1 & | & 1 \end{bmatrix} \xrightarrow[r_2'=r_2+\frac{3}{5}r_3]{r_1'=r_1-\frac{1}{5}r_3} \begin{bmatrix} 1 & 0 & 0 & | & 1 \\ 0 & 1 & 0 & | & -1 \\ 0 & 0 & 1 & | & 1 \end{bmatrix}$; Answer: $(1, -1, 1)$

13. $\begin{bmatrix} 1 & 0 & -3 & | & 10 \\ 2 & 1 & 0 & | & 6 \\ 0 & 2 & 1 & | & 5 \end{bmatrix} \xrightarrow{r_2'=r_2-2r_1} \begin{bmatrix} 1 & 0 & -3 & | & 10 \\ 0 & 1 & 6 & | & -14 \\ 0 & 2 & 1 & | & 5 \end{bmatrix} \xrightarrow{r_3'=r_3-2r_2} \begin{bmatrix} 1 & 0 & -3 & | & 10 \\ 0 & 1 & 6 & | & -14 \\ 0 & 0 & -11 & | & 33 \end{bmatrix} \xrightarrow{r_3'=-\frac{1}{11}r_3} \begin{bmatrix} 1 & 0 & -3 & | & 10 \\ 0 & 1 & 6 & | & -14 \\ 0 & 0 & 1 & | & -3 \end{bmatrix}$

$\xrightarrow[r_2'=r_2-6r_3]{r_1'=r_1+3r_3} \begin{bmatrix} 1 & 0 & 0 & | & 1 \\ 0 & 1 & 0 & | & 4 \\ 0 & 0 & 1 & | & -3 \end{bmatrix}$; Answer: $(1, 4, -3)$

14.

$\begin{bmatrix} 2 & -3 & 4 & | & 11 \\ 3 & 2 & -4 & | & -4 \\ 4 & 1 & -3 & | & -1 \end{bmatrix} \xrightarrow{r_1'=\frac{1}{2}r_1} \begin{bmatrix} 1 & -\frac{3}{2} & 2 & | & \frac{11}{2} \\ 3 & 2 & -4 & | & -4 \\ 4 & 1 & -3 & | & -1 \end{bmatrix} \xrightarrow[r_3'=r_3-4r_1]{r_2'=r_2-3r_1} \begin{bmatrix} 1 & -\frac{3}{2} & 2 & | & \frac{11}{2} \\ 0 & \frac{13}{2} & -10 & | & -\frac{41}{2} \\ 0 & 7 & -11 & | & -23 \end{bmatrix}$

$\xrightarrow{r_2'=\frac{2}{13}r_2} \begin{bmatrix} 1 & -\frac{3}{2} & 2 & | & \frac{11}{2} \\ 0 & 1 & -\frac{20}{13} & | & -\frac{41}{13} \\ 0 & 7 & -11 & | & -23 \end{bmatrix} \xrightarrow[r_3'=r_3-7r_2]{r_1'=r_1+\frac{3}{2}r_2} \begin{bmatrix} 1 & 0 & -\frac{4}{13} & | & \frac{10}{13} \\ 0 & 1 & -\frac{20}{13} & | & -\frac{41}{13} \\ 0 & 0 & -\frac{3}{13} & | & -\frac{12}{13} \end{bmatrix}$

$\xrightarrow{r_3'=-\frac{13}{3}r_3} \begin{bmatrix} 1 & 0 & -\frac{4}{13} & | & \frac{10}{13} \\ 0 & 1 & -\frac{20}{13} & | & -\frac{41}{13} \\ 0 & 0 & 1 & | & 4 \end{bmatrix} \xrightarrow[r_2'=r_2+\frac{20}{13}r_3]{r_1'=r_1+\frac{4}{13}r_3} \begin{bmatrix} 1 & 0 & 0 & | & 2 \\ 0 & 1 & 0 & | & 3 \\ 0 & 0 & 1 & | & 4 \end{bmatrix}$; Answer: $(2, 3, 4)$

15. The intercepts of $5x + 2y + 2.5z = 10$ are $(0, 0, 4)$, $(0, 5, 0)$, and $(2, 0, 0)$.

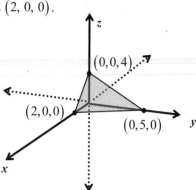

16. Let x be the weight of a pallet of bricks boat and y be the weight of a pallet of concrete blocks. To find these values, solve the following system.

$$\begin{cases} 2x + 3y = 18000 \\ 4x + y = 19600 \end{cases} \rightarrow \begin{bmatrix} 2 & 3 & | & 18000 \\ 4 & 1 & | & 19600 \end{bmatrix} \rightarrow \dots \rightarrow \begin{bmatrix} 1 & 0 & | & 4080 \\ 0 & 1 & | & 3280 \end{bmatrix}$$

Thus a pallet of bricks weighs 4,080 pounds and a pallet of concrete blocks weighs 3,280 pounds.

17. $\begin{cases} A + 2B + 5C = 156 \\ 2A + 4B + 8C = 294 \\ 3A + 3B + 7C = 321 \end{cases} \rightarrow \begin{bmatrix} 1 & 2 & 5 & | & 156 \\ 2 & 4 & 8 & | & 294 \\ 3 & 3 & 7 & | & 321 \end{bmatrix} \rightarrow \dots \rightarrow \begin{bmatrix} 1 & 0 & 0 & | & 61 \\ 0 & 1 & 0 & | & 25 \\ 0 & 0 & 1 & | & 9 \end{bmatrix}$

The prices are \$61.00 for calculator A, \$25.00 for calculator B, and \$9 for calculator C.

18. **a.** The graph of $f(x) = x^2$ has its vertex at the origin. Thus the graph is **B**.

  b. The graph of $f(x) = x^2 - 5$ is the graph of $y = x^2$ shifted down 5 units. Thus the graph is **A**.

  c. The graph of $f(x) = x^2 + 5$ is the graph of $y = x^2$ shifted up 5 units. Thus the graph is **C**.

19. **a.** The graph of $f(x) = \sqrt{x}$ passes through the origin. Thus the graph is **A**.

  b. The graph of $f(x) = \sqrt{x - 4}$ is the graph of $f(x) = \sqrt{x}$ shifted right 4 units. Thus the graph is **C**.

  c. The graph of $f(x) = \sqrt{x + 4}$ is the graph of $f(x) = \sqrt{x}$ shifted left 4 units. Thus the graph is **B**.

20. **a.** The graph of $f(x) = |x - 1| + 2$ is the graph of $y = |x|$ shifted right 1 unit and up two units. Thus the graph is **B**.

  b. The graph of $f(x) = |x - 2| + 1$ is the graph of $y = |x|$ shifted right 2 units and up 1 unit. Thus the graph is **A**.

  c. The graph of $f(x) = |x + 2| - 1$ is the graph of $y = |x|$ shifted left 2 units and down one unit. Thus the graph is **C**.

21. **a.** The graph of $y = f(x-3)$ is the graph of $y = f(x)$ shifted right 3 units.

b. The graph of $y = f(x)+4$ is the graph of $y = f(x)$ shifted up 4 units.

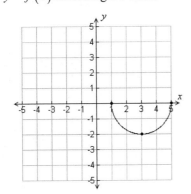

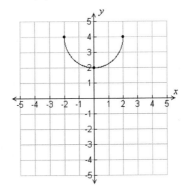

c. The graph of $y = f(x-3)+4$ is the graph of $y = f(x)$ shifted right 3 units and up 4 units.

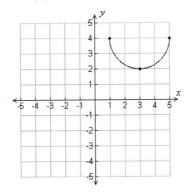

22. **a.** The graph of $f(x) = x^2 + 7$ is obtained by shifting the graph of $f(x) = x^2$ up 7 units. Thus the vertex is $(0, 7)$.

b. The graph of $f(x) = (x-9)^2$ is obtained by shifting the graph of $f(x) = x^2$ right 9 units. Thus the vertex is $(9, 0)$.

c. The graph of $f(x) = (x+11)^2 - 12$ is obtained by shifting the graph of $f(x) = x^2$ left 11 units and down 12 units. Thus the vertex is $(-11, -12)$.

23. **a.**

x	$y = f(x)+5$
-2	$5+5 = 10$
-1	$9+5 = 14$
0	$3+5 = 8$
1	$-4+5 = 1$
2	$0+5 = 5$

b.

x	$y = f(x+5)$
-7	5
-6	9
-5	3
-4	-4
-3	0

24. **a.** The graph of $y = f(x)-17$ is obtained by shifting the graph of $y = f(x)$ down 17 units. Answer: **D.**

b. The graph of $y = f(x-17)$ is obtained by shifting the graph of $y = f(x)$ right 17 units. Answer: **A.**

    c. The graph of $y = f(x) + 17$ is obtained by shifting the graph of $y = f(x)$ up 17 units. Answer: **B**.

    d. The graph of $y = f(x+17)$ is obtained by shifting the graph of $y = f(x)$ left 17 units. Answer: **C**.

25. **a.** To find the table for $y = f(x) + 2$ we add 2 units to every y value in the table for $f(x)$. Answer: **D**.

    b. To find the table for $y = f(x+2)$ we subtract 2 units to every x value in the table for $f(x)$. Answer: **B**.

    c. To find the table for $y = f(x-1) + 3$ we add 1 unit to every x value and add 3 units to every y value in the table for $f(x)$. Answer: **C**.

    d. To find the table for $y = f(x+3) - 1$ we subtract 3 units from every x value and subtract 1 unit from every y value in the table for $f(x)$. Answer: **A**.

26. **a.** The graph of $y = -f(x)$ is obtained by reflecting the graph of $y = f(x)$ across the x-axis. Answer: **B**.

    b. The graph of $y = 2f(x)$ is obtained by vertically stretching the graph of $y = f(x)$ by a factor of 2. Answer: **C**.

    c. The graph of $y = -2f(x)$ is obtained by vertically stretching the graph of $y = f(x)$ by a factor of 2 and reflecting the graph across the x-axis. Answer: **D**.

    d. The graph of $y = \dfrac{1}{2} f(x)$ is obtained by vertically shrinking the graph of $y = f(x)$ by a factor of $1/2$. Answer: **A**.

27. **a.** The graph of $y = -f(x)$ is obtained by reflecting the graph of $y = f(x)$ across the x-axis. Answer: **C**.

    b. The graph of $y = -\dfrac{1}{3} f(x)$ is obtained by vertically shrinking the graph of $y = f(x)$ by a factor of $1/3$ and reflecting the graph across the x-axis. Answer: **D**.

    c. The graph of $y = \dfrac{1}{3} f(x)$ is obtained by vertically shrinking the graph of $y = f(x)$ by a factor of $1/3$. Answer: **A**.

    d. The graph of $y = 2f(x)$ is obtained by vertically stretching the graph of $y = f(x)$ by a factor of 2. Answer: **B**.

28. **a.**

x	$y = -f(x)$
0	$-(0) = 0$
1	$-(8) = -8$
2	$-(4) = -4$
3	$-(12) = -12$
4	$-(24) = -24$

  b.

x	$y = \dfrac{1}{4} f(x)$
0	$\dfrac{1}{4}(0) = 0$
1	$\dfrac{1}{4}(8) = 2$
2	$\dfrac{1}{4}(4) = 1$
3	$\dfrac{1}{4}(12) = 3$
4	$\dfrac{1}{4}(24) = 6$

  c.

x	$y = 4f(x)$
0	$4(0) = 0$
1	$4(8) = 32$
2	$4(4) = 16$
3	$4(12) = 48$
4	$4(24) = 96$

  d.

x	$y = -3f(x)$
0	$-3(0) = 0$
1	$-3(8) = -24$
2	$-3(4) = -12$
3	$-3(12) = -36$
4	$-3(24) = -72$

29. **a.** The graph of $y = 2f(x)$ is obtained by vertically stretching the graph of $y = f(x)$ by a factor of 2. Answer: **D**.

    b. The graph of $y = -f(x)$ is obtained by reflecting the graph of $y = f(x)$ across the x-axis. Answer: **A**.

c. The graph of $y = f(x+2)$ is obtained by shifting the graph of $y = f(x)$ left 2 units. Answer: **B**.

d. The graph of $y = f(x)+2$ is obtained by shifting the graph of $y = f(x)$ up 2 units. Answer: **C**.

30. a. $f(10) = (3(10)-7) = 23$

b. $g(10) = 2(10)^2 + 1 = 201$

c. $(f+g)(10) = f(10) + g(10) = 23 + 201$
$$= 224$$

d. $(f-g)(10) = f(10) - g(10) = 23 - 201$
$$= -178$$

31. a. $(f \cdot g)(2) = f(2) \cdot g(2)$
$$= (3(2)-7) \cdot (2(2)^2 + 1)$$
$$= (-1) \cdot (9) = -9$$

b. $\left(\dfrac{f}{g}\right)(2) = \dfrac{f(2)}{g(2)} = \dfrac{(3(2)-7)}{(2(2)^2+1)}$
$$= \dfrac{-1}{9} = -\dfrac{1}{9}$$

c. $\left(\dfrac{g}{f}\right)(2) = \dfrac{g(2)}{f(2)} = \dfrac{(2(2)^2+1)}{(3(2)-7)}$
$$= \dfrac{9}{-1} = -9$$

d. $(g-f)(2) = g(2) - f(2)$
$$= \left(2(2)^2 + 1\right) - \left(3(2)-7\right)$$
$$= (9) - (-1) = 10$$

32. a. $(f \circ g)(2) = f(g(2))$
$$= f\left(2(2)^2 + 1\right)$$
$$= f(9) = 3(9) - 7 = 20$$

b. $(g \circ f)(2) = g(f(2))$
$$= g(3(2)-7)$$
$$= g(-1) = 2(-1)^2 + 1 = 3$$

c. $(f \circ f)(2) = f(f(2))$
$$= f(3(2)-7)$$
$$= f(-1) = 3(-1) - 7 = -10$$

d. $(g \circ g)(2) = g(g(2))$
$$= g\left(2(2)^2 + 1\right)$$
$$= g(9) = 2(9)^2 + 1 = 163$$

33. a.

x	$(f+g)(x)$
0	$-7+1 = -6$
1	$-4+3 = -1$
2	$-1+9 = 8$
3	$2+19 = 21$

b.

x	$(f-g)(x)$
0	$-7-1 = -8$
1	$-4-3 = -7$
2	$-1-9 = -10$
3	$2-19 = -17$

c.

x	$(f \cdot g)(x)$
0	$(-7) \cdot (1) = -7$
1	$(-4) \cdot (3) = -12$
2	$(-1) \cdot (9) = -9$
3	$(2) \cdot (19) = 38$

d.

x	$\left(\dfrac{f}{g}\right)(x)$
0	$\dfrac{-7}{1} = -7$
1	$\dfrac{-4}{3} = -\dfrac{4}{3}$
2	$\dfrac{-1}{9} = -\dfrac{1}{9}$
3	$\dfrac{2}{19} = \dfrac{2}{19}$

34. a.

x	$(f+g)(x)$
−3	$-3+(-1)=-4$
−1	$-1+(-1)=-2$
1	$1+(-1)=0$
2	$2+(-1)=1$
3	$3+(-1)=2$

$f+g=\{(-3,-4),(-1,-2),(1,0),(2,1),(3,2)\}$

b.

x	$(f-g)(x)$
−3	$-3-(-1)=-2$
−1	$-1-(-1)=0$
1	$1-(-1)=2$
2	$2-(-1)=3$
3	$3-(-1)=4$

$f-g=\{(-3,-2),(-1,0),(1,2),(2,3),(3,4)\}$

c.

x	$(f\cdot g)(x)$
−3	$(-3)(-1)=3$
−1	$(-1)\cdot(-1)=1$
1	$(1)\cdot(-1)=-1$
2	$(2)\cdot(-1)=-2$
3	$(3)\cdot(-1)=-3$

$f\cdot g=\{(-3,3),(-1,1),(1,-1),(2,-2),(3,-3)\}$

d.

x	$\left(\dfrac{f}{g}\right)(x)$
−3	$\dfrac{-3}{-1}=3$
−1	$\dfrac{-1}{-1}=1$
1	$\dfrac{1}{-1}=-1$
2	$\dfrac{2}{-1}=-2$
3	$\dfrac{3}{-1}=-3$

$\dfrac{f}{g}=\{(-3,3),(-1,1),(1,-1),(2,-2),(3,-3)\}$

35.

$$x \xrightarrow{\ g\ } g(x) \xrightarrow{\ f\ } f(g(x)) \qquad x \longrightarrow f(g(x))$$

$-1 \longrightarrow 4 \longrightarrow 5$	$-1 \longrightarrow 5$
$2 \longrightarrow 6 \longrightarrow 11$	$2 \longrightarrow 11$
$3 \longrightarrow 2 \longrightarrow 7$	$3 \longrightarrow 7$
$5 \longrightarrow 0 \longrightarrow 9$	$5 \longrightarrow 9$

36.

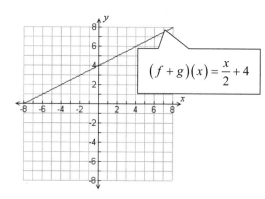

$$(f+g)(x)=\frac{x}{2}+4$$

37. a. $(f+g)(x)=(4x-2)+(1-2x)=2x-1;$ Domain: $(-\infty,\infty)$ or $\mathbb{R}$

b. $(f\cdot g)(x)=(4x-2)\cdot(1-2x)=-8x^2+8x-2;$ Domain: $(-\infty,\infty)$ or $\mathbb{R}$

c. $(f\circ g)(x)=f(g(x))=f(1-2x)=4(1-2x)-2=-8x+2;$ Domain: $(-\infty,\infty)$ or $\mathbb{R}$

38. a. $(f-g)(x)=(4x-2)-(1-2x)=6x-3;$ Domain: $(-\infty,\infty)$ or $\mathbb{R}$

b. $\left(\dfrac{f}{g}\right)(x)=\dfrac{4x-2}{1-2x}=\dfrac{2(2x-1)}{(-1)(2x-1)}=-2;$ Domain: $\left(-\infty,\dfrac{1}{2}\right)\cup\left(\dfrac{1}{2},\infty\right)$ or $\mathbb{R}\sim\left\{\dfrac{1}{2}\right\}$

c. $(g\circ f)(x)=g(f(x))=g(4x-2)=1-2(4x-2)=-8x+5;$ Domain: $(-\infty,\infty)$ or $\mathbb{R}$

39. f and g are not equal. $f(3)$ is defined and $g(3)$ is not defined. (The functions do not have the same domains.)

40. First, replace $f(x)$ with y.

$$f(x) = 4x + 3$$
$$y = 4x + 3$$

Next, exchange x and y, then solve for y.

$$x = 4y + 3$$
$$x - 3 = 4y$$
$$y = \frac{x-3}{4}$$

Rewrite the inverse using functional notation.

$$f^{-1}(x) = \frac{x-3}{4}$$

$$\left(f \circ f^{-1}\right)(x) = f\left(f^{-1}(x)\right)$$
$$= f\left(\frac{x-3}{4}\right) = 4\left(\frac{x-3}{4}\right) - 3$$
$$= (x - 3) + 3 = x$$

41. **a.** $F(100) = 400$

b. $V(100) = 1.5(100) = 150$

c. $C(x) = V(x) + F(x) = 1.5x + 400$

d. $A(x) = \dfrac{C(x)}{x} = \dfrac{1.5x + 400}{x}$

42. **a.** $N(40) = 3(40) = 120$; The factory can produce 120 desks in 40 hours.

b. $C(120) = \left(150 - \dfrac{120}{4}\right)(120) = 14,400$; The cost of producing 120 desks is \$14,400.

c. $(C \circ N)(40) = C\left(N(40)\right) = C(120) = 14,400$; The cost of operating the factory for 40 hours is \$14,400.

d. $(C \circ N)(t) = C\left(N(t)\right) = C(3t) = \left(150 - \dfrac{3t}{4}\right)(3t)$

e. There are only 168 hours in a week.

43. **a.** 5, 9, 13, 17, 21, 25,...

b. 5, 1, −3, −7, −11, −15,...

c. 5, 8, 11, 14, 17, 20,...

d. 5, 8, 11, 14, 17, 20,...

44. **a.** 3, 6, 12, 24, 48, 96,...

b. 3, −6, 12, −24, 48, −96,...

c. 3, 12, 48, 192, 768, 3072,...

d. 1, 3, 9, 27, 81, 243,...

45. **a.** 9, 11, 13, 15, 17,...

b. 4, 7, 12, 19, 28,...

c. 32, 16, 8, 4, 2,...

d. 3, 10, 17, 24, 31,...

46. $a_n = a_1 + (n-1)d$

$$a_{101} = 11 + (101 - 1)3 = 311$$

47. $a_n = a_1 r^{n-1}$

$$a_{11} = \left(\frac{1}{64}\right)2^{11-1} = 16$$

48. $a_n = a_1 + (n-1)d$

$$300 = -20 + (n-1)8$$
$$320 = (n-1)8$$
$$n - 1 = 40$$
$$n = 41$$

49.
$$a_n = a_1 r^{n-1}$$
$$78125 = \frac{1}{15625} 5^{n-1}$$
$$1220703125 = 5^{n-1}$$
$$\ln 1220703125 = \ln 5^{n-1}$$
$$\ln 1220703125 = (n-1)\ln 5$$
$$n = \frac{\ln 1220703125}{\ln 5} + 1 = 14$$

50. a. $\displaystyle\sum_{i=1}^{6}(3i-2) = (3(1)-2)+(3(2)-2)+(3(3)-2)+(3(4)-2)+(3(5)-2)+(3(6)-2)$
$$= 1+4+7+10+13+16 = 51$$

b. $\displaystyle\sum_{k=3}^{7}(k^2-2k) = \left((3)^2-2(3)\right)+\left((4)^2-2(4)\right)+\left((5)^2-2(5)\right)+\left((6)^2-2(6)\right)+\left((7)^2-2(7)\right)$
$$= 3+8+15+24+35 = 85$$

c. $\displaystyle\sum_{j=1}^{5} j^3 = (1)^3+(2)^3+(3)^3+(4)^3+(5)^3 = 1+8+27+64+125 = 225$

d. $\displaystyle\sum_{i=1}^{6} 10 = 10+10+10+10+10+10 = 60$

51. $\displaystyle S_n = \frac{n}{2}(a_1+a_n)$
$$S_{50} = \frac{50}{2}(23+366) = 9,725$$

52.
$$0.12121212... = 0.12+0.0012+0.000012+...$$
$$= 12(0.01)+12(0.01)^2+12(0.01)^3+...$$
$$S = \frac{a_1}{1-r} = \frac{0.12}{1-0.01} = \frac{4}{33}$$

53. Since $|r|<1$ we may use the following formula to evaluate the infinite geometric series.
$$S = \frac{a_1}{1-r}$$
$$S = \frac{\left(\dfrac{3}{5}\right)}{1-\left(\dfrac{3}{5}\right)} = \frac{3}{2}$$

54. $\displaystyle S_n = \frac{n}{2}(a_1+a_n)$
$$S_{17} = \frac{17}{2}(46+80) = 1,071 \text{ cm}$$

55. The perimeter of the third square is $4(10) = 40$ cm. The total perimeter of all the squares is

$$4(20)+4(10\sqrt{2})+4(10)+... = 4(20+10\sqrt{2}+10+...) = 4\left(20+20\frac{\sqrt{2}}{2}+20\left(\frac{\sqrt{2}}{2}\right)^2+20\left(\frac{\sqrt{2}}{2}\right)^3+...\right) =$$

$$S = 4\left(\frac{a_1}{1-r}\right) = 4\left(\frac{20}{1-\dfrac{\sqrt{2}}{2}}\right) = 80(\sqrt{2}+2) = 160+80\sqrt{2} \text{ cm}$$

56. Distance:

$$d = \sqrt{(x_2 - x_1)^2 + (y_2 - y_1)^2}$$
$$= \sqrt{(1-(-4))^2 + (-5-7)^2}$$
$$= \sqrt{(5)^2 + (12)^2} = \sqrt{25 + 144} = \sqrt{169} = 13$$

57. Midpoint: $\left(\dfrac{x_1 + x_2}{2}, \dfrac{y_1 + y_2}{2}\right) = \left(\dfrac{-5+7}{2}, \dfrac{2+12}{2}\right)$

$$= \left(\dfrac{2}{2}, \dfrac{14}{2}\right) = (1,\ 7)$$

58. To find the center we use the midpoint formula with the given points:

$$\left(\dfrac{x_1 + x_2}{2}, \dfrac{y_1 + y_2}{2}\right) = \left(\dfrac{1+5}{2}, \dfrac{-3+(-3)}{2}\right)$$
$$= \left(\dfrac{6}{2}, \dfrac{-6}{2}\right) = (3,\ -3)$$

59. The radius is 2 (half the distance between the given points).

60. Substitute: $(h, k) = (3, -3)$ and $r = 2$ in the standard form of the equation of a circle.

$$(x-h)^2 + (y-k)^2 = r^2$$
$$(x-3)^2 + (y-(-3))^2 = 2^2$$
$$(x-3)^2 + (y+3)^2 = 4$$

61. The equation $y = 2x - 4$ is in the slope intercept form of a line. Thus the graph is **C**.

62. The equation $y = 2(x-1)^2$ is in the standard form of a parabola. Thus the graph is **D**.

63. The equation $(x-1)^2 + (y+2)^2 = 4$ is in the standard form of a circle. Thus the graph is **A**.

64. The equation $\dfrac{(x-1)^2}{9} + \dfrac{(y+2)^2}{4} = 1$ is in the standard form of an ellipse. Thus the graph is **F**.

65. The equation $\dfrac{(x-1)^2}{9} - \dfrac{(y+2)^2}{4} = 1$ is in the standard form of a hyperbola. Thus the graph is **E**.

66. The equation $y = \sqrt{4 - x^2}$ is the upper half of the circle $x^2 + y^2 = 4$. Thus the graph is **B**.

67.

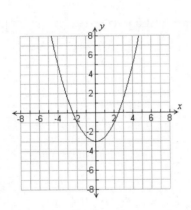

68.

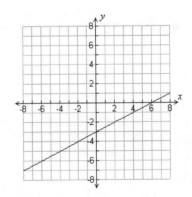

69.

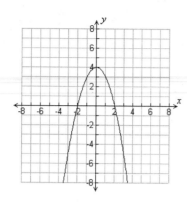

70. The equation $x^2 + y^2 = 36$ is a circle centered at the origin with a radius of 6.

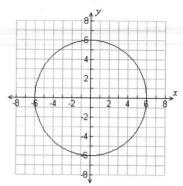

71. The equation $(x+3)^2 + (y-2)^2 = 9$ is a circle centered at the origin with a radius of 3.

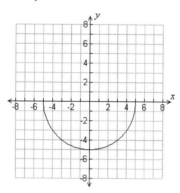

72. The equation $y = \sqrt{25 - x^2}$ is the upper half of the circle $x^2 + y^2 = 25$.

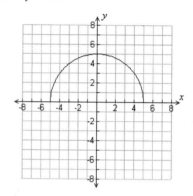

73. The equation $y = -\sqrt{25 - x^2}$ is the lower half of the circle $x^2 + y^2 = 25$.

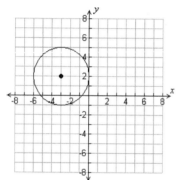

74. The equation $\dfrac{x^2}{49} + \dfrac{y^2}{16} = 1$ is a horizontally positioned ellipse centered at the origin. The length of the major axis is 14 and the length of the minor axis is 8.

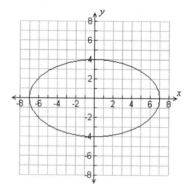

75.
The equation $\dfrac{(x-1)^2}{4}+\dfrac{(y+3)^2}{9}=1$ is a vertically positioned ellipse centered at the point $(1,\,-3)$. The length of the major axis is 6 and the length of the minor axis is 4.

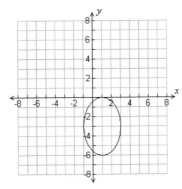

76. The equation $\dfrac{x^2}{36}-\dfrac{y^2}{9}=1$ is a horizontally positioned hyperbola centered at the origin. The length of the fundamental rectangle is 12 and the height of the fundamental rectangle 6.

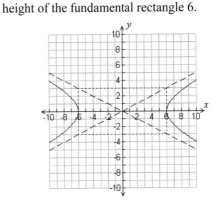

77. The solutions to the system of equations are the points of intersection: $(-2,\,3)$ and $(2,\,3)$.

78.

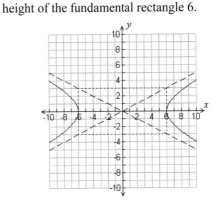

1. a. Answer: $(-2,\,7)$

b. The last row is a contradiction. Thus there is no solution.

c. Solving for x in the first equation we obtain: $x=6-2y$. Thus the general solution of the system is $(6-2y,\,y)$. For $y=0$, $y=2$, and $y=-1$, we obtain the following particular solutions: $(6,\,0),\,(2,\,2),$ and $(8,\,-1)$.

d. $\begin{bmatrix} 2 & 4 & | & -6 \\ 3 & -5 & | & 68 \end{bmatrix} \xrightarrow{r_1'=\frac{1}{2}r_1} \begin{bmatrix} 1 & 2 & | & -3 \\ 3 & -5 & | & 68 \end{bmatrix} \xrightarrow{r_2'=r_2-3r_1} \begin{bmatrix} 1 & 2 & | & -3 \\ 0 & -11 & | & 77 \end{bmatrix} \xrightarrow{r_2'=-\frac{1}{11}r_2} \begin{bmatrix} 1 & 2 & | & -3 \\ 0 & 1 & | & -7 \end{bmatrix}$

$\xrightarrow{r_1'=r_1-2r_2} \begin{bmatrix} 1 & 0 & | & 11 \\ 0 & 1 & | & -7 \end{bmatrix}$; Answer: $(11,\,-7)$

2.   a.

$$\begin{bmatrix} 1 & 3 & 2 & | & 13 \\ 3 & 3 & -2 & | & 13 \\ 6 & 2 & -5 & | & 13 \end{bmatrix} \xrightarrow[\substack{r_3'=r_3-6r_1}]{r_2'=r_2-3r_1} \begin{bmatrix} 1 & 3 & 2 & | & 13 \\ 0 & -6 & -8 & | & -26 \\ 0 & -16 & -17 & | & -65 \end{bmatrix} \xrightarrow{r_2'=-\frac{1}{6}r_2} \begin{bmatrix} 1 & 3 & 2 & | & 13 \\ 0 & 1 & \frac{4}{3} & | & \frac{13}{3} \\ 0 & -16 & -17 & | & -65 \end{bmatrix}$$

$$\xrightarrow[\substack{r_3'=r_3+16r_2}]{r_1'=r_1-3r_2} \begin{bmatrix} 1 & 0 & -2 & | & 0 \\ 0 & 1 & \frac{4}{3} & | & \frac{13}{3} \\ 0 & 0 & \frac{13}{3} & | & \frac{13}{3} \end{bmatrix} \xrightarrow{r_3'=\frac{3}{13}r_3} \begin{bmatrix} 1 & 0 & -2 & | & 0 \\ 0 & 1 & \frac{4}{3} & | & \frac{13}{3} \\ 0 & 0 & 1 & | & 1 \end{bmatrix} \xrightarrow[\substack{r_2'=r_2-\frac{4}{3}r_3}]{r_1'=r_1+2r_3} \begin{bmatrix} 1 & 0 & 0 & | & 2 \\ 0 & 1 & 0 & | & 3 \\ 0 & 0 & 1 & | & 1 \end{bmatrix}$$

Answer: $(2, 3, 1)$

b.

$$\begin{bmatrix} 1 & 3 & -2 & | & 2 \\ 2 & -1 & 1 & | & -1 \\ -5 & 6 & -5 & | & 5 \end{bmatrix} \xrightarrow[\substack{r_3'=r_3+5r_1}]{r_2'=r_2-2r_1} \begin{bmatrix} 1 & 3 & -2 & | & 2 \\ 0 & -7 & 5 & | & -5 \\ 0 & 21 & -15 & | & 15 \end{bmatrix} \xrightarrow{r_2'=-\frac{1}{7}r_2} \begin{bmatrix} 1 & 3 & -2 & | & 2 \\ 0 & 1 & -\frac{5}{7} & | & \frac{5}{7} \\ 0 & 21 & -15 & | & 15 \end{bmatrix}$$

$$\xrightarrow[\substack{r_3'=r_3-21r_2}]{r_1'=r_1-3r_2} \begin{bmatrix} 1 & 0 & \frac{1}{7} & | & -\frac{1}{7} \\ 0 & 1 & -\frac{5}{7} & | & \frac{5}{7} \\ 0 & 0 & 0 & | & 0 \end{bmatrix}$$

Solving for x in the first equation we obtain: $x = -\dfrac{1}{7} - \dfrac{1}{7}z$. Solving for y in the second equation we obtain:

$y = \dfrac{5}{7} + \dfrac{5}{7}z$. Thus the general solution of the system is $\left(-\dfrac{1}{7} - \dfrac{1}{7}z,\ \dfrac{5}{7} + \dfrac{5}{7}z,\ z\right)$.

c.

$$\begin{bmatrix} 1 & 1 & 1 & | & 1 \\ -2 & 1 & 1 & | & -2 \\ 3 & 6 & 6 & | & 5 \end{bmatrix} \xrightarrow[\substack{r_3'=r_3-3r_1}]{r_2'=r_2+2r_1} \begin{bmatrix} 1 & 1 & 1 & | & 1 \\ 0 & 3 & 3 & | & 0 \\ 0 & 3 & 3 & | & 2 \end{bmatrix} \xrightarrow{r_2'=\frac{1}{3}r_2} \begin{bmatrix} 1 & 1 & 1 & | & 1 \\ 0 & 1 & 1 & | & 0 \\ 0 & 3 & 3 & | & 2 \end{bmatrix} \xrightarrow{r_3'=r_3-3r_2} \begin{bmatrix} 1 & 1 & 1 & | & 1 \\ 0 & 1 & 1 & | & 0 \\ 0 & 0 & 0 & | & 2 \end{bmatrix}$$

The last row is a contradiction. Thus there is no solution.

3.   a. The graph of $f(x) = |x| - 2$ is the graph of $y = |x|$ shifted down 2 units. Thus the graph is **A**.

   b. The graph of $f(x) = |x| + 2$ is the graph of $y = |x|$ shifted up 2 units. Thus the graph is **C**.

   c. The graph of $f(x) = (x-3)^2$ is the graph of $y = x^2$ shifted right 3 units. Thus the graph is **D**.

   d. The graph of $f(x) = (x+3)^2$ is the graph of $y = x^2$ shifted left 3 units. Thus the graph is **B**.

4.   a.

x	$f(x+3)$
-3	-5
-2	-4
-1	3
0	22
1	59

b.

x	$f(x)-2$
0	$-5-2=-7$
1	$-4-2=-6$
2	$3-2=1$
3	$22-2=20$
4	$59-2=57$

c.

x	$f(x-3)$
3	-5
4	-4
5	3
6	22
7	59

d.

x	$f(x)+2$
0	$-5+2=-3$
1	$-4+2=-2$
2	$3+2=5$
3	$22+2=24$
4	$59+2=61$

5.   **a.**

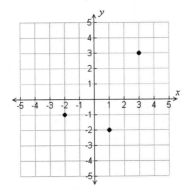

b.

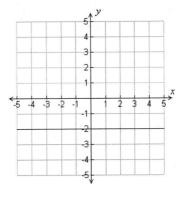

c.

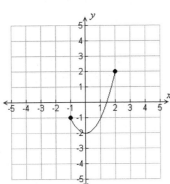

d.

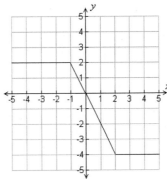

6.   **a.** The graph of $y = 2f(x)$ is the graph of $y = f(x)$ stretched vertically by a factor of 2. Thus the graph is **C**.

   b. The graph of $y = -2f(x)$ is the graph of the refection of $y = f(x)$ stretched vertically by a factor of 2. Thus the graph is **D**.

   c. The graph of $y = \dfrac{1}{2}f(x)$ is the graph of $y = f(x)$ compressed vertically by a factor of 1/2. Thus the graph is **A**.

   d. The graph of $y = -\dfrac{1}{2}f(x)$ is the graph of the reflection of $y = f(x)$ compressed vertically by a factor of 1/2. Thus the graph is **B**.

7.   **a.** $(f+g)(x) = (3x-5) + (x+2) = 4x - 3$

   b. $(f-g)(x) = (3x-5) - (x+2) = 2x - 7$

   c. $(f \cdot g)(x) = (3x-5) \cdot (x+2) = 3x^2 + x - 10$

   d. $\left(\dfrac{f}{g}\right)(x) = \dfrac{f(x)}{g(x)} = \dfrac{3x-5}{x+2}$ for $x \neq 2$

8.   **a.** $(f \circ g)(5) = f(g(5))$
$= f(2(5)-1)$
$= f(9) = (9)^2 + 1 = 82$

   b. $(g \circ f)(5) = g(f(5))$
$= g\left((5)^2 + 1\right)$
$= g(26) = 2(26) - 1 = 51$

   c. $(f \circ g)(x) = f(g(x))$
$= f(2x-1) = (2x-1)^2 + 1$
$= 4x^2 - 4x + 2$

   d. $(g \circ f)(x) = g(f(x))$
$= g(x^2 + 1) = 2(x^2 + 1) - 1$
$= 2x^2 + 1$

9. **a.** 4, 7, 10, 13, 16, 19,...

   b. 4, 12, 36, 108, 324, 972,...

   c. 2, 8, 14, 20, 26, 32,...

   d. 2, 8, 32, 128, 512, 2048,...

10. **a.** $S_n = \dfrac{n}{2}\left(2a_1 + (n-1)d\right)$

$$S_5 = \frac{5}{2}\left(2(2) + (5-1)5\right) = 60$$

   b. $S_n = \dfrac{a_1\left(1-r^n\right)}{1-r}$

$$S_5 = \frac{2\left(1-5^5\right)}{1-5} = 1{,}562$$

   c. $S_n = \dfrac{n}{2}\left(a_1 + a_n\right)$

$$S_{100} = \frac{100}{2}\left(10 + 21\right) = 1{,}550$$

   d. $S_n = \dfrac{a_1\left(1-r^n\right)}{1-r}$

$$S_{21} = \frac{6\left(1-(-2)^{21}\right)}{1-(-2)} = 4{,}194{,}306$$

   e. $\displaystyle\sum_{i=1}^{6}\left(3i^2 + i\right) = \left(3(1)^2 + (1)\right) + \left(3(2)^2 + (2)\right) + \left(3(3)^2 + (3)\right) + \left(3(4)^2 + (4)\right) + \left(3(5)^2 + (5)\right) + \left(3(6)^2 + (6)\right)$

$$= 4 + 14 + 30 + 52 + 80 + 114 = 294$$

11. **a.** $S = \dfrac{a_1}{1-r}$

$$S = \frac{1}{1 - \dfrac{1}{2}} = 2$$

   b. $0.888... = 0.8 + 0.08 + 0.008 + ...$

$$= 8(0.1) + 8(0.1)^2 + 8(0.1)^3 + ...$$

$$S = \frac{a_1}{1-r} = \frac{0.8}{1 - 0.1} = \frac{8}{9}$$

   d. $0.545454... = 0.54 + 0.0054 + 0.000054 + ...$

$$= 54(0.01) + 54(0.01)^2 + 54(0.01)^3 + ...$$

$$S = \frac{a_1}{1-r} = \frac{0.54}{1 - 0.1} = \frac{6}{11}$$

12. **a.** The equation $y = (x+3)^2 - 4$ is a parabola shifted left three units and down 4 units.

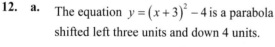

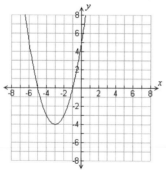

   b. The equation $(x-3)^2 + (y+4)^2 = 16$ is a circle with a radius 4 centered at the point $(3, -4)$.

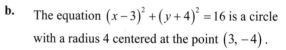

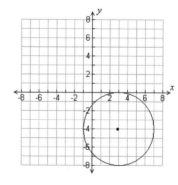

560

c.   The equation $\dfrac{(x-3)^2}{25}+\dfrac{(y+4)^2}{16}=1$ is a horizontally positioned ellipse centered at $(3,-4)$ with a major axis of length 10 and minor axis of length 8.

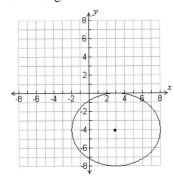

d.   The equation $\dfrac{x^2}{25}-\dfrac{y^2}{16}=1$ is a horizontally positioned hyperbola centered at the origin with a fundamental rectangle with length of 10 and height of 8.

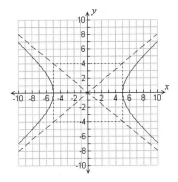

13.   a.   The graph is a parabola reflected across the x axis shifted up 4 units. Thus the equation is
$$y=-x^2+4$$

b.   The graph is a circle centered at the point $(0,5)$ and radius 5. Thus the equation is
$$(x-h)^2+(y-k)^2=r^2$$
$$(x-0)^2+(y-5)^2=5^2$$
$$x^2+(y-5)^2=25$$

c.   The graph is a horizontally positioned ellipse centered at the origin with a major axis of length 14 $(a=7)$ and minor axis of length 10 $(b=5)$. Thus the equation is
$$\frac{(x-h)^2}{a^2}+\frac{(y-k)^2}{b^2}=1$$
$$\frac{(x-0)^2}{7^2}+\frac{(y-0)^2}{5^2}=1$$
$$\frac{x^2}{49}+\frac{y^2}{25}=1$$

d.   The graph is a horizontally positioned hyperbola centered at the origin. It has a fundamental rectangle with a length of 14 $(a=7)$ and a height of 10 $(b=5)$. Thus the equation is
$$\frac{(x-h)^2}{a^2}-\frac{(y-k)^2}{b^2}=1$$
$$\frac{(x-0)^2}{7^2}-\frac{(y-0)^2}{5^2}=1$$
$$\frac{x^2}{49}-\frac{y^2}{25}=1$$

Notes

Notes

Notes

Notes

Notes

Notes

Notes

Notes

Notes